Grace & POWER

Grace
&
POWER

Charles Spurgeon

Whitaker House

GRACE AND POWER

ISBN: 0-88368-589-2
Printed in the United States of America
Copyright © 2000 by Whitaker House

Whitaker House
30 Hunt Valley Circle
New Kensington, PA 15068

Library of Congress Cataloging-in-Publication Data

Spurgeon, C. H. (Charles Haddon), 1834–1892.
    Grace and power / by Charles Haddon Spurgeon.
        p. cm.
    Includes bibliographical references.
    ISBN 0-88368-589-2 (tradepaper)
    1. Grace (Theology) 2. Power (Christian theology) 3. Christian life—Baptist authors. I. Title.

BT761.2 .S683 2000
234—dc21   00-023334

2 3 4 5 6 7 8 9 10 11 12 / 08 07 06 05 04 03 02 01

Contents

About the Author

Charles Haddon Spurgeon was born on June 19, 1834, at Kelvedon, Essex, England, the firstborn of eight surviving children. His parents were committed Christians, and his father and grandfather were both preachers. Spurgeon was converted in 1850 at the age of fifteen. He began to help the poor and to hand out tracts; he was known as "The Boy Preacher."

He preached his first sermon at the age of sixteen. At age eighteen, he became the pastor of Waterbeach Baptist Chapel, preaching in a barn. Spurgeon preached over six hundred times before he reached the age of twenty. By 1854, he was well-known and was asked to become the pastor of New Park Street Chapel in London.

In 1856, Spurgeon married Susannah Thompson; they had twin sons, both of whom later entered the ministry.

Spurgeon's compelling sermons and lively preaching style drew multitudes of people, and many came to Christ. Soon, the crowds had grown so large that they blocked the narrow streets near the church. Services eventually had to be held in rented halls, and he often preached to congregations of more than ten thousand. The Metropolitan Tabernacle was built in 1861 to accommodate the large numbers of people.

Spurgeon published over thirty-five hundred sermons, which were so popular that they sold by the ton. At one point, his sermons sold twenty-five thousand copies every week. The prime minister of England, members of the royal family, and Florence Nightingale, among others, went to hear him preach. Spurgeon preached to an estimated ten million people throughout his life. Not surprisingly, he is called the "Prince of Preachers."

In addition to his powerful preaching, Spurgeon founded and supported charitable outreaches, including educational institutions. His pastors' college, which is still in existence today, taught nearly nine hundred students in Spurgeon's time. He also founded the famous Stockwell Orphanage.

Charles Spurgeon died in 1892, and his death was mourned by many.

Book One

Grace: God's Unmerited Favor

Contents

Chapter 1

The Covenant of Grace

He will ever be mindful of His covenant.
—Psalm 111:5

That God would enter into gracious covenant with men is an amazing thing. That He would create man and be gracious to him is barely conceivable. However, that God would shake hands with His creation and would subject His august majesty to an unbreakable bond with man by His own pledge is astonishing.

Once I know that God has made a covenant with man, then, I am not surprised that He is mindful of it, for He is *"God, who cannot lie"* (Titus 1:2). *"Has He said, and will He not do?"* (Num. 23:19). Has he not given His promise? Thus, it is inconceivable that He would ever depart from it.

Our text verse commends itself to every reasonable, thoughtful man: if God has made a covenant, *"He will ever be mindful of* [that] *covenant."* For God to make a gracious covenant with us is so great a blessing that I hope everyone is saying in his heart, "Oh, may the Lord enter into covenant with me!"

I call your attention to this point with the desire to explore it effectively. We will practically look into this matter by first answering the question, What is this covenant? Then we will consider the inquiry, Am I personally included in the covenant? Finally, we will reflect on what a person's normal response to God's pledge should be: "If indeed I am in covenant with God, then every part of that covenant will be carried out, for God is ever mindful of it."

What Is This Covenant?

If you go to a lawyer and inquire about a deed, he may reply, "I can give you an abstract, but it is better if you read the deed thoroughly." He can tell you the essence of it; but if you want to be very

9

accurate, and if it is a very important transaction, you will want to read the document for yourself.

These passages of Scripture contain the covenant of grace, or an abstract of it. First, turn to Jeremiah:

> *Behold, the days are coming, says the LORD, when I will make a new covenant with the house of Israel and with the house of Judah; not according to the covenant that I made with their fathers in the day that I took them by the hand to lead them out of the land of Egypt, My covenant which they broke, though I was a husband to them, says the LORD. But this is the covenant that I will make with the house of Israel after those days, says the LORD: I will put My law in their minds, and write it on their hearts; and I will be their God, and they shall be My people. No more shall every man teach his neighbor, and every man his brother, saying, "Know the LORD," for they all shall know Me, from the least of them to the greatest of them, says the LORD. For I will forgive their iniquity, and their sin I will remember no more.* (Jer. 31:31–34)

Set every word of that passage in diamonds, for its significance is precious beyond measure.

Written on Hearts

God makes a covenant promise to His people that, instead of writing His law upon tablets of stone, He will write it on the tablets of their hearts. Instead of the law coming as a hard, crushing command, it will be placed within them as the object of love and delight, written on the transformed natures of His chosen, beloved people: *"I will put My law in their minds, and write it on their hearts"* (v. 33). What a covenant privilege this is!

A Sense of Belonging

"And I will be their God" (v. 33). Therefore, all that there is in God will belong to those who are in covenant with Him. *"And they shall be My people"* (v.33). He is saying, "They will belong to Me; I will love them as Mine; I will keep them, bless them, honor them, and provide for them as My people. I will be their portion, and they will be My portion." What security this promise provides!

Heavenly Instruction

Note the next privilege. God's people will all receive heavenly instruction about a most vital point: *"They all shall know Me"* (v. 34). Once again, God is saying, "There may be some things they do not know, but *'they all shall know Me.'* They will know Me as their Father; they will know Jesus Christ as their Brother; they will know the Holy Spirit as their Comforter. They will have communion and fellowship with Me." What a privilege it is to know God!

Forgiven and Forgotten

Then comes pardon: *"For I will forgive their iniquity, and their sin I will remember no more"* (v. 34). What a clean sweep of sin! God will forgive and forget; the two go together. *"I will forgive their iniquity, and their sin I will remember no more."* All of their transgressions and iniquities will be blotted out, never to be mentioned against them again. What an indescribable favor!

An Unconditional Grant

This is the covenant of grace. I call your attention to the fact that there is no *if* in it; there is no *but* in it; there is no requirement of man made by it. It is all *"I will"* and *"they shall."* *"I will be their God, and they shall be My people"* (v. 33). This gracious charter is written in a royal tone, and the majestic strain is not marred by a *perhaps* or a *maybe,* but dwells always on *shall* and *will.* These are two prerogative words of the Divine Majesty. In this wondrous deed to the gift, not only does the Lord bestow a heaven of grace on guilty sinners, but He also presents it according to the sovereignty of His own will, without anything to put the gift in jeopardy or to make the promise unsure.

More of the Covenant

Thus, we have read the covenant in one form, but if you turn a few pages in your Bible, you will come to a passage in Ezekiel. As we read, we find the bright-eyed prophet—he who lived among the wheels and the seraphim (see Ezekiel 1:15–16; 10:9–17)—telling us what the covenant of grace is:

> *Then I will give them one heart, and I will put a new spirit within them, and take the stony heart out of their flesh, and give them a heart of flesh, that they may walk in My statutes and keep My judgments and do them; and they shall be My people, and I will be their God.* (Ezek. 11:19–20)

You will find another form of the covenant further on in the thirty-sixth chapter of Ezekiel. How intently ought you to pay attention to this! So much better than hearing any preaching of mortal man is listening to the very words of God's own covenant, a covenant that saves all those who are touched by it. Let us read it:

> *Then I will sprinkle clean water on you, and you shall be clean; I will cleanse you from all your filthiness and from all your idols. I will give you a new heart and put a new spirit within you; I will take the heart of stone out of your flesh and give you a heart of flesh. I will put My Spirit within you and cause you to walk in My statutes, and you will keep My judgments and do them. Then you shall dwell in the land that I gave to your fathers; you shall be My people, and I will be your God.* (Ezek. 36:25–28)

This promise always comes in at the close: *"I will be your God."* In this form of the covenant, I urge you again to witness that God demands nothing, asks no price, and exacts no payment. But to the people with whom He enters into covenant, He makes promise after promise—all free, all unconditional, all made according to the bounty of His royal heart.

Transformed by Grace

Let us explore this point in more detail. God has made a covenant with certain people that He will do all this for them, and in each case it is pure grace. He will take away their stony hearts: it is clear from the promise that, when He began with them, they had stony hearts. He will forgive their iniquities: when He began with them, they had many iniquities. He will give them hearts of flesh: when He began with them, they did not have hearts of flesh. He will teach them to keep His statutes: when He began with them, they did not keep His statutes. They were a sinful, willful, wicked, degenerate people.

12

God had called to them many times to come to Him and repent, but they would not. In this passage He speaks like a king, no longer pleading, but instead decreeing. He declares, "I will do this and that for you, and you shall be this and that in return." Oh, blessed covenant! Oh, mighty, sovereign grace!

A Comparison of Covenants

How did all of this come about? We can find out as we learn the doctrine of the two covenants. The first covenant—made with our first father, Adam—was the covenant of works. This was not first in purpose, but it was the first to be revealed. It went like this: God Almighty declared, "Adam, you and your posterity will live and be happy *if* you will keep My law. To test your obedience to Me, there is a certain tree: *if* you let that alone, you will live; but *if* you eat of it, you will die, as well as those whom you represent."

Our first covenant head snatched greedily at the forbidden fruit and fell. And what a fall it was, my beloved! There you and I and all of us fell, while it was proven once and for all that *"by the deeds of the law no flesh will be justified in His sight"* (Rom. 3:20). If perfect Adam broke the law so readily, you can depend on it that you and I would break any law that God has ever made. There was no hope of happiness for any of us by a covenant that contained an *if* in it. The old covenant has been put away, for it has utterly failed. It brought nothing to us but a curse, and we are glad that it has abated and—as far as believers are concerned—has vanished.

Then came the Second Adam. You know His name; He is the ever blessed Son of the Highest. This Second Adam entered into covenant with God somewhat after this fashion: God the Father said to the Son, "I give You a people; they will be Yours. You must die to redeem them. When You have done this—when for their sakes You have kept My law and made it honorable, when for their sakes You have borne My wrath against their transgressions— Then I will bless them. Then they shall be My people; I will forgive their iniquities; I will change their natures; I will sanctify them and make them perfect."

There was an apparent *if* in this covenant at first. That *if* hinged on the question of whether Jesus would obey the law and pay the ransom, a question that His faithfulness placed beyond doubt. There is no *if* in it now. When Jesus bowed His head and said, *"It is finished!"* (John 19:30), there remained no *if* in the covenant.

13

Therefore, the covenant now stands, entirely one-sided: a covenant of promises that must be kept because the Father's side of it must stand, the other part of the covenant having been fulfilled by the Son. God cannot, and He will not, draw back from doing what He covenanted with Christ to do. The Lord Jesus will receive *"the joy that was set before Him"* (Heb. 12:2). *"He shall see the labor of His soul, and be satisfied. By His knowledge My righteous Servant [Jesus Christ] shall justify many, for He shall bear their iniquities"* (Isa. 53:11). How could it be otherwise than that they should be accepted for whom He was the Surety!

Do you see why it is that the covenant, as we have read it, stands so absolutely without *if*s, *but*s, or *maybe*s, and runs only on *shall*s and *will*s? It is because the one side of it that did look uncertain was committed into the hands of Christ, who cannot *"fail nor be discouraged"* (Isa. 42:4). He has completed His part of it. Now it stands fast, and so it must stand forever and ever.

This is now a covenant of pure grace and nothing else but grace. Let no man attempt to mix works with it, or anything else of human merit. God saves now because He chooses to save. Over the head of us all, there comes a sound as of a martial trumpet, and yet with a deep, inner, peaceful music to it: *"I will have mercy on whomever I will have mercy, and I will have compassion on whomever I will have compassion"* (Rom. 9:15). God observes us, all lost and ruined, and in His infinite mercy comes with absolute promises of grace to those whom He has given to His Son Jesus. So much, then, in regard to the doctrine of the covenant.

Are You Included in the Covenant?

Now comes the important question, Are you personally included in this covenant? May the Holy Spirit help each of us to ascertain the truth on this point. I would earnestly urge you, who are really anxious of heart to know the answer, to read the epistle to the Galatians. Read that through if you want to know whether you have any share in the covenant of grace.

Perhaps you are asking, "Did Christ fulfill the law for me? Are the promises of God absolutely and unconditionally made to me?" You can know by answering the following three questions.

In Christ

First, Are you in Christ? Did you notice that we were all in Adam, and in Adam we all fell? Now, *"as by one man's disobedience many were made sinners, so also by one Man's obedience many will be made righteous"* (Rom. 5:19). Are you in the Second Adam? You certainly were in the first one, for so you fell. Are you in the Second? Because, if you are in Him, you are saved in Him. He has kept the law for you.

The covenant of grace made with Christ was made with you if you are in Him. As surely as the sons of Levi were in the loins of Abraham when Melchizedek met him (see Hebrews 7:1, 5), so were all believers in the loins of Christ when He died on the cross. If you are in Christ, you are a part of the seed to whom the promise was made. However, there is only one seed, as the apostle Paul said, *"He does not say, 'And to seeds,' as of many, but as of one, 'And to your Seed,' who is Christ"* (Gal. 3:16).

Faith in Jesus

The second question is, Do you have faith? By ascertaining your response to this question you will be helped to answer the previous one, because believers are in Christ. In the epistle to the Galatians, you will find that the mark of those who are in Christ is their belief in Christ. The mark of all who are saved is not confidence in works, but faith in Christ. In writing Galatians, Paul insisted on it: *"But that no one is justified by the law in the sight of God is evident, for 'the just shall live by faith'"* (v. 11), and the law is not of faith. Over and over again he stated it.

Come, then, do you believe in Jesus Christ with all your heart? Is He your sole hope for heaven? Do you lean your whole weight, the entire strength of your salvation, on Jesus? Then you are in Him, and the covenant is yours. There is not one blessing God has decreed to give that He will not give to you. There is not a benefit that He has determined, out of the grandeur of His heart, to bestow on His elect, which He will not bestow upon you. You have the mark, the seal, the badge of His chosen if you believe in Christ Jesus.

Born Again

Another question that should help you is, Have you been born again? I refer you again to Galatians, which I would like every person anxious for his salvation to read through very carefully. You will see that Abraham had two sons. One of them, Ishmael, the child of the bondwoman, was born according to the flesh. Although he was the firstborn son, he was not the heir, for Sarah said to

15

Abraham, *"Cast out the bondwoman and her son, for the son of the bondwoman shall not be heir with the son of the freewoman"* (Gal. 4:30). He who was born after the flesh did not inherit the covenant promise.

Is your hope of heaven fixed on the fact that you have a good mother and father? Then your hope is born after the flesh, and you are not in the covenant. I constantly hear it said that children of godly parents do not need to be converted. Let me denounce that wicked falsehood. *"What is born of the flesh is flesh"* (John 3:6), and nothing better. Those who are born after the flesh are not the children of God. Do not trust in gracious descent or in holy ancestors. *"You must be born again"* (v. 7), every single one of you, or you will perish forever, whoever your parents may be.

Abraham had another son, Isaac, who was not born of the strength of his father, nor after the flesh at all, for we are told that both Abraham and Sarah had become old. Rather, Isaac was born by God's power, according to promise. He was the child given by grace. Now, have you ever been born like that—not by human strength but by power divine? Is the life that is in you a life given by God? The true life is not born of the will of man, nor of blood, nor of natural excellence (John 1:13). Instead, eternal life comes by the working of the Holy Spirit, and it is *"the gift of God...through Jesus Christ our Lord"* (Rom. 6:23 KJV). If you have this life, you indeed are included in the covenant, for it is written,

> *Nor are they all children because they are the seed of Abraham; but, "In Isaac your seed shall be called." That is, those who are the children of the flesh, these are not the children of God; but the children of the promise are counted as the seed.*
>
> (Rom. 9:7–8)

God said to Abraham, *"In your seed all the nations of the earth shall be blessed"* (Gen. 22:18). That was because He meant to justify the Gentiles by faith, so that the blessing given to believing Abraham might come on all believers (Gal. 3:14). Abraham is often called the father of the faithful, or *"the father of all those who believe"* (Rom. 4:11). With such is the covenant established.

Blessed Assurance

Here, then, are the test questions: Am I in Christ? Do I have faith in Jesus? Am I born again by the Spirit of God according to the promise, and not according to my works or to my fleshly birth? If you can answer in the affirmative, then, you are in the covenant, and your name stands in the eternal record. Before the stars began to shine, the Lord had covenanted to bless you. Before evening and morning made the first day, your name was in His book. Before the world's foundation was laid (see Ephesians 1:4), Christ shook hands with the Father in the council chamber of eternity and pledged Himself to redeem you and to bring you and multitudes of others into His eternal glory. Christ will do it, too, for He never breaks His guaranteed pledge any more than the Father breaks His covenant word.

I want you to be quite sure about these points, for what peace it will nurture in your soul, what a restfulness of heart it will be for you to understand the covenant and to know that your name is in it!

Are the Covenant Blessings for Me?

If indeed we can believe the good evidence of God's Word that we are of the seed with whom the covenant was made in Christ Jesus, then, every blessing of the covenant will come to us. I will put it in a little more personal terms: if you are of the covenanted seed, every blessing of the covenant will come to you.

The Devil says, "No, it won't." Why not, Satan? "Why," says he, "you are not able to do this or that." Refer the Devil to our text; tell him to read those passages that we have read, and ask him if he can spy an *if* or a *but* in them. I cannot.

"But, but, but," Satan sputters, "you cannot do enough. You cannot feel enough." Does it say anything about feeling there? It only says, *"I will give them...a heart of flesh"* (Ezek. 11:19). They will feel enough then.

"But," the Devil says, "you cannot soften your hard heart." Does it say that you are to do so? Does it not say *"I will...take the stony heart out of their flesh"* (v. 19)? The whole tone of the passage is that God will do it; therefore, God will do it! The Devil dares not say that God cannot do it, because he knows that God can even enable us to tread him under our feet (Luke 10:19).

Satan says, "You will never be able to keep on the right path if you become a Christian." Does it say anything about that in the covenant further than this: *"I will...cause you to walk in My statutes"* (Ezek. 36:27)? What if we do not have the power in and of ourselves to continue in God's statutes? God has the power to make us

17

continue in them. He can work obedience and final perseverance in holiness in us; His covenant promises these blessings to us.

Wholly the Gift of God

To come back to what we said before, God does not ask of us, but He gives to us. He sees us *"dead in trespasses and sins"* (Eph. 2:1), and He loves us even when we are so. He sees us feeble, unable to help ourselves, yet He comes in and works in us *"to will and to do for His good pleasure"* (Phil. 2:13). Only then can we *"work out* [our] *own salvation with fear and trembling"* (v. 12).

The bottom of it, the very foundation of it, is Christ Himself, and He finds nothing in us to help Him. There is neither fire nor wood in us, much less *"the lamb for a burnt offering"* (Gen. 22:7), but all is emptiness and condemnation. He comes in with "I will do" and "you shall be," like a royal Helper affording free aid to destitute, helpless sinners, according to the riches of His grace. Now be assured that, having made such a covenant as this, God *"will ever be mindful"* of it.

God Gave His Word

He will do so, first, because He cannot lie. If He says He will, He will. His very name is *"God, who cannot lie"* (Titus 1:2). If I am a believer in Christ, I must be saved; none can prevent it. If I am a believer in Christ, I must be saved; all the devils in hell cannot stop it, for God has said, *"He who believes in Him is not condemned"* (John 3:18). *"He who believes and is baptized will be saved"* (Mark 16:16).

God's word is not first "yes" and then, "no": *"For all the promises of God in Him are Yes, and in Him Amen, to the glory of God through us"* (2 Cor. 1:20). He knew what He said when He spoke the covenant. He has never changed it, nor has He contradicted it.

Promised to You through Christ

If, then, you are a believer, you must be saved, because you are in Christ to whom the promise is made. If you have the new life within, you must be saved, for is not this spiritual life *"having been born again, not of corruptible seed but incorruptible, through the word of God which lives and abides forever"* (1 Pet. 1:23)?

18

Jesus said, *"The water that I shall give him will become in him a fountain of water springing up into everlasting life"* (John 4:14). You have drunk the water Christ gave you; therefore, it must spring up into everlasting life. It is not possible for death to kill the life that God has given you, nor for all the fallen spirits to tread out the divine fire that Christ's own Spirit has cast into your bosom. You must be saved, for God *"cannot deny Himself"* (2 Tim. 2:13).

Freely Made

Next, God made the covenant freely. If He had not meant to keep it, He would not have made it.

When a man is driven into a corner by someone who says, "You must pay me now," the debtor is apt to promise more than he can perform. He solemnly declares, "I will pay you in two weeks." Poor fellow, he has no money now and will not have any then, but he made a promise because he could not help himself.

No such necessity can be imagined with God Almighty. The Lord was under no compulsion whatever. He could have left men to perish because of sin. There was no one to prompt Him to make the covenant of grace or even to suggest the idea.

Who has directed the Spirit of the LORD, or as His counselor has taught Him? With whom did He take counsel, and who instructed Him, and taught Him in the path of justice? Who taught Him knowledge, and showed Him the way of understanding? (Isa. 40:13–14)

He made the covenant of His own royal will. Be assured that, once having made it, God will never turn back from it. A covenant so freely made must be fully carried out.

Sealed in Blood

Moreover, on the covenant document is a seal. Did you see it? The grand thing in a deeded gift is the signature or seal. What is this, this red splash at the bottom of it? Is it blood? Yes, it is. Whose blood? It is the blood of the Son of God. This mark has ratified and sealed the covenant. Jesus' shed blood in His death has made the covenant sure. Can God forget the blood of His dear Son or show contempt for His sacrifice? Impossible. All for whom Christ died as a covenant substitute He will save. The redeemed will not be left in captivity as if the ransom price had brought about nothing. Has He not said, *"All that the Father gives Me will come to Me, and the one who comes to Me I will by no means cast out"* (John 6:37)? That covenant stands secure, though the earth pass away, because rejection of Christ's shed blood can never be possible on the part of the Father.

God's Delight

God delights in the covenant, and so we are sure He will not turn back from it. It is the joy of His holy heart. He delights to do His people good. To pass over transgression, iniquity, and sin is the recreation of Jehovah. Did you ever hear of God singing? It is extraordinary that the Divine One would solace Himself with song, yet a prophet has thus revealed the Lord to us:

> *The LORD your God in your midst, The Mighty One, will save;*
> *He will rejoice over you with gladness, He will quiet you with*
> *His love, He will rejoice over you with singing.*   (Zeph. 3:17)

The covenant is the heart of God written out in the blood of Jesus. Since the whole nature of God runs parallel with the tenor of the everlasting covenant, you may rest assured that even its tiniest point stands secure.

God's Solemn Oath

Finally, you who are in the covenant dare not doubt that God will save you, keep you, and bless you, assuming you have believed on Jesus, are in Jesus, and are quickened into newness of life! You will not doubt when I explain one more thing. If your father, your brother, or your dearest friend had solemnly stated a fact, would you allow anybody to say that he had lied? No, I know you would be indignant at such a charge. Now, suppose your father in his most solemn manner had taken an oath. Would you for a moment think that he had perjured himself and had sworn a lie? You would never for a moment think such a thing.

Now, turn to the book of Hebrews, and you will find that God, because He knew that an oath among men is the end of strife (Heb. 6:16), was pleased to seal the covenant with His oath:

> *Thus God, determining to show more abundantly to the heirs*
> *of promise the immutability of His counsel, confirmed it by an*

20

*oath, that by two immutable things, in which it is impossible
for God to lie, we might have strong consolation, who have
fled for refuge to lay hold of the hope set before us.*
                                                (Heb. 6:17–18)

God has raised His hand and sworn that Christ will have the
reward of His passion; that His purchased ones will be brought under His sway; that having borne sin and put it away, it will never
be a second time charged against His redeemed. His oath is unbreakable.

This is all of it. Do you believe in Christ? Then God will work
in you *"to will and to do for His good pleasure"* (Phil. 2:13). God
will conquer your sin; God will sanctify you; God will save you; God
will keep you; God will bring you to Himself. Rest in the covenant.
Then moved by intense gratitude, go forward to serve your Lord
with all your heart and soul and strength. Being saved, live to
praise Him. Do not work so that you may be saved, but serve Him
because you are saved, for the covenant has secured your safety.
Delivered from the servile fear that an Ishmael might have known,
live the joyous life of an Isaac. Moved by love of the Father, spend
and be spent for His sake. If the selfish hope of winning heaven by
works has moved some men to great sacrifice, so much more should
the godly motive of gratitude to Him, who has done all this for us,
move us to the noblest service and make us feel that it is not a sacrifice at all.

*For the love of Christ compels us, because we judge thus: that
if One died for all, then all died; and He died for all, that
those who live should live no longer for themselves, but for
Him who died for them and rose again.*   (2 Cor. 5:14–15)

*Or do you not know that your body is the temple of the Holy
Spirit who is in you, whom you have from God, and you are
not your own? For you were bought at a price; therefore glorify
God in your body and in your spirit, which are God's.*
                                                (1 Cor. 6:19–20)

If you are saved under the covenant of grace, the mark of the
covenanted ones is upon you, and the sacred character of the covenanted ones should be displayed in you. Bless and magnify your
covenant God. Take the cup of the covenant, and call on His name.
Plead the promises of the covenant, and have whatever you need.

21

Chapter 2

Salvation Altogether by Grace

*[God] has saved us and called us with a holy calling, not according
to our works, but according to His own purpose and grace which
was given to us in Christ Jesus before time began.*
—2 Timothy 1:9

To influence persons of thought, we must do so by solid reasoning. Shallow minds may be impressed by mere warmth of
emotion and force of excitement, but the more intellectual
part of the community must be dealt with in quite another manner.
When the apostle Paul desired to influence Timothy, his son in the
faith, who was a diligent and earnest student and a man of gifts as
well as of grace, he did not attempt to persuade him by mere appeals to his feelings. Instead, Paul felt that the most effective way
to appeal to him was to remind him of solid doctrinal truth, which
he knew Timothy believed.

The ministry at large needs to heed this lesson. Certain earnest preachers are incessantly exciting the people but seldom, if
ever, instructing them. They carry much fire and very little light.
God forbid that we should say a word against appealing to the
feelings—this is definitely needed in its place—but there is a balance to be observed with it. A religion that is based on, sustained,
and maintained simply by excitement will necessarily be flimsy and
insubstantial; it will yield very speedily to the crush of opposition
or to the crumbling hand of time. The preacher may touch the
feelings by rousing appeals, just as the harpist touches the harpstrings. He would be very foolish if he neglected such an admirable
instrument. Still, as he is dealing with reasonable creatures, he
must not forget to enlighten the intellect and instruct the understanding.

How can an evangelist appeal to the understanding better than
by presenting the truth that the Holy Spirit teaches? Scriptural

doctrine must furnish us with powerful motives to urge upon the minds of Christians. It seems to me that if I could, by some unreasoning impulse, move you to a certain course of action, it might be good in its own way for the immediate gain. However, in the long run, it would prove to be unsafe and untrustworthy, because you would be equally open to be moved in an opposite direction by other persons more skillful in such operations. Only when God enables us by his Spirit to influence your minds by solid truth and arguments of substance will you then move with a constancy of power that nothing can turn aside.

A feather floats on the wind, but it has no inherent power to move. Consequently, when the gale is over, it falls to the ground. Such is the religion of excitement. In contrast, the eagle has life within itself, and its wings bear it aloft and onward whether the breeze favors it or not. Such is religion when sustained by a conviction of the truth. The well-taught man in Christ Jesus stands firm where the uninstructed infant would fall or be carried away. *"We should no longer be children, tossed to and fro and carried about with every wind of doctrine"* (Eph. 4:14), wrote Paul. Those who are well established in the truth as it is in Jesus are least likely to be so carried away.

It is somewhat remarkable—at least it may seem so to people who are not accustomed to thinking about the subject—that Paul, in order to excite Timothy to boldness and to keep him constant in the faith, reminded him of the great doctrine that the grace of God reigns in the salvation of men. He gave in this verse—this parenthetical verse as some call it, but which seems to me to be fully in the flow of the passage—a brief summary of the Gospel, showing the great prominence that it gives to the grace of God. Paul did so with the intention of maintaining Timothy in the boldness of his testimony for Christ.

I do not doubt that a far greater power for usefulness lies concealed within the doctrines of grace than some men have ever dreamed of. It has been prevalent to look on doctrinal truth as being nothing more than impractical theory, yet many have spoken of the ordinances of God's Word as being more practical and more useful. The day may come when in clearer light we will perceive that sound doctrine is the very root and vital energy of practical holiness and that to teach the people the truth that God has revealed is the readiest and surest way of leading them to obedience and persevering holiness.

May the Holy Spirit assist us as we consider, first, the doctrine taught in this text, and second, the applications of that doctrine.

The Doctrine Explained

Readers, please remember that it is not my objective to extol doctrine that is the most popular or most palatable, nor do I desire to set forth the views of any one individual. My one aim is to give what I judge to be the meaning of the text. I probably deliver doctrinal principles that many of you may not like. Truly, I would not be at all surprised if you did not like them. Even if you become vexed and angry, I will not be at all alarmed, because I have never believed that I was commissioned to teach what would please my readers or that I was expected by sensible and gracious people to shape my views to suit the notions of my audience. I count myself responsible to God and to the text. If I explain the meaning of the text, I believe that I will give the mind of God and will be likely to have His favor, which will be sufficient for me—whoever may contradict me. However, let every candid mind be willing to receive the truth if what I am expressing is clearly in the inspired Word.

The Author of Salvation

In stating his doctrine in the following words, "[God] *has saved us and called us with a holy calling, not according to our works, but according to His own purpose and grace which was given to us in Christ Jesus before time began,"* the apostle Paul declared God to be the Author of salvation, "[God] *has saved us and called us."* The whole tenor of the verse is directed toward a strong affirmation of Jonah's doctrine: *"Salvation is of the LORD"* (Jonah 2:9). To rationalize salvation by man from this text would require a very great twisting, involving more than ingenuity—indeed, it would require out-and-out dishonesty. But to find salvation altogether of God in this verse is to perceive the truth that rests at the very surface. There is no need for profound inquiry into such an evident truth. *"Whoever walks the road, although a fool, shall not go astray"* (Isa. 35:8).

The text says as plainly as any words can say that "[God] *has saved us and called us with a holy calling."* The apostle Paul, then, in order to bring forth the truth that salvation is of grace, declared that it is of God, that it springs directly and entirely from Him, and that it is from Him only. Is this not according to the teaching of the Holy Spirit in other places, where He affirms repeatedly that the Alpha and Omega of our salvation must be found, not in ourselves, but in our God?

In saying that God has saved us, Paul was referring to all the persons of the Divine Trinity. The Father has saved us. *"God has given us eternal life"* (1 John 5:11). *"The Father Himself loves you"* (John 16:27). It was He whose gracious mind first conceived the thought of redeeming His chosen from the ruin of the Fall. It was His mind that first planned the way of salvation by substitution. From His generous heart the thought first sprang that Christ should suffer as the Covenant Head of His people, as the apostle Paul said,

> *Blessed be the God and Father of our Lord Jesus Christ, who has blessed us with every spiritual blessing in the heavenly places in Christ, just as He chose us in Him before the foundation of the world, that we should be holy and without blame before Him in love, having predestined us to adoption as sons by Jesus Christ to Himself, according to the good pleasure of His will, to the praise of the glory of His grace, by which He has made us accepted in the Beloved.* (Eph. 1:3–6)

From the depths of divine compassion came the gift of the only begotten Son: *"For God so loved the world that He gave His only begotten Son, that whoever believes in Him should not perish but have everlasting life"* (John 3:16). The Father selected the people who would receive an interest in the redemption of His Son, for these are described as *"called according to His purpose"* (Rom. 8:28). The plan of salvation in all its details came forth from the Father's wisdom and grace.

The apostle Paul did not, however, overlook the work of the Son. It is most certainly through the Son of God that we are saved, for is not His name Jesus, the Savior? Incarnate in the flesh, His holy life is the righteousness in which saints are arrayed, while His ignominious and painful death has filled the sacred bath of blood in which the sinner must be washed so that he may be made clean. Through the redemption that is in Christ Jesus, the people of God become *"accepted in the Beloved"* (Eph. 1:6). With one voice before the eternal throne, they sing, *"To Him who loved us and washed us from our sins in His own blood...to Him be glory"* (Rev. 1:5–6). They chant that hymn because He deserves the glory that they ascribe to Him. It is the Son of God who is the Savior of men; men are not the saviors of themselves.

Nor did the apostle Paul, I am persuaded, forget the third person in the blessed Trinity, the Holy Spirit. Who but the Holy Spirit first gives us power to understand the Gospel?

> *Now we have received, not the spirit of the world, but the Spirit who is from God, that we might know the things that have been freely given to us by God. These things we also speak, not in words which man's wisdom teaches but which the Holy Spirit teaches, comparing spiritual things with spiritual. But the natural man does not receive the things of the Spirit of God, for they are foolishness to him; nor can he know them, because they are spiritually discerned.* (1 Cor. 2:12–14)

Does not the Holy Spirit influence our wills, turning us from the obstinacy of our former rebellion to the obedience of the truth? Does not the Holy Spirit renew us, creating us *"in Christ Jesus for good works"* (Eph. 2:10)? Is it not by the Holy Spirit's breath that we live the spiritual life? Is He not to us Instructor, Comforter, and Quickener? Is He not everything, in fact, through His active operations upon our minds?

Thus, the Father in planning, the Son in redeeming, and the Spirit in applying the redemption must be spoken of as the one God *"who has saved us"* (2 Tim. 1:9).

To say that we save ourselves is to utter an absurdity. In Scripture each of us is called the *"temple of God"* (1 Cor. 3:16), a holy temple of the Lord. However, will anyone assert that the stones of the edifice in which he now resides were their own architect? Would anyone dare say that the stones of the building in which he now abides cut themselves into their present shape, spontaneously came together, and then piled themselves up into a spacious edifice? If someone were to assert such a foolish thing, we would be inclined to doubt his sanity. Much more may we suspect the spiritual sanity of any man who would venture to affirm that the great temple of the church, the body of Christ, designed and erected itself. No, we believe that God the Father was the architect, sketched the plan, supplied the materials, and will complete the work.

Will it also be said that those who are redeemed have redeemed themselves? Or that slaves of Satan break their own fetters? If that were true, then why was a redeemer needed at all? Why would there be any need for Jesus to descend into the world to redeem those who could redeem themselves? Do you believe that the sheep of God, whom He has taken from between the jaws of the lion, could have rescued themselves? It would be a strange thing if such were the case. Our Lord Jesus did not come to do an unessential work. However, if He had come to save persons who might have saved themselves, He certainly came without a necessity for so doing. We cannot believe that Christ came to do what sinners might have done themselves. No, He said of Himself, *"I have trodden the winepress alone, and from the peoples no one was with Me"* (Isa. 63:3). The redemption of His people will give glory to Himself only.

Will it be asserted that those who were once dead spiritually have quickened themselves? Can the dead make themselves alive? Who will assert that Lazarus, rotting in the grave, came forth to life by himself?

Even if that is accepted, still we will not believe that the dead in sin have ever quickened themselves. Those who are saved by God the Holy Spirit are created anew according to Scripture, but who ever dreamed of creation creating itself? God spoke the world into existence out of nothing, but nothing did not aid in the creation of the universe. Divine energy can do everything, but what can nothing do?

"Therefore, if anyone is in Christ, he is a new creation; old things have passed away; behold, all things have become new" (2 Cor. 5:17). If we have become new creations, there must have been a Creator. Further, it is clear that, having then been spiritually dead, we could not have assisted in our own new creation, unless, indeed, death can assist life and nonexistence can aid in creation. The carnal mind does not assist the Spirit of God in creating a new man, but regeneration is altogether the work of the Holy Spirit. Thus, the work of renewal is from His unassisted power.

Father, Son, and Spirit, we then adore. Putting these thoughts together, we humbly prostrate ourselves at the foot of the throne of the august Majesty and acknowledge that, if we are saved, He alone has saved us. To Him be all the glory.

God's Unique Methodology

Next, we find in our text that grace becomes conspicuous when we see that God pursues a remarkable method: "[God] *has saved us*

27

and called us." The singularity of the manner lies in three things, which we will examine in turn.

In Totality

The first characteristic of God's methodology is the completeness of it. The apostle used the perfect tense when he wrote, *"Who has saved us"* (2 Tim. 1:9). Believers in Christ Jesus are saved. They are not looked on as persons who are in a hopeful state and may ultimately be saved, but they are already saved. This is not according to the common talk of some believers, for many of them speak of being saved when they come to die. However, it is according to the usage of Scripture to speak of us who are saved. Be it known right now that at this present moment every man and woman is either saved or lost. Salvation is not a blessing just to be enjoyed on the deathbed and to be sung of in a future state above, but a matter to be obtained, received, promised, and enjoyed now.

God has saved His saints—not partly saved them, but perfectly and completely saved them. The Christian is perfectly saved in God's purpose. God has ordained him unto salvation, and that purpose is complete.

The Christian is also saved as to the price that has been paid for him, for this is done, not in part, but in whole. The substitutionary work that Christ has offered is not a certain proportion of the work to be done. *"It is finished!"* (John 19:30) was the cry of the Savior before He died, and so it is complete.

The believer is also perfectly saved in his Covenant Head. Just as we were utterly lost as soon as Adam fell, before we had committed any actual sin, so also every man in Christ was saved in the Second Adam when He finished His work. The Savior completed His work, and He did so in the sense in which Paul used that expression, *"who has saved us."*

Singular Order

This completeness is one facet of God's method, but we must move on to the next. I want you to notice the order as well as the completeness in our text: "[God] *has saved us and called us.*" What? He saved us before He called us? Yes, so the text says. But is a man saved before he is called by grace? Not in his own experience, not as far as the work of God the Holy Spirit goes, but he is saved in God the Father's purpose, in God the Son's redemptive payment, and in the person's relationship to his Covenant Head. Moreover, he is saved in this respect: the work of his salvation has been completed, and he has only to receive it as a finished work.

In past times when men were imprisoned for debts they could not pay, it would have been quite correct for you to step into the cell of a debtor and say to him, "I have freed you," if you had paid his debts and obtained an order for his discharge. He was still in prison at that moment, but you really had liberated him as soon as you paid his debts. It is true he was still in prison when you visited him, but he was not legally there. No sooner did he know that the debt had been paid and the receipt pleaded before proper authorities than the man obtained his liberty.

Likewise, the Lord Jesus Christ paid the incalculable debts of His people before they knew anything about it. Did He not pay them on the cross almost two thousand years ago to the utmost penny? Is this not the reason why, as soon as He meets with us in grace, He cries, "I have saved you. I have paid your debt. Take hold of the eternal life I am offering to you"? We are, then, virtually, though not actually, saved before we are called. "[God] *has saved us and called us.*"

With a Holy Calling

There is yet a third characteristic, and that is in connection with our holy calling. God has *"called us with a holy calling."* Those whom the Savior saved on the tree are in due time effectively called to holiness by the power of God the Holy Spirit. They leave their sins; they endeavor to be like Christ; they choose holiness, not out of any compulsion, but from the influence of a new nature. This leads them to rejoice in holiness, just as naturally as they had before delighted in sin. The old nature loved everything that was evil, but the new nature cannot sin because it is *"born of God"* (1 John 3:9) and loves everything that is good.

Did Paul mention this result of our calling in order to address those who say that God calls His people because He foresees their holiness? No, God calls them to that holiness (1 Thess. 4:7). That holiness is not a cause, but an effect. It is not the motive of His purpose, but the result of His purpose. He neither chose them nor called them because they were holy, but He called them so that they might be holy. Holiness is the beauty produced by His workmanship

29

in them (Eph. 2:10). The excellence that we see in a believer is as much the work of God as is the Atonement itself.

Altogether by Grace

This second point brings out very sweetly the fullness of the grace of God. First, salvation must be of grace, because the Lord is the Author of it. What motive but grace could move Him to save the guilty? In the next place, salvation must be of grace because the Lord works in such a manner that our righteousness is forever excluded. Salvation is completed by God. Therefore, it is not of man, neither is it by man. Salvation is generated by God in an order that puts our holiness as a consequence and not as a cause. Thus, merit is forever disowned.

Not by Our Works

When a speaker desires to strengthen his point and to make himself clear, he generally includes a negative for contrast. Thus, the apostle Paul added a negative: *"not according to our works."* The world's preaching is, "Do as well as you can, live a moral life, and God will save you." The gospel preaching is this: "You are a lost sinner and deserve nothing of God but His displeasure; if you are to be saved, it must be by an act of sovereign grace. God must freely extend the silver scepter of His love to you, for you are a guilty wretch who deserves to be sent to the lowest hell. Your best works are so full of sin that they can in no way save you. To the free mercy of God, you owe all."

Someone says, "Are good works of no use?" God's works are of use when a man is saved. They are the evidences of his being saved, but good works do not save a man. Good works do not influence the mind of God to save a man. If it were so, salvation would be a matter of debt and not of grace. The Lord has declared repeatedly in His Word, *"Not of works, lest anyone should boast"* (Eph. 2:9).

In his epistle to the Galatians, Paul was very strong about this point. Indeed, he thundered it out again and again. Paul denied that salvation is even so much as in part due to our works:

> *Knowing that a man is not justified by the works of the law but by faith in Jesus Christ, even we have believed in Christ Jesus, that we might be justified by faith in Christ and not by*

the works of the law; for by the works of the law no flesh shall be justified. (Gal. 2:16)

Paul assured us that the two principles of grace and merit can no more mix together than fire and water; that if man is to be saved by the mercy of God, it must be by the mercy of God and not by works; but if man is to be saved by works, it must be by works entirely and not by mercy mixed in, for mercy and works will not blend together.

And if by grace, then it is no longer of works; otherwise grace is no longer grace. But if it is of works, it is no longer grace; otherwise work is no longer work. (Rom. 11:6)

Jesus saves, but He does all the work or none. He is Author and Finisher, and works must not rob Him of His due. Sinner, you must either receive salvation freely from the hand of Divine Bounty, or else you must earn it by your own unassisted merits, the latter being utterly impossible for any human being. Oh, may you yield to the first.

Friends, this is the truth that still needs to be preached. This is the truth that shook all of Europe from end to end when Luther first proclaimed it. Is this not one of the thunderbolts that the great reformer hurled at Rome: *"Being justified freely by His grace through the redemption that is in Christ Jesus"* (Rom. 3:24)?

But why did God make salvation to be by faith? Scripture tells us, *"Therefore it is of faith that it might be according to grace"* (Rom. 4:16). If it had been by works, it must have been from debt; but since it is of faith, we can clearly see that there can be no deserving work in faith. It must be therefore by grace.

His Eternal Purpose

The text becomes even more explicit, for we find that God's eternal purpose is now mentioned. The next thing the apostle Paul said was this: *"[God] has saved us and called us with a holy calling, not according to our works, but according to His own purpose."* Mark those words, *"according to His own purpose."* Oh, how some people squirm over those words, as if they were worms on a fisherman's hook! Yet there it stands, and it cannot be eradicated. God saves His people *"according to His purpose"*—no, *"according to His*

31

own purpose." Friends, do you not see how all the merit and the power of the creature are eliminated when you are saved, not according to your purpose, but *"according to His own purpose"*?

If anyone is saved, it is not because he purposed to be saved, but because God purposed to save him. Have you never read the Holy Spirit's testimony: *"It is not of him who wills, nor of him who runs, but of God who shows mercy"* (Rom. 9:16)?

The Savior said to His disciples what He in effect says also to us: *"You did not choose Me, but I chose you and appointed you that you should go and bear fruit"* (John 15:16). Some people have one viewpoint and some hold another concerning the freedom of the will, but our Savior's statement was this: *"But you are not willing to come to Me that you may have life"* (John 5:40). You will not come by your own will, because your will would never bring you. If you do come, it is only because you are so inclined by grace: *"No one can come to Me unless the Father who has sent Me draws him"* (John 6:44). *"The one who comes to Me I will by no means cast out"* (v. 37) is a great and precious general Scripture, but it is quite consistent with the rest of the same verse: *"All that the Father gives Me will come to Me."*

Our text tells us that our salvation is *"according to His own purpose."* It is a strange thing that men should be so angry about the purpose of God. We ourselves have a purpose. We permit our fellow creatures to have some will of their own, especially in giving away their own goods, but supposedly God is to be bound and fettered by men and not permitted to do as He wills with His own. However, know this, you who *"reply against God"* (Rom. 9:20): He pays no attention to your arguments, but He asks you, "Can I not do as I will with My own?"

> *All the inhabitants of the earth are reputed as nothing; He does according to His will in the army of heaven and among the inhabitants of the earth. No one can restrain His hand or say to Him, "What have You done?"* (Dan. 4:35)

Dependent on Grace Alone

Lest we should make any mistake, the text then adds, *"According to His own purpose and grace."* The purpose of God is not founded on any foreseen merit of ours, but on His grace alone. It is grace, all grace, and nothing but grace from first to last. Man

32

stands shivering outside, a condemned criminal, and God, sitting upon the throne, sends the messenger to tell him that He is willing to receive sinners and to pardon them. The sinner replies, "Well, I am willing to be pardoned if I am permitted to do something in order to earn pardon. If I can stand before the King and claim that I have done something to win His favor, I am quite willing to come."

However, the messenger replies, "No, if you are pardoned, you must understand that it is entirely and wholly as an act of grace on God's part. He sees absolutely nothing good in you. He knows that there is nothing good in you. He is willing to take you just as you are—bad, wicked, and undeserving. He is willing to give you graciously what He would not sell to you for any price (Isa. 55:1) and what He knows you cannot earn from Him. Will you receive His gift?"

In the natural state, every man says, "No, the very idea is abhorrent to me. I will not be saved in that style." Well then, misguided soul, remember that you will never be saved at all, for God's way is salvation by grace. If ever you are saved, my dear one, you will have to confess that you never deserved or merited one single blessing from the God of grace. You will have to give all the glory to His holy name if you ever get to heaven.

Note that even in the matter of the acceptance of this offered mercy, you will never receive it unless He makes you willing. He does freely present it to every one of you, and He honestly bids you to come to Christ and live. However, I know that you will never come of your own accord, unless the effectual grace that first provided mercy makes you willing to accept that mercy by the working of the Holy Spirit. Thus, our text tells us it is *according to His own purpose and grace.*

A Free Gift

Again, in order to shut out everything that might lead to boasting, notice that the whole is spoken of as a gift. Lest we should still slip away from the fold—for we are such straying sheep in this matter—it is added, *His own purpose and grace which was given to us.* The wording was not "which was sold to us," "which we earned," or "which was offered to us," but *which was given to us.* The apostle Paul stated it here in such a way that it would be a deathblow to all of our supposed merit: *which was given to us.* It was given to us. What can be freer than a gift, and what is more evidently of grace?

The Medium of Bestowal

Further, the gift is bestowed through a medium that glorified Christ. It is written, *"Which was given to us in Christ Jesus."* We ask to have mercy from the fountainhead of grace, but we dare not ask even to make the bucket in which the precious draught of grace is to be brought to us. Christ is to be the sacred vessel in which the grace of God is to be presented to our thirsty lips. Now, where is boasting? Why surely, there it sits at the foot of the cross and sings,

God forbid that I should glory
Save in the cross of our Lord Jesus Christ.

Is this not grace and grace alone? No room exists here for merit or works or boasting, but only for grateful, humble hearts to receive the *"grace which was given to us in Christ Jesus."*

From Eternity Past

Still further, a time frame is given in the text: *"before time began."* These last words seem to me to lay prostrate forever all idea of anything of our own merits in saving ourselves, because it is here witnessed that God gave us grace *"before time began."* Where were you then? What hand held you in it *"before time began"*?

If you can, go back in your imagination to those ancient years when the venerable mountains were not yet formed, when world and sun and moon and stars were all in embryo in God's great mind, when the unnavigated sea of space had never been disturbed by wings of seraphim, when the awesome silence of eternity had never been startled by the song of cherubim—when God dwelt alone. If you can conceive that time before all time, that vast eternity, it was then God extended His *"grace which was given to us in Christ Jesus."* What, O soul, did you have to do with that? Where were your merits then? Where were you yourself? You who *"are counted as the small dust on the scales"* (Isa. 40:15), where were you? See how Jehovah reigned, dispensing mercy as He would and ordaining unto eternal life without taking counsel of man or angel, for neither man nor angel then had an existence. So that it might be all of grace, He gave us grace *"before time began."*

I have honestly explained the doctrine of the text, and nothing more. If such is not the meaning of our text, I do not know the meaning of it, and I cannot therefore tell you what it is, but I believe that I have given the natural and grammatical teaching of the verse. If you do not like the doctrine, I cannot help it. I did not write the text, and if I have to expound it, I must expound it honestly as it is in my Master's Word. Whatever you may do with what I say, I pray that you may receive what He says.

The Efficacy of the Doctrine

Now, I will try to show some of the effects of the doctrine of grace, which has been set in the storeroom of religious remnants by many. It is acknowledged to be true, for it is confessed in most creeds: it is in the Church of England articles, and it is in the confessions of all sorts of Protestant Christians, except those who are avowedly Arminian.* Yet how little is it ever preached or taught! It has been put among the relics of the past, considered to be a respectable sort of retired officer who is not expected to see any more active service. I believe that it is not an antiquated officer in the Master's army, but rather that it is as full of force and vigor as ever. So what is the purpose of this doctrine of grace?

Boldness

First, it is clear from the context that grace has a tendency to embolden the one who receives it. Paul told Timothy, *"Do not be ashamed of the testimony of our Lord"* (2 Tim. 1:8). He then gave this as the motive and reason: how could a man be ashamed when he believes that God has given him grace in Christ Jesus before the world existed?

Suppose a man is very poor. "What does it matter?" says he. "Though I have but a little oil in my cruet and a little meal in my barrel, yet I have a lot and a portion in everlasting things. My name is not in Burke's *Peerage,* but it is in the book of God's election and was there before the world began." Such a man dares to look the proudest of his friends in the face.

---

* Jacobus Arminius (1560–1609) was a Dutch Reformed theologian whose teachings opposed Calvin's strict doctrine of absolute predestination. Arminius denied the Calvinistic doctrine of irresistible grace by asserting the compatibility of divine sovereignty and human free will, thus maintaining the possibility of salvation for all.

This was the doctrine on which the brave old Ironsides, the soldiers under Oliver Cromwell's leadership, fed—the men who, when they rode to battle with the war cry of "The Lord of Hosts!" made the cavaliers fly before them like chaff before the wind. There is no doctrine like it for putting a backbone into a man and making him feel that he is made for something better than to be trodden down like straw for the dunghill beneath a despot's heel. Sneer whoever will, the elect of God derive a nobility from the divine choice that no royal lineage can outshine.

Confident Belief

I pray that free grace would be preached more often, because it gives men something to believe with confidence. The great mass of professing Christians know nothing of doctrine. Their religion consists in going a certain number of times to a place of worship, but they have no care for truth one way or another. I have talked with a large number of people who have been members of other churches for years. When I have asked them a few questions about doctrinal matters, it did not seem to me that they were in error. They were perfectly willing to believe almost anything that any earnest man might teach them, but they did not know anything. They had no minds of their own and no definite opinions. Our children who have learned *The Westminster Assembly's Confession of Faith* know more about the doctrines of grace and the doctrines of the Bible than hundreds of grown-up people who attend a ministry that very eloquently teaches nothing.

It was observed by a very excellent critic not long ago that if you were to hear thirteen lectures on astronomy or geology, you might get a pretty good idea about the science and the theoretical position of the person who gave the lectures; however, if you were to hear thirteen hundred sermons from some ministers, you would not know anything at all about what they were preaching or what their doctrinal sentiments were. It should not be so.

The reason Puseyism[*] spreads so, and all sorts of other errors have such a foothold, is that our people as a whole do not know what they believe. In contrast, the doctrines of the Gospel, if they have been well received, give to a man something that he knows,

---

[*] A system of High Church principles set forth in a series of tracts by Oxford theologian, Edward Pusey (1800–1882).

something that he holds on to, something that will become dear to him, and something for which he would be prepared to die if the fires of persecution were again kindled.

Keeping Power

Even better is the fact that this doctrine not only gives a man something to hold on to, but it also holds the man. Let a man once have it etched in his heart that salvation is of God, not of man, and that God's grace, not human merit, is to be glorified, and you will never get that belief out of him. It is the rarest thing in all the world to hear of such a man ever becoming an apostate.

Other doctrine is slippery ground, like the slope of a mountain composed of loose earth and rolling stones, down which the traveler may slide long before he can even get a transient foothold. However, this is like a granite step upon the eternal pyramid of truth. Get your feet on this, and there is no fear of slipping so far as doctrinal standing is concerned. If we want to have our churches well instructed and holding fast to the truth, we must bring out the grand old gospel doctrine of the eternal purpose of God in Christ Jesus before the world began. Oh, may the Holy Spirit write it on our hearts!

Moreover, friends, this doctrine overwhelms, as with an avalanche, all the claims of the priesthood. Let it be told to men that they are saved by God, and they say at once, "Then what is the need of the priest?" If they are told it is God's grace, they reply, "Then the priest does not need our money to buy masses and absolutions," and the truth of the Gospel becomes clear.

Beloved, this is the battering ram that God uses with which to shake the gates of hell. How much more forcible this truth is than the pretty essays of many religious writers, which have no more power than bulrushes, no more light than smoking flax. Why do you suppose people met in the woods during times of persecution, assembled by the thousands outside the town of Antwerp and such places on the Continent, in jeopardy of their lives? Do you suppose they would ever have come together to hear the poor milk-and-water theology of this age, or to receive the lukewarm, insipid pabulum of our modern anti-Calvinists? Not they, my friends. They needed stronger meat and a more savory diet to attract them. Do you imagine that, when it was death to listen to the preacher, people, under the cover of night and amid the winds of tempest, would then listen to philosophical essays or to mere moral precepts or to diluted, adulterated, soulless, theological suppositions? No, there is no energy in that kind of thing to draw people together when they fear for their lives.

But what did bring them together in the dead of night amid the glare of lightning and the roll of thunder? What idea brought them together? Why, the doctrine of the grace of God, the doctrine of Jesus, the doctrine of His servants: Paul, Augustine, Luther, and Calvin. Something in the doctrine touches the heart of the Christian and gives him the kind of food that his soul loves—savory meat, suitable to his heaven-born appetite. To hear this, men braved death and defied the sword.

If we are to see once again the scarlet hat plucked from the wearer's head and the shaved crowns with all the gaudy trumpery of Rome sent back to the place from where they came—and may heaven grant that they take our Puseyite Established Church with them—it must be by declaring the doctrines of the grace of God. When these are declared and vindicated in every place, we will yet again make these enemies of God and man know that they cannot stand their ground for a moment. There is no room for these enemies where men of God wield *"the sword of the LORD and of Gideon"* (Judg. 7:20) by preaching the doctrines of the grace of God.

Change of Focus

Beloved, let a man receive these truths, let them be written in his heart by the Holy Spirit, and they will make him look up. He will say, "God has saved me!" and he will walk with a constant eye toward God. He will not forget to see the hand of God in nature and in providence. He will, on the contrary, discern the Lord working in all places and will humbly adore Him. He will not give the glory due to the Most High to laws of nature or schemes of government, but he will have respect for the unseen Ruler. "What the Lord says to me, that will I do" is the believer's language. "What is His will, that will I follow; what is His word, that will I believe; what is His promise, on that I will live." It is a blessed habit to teach a man to look up to God in all things.

At the same time, this doctrine makes a man look down on himself. "Ah," says he, "I am nothing; there is nothing in me to merit esteem. I have no goodness of my own. If I am saved, I cannot praise myself. I cannot in any way honor myself. God has done it. God alone has done it." Nothing makes the man so humble, but nothing makes him so glad. Nothing lays him so low at the mercy seat, but nothing makes him so brave to look his fellowman in the face. It is a grand truth. I pray to God that you all would know its mighty power!

Comfort

Last, this precious truth is full of comfort to the sinner, and that is why I love it. As it has been preached by some, it has been exaggerated and made into a source of dread. Why, there are some who preach the doctrine of election as though it were a line of sharp spikes to keep a sinner from coming to Christ, or as though it were a menacing battle-ax to be pushed into the breast of a sinner to keep him away from mercy. It is not so.

Sinner, whoever you may be, wherever you may be, your greatest comfort should be to know that salvation is by grace. Why, if it were by merit, what would become of you? Suppose that God saved men on account of their merits. Where, then, would you drunkards be? Where would you swearers be? You who have been unclean and unchaste, you whose hearts have cursed God, and you who even now do not love Him, where would you be?

However, when salvation is all of grace, then all of your past life, however black and filthy it may be, does not need to keep you from coming to Jesus. Christ receives sinners. God has elected sinners. He has elected some of the blackest of sinners, so why not you? He receives everyone who comes to Him; He will not cast you out. (See John 6:37.) There have been some who have hated Him, insulted Him to His face, burned His servants alive, and persecuted Him through His members. Yet as soon as they have cried, *"God, be merciful to me a sinner"* (Luke 18:13), He has given them mercy at once. He will give it to you if you are led to seek it.

If I had to tell you that you were to work out your own salvation apart from His grace, it would be an impossible prospect for you. Instead, it comes to you in this way: Filthy, there is washing for you! Dead, there is life for you! Naked, there is raiment for you! All undone and ruined, here is complete salvation for you! O soul, may you have the grace given to you to grasp it, and then you and I together will sing the praises of the glory of divine grace.

Chapter 3

Grace, the One Way of Salvation

We believe that through the grace of the Lord Jesus Christ we shall
be saved in the same manner as they.
—Acts 15:11

Y ou who are familiar with Scripture will recall that these are
the words of the apostle Peter. Paul and Barnabas had been
preaching the Gospel among the Gentiles with great success,
but *"some of the sect of the Pharisees who believed"* (Acts 15:5)
could not get rid of their old Jewish bigotry and legalism. They ve-
hemently urged that the converted Gentiles ought to be circumcised or else they could not be saved. They made a great clamor
over this, causing no small dissension and disputing (v. 2). The
children of the bondwoman (see Genesis 21:9–10; Galatians 4:22–
23, 30–31) mustered all their forces, while the champions of
glorious liberty arrayed themselves for the battle.

Paul and Barnabas, those valiant soldiers of the Cross, stood
out stoutly against the ritualistic brothers, telling them that the
rite of circumcision did not belong to the Gentiles at all and ought
not to be forced upon them. They would not yield their principles of
freedom to the dictation of the Judaizers; they scorned to bow their
necks to the yoke of bondage.

It was agreed to bring the matter up for decision at Jerusalem
before the apostles and elders. When all the elders had assembled,
there seems to have been a considerable dispute. During the midst
of it, Peter, speaking with his usual boldness and clearness, declared that it would be wrong to put a heavy yoke upon the necks of
the Gentiles, which neither that generation of Jews nor their fathers had been able to bear (Acts 15:10). He then concluded his address by saying, in effect, "Although these people are not
circumcised and ought not to be, yet we believe that there is no difference between the Jew and the Gentile, and *'through the grace of*

the Lord Jesus Christ we shall be saved in the same manner as they.'" Peter was not to be blamed for his words, but to be greatly commended, for he spoke under the influence of the Spirit of God.

An Apostolic Confession of Faith

We will use our study text, *"We believe that through the grace of the Lord Jesus Christ we shall be saved in the same manner as they,"* as concisely as we can for three important purposes. In the first place, we will look on it as an apostolic confession of faith.

Notice it begins with, *"We believe."* Thus, we will call it the "Apostles' Creed," and we may rest assured that it has quite as clear a right to that title as the highly esteemed composition that is commonly called the "Nicene Creed" or "Apostles' Creed."

Here, we find that Peter was speaking for the rest, for he declared, *"We believe."* Well, Peter, what do you believe? We are all at attention. Peter's statement of faith was this: *"We believe that through the grace of the Lord Jesus Christ we shall be saved in the same manner as they."*

There is a great deal of talk in our day—foolish, vainglorious, idiotic, senseless talk—on the subject of apostolic succession. Some people think they have the direct line from the apostles running right to their feet, and others believe that those who make the greatest boast about it have the least claim to it.

Some clergymen imagine that because they happen to be in a church that is in open alliance with the state government, they must necessarily be ministers of the church, but Christ said, *"My kingdom is not of this world"* (John 18:36). I think that their union with the state is in itself a conclusive reply to all such claims to apostolic succession.

Moreover, I find many fatal points of difference between the apostles and their professed successors. When did Peter or Paul ever become state-paid ministers? In what state church did they enroll themselves? What tithes did they receive? What rates did they levy? What constraints did they make on the Jews and the Gentiles? Were they rectors or vicars, chaplains or deans, canons or curates? Did they sit in the Roman House of Lords dressed in fancy clothes? Were they titled Right Reverend Fathers in God? Were they appointed by the prime minister of the day? Did they put on gowns and read prayers out of a book? Did they christen children and call them regenerate, and did they bury wicked reprobates in sure and certain hope of a blessed resurrection?

41

As opposite as light is from darkness were those apostles from the men who pretend to be their divinely-appointed successors. When will men cease to thrust their arrogance into our faces? Only when common sense, to say nothing of the religion of our country, has rebuked their presumption.

Ritualism or Grace?

One thing is clear from this "Apostles' Creed" that we have before us: the apostles did not believe in ritualism. Peter—why, they make him out to be the head of the church! Do they not say that he was the first pope? I am sure that if Peter were here, he would grow very angry with them for slandering him so scandalously. In his first epistle Peter expressly warned others against *"being lords over God's heritage"* (1 Pet. 5:3 KJV), and you may be sure he did not fall into that sin himself.

When he was asked for his confession of faith, Peter stood up and declared that he believed in salvation *"through the grace of the Lord Jesus Christ"* alone. *"We believe."* O bold apostle, what do you believe? Now we can still hear his statement. Did Peter say, "We believe in circumcision; we believe in regeneration by baptism; we believe in the sacramental efficacy of the Lord's Supper; we believe in pompous ceremonies; we believe in priests and altars and robes and rubrics and incense and the mass"? Absolutely not! He did not utter a syllable concerning anything of the kind. He declared, *"We believe that through the grace of the Lord Jesus Christ we* [who have been circumcised] *shall be saved in the same manner as they* [who have not been circumcised]."

Peter made very small account, it seems, of ceremonies in the matter of salvation. He took care that no iota of Sacramentarianism would mar his explicit confession of faith. He gloried in no rite and rested in no ordinance. All of Peter's testimony concerned the grace of the Lord Jesus Christ. He said nothing whatsoever about ordinances, ceremonies, apostolic gifts, or ecclesiastical unction—his theme was grace, and grace alone.

My beloved, the true successors of the apostles are those who teach you that you are saved through the unmerited favor and free mercy of God, those who agree with Peter in their testimony, *"We believe that through the grace of the Lord Jesus Christ we shall be saved."* These are the men who preach to you the Gospel of salvation through the blood and righteousness of Jesus.

However, the false ministers who boast about their priesthood preach *"a different gospel, which is not another; but there are some who trouble you and want to pervert the gospel of Christ"* (Gal. 1:6–7). On their heads will be the blood of deluded souls. They profess to regenerate others, but they will perish themselves. They talk of sacramental grace but will receive eternal destruction. Woe to them, for they are deceivers. May the Lord deliver this land from their superstitions.

Merit versus Grace

Another thing is very clear here. The apostle did not believe in self-righteousness. The creed of the world is, "Do your best, and it will be all right with you." To question this maxim is treason against the pride of human nature that forever clings to salvation by its own merits. Every man is born a Pharisee. Confidence in the self and reliance on the self are bred in the bone—and will come out in the flesh.

"What," says a man, "do you not believe that if a man does his best, he will fare well in the next world? Why, surely you know that we must all live as well as we can, every man according to his own light; and if every man follows his own conscience, as closely as possible, certainly it will be well with him here and in the world to come. How could you possibly believe otherwise?"

That is not what Peter said. Peter did not say, "We believe we will be saved like other people through doing our best." He did not even say, "We believe if we act according to our own light, God will accept that little light for what it was." No, the apostle struck out on quite another track and solemnly affirmed, *"We believe that through the grace of the Lord Jesus Christ we shall be saved,"* not through our good works, not through anything that we do, not by the merit of anything that we feel or that we perform or that we promise to perform, but by grace, that is to say, by the free favor of God.

> Perish each thought of human pride,
> Let God alone be magnified.

We believe that if we are ever saved at all, we must be saved without cost; saved as the gratuitous act of a bountiful God; saved by a gift, not by wages; saved by God's love, not by our own works

43

or merits. This is the apostles' creed: salvation is all of grace from first to last, and the channel of that grace is the Lord Jesus Christ, who loved and lived and died and rose again for our salvation.

Those who preach mere morality, or set up any way except that of trusting in the grace of God through Christ Jesus, preach another gospel. They will be accursed, even though they preach it with an angel's eloquence. (See Galatians 1:8–9.) When the Lord comes to discern between the righteous and the wicked, their work will be burned in the fire as wood, hay, and straw. But those who preach salvation by grace through Jesus Christ will find that their work, like gold and silver and precious stones, will endure the fire, and great will be their reward. (See 1 Corinthians 3:10–15.)

The Question of Free Will

I think it is very clear, again, from the text, that the apostles did not believe in salvation by the natural force of free will. I fail to detect a trace of the glorification of free will here. Peter put it, *"We believe that...we shall be saved."* Through what? Through our own unbiased will? Through the volition of our own well-balanced nature? Not at all, but *"We believe that through the grace of the Lord Jesus Christ we shall be saved."*

Peter took the crown off the head of man in all respects and gave all glory to the grace of God. He extolled God, the gracious Sovereign, who *"will have mercy on whomever* [He] *will have mercy, and* [who] *will have compassion on whomever* [He] *will have compassion"* (Rom. 9:15). I wish I had a voice of thunder to proclaim in every street of London this glorious doctrine:

> *For by grace you have been saved through faith, and that not of yourselves; it is the gift of God, not of works, lest anyone should boast.* (Eph. 2:8–9)

Here is the old Reformation doctrine. This is the doctrine that will shake the very gates of hell if it is but faithfully preached. Oh, for an army of witnesses to publish abroad the Gospel of grace in its sovereignty, omnipotence, and fullness. If you are ever to have comfort, believe me, dear one, you must receive the doctrine of salvation by free grace into your soul as the delight and solace of your heart, for it is the living truth of the living God. Not by ritualism, not by good works, not by our own unaided free will, but by the grace of God alone are we saved.

> Not for the works which we have done,
> Or shall hereafter do,
> Hath God decreed on sinful worms
> Salvation to bestow.
>
> The glory, Lord, from first to last,
> Is due to Thee alone:
> Aught to ourselves we dare not take,
> Or rob Thee of Thy crown.

Human Ruin

Were I now to divide this apostles' creed into small pieces and examine it in detail, it would be easy to show that many important truths are contained within it. Most evidently, it implies the doctrine of human ruin. *"We believe that...we shall be saved."* That statement assuredly implies that all of us need to be saved. The apostle Peter was as sound in the faith concerning the total depravity of human nature as was the apostle Paul. Peter viewed man as a lost creature, needing to be saved by grace. He believed in those three great Rs—ruin, redemption, and regeneration. He saw most clearly man's ruin, or he would not have been so explicit about man's salvation.

If Peter were here preaching to us, he would not tell us that man, though he is a little fallen, is still a noble creature, who needs only a little assistance to be able to right himself. From some pulpits that awful false teaching has oozed, anointing corruption with the oil of hypocrisy, besmearing the abomination of our depravity with sickening flattery!

Peter would not give any sanction to such false prophets. No, he would faithfully testify that man is dead in sin; that life is a gift; and that man is lost, utterly fallen, and completely ruined. He wrote about the former lusts of our ignorance (1 Pet. 1:14), of our *"aimless conduct received by tradition from [our] fathers"* (v. 18), and of the *"corruption that is in the world through lust"* (2 Pet. 1:4). In our present text, he declared that the best of men, men such as himself and the other apostles, had need of salvation. Consequently, they must have been originally among the lost—heirs of wrath just as all other men are.

I am sure that he was a firm believer in what are called the doctrines of grace, as he was certainly in his own person an illustrious trophy and everlasting monument of grace.

What a ring there is in that word *grace*. Why, it does one good to speak it and to hear it; it is, indeed, a charming sound, harmonious to the ear. When one feels the power of it, it is enough to make the soul leap out of the body for joy.

> Grace! How good, how cheap, how free,
> Grace, how easy to be found!
> Only let your misery
> In the Savior's blood be drowned!

Grace, how it suits a sinner! How it cheers a poor forlorn wanderer from God! Peter was not in a fog about this; his witness was as clear as crystal, decisive as the sentence of a judge. He believed that salvation was of God's free favor and God's almighty power. He spoke out like a man, *"We believe that through the grace of the Lord Jesus Christ we shall be saved."*

Christ's Atonement for Sins

Our apostle was also most decided and explicit concerning the Atonement. Can you see the Atonement in the text, sparkling like a jewel in a well-made ring? We are saved *"through the grace of the Lord Jesus Christ."* What did the apostle mean but the grace that came streaming from those wounds when the Savior hung on the cross? What did he mean but the grace that is revealed to us in the bleeding Sufferer who took our sins and carried our sorrows (Isa. 53:4), so that we might be delivered from wrath through Him? Oh, that all were as clear about the Atonement as Peter was!

Peter had seen his Master. No, even more, his Master had looked at him and broken his heart, and afterward Christ had bound it up and given him much grace. Thus, Peter was not content to state, "We believe that we shall be saved through grace." Rather, he was careful to word it: *"We believe that through the grace of the Lord Jesus Christ we shall be saved."*

Dear ones, never have any questions on the vital point of redemption by the shed blood of Jesus Christ. This is a fundamental truth. He who is in darkness on this subject has no light in him. What the sun is to the heavens, the doctrine of a vicarious satisfaction is to theology. Atonement is the brain and spinal cord of

Christianity. Take away the cleansing blood, and what is left for the guilty? Deny the substitutionary work of Jesus, and you have denied all that is precious in the New Testament. Never let us endure one wavering, doubtful thought about this all-important truth.

Eternal Security

It seems to me, too, that without straining the text, I might easily prove that Peter believed in the doctrine of the final perseverance of the saints. They were not, in a certain sense, it seems, perfectly saved when he spoke, but he said, *"We believe that...we shall be saved."* But, Peter, could someone not fall away and perish? "No," Peter would reply. *"We believe that through the grace of the Lord Jesus Christ we shall be saved."* How positively he expressed it!

I desire that you grasp a firm and intelligent hold of the doctrine of the safety of the believer, which is as clear as noonday in the Scriptures. On the whole, you have learned it and can defend it well, but all of you should *"be ready to give a defense to everyone who asks you a reason for the hope that is in you"* (1 Pet. 3:15).

One of my congregation was met by those who do not believe this doctrine. They said to him, "You will fall away; look at your own weakness and tendency to sin." He responded, "No, I know I would if I were left to myself, but then Christ has promised that He will never leave me or forsake me" (Heb. 13:5). Then they questioned, "But might you be a believer in Christ today, yet perish tomorrow?" The question was met with this reply: "Do not tell me that falsehood! God's saints will never perish, neither will anyone pluck them out of Jesus' hand (John 10:28). As for your doctrine of the final falling of the Lord's blood-bought ones, if that is the Gospel, go and keep it to yourselves. As for me, I would not go two inches to listen to it; there is nothing in it to lay hold of; it is a bone without marrow; there is no strength, no comfort for the soul in it!"

If I know when I trust Christ that He will save me at the last, then I have something to rest on, something worth living for, but if it is all a mere *if* or *but* or *maybe* or *perhaps*, a little of myself and a little of Christ, I am in a poor state indeed. A gospel that proclaims an uncertain salvation is a miserable deception. Away with such a gospel; it is a dishonor to Christ, and it is a discredit to God's people. It neither came from the Scriptures of truth, nor does it bring glory to God.

Thus, I have tried to reveal to you the apostles' fundamental belief: *"We believe that through the grace of the Lord Jesus Christ we shall be saved in the same manner as they."*

The Statement of a Moral Convert

Having used the text as the apostles' confession of faith, I will explain it as the statement of a convert who had lived a moral life. Let me show you what I mean. Observe the way in which Peter handled the case. A company of Jews had assembled to discuss a certain matter, and some of them looked very wise and brought up suggestions that were rather significant. Their discussion went something like this: "Well, perhaps these Gentile dogs may be saved. Yes, Jesus Christ told us to go and preach the Gospel to every creature; therefore, He must have included these Gentile dogs. We do not like them, though, and must keep them as much under our rules and regulations as we can; we must compel them to be circumcised; we must have them brought under the full rigor of the law; we cannot excuse them from wearing the yoke of bondage."

After that, the apostle Peter got up to speak. These gentlemen expected him to affirm them by saying, "Why, these 'Gentile dogs,' as you call them, can be saved, even as you." Instead, he adopted quite a different tone. He turned the tables and said to them, "We believe that you may be saved, even as they."

A modern parallel would be if I located twenty people who had been very bad and wicked, who had plunged into the deepest sin, but God's grace has met with them and made them new creations in Christ Jesus (2 Cor. 5:17). Suppose I brought these people before a church meeting, and there were some of the members who said, "Well, yes, we believe that a drunkard may be saved, and a person who has been a harlot may, perhaps, be saved, too." But imagine, now, that I were to stand up and reply, "Now, my dear friends, I believe that you may be saved even as these." What a rebuke it would be! And that is precisely what Peter meant: "Do not raise the question about whether they can be saved—the question is whether you, who have raised such a question, will be saved. *'We believe that, through the grace of the Lord Jesus Christ, we shall be saved in the same manner as they.'"* Thus, Peter seemed to take the objectors aback and to put the Gentile believers first, in order to cast out the bad, proud, wicked, devilish spirit of self-righteousness.

48

The Favor of Christian Heritage

Now, beloved, some of us were favored by providence with the great privilege of having Christian parents; consequently, we never did know a great deal of the open sin into which others have fallen. Some reading this, perhaps, have never frequented a tavern, do not know a lascivious song, and have never uttered an oath. This is cause for great thankfulness, very great thankfulness indeed. But, you excellent moralists, mind that you do not say in your hearts, "We are quite sure to be saved," for you do not have before God any advantage over the outward transgressor so as to entitle you to be saved in any less humbling manner. If you ever are saved, you will have to be saved in the same way as those who have been permitted to plunge into the most outrageous sin.

Your being restrained from overt offenses is a favor for you to be grateful for, but not a virtue for you to trust in. Ascribe it to God's providential goodness, but do not wrap it about you as though it were to be your wedding garment. If you do, your self-righteousness will be more dangerous to you than some men's open sins are to them. As the Savior put it, *"Tax collectors and harlots enter the kingdom of God before you"* (Matt. 21:31).

Only One Way for All

You moral people must be saved by the grace of our Lord Jesus Christ—*"saved in the same manner as they,"* the outcasts, the wanderers. You will not, you cannot, be saved in any other way, and you will not be saved at all if you do not submit to this way. You will not be permitted to enter heaven, good as you think yourselves to be, unless you accept the terms and conditions that sovereign grace has laid down, namely, that you should trust Christ, and be saved by grace, *"in the same manner as they."*

To prove to you, dear friends, that this must be the case, I will suppose that you have picked out twenty people who have been good, in a moral sense, from their youth up. Now, these people must be saved just the same as those other twenty that I have picked out, who have been as bad as bad can be from their earliest childhood. The reason is that these amiable persons fell in Adam just as surely as the outcasts did. They are as fully partakers of the curse of the Fall as the profane and drunken, and they were born in sin and shaped in iniquity just as the dissolute and the dishonest

49

were. There is no difference in the blood of humanity; it flows from one polluted source and is tainted in all its channels.

The depravity of human nature does not belong merely to those who are born in dirty back courts and alleys, but it is as certainly manifest in those of you who were born in the best parts of the city. The west side of town is as sensual as the east. The corruption of those born in the castle at Windsor is as deep as the depravity of flagrant sinners.

The elite of society are born with hearts as bad and as black as the poorest of the poor. Sons of Christian parents, do not imagine, because you spring from a godly ancestry, that your nature is not polluted like the nature of others. In this respect, we are all alike: we are born in sin (Ps. 51:5), are *"dead in trespasses and sins"* (Eph. 2:1), and are *"by nature children of wrath"* (v. 3).

Remember, too, that although you may not have sinned openly, as others have done, yet in your hearts you have, and it is by your hearts that you will be judged. How often a man may commit adultery or incur the guilt of theft in his soul, while his hand lays idly by his side! Do you not know that a look may have in it the essence of an unclean act (Matt. 5:28) and that a thought may commit murder as well as a hand? God takes note of heart sin as well as hand sin. If you have been outwardly moral, I am thankful for it, and I ask you to be thankful for it, too; but do not trust in it for justification, seeing that you must be saved, even as the worst of criminals are saved, because in heart, if not in life, you have been as bad as they.

The Same Pardon for All

Moreover, the method of pardon is the same in all cases. If you moralists are to be washed, where must you find the purifying bath? I have never discovered a fountain with the capacity except this one:

> There is a fountain filled with blood,
> Drawn from Immanuel's veins.

That fountain is for the dying thief as much as for you, and for you as much as for him. There is a robe of righteousness to cover the best among the living who profess Christ; that same robe of righteousness covered Saul of Tarsus, the bloody persecutor. If you of unspotted outward character are ever to have a robe of righteousness, you must wear the same one as he wore. There cannot be another or a better one.

You who are conscious of outward innocence, humble yourselves at the foot of the cross, and come to Jesus just as empty-handed, just as brokenhearted, as if you had been outwardly among the vilest of the vile, and *"through the grace of the Lord Jesus Christ* [you] *shall be saved in the same manner as they."* May the Holy Spirit bring you to this place.

I do not know whether anybody reading this book has ever fallen into such an unwise thought as I have known some entertain. I met with a case of this sort only the other day. A very excellent and amiable young woman, when converted to God, said to me, "You know, sir, I used almost to wish that I were one of those very bad sinners whom you so often speak to and invite to come to Jesus, because I thought then I should feel my need more. That was my difficulty: I could not feel my need." But see, dear friends, we believe that through the grace of our Lord Jesus Christ, we who have not plunged into black sin shall be saved even as they who have done so. Do not make this a difficulty for yourselves.

Others take the opposite excuse: "I could trust Christ if I had been kept from sin." The fact is that you unbelieving souls will not trust Christ whichever way you have lived, for from some quarter or other, you will find cause for your doubting. But when the Holy Spirit gives you faith, you big sinners will trust Christ quite as readily as those who have not been great open offenders, and you who have been preserved from open sin will trust Him as joyfully as the great transgressors.

Come, you sick souls; come to my Master! Do not say, "We would come if we were worse." Do not say, "We would come if we were better," but come as you are; come just as you are. If you are a sinner, Christ invites you. If you are lost, remember Christ came to save the lost. Do not single out your case and make it to be different from others, but come to the foot of the cross. You are welcome!

> Just as you are, without one trace
> Of love, or joy, or inward grace,
> Or goodness for the heavenly place,
> O guilty sinner, come!
>
> Come, hither bring your boding fears,
> Your aching heart, your bursting tears;

51

'Tis mercy's voice salutes your ears,
O trembling sinner, come.

The Spirit and the Bride say, "Come,"
Rejoicing saints re-echo, "Come";
Who faints, who thirsts, who will, may come:
Your Savior bids you come.

A Converted Sinner's Confession

So far, I have illustrated that the text is the creed of an apostle and the statement of faith of a moral person upon conversion. But our text would not be fairly treated if I did not use it as the confession of the great outward sinner when converted.

I will now address those who, before conversion, indulged in gross sin. Such were some of you. You have been washed; you have been cleansed. Glory be to God! My dear brothers and sisters, I can rejoice over you. More precious are you by far in my eyes than all the precious gems that kings delight to wear, because you are my eternal joy and *"crown of rejoicing"* (1 Thess. 2:19). You have experienced a divine change. You are not what you once were. You are new creations in Christ Jesus (2 Cor. 5:17).

Now, I will explain our text in terms that apply to you. *"We believe that through the grace of the Lord Jesus Christ we shall be saved in the same manner as they."* What do we mean? Why, we believe that we will be saved, even as the best are saved. I will divide that thought, as it were, into individual instances.

Earthly Poverty

In many churches in the back pew or off to the side sits a very poor believer. I am always glad to see such a person in my church. He probably had thoughts that his clothes were not good enough to come in, but I hope none of you will ever stay away from church because of your clothes. Attend services anyhow. The poor are always welcome, and I am glad to see them.

But indeed, my poor friend is in dire financial straits. He perhaps would not like anybody to see the room where he lives. Yet, my brother, do you expect to have a poor man's salvation? Do you expect that when you get to heaven, you will be placed in a distant corner as a pauper pensioner? Do you think that Jesus will only give you the crumbs that fall from His table? (See Matthew 15:22–28.) "Oh, no!" I think I hear you say, "Oh, no! I will leave my poverty when I get to glory."

Some of our friends are rich. They have an abundance of this world's goods. We rejoice to think they have, and hope that they will have, grace to make a proper use of this mercy. Nevertheless, we poor people believe that *"we shall be saved in the same manner as they."* We do not believe that our poverty will make any difference in our share in divine grace, but that we will be as much loved by God as the earthly rich are, as much blessed in our poverty as they are in their riches, and as much enabled by divine grace to glorify God in our sphere as they are in theirs. We do not envy them. On the contrary, we ask grace from God that we may feel that if we are poor in pocket, yet we are rich in faith, and *"shall be saved in the same manner as they."*

Lack of Talent

Others of you are not so much poor in money as you are poor in useful talent. You come to church and fill your seat, and that is about all you can do. You drop your weekly offering in the basket. When that is done, you have done all, or nearly all, in your power. You cannot preach; you could not conduct a prayer meeting; you have hardly courage enough to give away a tract. Well, my dear friend, you are one of the timid ones, of whom there are many.

Now, do you expect that the Lord Jesus Christ will give you a secondhand robe to wear at His wedding feast? When you sit at the banquet, do you think He will serve you from cold and inferior dishes? "Oh, no!" you say. "Some of our friends have great talents, and we are glad that they have. We rejoice in their talents, but we believe that *'we shall be saved in the same manner as they.'* We do not think that there will be any difference made in the divine distribution of mercies because of our degree of ability."

Here on earth, very clear distinctions are made between rich and poor, and between those who are learned and those who are unlearned. However, we believe that there is no distinction in the matter of salvation: *"we shall be saved in the same manner as they."*

Many of you would preach ten times better than I do if you could get your tongues loosened to say what you feel. What red-hot sermons you would preach, and how earnest you would be in their

53

delivery! The sermon that you could not preach will be set down to your account, while perhaps that discourse of mine will be a failure because I may not have preached it as I should have done, with pure motives and a zealous spirit. God knows what you would do if you could, and He judges, not so much according to what you do, as according to your will to do it. He takes the will for the deed, and you *"shall be saved in the same manner as they"* who proclaim the truth with tongues of fire.

Weak in the Faith

Most likely, some doubting person is reading this. Whenever you sing or pray, you probably seldom focus on the victorious celebration of our Lord, but generally you cry out words of contrition. Well, my dear friend, you are a weakling. You are Mr. Much-afraid or Mr. Little-Faith. But how is your heart? What are your prospects? Do you believe that you will be put off with a second-rate salvation, that you will be admitted by the back door into heaven instead of through the gates of pearl (Rev. 21:21)? "Oh, no!" you say. "I am the weakest lamb in Jesus' fold, but I believe that I *'shall be saved in the same manner as they'*—that is, even as they who are the strongest in grace, most useful in labor, and mighties in faith."

Soon, dear friends, I will be crossing the channel. I will suppose that a good stiff wind may arise and that the vessel may be driven off her course and be in danger. I imagine that as I walk the deck, I see a poor girl on board. She is very weak and ill, quite a contrast to the strong, burly passenger who is standing beside her, enjoying the salt spray and the rough wind. Now, suppose a storm comes up. Who of these two is safer? Well, I cannot see any difference, because if the ship goes to the bottom, they will both go, and if the ship gets to the other side of the channel, they will both land in security. The safety is equal when the thing on which they depend is the same.

Likewise, if the weakest Christian is in the boat of salvation— that is, if he trusts Christ—he is as safe as the strongest Christian. If Christ failed the frail one, He would fail the strong one, too. If the weakest Christian who believes in Jesus does not get to heaven, then Peter himself will not get there. I am sure of this: if the smallest star that Christ ever kindled does not blaze in eternity, neither will the brightest one. If any of you who have given yourselves to

Jesus would be cast away, this would prove that Jesus is not able to save; then all of us must be cast away, too. Oh, yes! *"We believe that...we shall be saved in the same manner as they."*

Suppose for a moment that there has been a work of grace in a prison. Out of all the inmates, perhaps six thorough criminals have been redeemed and made new creations by the grace of God. If they have understood the text, as they look in Scripture at the lives of half a dozen apostles—let us say Peter, James, John, Matthew, Mark, and Paul—they might exclaim, *"'We believe that through the grace of our Lord Jesus Christ we shall be saved in the same manner as they,'* even as those apostles are."

Can you catch the idea and make it your own? When artists have drawn pictures of the apostles, they have often put halos around their heads, much like a brass pan or something of that kind, as if to signify that they were some particular and special saints. But in reality, there was no such halo there; the painter is far from the fact. Seriously and thoughtfully, we say that twelve souls picked from the scum of creation who look to Christ shall be saved, even as the twelve apostles are saved. Halo or no halo, they will join in the same hallelujah to God and the Lamb.

Let us select three holy women: the three Marys that we read about in the Gospels, the three Marys whom Jesus loved and who loved Jesus. These holy women, we believe, shall be saved. Now, suppose that I go to one of our refuges for the wayward and find three girls there who were once of evil fame. The grace of God has met with them, and they are now three weeping Magdalenes, penitent for sin. These three might say, humbly, but positively, *"'We believe that through the grace of the Lord Jesus Christ we* [three reclaimed harlots] *shall be saved in the same manner as they,'* the three holy matrons who lived near Christ and were His delight." "Oh!" says one, "This is grace indeed! This is plain speech and wonderful doctrine, that God should make no distinction between one sinner and another when we come to Him through Christ."

Dear friend, if you have understood this very simple statement, come to Jesus at once. May God enable you to obtain complete salvation at this very moment. I pray that you will come in faith to the cross. I pray that my Master's grace will compel you to enter into a state of full dependence on Jesus, and so into a state of salvation. If you are now led to believe on the Lord Jesus Christ, no matter how black your past may have been, please know that *"the blood of Jesus Christ His Son cleanses us from all sin"* (1 John 1:7).

Chapter 4

All of Grace

For by grace you have been saved through faith, and that not of
yourselves; it is the gift of God.
—Ephesians 2:8

O f the things that I have written about over the years, this is
the sum. My theology, as it pertains to salvation, is contained within the circle of these words. I rejoice also to remember that those of my family who were ministers of Christ before me preached this doctrine and none other. My father, who is
still able to bear his personal testimony for his Lord, knows no
other doctrine, and neither did his father before him.

I remember this by a circumstance, recorded in my memory,
that connects this text with my grandfather and me. The event occurred many years ago. It was announced that I was going to
preach in a certain country town in the Eastern counties. I am not
often late, for I feel that punctuality is one of those little virtues
that may prevent great sins. But I have no control over railway delays and breakdowns. Thus, I was considerably tardy when I
reached the appointed place. Like sensible people, they had begun
their worship and had proceeded as far as the sermon.

As I neared the chapel, I perceived that someone was in the
pulpit preaching, and who should the preacher be but my dear,
venerable grandfather? He saw me as I came in the door and made
my way up the aisle. At once he said, "Here comes my grandson! He
may preach the Gospel better than I can, but he cannot preach a
better Gospel—can you, Charles?"

As I made my way through the throng, I answered, "You can
preach better than I can. Do, I pray, go on." But he would not agree
to that.

He insisted that I must take the sermon, and so I did, continuing with the subject just where he left off. "There," said he, "I

was preaching on *'For by grace you have been saved.'* I have been setting forth the source and fountainhead of salvation, and I am now showing them the channel of it, through faith. Now, you take it from there and go on."

I am so much at home with these glorious truths that I did not feel any difficulty in taking from my grandfather the thread of his message and joining my thread to it, so as to continue without a break. Our agreement in the things of God made it easy for us to be joint-preachers of the same topic. I went on with *"through faith,"* and then I proceeded to the next point, *"and that not of yourselves."*

Based on this essential phrase, I was explaining the weakness and inability of human nature and the certainty that salvation could not be of ourselves, when I had my coattail pulled, and my beloved grandfather took his turn again. When I spoke of our depraved human nature, the good old man said, "I know most about that, dear friends." So he took up the parable, and for the next five minutes set forth a solemn and humbling description of our lost estate, the depravity of our natures, and the spiritual death under which we were found.

When he had said his say in a very gracious manner, his grandson was allowed to go on again, to the dear old man's great delight, for now and then he would say in a gentle tone, "Good! Good!" Once he said, "Tell them that again, Charles," and, of course, I did tell them once again. It was a happy exercise for me to share in bearing witness to truths of such vital importance that are so deeply impressed on my heart.

While selecting this text, I seemed to hear that dear voice, which has been so long lost to the earth, saying to me, "Tell them that again." I am not contradicting the testimony of forefathers who are now with God. If my grandfather could return to Earth, he would find me where he left me, steadfast in the faith and true to that form of doctrine *"which was once for all delivered to the saints"* (Jude 3).

I expound on the doctrines of grace because I believe them to be true, because I see them in the Scriptures, because my experience endears them to me, and because I see the holy result of them in believers. I confess they are nonetheless dear to me because the new intellectual school despises them. I would never consider the fact that a doctrine was new as a recommendation for it. Those truths that have enlightened so many ages appear to me to be ordained to remain throughout eternity.

The doctrine that I preach to you is that of the Puritans. It is the doctrine of Calvin, the doctrine of Augustine, the doctrine of Paul, the doctrine of the Holy Spirit. *"The author and finisher of our faith"* (Heb. 12:2) Himself taught blessed truth that well agreed with our text; the doctrine of grace is the substance of the testimony of Jesus.

A Present Salvation

I will handle the text briefly, by way of making a few statements. The first statement is clearly contained in the text: there is *present* salvation.

When Paul wrote this epistle, he declared, *"You have been saved,"* not "shall be" or "may be," but *"have been."* He did not write, "partly saved" or "on the way to being saved" or "hopeful of salvation," but *"By grace you have been saved."* Let us be as clear on this point as he was, and let us never rest until we know that we are saved. At this moment we are either saved or unsaved. That is clear. To which class do we belong? I hope that, by the witness of the Holy Spirit, we may be so assured of our safety as to sing, *"The LORD is my strength and song, and He has become my salvation"* (Exod. 15:2).

Present Salvation Must Be by Grace

If we can say of any man or of any group of people, *"You have been saved,"* we must preface or follow it with the words, *"by grace."* There is no other present salvation except what begins and ends with grace. As far as I know, I do not think that anyone in the wide world pretends to preach or to possess a present salvation except those who believe salvation to be all of grace. No one in the Church of Rome claims to be presently saved—completely and eternally saved. Such a profession would be heretical to them. Many Catholics hope to enter heaven when they die, but most of them have the miserable prospect of purgatory before their eyes. We see constant requests for prayers for departed souls; this would not be if those souls were saved and glorified with their Savior. Masses for the repose of the soul indicate the incompleteness of the salvation that Rome has to offer. Well may it be so, since papal salvation is by works. Even if salvation by good works were possible, no man could ever be sure that he has performed enough of them to secure his salvation.

Among those who dwell around us, we find many who are complete strangers to the doctrine of grace. These poor souls never dream of present salvation. Possibly they trust that they may be saved when they die; they half hope that, after years of watchful holiness, they may, perhaps, be saved at last. But to be saved now, and to know that they are saved, is quite beyond them, and they believe it is presumptuous to think so.

There can be no present salvation unless it is on this foundation: *"By grace you have been saved."* It is a very singular thing that no one has risen up to preach a present salvation by works. I suppose it would be too absurd. The works being unfinished, the salvation would be incomplete; or the salvation being complete, the main motive of the legalist would be gone.

Salvation must be by grace. If man is lost by sin, how can he be saved except through the grace of God? If he has sinned, he is condemned; how could he, of himself, reverse that condemnation? Suppose that he should keep the law all the rest of his life; he will then only have done what he was always bound to have done, and he will still be an unprofitable servant (Luke 17:10). What is to become of the past? How can old sins be blotted out? How can the old ruin be rebuilt? According to Scripture and according to common sense, salvation can only be through the free favor of God.

Salvation in the present tense must be by the free favor of God. People may contend for salvation by works, but you will not hear anyone support his own argument by saying, "I am myself saved by what I have done." Few men would dare to express such inordinate arrogance. Pride could hardly control its swelling with such extravagant boasting. No, if we are now saved, it must be by the free favor of God. No one professes to be an example of the opposite view.

To be complete, salvation must be by free favor. When they come to die, saints never conclude their lives by hoping in their good works. Those who have lived the most holy and useful lives invariably look to free grace in their final moments. I have never stood by the bedside of a godly man who placed any confidence whatsoever in his own prayers, repentance, or piety. I have heard eminently holy men on their deathbeds quoting the words, *"Christ Jesus came into the world to save sinners"* (1 Tim. 1:15). In fact, the nearer men come to heaven, and the more prepared they are for it, the simpler their trust is in the merit of the Lord Jesus, and the more intensely they abhor all trust in themselves.

If this is the case in our last moments, when the conflict is almost over, how much more ought we to feel it to be so while we are in the thick of the fight. If a man is completely saved in this present time of warfare, how can it be except by grace? While he has to mourn over sin that dwells in him, while he has to confess innumerable shortcomings and transgressions, while sin is mixed with all he does, how can he believe that he is completely saved except that it is by the free favor of God?

Paul spoke of this salvation as belonging to the Ephesians: *"By grace you have been saved."* The Ephesians had been given to curious arts and works of divination. They had thus made a covenant with the powers of darkness. Now, if people such as these were saved, it must have been by grace alone. So is it with us also. Our original condition and character render it certain that, if saved at all, we must owe it to the free favor of God. I know it is so in my own case, and I believe the same principle holds true for the rest of believers.

By Grace through Faith

A present salvation must be by grace, and salvation by grace must be through faith. You cannot understand salvation by grace by any other means than through faith. This live coal from off the altar needs the golden tongs of faith with which to carry it.

I suppose that it would have been possible, if God had so willed it, that salvation might have been through works and yet still by grace. If Adam had perfectly obeyed the law of God, he would only have done what he was bound to do. So, if God had rewarded him, the reward itself must have been according to grace, since the Creator owes nothing to the creature. This system would have been very difficult to work on a practical level, even though its objective was perfect. However, in our case it would not work at all. Salvation in our case means deliverance from guilt and ruin, and this could not have been secured by a measure of good works, since we are not in a condition to perform any.

Suppose I had to preach that you as sinners must do certain works, and then you would be saved. Further, suppose that you could perform them. Such a salvation would not then be seen to be all of grace; it would soon appear to be of debt. Understood in such a fashion, it would have come to you in some measure as the reward of work done, and its whole appearance would have been changed. Salvation by grace can only be gripped by the hand of faith. The attempt to lay hold of it by the performance of certain acts of law would cause the grace to evaporate.

Therefore it is of faith that it might be according to grace.
(Rom. 4:16)

And if by grace, then it is no longer of works; otherwise grace is no longer grace. But if it is of works, it is no longer grace; otherwise work is no longer work. (Rom. 11:6)

Some try to lay hold of salvation by grace through the use of ceremonies, but it will not do. You are christened, confirmed, and caused to receive "the holy sacrament" from priestly hands. Does this bring you salvation? I ask you, "Do you have salvation?" You dare not say "Yes." If you did claim salvation of a sort, I am sure it would not be in your minds as salvation by grace, for those who are most addicted to the performance of outward rites are usually the last persons to enjoy any assurance of being saved by grace. They do not even think to look for such a thing. The more they multiply their rites and ceremonies, the more they quit the notion of grace, and the more they lose the true idea of salvation.

Again, you cannot lay hold of salvation by grace through your feelings. The hand of faith is constructed for the grasping of a present salvation by grace, but feeling is not adapted for that end. If you say, "I must feel that I am saved; I must feel so much sorrow and so much joy, or else I will not admit that I am saved," you will find that this method will not suffice. You might as well hope to see with your ears or taste with your eyes or hear with your nose as to believe by feeling: it is the wrong organ. After you have believed, you can enjoy salvation by feeling its heavenly influences, but to dream of getting a grasp of it by your own feelings is as foolish as to attempt to carry the sunlight in the palm of your hand or the breath of heaven between the lashes of your eyes. There is an essential absurdity in the whole affair.

Moreover, the evidence yielded by feeling is distinctly fickle. When your feelings are peaceful and delightful, they are soon broken in upon and become restless and melancholy. The most fickle of elements, the most feeble of creatures, or the most contemptible of circumstances may sink or raise our spirits. Mature men come to think less and less of their present emotions as they reflect on the little reliance that can be safely placed in them.

Faith receives the statement of God concerning His way of gracious pardon, and thus it brings salvation to the person believing it. In contrast, feeling, warming under passionate appeals, yielding itself deliriously to a hope that it dares not examine, whirling round and round in a sort of dervish dance of excitement that has become necessary for its own sustaining, is all astir like the troubled sea that cannot rest. From its boiling and raging, feeling is apt to drop to lukewarmness, despondency, despair, and all similar states. Feelings are a set of cloudy, windy phenomena that cannot be trusted in reference to the eternal truths of God.

Not of Ourselves

We now take this discussion a step further. The present salvation and the faith and the whole gracious work altogether are not of ourselves. First of all, they are not deserved because of our prior performance. They are not the reward of former good endeavors. No unregenerate person has lived so well that God is bound to give him further grace and to bestow on him eternal life. Otherwise, it would be no longer of grace, but of debt. Salvation is given to us, not earned by us. Our first life is always a wandering away from God, and our new life of return to God is always a work of undeserved mercy, performed in those who greatly need, but never deserve, such gracious favor.

It is not of ourselves, in the further sense that it is not out of our internal excellence. Salvation comes from above. It is never evolved from within. Can eternal life be evolved from the bare ribs of death? Some dare to tell us that faith in Christ and the new birth are only the development of good things that lay hidden in us by nature. But in this, like their father the Devil, they speak of their own (John 8:44). Beloved, if an heir of wrath is left to develop on his own, he will become more and more fit for the place prepared for the Devil and his angels! You may educate an unregenerate man to the highest degree. Yet he remains, and must forever remain, dead in sin unless a higher power comes in to save him from himself.

Grace brings into the heart an entirely foreign element. That element does not improve and perpetuate. It kills and then makes alive. There is no continuity between the state of nature and the state of grace: the one is darkness, and the other is light; the one is death, and the other is life. Grace, when it comes to us, is like a firebrand dropped into the sea, where it would certainly be quenched were it not of such a miraculous quality that it baffles the waters and sets up its reign of fire and light even in the depths.

Salvation by grace, through faith, is not of ourselves in the sense of being the result of our own power. We are bound to view salvation as being a divine act as surely as we do creation or providence or resurrection. In every point of the process of salvation, this word is appropriate: *"not of yourselves."* From the first desire for it to the full reception of it by faith, it is forever of the Lord alone, and not of ourselves. The man believes, but that belief is only one result among many of the implantation of divine life within the man's soul by God Himself.

Even the very will or desire to be saved by grace is *"not of yourselves; it is the gift of God."* Here lies the emphasis of the discussion. A man ought to believe in Jesus. It is his duty to receive Him whom God has set forth to be a propitiation for sins. Yet man will not believe in Jesus. He prefers anything to faith in his Redeemer. Unless the Spirit of God convinces his judgment and constrains his will, man has no heart to believe in Jesus unto eternal life.

I ask any saved man to look back on his own conversion and explain how it came about. You turned to Christ and believed on His name; these were your own acts and deeds. But what caused you to turn that way? What sacred force was it that turned you from sin to righteousness? Do you attribute this singular renewal to the existence of something better in you than has been yet discovered in your unconverted neighbor? No, you confess that you might have been what he is now if it had not been that there was a potent something that touched the spring of your will, enlightened your understanding, and guided you to the foot of the cross. Gratefully we confess the fact; it must be so. Salvation by grace, through faith, is not of ourselves. None of us would dream of taking any honor to ourselves from our conversion or from any gracious effect that has flowed from the first divine cause.

It Is the Gift of God

Finally, salvation may be called, *Theodora,* or God's gift, and each saved soul may be surnamed *Dorothea,* which is another form of the same expression. Multiply your phrases and expand your expositions as you will, but salvation truly traced to its fountainhead is all contained in the unspeakable gift, the free, unmeasured blessing of love.

Salvation is the gift of God, in opposition to wages. When a man pays another his wages, he does what is right. No one would dream of praising him for it. Yet we praise God for salvation because it is not the payment of debt but the gift of grace. No man enters eternal life on Earth or in heaven as his due: *"It is the gift of God."* We say, "Nothing is freer than a gift." Salvation is so purely, so absolutely, a gift of God that nothing can be freer.

God gives salvation because He chooses to give it, according to that grand text that has made many a man bite his lip in wrath: *"I will have mercy on whomever I will have mercy, and I will have compassion on whomever I will have compassion"* (Rom. 9:15). You are all guilty and condemned, and the Great King pardons whom He chooses from among you. This is His royal prerogative. He saves in infinite sovereignty of grace.

At the same time, the Lord Himself has declared, *"Whoever calls on the name of the LORD shall be saved"* (Acts 2:21). This sweeping statement in no way conflicts with the statement that no one receives salvation except as a gift. You must stand obliged to God's mercy for it, or else you will die without it. To pretend a right to it will be to insult God, whose heart is set upon the exercise of His free bounty. He will not barter and bargain with you—so much grace for so many tears, so much mercy for so much repentance, so much love for so many works—the idea is contemptible! Salvation is not available except under these explicit terms: *"without money and without price"* (Isa. 55:1). Freely you may be saved if you will cast out of your soul the last thought of making God your debtor.

Salvation is the gift of God—that is to say, it is completely so, in opposition to the notion of growth. Salvation is not a natural production from within; it is brought from a foreign zone and planted within the heart by heavenly hands. Salvation is a gift from God in its entirety. If you will receive it, there it is, complete.

Will you accept it as a perfect gift? "No, I will produce it in my own workshop." You cannot forge a work so rare and costly, upon which even Jesus spent His life's blood. Here is a garment without seam, woven from the top down in one piece. It will cover you and make you glorious. Will you take it and wear it? "No, I will sit at the loom, and I will weave a raiment of my own!" Proud fool that you are! You spin cobwebs. You weave a dream. Oh, that you would freely take what Christ upon the cross declared to be finished!

"It is the gift of God" in the sense that it is eternally secure, in opposition to the gifts of men, which soon pass away. *"Not as the world gives do I give to you"* (John 14:27), said our Lord Jesus. If my Lord Jesus gives you salvation at this moment, you have it, and you have it forever. He will never take it back again. And if He does not take it from you, who can? If He saves you now through faith, you are saved—so saved that you will never perish, neither will anyone snatch you out of His hand (John 10:28).

I pray that you may know, at this moment and always, the joy of being eternally secure as you *"abide under the shadow of the Almighty"* (Ps. 91:1), because you have accepted His free, merciful gift of salvation by His precious grace.

Chapter 5

Grace for the Covenanter

All the paths of the LORD are mercy and truth, to such as keep His
covenant and His testimonies.
—Psalm 25:10

The Twenty-fifth Psalm is intensely earnest. *"To You, O LORD, I lift up my soul"* (v. 1). The sentences are bars of gold. Every word is exceedingly weighty with feeling and sincerity. One reason for this weightiness is the fact that David was suffering affliction. He said, *"I am desolate and afflicted....Look on my affliction and my pain"* (vv. 16, 18).

Pain can be a great disenchanter. Flowery speeches suit the summer of our health, but we do not find them in the winter of our grief. Pain kills fine phrases as a mighty frost kills butterflies and moths. You can play with religion until you are laid low, and then it becomes serious work. The romance of religion is one thing; the reality of it is another. It would be a great blessing to some if they were shriveled with a little pain, or else they will grow unbearable in their pride. Often the best thing that can happen to us is that we are reduced to our true selves and not left to strut about as noble somebodies. May our meditations be solid and leave no tinge of unreality in our minds!

Also mixed with David's suffering was a sense of sin. Read the eleventh verse of that same Psalm: *"For Your name's sake, O LORD, pardon my iniquity, for it is great."* A little further we find: *"Forgive all my sins"* (v. 18). No one can experience a worse troubling of soul than when under conviction of sin. A thorn in the flesh is nothing in comparison to a thorn in the conscience.

A sense of sin is another great disenchanter. This knowledge bursts the bubbles of conceit. When the heart is awakened and sin is laid bare by the Spirit of God so that we are truly humbled by it, life ceases to be sport, and an awful earnestness pervades the core of our being. To carry burning coals in the bosom is nothing compared with bearing sin in an awakened conscience. There is no cheating the soul when sin lies hard on it, and no attempt is then made at dealing with God in a dishonest or superficial manner. Crushed into the dust, we pine for a real atonement, a real faith, and the true seal of the Spirit to make our pardon sure. When sin is truly felt, we come before the great Father, not with mimicking sorrow, but with downright, soul-felt weeping and breaking hearts. Thus, we cry to Him, *"God, be merciful to me a sinner"* (Luke 18:13).

If we feel either of these two things, pain or sin—and who among us can hope to be without them at all times?—then we will see the solemn side of life and look for those sure consolations by which we may be sustained. I hope that this subject of discussion may help in that direction.

One other thing is notable about David in writing the Twenty-fifth Psalm in which our text is found: whatever his trouble might have been and however deep his sense of sin was, he always looked toward God. He cried, *"To You, O LORD, I lift up my soul"* (v. 1), and *"Remember me, for your goodness' sake, O LORD"* (v. 7). In our text verse, his mind focused on *"the paths of the LORD."*

The ungodly flee from God when He chastens them, but saints kiss the chastening rod. The child of God goes home when it grows dark. We seek our healing from the hand that has wounded us.

Which way do you look in a storm? If the Lord is now your haven, you will look to Him in the final dreadful storm, for that is the way your eye has turned all these years. If you look to God for everything, you are looking out the right window. When your eyes look toward the great sea of divine all-sufficiency, you do not look in vain. You may have to come again seven more times before you see your deliverance; and when you do see it, it may seem no bigger than a man's hand. (See 1 Kings 18:41–45.) However, you will not be ashamed in the end.

I trust this mark and evidence of being a child of God is on you. If it is, you are among the Lord's army whom I would call to the battle. With your face set straight ahead and your eyes focused on our Captain, come with me to the rallying place of the Lord of Hosts.

In our text verse I want to point out two things. The first is the character of people who are in covenant with God: *"such as keep His covenant and His testimonies."* The second is the notable experience of such individuals: *"All the paths of the LORD are mercy and truth, to such as keep His covenant."*

The Spiritual Covenanter

Observe in the text the footprint of the spiritual covenanter. We may define spiritual covenanters as people who enter into covenant with God, who are the recipients of His grace, who are the beneficiaries of the Lord's last will and testament, and who are *"such as keep His covenant and His testimonies."*

You may have heard of the old Covenanters of Scotland, their decisiveness of mind and force of character. Their theory of government for the kingdom of Scotland was quaintly impractical, but it grew out of a true and deep fear of the Lord. The Old Testament combative spirit in them was not balanced enough with the meekness of Christ, or else they would not have touched the weapon of steel. Yet in this mistake they were very far from being alone.

In my bedroom I have hung up a painting of an old Covenanter. He sits in a wild glen with his Bible open before him on a huge stone. He leans on his great broad sword, and his horse stands quietly at his side. Evidently he senses the battle afar off and is preparing for it by drinking in some mighty promise. As I look into the old man's face, I can almost hear him saying to himself, "For the crown of Christ and the Covenant, I would gladly lay down my life this day."

The Covenanters did lay down their lives, too, very gloriously, and Scotland owes to her covenanting fathers far more than she knows. It was a grand day in which they spread the Solemn League and Covenant on the tombstones of the old churchyard in Edinburgh, and all sorts of men came forward to set their names to it. Glorious was that roll of worthy men. There were the lords of the Covenant and the common men of the Covenant. Some pricked a vein and dipped the pen into their blood, so that they might write their names with the very fluid of their hearts.

All over England there were also men who entered into a similar solemn league and covenant; they met together to worship God according to the light they were given and not according to human order-of-service books. They were united in resolution about this one thing: that Rome should not come back to power while they could lift a hand against her, and neither should any other power in throne or Parliament prevent the free exercise of their consciences for Christ's cause and covenant.

These stern old men with their stiff notions have gone, but what do we have in their places? Indifference and frivolity. We have no Roundheads and Puritans, but we arrange flowers and play tennis! We have no contentions for the faith because our amusements occupy all our time. This wonderful age has become a child and put away mature things. (See 1 Corinthians 13:11.) Self-disciplined men, men of integrity and true grit, are now very few and far between as compared with the old covenanting days.

In Right Relationship with God

However, I want to discuss, not the old Covenanters, but rather those who at this time keep the covenant of the Lord. I pray to God that we have among us great companies of believers, *"such as keep His covenant, and...remember His commandments to do them"* (Ps. 103:18).

The true covenanter is one who has found God, and in that has made the greatest discovery that was ever made. He has discovered, not only a god, but the living and true God, and has resolved to be on living terms with Him for time and for eternity. Henceforth, he will never shut his eyes to God, for his longing is to see more and more of Him. He is determined to be right with God; he knows that if he were right with all his fellowmen and yet were wrong with God, he would be out of order in the main point. He has settled in his own soul that he will know the Lord, be right with Him, at peace with Him, and in league with Him.

It is not natural for men thus to cling to God and seek after Him, but it has become natural for this man, so that he hungers and thirsts for the living God. By this very fact the man is ennobled. He is lifted up above the brutes that perish. A man capable of the idea of covenant with God, and caught up with a passion for it, must surely be born from above. There must be a divine nature within him, or he would not be drawn toward the Divine One above him. It is true: the Spirit of God has been working in his heart.

Experience with the First Covenant

Already, too, the man has discovered a prior covenant, whose ruins lay between him and God and blocked the road. Turning to his Bible, the believer finds that we had been under the first covenant in our relationship toward God. He reads of the first covenant, the covenant with our first father, Adam, which was broken by his disobedience, whose fatal breach has brought upon us losses and woes innumerable.

The true believer has not ignored this first covenant or made quick work of it, for he himself has felt his share in its failure and has come under its condemnation. His very desire to be right with God has brought home to him the judgment of the law; he has smarted under the lash of it. He has seen the Lord arrayed in robes of justice, avenging the breaches of His covenant, and he has thought to himself, "What shall I do? The law is holy, and the commandment holy, just, and good; *"but I am carnal, sold under sin"* (Rom. 7:14).

Beloved, we are condemned under the first covenant, not only by the act of our representative, Adam, but also through our personal endorsement of his rebellion by our own actual sin. That covenant, which should have been a covenant of life, has become a covenant of death to us.

You know what I mean. Many of you know by deep personal experience what it is to be the prisoners of the covenant, shut up in soul despair and numbered for destruction. The future was against you; you knew you could not keep the law, even though you wished and prayed that you could. The past was against you; as for former violations of the law, you could find no way to make amends for them. The present was against you; your inward corruptions were continually gnawing at your heart like the worm that never dies (Isa. 66:24) and the leech that is never satisfied (Prov. 30:15). Yet despite all of this, you still followed after the Lord and could not live without Him.

Perception of a Better Covenant

The covenanter is one who has, through divine enlightenment, perceived a better covenant and the sure salvation contained therein. He has seen in the Lord Jesus a Second Adam, greater than the first, and he has heard the glorious Lord exclaim, *"I, the LORD,...give* [Him] *as a covenant to the people"* (Isa. 42:6). He has seen Jesus pledge to God to make good the breaches of the broken covenant. The believer has seen the Son of God arrayed in blood-stained garments coming from Gethsemane. He has seen Him answering at the bar for the broken law, scourged with *"the chastisement for our peace"* (Isa. 53:5) and bound with the chains of our condemnation. He has seen the beloved Surety of the new covenant meeting the law's demands at Calvary, surrendering His hands to be nailed for our evildoing, His feet to be fastened up for our wanderings, and His heart to be pierced for our wantonness.

O my dear souls, have you seen our Lord stripped for sin amid the tempest of divine wrath? Have you heard Him cry, *"My God, My God, why have You forsaken Me"* (Matt. 27:46)? If so, you have seen how out of the old covenant, the new was born like life from between the jaws of death. Our souls have stood in the midst of the horrible tempest, half-blinded by the lightning and deafened by the thunder. At last there has been a tear in the black mantle; a shower of wondrous love has followed the black tempest; and a voice has been heard, sweeter than the harps of angels, crying, *"It is finished!"* (John 19:30).

Thus have the Lord's covenanted ones come forth from under the old covenant into the new covenant of grace in which peace and joy abound. Now are we in happy league with God. Now we can think, feel, and act in harmony with God. Our covenant with Him will encompass all our lives. We are His, and He is ours: *"'The LORD is my portion,' says my soul"* (Lam. 3:24). Yet on the other hand, *"The Lord's portion is His people"* (Deut. 32:9). Henceforth, we have no life apart from the living God; He is our ambition and our expectation, our end and our way, our desire and our delight. He rejoices over us (Zeph. 3:17) to do us good, and we rejoice in Him and seek His glory.

A Heart Covenant with God

The spiritual covenanter has the covenant with God written on the tablets of his heart. I have known believers, when first converted, who have followed a hint given them by Dr. Doddridge in his *Rise and Progress of Religion,* where he drew up a covenant that he invited readers to sign. Some have executed a deed with great solemnity and have also observed the day of its signature from year to year. Very proper, no doubt, for some natures, but I fear that to the more timid and conscientious such covenants are apt to cause bondage. When they find that they have not, in all things, lived up to their own pledges, they are apt to cut themselves off from all part and lot in the matter. This is the covenant of works and not of grace, a covenant on paper and not the covenant written on the heart and mind.

The true covenanter wills the will of God. It is not merely that God commands him to do right, but he longs to do it. God's law is his love. (See Psalm 119:97.) What is pleasing to God is pleasing to His people, because their hearts are made like His own. The divine likeness is restored by the Spirit of grace; hence, the will of the Lord is written on the newly born nature. Holiness is the passion of a true believer. He consents and assents to the law that it is good, and the divine life within him delights itself in the law of the Lord (Ps. 1:2).

The surest sort of covenant is this divine writing in the new nature, according to these gracious promises:

> *I will give you a new heart and put a new spirit within you; I will take the heart of stone out of your flesh and give you a heart of flesh.* (Ezek. 36:26)

> *But this is the covenant that I will make with the house of Israel after those days, says the LORD: I will put My law in their minds, and write it on their hearts; and I will be their God, and they shall be My people.* (Jer. 31:33)

Happy is the man whose covenant with God is the covenant of his own desire—who wills, wishes, longs, and labors to yield himself fully and wholly to the law of his God!

United with the Lord

This covenanting man no longer regards himself as one by himself, because he *"is joined to the Lord"* (1 Cor. 6:17) and has entered into the closest fellowship with Him. None can separate him from God; the union is vital and complete. He has thrown his little all into God's great all, and he has taken God's great all unto himself to be his heritage forever. Now, henceforth, he is in God and God in him. (See John 14:20.)

You ask me what it is that thus binds a man to God. My answer is that he feels he is henceforth joined to the Lord for many reasons, among them being that the Lord has chosen him to be His own. He is old-fashioned enough to believe that God has a choice in the salvation of men, and he perceives that the Lord has evidently chosen him for salvation, for faith has been granted to him. He often cries, "Why me? Why me?" Yet he knows that those whom the Lord calls by grace He first predestined to that end (Rom. 8:30), and he is not ashamed to believe in his election. The man who believes that God has chosen him is the man who enters into covenant with God and keeps that covenant. He who is chosen by God chooses God; he chooses God because he has been chosen. The vows of God are upon him. Such amazing grace compels him to a consecrated life.

The Mark of Redemption

Moreover, in addition to the choice of God, this covenanter sees the mark of Christ's blood upon his body, soul, and spirit. The redemption made on the cross, whatever its other directions, is seen by the believer to be especially for him. He cries, "For me was the bloody sweat; for me the spitting and the scourging; for me the nails and the spear. Truly I am not my own, for I am bought with a price." (See 1 Corinthians 6:20.)

This blood-bought man feels that he cannot be as other men are. He must pledge with his hand to the God of Jacob, and he must cling to and confess that he belongs to the Lord alone.

Others may be their own lords. But as for us, we have been redeemed, not *"with corruptible things, like silver or gold,...but with the precious blood of Christ"* (1 Pet. 1:18–19). O beloved, if you know your election and your redemption, you must and will dedicate yourselves to the Lord by a covenant that cannot be broken. If the choice of the Father and the redemption of the Son do not supply us with a potent force toward holiness, what can do so? Well may we be the covenanted ones of God when we are thus distinguished.

The Subject of a Special Calling

In addition, the covenanting believer feels that he has been the subject of a special call. Whatever God may have done with others, he knows that God has dealt specially with him according to His grace and mercy. The Lord has said to him,

> *Fear not, for I have redeemed you; I have called you by your name; you are Mine....Since you were precious in My sight, you have been honored, and I have loved you.* (Isa. 43:1, 4)

A voice has called him from his kindred and from his father's house just as surely as Abraham was called. The Lord Himself has brought him *"out of darkness into His marvelous light"* (1 Pet. 2:9). Whatever the Gospel may be to the congregation at large, it has

73

been *"the power of God to salvation"* (Rom. 1:16) for him. In it he has felt the touch of a hand unfelt before and heard the sound of a voice unheard in all the days gone by. Omnipotent grace has aroused the response of his soul: *"When You said, 'Seek My face,' my heart said to You, 'Your face, LORD, I will seek'"* (Ps. 27:8).

This special, authoritative calling is another mighty reason for entering into league and covenant with God. Let your prayer be, "By that omnipotent call, O Lord, I give myself to You. Let the world do as it wants—I cannot account for its folly—*'but as for me and my house, we will serve the LORD'"* (Josh. 24:15). Our bonds of friendship with the world are broken, whatever it may do or say. We are bound to the Lord forever by the same power that has pulled us out of our former slavery. With election, redemption, and calling, what more can I say?

United to God in Christ Jesus

Yes, I can add something more, for the true covenanter feels that he is now united to God in Christ Jesus. What a matchless doctrine is unity with God through Jesus Christ! No man knows the lineage and the nature of the man who has been quickened by the Spirit. You cannot tell his ancestry or his progeny. We talk of aristocrats, but believers are the aristocrats of heaven and Earth. We often hear the words *royalty* and *royal blood*. The true royal blood of the universe is in the man who believes in Jesus. He has *"made us kings and priests to our God"* (Rev. 5:10). By virtue of our union with Christ, we are one with God and *"partakers of the divine nature"* (2 Pet. 1:4).

The day will come when all the baubles and trappings of courts will be laid aside as the faded tawdriness they are. When that happens, the real dignity and honor of the twice-born, the quickened by the Holy Spirit, will truly be seen. To be members of the body of Christ means glory indeed. To be married to the King's Son, to the Lord Jesus, means such a state of bliss that even angels cannot reach. Given such an immeasurable privilege, do you question that a man enters into a sure covenant with God?

Zeal for the Gospel

There are several more things I would like to say briefly about this true covenanter. May the Lord make each one of us to be of his

74

character! You may know him by his attachment to the Lord Jesus, who is the Sum, Substance, Surety, and Seal of the covenant. The committed believer is known also by his zeal for the Gospel, through which the covenant is revealed to the sons of men. He will not hear anything that is not according to the old Gospel, for he counts any other gospel to be a deadly evil. He is very fond of the word *grace,* and with grace itself he is altogether enamored.

The person who is in covenant with God cannot bear the idea of human merit—he loathes it. It raises his indignation. I have known some Christians who come out from hearing certain apathetic sermons with their souls on fire with holy wrath. I feel, in casting my eye over many modern writings, as if I were about to die from breathing poisonous gas. We cannot endure the smell of false piety and human righteousness. Others may feed on philosophical morality, but nothing but the grace of God will do for us. Stray dogs may feed on any rubbish, but men of God must live on the grace of God and nothing else. Our keeping the covenant and the testimonies binds us to a firm adherence to the inspired Gospel and to the grace of God, which is the glory of it.

A Person of Faith

He who is indeed in covenant with God is known by his continual regard for the life, walk, and triumph of faith. He has faith, and by that faith he lives and grows. He is, has, and does all things by faith. No one can tempt him away from the faith in which he stands. Carnal sense and fleshly feeling are not able to tempt him from believing. The highest enjoyment offered by a fancied perfection cannot charm him from standing by faith. "No," he says, "I must trust, or else it is all over with me. My element is faith. Just as a fish out of water dies, so do I die—and all my covenanting with God dies, too—unless I cling by faith to the promise of a faithful God." Even if all other men should live by their senses and emotions, the true covenanter will not quit the hallowed way of faith in the Lord.

Proclaiming the Pure Gospel

This covenanting man will also be known by his stern resolve to preserve the Gospel in its purity and hand it on to others. When the truth of God was made known to Abraham, it was committed to him and to his descendants as a sacred deposit, of which they were to be the guardians and trustees. It was theirs to keep that lamp burning by which the rest of the world would, in due time, be saved from darkness. The eternal truths of the Gospel of our Lord Jesus Christ are given over to certain chosen men and women to be preserved by them until the coming of the Lord. This keeping is to be accompanied with a constant proclamation, so that the truth may spread as well as live, and may continue to conquer.

You who are the covenanted ones of God, do not let His Gospel suffer damage. I charge you who love the Lord to bind the Gospel about you more firmly than ever. Bear aloft the standard of our grand army. The blood-stained colors of the cross—carry them to the front, spread them on every wind, uplift them on every hill! And if you cannot spread the truth, but are shut up to defend it, then do so even to the death. Wrap the colors about your heart. If you cannot live to bear them as your flag, be wrapped in them as your shroud!

A true covenanter says, "Sooner death than to be false of faith." The crown of our Lord Jesus will never suffer loss. We will do everything for Jesus. We will bear reproach for His sake (Heb. 13:13), and for His sake we will labor to win souls to God. We vow that He will be glorified in our mortal bodies (1 Cor. 6:20). We further state that by some means His great name will be made known *"to the ends of the earth"* (Ps. 48:10).

O my fellow warriors! I am invigorated by the very thought of you. God still has His faithful covenanters who have not bowed the knee to Baal, to whom the Lord is God and King forever and ever.

The Experience of the Covenanter

For our second part of this study, let us now consider the covenanter's extraordinary experience. Our text verse says, *"All the paths of the LORD are mercy and truth, to such as keep His covenant and His testimonies."* Those who keep the covenant walk in blessing.

The Lord Approaches in Many Ways

Observe, first, that the Lord makes many approaches to covenanting men. He does not leave them alone, but He comes to them and manifests Himself to them. By the expression, *"All the paths of the LORD,"* I learn that the Lord has many ways of drawing near to His chosen. Not only in the public highways of grace does He meet those with whom He is on terms of peace, but in many private and secret paths. In a grassy field a path is made by constant treading, and God makes paths to His people by continually drawing near to their souls and communing with them. The Lord has many paths, for He comes to them from different points of the compass as their experience requires. He sometimes uses one way and sometimes another, in order that He may commune with us. He will never leave His covenanted ones alone for long. He often says, *"Gather My saints together to Me, those who have made a covenant with Me by sacrifice"* (Ps. 50:5).

I like the word *"paths"* as it is translated in our text verse, for it seems to say that the Lord has walks of His own. He makes ways for Himself and goes along them quietly, taking His people unaware. All of a sudden He whispers a word of heavenly promise, and then He is gone again. However, He is not gone for long. He makes another path and comes to us with new anointing and fresh revelation. His visits to us are many and gracious.

O beloved, if you will give yourself to God, God will give Himself to you. Youthful one, I invite you to the grand destiny of one who will henceforth live with God, to whom God will manifest Himself. Would this not be a distinguished honor? Do not think it unattainable. God may be reached; if you will consecrate yourself to Him this day by a covenant through Jesus Christ, the ever-blessed Sacrifice, you will know the visitations of the Almighty. You will, like Enoch, walk with God (Gen. 5:24).

Believe me, this is the solemn truth. Between this place and the pearly gates, the Lord will come to you and will take up His abode with you. When you cannot get to Him, He will come to you, for He is a great pathmaker. His ways are in the sea, and He leaps over the mountains. He has a desire for the work of His hands, and that desire will break through stone walls to reach you. How blessed is the one to whom the Lord makes innumerable paths! What happiness floods that soul!

Merciful Treatment

Note, next, that all the dealings of God with His people are in mercy: *"All the paths of the LORD are mercy."* This is fitting, for the best of the saints will always need mercy. Those who keep His covenant are still kept by His mercy. When they grow in grace and come to be fully developed Christians, they still need mercy for their sins, their weaknesses, and their needs. The Lord exercises mercy to the most highly instructed believer as well as to the babe in grace, mercy to the most useful worker as much as to the most weary sufferer. *"Oh, give thanks to the LORD, for He is good! For His mercy endures forever"* (Ps. 107:1).

That mercy will always be *"tender mercy"* (Luke 1:78), abiding mercy, and *"abundant mercy"* (1 Pet. 1:3). His mercy is as constant as the day, as fresh as the hour, and *"new every morning"* (Lam. 3:23). Mercy covers all His works (Ps. 145:9). In every gift of providence and in every way of predestination, mercy may be seen. It would be greatly advantageous for us to meditate more on the mercy of God to us. So much of His mercy comes and goes without our noticing it. It is a shame that the Lord should thus be deprived of the revenues of His praise!

The original Hebrew word that has been translated *"paths"* means "well-worn roads" or "wheel tracks," such ruts as wagons make when they go down grassy roads in wet weather and sink in up to the axles. God's ways are at times like heavy wagon tracks that cut deep into our souls, yet all of them are merciful. Whether our days trip along like the angels mounting on Jacob's ladder to heaven (Gen. 28:12) or grind along like the wagons that Joseph sent for Jacob (Gen. 45:27), they are in each case ordered by God's mercy.

When I recall the happy memories of a tried past, as I walk down a summery green lane and look at the deep ruts that God's providence made long ago, I see flowers of mercies growing in them. All of the crushing and crashing was in goodness. *"Surely goodness and mercy* [have] *follow*[ed] *me all the days of my life"* (Ps. 23:6)— yes, in *"all the days of my life,"* the dark and cloudy, the stormy and the wintry, as surely as in *"the days of the heavens above the earth"* (Deut. 11:21). Beloved, we may sing a song of untainted mercy. The paths of God have been to us nothing else but mercy. Mercy, mercy, mercy! *"I will sing of the mercies of the LORD forever"* (Ps. 89:1).

Grace in His Truth

The psalmist said, *"All the paths of the LORD are mercy and truth."* That is to say, God has always shown the truth of His Word. He has never been false to His pledge. He has done according to His

Word. Moreover, the blessings that God has promised have always turned out to be as He represented them. We have followed no cunningly devised fables. The blessings of grace are not fancies or frenzies, exaggerations or mere sentiments. The Lord has never fallen short of His promise. He has never kept His Word to the ear and broken it to the heart.

All the ways of God have not only been merciful and true, but they have been essential *"mercy and truth."* We have had truth-filled mercy; authentic mercy; substantial, solid, essential mercy.

I have found no delusion in trusting in God. I may have been a dreamer in some things, but when I have lived for God, I have then exercised the shrewdest common sense and have walked after the rule of prudence. It is no vain thing to serve God; the vanity lies on the other side.

Many think the Christian experience leans toward the area of sentiment, if not of imagination, but indeed it is not so. The surest fact in a believer's life is God's nearness to him, care for him, love for him. Other things are shadows or impressions that come and go, but the goodness of God is the substance, the truth, the reality of life. How much I desire to persuade you of this! But, alas, the natural mind cannot receive spiritual things (1 Cor. 2:14). I may bear witness of what I taste and handle, but you will not believe me. Divine Spirit, come and open blind eyes.

No Exceptions

There is no exception to this rule: *"All the paths of the LORD are mercy and truth to such as keep His covenant."* They say there is no rule without an exception, but there is an exception to that rule. All God's dealings with His people are gracious and faithful. Sometimes the ways of God are full of truth and mercy manifestly; they have been so to me in many notable instances.

I hope I do not trouble you too often with personal experiences. I do not write of them out of egotism, but I do so because it seems to me that every Christian should add his own personal testimony to the great evidence that proves the truth of our God. If I tell you about John Newton, you may answer, "He is dead, and you did not know him." However, if I tell you of Charles Haddon Spurgeon, I know him and can give his account truthfully.

About ten days ago I was called to bear a baptism of pain. I had a night of anguish, and the pangs did not cease in the morning.

How gladly I would have escaped from these acute attacks, but it seemed I might not hope it. I felt worn down and spent. Late in the morning, my ever-thoughtful secretary came by my bedside and cheered me greatly by the news that the mail brought tidings of considerable help for the various ministries. In fact, there was far more coming in than is at all usual at this season. A generous legacy was reported that was to be shared between the orphanage and the college. Another will named the orphanage as a secondary beneficiary. Friends had also sent large sums in what seemed to be a directed concert of liberality. They had no way of knowing that their friend was going to be very ill that morning, but the Lord knew, and He moved them to take away every care from me. It seemed to me as if my Lord said, "Now, you are not going to fret and worry while you are ill. You will have no temptation to do so, for I will send you n so much help for all My work that you will not dare to be downcast." Truly in this, the paths of the Lord were mercy and truth to me.

Many times have I been lost in wonder at the Lord's mercy to His unworthy servant. I bow my head and bless the name of the Lord and cry, "Why is this to me?" Beloved, one can bear rheumatism or gout when mercy flows in as a flood. *"Shall we indeed accept good from God, and shall we not accept adversity?"* (Job 2:10). Seeing that it all comes from the same hand, we should receive it with equal cheerfulness. I am thus enabled to suffer with patience and endure with tranquillity, *"because God has dealt graciously with me"* (Gen. 33:11).

I have often found that His comfort abounds to me in proportion to my tribulations. Of course, I am on the lookout for the mercy when I begin to feel the pain, even as a child looks for the sweet when he finds himself called upon to take medicine. Those more closely around me say, "Now that you have a bad time of personal suffering, you will see the Lord doing wonderfully for you." They are not disappointed.

Indeed, I serve a good Master. I can speak well of Him at all times, but I find Him especially kind when the weather is rough around His pilgrim child! Have you not found it so in your life? Come, dear friends, you may not be able to tell me what the Lord has done personally in your lives, but I exhort you to speak at mealtime when your children are gathered around you. Tell them how gracious God has been to you in your times of trouble. I urge you to recall your memories of His great goodness often.

Unseen Mercies

Be aware that even when we cannot see it, the Lord is just as merciful in His ways to us. We may not expect to be indulged and pampered by always being allowed to see the mercy of God, like silly children who pout unless their father stuffs their mouths with sweets and their hands with toys. God is as good when He denies as when He grants. Though we often see the marvelous tenderness of our God, it is not necessary that we see it to make it true. Our God is wise as a father and tender as a mother. While we cannot comprehend His methods, we still believe in His love. This is not false trust, but a solid confidence to which the Lord is fully entitled. There can be no doubt that *"all the paths of the LORD are mercy and truth to such as keep His covenant."*

I hear some say, "These things do not happen to me. I find myself struggling alone and full of sorrow." Do you keep the covenant? Some of you professing Christian people live however you please and not by covenant rule. You do not live for God, you do not keep His covenant, you do not observe His testimonies, and you are not living consecrated lives. Therefore, if you do not enjoy His mercy and His truth, do not blame the Lord. The verse says that all His paths are mercy and truth *"to such as keep His covenant."* Remember the character, and do not expect the blessing apart from it. O child of God, be more careful to keep the way of the Lord, more concentrated in heart in seeking His glory, and you will see the loving-kindness and the tender mercy of the Lord in your life. God bless this feeble testimony of mine to all who learn of it!

The Joy of Being in Covenant with God

I have this much to add to it: what a bliss it is to have entered upon the spiritual life and to be in covenant with God! Even if there were no mercy of a providential character joined to the covenant, it would nevertheless be the grandest thing that could ever happen to any one of us to be living for God. What a solid foundation we have in godliness! It puts eternal rock beneath our feet.

There are fascinating things in life about which you are almost afraid to inquire, for fear they should not prove to be what they seem. All earthborn joys are of this kind: their charms are on the surface; their beauty is skin deep. But regarding the life consecrated to God by covenant and then enriched by His mercy, you may pry and dig and search, and the more you do so, the more you will be certain that now you are in the land of realities.

Though we do not see physically, we perceive with a perception clearer than sight, and so we will perceive through life. When those golden gates fling open and we peer into the spiritual realm, then we will value, most of all, the life that observes the covenant and is surrounded with mercy and truth. What a wondrous thing the life of a consecrated person will seem to be when we will view it in its completeness, in the light of the eternal throne! Then will the embroidery of love be seen in its beauty, and the fabric of life will be admitted to be worthy of God. Things not seen as yet will be seen then, and things known in part will be seen in all their fullness (1 Cor. 13:12). I suppose that one of the engagements of heaven will be to observe how kindly our God has dealt with us upon the road. At any rate, when we come to the glory land, only the life that was spent in communion with God will we deem to have been true life. Link us with God, and we live; divide us from Him, and we are dead.

A Vision of Life without Grace

I hear worldlings mutter, "Where is this man coming from? We know nothing and care nothing about being in covenant with God." You who live for gain or pleasure, truly you despise the life I set before you, but it is your own way of life that most deserves scorn! I will sketch for you with the pencil of truth. It is a country scene that passed by my mind's eye but a few hours ago. I sat by the water's edge, at a point where abundant springs poured forth new streams. It was a brook, wide but shallow, and the pure water glided along refreshingly under the overhanging boughs. Little children were there, wading into the stream and enjoying its cool waters.

One of them was a true representative of many wealthy merchants. He went fishing with a bright green glass bottle, and his ventures were successful. Again and again, I heard his voice ring out most joyously and impressively, "Look here! Look here! Such a big 'un! I have caught such a big 'un!" It was by no means a whale that he held up, but a fish that might have been an inch long at most. How he triumphed: "Such a big 'un!" To him the affairs of nations were nothing when compared with the great spoil that he had taken.

This lad symbolizes the gentleman who has made a successful speculation in the stock exchange. For the next few days, he astonishes everybody as they hear that it was "Such a big one!" Earth and heaven and hell, time and eternity, may all admire the accomplishment now that the glass bottle contains its prey.

His brother, not far off, changed the picture for me. He was less richly endowed, yet he had a very serviceable tin can with which he fished most diligently. Soon I heard his voice, pitched in another key: "Nasty little things! They won't come here! I can't catch 'em! They're good for nothing! I won't try any more." Then the impetuous genius threw his tin can with a splash into the water, and his enterprise was ended.

This boy represents the merchant whose business has closed or whose goods will not command a market. Things will not come his way. He cannot get ahead. He has failed miserably, and it has been published in the newspaper. He is convinced that all society is out of order, or he would have been sure to succeed. He is sick of it all for the present.

You smile at my boys! O worldlings, they are yourselves! You are those children, and your ambitions are their little amusements.

> O happy man that lives on high,
> While men lie groveling here.

Without God you are paddling in the stream of life, fishing for minnows. If you get a hold on God, because He has laid hold on you, blessed one, there is then a soul in you. Then you have come to be allied with angels and akin to seraphim. Apart from God, you subside into shameful littleness.

O Lord Jesus, have compassion on those who do not know You!

Chapter 6

Twelve Covenant Mercies

Incline your ear, and come to Me. Hear, and your soul shall live;
and I will make an everlasting covenant with you;
the sure mercies of David.
—Isaiah 55:3

So far, I have pleaded with all to come to God, to hear what He has to say, to give diligent and earnest heed to His teaching about their souls and about salvation. As I have pleaded—and I can truly say, with all the strength I have—I have made this one of the master arguments: that, in hearing, their souls would live, and in coming to God, they would find Him ready to enter into *"an everlasting covenant...the sure mercies of David"* with them.

This seems to me to be one of the most astonishing truths that was ever given to men to realize: that God would be a high contracting party with poor, insignificant, guilty man; that He would make a covenant with man, with you and me; and that He would bind Himself by a solemn promise, give His sacred pledge, and enter into a holy contract of mercy with the guilty sons of Adam. I believe that if men were in their right minds and God had taught their reason to be reasonable, they would be drawn to the Lord by such a wonderful promise as this: *"I will make an everlasting covenant with you; the sure mercies of David."*

Remember, there was a covenant of old that men broke. The covenant of works was essentially as follows: Do this, and you will live; keep this and that commandment, and you will be rewarded. That covenant failed because man did not keep God's commands, and so he did not earn the promised reward. We broke the terms of that contract, and it is no longer valid, except that we come under penalty for the breach of it. The penalty is that we are to be cast away from God's presence and to perish without hope, as far as that broken covenant is concerned.

Now, rolling up that old covenant as a useless thing out of which no salvation can ever develop, God comes to us in another way and says, "I will make a new covenant with you, not like the old one at all." (See Hebrews 8:8–13.) It is a covenant of grace, a covenant made, not with the worthy, but with the unworthy; a covenant not made upon conditions, but unconditionally, every supposed condition having been fulfilled by our great Representative and Surety, the Lord Jesus Christ; a covenant without an *if* or a *but* in it; *"an everlasting covenant, ordered in all things and secure"* (2 Sam. 23:5); a covenant of *shall*s and *will*s, in which God says, "I will, and you shall"; a covenant suited to our broken-down, helpless condition; a covenant that will land everyone who has an interest in it in heaven. No other covenant will ever do this.

In earlier chapters I discussed the covenant of grace. Now I would like to show to any who desire to be in this covenant of grace what the blessings are that God promises to give to guilty men when they come to Him, when they accept His love and His mercy. What are these blessings? I have little else to do but to refer you again to God's Word.

Beloved, if you had met together after the death of some wealthy relative and his will were about to be read to you, you would not require an eloquent lawyer. You would all be very attentive, and some of you who are a little deaf would recover your hearing. An important question would be, What has he bequeathed? A still more important inquiry would be, What has he left to me?

I hope you feel right now that you do not want an eloquent teacher, because I am only going to read God's will with you, His covenant, which is virtually the testament or will of Christ. All that you have to do is to pay attention and say, "What has He left? What has He bequeathed to me? What did He covenant to give to me?"

Remember that, whoever you may be, if you are willing to be saved by grace, you may be saved by grace. If you give up all hope of being saved any other way, you may be saved by the free mercy and love of God. *"If you are willing and obedient, you shall eat the good of the land"* (Isa. 1:19). If you come and take Christ as your Savior, then *"all the promises of God in Him are Yea, and in Him Amen"* (2 Cor. 1:20) are made to you. If you take Him, you take all that is in the covenant, for He is the covenant. Embodied in Him is the whole covenant of grace, and the person who has Christ has all it contains.

I am simply going to point out to you some of the passages in which we have this covenant written out at length. I will not say much about any one promise, but I will refer you to twelve wonderful mercies of the covenant of grace. I encourage you to look up each Scripture in your Bible as we progress through these passages so that you may see for yourself.

As an aside, no music is sweeter to a gospel preacher than the rustle of Bible pages in the congregation. Many times when I have been in the pulpit and I have read a passage of Scripture, nobody has followed me to see if I was quoting correctly. I strongly urge you to take your Bibles with you when you go to church. What is the best way of hearing the Word? Is it not to search and see whether what the preacher says is really according to the Word of God? Thus, I entreat you to search the Scriptures to see if what is being taught to you is true. (See Acts 17:11.)

Saving Knowledge

The first mercy of the covenant we will look at is that of saving knowledge. Let us read from Jeremiah:

> *Behold, the days are coming, says the LORD, when I will make a new covenant with the house of Israel and with the house of Judah; not according to the covenant that I made with their fathers in the day that I took them by the hand to lead them out of the land of Egypt, My covenant which they broke, though I was a husband to them, says the LORD. But this is the covenant that I will make with the house of Israel after those days, says the LORD: I will put My law in their minds, and write it on their hearts; and I will be their God, and they shall be My people. No more shall every man teach his neighbor, and every man his brother, saying, "Know the LORD," for they all shall know Me, from the least of them to the greatest of them, says the LORD. For I will forgive their iniquity, and their sin I will remember no more.* (Jer. 31:31–34)

Saving knowledge is one of the first blessings of the covenant of grace. By nature man does not know God; he does not want to know God; and when he is aroused to think of God at all, God seems a great mystery, a being invisible and unreasonable. The man asks, "Who will make me be able to know God?" It may be that he reads his Bible, but even that he does not understand. He hears the preacher, but the Lord's servant seems to talk a jargon that the unconverted man cannot comprehend.

Beloved, there is no knowing God except through God. A man's neighbor cannot teach him, even though he may attempt it. Though the neighbor may say, *"Know the LORD"* (Jer. 31:34), yet he cannot give knowledge of God. By nature, our eyes are blinded; we cannot see. You may even hold an electric light to a blind man's sightless eyes, but it will not give him sight. Blind Bartimaeus saw no light until Jesus spoke to him. (See Mark 10:46–52.) By his bigotry and self-righteousness, Saul of Tarsus was blind enough, until God shined a glorious light into his soul. (See Acts 9:1–6.)

Now, here is a covenant that God will give the knowledge of Himself to the lost, the guilty, the ruined, to those who have provoked Him and gone astray from Him. Who, reading this, are those to whom this covenant will be fulfilled right now? I cannot tell except by marks and tokens, and this is one of the marks: Do you know that you are blind? Do you know that you cannot see apart from divine grace? Do you long to see? He is not totally blind, in a spiritual sense, who knows that he is so. He is not in the dark who senses that he is in the dark, because there is already some degree of light that makes him perceive the presence of darkness.

O soul, if you desire to know God, here is the covenant: *"They all shall know Me, from the least of them to the greatest of them"* (Jer. 31:34). All God's chosen will know Him. Not one will abide in ignorance, neither will they die in ignorance. They will come to know the Lord and will *"grow in the grace and knowledge of our Lord and Savior Jesus Christ"* (2 Pet. 3:18). What a privilege this is!

"If any of you lacks wisdom, let him ask of God, who gives to all liberally and without reproach, and it will be given to him" (James 1:5). If any person is ignorant of God, let him hear the Word of the Lord, and let him seek the Lord. God will give him instruction concerning Himself and will make that person to know the great Jehovah, the Father of our spirits, who passes over iniquity, transgression, and sin.

God's Law Written in Men's Hearts

I must not linger on any one blessing. The first covenant mercy is saving knowledge; the next is that God's law will be written on the hearts of men. Let us read Jeremiah 31:33 again: *"After*

87

those days, says the LORD: I will put My law in their minds, and write it on their hearts; and I will be their God, and they shall be My people."

You know that the Law of Moses was written on two tablets of stone. Wonderfully precious those two slabs of marble must have been when the divine finger had traced the solemn lines. Moses had a great charge to keep when he had those two divinely-written tablets, but he broke them because the people had broken them in spirit. It could not be that such divine writing should ever be handled or looked at by such an unholy people.

Now, friends, it was of no use writing the Commandments on tablets of stone except to serve as condemnation of the people. However, when God comes in the covenant of grace, He does not merely give us the law in a book—the law written in legible characters—but He comes and writes on the fleshly tablets of our hearts. That way, the man knows the law by heart. What is even better, he loves the law. That law accuses him, but he would not have it altered. He bows and confesses the truthfulness of the accusation. He cries, "Lord, have mercy on me; incline my heart to Yourself, to walk in all Your ways, and to keep Your commandments and Your statutes." (See 1 Kings 8:58.) This is the covenant blessing: God makes men to love His commandments and to delight themselves in truth, righteousness, and holiness.

This writing on our hearts is a very wonderful thing. Nobody but God can write on human hearts. I can write certain thoughts on your minds as I appeal to your eyes and ears, but to reach the heart is another thing. Only He who has the keys of heaven, He who has the keys of the heart, He who shuts and no man opens, or opens and no man shuts (Rev. 3:7), only He can really access the human heart. Yet God does so reach the human heart that He writes His commandments there. Moreover, He does this to men who formerly hated those commandments; He makes them love His law. He makes men who despised His commandments honor them. As for men who forgot His commandments, He writes them in their hearts so that they cannot get away from them. As for men who would have changed the commandments, He changes their hearts instead. Then their hearts and the commandments agree.

This is a second covenant blessing. Do any of you want it? Would you like to know the Lord? Do you wish to have His law written on your hearts? *"According to your faith let it be to you"* (Matt. 9:29). Believe that God can do this for you, trust in Christ that it may be done unto you, and it will be so.

Free Pardon

The third covenant mercy is free pardon. You will find this at the end of Jeremiah 31:34: *"For I will forgive their iniquity, and their sin I will remember no more."* This is such a great blessing of the covenant. You people who think that you have never sinned, you who believe yourselves to have been always good—or at least as good as you could be—and far above the average of mankind, you exceedingly excellent people, who have never done anything that you need to repent of very greatly, I have nothing for you here. Only remember what Mary sang: *"He has filled the hungry with good things, and the rich* [that is you] *He has sent away empty"* (Luke 1:53).

However, if one of you feels the burden of his guilt, if one soul is bowed down with grief because of the heavy load of past iniquity that lies upon it, surely, if you have the faith, you will jump for joy as you read these words: *"I will forgive their iniquity, and their sin I will remember no more."* First, the Lord will forgive and blot it out. He calls you by name and says, "Be as if you had never offended. Come to Me, come to My heart, as if you had always loved Me. Guilty though you are, I will not impute iniquity to your charge. I forgive it all." The great Judge will put on the white gloves, signifying mercy, and not the black cap, which indicates a death sentence. You are forgiven.

Then the Lord says, *"Their sin I will remember no more."* It is a wonderful thing when omnipotence overcomes omniscience, when omnipotent love will not allow omniscience to recall: *"Their sin I will remember no more."* Satan comes and pleads against the sinner, "God, this man did so-and-so." God says, "I do not remember it." And He does not remember it because He laid it all on Christ. Christ has suffered the penalty due for it; therefore, it is gone. It will never be recalled; it does not stand in the Book of Remembrance. As the Lord looks over this man's life, when He comes to the black pages, they are blank. Not a line is left, for He who died has made the scarlet sins as white as snow (Isa. 1:18). *"Their sin I will remember no more."*

Oh, what a precious covenant mercy is this! I do not feel as if I want to elaborate or embellish it in any way or give you any illustrations or tell you any anecdotes. Was there ever set before you such a glorious gift? Will you accept it, the perfect pardon of every sin and a divine act of amnesty and oblivion for every crime of every sort, published in the covenant of grace to every soul that is willing to receive it through Christ Jesus the Savior?

Reconciliation

Reconciliation is the next covenant mercy. In Jeremiah 32:38 we read: *"They shall be My people, and I will be their God."* The offense is put away; the sin is pardoned, and God says, *"They shall be My people."*

"But, Lord, they are the people who worshipped Baal; they are the horrid wretches who gave their children up to be burned in the red-hot arms of Molech," someone objects. (See 2 Kings 23:10.)

"Nevertheless," says the Lord, *"they shall be My people."*

"But, Lord, these are the men and women who committed adultery and fornication, and were even guilty of murder."

"They shall be My people," says the Lord.

"But, Lord, they provoked You to anger year after year and would not listen to Your prophets."

"They shall be My people, and I will be their God."

Did you ever think how much there is involved in that expression, *"I will be their God"*? God is everything. When God gives Himself to us, He gives us more than all time and all eternity, all Earth and all heaven. *"Do not be afraid, Abram,"* said the Lord to the patriarch. *"I am your shield, your exceedingly great reward"* (Gen. 15:1), as if it were reward enough for any man to have God to be his God—and so it is. More riches than the wealthiest king, more honor than the greatest conqueror, has the man who has this God to be his God forever and ever.

"They shall be My people, and I will be their God" (Jer. 32:38). You might look up that promise and find how many times it occurs in the Scriptures. I know that many times God puts it similarly: *"They shall be My people, and I will be their God."* (See Jeremiah 24:7; 31:1; 31:33; Ezekiel 11:20; 37:23, 27; Zechariah 8:8; 2 Corinthians 6:16; Hebrews 8:10.) This is another covenant blessing.

Are you willing to be the people of God? Are you willing to take Him, even this God, to be yours forever and ever? If so, then our chapter text is true concerning you: *"I will make an everlasting covenant with you; the sure mercies of David."*

True Godliness

Will you follow me to the next verse for a fifth covenant mercy, the blessing of true godliness? *"I will give them one heart and one*

Twelve Covenant Mercies

way, that they may fear Me forever, for the good of them and their children after them" (Jer. 32:39). Do you see here that *"the fear of the LORD is the beginning of wisdom"* (Prov. 9:10)?

"The fear of the LORD" is a description of true godliness, and God says that He will give this to men. He might have asked it of you—and rightly, too—but you could never have produced it on your own. However, when He says that He will give it, that is a very different thing. He is willing to give you fear of Him, to give you true religion, to bestow upon you the veneration of His sacred name that lies at the bottom of all godliness.

God will give His fear to you who never had it, or even despised it, and to any of you who have lived all your lives without it but who are willing to come and take it, right now, as the gift of His grace through Jesus Christ. May the Lord make you *"volunteers in the day of* [His] *power"* (Ps. 110:3), for that is a part of the covenant blessing! The willingness itself is His gift, and this He gives freely to His own.

Continuance in Grace

Now look, dear friends, at the next verse, which is more wonderful than anything that I have yet read. In it we find the sixth covenant mercy, continuance in grace: *"And I will make an everlasting covenant with them, that I will not turn away from doing them good; but I will put My fear in their hearts so that they will not depart from Me"* (Jer. 32:40).

Perseverance to the end, is it not granted here? *"I will not turn away from doing them good...*[and] *they will not depart from Me."* What a covenant blessing this is! It reminds me of the words of the Lord Jesus concerning His sheep: *"And I give them eternal life, and they shall never perish; neither shall anyone snatch them out of My hand"* (John 10:28).

A man who did not believe what this verse teaches said to me, "Well, no man may be able to snatch them out of His hand, but they can crawl away from between His fingers." No, they will not. See how this text secures them both ways: *"I will not turn away from doing them good; but I will put My fear in their hearts so that they will not depart from Me."* Here both gaps are blocked; there is no getting out either way. God will not leave you, and He will not let you leave Him. This is a covenant blessing indeed. Oh, for faith to lay hold of it! The soul who comes to Christ and rests wholly on

Him will find two hands with which to grasp these two gracious words: *"I will not turn away from doing them good,"* and *"they will not depart from Me."* And this is spoken of the guilty, of the very men who provoked God.

> Wonders of grace to God belong,
> Repeat His mercies in your song.

If God saved the good, the meritorious, and the righteous, then the proud Pharisees would swarm over every street in heaven, and God would have no glory. But since He saves the vilest of the vile, and the publicans, who are afraid to lift their eyes to heaven whenever they think of their own unworthiness, gather near the throne and sing of His free grace and dying love!

This covenant would be great enough if there were nothing more in it than the six blessings that I have already mentioned, but there are more. Let us look at another prophetic Scripture in order to read about more of the mercies of this covenant:

> *Then I will sprinkle clean water on you, and you shall be clean; I will cleanse you from all your filthiness and from all your idols. I will give you a new heart and put a new spirit within you; I will take the heart of stone out of your flesh and give you a heart of flesh. I will put My Spirit within you and cause you to walk in My statutes, and you will keep My judgments and do them. Then you shall dwell in the land that I gave to your fathers; you shall be My people, and I will be your God....Then you will remember your evil ways and your deeds that were not good; and you will loathe yourselves in your own sight, for your iniquities and your abominations.*
>
> (Ezek. 36:25–28, 31)

Cleansing

In the above passage we find the seventh covenant mercy, namely that of cleansing. I can hear some poor soul saying, "Well, I can see that God is going to do great things, but I feel that I am so unclean I dare not come near to God. Why, I am polluted all over, inside and out. I am altogether like a leprous man!" Come then, let me read this verse to you: *"Then I will sprinkle clean water on you, and you shall be clean; I will cleanse you from all your filthiness and from all your idols"* (v. 25).

God's Word elsewhere commands, *"Wash yourselves, make yourselves clean"* (Isa. 1:16). That is your duty. However, here you are told that the Lord will wash you and make you clean. This is your privilege. *"You are already clean,"* Christ said to His disciples, *"because of the word which I have spoken to you"* (John 15:3). That is *"the washing of water by the word"* (Eph. 5:26) of which Paul wrote to the church at Ephesus.

The free-grace covenant states, *"Then I will sprinkle clean water on you, and you shall be clean"* (Ezek. 36:25). The Lord sprinkles this *"clean water"* on the leprous and the polluted sinner, on the man who lies covered with his own blood, a filthy thing in the sight of God, and loathsome to Him. When God Himself says, *"You shall be clean,"* I know that we are clean, for He is the best judge of true cleanliness. His pure and holy eyes detect every spot of sin and every latent trace of disease. Though it may be deep within the heart, He can spy it out; but He says, *"I will sprinkle clean water on you, and you shall be clean."*

Then the Lord goes on to enumerate that from which He will cleanse us: *"I will cleanse you...from all your idols"* (v. 25). Is drink your idol? Is some lust of the flesh your idol? "Oh!" you say, "I cannot get rid of these things." No, but the Lord can cleanse you from them. Only come to Him, listen diligently to Him, trust Him, yield to Him, surrender yourself to Him, and He will dash your idols in pieces and tear them from their thrones. He will also cleanse you from whatever else there may be that is unmentionable: *"from all your filthiness"* (v. 25), things not to be spoken of, those things that are done in secret. "I will cleanse you from them," says the Lord.

I may be addressing somebody who, as he reads this, thinks that I am delusional. "Why," says he, "I am a contemptible creature. I am a great sinner. Can God bless me?" Yes, He can bless even you.

Such was the case of Colonel Gardiner. On the very night that he had planned to commit a vile sin, Christ appeared to him, and he thought that he heard Him say, "I have done all this for you; will you never turn to Me?" At that moment he did turn to Jesus. He became noted as an eminent Christian man, more noted than he had formerly been as a debauched officer in the army.

The Lord Jesus Christ still works these wonders of grace. He meets men often when they are desperately set on mischief, just as a horse that is rushing headlong into battle. Christ comes and lays His hand on the reins, turns the steed, and leads it back wherever

He desires. Such is the power of His almighty love. I pray that He will do the same for you, according to this wondrous promise: *"I will sprinkle clean water on you, and you shall be clean; I will cleanse you from all your filthiness and from all your idols"* (Ezek. 36:25).

A Renewed Nature

Nor is that all. When a man is once made clean, he would soon become foul again if left to himself. So here follows the next astounding covenant mercy, a renewal of nature: *"I will sprinkle clean water on you, and you shall be clean; I will cleanse you from all your filthiness and from all your idols"* (v. 25).

God did not say, "I will help you to this," but "I will do it." His words were not, "I will help you to make yourself a new heart"— no, nothing of the kind—but *"I will give you a new heart"* (v. 26).

You know that if you cut off the branches of a tree, it will grow fresh ones. However, if you could tear out its heart, it would never grow a new one. There are some creatures such as the lobster that will shed their claws, and the claws will grow again, but a lobster can never grow a new heart. If the center of animal or vegetable life is once destroyed, there is no renewing it. Even so, God can work this miracle in human hearts. He can strike at the very center of man's nature and change it. It takes little to purify the flowing streams, but it is a great marvel to cleanse an impure spring so that the bitter water suddenly turns sweet. This is a miracle that can only be brought about by the finger of God, yet there is nothing except this renewal of the inward nature that is worth having.

Some people imagine that we Christians, when we do not attend or participate in certain worldly amusements, are very much denying ourselves. It is nothing of the kind. Contrary to their thinking, it would be an awful denial for us if we had to go with the worldlings to pollute our minds and hearts with their immoral amusements. Those who frequent such places perhaps assume that it is a denial for us not to go with them. How little they know us!

When I go down to a friend's farm, I see a man carrying a couple of buckets of food to the pigs, but I never envy the pigs. I like them to have all that they can and to enjoy themselves, but do not suppose that I am denying myself in not wanting their food. My taste does not lie that way.

But suppose that a man has a hog's heart. What is the way to deal with him—to deny him his swill? Certainly not, let him have it while he is like the hogs. The thing that is needed is a change of heart. When his heart is turned into a renewed man's heart and is made to be a godlike heart, then it is no denial to him to loathe the things that once gave him so much pleasure. His tastes are entirely changed, according to the promise of the covenant: *"I will give you a new heart and put a new spirit within you"* (Ezek. 36:26).

The old heart is very hard. In some poor souls, it seems to be altogether petrified. You cannot make any impression upon it. You are received with ridicule, however earnest you may be in your testimonies for God. Yet the Lord can change that stony heart to a heart of flesh.

> Our heart, that flinty, stubborn thing,
> That terrors cannot move,
> That fears no threat'nings of His wrath,
> Shall be dissolved by love.
> Or He can take the flint away,
> That would not be refined;
> And from the treasures of His grace,
> Bestow a softer mind.

Then the man, who had just previously been as hard as flint, sits and weeps over his sins. See how watchful he is in the presence of all kinds of temptations. He is half afraid to put one foot in front of the other. The very man with the devil-may-care attitude is now the one who does care and who trembles lest he should in any way grieve the living God. What a blessed covenant mercy this is!

Holy Conduct

Moving on, we find that the ninth covenant mercy is holy conduct. Let us continue reading in Ezekiel: *"I will put My Spirit within you and cause you to walk in My statutes, and you will keep My judgments and do them"* (Ezek. 36:27).

When God deals with a man through His grace, He not only calls him to holiness, but also gives him holiness; He not only bids him walk in His way, but also makes him walk in His way. He does so, not by compulsion, not by any kind of physical force, but by the sweet constraints of infinite love. The man's entire life is changed externally, just as his heart is changed internally. "Oh," says one, "this is very wonderful!" Yes, it is the steadfast wonder of the Gospel. Certain miracles may have ceased, but the miracles of turning men from darkness to light and from the power of Satan unto God are being accomplished every day.

I rejoice that they are constantly being brought about in houses of prayer around the world, and I believe that they are going to be produced in some who are now reading this book. If this miracle is accomplished, do not attribute it to me, for I ask you to remember how feeble I am. Rather, understand that the power of God works through the teaching of the Gospel, making dry bones live and turning black sinners into bright saints, *"to the praise of the glory of His grace"* (Eph. 1:6).

Happy Self-Loathing

This will be the tenth covenant mercy, happy self-loathing. Perhaps you wonder that I called this a mercy. But read the following: *"Then you will remember your evil ways and your deeds that were not good; and you will loathe yourselves in your own sight, for your iniquities and your abominations"* (Ezek. 36:31).

Free grace makes men loathe themselves. After God has done so much for them, they feel ashamed that they do not know what to do. "O Lord," says the saint, "to think that I could have ever sinned against One who loved me so much! That I, the elect of God, could have ever acted like the elect of hell! That I, who am Your own, ever called myself the Devil's own! That I, who was chosen unto holiness and eternal life, passed it all by as if it were no concern of mine!" May God grant us this holy loathing, as He will do when we have once tasted of His infinite love!

Communion with God

The next covenant mercy is the blessing of communion with God:

> *Moreover I will make a covenant of peace with them, and it shall be an everlasting covenant with them; I will establish them and multiply them, and I will set My sanctuary in their midst forevermore. My tabernacle also shall be with them; indeed I will be their God, and they shall be My people. The nations also will know that I, the LORD, sanctify Israel, when My sanctuary is in their midst forevermore.* (Ezek. 37:26–28)

God promises to set up His tabernacle and His temple in the midst of His people and to make them His priests, His servants, His children, His friends. God will no longer be absent from you when this covenant work has been accomplished in you. You will be brought to dwell in His presence and to abide in His house, no more to go out, until the day when He takes you to His palace home above to be forever in His presence and to serve Him in His temple. All of this is promised to the worthless, to the most vile; all of this is given without asking of you anything but that you will be willing to receive Him; all of this is yours without requiring of you anything but just your emptiness that He may fill it, your sinfulness that He may cleanse it, and your surrender to Him. What do you have to surrender? Nothing but a lot of rubbish of your own—your self-righteousness especially, which is but *"filthy rags"* (Isa. 64:6) to Him. May the Lord bring you to this place of surrender even now!

Necessary Chastisement

There is one more covenant mercy for me to mention, and I put it last because you will be surprised, perhaps, when I state it. It is about needed chastisement. For this I ask you to turn to Psalm 89:

If his sons forsake My law and do not walk in My judgments, if they break My statutes and do not keep My commandments, then I will punish their transgression with the rod, and their iniquity with stripes. Nevertheless My lovingkindness I will not utterly take from him, nor allow My faithfulness to fail.
(Ps. 89:30–33)

There is a rod of grace in the covenant. Children of God, you do not like it; it would be no rod if you did. However, it is good for you when you come under the fatherly discipline of God. Though He will never take His everlasting love from you nor allow His faithfulness to fail, yet when you transgress, His rod will be sure to fall upon you. Sometimes its strokes will come upon you before you transgress to keep you from sinning.

I often hear of some of God's dearest servants suffering. I heard of one whom I am sure God loves very much. He is very useful in the Lord's kingdom and spends himself in his Master's work.

He is also very prosperous; God has given to him great wealth that he discreetly and wisely uses. With all of that, however, he has had a very sharp affliction come upon him lately that is enough to break his heart. When I heard about it, I said, "Yes, yes, God loves him; God loves him."

If you are a child of God, note this truth, and accept it with joy: our heavenly Father never pampers His children. We may spoil our sons and daughters, but our Father never spoils His children. If He gives you great happiness and great success and makes you useful, He will every now and then give you a whipping behind the door.

You may think sometimes, "That man is very happy; he has great blessing resting on his work." Yes, this man is very happy to tell you that he does not have all sweets to drink, which would make him weak and sickly; but there are bitter tonics in his life, sharp blows of the rod, to keep him right. If we have to bless God more for any one thing than for everything else, it is to thank Him that we have not escaped the rod. Infirmity can be a choice blessing from God. I cannot measure the unutterable good that comes to us often in that way. Losses in business and crosses and bereavements and depressions of spirit are all covenant mercies when we see them in the light of eternity.

The true child of God cannot escape the rod, and would not if he could. He becomes afraid when he does not sometimes feel it. He will not have to be afraid about it for long, for it will come in due time.

I think that I hear somebody say, "I do not want that." Rightly said, because you want worldly pleasure. Perhaps God will let you have it until you have spent all your substance on it, as the Prodigal Son did. (See Luke 15:11–32.) Then you will find that it is all weariness and sorrow, and you will want something better.

However, if you will say, "I will accept the covenant of grace, rod and all; for if I can be God's child, I will very gladly take the rod as part of the mercies of the covenant," come, and you shall have it. Seek the Lord this moment. Do not give sleep to your eyes nor allow your eyelids to close until you have found Him.

May God grant you all the mercies of the everlasting covenant, for Jesus' sake!

Book Two

Power in the Blood

Contents

Chapter 1

Healing by the Stripes of Jesus

By His stripes we are healed.
—Isaiah 53:5

One evening in Exeter Hall, I heard a speech by the late Mr. Mackay. He told of a person who was very concerned about his soul and felt that he could never rest until he found salvation. So, taking the Bible in his hand, he said to himself, "Eternal life is to be found somewhere in the Word of God; and if it is here, I will find it, for I will read the Book right through. I will pray to God over every page of it. Possibly, it may contain some saving message for me."

He told us that the earnest seeker read on through Genesis, Exodus, Leviticus, and so on; and though Christ is there very evidently, he could not find Him in the types and symbols. The holy histories did not yield him comfort, nor did the book of Job. He passed through Psalms but did not find his Savior there, and the same was the case with the other books, until he reached Isaiah. In this book he read on until near the end, and then in the fifty-third chapter these words arrested his delighted attention: *"By His stripes we are healed."*

"Now I have found it," he said. "Here is the healing that I need for my sin-sick soul, and I see how it comes to me through the sufferings of the Lord Jesus Christ. Blessed be His name, I am healed!" It was well that the seeker was wise enough to search the Sacred Volume; it was better still that in that volume there was a life-giving word that the Holy Spirit revealed to the seeker's heart.

I have decided that Isaiah 53:5 is a fine text on which to write. Perhaps a voice from God may speak through it yet again to some other awakened sinner. By this verse God spoke to the treasurer of the Ethiopian queen; he was impressed by it while searching the

Scriptures. (See Acts 8:26–38.) May God also speak to many who will read this book! Let us pray that it may be so. God is very gracious, and He will hear our prayers.

The purpose of this chapter is very simple: I want to explain my text, Isaiah 53:5. May the Holy Spirit give me power to do so to the glory of God!

The Disease of Sin

In endeavoring to explain the full meaning of the text, I would remark first that God, in His infinite mercy, here treats sin as a disease. *"By His stripes"*—that is, the stripes of the Lord Jesus— *"we are healed."* Through the sufferings of our Lord, sin is pardoned, and we are delivered from the power of evil. We are healed of the deadly malady of sin.

In this present life, the Lord treats sin as a disease. If He were to treat it at once as sin and summon us to His court to answer for it, we would immediately sink beyond the reach of hope, for we could neither answer His accusations nor defend ourselves from His justice. In His great mercy He looks on us with pity, and for now He treats our ill manners as if they were diseases to be cured rather than rebellions to be punished.

It is most gracious on His part to do so, for while sin is a disease, it is also a great deal more. If our iniquities were the result of an unavoidable sickness, we might claim pity rather than scolding. However, we sin willfully; we choose evil; we transgress in heart. Therefore, we bear a moral responsibility that makes sin an infinite evil. Our sin is our crime rather than our calamity.

However, God looks at our sin as a disease for a season. So that He can deal with us on hopeful grounds, He looks at the sickness of sin and does not look yet at the wickedness of sin. This is not without reason, for men who indulge in gross vices are often charitably judged by their fellowmen to be not only wholly wicked, but partly mad. Propensities to evil are usually associated with some degree of mental disease and, perhaps, also, of physical disease. At any rate, sin is a spiritual malady of the worst kind.

The Abnormality of Sin

Sin is a disease, for it is neither essential to manhood nor an integral part of human nature as God created it. Man was never more

102

fully and truly man than he was before he fell. He who is specially called *"the Son of Man"* (Matt. 8:20) *"committed no sin, nor was deceit found in His mouth"* (1 Pet. 2:22), yet He was perfectly man.

Sin is abnormal, a sort of cancerous growth that should not be in the soul. Sin is disturbing to manhood: sin unmans a man. Sin is sadly destructive to man; it takes the crown from his head, the light from his mind, and the joy from his heart. We may name many grievous diseases that are destroyers of our race, but the greatest of these is sin. Sin, indeed, is the fatal egg from which all other sicknesses have been hatched. It is the fountain and source of all mortal maladies.

The Disorder of Sin

Sin is a disease because it puts the man's whole system out of order. It places the lower faculties in the higher place, for it makes the body master over the soul. The man should ride the horse, but in the sinner the horse rides the man. The mind should keep the animal instincts and propensities in check, but in many men the animal crushes the mental and the spiritual. For instance, many live as if eating and drinking were the chief objects of existence; they live to eat, instead of eating to live!

The faculties are thrown out of gear by sin, so that they act fitfully and irregularly; you cannot depend on any one of them to keep its place. The equilibrium of the life forces is grievously disturbed. Even as a sickness of the body is called a disorder, so sin is the disorder of the soul. Human nature is out of joint and out of health, and man is no longer man. He is dead through sin (Eph. 2:1), even as he was warned of old, *"In the day that you eat of it you shall surely die"* (Gen. 2:17). Man is marred, bruised, sick, paralyzed, polluted, and rotten with disease, to the same degree that sin has shown its true character.

The Undermining Nature of Sin

Sin, like disease, weakens man. The moral energy is so broken down in some people that it scarcely exists. The conscience labors under a fatal disease and is gradually ruined by a decline. The understanding has been lamed by evil, and the will is rendered feeble for good, though forcible for evil. The principle of integrity, the resolve of virtue—in which a man's true strength really lies—is sapped and undermined by wrongdoing.

Sin is like a secret bleeding that robs the vital parts of their essential nourishment. How near to death in some people is even the power to discern between good and evil! The apostle tells us that *"when we were still without strength, in due time Christ died for the ungodly"* (Rom. 5:6). This being without strength is the direct result of the sickness of sin, which has weakened our whole manhood.

The Numbing Nature of Sin

Sin is a disease that in some cases causes extreme pain and anguish, but in other cases deadens sensibility. It frequently happens that the more sinful a man is, the less he is conscious of it.

It was remarked of a certain notorious criminal that many thought him innocent because when he was charged with murder, he did not betray the least emotion. In that wretched self-possession there was, to my mind, presumptive proof of his great familiarity with crime. If an innocent person is charged with a great offense, the mere charge horrifies him. It is only by weighing all the circumstances and distinguishing between sin and shame that he recovers himself. It is he who can do the deed of shame that does not blush when he is charged with it.

The deeper a man goes into sin, the less he concedes that it is sin. Like a man who takes drugs, he acquires the power to take larger and larger doses, until what would kill a hundred other men has only a slight effect on him. A man who readily lies is scarcely conscious of the moral degradation involved in being a liar, though he may think it shameful to be called one. It is one of the worst points of this disease of sin that it stupefies the understanding and causes a paralysis of the conscience.

By and by, sin is sure to cause pain, like other diseases that flesh is heir to; and when awakening comes, what a start it gives! Conscience one day will awaken and fill the guilty soul with alarm and distress, if not in this world, certainly in the next. Then the sinner will see what an awful thing it is to offend the Lord's law.

The Impurity of Sin

Sin is a disease that pollutes a man. Certain diseases render a man horribly impure. God is the best judge of purity, for He is exceedingly holy and cannot endure sin. The Lord puts sin from Him with abhorrence, and He prepares a place where the forever unclean will be shut up by themselves. He will not dwell with them here, nor can they dwell with Him in heaven. Justice must put out of heaven everything that defiles. Oh, my reader, will the Lord be compelled to put you out of His presence because you persist in wickedness?

The disease of sin, which is so polluting, is, at the same time, most injurious to us, for it prevents the higher enjoyment and employment of life. People can exist in sin, but they do not truly live. As the Scripture says, such a person is *"dead while* [he] *lives"* (1 Tim. 5:6). While we continue in sin, we cannot serve God on earth or hope to enjoy Him forever above. We are incapable of communion with perfect spirits and with God Himself, and the loss of this communion is the greatest of all evils. Sin deprives us of spiritual sight, hearing, feeling, and taste, and thus deprives us of those joys that turn existence into life. It brings true death upon us, so that we exist in ruins, deprived of all that can be called life.

The Fatality of Sin

This disease is also fatal. Is it not written, *"The soul who sins shall die"* (Ezek. 18:4)? *"Sin, when it is full-grown, brings forth death"* (James 1:15). There is no hope of eternal life for any man unless sin is put away. This disease never exhausts itself or destroys itself. *"Evil men...will grow worse and worse"* (2 Tim. 3:13). In another world, as well as in this present world, character will go on to develop and ripen, and so the sinner will become more and more corrupt as the result of his spiritual death.

Oh, my friends, if you refuse Christ, sin will be the death of your peace, your joy, your prospects, your hopes, and thus the death of all that is worth having! In the case of other diseases, nature may conquer the malady, and you may be restored; but in this case, apart from divine intervention, nothing lies before you but eternal death.

God, therefore, treats sin as a disease because it is a disease. And I want you to believe that it is so, for then you will thank the Lord for treating your sin this way. Many of us have felt that sin is a disease and have been healed of it. Oh, that others could see what an exceedingly evil thing it is to sin against the Lord! It is a contagious, defiling, incurable, mortal sickness.

Perhaps somebody is saying, "Why do you raise these points? They fill us with unpleasant thoughts." I do it for the reason given by the engineer who built the great Menai Tubular Bridge. When it was being erected, some engineer friends said to him, "You raise all kinds of difficulties."

"Yes," he said, "I raise them so that I may solve them."

That is why I expound on the sad state of man, so that I may present the glorious remedy of which our text so sweetly speaks.

The Remedy for Sin

God treats sin as a disease, and He here declares the remedy that He has provided: *"By His stripes we are healed."* I ask you very solemnly to accompany me in your meditations for a few minutes, while I bring before you the stripes of the Lord Jesus.

The Lord resolved to restore us; therefore, He sent His only begotten Son (John 3:16), very God of very God. God's Son descended into this world to take upon Himself our nature (Heb. 2:17) in order to redeem us. He lived as a man among men (Phil. 2:8); and, in due time, after thirty years or more of service, the time came when He should do us the greatest service of all. Namely, He stood in our stead and bore *"the chastisement for our peace"* (Isa. 53:5). He went to Gethsemane, and there, at the first taste of our bitter cup, *"His sweat became like great drops of blood"* (Luke 22:44). He went to Pilate's hall and Herod's judgment seat, and there He suffered a great deal of pain and scorn in our place. Last of all, they took Him to the cross and nailed Him there to die—to die in our stead—*"the just for the unjust, that He might bring us to God"* (1 Pet. 3:18).

The word *stripes* is used to set forth His sufferings, both of body and of soul. The whole of Christ was made a sacrifice for us: His whole manhood suffered. His body and His mind shared in a grief that can never be fully described. In the beginning of His passion, when He emphatically suffered instead of us, He was in agony, and from His body a bloody sweat flowed so heavily that it fell to the ground (Luke 22:44). It is very rare for a man to sweat blood. There have been one or two instances of it, and they have been followed by almost immediate death. But our Savior lived—lived after an agony that, to anyone else, would have proved fatal.

Before He could cleanse His face from this dreadful crimson, they hurried Him to the high priest's hall. In the dead of night they bound Him and led Him away. Then they took Him to Pilate and to Herod. They scourged Him (Matt. 27:26), the soldiers spat on Him and struck Him (v. 30), and they put a crown of thorns on His head (v. 29).

Scourging is one of the most awful tortures that can be inflicted. It is to the eternal disgrace of Englishmen that they permitted the cat-o'-nine-tails to be used on the soldier; but to the Romans, cruelty was so natural that they made their common punishments worse than brutal. The Roman scourge is said to have been made of the sinews of oxen, twisted into knots, and into these knots were inserted both slivers of bone and the hipbones of sheep. Every time the scourge fell on the bare back, *"the plowers...made their furrows long"* (Ps. 129:3). Our Savior was called upon to endure the fierce pain of the Roman scourge, and this not as the end of His punishment, but as a preliminary to crucifixion.

In addition to this, they struck Him and plucked out His hair; they spared Him no form of pain. In all His faintness, through bleeding and fasting, they made Him carry His cross (John 19:17). Then another was forced, by the forethought of their cruelty, to bear the cross (Matt. 27:32), lest their victim should die on the road. They stripped Him, threw Him down, and nailed Him to the wood. They pierced His hands and His feet (Ps. 22:16). They lifted up the cross with Him on it, and then they dashed it down into its place in the ground, so that all His limbs were dislocated. This was done in accordance with the Scripture: *"I am poured out like water, and all My bones are out of joint"* (v. 14). He hung in the burning sun until the fever dissolved His strength, and He said, *"My heart is like wax; it has melted within Me. My strength is dried up like a potsherd, and My tongue clings to My jaws; You have brought Me to the dust of death"* (vv. 14–15). There He hung, in the sight of God and men.

The weight of His body was first sustained by His feet, until the nails tore through the tender nerves; then the painful load began to weigh on His hands and tear that sensitive flesh. How awful must have been the torment caused by that dragging iron tearing through the delicate parts of the hands and feet! Now every kind of bodily pain tortured His body.

All the while His enemies stood around, pointing at Him in scorn, mocking Him, scoffing at His prayers, and gloating over His sufferings. He cried, *"I thirst"* (John 19:28), and they gave Him vinegar *"mingled with gall"* (Matt. 27:34). After a while He said, *"It is finished!"* (John 19:30). He had endured the utmost of appointed grief and had made full vindication to divine justice. Then, and not until then, He *"gave up His spirit"* (v. 30).

107

Holy men of old have expounded most lovingly on the bodily sufferings of our Lord, and I have no hesitation in doing the same. I trust that trembling sinners may see salvation in these painful stripes of the Redeemer.

To describe the outward sufferings of our Lord is not easy: I acknowledge that I have failed. But His soul sufferings, which were the soul of His sufferings, who can even conceive, much less express? At the very first I told you that *"His sweat became like great drops of blood"* (Luke 22:44). That was His heart driving out its life to the surface because of His terrible depression of spirit. He said, *"My soul is exceedingly sorrowful, even to death"* (Matt. 26:38). The betrayal by Judas (vv. 47–49) and the desertion of the Twelve (v. 56) grieved our Lord, but the weight of our sin was the real pressure on His heart. Our guilt was the olive press that forced from Him the moisture of His life.

No language can ever tell His agony in the prospect of His passion; how little, then, can we comprehend the passion itself? When nailed to the cross, He endured what no martyr ever suffered; for martyrs, when they have died, have been so sustained by God that they have rejoiced amid their pain. But our Redeemer was forsaken by His Father, and He cried, *"My God, My God, why have you forsaken Me?"* (Matt. 27:46). That was the bitterest cry of all, the utmost depth of His unfathomable grief. Yet it was necessary for Christ to be deserted because God must turn His back on sin, and consequently on Him who was made *"to be sin for us"* (2 Cor. 5:21).

The soul of the great Substitute suffered a horror of misery so that sinners would not have to experience the horror of hell. We would have been plunged into hell, but Jesus took our sin upon Himself. He became *"a curse for us (for it is written, 'Cursed is everyone who hangs on a tree')"* (Gal. 3:13). But who can comprehend what that curse means?

The remedy for your sins and mine is found in the substitutionary sufferings of the Lord Jesus, and in these alone. These stripes of the Lord Jesus Christ were on our behalf. Do you ask, "Is there anything for us to do to remove the guilt of sin?" I answer, There is nothing whatsoever for you to do. *"By His stripes we are healed."* All those stripes He has endured, and He has not left one of them for us to bear.

"But do we not have to believe on Him?" Yes, certainly. If I claim that a certain ointment heals, I do not deny that you need a bandage with which to apply it to the wound. Faith is the bandage that binds the ointment of Christ's reconciliation to the sore of our sin. The bandage does not heal; that is the work of the ointment. Likewise, faith does not heal; that is the work of the Atonement.

Do I hear someone say, "But surely I must do something or suffer something"? I answer, You must not try to add anything to Christ's atonement, or you greatly dishonor Him. For your salvation, you must rely on the wounds of Jesus Christ and nothing else. The text does not say, "His stripes help to heal us," but *"By His stripes we are healed."*

"But we must repent," cries another. Assuredly we must, and will, for repentance is the first sign of healing; but the stripes of Jesus heal us, not our repentance. These stripes, when applied to the heart, work repentance in us: we hate sin because it made Jesus suffer.

When you believe that Jesus suffered for you, then you discover the fact that God will never punish you for the same offense for which Jesus died. His justice will not permit Him to see the debt paid first by the surety, and then again by the debtor. Justice cannot demand a recompense twice; if my bleeding Substitute has borne my guilt, then I cannot bear it. Accepting Christ Jesus as having suffered for me, I have accepted a complete discharge from judicial liability. I have been condemned in Christ, and *"there is therefore now no condemnation"* (Rom. 8:1) to me anymore.

This is the groundwork of the security of the sinner who believes in Jesus. He lives because Jesus died in his place, and he is acceptable before God because Jesus is accepted. The person for whom Jesus is an accepted Substitute must go free. None can touch him; he is clear. Oh, my reader, will you take Jesus Christ as your Substitute? If so, you are free. *"He who believes in Him is not condemned"* (John 3:18). Thus, *"by His stripes we are healed."*

The Power of This Remedy

I have tried to put before you the disease and the remedy. I now desire to explain the fact that this remedy is effective immediately wherever it is applied. The stripes of Jesus do heal men; they have healed many of us. It does not look as if they could cause so great a cure, but the fact is undeniable.

I often hear people say, "If you preach this faith in Jesus Christ as the means of salvation, people will be careless about holy living." I am as good a witness on that point as anybody, for I live every day in the midst of men who are trusting in the stripes of Jesus for their salvation. I have seen no bad effect from such a trust, but I have seen the reverse. I bear testimony that I have seen the very worst of men become the very best of men by believing in the Lord Jesus Christ. It is surprising how these stripes heal the moral diseases of those who seem past remedy.

I have seen a sinner's character healed. I have seen the drunkard become sober, the harlot become chaste, the angry man become gentle, the covetous man become generous, and the liar become truthful, simply by trusting in the sufferings of Jesus. If trusting in Jesus did not make a person righteous, it would not really do anything for him. You must judge a person by his fruits (Matt. 7:20). If the fruits are not changed, the tree is not changed. Character is everything; if the character is not set right, the person is not saved.

I say without fear of contradiction that the atoning sacrifice, applied to the heart, heals the disease of sin. If you doubt it, try it. He who believes in Jesus is sanctified (Heb. 10:10) as well as justified (Rom. 3:24); by faith he becomes an altogether changed person.

Not only is the character healed, but the conscience is healed of its sting. Sin crushes a person's soul; he is spiritless and joyless. But the moment he believes in Jesus, he leaps into the light. You can often see a change even in the person's face; the cloud flies from the countenance when guilt goes from the conscience. Dozens of times, when I have been talking with those bowed down with sin's burden, they have looked as though they qualified for an asylum because of their inward grief. But they have caught the thought, "Christ stood for me; and if I trust in Him, I have the sign that He did so, and I am clear," and their faces have lit up as if they had glimpsed heaven.

Gratitude for such great mercy causes a change of thought toward God, and so it heals the judgment. By this means, the affections are turned in the right way, and the heart is healed. Sin is no longer loved, but God is loved, and holiness is desired. The whole man is healed, and the whole life is changed. How lighthearted a person is made by faith in Jesus! How the troubles of life lose their weight! How the fear of death is gone! A convert rejoices in the Lord, for the blessed remedy of the stripes of Jesus is applied to his soul by faith in Him.

The fact that *"by His stripes we are healed"* has plenty of evidence. I will take the liberty of giving my own testimony. If it were necessary, I could call thousands of people, my daily acquaintances, who can say that with the stripes of Christ they are healed. Even so, I must not withhold my personal testimony. Suppose I had suffered from a dreadful disease and a physician had given me a remedy that had healed me. I would not be ashamed to tell you all about it. I would use my own case as an argument to persuade you to use my physician.

Years ago, when I was a youth, the burden of my sin was exceedingly heavy upon me. I had not fallen into any great sins, and I was not regarded by anyone as an especially evil transgressor. However, I regarded myself as such, and I had good reason for doing so. My conscience was sensitive because it was enlightened; and I judged that, having a godly father and a praying mother, and having been trained in the ways of piety, I had sinned against much light. Consequently, there was a greater degree of guilt in my sin than in that of others who were my youthful associates, who had not enjoyed my advantages.

I could not enjoy the fun of youth because I felt that I had damaged my conscience. I would go to my room and sit there alone, read my Bible, and pray for forgiveness, but peace did not come to me. Books such as Baxter's *Call to the Unconverted* and Doddridge's *Rise and Progress* I read over and over again. Early in the morning I would awaken and read the most earnest religious books I could find, desiring to be eased of my burden of sin. I was not always this dull, but at times my misery of soul was very great. The words of the weeping prophet and of Job suited my mournful case. I would have chosen death rather than life. I tried to do as well as I could and behave myself, but in my own judgment I grew worse and worse. I felt more and more despondent.

I attended every place of worship within my reach, but I heard nothing that gave me lasting comfort. Finally, one day I heard a simple preacher of the Gospel speak from the text, *"Look to Me, and be saved, all you ends of the earth!"* (Isa. 45:22). When he told me that all I had to do was look to Jesus—to Jesus the Crucified One—I could scarcely believe it. He went on and said, "Look, look, look!" He added, "There is a young man, under the left-hand gallery there, who is very miserable. He will have no peace until he looks to Jesus." Then he cried, "Look! Look! Young man, look!" I did look. In that·moment relief came to me, and I felt such overflowing joy that I could have stood up and cried, "Hallelujah! Glory be to God! I am delivered from the burden of my sin!"

Many days have passed since then, but my faith has held me up and compelled me to tell the story of free grace and dying love. I can truly say,

> E'er since by faith I saw the stream
> Thy flowing wounds supply,
> Redeeming love has been my theme,
> And shall be till I die.

I hope to sit up in bed during my last hours and tell of the stripes that healed me. I hope some young men, yes, and old men, will at once try this remedy. It is good for all characters and all ages. *"By His stripes we are healed."* Thousands upon thousands of us have tried and proven this remedy. *"We speak what We know and testify what We have seen"* (John 3:11). God grant that others may receive our witness through the power of the Holy Spirit!

I want to write a few lines to those who have not tried this marvelous cure. Let my words speak directly to you. Friend, you are by nature in need of soul healing as much as anybody, and one reason that you do not care about the remedy is that you do not believe you are sick. I saw a salesman one day as I was taking a walk; he was selling walking sticks. He followed me and offered me one of the sticks. I showed him mine—a far better one than any he had to sell—and he left at once. He could see that I was not likely to be a purchaser.

I have often thought of that when I have been preaching. I show men the righteousness of the Lord Jesus, but they show me their own, and all hope of dealing with them is gone. Unless I can show them that their righteousness is worthless, they will not seek *"the righteousness which is from God by faith"* (Phil. 3:9). Oh, that the Lord would show you your disease, and then you would desire the remedy!

It may be that you do not care to hear of the Lord Jesus Christ. Ah, my dear friends! You will have to hear of Him one of these days, either for your salvation or your condemnation. The Lord has the key to your heart, and I trust He will give you a better mind. Then, your memory will recall my simple words, and you will say, "I do remember. Yes, I read that there is healing in the wounds of Christ."

I pray you do not put off seeking the Lord; that would be great presumption on your part and a sad provocation to Him. But if you have put it off, I pray you do not let the Devil tell you it is too late. It is never too late while life lasts. I have read in books that very few people are converted after forty years of age. I am solemnly convinced that there is little truth in such a statement. I have seen as many people converted at one age as at another in proportion to the number of people who are living at that age. Any first Sunday in the month there are thirty to eighty new converts in our church who are given the right hand of fellowship. This selection of people represents every age, from childhood up to old age.

The precious blood of Jesus has power to heal long-rooted sin. It makes old hearts new. If you were a thousand years old, I would exhort you to believe in Jesus, and I would be sure that His stripes would heal you. Your hair is nearly gone, old friend, and wrinkles appear on your brow, but come to Jesus now! You are rotting away with sin, but this medicine heals desperate cases! Retiree, put your trust in Jesus, for *"by His stripes"* the old and the dying are healed!

Now, my dear friend, you are at this moment either healed or not. You are either healed by grace, or you are still in your natural sickness. Will you be so kind to yourself as to inquire which it is? Many say, "We know what we are"; but some more thoughtful ones reply, "We don't quite know." Friend, you ought to know. Suppose I asked a man, "Are you bankrupt or not?" and he said, "I really have no time to look at my books; therefore, I am not sure." I would suspect that he was in financial trouble; wouldn't you? Whenever a man is afraid to look at his books, I suspect that he has something to be afraid of. So whenever a person says, "I don't know my condition, and I don't care to think much about it," you may pretty safely conclude that things are not right between him and God. You ought to know whether you are saved or not.

"I hope I am saved," says one, "but I do not know the date of my conversion." That does not matter at all. It is a pleasant thing for a person to know his birthday; but when a person is not sure of the exact date of his birth, he does not, therefore, infer that he is not alive! If a person does not know when he was converted, that is no proof that he is not converted.

The point is, do you trust Jesus Christ? Has that trust made a new person out of you? Has your confidence in Christ made you feel that you have been forgiven? Do you love God for forgiving you, and has that love become the mainspring of your being, so that out of love to God you delight to obey Him? Then you are healed. If you do not believe in Jesus, be sure that you are still not healed, and I pray you will look at my text until you are led by grace to say, "I am healed, for I have trusted in the stripes of Jesus."

Suppose, for a moment, you are not healed; let me ask the question, "Why aren't you?" You know the Gospel; why are you not healed by Christ? "I don't know," says one. But, my dear friend, I entreat you not to rest until you do know.

"I can't find the way," says another. The other day a young girl was putting a button on her father's coat. She was sitting with her back to the window, and she said, "Father, I can't see. I am blocking my own light."

He replied, "Ah, my daughter, that is what you have been doing all your life!"

This is the position of some of you spiritually. You are blocking your own light; you think too much of yourselves. There is plenty of light in the Sun of Righteousness, but you get in the dark by putting self in the way of that Sun. Oh, that your self might be put away!

I read a touching story the other day about how one young man found peace. For some time he had been under conviction of sin, longing to find mercy, but he could not reach it. He was a telegraph clerk, and being in the office one morning, he had to receive and transmit a telegram. To his great surprise, he spelled out these words: *"Behold! The Lamb of God who takes away the sin of the world!"* (John 1:29). A gentleman on vacation was telegraphing a message to a friend whose soul was in distress. The message was meant for another, but he who transmitted it received eternal life as the words came flashing into his soul.

Oh, dear friends, get out of your own light, and at once *"Behold! The Lamb of God who takes away the sin of the world!"* I cannot telegraph the words to you, but I want to put them before you so plainly and distinctly that every troubled soul may know that they are meant for him. There lies your hope—not in yourself, but in the Lamb of God. Behold Him. And as you behold Him, your sin will be put away, and *"by His stripes"* you will be healed.

Words to the Healed

If, dear friend, you are healed, this is my word to you: get out of diseased company. Come away from the companions that have infected you with sin. *"Come out from among them and be separate, says the Lord. Do not touch what is unclean"* (2 Cor. 6:17).

If you are healed, praise the Healer, and acknowledge what He has done for you. There were ten lepers healed, but only one returned to praise the healing hand. Do not be among the ungrateful nine. (See Luke 17:12–19.)

If you have found Christ, confess His name. Confess it in His own appointed way: *"He who believes and is baptized will be saved"* (Mark 16:16). When you have thus confessed Him, speak out for Him. Tell what Jesus has done for your soul, and dedicate yourself to the holy purpose of spreading abroad the message by which you have been healed.

I had an experience related to me that pleased me. It shows how one man, being healed, may be the means of blessing to another. Many years ago I preached a sermon in Exeter Hall that was printed and entitled, "Salvation to the Uttermost." A friend who lives not very far from me was in the city of Para in Brazil. He heard of an Englishman in prison there who had, in a state of drunkenness, committed a murder for which he was confined for life. My friend went to see him and found him deeply penitent, but quietly restful and happy in the Lord. He had felt the terrible wound of bloodguiltiness in his soul, but it had been healed, and he felt the bliss of pardon. Here is the story of the poor prisoner's conversion in his own words:

A young man who had just completed his contract with the gasworks was returning to England, but before doing so he called to see me and brought with him a parcel of books. When I opened it, I found that they were novels; but, being able to read, I was thankful for anything. After I had read several of the books, I found a sermon (No. 84), preached by C. H. Spurgeon, in Exeter Hall, on June 8th, 1856, from the words, *"Therefore He is also able to save to the uttermost"* (Heb. 7:25). In his discourse, Mr. Spurgeon referred to Palmer, who was then lying under sentence of death in Stafford Gaol, and in order to bring home this text to his hearers, he said that if Palmer had committed many other murders, if he repents and seeks God's pardoning love in Christ, even he will be forgiven! I then felt that if Palmer could be forgiven, so might I. I sought, and blessed be God, I found. I am pardoned, I am free; I am a sinner saved by grace. Though a murderer, I have not yet sinned *"to the uttermost."* Blessed be his holy name!

It made me very happy to think that a poor condemned murderer could thus be converted. Surely, there is hope for every reader of this book, however guilty he may be!

If you know Christ, tell others about Him. You do not know what good there is in making Jesus known, even if all you can do is give a tract or repeat a verse. Dr. Valpy, the author of a great many books, wrote the following simple lines as his confession of faith:

> In peace let me resign my breath,
> And thy salvation see;
> My sins deserve eternal death,
> But Jesus died for me.

Valpy is dead and gone, but he gave those lines to dear old Dr. Marsh, the rector of Beckenham, who put them over his study mantelshelf. The earl of Roden came in and read them. "Will you give me a copy of those lines?" asked the good earl.

"I will be glad to," said Dr. Marsh, and he copied them. Lord Roden took them home and put them over his mantel. General Taylor, a Waterloo hero, came into the room and noticed them. He read them over and over again while staying with Earl Roden, until his lordship remarked, "I say, friend Taylor, I should think you know those lines by heart."

He answered, "I do know them by heart; indeed, my very heart has grasped their meaning." He was brought to Christ by that humble rhyme.

General Taylor handed those lines to an officer in the army, who was going out to the Crimean war. He came home to die; and when Dr. Marsh went to see him, the poor soul in his weakness said, "Good sir, do you know this verse that General Taylor gave to me? It brought me to my Savior, and I die in peace." To Dr. Marsh's surprise, he repeated the lines:

> In peace let me resign my breath,
> And thy salvation see;
> My sins deserve eternal death,
> But Jesus died for me.

Think of the good that four simple lines can do. Be encouraged, you who know the healing power of the wounds of Jesus. Spread this truth by all means. Never mind how simple the language. Tell it. Tell it everywhere and in every way, even if you cannot do it in any other way than by copying a verse out of a hymnbook. Tell others that by the stripes of Jesus we are healed. May God bless you, dear friends!

Chapter 2

The Beginning of Months

*Now the LORD spoke to Moses and Aaron in the land of Egypt,
saying, "This month shall be your beginning of months;
it shall be the first month of the year to you."*
—Exodus 12:1–2

When sinners put their trust in Jesus' blood, they begin a whole new life. Truly, they can count their day of salvation as the first day of a new year and, in fact, a new life. This is what happened with Israel: the day of their exodus from Egypt marked a new beginning, a new year, for them. In fact, they changed their calendar; the month they left Egypt became the first month of the new year. I will attempt to further explain how this happened.

In all probability, up to the time of the Exodus, the new year began in autumn. People have sometimes wondered at what season of the year God created man. Many have decided that it must have been in autumn, so that when Adam was placed in the garden, he might at once find fruits ripe and ready to eat. It does not seem probable that he began his life while all the fruits were still raw and green. Therefore, many have concluded that the first year of human history began in the time of harvest, when fruits were ripened for man's food.

For this reason, perhaps, in the old times the new year began when the feast of harvest was celebrated. However, here at the point of the Exodus, by a decree of God, the first day of the new year was changed. As far as Israel was concerned, the opening of the year would be in the time of our spring—in the month called Abib, or Nisan.

We know that a little before the barley was in the ear, and on the Sabbath after the Passover, the produce of the earth was so far advanced that the firstfruits were offered, and a sheaf of new barley was waved before the Lord. Of course, when I speak of spring and ears of barley, you must remember the difference of climate, for in that warm region the seasons are far in advance of ours. You must pardon me if my ideas become a little mixed; you can sort them easily at your leisure.

From the time when the Lord saved His people from destruction by passing them over, the ecclesiastical year began in the month Abib, in which the Passover was celebrated. The jubilee year was not altered but began in the autumnal equinox. The Jews seem to have had two or three beginnings of the year in relation to different purposes; but the ecclesiastical year, the great year by which Israel reckoned its existence, began henceforth in the month Abib, when the Lord brought His people *"out of Egypt with a mighty hand and with an outstretched arm"* (Deut. 26:8).

God can change times and seasons as He pleases, and He has done so for great, commemorative purposes. The change of the Sabbath is along the same lines; for whereas the day of rest was formerly the seventh, it is now merged with the Lord's Day, which is the first day of the week. As George Herbert, poet and pastor, said, "He did unhinge the day," and He set the Sabbath on golden hinges by consecrating the day of Christ's resurrection.

To every man God makes a similar change of times and seasons when He deals with him in a way of grace, for *"all things have become new"* (2 Cor. 5:17) within him. Therefore, he begins a new chronology. We used to think our birthdays fell at certain times of the year; but now we regard with much more delight another day as our true birthday, since on that second birthday we began to truly live. Our calendar has been altered and amended by a deed of divine grace.

I want to bring to your mind this fact. Just as the people of Israel, when God gave them the Passover, had a complete shifting of all their dates, so when God gives a person the spiritual Passover, a very wonderful change takes place in his chronology. Saved individuals date from the dawn of their true life—not from their first birthday, but from the day that they were born again. The Passover is, as we all know, a type of the great work of our redemption by the blood of Jesus, and it represents the personal application of Christ's blood to each believer. When we perceive the Lord's act of passing over us because of Christ's atoning sacrifice, then we begin to live, and from that day we date all future events.

This being said, I will, first, describe the Passover (see Exodus 12:1–32); second, mention varieties of its recurrence; and third, consider how the date of this grand event is to be regarded according to the law of the Lord.

The Meaning of the Passover

First, then, I will describe this remarkable event that was henceforth to stand at the head of the Jewish year and, indeed, at the commencement of Israel's chronology.

Salvation by Blood

First, the Passover was an act of salvation by blood. You know how the elders and heads of families each took a lamb and shut it up, that they might examine it carefully. Having chosen a lamb in the prime of its life, *"without blemish"* (Exod. 12:5), they kept it by itself as a separated and consecrated creature. After four days they slew it and caught its blood in a basin. When this was done, they took hyssop and dipped it in the blood and therewith sprinkled the lintel and the two side posts of their houses (v. 7). By this means the houses of Israel were preserved on that dark and dreadful night, when with unsheathed sword the angel of vengeance sped through every street of Pharaoh's domain and slew the firstborn of all the land, both of men and of cattle (v. 12).

You will remember, dear friends, the time when you yourselves perceived that God's vengeance was out against sin; you can even now recollect your terror and your trembling. Many of us can never forget the memorable time when we first discovered that there was a way of deliverance from the wrath of God. Memory may drop all else from her enfeebled grasp, but this is graven on the palms of her hands.

Moses described our mode of deliverance when he described the Passover. The angel cannot be restrained, his wing cannot be bound, and his sword cannot be sheathed. He must go forth, and he must smite. He must smite us among the rest, for sin is upon us, and there must be no partiality: *"The soul who sins shall die"* (Ezek. 18:4).

But do you remember when you discovered God's new way? Without abolishing the law, He has brought in a glorious, saving clause by which we can be delivered. The clause is this, that if another would suffer instead of us and there was evidence that he had suffered, that would be enough for our deliverance.

Do you remember your joy at that discovery? If so, you can appreciate the feelings of the Israelites when they understood that God would accept an unblemished lamb in the place of their firstborn. If the blood was displayed on the doorpost as the clear evidence that a sacrifice had suffered and died, then the angel would know that in that house his work was done and he could therefore pass over that habitation. The avenger was to demand a life, but if the life was already paid, and there was the blood to prove it, the avenger could go on his way. It was the night of God's Passover, not because the execution of vengeance was left undone in the houses passed over, but just the opposite. For in those houses the deathblow had been struck, and the victim had died, and, since the penalty could not be exacted twice, that family was clear.

I do not know whether there is any truth in the statement that lightning never strikes the same place twice. But whether it is true or not, it is certain that wherever the lightning of God's vengeance has struck, it will not strike again. In each case where God's vengeance has struck the sinner's Substitute, it will not strike the sinner.

The best preservative for the Israelite's house was this: vengeance had struck there and could not strike again. There was the insurance mark, the streak of blood. Death had been there. Even though it had fallen on a harmless lamb, it had still fallen on a victim of God's own appointment. In God's eyes it had fallen upon Christ Himself, the *"Lamb slain from the foundation of the world"* (Rev. 13:8). Because the claims of retribution had been fully met, there was no further demand, and Israel was secure. This is my eternal confidence, and here is my soul's sweet hymn:

> If Thou has my discharge procured,
> And freely in my room endured
> The whole of wrath divine:
> Payment God cannot twice demand,
> First at my bleeding Surety's hand,
> And then again at mine.
>
> Turn then, my soul, unto thy rest;
> The merits of thy great High Priest
> Have bought thy liberty:
> Trust in His efficacious blood,
> Nor fear thy banishment from God,
> Since Jesus died for thee.

For me, it was the beginning of my life, that day in which I discovered that judgment was passed upon me in the person of my Lord, and that *"there is therefore now no condemnation to* [me]*"* (Rom. 8:1). The law demands death: *"The soul who sins shall die"* (Ezek. 18:4). Christ gave what the law demands, and more. Christ, my Lord, has died, died in my place. It is written, *"Who Himself bore our sins in His own body on the tree"* (1 Pet. 2:24). Such a sacrifice is more than even the most rigorous law could demand. *"Christ, our Passover, was sacrificed for us"* (1 Cor. 5:7). *"Christ has redeemed us from the curse of the law, having become a curse for us"* (Gal. 3:13).

Therefore, we sit securely within doors, needing no guard outside to drive away the destroyer; for when God sees the blood of Jesus, He will pass over us. *"Now this is His name by which He will be called: THE LORD OUR RIGHTEOUSNESS"* (Jer. 23:6).

It was the beginning of life to me when I saw Jesus as dying in my place. I beheld the first sight that was worth beholding; let all the rest be darkness and like the shadow of death. Then my soul rejoiced when I understood and accepted the substitutionary sacrifice of the appointed Redeemer. That is my first observation of the Passover: *"the blood of sprinkling"* (Heb. 12:24) made Israel secure.

Refreshment from the Lamb

Here is my second observation: the night of the Passover, the Israelites received refreshment from the lamb. Being saved by its blood, the believing households stood and fed upon the lamb. They never ate as they ate that night. Those who spiritually understood the symbol must have partaken of every morsel with a mysterious awe mingled with an unfathomable delight. There must have been a singular seriousness around the table as they stood there eating in haste. Every now and then they were startled by the shrieks that rose from the Egyptian houses because of the slain of the Lord. It was a solemn feast, a meal of mingled hope and mystery.

Do you remember, brothers and sisters, when you first fed upon Christ, when your hungry spirit enjoyed the first morsel of that food of the soul? It was delicious food, was it not? It was better than angel's bread, for

Never did angels taste above
Redeeming grace and dying love.

I hope you have never risen from that table, but are daily feeding upon Jesus. It is a very instructive fact that we do not go to our Lord's table like the Israelites, to eat in haste with a staff in our hand (Exod. 12:11). But we come there to recline at ease with our heads on His bosom, reposing in His love. Christ Jesus is the daily bread of our spirits.

Observe that the refreshment Israel ate that night was the lamb *"roasted in fire"* (v. 8). The best refreshment to a troubled heart is the suffering Savior, the Lamb roasted in fire. A poor sinner under conviction of sin goes to a place of worship, and he hears Christ preached as an example. This may be useful to the saint, but it is little help to the poor sinner. He cries, "That is true, but it condemns rather than comforts me." It is not food for him; he wants the Lamb roasted in fire, Christ his substitute, Christ suffering in his place and stead.

We hear a great deal about the beauty of Christ's moral character, and assuredly our blessed Lord deserves to be highly exalted for His character, but that is not the aspect under which He is food to a soul conscious of sin. The chief relish about our Lord Jesus to a penitent sinner is His sin-bearing and His agonies. We need the suffering Savior, the Christ of Gethsemane, the Christ of Golgotha and Calvary, Christ shedding His blood in the sinner's stead and bearing for us the fire of God's wrath. Nothing short of this will suffice to be food for a hungry heart. Withhold this, and you starve the child of God.

The Israelites were not to eat any of the lamb raw (v. 9). Alas! There are some who try to do this with Christ, for they preach a half-atoning sacrifice. They try to make His person and His character to be food for their souls, but they have small liking for His passion. They cast His atonement into the background or represent it as an ineffective atonement that does not rescue any soul. What is this but to devour a raw Christ?

I will not touch their half-roasted lamb; I will have nothing to do with their half substitution, their half-redemption. No, no. Give me a Savior who has borne all my sins in His own body (1 Pet. 2:24) and so has been roasted in fire to the full. *"It is finished!"* (John 19:30) is the most charming note in all of Calvary's music. *"It is finished!"* The fire has passed upon the Lamb. He has borne the whole of the wrath that was due to His people. This is the royal dish of the feast of love.

There is a multitude of teachers who want to have the Lamb boiled with water, though the Scripture says, *"Do not eat it raw, nor boiled at all with water"* (Exod. 12:9). I have heard it said that a great number of sermons are about Christ and the Gospel yet neither Christ nor His Gospel are preached in them. If so, the preachers present the Lamb boiled in the water of their own thoughts, speculations, and notions.

Now, the harm in this boiling process is that the water takes away a good deal from the meat. Likewise, philosophical discourses on the Lord Jesus take away much of the essence and virtue of His person, offices, work, and glory. The real juice and vital nutrients of His glorious Word are carried off by interpretations that do not explain, but explain away. How many boil away the soul of the Gospel by their carnal wisdom!

What is worse still, when meat is boiled, not only does the meat get into the water, but the water gets into the meat. What truth these gospel-boilers do hand out is boiled with error, and you receive from them dishes made up partly of God's truth and partly of men's imaginings. We hear in some measure solid Gospel and in larger measure mere watery reasoning. When certain preachers preach atonement, it is not pure and simple substitution; one hardly knows what it is. Their atonement is not the vicarious sacrifice, but a performance of a long list of things. They have a theory that is like the remainders of meat after days of boiling, all strings and fibers.

People use all kinds of schemes to try to extract the marrow and fatness from the grand, soul-satisfying doctrine of substitution, which to my mind is the choicest truth that can ever be brought forth for the food of souls. I cannot figure out why so many preachers are afraid of the shedding of blood for the remission of sin (Heb. 9:22). Why do they have to stew down the most important of all the truths of revelation?

As the type could be correct only when the lamb was roasted with fire, so the Gospel is not truly presented unless we describe our Lord Jesus in His sufferings in the place of sinners. He was absolutely and literally a substitution for them. When it comes to the Gospel, I will allow no dilution: it is substitution. He bore our sins (1 Pet. 2:24). He was made sin for us (2 Cor. 5:21). *"The chastisement for our peace was upon Him, and by His stripes we are healed"* (Isa. 53:5). We must have no mystifying of this plain truth. It must not be *"boiled at all with water"* (Exod. 12:9). We must have Christ in His sufferings, fresh from the fire.

Now, this is the lamb the Israelites were to eat, and they were to eat all of it. Not a morsel was to be left (Exod. 12:10). Oh, that you and I would never cut and divide Christ so as to choose one part of Him and leave another! Let not a bone of Him be broken (v. 46), but let us take the whole Christ, up to the full measure of our capacity. Prophet, Priest, and King; Christ divine and Christ human; Christ loving and living, Christ dying, Christ risen, Christ ascended, Christ coming again; Christ triumphant over all His foes—the whole Lord Jesus Christ is ours. We must not reject a single morsel of what is revealed concerning Him, but we must feed on it all as we are able.

That night Israel had to feed on the lamb there and then. They could not save a portion for the next day; they had to consume it all one way or another (v. 10). Oh, my friend, we need a whole Christ at this very moment. Let us receive Him in His entirety. Oh, for a splendid appetite and good digestion to receive into my inmost soul the Lord Christ just as I find Him.

May you and I never think lightly of our Lord in any of His offices or aspects. All that you now know and all that you can find out concerning Christ, you should now believe, appreciate, feed on, and rejoice in. Make the most of all that is in the Word concerning your Lord. Let Him enter into your being to become part and parcel of your self. If you do this, the day in which you feed on Jesus will be the first day of your life, its day of days, the day from which you date all that follows. If once you have fed upon Christ Jesus, you will never forget it in time or in eternity.

Refreshment from the lamb was the second event that was celebrated in each succeeding Passover.

Purification from Leaven

The third event was the purification of their houses from leaven. (See Exodus 12:15.) This process was to go side by side with the sprinkling of the blood and the eating of the lamb. They were told that they must not eat leaven for seven days, for whoever ate leaven would be *"cut off from Israel"* (v. 15). This purification was deeply important, for it is put in equal position with the sprinkling of the blood. The two could not be separated. Anyone who divided the two faced the pain and penalty of being divided from the congregation of Israel.

Now, it is always a pity to preach justification by faith in a way that makes sanctification a part of justification. But it is also a horrible error to preach justification in a way that denies the absolute necessity of sanctification. The two are joined together by the Lord. There must be the eating of the lamb and the sprinkling of the blood, and there must be the purging out of the old leaven as well. Carefully, the Jews looked into every closet, corner, drawer, and cupboard to sweep out every crumb of stale bread. If they had any bread, even if it was new and they intended to eat it, they had to get rid of it, for there could not be a particle of leaven in the same house with the lamb.

When you and I first came to Christ, what a sweeping out there was of the leaven! I know I was fully delivered from the *"leaven of the Pharisees"* (Luke 12:1), for all trust in my own good works went, even the last crumb of it. All confidence in rites and ceremonies went, too. I do not have a crust left of these sour and corrupt confidences at the present moment, and I wish never to taste that old leaven again. Some people are always chewing on that leaven, glorying in their own prayers and giving and ceremonies; but when Christ comes in, this leaven all goes out. The *"leaven of the Pharisees, which is hypocrisy"* (v. 1), must be cleared out. *"Blessed is he whose transgression is forgiven, whose sin is covered. Blessed is the man to whom the LORD does not impute iniquity, and in whose spirit there is no deceit"* (Ps. 32:1–2).

Guile must go, or guilt will not go. The Lord sweeps the cunning, the craftiness, and the deceit out of His people. He makes His people true before His face. They wish that they were as clear of every sin as they are from insincerity. They once tried to dwell before the Lord with double-dealing, pretending to be what they were not. But as soon as they ate of Christ and the blood was sprinkled, then they humbled themselves in truth and laid bare their sinfulness. They stood before God in complete openness.

Christ has not saved the man who still trusts in falsehood. You cannot feed on Christ and at the same time hold love of sin or vain confidence in yourself. Self and sin must go. But, oh, what a day it is when the old leaven is thrown out. We will never forget it! That month is the beginning of months, the first month of the year to us, when the Spirit of truth purges out the spirit of falsehood.

A Mighty Deliverance

We come now to our fourth point about the Passover. On the Passover night there came, as the result of these other things, a wonderful, glorious, and mighty deliverance. That night every Israelite was promised immediate emancipation, and as soon as the morning dawned, he left his house and Egypt, too. He left the brick kilns forever, he washed the brick earth from his hands for the last time, and he left the yoke he used to carry when he worked amid the clay. He looked at the Egyptian taskmaster, remembered being struck often by him with a stick, and rejoiced that he would never be beaten again, for the taskmaster was at his feet begging him to leave lest all Egypt should die. Oh, what joy!

They marched out with their unleavened bread on their backs (Exod. 12:34), for they still had some days in which they were to eat it, and I think before the seventh day of unleavened bread was over (Exod. 13:6–7), they had reached the Red Sea. Still eating unleavened bread, they went into the depths of the Red Sea. Still with no flavor of leaven in their mouths, they stood on its shore to sing to the Lord the great hallelujah. God had *triumphed gloriously! The horse and its rider He has thrown into the sea!*" (Exod. 15:1).

Do you recollect when the Lord purged you from love of sin and trust in self, when He brought you completely out and set you free, and when He said, "Go on to the promised rest; go on to Canaan"? Do you remember when you saw your sins drowned forever, never to rise in judgment against you? Not merely was your destruction prevented, not merely was your soul fed with the finest food, not merely was your heart and your house cleansed of hypocrisy, but you, yourself, were delivered and emancipated, the Lord's free man! Oh, if you remember, I am sure you will acknowledge the wisdom of the Lord's decree: *"This month shall be your beginning of months; it shall be the first month of the year to you."*

This much will suffice in describing the event of the Passover.

How We Celebrate the Passover Today

Second, I want to mention the ways in which the Passover recurs among us today. There are three ways: the salvation of ourselves, our families, and our world.

Our Personal Salvation

The first recurrence is, of course, the personal salvation of each one of us. All of Exodus 12 was transacted in your heart and mine when we first knew the Lord.

A venerable elder in my church, Mr. White, said to me the other night, "Oh, sir, it is very precious to read the Bible, but it is infinitely more delightful to have it here in my own heart." Now, I find it very profitable to read about the Passover; but, oh, how sweet to have a Passover transacted in my own soul by the work of the Holy Spirit!

Moses wrote thousands of years ago about something that happened, but the substance of it has happened to me in all its details, and to thousands who are trusting in the Lord. Can we not read this story in Exodus and say, "Yes, it is so even now"? Every word of it is true, for it has all occurred to me, every detail of it, even to the eating of the bitter herbs (Exod. 12:8). For I recall that, at the very moment that I tasted the sweet flavor of my Lord's atonement, I also felt the bitterness of repentance from sin and the bitterness of struggling against the temptation to sin again. Even the minute touches of that festival are symbolic of salvation, as thousands of Christians can testify. This Passover record is not a story of olden times alone; it is the record of your life and mine. I hope it is. Thus, by each person who is saved, the Passover Feast is kept.

The Salvation of Our Families

In a certain sense, the Passover occurs again when a man's family is saved. Remember, the Passover was a family business. The father and mother were present when the lamb was slain. I imagine the oldest son helped to bring the lamb to the slaughter; another held the knife; a third held the basin; the little boy fetched the bunch of hyssop; and they all united in the sacrifice. They all saw the father strike the lintel and the doorposts, and they all ate of the lamb that night. Everyone who was in the house, all who were part of the family, partook of the meal. They were all protected by the blood, they were all refreshed by the feast, and they all started out the next morning to go to Canaan.

Have you ever held a family supper of that kind? "Oh," some fathers might say, "it would be the beginning of family life to me if all my sons and daughters sitting around my supper table were saved. Oh, that all my children truly belonged to Christ." A family begins to live in the highest sense when as a family, without exception, it has all been redeemed, all sprinkled with the blood, all made to feed on Jesus, all purged from sin, and all freed to leave the domains of sin, headed for the kingdom. What joy! *"I have no greater joy than to hear that my children walk in truth"* (3 John 1:4). If any of you enjoy the privilege of family salvation, you may well set up a monument of praise and make a generous offering to God, who favors you in this way. Engrave it on marble and set it up forever! This household is saved, and the day of its salvation is the beginning of its spiritual history.

The Salvation of Our World

Extend the thought: the Passover was not only a family ordinance, but it was for all the tribes of Israel. There were many families, but in every house the Passover lamb was sacrificed. It would be an impressive thing if you business owners could gather all your workers together and say, "All of these workers understand the sprinkling of the blood, and all of them feed on Christ." Dear men and women who are placed in such responsible positions, you could indeed say, "This will be the beginning of months to us." Labor for it, therefore, and make it your heart's desire.

If you live to see the area in which you labor permeated with the Gospel, what a joy! Oh, that we might live to see every house in our communities sprinkled with the redeeming blood! Oh, that we might live to see the whole country feasting. I do not mean the feasting done at Christmas, when many eat sweets to excess; I mean feasting spiritually upon Christ, where there can be no excess. Oh, what a beginning of years it would be for our country! What a paradise it would be! If it were so in any country, what a day to be remembered! Mark a nation's annals from its evangelization. Begin the chronicle of a people from the day when they bow at the feet of Jesus.

There will come a day to this poor earth when Jesus will reign over all of it (Rev. 11:15). It may be a long time yet, but the day will come when Christ will have *"dominion...from sea to sea"* (Ps. 72:8). The nations that are called Christian, although they so little deserve the title, already date their chronology from the birth of Christ. This is a sort of faint foreshadowing of the way in which people will one day date all things from the reign of Jesus. His kingdom will come. God has decreed His triumph, and on the wings of time it hastens. When He comes, that month will be the beginning of months to us.

How to Regard Our Passover

Now, for my last point, I will show how we should regard our Passover, the day of our salvation.

The Most Honorable Day

Primarily, the day in which we first knew the Savior as the Passover Lamb should always be the most honorable day that has ever dawned upon us. The Israelites placed the month Abib as the first month because it was the month of the Passover. Mark the date you came to know the Lord as the premier day, the noblest hour you have ever known. It eclipses your natural birthday, for then you were born in sin, then you were *"born to trouble, as the sparks fly upward"* (Job 5:7). But now you are born into spiritual life, born to eternal bliss.

Your salvation day eclipses your marriage day, for union to Christ will bring you greater joy than the happiest of marriage bonds. If you have ever received the honors of the State, gained distinction in learning, attained a position in society, or acquired great wealth, all these are but dim, cloudy, foggy days compared with this *"morning without clouds"* (2 Sam. 23:4). On that day, your sun rose, never to go down again. The die was cast. Your destiny for glory was openly declared.

I entreat you never to degrade that blessed day in your thoughts by thinking more of any pleasure, honor, or advancement than you do of the blessing of salvation by the blood of Jesus. I am afraid that some of you are striving and struggling after other distinctions, and you think that if you could only reach a certain event you would be satisfied. Is your salvation not worth vastly more than this? You feel that you would be set for life if a certain matter turned out right. Friend, you were set for life when you were made anew in Christ Jesus. You received your inheritance when you came to Christ. You were promoted when He invited you into His friendship. You gained all that you need when you found Christ. A saint of old said, "He is all my salvation, and all my desire."

If you should be elected to some high position in the government, do not think that the event would overshadow your conversion. Think of your salvation as the Lord thinks of it, for He says, *"Since you were precious in My sight, You have been honored, and I have loved you"* (Isa. 43:4). Honor belongs to those who believe in

Jesus. In Jesus you boast and glory, and so you should. The mark of blood is a believer's chief adornment and decoration, and his being cleansed and set free by grace is his noblest distinction. Glory in grace and in nothing else. Prize the work of grace beyond all the treasures of Egypt.

The Beginning of Life

The date of your salvation is to be regarded as the beginning of life. The Israelites reckoned that all their former existence as a nation had been death. The brick kilns of Egypt, the sitting around pots of meat, the mixing with idolaters, the hearing of a language they did not understand—all Egyptian life they considered to be death, and the month that ended it was to them the beginning of months. On the other hand, they looked on all that followed their Exodus as life. The Passover was the beginning, and only the beginning. A beginning implies that something is to follow.

Now then, Christians, whenever you speak about your existence before conversion, always do it with shamefacedness, as one risen from the dead might speak of the cemetery and the worm of corruption. I feel grieved when people stand up and talk about what they used to do before they were converted as an old sailor talks of his voyages and storms. No, no! Be ashamed of your *"former lusts, as in your ignorance"* (1 Pet. 1:14). If you must speak of them to the praise and glory of Christ, speak with tears and sighs and bated breath. Death, rottenness, and corruption are all most fitly left in silence; or if they demand a voice, let it be as solemn and mournful as a funeral service. Tell about your sinful past in a way that will show that you wish it had never happened. Let your conversion be the burial of the old existence. (See 2 Corinthians 5:17.) As for what follows, take care that you make it real life, worthy of the grace that has saved you.

Suppose these Israelites had loitered in Egypt. Suppose one of them had said, "Well, I did not finish that batch of bricks. I cannot leave just yet. I would like to see them thoroughly baked and prepared for the pyramid." What a foolish man he would have been! No, they left the bricks and the clay and the stuff behind; they left right away and let Egypt take care of itself.

Now, child of God, leave the ways of sin with determination. Leave the world; leave its pleasures; leave its cares; and cleave to Jesus and His leadership. You are now the Lord's free man. Will

131

the Lamb be slain and mean nothing? Will the blood be sprinkled for nothing? Will the leavened bread be purged out in vain? Will the Red Sea be crossed, and the Egyptians drowned, and you remain a slave? The thought is abhorrent.

That was the wrongdoing of the Israelites: they still had a craving for the leeks and garlic of Egypt (Num. 11:5). These strong-smelling things had scented their garments, and it is hard to get such vile odors out of one's clothes. Alas, the Egyptian garlic clings to us, and its smell is not always so abominable to us as it ought to be.

Besides, they pined for fish that they ate in plenty in Egypt (v. 5), muddy fish though it was. There were better fisheries for them in Jordan and Gennesaret and the Great Sea if they had gone ahead. Sweeter herbs were on Canaan's hills than ever grew in Egypt's mire. Because of this evil lusting, they were kept dodging about for forty years in the wilderness (Num. 32:13). They might have marched into Canaan in forty days had it not been for that stinking garlic of theirs. Their Egyptian habits and memories held them back. Oh, that God would cut us completely free and enable us to forget those *"things of which* [we] *are now ashamed"* (Rom. 6:21)!

Setting All Things Right

Inasmuch as the Passover became the beginning of the year to Israel, it set all things right. I told you that the year had formerly begun in autumn, according to most traditions. Was this really the best season to start the year? Was autumn the best season in which to begin life, with winter ahead and everything declining?

With the institution of the Passover, the year was made to begin in what is our spring. When could the year begin more fitly than in the springtime of early May? It seems to me that the year actually does begin in spring. I do not see that the year naturally begins in winter, though it does so arbitrarily. In the middle of winter, the year as yet lies dead. When the birds sing and the flowers rise from their beds of earth, then the year begins.

I think it is a wrong supposition that our first parents commenced life in autumn, amid lengthening nights and declining forces. No, by all means let the date be fixed in spring. Then the salutations of the new year will be sweet with fragrant flowers and rich with joyous songs. Moreover, the time of spring in the East is not a season without crops, for in April and May the first ears of corn are ready, and many other fruits are fit for food.

It was good for the Israelites to have the Feast of Firstfruits in the month Abib. Hence, they could bring the first ears to the Lord and not wait until they were ripe before they blessed the Giver of all good. We ought to be grateful for green mercies and not wait until everything comes to ripeness.

In some parts of the East there is fruit all year round, and why not in Eden? In my delightful country England, which bears a very close resemblance to the East, one tree or another bears fruit every month all year round. So if Adam had been created in the month of April, there would have been food for him, followed by a succession of fruits that would have supplied all his wants. Then he would have had summer before him with all its ripening beauties. This is a more paradisiacal outlook than winter.

It is right that the year should begin with the firstfruits, and I am sure it is quite right that the year should begin for you and me when we come to Christ and receive the *"firstfruits of the Spirit"* (Rom. 8:23). Everything is in disarray until a man knows Christ. Everything is disorderly and bottom upwards until the Gospel comes and turns everything upside down, and then the right side is up again. Man is all wrong until the Gospel puts him all right.

Though grace is above nature, it is not contrary to nature; rather, it restores true nature. Our nature is never so truly the nature of a man as when it is no longer man's sinful nature. We truly become men, such as God meant men to be, when we cease to be the kind of men that sin has made men to be.

Since our life begins at our spiritual Passover and at our feeding upon Christ, we ought to always regard our conversion as a festival and remember it with praise. Whenever we look back on it, the memory of it should excite delight in our hearts.

How long should a person thank God for forgiving his sins? Is life long enough? Is time long enough? Is eternity long enough? How long should a man thank God for saving him from going down to hell? Would fifty years suffice? Oh, no, that would never do; the blessing is too great to all be sung in a millennium.

Suppose you and I never had a single mercy except this one, that we were made the *"children of God...and joint heirs with Christ"* (vv. 16–17). Suppose we had nothing else to enjoy. We ought to sing about that alone forever and ever. Yes, if we were sick, cast on a bed of pain with a hundred diseases, with the bone wearing through the skin, yet since God's everlasting mercy would sanctify every pain, should we not still continue to lift up happy psalms to God and praise Him forever and ever? Therefore, let this be your slogan all through the year: "Hallelujah! Praise the Lord!"

The Israelites always closed the Passover with a hymn of praise; therefore, let us close this chapter with holy joy and continue our happy music until this year ends, yes, until time shall be no more.

Chapter 3

God's Watchful Care

The eyes of the LORD your God are always on it [the land of
Palestine], *from the beginning of the year to the very end of the year.*
—Deuteronomy 11:12

Truly, salvation does start a new year for the new believer.
And the eyes of the Lord are on His new child from the beginning of that new year to the end, and throughout every
year that follows. Our text assures us of this promise, but to fully
understand this verse, let us look at the land to which it refers:
Palestine.

Palestine was a land that was superior to Egypt. Egypt was a
land that produced food for its inhabitants only by the laborious
process of irrigating its fields. The Israelites, during their sojourn
in Egypt, mingled with the Egyptians as they watched with anxious
eyes the swelling of the river Nile. They shared in the incessant
labors of preserving water in reservoirs and then slowly eking it out
to nourish the various crops.

Moses told the Israelites in Deuteronomy 11 that the land of
Palestine was not at all like Egypt. It was a land that did not depend so much on the labor of the inhabitants as on the good will of
God. Moses called it a land of hills and valleys, a land of springs and
rivers, a land dependent not on the rivers of earth, but on the *"rain
of heaven"* (v. 11). He described it in conclusion as *"a land for
which the LORD your God cares; the eyes of the LORD your God are
always on it, from the beginning of the year to the very end of the
year"* (v. 12).

Egypt is a type of the natural man, and Canaan is a type of the
spiritual man. In this world the merely carnal man has to be his
own providence and look to himself for all his needs. Hence, his
cares are always many, and frequently they become so heavy that

135

they drive him to desperation. He lives a life of care, anxiety, sorrow, fretfulness, and disappointment. He dwells in Egypt, and he knows that there is no joy or comfort or provision if he does not wear out his soul in winning it.

But the spiritual man dwells in another country; his faith makes him a citizen of Canaan. It is true he endures the same toils and experiences and afflictions as the ungodly, but they affect him differently, for they come as a gracious Father's appointments, and they go at the bidding of loving wisdom. By faith the godly man casts his care upon God, who cares for him (1 Pet. 5:7). He walks without heavy cares because he knows he is the child of heaven's loving-kindness, for whom *"all things work together for good"* (Rom. 8:28). God is his great Guardian and Friend, and all his concerns are safe in the hands of infinite grace.

Even in the year of drought, the believer dwells in green pastures and lies down beside still waters (Ps. 23:2). As for the ungodly, he abides in the wilderness and hears the mutterings of that curse: *"Cursed is the man who trusts in man and makes flesh his strength....He shall be like a shrub in the desert, and shall not see when good comes"* (Jer. 17:5–6).

Do you disagree that Canaan is a fitting type of the present condition of the Christian? I have frequently insisted that it is a far better type of the Christian soldier on earth than of the glorified saint in heaven. Canaan is sometimes used in our hymns as the picture of heaven, but it is not so. A moment's reflection will show that Canaan is distinctly the picture of the present state of every believer.

While we are under conviction of sin, we are like Israel in the wilderness; we have no rest for our feet. But when we put our trust in Jesus, we do, as it were, cross the river and leave the wilderness behind. *"We who have believed do enter that rest"* (Heb. 4:3), for *"there remains therefore a rest for the people of God"* (v. 9).

Believers have entered into the finished salvation that is provided for us in Christ Jesus. The blessings of our inheritance are to a great extent already in our possession. The state of salvation is no longer a land of promise, but it is a land possessed and enjoyed. *"Having been justified by faith, we have peace with God"* (Rom. 5:1). *"Beloved, now we are children of God"* (1 John 3:2). We are sons right now! Covenant blessings are at this moment actually ours, just as the land of Canaan was actually possessed by Israel.

It is true there is an enemy in Canaan, an enemy to be driven out. There is indwelling sin, which is entrenched in our hearts like troops in walled cities. There are fleshly lusts, which are like chariots of iron with which we have to war. Even so, the land is ours. We have the covenanted heritage in our possession at this moment. The foes who would rob us of it will be utterly rooted out by the sword of faith and the weapon of prayer.

The Christian, like Israel in Canaan, is not under the government of Moses now; he is done with Moses once and for all. Moses was magnified and made honorable as he made his last climb to the top of the hill, and with a kiss from God's lips he was carried into heaven. (See Deuteronomy 34:1, 5.) Even so, the law has been magnified and made honorable in the person of Christ, and it has ceased to reign over the believer.

As Joshua was the leader of the Israelites when they came into Canaan, so Jesus is our leader now. It is He who leads us on from victory to victory. He will not sheathe His sword until He has given us all the holiness and happiness that the covenant promises us. For these and many other reasons, it is clear that the children of Israel in Canaan were a type of us believers.

Beloved, those of you who are believers will relish the text. It is to believers that the text is addressed. *"The eyes of the LORD your God are always on* [you, believer], *from the beginning of the year to the very end of the year."* You who trust in Jesus are under the guidance of the great Joshua. You are fighting sin. You have obtained salvation. You have left the wilderness of conviction and fear behind you, and you have come into the Canaan of faith. Now the eyes of God are upon you and on your state from the opening of the year to its close.

May the Holy Spirit bless us as we study the text in more detail. We will, first, take the text as we find it. Second, we will turn the text around. Third, we will blot the text out. Fourth, we will distill practical lessons from the text.

God's Watchful Eyes

First, we will consider the text as we find it. The first word that glitters before us like a jewel in a crown is that word *eyes*— *"the eyes of the LORD."* What is meant here? Surely not mere omniscience. In that sense, *"the eyes of the LORD are in every place, keeping watch on the evil and the good"* (Prov. 15:3). God sees Hagar as well as Sarah; He beholds Judas when he gives the traitorous kiss (Matt. 26:48–49) just as surely as He beholds the holy woman when she washes the Savior's feet with her tears (Luke 7:37–38).

No, our text is speaking of something more than omniscience; there is love in the text to sweeten observation. *"The LORD knows the way of the righteous"* (Ps. 1:6) with a knowledge that is over and above that of omniscience. The eyes of the Lord are upon the righteous, not merely to see them, but to view them with delight; not only to observe them, but to observe them with affectionate care and interest.

An Intense Affection

The meaning of the text is then, first, that God's love is always upon His people. Oh, Christians, think of this—it is rather to be thought of than to be spoken of—that God loves us! The big heart of Deity is set upon us poor, insignificant, undeserving, worthless beings. God loves us, always loves us, and never thinks of us without loving thoughts. He never regards us, nor speaks of us, nor acts toward us, except in love.

God is love in a certain sense toward all, for He is full of benevolence to all His creatures. Love is indeed His essence. But there is a depth unfathomable when the word *love* is used in reference to His elect ones. They are the objects of distinguishing grace, redeemed by blood, set free by power, adopted by condescension, and preserved by faithfulness. Beloved, do not ask me to write of this love, but implore God the Holy Spirit to speak of it to your inmost souls. The loving eyes of God are always upon you, the poorest and most obscure of His people, *"from the beginning of the year to the very end of the year."*

A Personal Interest

The text teaches us that the Lord takes a personal interest in us. It does not say that God loves us and therefore sends an angel to protect and watch over us, but the Lord does it Himself. The eyes that observe us are God's own eyes; the guardian under whose protection we are placed is God Himself. Some mothers give their children to others to feed and care for, but God never does. All His babes are fed by Him and are carried in His own arms.

We could do little if we had to perform everything personally; therefore, most things are done by proxy. The captain, when the vessel is to be steered across the deep, must have his hour of sleep; then the second in command, or someone else, must manage the vessel. But in times of emergency the captain himself is called up and takes personal responsibility. See him as he himself anxiously heaves the lead and stands at the helm or at the lookout, for he can trust no one else in perilous moments.

It seems from the text that it is always a time of emergency with God's people, for their great Lord always exercises a personal care over them. He has never said to His angels, "I will dispense with my own watching, and you will guard my saints." While He gives angels charge concerning His people (Ps. 91:11), yet He Himself is personally their keeper and their shield. *"I, the LORD, keep it, I water it every moment; lest any hurt it, I keep it night and day"* (Isa. 27:3).

Think of times when you have been very sick and have sent for a physician. Perhaps the doctor was busy with another patient and sent his assistant, who was probably just as skillful. Yet as soon as that assistant came, such was your confidence in the doctor himself that you felt quite disappointed. You wanted to see the man who treated you successfully in days gone by.

We need not fear that God will send someone else. Oh, beloved, when I think of the text, I am of the same mind as Moses when God said, *"I will send My Angel before you"* (Exod. 33:2). "No," Moses said, "that will not suffice. *'If Your Presence does not go with us do not bring us up from here'* (v. 15)." My Lord, I cannot be satisfied with Gabriel or Michael; I cannot be content with the brightest of the seraphim who stand before Your throne. It is Your presence I want, and blessed be Your name, it is Your presence that the text promises to give.

The anxious mother is glad to have a careful nurse on whom she can rely. But in the crisis of her baby's disease, when his life trembles in the balance, she says, "Nurse, I must sit up with the child myself tonight." And though it is perhaps the third or fourth night since the mother has had sleep, yet her eyes will not close as long as the point of danger is still in view.

See, my friends, see the loving tenderness of our gracious God. Never, never, never does He delegate the care of His people to others, no matter how good or powerful they are. His own eyes, without a substitute, must watch over us.

An Unwearied Power

Further, the text reminds us of the unwearied power of God toward His people. What? Can His eyes always watch us? This would not be possible if He were not God. To concentrate always on one object, man can scarcely accomplish that. But where there are ten thousand times ten thousand objects, how can the same eyes always be upon every one of them?

I know what unbelief has said to you. It has whispered, "He brings forth the stars. *'He calls them all by name'* (Ps. 147:4). How then can He notice an insignificant being like you?" Perhaps you have replied, "My way is unseen by God. God has forgotten me. My God has forsaken me." But this is where the text comes in. Not only has He not forgotten you, but He has never once taken His eyes off you! Though you are one among so many, yet He has observed you as narrowly, as carefully, as tenderly as if you were the only child in the divine family. He has heard you as if you were the only one whose prayers were to be heard and whose cares were to be relieved.

What would you think about yourself if you were the only saved soul in the world, the only elect one of God, the only one purchased on the bloody cross? Why, you would say, "How God must care for me! How He must watch over me! Surely, He will never take His eyes off such a special favorite." Beloved, though God's family is so large, it is the same as if you were the only one. The eyes of the Lord never grow weary. He *"shall neither slumber nor sleep"* (Ps. 121:4). Both by day and by night He observes each one of His people.

Accepted in Christ

If you put these things together—intense affection, personal interest, and unwearied power—and if you remember that God's heart is moved toward you by unchanging purposes of grace, surely there will be enough to make you lose yourself in wonder, love, and praise. You have sinned in the past, but your sin has never made Him love you less. He never looked at you as you are in yourself, naked and standing alone, but He saw you and loved you in Christ, even when you were *"dead in trespasses and sins"* (Eph. 2:1). He has seen you in Christ ever since and has never ceased to love you.

It is true you have been very faulty (what tears this ought to cost you!), but as He never loved you for your good works, He has never cast you away for your bad works. He has beheld you as washed in the atoning blood of Jesus until you have become whiter than snow (Ps. 51:7), and He has seen you clothed in the perfect righteousness of your Substitute. (See Isaiah 61:10.) Therefore, He has looked upon you and regarded you as though you were without *"spot or wrinkle or any such thing"* (Eph. 5:27).

Grace has always set you before the Lord's eyes as being in His dear Son, therefore, all fair and lovely—a pleasing prospect for Him to look upon. He has gazed on you, beloved, but never with anger. He has looked on you when your weakness, no, your willful wickedness, has made you hate yourself. Yet though He has seen you in this sad state, He has had such a regard for your relationship to Christ that you have still been *"accepted in the Beloved"* (Eph. 1:6).

I wish my mortal words could convey the full glory of that thought, but they cannot. You must eat this morsel alone. You must take it like a wafer made with honey and put it under your tongue and suck the sweetness out of it. The eyes of God, my God, are always upon His chosen. They are eyes of affection, delight, unwearied power, immutable wisdom, and unchanging love.

His Constant Care

The next word that seems to flash and sparkle in the text is that word *always*. *"The eyes of the LORD your God are always on it."* And it is added, as if that word were not enough for such dull ears as ours, *"from the beginning of the year to the very end of the year."* This is so plain and pointed that we cannot imagine we are removed from God's eyes even for a single day or a single hour of the day or a single minute of the hour.

I tried to discover the other day what time of life we could afford to be without God. Perhaps imagination suggests the time of prosperity, when business prospers, wealth is growing, and the mind is happy. Ah, beloved, to be without our God then would be like the marriage feast without the bridegroom! It would be the day of delight and no delight, a sea and no water in it, a day and no light. What? All these mercies and no God? Then there is only a shell but no kernel, a shadow but no substance.

When a person has earthly "joys" but none of the Lord's presence, his soul can hear satanic laughter. Satan laughs at the soul because it has tried to make the world its rest and is sure to be deceived. Do without God in prosperity, beloved? We cannot, for then we would grow worldly, proud, and careless; deep damnation would be our lot. The Christian in prosperity is like a man standing on a pinnacle. He must be divinely upheld, or his fall will be terrible. If you can do without God at all, it certainly is not when you are standing on the pinnacle.

What then? Could we do without Him in adversity? Ask the heart that is breaking! Ask the tortured spirit that has been deserted by its friend! Ask the child of poverty who has nowhere to lay his head! Ask the daughter of sickness, tossing by night and day on that uneasy bed! Ask them, "Could you do without your God?" And the very thought causes wailing and gnashing of teeth. With God pain becomes pleasure, and dying beds are elevated into thrones. But without God—ah, what could we do?

Well, then, is there no period during which we could do without God? Cannot the young Christian, full of freshness and vigor, elated with the novelty of piety, do without his God? Ah, poor puny thing, how can the lamb do without the shepherd to carry it in his arms? Cannot the man in midlife then, whose virtues have been strengthened, do without his God? No, he tells you that it is his day of battle and that the darts fly thickly in business and that the burdens of life are heavy. Without God, a man in midlife is like a naked man in the midst of a thicket of briars and thorns; he cannot hope to get through without being torn, scratched, and mangled.

Ask the elderly man with all the experience of seventy years whether he has attained an independence of grace. He will say to you that as his body grows weaker, it is his joy that his *inward man is being renewed day by day*" (2 Cor. 4:16). But take away God, who is the spring of that renewal, and old age would be utter wretchedness.

Ah, friend, there is not a moment in any one day that you or I have ever lived that we could have afforded to dispense with the help of God. For when we have thought ourselves strong, as, alas, we have been fools enough to do, in five minutes we have done what has cost us rivers of tears to undo. In an unguarded moment we have spoken a word that we could not recall, but that we would have recalled if we had to bite our tongues in halves to do so. We have thought a thought that has gone speeding through our souls like a hellish thunderbolt, making a fiery path along the spirit. The evil thought would have become a terrible act if God, whom we had forgotten, had forgotten us.

We need to *"set the LORD always before* [us]*"* (Ps. 16:8). When we wake in the morning, let us claim the promise of our text, and say, "Lord, You have said You will always be with us. Then do not leave us until the dew of evening falls and we return to our beds. Do not leave us even then, lest temptation is whispered in our ears in the night and we wake to defile our minds with unholiness. Do not leave us ever, O God, but always be our *very present help* (Ps. 46:1)!"

Perhaps you have had the gloomiest year of your life. Perhaps the latest newspapers have been like the prophetic scroll that was written within and without with lamentations. (See Ezekiel 2:9–10.) Take comfort; a new year is on its way. Yet there is no guarantee that next year will be an improvement. Who can tell?

Well, friends, let it be what God chooses it to be. Let it be what He appoints. For there is this comfort: not a moment from the first of January to the thirty-first of December will be without the tender care of heaven. Not even for a second will the Lord remove His eyes from any one of His people. Here is good cheer for us! We will march boldly into this wilderness, for the pillar of fire and cloud will never leave us. The manna will never cease to come. The rock that followed us will never cease to flow with living streams. Onward, onward, let us go, joyously confident in our God.

Jehovah's Eyes

The next word that springs from the text is that great word *Jehovah*. It is a pity that our translators did not give us the names of God as they found them in the original. The word LORD in capitals is good enough, but that grand and glorious name of Jehovah should have been retained. Then we would read in Deuteronomy 11:12, "The eyes of Jehovah are always on it." He who surveys us with love and care is none other than the one indivisible God. We should conclude that if we have His eyes to view us, we have His heart to love us. If we have His heart to love us, we have His wings to cover us (Ps. 91:4), and we have His hands to bear us up, and we have the everlasting arms underneath us (Deut. 33:27). We have all the attributes of the Deity at our command.

Oh, Christian, when God says He always looks at you, He means that He is always yours. There is nothing that you need that He will refuse to do. There is no wisdom stored up in Him that He will not use for you. God will not withhold even one attribute of all of His great splendor, but all that God is will be yours. He will be your God *"forever and ever"* (Ps. 48:14). *"The LORD will give* [you] *grace and glory"* (Ps. 84:11), and *"He will be* [your] *guide even to death"* (Ps. 48:14).

Your God

Perhaps the sweetest term of the text is that next one—the eyes of Jehovah *"your God."* Ah, there is a blessed secret! Why? He is ours in covenant, our God, for He has chosen us to be His portion, and by His grace He has made us choose Him to be our portion. We are His, and He is ours.

> So I my best Beloved's am,
> So He is mine.

"Your God." Blessed be the Lord, we have learned to view Him not as another man's God, but as our God. Christian, can you claim God as yours this day? Has your hand grasped Him by faith? Has your heart by love twisted its tendrils around Him? Do you feel that He is the greatest possession that you have, that all else is but a dream, an empty show, but that God is your substantial treasure, your all in all?

Oh, then it is not an absolute God whose eyes are upon you, but God in covenant relationship who regards you. *"Your God."* What a term this is! He who is watching me is my Shepherd. He who cares for me is my Father. He is not my God by way of power alone, but my Father by way of relationship.

He is so great that the heaven of heavens cannot contain Him, yet He deigned to visit this poor earth robed in mortal flesh. And He is now our God, the God of His people by near and dear relationship. In ties of blood, Jesus is one with sinners—our Husband, our Head, our all in all. We are His fullness, *"the fullness of Him who fills all in all"* (Eph. 1:23).

Thus, the eyes of God, as the covenant God of Israel, are upon His people *"from the beginning of the year to the very end of the year."*

Much more may be said about the words of this text, but it is better unsaid by me, if you let the text say it to you. Talk to the text, I pray you. Let it journey with you until you can say about it what the disciples said about Christ: *"Did not our heart burn within us while He talked with us on the road?"* (Luke 24:32).

Our Eyes upon God

We are now going to turn the text around. That is, we will misread it, yet read it rightly. Suppose the text were to go like this: "The eyes of the Lord's people are always on Him from the beginning of the year to the end of the year." Dear friends, I like the text as it stands, but I do not believe we will ever comprehend its full meaning unless we read it this other way, for we only understand God's sight of us when we get a sight of Him. God, unknown to us, is our protector, but He is not such a protector that we can comfortably repose upon Him. We must discern Him by the eyes of faith, or else the mercy, though given by God, is not spiritually enjoyed in our hearts.

Beloved, if God looks at us, how much more ought we to look at Him! When God sees us, what does He see? If He were to look at us in ourselves, He would see nothing but what is unworthy to be looked at. (I praise God that He sees us in Christ!) Now, on the contrary, when we look at Him, what do we see? Oh, such a sight that I am not surprised that Moses said, *"Please, show me Your glory"* (Exod. 33:18). What a vision it is! Is it not a vision of heaven itself to see God? Is it not the prerogative of the pure in heart that they will see God (Matt. 5:8)?

Yet I cannot figure something out. Some of us have had the right to see God for years, and we have occasionally seen Him face to face, *"as a man speaks to his friend"* (Exod. 33:11). By faith we have seen God. But, beloved, what I cannot figure out is why we see Him so little. Do you ever find yourself living all day without God? Not completely, perhaps, for you would not want to go to work without a little prayer in the morning. But do you not sometimes get through that morning's prayer without seeing God at all? I mean, is it not just the form of kneeling down and saying good words and getting up again? And all through the day have you not lived away from God?

This is a strange world to live in; there are not many things to make us happy. Yet somehow we forget the very things that could give us happiness, and we keep our eyes on the frivolous cares and teasing troubles, which distract us.

Do we even end the day with no taste of His love, no kisses from His lips, which are *"better than wine"* (Song 1:2)? And our evening prayer—poor moaning that it is—is hardly a prayer.

I fear it is possible to live not only days, but months at this dying rate, and it is horrible living. I would infinitely prefer to rot in a moldy dungeon and have the Lord's presence than to live in the noblest palace without God. After all, what makes life life is the enjoyment of the presence of God.

It is not so with the worldling: he can live without God. He is like the swine, who, being contented with their husks, lie down and sleep and wake again to feed. But the Christian cannot live on husks, for he has a stomach above them. If he does not get his God, he is miserable.

God has ordained that a spiritual man is wretched without the love of God in his heart. If you and I want present happiness without God, we had better be sinners outright and feed on this world, rather than trying to be happy in religion without communion with Jesus. For a genuine Christian, happiness apart from Christ is an absolute impossibility. We must have God, or *"we are of all men the most pitiable"* (1 Cor. 15:19).

Suppose that this year we were filled with the desire to have our eyes always upon God from the beginning of the year to the end of the year, to be always conscious that He is seeing us, to be always aware of His presence. More than that, suppose that this year we were always longing to be obedient to His commands, always wanting to win souls for His dear Son, from the beginning of the year to the end of the year. What a happy thing this would be! If we could abide in a spirit of prayerfulness and thankfulness—devout, consecrated, loving, and tender—it would be a high thing to attain.

Friends, we believe in a great God who *"is able to do exceedingly abundantly above all that we ask or think"* (Eph. 3:20). Why not expect great things from Him? If I think of a blessing and dare to ask for it, surely then He is able to give it. Let us not stand back because of unbelief; let us ask that as God's eyes are upon us, our eyes may be upon Him. What a blessed meeting of eyes when the Lord looks us full in the face, and we look at Him through the mediator Christ Jesus, and the Lord declares, "I love you," and we answer, "We also love You, O our God!"

Oh, that we may be in harmony with the Lord our God and find ourselves drawn upwards and bound to Him! May the Lord be the sun and we the dewdrops that sparkle in His rays and are evaporated and drawn upward by the heat of His love! May God look down from heaven, and we look up to heaven, and both of us be happy in the sight of each other, rejoicing in mutual affection!

This is what communion means. I have taken a long time to come to that definition, but that is what it means.

> Daily communion let me prove
> With Thee, blest object of my love.

That was Toplady's* desire. If I would express my own experience, I must close with the other two lines of the verse, where Toplady said,

> But oh, for this no strength have I,
> My strength is at Thy feet to lie.

A World without God's Watchful Care

In the third place, we will, in our imaginations, blot the text out altogether. Not that we could blot it out or would do so if we could. But suppose for a moment that it is blotted out of the Bible. Imagine that you and I have to live all year without the eyes of God upon us, not finding a moment from the beginning of the year to the end of the year in which we perceive the Lord to be caring for us. Imagine that there is no one to whom we may appeal for help except our fellowman.

Oh, miserable supposition! We would have to get through the year somehow. We would go muddling through the winter, groaning through the spring, sweating through the summer, fainting through the autumn, and groveling on through another winter. Imagine having no God to help us, no prayer because God is gone, no promise because God is no more. There could be no promise, no comfort, no spiritual help for us if there were no God. But, I hear you cry out, "Do not imagine such a thing, for I would be like a child without a father. I would be helpless—a tree with no water for its roots."

But I will imagine this in the case of you sinners. You know you have been living for twenty or thirty or forty years without God, without prayer, without trust, without hope. Yet if I were to tell you solemnly that God would not let you pray during the next year, and would not help you if you did pray, you would be greatly startled. Although I believe that the Lord will hear you from the

---

* Augustus Montague Toplady (1740–87) was an Anglican minister and a hymnwriter. He is best known for his hymn "Rock of Ages."

beginning of the year to the end of the year, although I believe that He will watch over you and bless you if you seek Him, yet I fear that most of you are despising His care and living without fellowship with Him. You are without God, without Christ, without hope, and will continue to be *"from the beginning of the year to the very end of the year."*

There is a story about a most eccentric minister. Walking outside one morning, he saw a man going to work and said to him, "What a lovely morning! How grateful we ought to be to God for all His mercies!" The man said he did not know much about God's mercies. "Why," said the minister, "I suppose you always pray to God for your wife and children, don't you?"

"No," he said, "I do not know that I do."

"What," said the minister, "do you never pray?"

"No."

"Then I will give you ten dollars if you will promise me you will never pray as long as you live."

"Oh," he said, "I will be very glad for ten dollars to get me some beer."

He took the money and promised never to pray as long as he lived. He went to work, and when he had been digging for a little while, he thought to himself, "That's a strange thing I have done this morning—a very strange thing. I've taken money and promised never to pray as long as I live." He thought it over, and it made him feel wretched. He went home to his wife and told her about it.

"Well, John," she said, "you may count on it that it was the Devil. You've sold yourself to the Devil for ten dollars." This so weighed the poor wretch down that he did not know what to do with himself. All he could think about was that he had sold himself to the Devil for money and would soon be carried off to hell. He started to attend places of worship, believing that it was of no use, for he had sold himself to the Devil. He was really ill, bodily ill, because of the fear and trembling that had come upon him.

One night at church, the sick man recognized the preacher. He was the very man who had given him the ten dollars! The preacher probably recognized him, for the text was, *"What will it profit a man if he gains the whole world, and loses his own soul?"* (Mark 8:36). The preacher remarked that he knew a man who had sold his soul for ten dollars. The poor man rushed forward and said, "Take it back! Take it back!"

"You said you would never pray," said the minister, "if I gave you ten dollars. Do you want to pray?"

"Oh, yes, I would give the world to be allowed to pray."

That man was a great fool to sell his soul for ten dollars. But some of you are even bigger fools, for no one gave you ten dollars, and yet you do not pray. I dare say you never will, but you will go down to hell having never sought God.

Perhaps, if I could say the opposite of this text to you—"the eyes of God will not be upon you from the beginning of this year to the end of this year, and God will not hear and bless you"—it might alarm and awaken you. But, though I suggest the thought, I long for you to say, "Oh, let not such a curse rest on me, for I may die this year, or I may die this day. O God, hear me now!" Ah, dear reader, if such a desire is in your heart, the Lord will hear you and bless you with His salvation.

Our Response to God's Promise

Let us close by using the text for a practical lesson. The way to use it is by answering this question: If the eyes of the Lord will be upon us His people, *"from the beginning of the year to the very end of the year,"* what should we be doing? Why, let us be as happy as we can during this year. Trials and troubles will come; do not expect to be free from them. The Devil is not dead, and sparks still fly upward (Job 5:7). Herein is your joy: the God and Father of our Lord Jesus Christ *"will never leave you nor forsake you"* (Heb. 13:5). Up with your flag now, and march on boldly! In the name of the Lord, set up your banner, and begin to sing. Away with burdensome care; God cares for us (1 Pet. 5:7). God feeds the sparrows; will He not feed His children (Matt. 6:26)? God clothes the lilies; will He not clothe the saints (vv. 28–30)? Let us roll all our burdens upon the Burden-bearer.

You will have enough to care for if you care for His cause as you should. Do not spoil your power to care for God by caring for yourself. This year let your motto be, *"Seek first the kingdom of God and His righteousness, and all these things shall be added to you"* (v. 33). By worrying you can neither add a cubit to your stature (v. 27), nor *"make one hair white or black"* (Matt. 5:36). *"Therefore do not worry about tomorrow, for tomorrow will worry about its own things"* (Matt. 6:34). Lean on your God, and remember His promise: *"As your days, so shall your strength be"* (Deut. 33:25).

The apostle said, *"I want you to be without care"* (1 Cor. 7:32). He did not mean, "I do not want you to use economy, prudence, or discretion," but he means, "I do not want you to have fretfulness or distrustful care. I do not want you to be concerned for yourself, because the Lord's eyes will be upon you."

Seek greater blessings and richer mercies than you have ever enjoyed. Blessed be God for His merciful kindness toward His church. His loving-kindnesses have been abundant. His compassion is new every morning (Lam. 3:22–23) and fresh every evening. However, we want more. Let us not be content to wait until we have revival services to get a blessing; let us seek that blessing today.

I hope you Sunday school workers and your classes will be blessed *"from the beginning of the year to the very end of the year."* Let there be no dullness, lethargy, and lukewarmness in our Sunday school classes. Let our teachers speak with fervor and earnestness: there must be no coldness in our classrooms. And I hope you who are preaching in the streets or going from house to house with tracts, or doing anything else, will have a blessing as you do so.

Will we grow cold as the year progresses? Not at all. We will serve God *"from the beginning of the year to the very end of the year."* Will we endeavor to get up a little excitement and have a revival for five or six weeks? No, blessed be God, we must have revival *"from the beginning of the year to the very end of the year."* Since we have a spring of water that never grows dry (Isa. 58:11), why should the pitcher ever be empty? Surely gratitude can find us fuel enough in the forests of memory to keep the fire of love always flaming. Why should we be weary when the glorious prize is worthy of our constant exertions, when the great crowd of witnesses keeps us in its sight (Heb. 12:1)?

May our Lord by His Spirit bring you and me to a high level of prayerfulness; then, let us continue in prayer *"from the beginning of the year to the very end of the year."* May God bring you and me to a high degree of generosity; then, may we always be giving *"from the beginning of the year to the very end of the year,"* every week from the first to the last, always giving money for His cause as God has prospered us (1 Cor. 16:2). May we be always active, always industrious, always hopeful, always spiritual, always heavenly, and always raised up and made to *"sit together in the heavenly places in Christ Jesus"* (Eph. 2:6). May God deal graciously with us *"from the beginning of the year to the very end of the year"* through Jesus Christ our Lord.

Chapter 4

A Tempted Savior—Our Best Help

For in that He Himself has suffered, being tempted,
He is able to aid those who are tempted.
—Hebrews 2:18

One important area in which God helps us from the beginning to the end of the year is that of temptation. Recently, a friend of mine, who is a clergyman of the Church of England, wrote to me and included this verse about temptation from Hebrews 2:18. This man is a venerable clergyman, who has always shown me the most constant and affectionate regard. This text is dear to this aged servant of the Lord because of his deep experience of both affliction and deliverance. Through these experiences he has learned his need of solid, substantial food, fit for the veteran warriors of the Cross. Having been tempted these many years, my friend finds that as his natural strength decays, he needs to cast himself more and more upon the tenderness of the Redeemer's love. And he is led to look more fully to Him who is his only help in the day of trouble, finding consolation alone in the person of Christ Jesus the Lord.

Hebrews 2:18 is a staff for old age to lean on in the rough places of the way. It is a sword with which the strong man may fight in all hours of conflict. It is a shield with which youth may cover itself in the time of peril. And it is a royal chariot in which spiritual babes may ride in safety. There is something here for every one of us, as Solomon put it: *"Cast your bread upon the waters, for you will find it after many days. Give a serving to seven, and also to eight"* (Eccl. 11:1–2). If we consider the Great Prophet and High Priest of our profession—Jesus Christ—who *"was in all points tempted as we are"* (Heb. 4:15), we will not grow weary or faint in our minds. No, we will prepare to run in our future journey, and like Elijah we will go in the strength of this food for many days to come (1 Kings 19:8).

151

You who are tempted—and I suppose most readers would fall into this category—read what I have tried to explain about your temptations and the temptations of Jesus. For Jesus, having known your trials, is able to help you at all times.

Christ Was Tempted

Our first point is this: many souls are tempted—even Christ was tempted. All the heirs of heaven have carried this burden. All true gold must feel the fire. All wheat must be threshed. All diamonds must be cut. All saints must endure temptation.

Saints are tempted from every direction. It is like Christ's parable about the house built on the rock. The Bible says, *"The rain descended, the floods came, and the winds blew and beat on that house; and it did not fall, for it was founded on the rock"* (Matt. 7:25). The descending rain may represent temptations from above. The floods pouring their devastating torrents over the land may denote the trials that spring from the world. And the howling winds may typify those mysterious influences of evil that issue from the *"prince of the power of the air"* (Eph. 2:2).

Now, whether we shudder at the descending rain, fear the uprising flood, or are amazed at the mysterious energy of the winds, we should remember that our blessed Lord *"was in all points tempted as we are"* (Heb. 4:15). This is to be our consolation: nothing has happened to the members of Christ's body that has not happened to Christ, the Head.

Tempted by God

Beloved friends, it is possible that we may be tempted by God. I know it is written that *"God cannot be tempted by evil, nor does He Himself tempt anyone"* (James 1:13). Yet I read in Scripture, *"It came to pass...that God did tempt Abraham"* (Gen. 22:1 KJV). Also, part of the prayer that we are taught to offer before God is, *"Do not lead us into temptation"* (Matt. 6:13). This verse clearly implies that God does lead into temptation, or why else would we be taught to entreat Him not to do so?

In one sense of the term *tempt*, a pure and holy God can have no share, but in another sense He does tempt His people. The temptation that comes from God is altogether that of trial. God's trials are not meant for evil like Satan's temptations, but they are trials meant to prove and strengthen our graces. All at once, God's trials illustrate the power of divine grace, test the genuineness of our virtues, and strengthen our character.

You remember that Abraham was tried and tested by God when he was bidden to go to a mountain that God would show him, there to offer up his son Isaac. (See Genesis 22:1–2.) You and I may have a similar experience. God may call us in the path of obedience to a great and singular sacrifice. The desire of our eyes may be demanded of us in an hour, or He may summon us to a duty far surpassing all our strength; we may be tempted by the weight of the responsibility, like Jonah, to flee from the presence of the Lord (Jonah 1:3).

We do not know which temptations we will face until we come to them; but, beloved, whatever they may be, our Great High Priest has felt them all (Heb. 4:15). His Father called Him to a work of the most terrific kind. He *"laid on Him the iniquity of us all"* (Isa. 53:6). He ordained Him as the second Adam, the bearer of the curse, the destroyer of death, and the conqueror of hell. Jesus was the seed of the woman, doomed to be wounded in the heel but elected to bruise the Serpent's head (Gen. 3:15). Our Lord was appointed to toil at the loom, and there, with ever-flying shuttle, to weave a perfect garment of righteousness for all His people. (See Isaiah 61:10.)

Now, beloved, this was a strong and mighty testing of Jesus' character. It is impossible that we could ever be thrust into a refiner's fire as hot as the one that tried this purest gold. No one else could be in the crucible so long or subjected to a heat so hot as what was endured by Christ Jesus. If, then, the trial is sent directly from our heavenly Father, we may solace ourselves with this reflection: *"In that* [Christ] *Himself has suffered, being tempted* [by God], *He is able to aid those who are* [likewise] *tempted."*

But, dear friends, our God tries us not only directly, but indirectly. Everything is under the Lord's control of providence. Everything that happens to us is meted out by His decree and settled by His purpose. We know that nothing can happen to us unless it is written in the secret book of providential predestination. Consequently, all the trials resulting from circumstances can be traced at once to the great First Cause. Out of the golden gate of God's ordinance, the armies of trial march forth in array. No shower falls from the threatening cloud unless God permits it; every drop has its orders before it hastens to the earth.

Consider poverty, for instance. So many people are made to feel its pinching necessities. They shiver in the cold for lack of clothes. They are hungry and thirsty. They are homeless, friendless, despised. This is a temptation from God, but Christ suffered the same: *"Foxes have holes and the birds of the air have nests, but the Son of Man has nowhere to lay His head"* (Matt. 8:20). When He had fasted forty days and forty nights, He was hungry, and it was then that He was tempted by the Devil. (See Matthew 4:2–3.)

It is not only the scant table and the ragged garment that invite temptation, for all blessings are doors to trials. Even our mercies, like roses, have their thorns. Men may be drowned in seas of prosperity as well as in rivers of affliction. Our mountains are not too high, and our valleys are not too low, for temptation to travel. Where can we go to get away from temptations? What wind is strong enough to carry us away from them? Everywhere, above and beneath, we are troubled and surrounded by dangers. Now, since all these trials are overseen and directed by the great Lord of providence, we may look at them all as temptations that come from Him.

Christ suffered every kind of temptation. Let us choose the special one of sickness. Sickness is a strong temptation to impatience, rebellion, and murmuring, but *"He Himself took our infirmities and bore our sicknesses"* (Matt. 8:17). His appearance was marred more than that of any man (Isa. 52:14) because His soul was sorely vexed; consequently, His body was greatly tormented.

Bereavement, too, is such a trial to the tender heart! You arrows of death, you kill, but you wound with wounds worse than death. *"Jesus wept"* (John 11:35) because His friend Lazarus slept in the tomb. That great loss taught Jesus to sympathize with the widow in her loss, with the orphan in his fatherless estate, and with the friend whose acquaintance has been thrust into darkness. Nothing can come from God to the sons of men unless the same thing or a similar thing also happened to the Lord Jesus Christ. Herein let us wrap the warm cloak of consolation around ourselves, since Christ was tempted like we are.

Tempted by Men

We are tempted more often by men than by God. God tries us now and then, but our fellowmen try us every day. Our foes are in our own household and among our own friends. Out of mistaken kindness, they would often lead us to prefer our own ease to the service of God. Links of love have made chains of iron for saints. It is hard to ride to heaven over our own flesh and blood. Relatives and acquaintances may greatly hinder the young disciple.

This, however, is no novelty to our Lord. You know how He had to say to Peter, well-beloved disciple though he was, *"Get behind Me, Satan!...You are not mindful of the things of God"* (Matt. 16:23). Poor, ignorant human friendship tried to keep Jesus back from the cross. It would have made Him miss His great purpose for being fashioned as a man, and it would have robbed Him of all the honor that only shame and death could win Him.

Not only true friends, but also false friends attempt our ruin. Treason creeps like a snake in the grass; falsehood, like an adder, *"bites the horse's heels"* (Gen. 49:17). If treachery assaults us, let us remember how Jesus was betrayed: *"He who eats bread with Me has lifted up his heel against Me"* (John 13:18). *"Even my own familiar friend in whom I trusted, who ate my bread, has lifted up his heel against me"* (Ps. 41:9). What should be done to you, false tongue? Eternal silence rest on you! And yet, you have spent your venom on my Lord; why should I marvel if you try your worst on me?

We are tempted by friends, and we are often assailed by enemies. Enemies will waylay us with subtle questions, seeking to trap us by our words. Oh, cunning devices of a generation of vipers! They did the same to Christ. The Sadducee, the Pharisee, the lawyer—each one had his riddle. And each one was answered—answered gloriously—by the Great Teacher, who cannot be trapped.

You and I are sometimes asked strange questions. Doctrines are set in controversy with other doctrines. Texts of Scripture are made to clash with other texts of Scripture. We hardly know how to reply to these things. Let us retire into the secret chamber of this great fact: in this point, also, Christ was tempted.

When Jesus' foes could not prevail against Him with questions, they slandered His character. They called Him *"a glutton and a winebibber, a friend of tax collectors and sinners"* (Matt. 11:19). He became the song of the drunkard, and their reproach broke His heart.

This may happen to us. People may accuse us of the very thing of which we are the most innocent. Our good deeds may be misrepresented, our motives misinterpreted, our words misreported, and our actions misconstrued. In this, also, we may shelter ourselves beneath the eagle wings of this great truth: our glorious Head has suffered, and, having been tempted, He can give us aid.

However, His foes did even more than this. When they found Him in agonizing pain, they taunted Him to His face (Matt. 27:39–40). Pointing their fingers, they mocked His nakedness. Thrusting out their tongues, they jeered at His claims. They hissed out that diabolical temptation: *"If He is the King of Israel, let Him now come down from the cross, and we will believe Him"* (v. 42).

How often the sons of men have mocked us and then accused us in like manner. They have caught us in some unhappy moment—when our spirits were broken, when our circumstances were unhappy—and then they have said, "Now where is your God? If you are what you profess to be, prove it." They ask us to prove our faith by a sinful action, which they know would destroy our characters—some rash deed that would be contrary to our profession of faith. Here, too, we may remember that, having been tempted, our High Priest is able to help those who are tempted.

Moreover, remember that there are temptations that come from neither friends nor foes, but from those with whom we are compelled to mix in ordinary society. Jesus ate at a Pharisee's table, even though most Pharisees reeked with infectious pride. He sat with the publicans, even though their characters were contagious with impurity. But whether it was in one difficult place or another, the Great Physician walked through the midst of moral plagues and leprosies unharmed. He associated with sinners but was not a sinner. He touched disease but was not diseased Himself. He could enter into the chambers of evil, but evil could not find a chamber in Him.

You and I are thrown by our daily duties into constant contact with evil. It is impossible, I suppose, to walk among men without being tempted by them. Men who have no preconceived plan to betray us entice us to evil and corrupt our good manners simply by the force of their ordinary behavior. We may cry, *"Woe is me, that I dwell in Meshech, that I dwell among the tents of Kedar!"* (Ps. 120:5). However, we may remember that our great Leader sojourned here, too; and being here, He was *"tempted as we are"* (Heb. 4:15).

Tempted by Satan

Dear friends, we will not complete the list of temptations if we forget that a vast host, and those of a most violent nature, can only be ascribed to satanic influence. Satan's temptations are usually threefold, for Christ's threefold temptation in the wilderness, if I read it right, was a true picture of all the temptations that Satan uses against God's people. The first temptation of Satan is usually made against our faith. When our Lord was hungry, Satan came to Him and said, *"If You are the Son of God, command that these stones become bread"* (Matt. 4:3). Here it was, that devilish *"if,"* that cunning suggestion that He was not God's Son, coupled with the enticement to commit a selfish act to prove that He was the Son.

Ah, how often Satan tempts us to unbelief! "God has forsaken you," he says. "God has no love for you. Your experience has been a delusion. Your profession of faith is a falsehood. All your hopes will fail you. You are only a poor, miserable fool. There is no truth in religion. If there is, why are you in this trouble? Why not do as you like, live as you want, and enjoy yourself?" Ah, foul fiend, how craftily you spread your net, but it is all in vain, for Jesus has passed through and broken the snare.

Dear reader, beware of interfering with divine providence. Satan tempts many believers to run before the guiding cloud, to carve their own fortunes, to build their own houses, to steer their own ships. Trouble will surely befall all who yield to this temptation. Beware of becoming the keepers of your own souls, for evil will soon overtake you. When you are thus tempted by Satan and your adoption seems to be in jeopardy and your experience appears to melt, fly at once to the Good Shepherd. Remember this: *"In that He Himself has suffered, being tempted, He is able to aid those who are tempted."*

The next foul temptation of Satan with Christ was not to unbelief, but to the very opposite—presumption. *"Throw Yourself down"* (Matt. 4:6), he said, as he poised the Savior on the pinnacle of the temple. Even so, he whispers to some of us, "You are a child of God; you know that. Therefore, you are safe to live as you like."

Oh, that foul temptation! It leads many an antinomian by the nose, and he is like *"an ox [going] to the slaughter, or as a fool to the correction of the stocks"* (Prov. 7:22). For many an antinomian will say, "I am safe; therefore, I may indulge my lusts with impunity."

You see, the Devil tries to use the doctrine of election or the great truth of the final perseverance of the saints to tempt you to soil your purity. He tries to use the mercy and love of God to tempt you to stain your innocency. However, you who know better, when you are thus tempted, console yourselves with the fact that Christ was tempted in this way, too, and He is able to help you even here.

The final temptation of Christ in the wilderness was that of idolatry. Actually, ambition was the temptation, but idolatry was the end at which the tempter aimed. *"All these things I will give You if You will fall down and worship me"* (Matt. 4:9). The old Serpent will suggest to us, "I will make you rich if you will only venture upon that one dishonest transaction. You will be famous; only tell that one lie. You will be perfectly at ease; only wink at one small evil. All these things will I give you if you will make me lord of your heart." Ah, then it will be a noble thing if you can look up to Him who endured this temptation and bid the fiend depart with, *"It is written, 'You shall worship the LORD your God, and Him only you shall serve'"* (v. 10). Then, Satan will leave you, and angels will minister to you as they did to the tempted One of old.

Tempted in All Positions

Not only are we tempted from all directions, but we are tempted in all positions. No man is too lowly for the arrows of hell; no man is too elevated for the arrows of hell. Poverty has its dangers: *"Lest I be poor and steal"* (Prov. 30:9). Christ knew these dangers. Contempt has its aggravated temptations. To be despised often makes men bitter; it often exasperates them into savage selfishness and wolfish revenge. Our Great Prophet knew from experience the temptations of contempt.

It is no small trial to be filled with pain. When all the strings of our personhood are strained and twisted, it is little wonder if they make a sour note. Christ endured the greatest amount of physical pain, especially upon the cross. And on the cross, where all the rivers of human agony met in one deep lake within His heart, He bore all that it was possible for the human frame to bear. Here, then, without limit, He learned the ills of pain.

Turn the picture around: Christ knew the temptations of riches. You may say, "How?" He had opportunities to be rich. Mary, Martha, and Lazarus would have been glad to give Him their substance. The honorable women who ministered to Him would have grudged Him nothing. There were many opportunities to make Himself a king. He could have become famous and great like other teachers and earned a high salary. However, knowing the temptations of wealth, He also overcame them.

The temptations of ease—and these are not small—Christ readily escaped. There always would have been a comfortable home for Him at Bethany. There were many disciples who would have felt highly honored to find for Him the softest couch ever made. But He who came not to enjoy but to endure spurned all, but not without knowing the temptation.

He learned, too, the trials of honor, popularity, and applause. "Hosanna, hosanna, hosanna," said the multitudes in the streets of Jerusalem, as palm branches were strewn in the way and He rode in triumph over the garments of His disciples. (See Matthew 21:6–9.) But, experiencing all this, He was still meek and lowly, and in Him was no sin (1 Pet. 2:21–22). When you are cast down or lifted up, when you are put into the strangest of positions, remember that Christ has made a pilgrimage over the least trodden of our paths and is therefore able to help those who are tempted.

Tempted at All Ages

Further, let me remark that every age has its temptations. Even children, if believers, will discover that there are particular snares for them. Christ knew these. It was no small temptation to a twelve-year-old boy to be found sitting in the midst of the doctors, hearing them and answering their questions. It would have caused pride in most boys, yet Jesus went down to Nazareth and was subject to His parents (Luke 2:51).

It says that "Jesus increased in wisdom and stature, and in favor with God and men" (v. 52). It would be dangerous to grow in favor with God and man if the word God were not included. To grow in favor constantly with men would be too much of a temptation for most teenagers. It is good for a man to bear the yoke in his youth; for youth, when honored and esteemed, is too apt to grow self-conceited, vain, and disobedient.

When a young man knows that he will become something great someday, it is not easy to keep him balanced. Suppose that he is born to an estate and knows that when he grows up he will be lord and master and will be popular with everybody. Why, he is apt to be very wayward and self-willed. Now, there were prophecies that went before concerning Mary's son. They pointed Him out as King of the Jews (Matt. 2:1–2) and "The Mighty One of Israel" (Isa. 30:29). Yet I do not find that the holy child Jesus was ever lured by His coming greatness into any evil actions. So, teenage believers, you who are like Samuel and Timothy, you can look to Christ and know that He can help you.

It is unnecessary for me to repeat the various afflictions that beat upon Jesus in His full manhood. You who today bear the burden and heat of the day will find an example here. Old age, also, does not need to look elsewhere, for we may view our Redeemer with admiration as He went up to Jerusalem to die. His last moments were obviously near at hand; He knew the temptations of an expected death. He saw death more clearly than any of you, even if your temples are covered with white hair. Yet whether in life or in death, on Tabor's summit or on the banks of the river of death, He is still the same—tempted ever, but never sinning; tried always, but never found failing. O Lord, You are able to help those who are tempted. Help us! I do not need to write more about this. Perhaps I have not mentioned your particular trial, but it may be included in one of the general descriptions. Whatever your trial may be, it cannot be so rare that it is not included somewhere in the temptations of our Lord Jesus Christ. I, therefore, now turn to the second topic of this chapter.

Christ Suffered

My second point is that as the tempted often suffer, Christ also suffered. Notice, our text does not say, "In that He Himself has also been tempted, He is able to help those who are tempted." It is better than that. The text tells us that Christ suffered: *"In that He Himself has suffered, being tempted, He is able to aid those who are tempted."* Temptation, even when overcome, brings to the true child of God a great deal of suffering.

The Shock of Sin

This suffering consists of two or three things. It lies, mainly, in the shock that sin gives to the sensitive, regenerate nature. A man who is clothed in armor may walk through tearing thorns and brambles without being hurt; but if he takes off his armor and attempts the same journey, how sadly he will be cut and torn. Sin, to the man who is used to it, brings no suffering. Being tempted causes him no pain. In fact, temptation frequently yields pleasure to the sinner. To look at the bait is sweet to the fish that plans to swallow it before long. But the child of God, who is spiritually new and alive, shudders at the very thought of sin. He cannot look at sin without abhorrence and without being alarmed at the possibility of falling into an abominable crime.

Now, dear friends, in this case Christ indeed has experience, and it far surpasses ours. His hatred of sin must have been much deeper than ours. A word of blasphemy, a sinful deed, must have cut Him to His very heart. We cannot even comprehend the wretchedness that Jesus must have endured in merely being on earth among the ungodly. For infinite purity to dwell among sinners must be something like the best educated, the purest, the most amiable person being condemned to live in a den of burglars, blasphemers, and filthy wretches. That man's life would be misery. No whip or chain would be needed. Merely associating with such people would be pain and torment enough. The Lord Jesus must have suffered a vast amount of woe just by being near to sin.

The Dread of Temptation

Suffering, too, comes to the people of God from the dread of a temptation. Dread arises in our hearts as the shadow of the temptation falls upon us, announcing its soon arrival. At times there is more dread in the prospect of a trial than there is in the trial itself. We feel a thousand temptations in fearing one.

Christ knew this. What an awful dread came over Him in the black night of Gethsemane! It was not the cup—it was the fear of drinking it. He cried, *"Let this cup pass from Me"* (Matt. 26:39). He knew how black, how foul, how fiery its contents were; and it was the dread of drinking it that bowed Him to the ground until He sweat, as it were, great drops of blood (Luke 22:44). When you have a similar overwhelming pressure on your spirit in the prospect of a trial, fly to the loving heart of your sympathizing Lord, for He has suffered all this.

The Source of Temptation

Temptation also causes suffering because of its source. Have you ever felt that you would not have minded the temptation if it had not come from where it did? "Oh," you say, "to think that my own friend, my dearly beloved friend, should tempt me!" Perhaps you are a teenager, and you have said, "I think I could bear anything but my father's frown or my mother's sneer." Perhaps you are a husband, and you have said, "My thorn in the flesh is too sharp, for it is an ungodly wife." Or you are a wife (and this is more frequently the case), and you think there is no temptation like yours, because it is your husband who assaults your religion and who speaks evil of your good.

It makes all the difference where the temptation comes from. If some scoundrel mocks us, we consider it an honor; but when it is an esteemed companion, we feel his taunt. A friend can cut under our armor and stab us the more dangerously.

Ah, but the Man of Sorrows knew all this, since it was one of the chosen twelve who betrayed Him. Moreover, *"it pleased the LORD to bruise Him; He has put Him to grief"* (Isa. 53:10). To find God to be in arms against us is a huge affliction. *"Eloi, Eloi, lama sabachthani?...My God, My God, why have You forsaken Me?"* (Mark 15:34) is the very epitome of woe. Jesus surely has suffered your grief, regardless of its source.

The Fear of Dishonoring God

I have no doubt, too, that a portion of the suffering of temptation lies in the fact that God's name and honor are often involved in our temptation. Those of us who are in the public eye are sometimes slandered. When the slander is merely against our own personal character, against our modes of speech or habit, we can receive it gratefully and thankfully, blessing God that He has counted us worthy to suffer for His name's sake (Acts 5:41). However, sometimes the attack is very plainly not against us, but against God. People say things that make us cry with the psalmist David, *"Indignation has taken hold of me because of the wicked, who forsake Your law"* (Ps. 119:53).

When direct blasphemies are uttered against the person of Christ, or against the doctrine of His holy Gospel, my heart has been very heavy because I have thought, "If I have opened this dog's mouth against myself, it does not matter; but if I have made him roar against God, then how will I answer, and what will I say?" This has often been the bitterness of it: "If I fall, God's cause is stained. If I slip through the vehemence of this assault, then one of the gates of the church will be carried off by storm. Harm comes not just to me, but to many of the Israel of God." David says this about grieving the saints: *"When I thought how to understand this, it was too painful for me"* (Ps. 73:16).

Jesus had to suffer for God, for it is written, *"The reproaches of those who reproached You fell on Me"* (Rom. 15:3). He was made the target for those arrows that were really shot at God, and so He felt this bitterness of sympathy with His ill-used God.

I cannot, of course, be specific enough to hit on the precise sorrow that you, beloved believer in Christ, are enduring as the result of temptation. But whatever phase your sorrow may have assumed, this should always be your comfort: Jesus suffered in temptation. He did not merely know temptation as you sometimes have known it, when it has hit you and fallen harmless to the ground, but it festered in His flesh. It did not make Him sin, but it made Him suffer. It did not make Him err, but it caused Him to mourn. Oh, child of God, I do not know a deeper well of purer consolation than this: *"He Himself has suffered, being tempted."*

Christ Helps the Tempted

Now for the third and last point. Those who are tempted have great need of help; and Christ, having been tempted Himself, is able to help them. Of course, Christ is able to help the tempted because Christ is God. Even if He had never endured any temptation, He would still be able to help the tempted because He is God. However, we are now speaking in our text of Christ as a high priest; we are to regard Him in His complex character as God-man. For Christ is not only God, but man, and not only man, but God. Christ, the Anointed One, the High Priest of our profession, is, in His complex character, able to help those who are tempted.

Because He Was Tempted

How can He help us? Why, first, the very fact that He was tempted has help in it for us. If we had to walk through the darkness alone, we would know the very extremity of misery. But having a companion, we have comfort; having such a companion, we have joy.

Darkness surrounds me, and the path is miry. I sink in it and can find no foothold. But I plunge onward, desperately set on reaching my journey's end. It worries me that I am alone. I can see nothing, but suddenly I hear a voice that says, *"Yea, though I walk through the valley of the shadow of death, I will fear no evil"* (Ps. 23:4). I cry out, "Who is there?" and an answer comes back to me:

"I, *'the Faithful and True Witness'* (Rev. 3:14), the *'Alpha and the Omega'* (Rev. 1:8), the sufferer who was *'despised and rejected by men'* (Isa. 53:3), I lead the way." Then, at once, light surrounds me, and there is a rock beneath my feet. If Christ my Lord has been here, then the way must be safe and must lead to the desired end. The very fact that He has suffered, then, consoles His people.

Because He Was Not Destroyed

But, further, the fact that He has suffered without being destroyed is inestimably comforting to us. Think about a block of ore just ready to be put into the furnace. Suppose that block of ore could look into the flames and could see the blast as it blows the coals to a vehement heat. If that ore could speak, it would say, "Ah, how awful that I should ever be put into such a blazing furnace as that! I will be burnt up! I will be melted with the slag! I will be utterly consumed!" But suppose another lump all bright and glistening could lie by its side and say, "No, no, you are just like I was, but I went through the fire and lost nothing. See how bright I am! See how I have survived all the flames!" Why, that piece of ore would anticipate, rather than dread, being exposed to the purifying heat. It would anticipate coming out all bright and lustrous like its companion.

I see You, Son of Mary, bone of our bone, flesh of our flesh (Gen. 2:23). You have felt the flames, but You are not destroyed. There is no smell of fire on You. Your heel has been bruised, but You have broken the Serpent's head (Gen. 3:15). There is no scar, nor spot, nor injury in You. You have survived the conflict. Therefore, I, bearing Your name, purchased with Your blood (Acts 20:28), and as dear to God as You are dear to Him, I will survive the conflict, too. I will tread the coals with confidence and bear the heat with patience. Christ's conquest gives me comfort, for I will conquer, too.

Because He Was a Great Gainer

Please remember, too, that Christ, in going through the suffering of temptation, not only did not lose anything, but He gained much. Through suffering, He was a great gainer. It is written that it pleased God *"to make the captain of their salvation perfect through sufferings"* (Heb. 2:10). It was through His suffering that He obtained the mediatory glory that now crowns His head. If He had never carried the cross, He would have never worn that crown. (It is a transcendently bright and glorious crown that He now wears as King in Zion and as leader of His people, whom He has redeemed by blood.) Had He not carried the cross, He would still have been God over all and blessed forever; however, He could never have been extolled as the God-man Mediator unless He had been *"obedient to the point of death"* (Phil. 2:8). Therefore, He was a gainer by His suffering.

Glory be to His name, we get comfort from this, too! For we also will be gainers by our temptations. We will come up out of Egypt enriched; as it is written, *"He also brought them out with silver and gold"* (Ps. 105:37). We will come forth out of our trials with great treasures. *"Blessed is the man who endures temptation; for when he has been approved, he will receive the crown of life"* (James 1:12). The deeper our sorrows, the louder our song. The more terrible our toil, the sweeter our rest. The more bitter the wormwood, the more delightful the wine of consolation. We will have glory for our shame; we will have honor for our contempt; we will have songs for our sufferings; and we will have thrones for our tribulations.

Because He Sends His Grace to Help Us

Moreover, because Christ has suffered temptation, He is able to help us who are tempted by sending His grace to help us. He was always able to send grace; but now as God and man, He is able to send just the right grace at the right time and in the right place. A doctor may have all the drugs that can be gathered, but an abundance of medicine does not make him a qualified practitioner. If, however, he has gone himself and seen the case, then he knows just at what crisis of the disease a certain medicine is needed. The medications are good, but the wisdom to use the medications—this is even more precious.

Now, *"it pleased the Father that in* [Christ] *all the fullness should dwell"* (Col. 1:19). But where would the Son of Man earn His diploma and gain the skills to use the fullness correctly? Beloved, He won it by experience. He knows what sore temptations mean, for He has felt the same. You know, if we had comforting grace given to us at the wrong point in our temptation, it would tempt us more than help us. It is just like certain medicines: given to the patient at one period of the disease, they would worsen the malady, though the same medicine would cure him if administered a little later.

165

Now, Christ knows how to send His comfort in the nick of time. He gives His help exactly when it will not be a superfluity. He sends His joy when we will not spend it upon our own lusts. How does He do this? Why, He recollects His own experience; He has passed through it all. *"Then an angel appeared to Him from heaven, strengthening Him"* (Luke 22:43). That angel came just when he was needed. Jesus knows when to send His angelic messenger to strengthen you, when to use the correcting rod, and when to refrain and say, "I have forgiven you. Go in peace."

Because He Prays for Us

I will not write much more on this subject. Having suffered Himself, having been tempted, Christ knows how to help us by His prayers for us. There are some people whose prayers are of no use to us because they do not know what to ask for. Christ is the intercessor for His people; He has success in His intercession; but how does He know what to ask for? How can He know this better than by His own trials? He has suffered temptation.

You hear some believers pray with such power, such unction, such fervor. Why? Part of the reason is that they pray from experience—they pray out of their own lives; they just tell of the great deep waters over which they themselves sail. Now, the prayer of our Great High Priest in heaven is wonderfully comprehensive. It is drawn from His own life, and it takes in every sorrow and every pang that ever tore a human heart, because He Himself has suffered temptation. I know you feel safe in committing your case into the hands of such an intercessor, for He knows the precise mercy for which to ask. And when He asks for it, He knows how to word it so that the mercy will surely come at the right time.

Ah, dear friends, it is not in my power to bring out the depth that lies in my text. However, I am certain of this: when He causes you to go through the deep waters, when you are made to pass through furnace after furnace, you will never need a better support or provision than my text: *"In that He Himself has suffered, being tempted, He is able to aid those who are tempted."* Hang this text up in your house; read it every day; take it before God in prayer every time you bend your knee. You will find it to be like the widow's cruse of oil, which did not go dry, and like her handful of meal, which did not run out (1 Kings 17:16). It will sustain you as much a year from now as it does when you begin to feed on it today.

Will my text not suit the awakened sinner as well as the saint? Perhaps you are a timid soul that cannot say that you are saved. Yet here is a loophole of comfort for you, you poor troubled one who is not yet able to get a hold of Jesus: *"He is able to aid those who are tempted."* Go and tell Him you are tempted—tempted, perhaps, to despair; tempted to self-destruction; tempted to go back to your old sins; tempted to think that Christ cannot save you. Go and tell Him that He Himself has suffered temptation and that He is able to help you. Believe that He will, and He will, for you can never believe in the love and goodness of my Lord too much. He will be better than your faith to you. If you can trust Him with all your heart to save you, He will do it. If you believe He is able to put away your sin, He will do it. Only honor Him by attributing to Him a good character of grace; you cannot give Him too good a name.

> Trust Him, He will not deceive you,
> Though you hardly on Him lean;
> He will never, never leave you,
> Nor will let you quite leave Him.

Receive, then, the blessing. May the grace of our Lord Jesus Christ, the love of God our Father, and the fellowship of the Holy Spirit be with you forever.

Chapter 5

True Unity Promoted

Endeavoring to keep the unity of the Spirit in the bond of peace.
—Ephesians 4:3

The people of the church are often tempted to spread strife and division. I hope our text verse will be useful to us all. It will remind us of our former faults and of our present duty in the matter of *"endeavoring to keep the unity of the Spirit in the bond of peace."*

In former days, the argument used against reformation was the necessity of maintaining unity. The argument went something like this: "You must bear with this ceremony and that dogma, no matter how anti-Christian and unholy it is. You must endeavor *'to keep the unity of the Spirit in the bond of peace.'*" That is what the old Serpent said in those early days. And the argument continued like this: "The church is one; woe to those who create division! It does not matter that Mary is set up in the place of Christ, that images are worshiped, that rotten rags are adored, and that pardons for every kind of crime are bought and sold. It does not matter that the so-called church has become an abomination and a nuisance on the face of the earth. Still, you must *'keep the unity of the Spirit in the bond of peace.'* You must lie down, restrain the testimony of the Spirit of God within you, keep His truth under a bushel, and let the lie prevail."

Believers, there is no force in this argument if you will look at the text for a moment. The text tells us to endeavor *"to keep the unity of the Spirit,"* but it does not tell us to maintain the unity of evil or the unity of superstition. The unity of error and false doctrine may have in them the spirit of Satan—we do not doubt it— but it is not the unity of the Spirit of God. We are to break down the unity of evil by every weapon that our hands can grasp. It is the unity of the Spirit that we are to maintain and foster.

Remember, we are forbidden to *"do evil that good m ay come"* (Rom. 3:8). The following things are evil: restraining the witness of the Spirit of God within us, concealing any truth that we have learned by the revelation of God, and holding back from testifying for God's truth against the sin and folly of man's inventions. This is sin of the blackest hue.

We dare not commit the sin of quenching the Holy Spirit (1 Thess. 5:19), even if we are trying to promote unity. The unity of the Spirit never requires any support of sin. This unity is maintained, not by suppressing truth, but by publishing it abroad. One of the pillars of the unity of the Spirit is witnessing about the one faith that God has revealed in His Word. This unity is quite different from the "unity" that would gag our mouths and turn us all into dumb, driven cattle, to be fed or slaughtered at the will of men.

Dr. McNeil has, very properly, said that a man can scarcely be an earnest Christian in the present day without being a controversialist. We are sent forth today *"as sheep in the midst of wolves"* (Matt. 10:16); can we have agreement with wolves? We are like lamps in the midst of darkness; can we have harmony with darkness (2 Cor. 6:14)? Did not Christ Himself say, *"Do not think that I came to bring peace on earth. I did not come to bring peace but a sword"* (Matt. 10:34)? You can understand how all this controversy is the truest method of trying *"to keep the unity of the Spirit"*; for Christ, the Man of War, is Jesus the Peacemaker. In order to create lasting, spiritual peace, the concord of evil must be broken, and the unity of darkness must be dashed to pieces.

I pray that God will always preserve us from a unity in which truth is considered valueless, in which principle gives place to policy, in which the masculine virtues of the Christian hero are supplemented by an effeminate, fake love. May the Lord deliver us from indifference to His Word and will, for this creates a cold unity—like masses of ice frozen into an iceberg, chilling the air for miles around; or like the unity of the dead as they sleep in their graves, contending for nothing because they no longer have a part in the land of the living.

There is a unity that is seldom broken: the unity of devils, who, under the service of their evil master, never disagree and quarrel. From this terrible unity keep us, O God of heaven! There is the unity of locusts, who have one common objective: the glutting of themselves to the ruin of all around. From this unity, also, save us, we pray! There is the unity of the waves of hell's fire, sweeping myriads into deeper misery. From this, also, O King of heaven, save us evermore!

May God perpetually send some prophet who will cry aloud to the world: *"Your covenant with death will be annulled, and your agreement with Sheol will not stand"* (Isa. 28:18). May there always be found some men, though they are as rough as Amos, or as stern as Haggai, who will denounce again and again all league with error and all compromise with sin. May they declare that these evil alliances and compromises are abhorred by God.

Never dream that holy contention is a violation of Ephesians 4:3: *"Endeavoring to keep the unity of the Spirit in the bond of peace."* We must destroy every union that is not based on truth before we can enjoy the unity of the Spirit. We must first sweep away these walls of untempered mortar—these tottering fences of man's building—before there can be room to lay the strong stones of Jerusalem's walls. It is these walls that will bring lasting prosperity. I have written these things in order to clear a path to reach my text.

Three things are clear from the text: first, there is a unity of the Spirit to be kept; second, it needs keeping; and third, a bond is to be used. When I have expounded on these points, I will give practical applications of the text, first to Christians in their connection with other churches, and then to members of the same church in their connection with each other.

A Unity Worth Keeping

First, there is a unity of the Spirit that is worthy to be kept. You will notice that it is not an ecclesiastical unity; it is not endeavoring to keep the unity of the denomination, the community, the diocese, or the parish. No, it is *"endeavoring to keep the unity of the Spirit."* Men speak of the Episcopal church, the Wesleyan church, or the Presbyterian church. Now, I do not hesitate to say that there is nothing whatsoever in Scripture that is even similar to such language, for there I read of the seven churches in Asia (Rev. 1:4): the church in Corinth, Philippi, Antioch, and so on.

In England there are thousands of churches adhering to the episcopal form of government; in Scotland there are thousands of churches adhering to the presbyterian form of government; among the Wesleyans there are churches adhering to Mr. Wesley's form of government. However, to speak of a whole cluster of churches as one church is not in accordance with Scripture, but only in accordance with human invention. Although I myself am inclined to a presbyterian union among our churches, I cannot help perceiving in Holy Scripture that each church is separate and distinct from every other church. All of them are connected by those various bonds and ligaments that keep all the separate churches together, but they are not so connected that they run into each another and lose their separateness and individuality. There is nothing in Scripture that says, "Endeavoring to keep up your ecclesiastical arrangements for centralization." No, the exhortation goes like this: *"Endeavoring to keep the unity of the Spirit."*

Again, you will observe that it does not say, "Endeavoring to keep the uniformity of the Spirit." The Spirit does not recognize uniformity. Take nature, for instance. The flowers are not all tinted with the same hue, nor do they give off the same odors. There is variety everywhere in the work of God. If I glance at providence, I do not perceive that any two events happen the same way; the page of history is varied.

If, therefore, I look at the church of God, I do not expect to find that all Christians speak the same way or see with the same eyes. We rejoice to recognize that there is *"one Lord, one faith, one baptism; one God and Father of all"* (Eph. 4:5–6). But as for uniformity in dress, liturgical verbiage, or form of worship, I find nothing of it in Scripture. Men may pray acceptably standing, sitting, kneeling, or lying with their faces to the ground. They may meet with Jesus by the river's side, in a church, in a prison, or in a house. They may be one in the same Spirit although *"one person esteems one day above another; [and] another esteems every day alike"* (Rom. 14:5).

What, then, is this unity of the Spirit? I trust, dear friends, that we know it by possessing it, for it is certain that we cannot *"keep the unity of the Spirit"* if we do not have it already. Let us ask ourselves the question, "Do we have the unity of the Spirit?" The only ones who can have it are those who have the Spirit, and the Spirit dwells only in born-again, believing souls. By virtue of his having the Spirit, the believer is in union with every other spiritual man, and this is the unity that he is to endeavor to keep.

This unity of the Spirit is manifested in love. A husband and wife may be, through providence, cast hundreds of miles from one another, but there is a unity of spirit in them because their hearts are one. I am divided many thousands of miles from the saints in Australia, Africa, and the South Seas; but loving them as brothers,

I feel the unity of the Spirit with them. I have never attended a church meeting in Africa; I have never worshiped God with the Samoans or with my brothers in New Zealand; but notwithstanding, I feel the unity of the Spirit in my soul with them, and everything that concerns their spiritual welfare is important to me.

This unity of the Spirit is caused by a similarity of nature. You may find a drop of water glittering in the rainbow, leaping in the waterfall, rippling in the stream, lying silent in the stagnant pool, or spraying against the ship's side. Each one of these drops of water claims kinship with every drop of water the whole world over, because it is the same in its elements. Similarly, there is a unity of the Spirit that we cannot fake. It consists of these things: being *"begotten...again to a living hope through the resurrection of Jesus Christ from the dead"* (1 Pet. 1:3), bearing in us the Holy Spirit as our daily quickener, and walking in the path of faith in the living God. Here is the unity of spirit; it is a unity of life, nature working itself out in love. This unity is sustained daily by the Spirit of God. He who makes us one, keeps us one.

Every member of my body must have communion with every other member of my body. I say must. As far as I know, the members of my body never ask each other whether they will be in harmony or not. As long as there is life in my body, every separate portion of my body must have communion with every other portion of it. Take, for example, my finger. Imagine that I discolor it with some noxious drug. My head may not approve of the staining of my finger, and my head may suggest a thousand ways to clean that finger. However, my head never says, "I will cut off that finger." My tongue speaks loudly against the noxious fluid that has blistered my finger and caused pain to my entire body. Yet my tongue cannot say, "I will have that finger cut off," unless my body is willing to be forever mutilated and incomplete.

Now, it is impossible to mutilate the body of Christ. Christ does not lose His members or cast off parts of His body. Therefore, a Christian should never ask himself whether he should have communion in spirit with a certain Christian, for he cannot do without it. As long as he lives, he must have it. This does not stop him from boldly denouncing the error into which his brother may have fallen, or from avoiding his intimate acquaintance while he continues to sin. However, we can never really sever any true believer from Christ, or from ourselves if we are in Christ Jesus.

The unity of the Spirit is preserved, then, by the Holy Spirit's infusing life daily into the one body. As the life become stronger, that union becomes more manifest. Let a spirit of prayer be poured out on all our churches—then conventionalities will be dashed down; divisions will be forgotten; and, arm in arm, the people of God will show to the world that they are one in Christ Jesus. (See Galatians 3:28.)

There are some activities during which this unity of the Spirit is certain to show itself. One is prayer. How truly Montgomery put it:

> The saints in prayer appear as one
> In word, and deed, and mind,
> While with the Father and the Son,
> Sweet fellowship they find.

There is a unity of praise, too. Our hymnbooks differ very little after all. We still sing the same song, the praise of the same Savior. Then there is a unity of working together: we have a union in our conflict with the common foe, and in our contention for the common truth. This leads to communion. I do not mean sitting down to the same table to eat bread and drink wine; that is only the outward union. I mean the communion in which many hearts beat as one and there is a feeling that we are all one in Christ Jesus.

Bucer's motto was to love everyone in whom he could see anything of Christ Jesus. Let this be your motto, too, fellow believer. Do not make your love an excuse for not offering stern rebuke, but rebuke because you love. Some people think that unless you cover your words with sugar, unless you cringe and compliment and conceal, there is no love in your heart. But I trust it will be our privilege to show that we can sternly disapprove and yet love; that we can shun our brother's error and yet, in our very shunning, prove our affection to him and to our common Master.

It is said of some men that they were born on the mountains of Bether, for they do nothing but cause division, or that they were baptized in the waters of Meribah, for they delight in causing strife. (See Exodus 17:7.) This is not the case with the genuine Christian; he cares only for the truth, for his Master, for the love of souls. When these things are not in danger, his own private likes or dislikes never hinder his communion with other Christians. He loves to see another church prosper as much as his own. As long as he knows that Christ is glorified, it does not matter to him which minister God uses, where souls are converted, or what form of worship is used.

Yet the genuine Christian always holds to this: there is no unity of the Spirit where there is a lie involved. Where the souls of men are concerned, he would be a traitor to God if he did not witness against the damning error and testify for the saving truth. Where the crown jewels of his Master's kingdom are concerned, he dares not traitorously hold his tongue. No, though his fellow subjects throw his name out as evil, he counts it all joy, as long as he is faithful to his Master and obeys his conscience as before the *"Judge of the living and the dead"* (Acts 10:42).

Keeping the Unity

Now that we know that there is a unity of the Spirit worthy to be kept, I want to point out that it needs to be kept. It is a very difficult thing to maintain, for several reasons. First of all, our sins would, very naturally, break it. If we were all angels, we would keep the unity of the Spirit and not even need the exhortation to do so. But, alas, we are proud, and pride is the mother of division. Diotrephes, who loves to have preeminence (3 John 1:9), is very sure to head a faction. How envy, too, has separated good friends! When I cannot be satisfied with anything that is not hammered on my workbench, when another man's candle grieves me because it gives more light than mine, and when another man troubles me because he has more grace than I have—oh, there is no unity in this case. Anger—what a deadly foe that is to unity! When we cannot overlook the smallest disrespect, when the slightest thing turns our faces red, when we speak unadvisedly with our lips—surely then there is no unity. But I do not need to read the long list of sins that spoil the unity of the Spirit, for it is lengthy. Oh, may God cast them out of us, for only then can we *"keep the unity of the Spirit."*

But, beloved, our very virtues may make it difficult for us to keep this unity. Luther was brave and bold, hot and impetuous; he was just the man to clear the way for the Reformation. Calvin was logical, clear, cool, precise; he seldom spoke rashly. It was not natural for Luther and Calvin to always agree. Their very virtues caused them to argue. Consequently, Luther, in a bad temper, called Calvin a pig and a devil. And although Calvin once replied, "Luther may call me what he will, but I will always call him a dear servant of Christ," John Calvin knew how to pierce Luther under the fifth rib when he was angry.

In those days the courtesies of Christians to one another were generally of the iron glove kind, rather than the naked hand. They were all called to war for the sake of the truth, and they were so intent on their task that they were even suspicious of their fellow soldiers. It may be the same way with us: the very watchfulness of truth, which is so valuable, may make us suspicious where there is no need for suspicion. And our courage may take us where we should not go, like a fiery horse that carries a young warrior beyond where he intended to go, where he may be taken prisoner. We must watch—the best of us must watch—lest we fight the Lord's battles with Satan's weapons and thereby, even from love for God and His truth, violate the unity of the Spirit.

The unity of the Spirit ought to be kept, dear friends, because Satan is so busy trying to mar it. He knows that the greatest glory of Christ will spring from the unity of His church. *"That they all may be one, as You, Father, are in Me, and I in You; that they also may be one in Us, that the world may believe that You sent Me"* (John 17:21). There is no church happiness where there is no church unity. If a church is divided, the schism is death to all sacred fellowship. We cannot enjoy communion with each other unless our hearts are one. How feeble is our work for God when we are not in agreement!

The enemy cannot desire a better ally than strife in the midst of our camp. "Can you not agree," said a warrior of old, "when your enemy is in sight!" Christians, can you not agree *"to keep the unity of the Spirit"* when a destroying Satan is ever on the watch, seeking to drag immortal souls down to perdition? (See 1 Peter 5:8.) We must be more diligent in this matter. We must purge ourselves of everything that would divide us, and we must equip our hearts with every holy thought that would unite us. When I join a Christian church, I should not say, "I am sure I will never break this church's unity." I am to suspect myself of tending toward that evil, and I am to watch with all diligence that I keep the unity of the Spirit.

The Bond of Peace

I have now come to my third point. In order to *"keep the unity of the Spirit,"* there is a bond provided—the bond of peace. Beloved, there should be much peace, perfect peace, and unbounded peace among the people of God. We are not strangers; we are *"fellow citizens with the saints and members of the household of God"* (Eph.

2:19). Realize your fellow citizenship, and do not treat Christian people as foreigners; then this common bond of citizenship will be a bond of peace.

Men may be fellow citizens and still be enemies, but you are friends. You are all friends to Christ, and in Him you are all friends to one another. Let that be another bond. But your relationship goes even deeper. You are not just friends, you are brothers, born of the same Parent, filled with the same life. Will this not bind you together? *"See that you do not become troubled along the way"* (Gen. 45:24). Do not contend with one another, for you are brothers. (See Acts 7:26.)

But this is not all. You are even closer than brothers, for you are members of the same body! Will this mysterious union fail to be a bond of peace to you? Will you, being the foot, contend with the eye, or will you, being the eye, contend with the hand and say, *"I have no need of you"* (1 Cor. 12:21)? The joints and bones in a person's body do not disagree. If it is really true that we are members of Christ's body, let it never be said that the various parts of Christ's body would not work together but instead battled one another. What a monstrous thing to be said!

I believe I have brought out the meaning of the text. There is a unity of the Spirit that is worthy to be kept. We ought to keep it. We must try to keep it in the bond of peace.

Practical Conclusions

Now I will come to the practical conclusions of the subject—first, in the connection of one church with another; second, in the connection of one church member with another.

Church to Church

It is not a desirable thing for all churches to melt into one another and become one. The complete fusion of all churches into one ecclesiastical corporation would inevitably produce another form of popery, since history teaches us that large ecclesiastical bodies grow more or less corrupt as a matter of course. Huge spiritual corporations are, as a whole, the strongholds of tyranny and the refuges of abuse; and it is only a matter of time until they will break into pieces. Disruption and secession must occur, and will occur, where a unity is attempted that is not meant in God's Word.

However, it will be a blessed thing when all the churches walk together in the unity of the Spirit. What a wonderful thing when that church over there, although it baptizes its members and laments the neglect of that ordinance by other churches, yet feels that the unity of the Spirit must not be broken and holds out its right hand to all who love our Lord Jesus Christ in sincerity. What a refreshing thing when this church over here, governed by its elders, feels a unity with another church that is presided over by its bishop. What an inspiring thing when a church that believes in mutual edification is not quarrelsome toward those in another church that loves the ministry of the Word as it is preached by their minister.

What a great thing when churches have agreed about this one thing: we will search the Word independently and act out, according to our light, what we find to be true. Having done so, we will *"keep the unity of the Spirit in the bond of peace."* Yes, these things are most desirable; we should seek after them. We should not seek to fuse all churches into one denomination, but we should seek to keep each distinct church in love with every other church.

Now, in order to do this, I have a few suggestions to offer. It is quite certain we will never *"keep the unity of the Spirit"* if each church declares that it is superior to every other. If a church says, "We are the church, and all others are mere sects; we are established, and others are only tolerated," then it is a troublemaker and must hide its head when the unity of the Spirit is so much as hinted at. Any church that lifts its head and boasts that it is better than other churches has violated the unity of the Spirit. On the other hand, if a group of churches says, "Christ is our Master, and we are all brothers," they do not violate the unity of the Spirit, for they simply claim their rights and speak the truth. The church that forgets its true position as one in the family and begins to set itself up as master and claim preeminence over its fellow servants has violated the unity of the Spirit once and for all.

Again, a church that wants to keep the unity of the Spirit must not consider itself to be so infallible that not to belong to its membership is sin. What right has any one church to set itself up as the standard, so that those who do not join it are dissenters? It is true my Episcopal brother is a dissenter, for he dissents from me; it is true he is a nonconformist, for he does not conform to me. I would not, however, call him by such names, lest I should arrogantly imply that my own church is the church, and so break the unity of the Spirit.

You may believe that your church can claim a long line of ancestors descending from the apostles, without ever running through the Church of Rome, but should you therefore call a brother who does not quite see this succession, a schismatic, and call his assembly a cult? If he is a schismatic because he does not go to your church, why are you not a schismatic because you do not go to his? You say, "Well, but he divides the church! He ought to come and worship with me." Ought you not to go and worship with him? You say, "Ah, but there are more of us!" Are divine things to be ruled by the majority? Where would the church of God be if it came to polling? I am afraid the Devil would always be at the head of the poll. We wish *"to keep the unity of the Spirit,"* and if we have a smaller sister church, we will treat her all the more kindly, owing to the fewness of her members.

If I want *"to keep the unity of the Spirit in the bond of peace,"* I must never call in the magistrate to force my brother to pay my church so that it can buy choir robes, ring the church bell, and keep the building clean. I must not tell my brother that he is bound to pay for the support of my worship. If I do, he will say, "Oh, my dear friend, I pay for the maintenance of the worship that I believe to be correct, and I am quite willing that you should do the same for yours. I would voluntarily assist you if you were poor, but you tell me you will put me in prison if I do not pay, and yet you tell me *'to keep the unity of the Spirit.'* My dear friend, it is not keeping the unity of the Spirit to take away my stool, my table, and my candlestick, and say you will put me in jail or drag me before an ecclesiastical court. You send the police after me; then if I say a word about it, you say, '[Love] *hopes all things'* (1 Cor. 13:7). Yes, among the rest, it hopes that you will give up your sin in this matter."

If we should own a piece of ground where we bury our dead, and if there should happen to come a member of another Christian church who would wish to lay his poor dead baby in our ground, there being no other convenient spot anywhere, and he asks the favor, I think we can hardly be thought of as keeping the unity of the Spirit if we tell him, "No, nothing of the kind. You had your child sprinkled; therefore, it cannot be buried with us Christians. We will not have your sprinkled baby lying alongside our baptized dead." I do not think that is keeping the unity of the Spirit. When some churches have sent away from their graveyard gate the mourners who have brought an unbaptized infant, and the mourners have gone back weeping to their homes, I do not think such churches have been *"endeavoring to keep the unity of the Spirit in the bond of peace."*

Again, if churches are to agree with one another, they must not make rules that ministers who are not of their own denomination cannot occupy their pulpits. I should be ashamed if my congregation would pass a resolution that no one dissenting from us could stand in my pulpit. But we know a church that says, "We will not allow in our pulpit any minister who is not of our denomination, no matter how good a man he may be. He may be a man as venerated as John Angell James or have all the excellencies of a William Jay, and we would not, perhaps, mind hearing him in a town hall, but into the sacredness of our particular pulpit, these intruders must not come. For we have ministers; you have only lay teachers. We have the sacraments; the cup of blessing that we bless is the blood of Christ, and the bread that we break is the body of Christ. You have no sacramental power with you; you are not a church, but only a body of schismatics, meeting together to carry out what you think to be right. We tolerate you; that is all we can do." Where is the unity of the Spirit there?

It is wrong for any church to stand up and say, "We are the church; our ministers are the ministers; our people are the people. Now, dear brothers, shake hands, and endeavor *'to keep the unity of the Spirit'* of God." Why, it is preposterous! Let us meet on equal ground; let us lay aside all pretenses to superiority; let us really aid and not oppress each other; let us mingle in prayer; let us unite in confession of sin; let us join heartily in reforming our errors; and a true evangelical alliance will cover our land.

If any church will take the Bible as its standard, and in the power of the Spirit of God preach the name of Jesus, thousands of us will rejoice to give them the right hand of fellowship. Every day, we are striving to get other churches and ourselves more and more into that condition in which, while holding our own, we can still *"keep the unity of the Spirit in the bond of peace."*

Church Member to Church Member

Now I will write to you in regard to your relationship to one another as members of the same church. If we are to endeavor *"to keep the unity of the Spirit in the bond of peace"* in the same church, then we must avoid everything that would mar it. Gossip is a very ready means of separating friends from one another. Let us endeavor to talk of something better than each other's characters.

Dionysius went to Plato's academy, and Plato asked what he came for. "Why," said Dionysius, "I thought that you, Plato, would be talking against me to your students." Plato answered, "Do you think, Dionysius, we are so destitute of matter to discuss that we talk about you?" Truly, we must be very short of subjects when we begin to talk of one another. It is far better to magnify Christ than to detract from the honor of His members.

We must lay aside all envy. Multitudes of good people liked the Reformation, but they said they did not like that it was done by a poor miserable monk like Martin Luther. Many like to see good things done, but they do not care to see them done by a young, up-start brother or a poor man or woman who has no particular rank. As a church, let us shake off envyings; let us all rejoice in God's light.

As for pride, if any of you have grown vain lately, shake it off. I hope to have a ministry that will drive out those who will not acknowledge their brothers when they are poorer or less educated than themselves. So what if a person mars the English language when he talks? What does that matter, as long as his heart is right? As long as you can feel he loves the Master, surely you can put up with his faults of speech, if he can put up with your faults of action.

Let us cultivate everything that would tend to unity. Are any sick? Let us care for them. Are any suffering? Let us weep with them. Do we know someone who has less love than others? Then let us have more to make up the deficiency. Do we perceive faults in a brother? Let us admonish him in love and affection. I implore you to be peacemakers, everyone. Let the church go on in holy accord and blessed unity.

Let us remember that we cannot *"keep the unity of the Spirit"* unless we all believe the truth of God. Let us search our Bibles, therefore, and conform our views and sentiments to the teaching of God's Word. I have already told you that unity in error is unity in ruin. We want unity in the truth of God through the Spirit of God. Let us seek after this; let us live near to Christ, for this is the best way of promoting unity.

Divisions in churches never begin with those full of love for the Savior. Cold hearts, unholy lives, inconsistent actions, neglected prayer closets—these are the seeds that sow schisms in the body. However, he who lives near to Jesus wears His likeness and copies His example. He will be, wherever he goes, a sacred bond, a holy link, to bind the church together more closely than ever. May God give us this bond, and from now on let us endeavor *"to keep the unity of the Spirit in the bond of peace."*

I commend the text to all believers to be practiced throughout the coming year. Those of you who are not believers, I trust your unity and your peace may be broken forever, and that you may be led to Christ Jesus to find peace in His death. May faith be given to you, and then love and every grace will follow, so that you may be one with the church of Christ Jesus our Lord.

Chapter 6

Creation's Groans and Saints' Sighs

For we know that the whole creation groans and labors with birth
pangs together until now. Not only that, but we also who have the
firstfruits of the Spirit, even we ourselves groan within ourselves,
eagerly waiting for the adoption, the redemption of our body.
—Romans 8:22–23

Our sighs should never come from having a disunited
church. But even if the church is perfectly united, we will
still have other reasons to sigh. Our text attests to this.
Unfortunately, this text is far from easy to handle. The more I read
it, the more I am certain that this is one of the things to which Peter referred when he wrote about Paul's epistles and said, *"In*
which are some things hard to understand" (2 Pet. 3:16). However,
dear friends, we have often found that the nuts that are hardest to
crack have the sweetest kernels, and the bones that are hardest to
break have the richest marrow. So it may be with this text; so it
will be if the Spirit of God is our instructor, for He will fulfill His
gracious promise to *"guide* [us] *into all truth"* (John 16:13).

The whole creation is fair and beautiful even in its present
condition. I have no sympathy with those who cannot enjoy the
beauties of nature. Climbing the lofty Alps, wandering through the
charming valley, skimming the blue sea, or walking through the
green forest, I have felt that this world, however desecrated by sin,
was built to be a temple of God; and the grandeur and the glory of
it plainly declare that *"the earth is the Lord's, and all its fullness"*
(Ps. 24:1). Like the marvelous structures of Palmyra of Baalbek,
the earth in ruins reveals a magnificence that speaks of a royal
founder and an extraordinary purpose.

Creation glows with a thousand beauties, even in its present
fallen condition; clearly, it is not the same as when it came from the
Maker's hand. The slime of the Serpent is on it all, and this is not

182

the world that God pronounced to be *"very good"* (Gen. 1:31). We hear of tornadoes, earthquakes, tempests, volcanoes, avalanches, and the sea that kills thousands; there is sorrow on the sea, and there is misery on the land. Into the highest palaces as well as the poorest cottages, Death, the insatiable, is shooting his arrows, while his quiver is still full to bursting with future woes.

It is a sad, sad world. The curse has fallen on it since the Fall, and it brings forth thorns and thistles. Earth wears on her brow, like Cain of long ago, the brand of transgression. (See Genesis 4:15.) It would be sad to think that this were always to be so. If there were no future for this world, as well as for ourselves, we would be glad to escape from this world, considering it nothing better than a huge prison from which we long to be freed.

Presently, the groaning and travailing that are prevalent throughout creation are deeply felt among the sons of men. The dreariest thing you can read is the newspaper. I heard of a person who sat up at the end of last year to groan last year out; he was not good at groaning, from what I hear, but in truth it was a year of groaning, and the present one opens amid turbulence and distress. We heard of abundant harvests, but we soon discovered that they were all a dream and that there would be scarcity in the worker's home. And now, what with conflicts between men and masters, which are banishing trade from England, and political convulsions, which unhinge everything, the ship of the state is drifting fast to shipwreck. May God in His mercy put His hand to the helm of the ship and steer her safely. There is a general wail among nations and peoples. You can hear it in the streets of the city. If we did not know that *"the LORD reigns"* (1 Chron. 16:31), we might lament bitterly.

Our text tells us that not only is there a groan from creation, but this is shared by God's people. We notice in our text, first, what the saints have already attained; second, where they are deficient; and third, what the saints' state of mind is in regard to the whole matter.

What the Saints Have Already Attained

Before we were saved, we were an undistinguished part of the creation, subject to the same curse as the rest of the world, *"children of wrath, just as the others"* (Eph. 2:3). But distinguishing grace has made a difference where no difference naturally was; we are now no longer treated as condemned criminals, but as children and heirs of

God (Rom. 8:16–17). We have received a divine life, by which we are made *"partakers of the divine nature, having escaped the corruption that is in the world through lust"* (2 Pet. 1:4). The Spirit of God has come to us so that our bodies are the temples of the Holy Spirit (1 Cor. 6:19). God dwells in us, and we are one with Christ.

We have in us at this present moment certain priceless things that distinguish us as believers in Christ from all the rest of God's creatures. "[We] **have the firstfruits of the Spirit**" (italics added), not "we hope and trust we have" or "possibly we may have," but "we have, we know we have, and we are sure we have." Believing in Jesus, we speak confidently; we have unspeakable blessings given to us by the Father of spirits. Not we will have, but we have. True, many things are yet in the future, but even at this present moment *"we have obtained an inheritance"* (Eph. 1:11); we already have in our possession a divine heritage that is the beginning of our eternal portion.

This divine heritage is called *"the firstfruits of the Spirit,"* which I understand to mean the first works of the Spirit in our souls. Beloved, we have repentance, that first gem of the Spirit. We have faith, that priceless, precious jewel. We have hope, which sparkles, a hope most sure and steadfast. We have love, which sweetens all the rest. We have that work of the Spirit within our souls that always comes before admittance into glory. We are already made new creations in Christ Jesus (2 Cor. 5:17) by the effective working of the mighty power of God the Holy Spirit.

These are called the firstfruits because they come first. They are like the first sheaf of the harvest, which was waved before the Lord:

> *Speak to the children of Israel, and say to them:* "When you come into the land which I give to you, and reap its harvest, then you shall bring a sheaf of the firstfruits of your harvest to the priest. He shall wave the sheaf before the LORD, to be accepted on your behalf; on the day after the Sabbath the priest shall wave it." (Lev. 23:10–11)

Our spiritual lives are similar to this first sheaf, for all the graces that adorn the spiritual life are the first gifts, the first operations of the Spirit of God in our souls.

They are called firstfruits, again, because the firstfruits were always the pledge of the harvest. As soon as the Israelite had plucked the first handful of ripe ears, they were proof to him that the harvest was already come. He looked forward with glad anticipation to the time when the wagon would creak beneath the sheaves, and when "Harvest home" would be shouted at the door of the barn. So, beloved, when God gives us *"faith, hope, love, these three"* (1 Cor. 13:13), when He gives us *"whatever things are pure...lovely...of good report"* (Phil. 4:8), as the work of the Holy Spirit, these are to us the forerunners of the coming glory. If you have the Spirit of God in your soul, you may rejoice over it as the pledge and token of the fullness of bliss and perfection *"which God has prepared for those who love Him"* (1 Cor. 2:9).

They are called firstfruits, again, because these were always holy to the Lord. The first ears of corn were offered to the Most High, and surely our new nature, with all its powers, must be regarded by us as a consecrated thing. The new life that God has given to us is not ours, that we should ascribe its excellence to our own merit; the new nature comes only from Christ. Since it is Christ's image and Christ's creation, so it is for Christ's glory alone. That new nature we must keep separate from all earthly things; that treasure that He has committed to us we must watch both night and day against those profane intruders who would defile the consecrated ground. We must stand on our watchtower and cry aloud to our strong Lord for strength (1 Chron. 16:11), so that the adversary may be repelled, so that the sacred castle of our hearts may be for the habitation of Jesus, and Jesus alone. We have a sacred secret that belongs to Jesus, as the firstfruits belong to Jehovah.

Beloved, the work of the Spirit is called firstfruits because the firstfruits were not the harvest. No Jew was ever content with the firstfruits. He was glad to have the firstfruits, but they enlarged his desires for the harvest. If he had taken the firstfruits home and said, "I have all I want," and had rested satisfied month after month, he would have proved that he was mad, for the firstfruits only whet the appetite—only stir up the desire that they cannot satisfy by themselves.

Therefore, when we get the first works of the Spirit of God, we are not to say, "I have attained my goal; I am already perfect; there is nothing further for me to do or to desire." No, my beloved, everything that the most advanced of God's people know now should excite in them an insatiable thirst for more. My brother with great experience, my sister with a close friendship with Christ, you have not yet known the harvest; you have only reaped the first handful of corn. *"Open your mouth wide, and* [God] *will fill it"* (Ps. 81:10)! Enlarge your expectations, seek great things from the God of heaven, and He will give them to you. Do not, by any means, fold your arms in sloth and sit down on the bed of carnal security. Forget the steps you have already trodden, and reach forward toward what is ahead (Phil. 3:13), *"looking unto Jesus"* (Heb. 12:2).

Even this first point, about the saint receiving only the firstfruits of the Spirit, will help us understand why he groans. As I have already stated, we have not received all of our portion. In fact, what we have received is to the whole no more than one handful of wheat is to the whole harvest—a very gracious pledge, but nothing more. Therefore, we groan. Having received something, we desire more. Having reaped handfuls, we long for sheaves. It is because of this very fact, the fact that we are saved, that we groan for something beyond.

Did you hear that groan just now? It is a traveler lost in the deep snow on the mountain pass. No one has come to rescue him, and indeed he has fallen into a place from which escape is impossible. The snow is numbing his limbs, and his soul is breathed out with many a groan. Keep that groan in your ear, for I want you to hear another.

Suppose the traveler has been rescued and taken to the lodge. He has been hospitably received; he has warmed himself at the fire; he has received abundant provision; he is warmly clothed. There is no fear of storm; that grand old lodge has outlasted many thundering storms. The man is perfectly safe, and quite content, so far as that goes, and exceedingly grateful to think that he has been rescued.

Yet I hear him groan because he has a wife and children on the plain down below, and the snow is too deep to travel in. The wind is howling, and the blinding snowflakes are falling so thickly that he cannot pursue his journey. Ask him whether he is happy and content. He says, "Yes, I am happy and grateful. I have been saved from the snow. I do not wish for anything more than I have here; I am perfectly satisfied, so far as this goes. But I long to see my family and to be once more in my own sweet home. And until I reach it, I will not stop groaning."

Now, the first groan that you heard was deep and dreadful, as though it were fetched from the abyss of hell; that is the groan of the ungodly man as he perishes and leaves all his dear delights. But the second groan is so soft and sweet that it is rather the note of desire than of distress. Such is the groan of the believer, who, though rescued and brought into the lodge of divine mercy, is longing to see his Father's face without a veil between. He is longing to be united with the happy family on the other side of the Jordan, where they will rejoice forevermore.

When the soldiers of Godfrey of Bouillon came in sight of Jerusalem, it is said they shouted for joy at the sight of the holy city. For that very reason they also began to groan. Do you ask why? It was because they longed to enter it. Having once looked upon the city of David, they longed to take the holy city by storm, to overthrow the crescent and place the cross in its place. He who has never seen the New Jerusalem has never clapped his hands with holy ecstasy; he has never sighed with the unutterable longing that is expressed in words like these:

> O my sweet home, Jerusalem,
> Would God I were in thee!
> Would God my woes were at an end,
> Thy joys that I might see!

I will give another illustration to show that the obtaining of something makes us groan after more. An exile, far away from his native country, has been long forgotten, but suddenly a ship brings him the pardon of his king and gifts from his friends who have remembered him. As he turns over each of these tokens of love, and as he reads the words of his reconciled prince, he asks, "When will the ship sail to take me back to my native shore?" If the ship waits, he groans over the delay; if the voyage is tedious and adverse winds toss the ship, his longing for his own sweet land compels him to groan.

It is the same way with your children when they look forward to their holidays; they are not unhappy or dissatisfied with school, yet they long to be at home. Do you remember how, in your school days, you used to make a little calendar with a square for every day, and how you always crossed off the day as soon as it began, as though you were trying to make the time pass as quickly as possible? You groaned for it, not with the unhappy groan that marks one who is going to perish, but with the groan of one who, having tasted of the sweets of home, is not content until he can feast on them again.

So you see, beloved, it is because we have the firstfruits of the Spirit that we groan. We cannot help but groan for that blissful period that is called *"the adoption, the redemption of our body."*

187

What the Saints Are Lacking

I now come to my second point, which is what the saints are lacking. We are deficient in those things for which we groan and wait. And there appear to be at least four of them.

Our New Bodies

The first is that these bodies of ours are not delivered. Beloved, as soon as a man believes in Christ, he is no longer under the curse of the law. (See Galatians 3:13.) As to his spirit, sin has no more dominion over him, and the law has no further claims against him. His soul is translated from death to life. But the body, this poor flesh and blood, does it not remain as before? Not in one sense, for the members of our bodies, which were instruments of unrighteousness, become by sanctification the instruments of righteousness to the glory of God. (See Romans 6:13.) The body that was once a workshop for Satan becomes a temple for the Holy Spirit, in which He dwells (1 Cor. 6:19).

However, we are all perfectly aware that the grace of God makes no change in the body in other respects. It is just as subject to sickness as before; pain throbs quite as sharply in the heart of the saint as in the heart of the sinner; and he who lives near to God is no more likely to enjoy bodily health than he who lives at a distance from Him. The greatest piety cannot preserve a man from growing old; although in grace he may be like a young cedar, fresh and green, yet the body will have its gray hairs, and the strong man will be brought to totter on a cane. The body is still subject to the evils that Paul mentioned when he said that it is subject to corruption, dishonor, and weakness, and is still a natural body. (See 1 Corinthians 15:42–44.)

These are not little things, for the body has a depressing effect on the soul. A man may be full of faith and joy spiritually, but I would challenge him to feel the same way under the ill effects of some diseases. The soul is like an eagle, and the body is like a chain that prevents its mounting. Moreover, the appetites of the body have a natural affinity to what is sinful. The natural desires of the human frame are not in themselves sinful, but through the degeneracy of our nature, they very readily lead us into sin. Through the corruption that is in us, even the natural desires of the body become a very great source of temptation. The body is redeemed with the precious blood of Christ; it is redeemed by price, but it has not as yet been redeemed by power. It still lingers in the realm of bondage and is not brought into *"the glorious liberty of the children of God"* (Rom. 8:21).

This is the cause of our groaning and mourning, for the soul is so married to the body that when it is itself delivered from condemnation, it sighs to think that its poor friend, the body, is still under the yoke. Suppose that you were a free man who had married a slave. You could not feel perfectly content; but the more you enjoyed the delights of freedom yourself, the more you would mourn that she was still in slavery. So it is with the spirit: it is free from corruption and death, but the poor body is still under the bondage of corruption; therefore, the soul groans until the body itself is set free.

Will it ever be set free? Oh, my beloved, do not ask that question. This is the Christian's brightest hope. Many believers make a mistake when they long to die and go to heaven. That may be desirable, but it is not the ultimate satisfaction for the saints. The saints in heaven are perfectly free from sin, and, so far as they are capable of it, they are perfectly happy; but a disembodied spirit can never be perfect until it is reunited with its body. God made man not pure spirit, but body and spirit, and the spirit alone will never be content until it sees its physical body raised to its own condition of holiness and glory. Do not think that our longings here below are not shared by the saints in heaven. They do not groan because of any pain, but they long with greater intensity than you and I for *"the adoption, the redemption of our body."*

People have said there is no faith in heaven and no hope; they do not know what they say. In heaven faith and hope have their fullest strength and their brightest sphere, for glorified saints believe in God's promise and hope for the resurrection of the body. The apostle tells us that *"they should not be made perfect apart from us"* (Heb. 11:40); that is, until our bodies are raised, theirs cannot be raised; until our adoption day comes, neither can theirs. *"The Spirit and the bride say, 'Come!'"* (Rev. 22:17). Not only the bride on earth, but also the bride in heaven says, "Come," telling the happy day to hurry, the day when *"the trumpet will sound, and the dead will be raised incorruptible, and we shall be changed"* (1 Cor. 15:52). For it is true, beloved, the bodies that have decayed will rise again; the fabric that has been destroyed by the worm will suddenly form a nobler being; and you and I, though the worm may devour our bodies, will in our flesh behold our God (Job 19:26).

> These eyes shall see Him in that day,
> The God who died for me;
> And all my rising bones shall say,
> "Lord, who is like to thee?"

Thus, we desire that our entire manhood, in its trinity of spirit, soul, and body, may be set free from the last vestige of the Fall. We long to put off corruption, weakness, and dishonor, and to wrap ourselves in incorruption, in immortality, in glory, in the spiritual body that the Lord Jesus Christ will bestow on all His people. (See 1 Corinthians 15:42–44.) You can understand in this sense why we groan, for if this body, though redeemed, is really still a captive, and if it is to be completely free and rise to amazing glory one day, those who believe in this precious doctrine may very well groan after it as they wait for it.

Our Public Adoption

Another point in which the saint is deficient right now is, namely, in the manifestation of our adoption. Observe, the text speaks of waiting for the adoption; and another text, further back, explains what that means: *"wait*[ing] *for the revealing of the sons of God"* (Rom. 8:19). In this world, saints are God's children, but you cannot see that they are, except by certain moral characteristics. The man who has been saved is God's child, a prince of the royal blood, even though he wears workman's clothes. The woman who has accepted God's gift of salvation is one of the daughters of the King, but see how pale she is; what wrinkles are on her brow! Many of the daughters of pleasure are far more attractive than she! Why is this? The adoption is not yet manifested; the children are not yet openly declared.

Among the Romans a man could have adopted a child, and that child might have been treated as his for a long time; however, there was a second adoption in public. The child was brought before the authorities and the public, his ordinary garments were taken off, and the adoptive father put on him garments suitable to his new station in life.

"Beloved, now we are the children of God; and it has not yet been revealed what we shall be" (1 John 3:2). We do not yet have the royal robes that distinguish the princes of the blood; we are wearing in this flesh and blood just what we wore as the sons of

Adam. However, we know that when He who is the *"firstborn among many brethren"* (Rom. 8:29) appears, we will be like Him; that is, God will dress us all as He dresses His eldest Son. *"We shall be like Him, for we shall see Him as He is"* (1 John 3:2).

Can you not imagine that a child taken from the lowest ranks of society and adopted by a Roman senator would be saying to himself, "I wish the day were here when I will be publicly revealed as the child of my new father. Then I will take off these plebeian garments, and I will be robed with garments that become my senatorial rank." He is already happy in what he has received, but for that very reason he groans to experience the fullness of what is promised him.

It is the same with us today. We are waiting for the day when we will put on our proper garments and be manifested as the children of God. You are young princes, and you have not yet been crowned. You are young brides, and the marriage day has not yet come. And because of the love your fiancé shows you, you long and sigh for the marriage day. Your very happiness makes you groan; your joy, like a swollen spring, longs to leap up like some Iceland geyser, climbing to the skies. Your joy heaves and groans deep within your spirit because it does not have enough room to express itself to others.

Our Liberty

A third thing in which we are deficient is liberty, *"the glorious liberty of the children of God"* (Rom. 8:21). The whole creation is said to be groaning for its share in that freedom. You and I are also groaning for it.

Beloved, we are free. *"If the Son makes you free, you shall be free indeed"* (John 8:36). But our liberty is incomplete. When Napoleon was on the island of St. Helena, he was watched by many guards; but after many complaints, he enjoyed comparative liberty and walked alone. Yet what liberty did he have? Liberty to walk around the rock of St. Helena, nothing more.

You and I are free, but what is our liberty? As for our spirits, they have liberty to soar into the third heaven and *"sit together in the heavenly places in Christ Jesus"* (Eph. 2:6). But as for our bodies, we can only roam about this small prison cell of earth, feeling that it is not the place for us. Napoleon had been accustomed to gilded halls and all the pomp and glory of imperial state, and it was hard to be reduced to a handful of servants. Even so, we are kings (Rev. 1:5–6)—we are of the imperial blood—but we do not have our proper state as dignities yet; we do not have our privileges of royalty here.

We meet with our brothers and sisters here in their earthen temples. We go to our lowly homes, and we are content, so far as these things go. Still, how can kings be content until they ascend their thrones? How can a heavenly one be content until he rises to heaven? How can a celestial spirit be satisfied until it sees celestial things? How can the heir of God be content until he rests on his Father's bosom and is *"filled with all the fullness of God"* (Eph. 3:19)?

I want you to now observe that we are linked with the creation. Adam was in liberty, perfect liberty; nothing confined him; Paradise was exactly fitted to be his seat. There were no wild beasts to tear him apart, no rough winds to cause him injury, no blighting heat to bring him harm. But in this present world, everything is contrary to us. Evidently, we are foreigners here. Ungodly men prosper well enough in this world. They root themselves and spread themselves like *"green bay tree[s]"* (Ps. 37:35 KJV): it is their native soil. But the Christian needs the greenhouse of grace to keep himself alive at all. Out in the world he is like some strange, foreign bird, native of a warm and sunny climate; being let loose here under our wintry skies, he is ready to perish.

Now, God will one day change our bodies and make them fit for our souls, and then He will change this world itself. I must not speculate, for I know little about this new world. However, it is no speculation to say that we *"look for new heavens and a new earth in which righteousness dwells"* (2 Pet. 3:13), and that there will come a time when *"the leopard shall lie down with the young goat...and the lion shall eat straw like the ox"* (Isa. 11:6–7).

We expect to see this world, which is now so full of sin that it is a field of blood, turned into a paradise, a garden of God. We believe that *"the tabernacle of God* [will be] *with men, and He will dwell with them"* (Rev. 21:3), and *"they shall see His face, and His name shall be on their foreheads"* (Rev. 22:4). We expect to see the New Jerusalem descend out of heaven from God (Rev. 3:12). In this very place, where sin has triumphed, we expect that *"grace* [will] *much more abound"* (Rom. 5:20 KJV). Perhaps after those great fires of which Peter spoke when he said, *"The heavens will be dissolved, being on fire, and the elements will melt with fervent heat"* (2 Pet.

3:12), the earth will be renewed and will be more lovely than it was originally. Perhaps, since matter cannot be annihilated but will be as immortal as spirit, this very world will become the place of an eternal jubilee, from which perpetual hallelujahs will go up to the throne of God. If such is the bright hope that cheers us, we may well groan for its realization, crying out,

> O long-expected day, begin;
> Dawn on these realms of woe and sin.

The Unveiling of Our Glory

I will not elaborate further, except to say that our glory is not yet revealed, and that is another subject of sighing. *"The glorious liberty"* (Rom. 8:21) may be translated, "The liberty of glory." Beloved, we are like warriors fighting for the victory; we do not yet share in the shout of triumph. Even up in heaven they do not yet have their full reward. When a Roman general came home from war, he entered Rome secretly; he stayed, perhaps for a week or two, among his friends. He went through the streets, and people whispered, "That is the general, the valiant one," but he was not publicly acknowledged. But on the appointed day, the gates were thrown wide open; and the general, victorious from the wars in Africa or Asia, with his snow-white horses bearing the trophies of his many battles, rode through the streets, which were strewn with roses, while the music sounded. The multitudes, with glad acclaim, accompanied him to the capitol. That was his triumphant entry.

Those in heaven have, as it were, secretly entered there. They are blessed, but they have not had their public entrance. They are waiting for their Lord to *"descend from heaven with a shout, with the voice of an archangel, and with the trumpet of God"* (1 Thess. 4:16). Then their bodies will rise; then the world will be judged; then the righteous will be divided from the wicked (Matt. 13:49). The whole blood-washed host will stream upwards in marvelous procession; the Prince will be at their head, leading *"captivity captive"* (Ps. 68:18) for the last time. Wearing their white robes and bearing their palms of victory (Rev. 7:9), the saints will march up to their crowns and to their thrones to reign forever and ever! The believing heart is panting, groaning, and sighing for this consummation.

Now, I think I hear somebody say, "You see these godly people who profess to be so happy and so safe; they still groan, and they must confess it." To which I reply, "Yes, that is quite true, and it would be a great mercy for you if you knew how to groan in the same way. If you were half as happy as a groaning saint, you might be content to groan on forever."

I showed you the difference between a hopeless groan and a hopeful groan. I will show you yet again. Go into that house over there, and listen at that door on the left; there is a deep, hollow, awful groan. Go to the next house, and hear another groan. It seems to be, so far as we can judge, much more painful than the first, and it has the severest anguish in it. How are we to judge between them? We will come again in a few days. As we enter the first house, we see weeping faces, flowing tears, and a coffin. Ah, it was the groan of death! We will go into the next. Ah, what is this? Here is a smiling baby, and a father with a glad face; if you venture to look at the mother, see how her face smiles for joy that a child is born into the world. The family is happy and rejoicing. There is all the difference between the groan of death and the groan of life.

Now, the apostle set the whole matter before us when he said, *"The whole creation groans"*—you know what words come next— *"and labors."* Your groaning and travailing will result in a blessing of the best kind. We are panting, longing after something greater, better, nobler; and it is coming. It is not the pain of death we feel, but the pain of life. We are thankful to have such a groaning. One night, just before Christmas, two men who were working very late were groaning in two very different ways. One of them said, "Ah, a poor Christmas day is in store for me; my house is full of misery." He had been a drunkard and a spender and did not have a penny to bless himself with, and his house had become a little hell. He was groaning at the thought of going home to such a scene of quarreling and distress. Now, the man who worked beside him, since it was getting very late, wished to be at home; therefore, he groaned. A coworker asked, "What's the matter?" "Oh, I want to get home to my dear wife and children. I have such a happy house; I do not like to be away from it." The other might have said, "Ah, you pretend to be a happy man, and here you are groaning." "Yes," he could say, "and you would be blessed if you had the same thing to groan about that I have."

Similarly, the Christian has a good Father and a blessed, eternal home, and he groans to get to it. Ah, there is more joy even in the groan of a Christian, than in all the mirth, merriment, dancing, and lewdness of the ungodly when their mirth is at its greatest height. We are like the dove that flutters and is weary, but thank God, we have an ark to go to. (See Genesis 8:6, 8–9.) We are like Israel in the wilderness: our feet are sore, but blessed be God, we are on the way to Canaan. We are like Jacob looking at the wagons: the more he looked at the wagons, the more he longed to see Joseph's face. (See Genesis 45:25–28.) Our groaning after Jesus is a blessed groan, for

'Tis heaven on earth, 'tis heaven above,
To see His face, and taste His love.

The Saints' State of Mind

Now I will conclude with what our state of mind is. A Christian's experience is like a rainbow: it is made up of drops of earth's sorrows and beams of heaven's bliss. It is a checkered scene, a garment of many colors. A Christian is sometimes in the light and sometimes in the dark. The text says, *"We ourselves groan."* I have told you what that groan is; I need not explain it further. But, it is added, *"We ourselves groan within ourselves."* It is not the hypocrite's groan, who goes mourning everywhere, wanting to make people believe that he is a saint because he is wretched. We groan within ourselves. Our sighs are sacred things; these sorrows and sighs are too hallowed for us to announce in the streets. We tell our longings to our Lord, and to our Lord alone. We groan within ourselves.

It appears from the text that this groaning is universal among the saints; there are no exceptions. We all feel it to some extent. He who is rich with worldly goods and he who is poor, he who is blessed in health and he who suffers with sickness—we all have some measure of an earnest, inward groaning for the redemption of our bodies.

In our text the apostle said we are *"waiting,"* by which I understand that we are not to sulk, like Jonah or Elijah, when they said, "Let me die." (See Jonah 4:8; 1 Kings 19:4.) Nor are we to sit still and look for the end of the day because we are tired of work; nor are we to become impatient and wish to escape from our present pains and sufferings. We are to groan after perfection, but we are to wait patiently for it, knowing that what the Lord appoints is best. Waiting implies being ready. We are to stand at the door, expecting the Beloved to open it and take us away to Himself.

In the verse that follows our text, Romans 8:24, we are described as hoping. The verse says, *"We are saved by hope"* (KJV). The believer continues to hope for the time when death and sin will no longer torment his body. As his soul has been purified, so will his body be; this will be an answer to his prayer that the Lord would sanctify him wholly—body, soul, and spirit. (See 1 Thessalonians 5:23.)

A Practical Application

Now, beloved, I will give you a practical application for this somewhat rambling writing. Here is a test for us all. You may judge a man by what he groans after. Some men groan after wealth; they worship money. Some groan continually under the troubles of life; they are merely impatient—there is no virtue in that. Some men groan because of their great losses or sufferings; well, this may be nothing but a rebellious complaining under God's rod, and if so, no blessing will come of it.

But the man who yearns after more holiness, the man who sighs after God, the man who groans after perfection, the man who is discontented with his sinful self, the man who feels he cannot be at rest until he is made like Christ—he is the man who is blessed indeed. May God help us to groan all our days with that kind of groaning. As I have said before, there is heaven in this groaning, and though the word denotes sorrow, there is a depth of joy concealed within.

> Lord, let me weep for nought but sin,
> And after none but Thee;
> And then I would, O that I might,
> A constant weeper be.

I do not know a more beautiful sight on earth than a man who has served his Lord many years and who, having grown gray in service, feels that he will soon be called home. He is rejoicing in the *"firstfruits of the Spirit"* that he has obtained, but he is panting after the full harvest of the Spirit that is guaranteed to him. I see him sitting on a jutting crag by the edge of Jordan, listening to the harpers on the other side and waiting until *"the pitcher [will] be broken at the fountain, or the wheel broken at the cistern...and the spirit shall return unto God who gave it"* (Eccl. 12:6–7 KJV).

A wife waiting for her husband's footsteps, a child waiting in the dark until his mother comes to give him a goodnight kiss—these are portraits of our waiting. It is a pleasant and precious thing to experience this waiting and hoping.

I fear for some of you who have never come and put your trust in Christ. When your time comes to die, you will have to say what Wolsey said, with only one word of alteration:

> O Cromwell, Cromwell!
> Had I but served my God with half the zeal
> I served the world, he would not, in mine age,
> Have left me naked to mine enemies.

Oh, before your day to die comes, quit serving the master who can never reward you except with death! Throw your arms around the cross of Christ, and give up your heart to God. Then, come what may,

> *neither death nor life, nor angels nor principalities nor powers, nor things present nor things to come, nor height nor depth, nor any other created thing, shall be able to separate us from the love of God which is in Christ Jesus our Lord.* (Rom. 8:38–39)

Although you will sigh for a while for more of heaven, you will soon come to the home of blessedness, where *"sorrow and sighing shall flee away"* (Isa. 35:10).

May the Lord bless you for Christ's sake.

Book Three

Being God's Friend

Contents

Chapter 1

The Obedience of Faith

*By faith Abraham obeyed when he was called to go out to the place
which he would receive as an inheritance. And he went out, not
knowing where he was going.*
—Hebrews 11:8

Obedience—what a blessing it would be if we were all
trained to it by the Holy Spirit! If we were perfectly obedient, we would be fully restored. If the whole world would
obey the Lord, it would be heaven on earth. Perfect obedience to
God would mean love among men, justice to all classes, and peace
in every land. Our wills bring envy, malice, war. But if we would
only obey the Lord's will, we would receive love, joy, rest, bliss.
Obedience—let us pray for it for ourselves and others!

> Is there a heart that will not bend
> To Thy divine control?
> Descend, O sovereign love, descend,
> And melt that stubborn soul!

I want to emphasize part of the verse from Hebrews 11 that
starts this chapter: *"By faith Abraham obeyed."* It is certainly true
that although we have had to mourn our disobedience with many
tears and sighs, we now find joy in yielding ourselves as servants of
the Lord: our deepest desire is to do the Lord's will in all things.
Oh, for obedience! It has been supposed by many badly instructed
people that the doctrine of justification by faith is opposed to the
teaching of good works, or obedience. There is no truth in the supposition. We who believe in justification by faith teach the obedience of faith.

Faith is the fountain, the foundation, and the fosterer of obedience. Men do not obey God until they believe Him. We preach faith
so that men may be brought to obedience. To disbelieve is to disobey.

One of the first signs of practical obedience is found in the obedience of the mind, the understanding, and the heart. This is expressed in believing the teachings of Christ, trusting in His work, and resting in His salvation. Faith is the morning star of obedience. If we want to work the work of God, we must believe on Jesus Christ whom He has sent.

Beloved, we do not give a secondary place to obedience, as some suppose. We look on the obedience of the heart to the will of God as salvation. The attainment of perfect obedience would mean perfect salvation. We regard sanctification, or obedience, as the great purpose for which the Savior died. He shed His blood so that He might cleanse us from dead works and purify to Himself a people *"zealous for good works"* (Titus 2:14).

It is for this that we were chosen: we are *"elect...for obedience"* (1 Pet. 1:2) and holiness. We know nothing of an election in which we would continue in sin. It is for this that we have been called: we are *"called to be saints"* (Rom. 1:7). Obedience is the principal objective of the work of grace in the hearts of those who are chosen and called. We are to become obedient children, conformed to the image of Jesus, our Elder Brother, with whom the Father is *"well pleased"* (Matt. 3:17).

The Obedience That Comes from Faith

The obedience that comes from faith is a noble obedience. The obedience of a slave ranks only a little higher than the obedience of a well-trained horse or dog, for it is tuned to the crack of the whip. Obedience that is not cheerfully rendered is not the obedience of the heart; consequently, it is of little worth before God. If a person obeys because he has no choice in the matter, and would rebel if he had the opportunity, there is nothing in his obedience. The obedience of faith springs from an internal principle and not from external compulsion. It is sustained by the mind's most sober reasoning and the heart's warmest passion.

It happens in this way: A person reasons with himself that he ought to obey his Redeemer, his Father, his God; at the same time, the love of Christ constrains him to do so. Therefore, what argument suggests, affection performs. A sense of great obligation, an understanding of the justness of obedience, and a spiritual renewal of the heart produce an obedience that becomes essential to the sanctified soul. Therefore, he is not relaxed in the time of temptation or destroyed in the hour of losses and sufferings. There is no trial of life that can turn the gracious soul from his passion for obedience, and death itself will only enable him to render an obedience that will be as blissful as it will be complete. A chief ingredient of heaven is that we will see the face of our Lord and *"serve Him day and night in His temple"* (Rev. 7:15). Meanwhile, the more fully we obey while we are still on earth, the nearer we will be to His temple gate. May the Holy Spirit work in us, so that, by faith—like Abraham—we may obey!

The Obedience of a Child

I am writing to you about absolute obedience to the Lord God. Yet I am referring to the obedience of a child, not the obedience of a slave; the obedience of love, not of terror; the obedience of faith, not of dread. As God helps me, I will urge you to seek a stronger faith so that you may reach this obedience. *"By faith Abraham obeyed."* In every case where the father of the faithful obeyed, it was the result of his faith. And in every case in which you and I will render true obedience, it will be the product of our faith.

Obedience that God can accept never comes out of a heart that thinks that God is a liar. It is worked in us by the Spirit of the Lord, through our belief in the truth, love, and grace of our God in Christ Jesus. If you are currently being disobedient, or have been so, the road to a better state of things is trust in God. You cannot hope to render obedience by merely forcing your conduct into a certain groove or by unaided, determined effort. There is a free-grace road to obedience, and that is receiving, by faith, the Lord Jesus, who is the gift of God, and *"who became for us...sanctification"* (1 Cor. 1:30).

We accept the Lord Jesus by faith, and He teaches us obedience, and creates it in us. The more faith in Him that you have, the more obedience to Him you will manifest. Obedience naturally flows out of faith, *"for as* [a man] *thinks in his heart, so is he"* (Prov. 23:7); the holy obedience of a person's life will be in proportion to the strength and purity of his faith in God, as He is revealed in Christ Jesus.

So that we can best understand how to apply these truths to our lives, let us consider several important aspects of obedience to God: the kind of faith that produces obedience, the kind of obedience that faith produces, and the kind of life that comes out of this faith and obedience. Let us trust the Holy Spirit for His gracious illumination.

Faith That Produces Obedience

Beloved in the Lord, we know that God is sovereign, and that His will is law. We feel that God, our Maker, our Preserver, our Redeemer, and our Father, should have our unswerving service. We unite, also, in confessing that we are not our own, for we are bought with a price (1 Cor. 6:19–20). The Lord our God has a right to us that we would not wish to question. He has a greater claim on our fervent service than He has on the services of angels, for, while they were created as we have been, still they have never been redeemed by precious blood.

Faith in God's Right to Command

Faith that produces obedience is therefore faith in God and His right to command our obedience. Our glorious, incarnate God has an unquestioned right to every breath we breathe, to every thought we think, to every moment of our lives, and to every capacity of our beings. We believe that it is right and just that Jehovah is our Lawgiver and our Ruler. This loyalty of our minds is based on faith and is a chief factor that persuades us to obey. Always cultivate this feeling. The Lord is our Father, but He is *our Father in heaven* (Matt. 6:9). He draws near to us in condescension; but it is condescension, and we must not presume to think of Him as though He were like us.

There is a holy familiarity with God that cannot be enjoyed too much, but there is a flippant familiarity with God that cannot be abhorred too much. The Lord is King; His will is not to be questioned; His every word is law. Let us never question His sovereign right to decree what He pleases and to fulfill the decree, to command what He pleases and to punish every shortcoming. Because we have faith in God as Lord of all, we gladly pay Him our homage, and we desire in all things to say, *Your will be done on earth as it is in heaven* (v. 10).

Faith in the Justness of God's Commands

Next, we must have faith in the rightness of all that God says or does. I hope that you do not think of God's sovereignty as tyranny or imagine that He ever could or would will anything except what is right. Neither should we admit into our minds a suspicion that the Word of God is incorrect in any matter whatsoever, as though the

Lord Himself could err. We will not have it that God, in His Holy Book, makes mistakes about matters of history or science any more than He does about the great truths of salvation. If the Lord is God, He must be infallible; and if He can be described as being in error in the little respects of human history and science, He cannot be trusted in the greater matters.

Beloved, Jehovah never errs in deed or in word. And when we find His law written either in the Ten Commandments or anywhere else, we believe that there is not a precept too many or too few. Whatever the precepts of the law or the Gospel may be, they are pure and altogether holy. The words of the Lord are like *"fine gold"* (Ps. 19:10), pure, precious, and weighty—not one of them may be neglected.

We hear people talking about "minor points of the law" and so on. However, we must not consider any word of our God as a minor thing, if by that expression it is implied that it is of small importance. We must accept every single word of precept or prohibition or instruction as being what it ought to be, neither to be diminished nor increased. We should not reason about the command of God as though it might be set aside or amended. He commands: we obey. May we enter into that true spirit of obedience, which is the unshakable belief that the Lord is right! Nothing short of this is the obedience of the inner man—the obedience that the Lord desires.

Faith in Our Personal Obligation to Obey

Furthermore, we must have faith in the Lord's call upon us to obey. Abraham went out from his father's house because he felt that, whatever God may have said to others, He had spoken to him and said, *"Get out of your country, from your family and from your father's house, to a land that I will show you"* (Gen. 12:1). Whatever the Lord may have said to the Chaldeans or to other families in Ur, Abraham was not so much concerned with that as with the special word of command that the Lord had sent to his own soul.

Oh, if only we were earnest to render personal obedience most of all! It is very easy to offer to God a sort of "other people's obedience"—to imagine that we are serving God when we are finding fault with our neighbors and complaining that they are not as godly as they ought to be. It is true that we cannot help seeing their shortcomings, but we would do well to be less observant of these shortcomings than we are. Let us turn our magnifying glasses on ourselves. It is not so much our business to be weeding other people's gardens as it is to be keeping our own vineyards. Each person should pray, *"Lord, what do You want me to do?"* (Acts 9:6).

We who are His chosen, redeemed from among men, and called out from the rest of mankind, ought to feel that if no other ears hear the divine call, our ears must hear it; and if no other hearts obey, our souls rejoice to do so. The apostle Paul wrote that we are to present ourselves to God as *"a living sacrifice, holy, acceptable to God, which is* [our] *reasonable service"* (Rom. 12:1). The strongest ties of gratitude hold us to the service of Jesus. We must be obedient in life to Him who, for our sakes, was *"obedient to the point of death"* (Phil. 2:8).

Our service to our Lord is freedom. We want to yield to His will. To delight Him is our delight. It is a blessed thing when the inmost nature yearns to obey God, when obedience grows into a habit and becomes the very element in which the spirit breathes. Surely this should be the case with every one of the blood-washed children of the Most High, and their lives will prove that it is so. Others are also bound to obey, but we should attend most to our own personal obligations and set our own houses in order. Obedience should begin at home, and it will find its hands full enough there.

Faith That Is Our Chief Authority

Genuine obedience arises out of a faith that is the chief authority over all our actions. The kind of faith that produces obedience is lord of the understanding; it is a royal faith. The true believer believes in God more than he believes in anything else and everything else. He can say, *"Let God be true but every man a liar"* (Rom. 3:4). His faith in God has become the crown of all his belief, the most assured of all his confidences.

As gold is to inferior metals, so is our trust in God to all our other trusts. To the genuine believer, the eternal is as much above the temporal as the heavens are above the earth. The infinite rolls, like Noah's flood, over the tops of the hills of the present and the finite. If a truth is infused with the glory of God, the believer will value it. However, if God and eternity are not in it, he will leave trifles to those who choose them. You must have a paramount faith in God, or else the will of God will not be a sovereign rule to you. Only a reigning faith will make us subject to its power, so that we will be obedient to the Lord in all things.

The chief thought in life with the true believer is: How can I obey God? His greatest concern is to do the will of God, or to yield to that will in a way that is pleasing to God. And if he can obey, he will not negotiate with God or be distracted with any reservations on his part. He will pray, "Refine me from the dross of rebellion, and let the furnace be as fierce as you will." His choice is neither wealth nor ease nor honor, but that he may *"glorify God in* [his] *body and in* [his] *spirit, which are God's"* (1 Cor. 6:20). Obedience has become as much his rule as self-will is the rule of others. His cry to the Lord is, "By your command I stay or go. Your will is my will; Your pleasure is my pleasure; Your law is my love."

May God grant us a supreme, overmastering faith, for this is the kind of faith that we must have if we are to lead obedient lives. We must have faith in God's right to rule, faith in the justness of His commands, faith in our personal obligation to obey, and faith that His commands must be the chief authority of our lives. With the faith that belongs to God's elect, we will realize the purpose of our election, namely, *"that we should be holy and without blame before Him in love"* (Eph. 1:4).

Faith in Action

Dear friend, do you have this kind of faith? I will withdraw the question and ask it of myself: Do I have that faith that leads me to obey my God? For obedience, if it is the kind of which we are speaking, is faith in action—faith walking with God, or, shall I say, walking *"before the LORD in the land of the living"* (Ps. 116:9)? If we have a faith that is greedy in hearing, severe in judging, and rapid in self-congratulation, but not inclined to obedience, we have the faith of hypocrites. If our faith enables us to set ourselves up as patterns of sound doctrine and qualifies us to crack the heads of all who differ from us, yet lacks the fruit of obedience, it will leave us among the *"dogs"* mentioned in the book of Revelation, who are outside the city of God. (See Revelation 22:15.)

The only faith that distinguishes the children of God is the faith that makes us obey. It is better to have the faith that obeys than the faith that moves mountains. I would rather have the faith that obeys than the faith that heaps the altar of God with sacrifices and perfumes His courts with incense. I would rather obey God than rule an empire. For, after all, the loftiest sovereignty a soul can inherit is to have dominion over self by rendering believing obedience to the Most High. Therefore, this is the kind of faith we need: *"By faith Abraham obeyed."* The only way you and I can obey is by faith alone.

The Obedience That Faith Produces

Let us now consider the kind of obedience that faith produces. I will illustrate this by what we can learn from taking the verse as a whole.

Immediate Obedience

Genuine faith in God creates a prompt obedience. *"By faith Abraham obeyed when he was called to go out to the place which he would receive as an inheritance."* Abraham immediately responded to the command. Delayed obedience is disobedience. I wish some Christians who put off duty would remember this. Continued delay of duty is a continuous sin. If I do not obey the divine command, I sin; and every moment that I continue in that condition, I repeat the sin. This is a serious matter. If a certain act is my duty at this hour, and I leave it undone, I have sinned. But it will be equally incumbent upon me during the next hour, and if I still refuse, I disobey again, and so on, until I do obey.

Neglect of a standing command must grow very grievous if it is persisted in for years. To the extent that the conscience becomes callous on the subject, the guilt becomes even more provoking to the Lord in proportion. To refuse to do right is a great evil. However, it is far worse to continue in that refusal until the conscience grows numb on the matter.

I remember a person who came to be baptized. He said that he had been a believer in the Lord Jesus for forty years and had always believed that the ordinance was scriptural. I felt grieved that he had been disobedient to a known duty for so long, and I proposed to him that he should be baptized at once. It was in a village, and he said that there was no place convenient for it. I offered to go with him to the brook and baptize him, but he said, "No, *'whoever believes will not act hastily'*" (Isa. 28:16).

Here was someone who had willfully disobeyed his Lord for as many years as the Israelites were in the wilderness, in a matter that was very easy to fulfill. Yet after confessing his fault, he was not willing to amend it; instead, he perverted a passage of Scripture to excuse himself in further delay. David said, *"I made haste, and did not delay to keep Your commandments"* (Ps. 119:60). I give this case as a typical illustration; there are a hundred spiritual, moral, domestic, business, and religious duties that men put off in the same manner, as if they thought that any time would do for God and that He must take His turn with the rest.

What would you say to your son if you told him to go on an errand, and he answered you, "I will go tomorrow." Surely, you would give him "tomorrow" in a way that he would not soon forget. Your tone would be sharp, and you would tell him to go at once. If he then promised to go in an hour, would you call that obedience? It would be impudence. Obedience is for the present tense; it must be prompt, or it is nothing. Obedience respects the time of the command as much as any other part of it. To hesitate is to be disloyal. To stop and consider whether or not you will obey is rebellion in the seed. If you believe in the living God for eternal life, you will be quick to do your Lord's commands, even as a maid obeys her mistress. You will not be like a horse, which needs a whip and spur to ensure its obedience. Your love will do more for you than compulsion could do for slaves. You will have wings on your heels to speed you along the way of obedience. *"Today, if you will hear His voice: 'Do not harden your hearts'"* (Ps. 95:7–8).

Exact Obedience

Next, obedience should be exact. Even Abraham's obedience failed somewhat in this at first. He started at once from Ur of the Chaldees, but he went only as far as Haran, and he stayed there until his father died. Then the command came to him again, and he set off for the land that the Lord had promised to show him. If you have only half obeyed, I pray that you may pay close attention to this. Do all that the Lord commands, and be very careful not to withhold any part of the revenue of obedience.

Yet the great Patriarch's error was soon corrected, for we read that *"Abraham obeyed when he was called to go out...and he went out."* I have omitted only intermediate words, which do not alter the meaning. This is exactly how we should obey. We should do what the Lord commands—just that, and not another thing of our own devising.

It is very interesting how people try to give God something other than what He asks for! The Lord says, *"My son, give me your*

209

heart" (Prov. 23:26), and they give Him ceremonies. He asks for obedience, and they give Him man-made religion. He asks for faith, love, and justice, and they offer meaningless sacrifices. They will give everything except the one thing that He will be pleased with: *"To obey is better than sacrifice, and to heed than the fat of rams"* (1 Sam. 15:22).

If the Lord has given you true faith in Himself, you will not be concerned so much about doing a notable thing as about doing exactly what God would have you to do. Pay attention to even the smallest parts of the Lord's precepts. Attention to little things is a fine feature of obedience. The essence of obedience lies much more in the little things than in the great ones. Few dare to rush into great crimes, yet people will indulge in secret rebellion, for their hearts are not right with God. Therefore, too many mar what they call obedience by forgetting that they serve a God who searches the heart and tries the mind, who observes thoughts and motives. He wants us to obey Him with the heart. This will lead us not merely to regard a few pleasing commands, but also to have respect for His entire will. Oh, for a tender conscience that will not willfully neglect or presumptuously transgress!

Practical Obedience

Next, make a special note of the fact that Abraham rendered practical obedience. When the Lord commanded Abraham to leave his father's house, he did not say that he would think it over; he did not discuss the pros and cons in an essay; he did not ask his father, Terah, and his neighbors to consider it. Rather, as he was called to go out, he went out. Dear friends, we have so much talk and so little obedience! The religion of mere brain and jaw does not amount to much. We lack the religion of hands and feet.

I remember a place in Yorkshire, England, where, years ago, a good man said to me, "We have a real good minister." I said, "I am glad to hear it." "Yes," he said, "he is a fellow who preaches with his feet." Well, now, it is an excellent thing if a preacher preaches with his feet by walking with God and with his hands by working for God. A person does well if he glorifies God by where he goes and by what he does. He will surpass fifty others who preach religion only with their tongues. You, dear readers, are not good hearers as long as you are only hearers. But when the heart is affected by the ear and the hand follows the heart, then your faith is proved. That kind of obedience, which comes from faith in God, is real obedience, since it shows itself by its works.

Farseeing Obedience

Moreover, faith produces a farseeing obedience. Note this: *"By faith Abraham obeyed when he was called to go out to the place which he would receive as an inheritance."* How many people would obey God if they were paid for it on the spot! They *"[look] to the reward"* (Heb. 11:26), but they must have it in the palms of their hands. With them, "A bird in hand is better far than two which in the bushes are." When they are told that there is heaven to be gained, they answer that, if heaven were to be had here, as an immediate freehold, they might attend to it, but they cannot afford to wait. To inherit a country after this life is over is too much like a fairy tale for their practical minds.

There are many who inquire, Will religion pay? Is there anything to be made out of it? Will I have to close my shop on Sundays? Must I alter the way I do business and curtail my profits? When they have totaled up the cost and have taken all things into consideration, they come to the conclusion that obedience to God is a luxury that they can dispense with, at least until close to the end of their lives.

Those who practice the obedience of faith look for the future reward and set the greatest store by it. To their faith alone, the profit is exceedingly great. For them to take up the cross will be to carry a burden, but it will also be to find rest. They know the saying, "No cross, no crown." They recognize the truth that, if there is no obedience here on earth, there will be no future reward. This requires a faith that has eyes that can *"see afar off"* (2 Pet. 1:9 KJV), across the black torrent of death and within the veil that separates us from the unseen. A person will not obey God unless he has learned to endure *"as seeing Him who is invisible"* (Heb. 11:27).

Unquestioning Obedience

Also, remember that the obedience that comes from true faith is often required to be unhesitating and unquestioning, for it is written, *"He went out, not knowing where he was going."* God commanded Abraham to journey, and he moved his camp at once. Into the unknown land he made his way; through fertile regions or across a wilderness, among friends or through the midst of foes, he pursued his journey. He did not know where his way would take him, but he knew that the Lord had commanded him to go. Even bad men will obey God when they agree with Him, but good men will obey His commands even when they do not know what to think of them. It is not ours to judge the Lord's commands, but to follow them. I am weary of hearing people say, "Yes, we know that such a course would be right, but then the consequences might be painful: good men would be grieved, the cause would be weakened, and we ourselves would get into a world of trouble and put our hands into a hornet's nest." There is not much need to preach caution nowadays. Those who are willing to run any risk for the truth's sake are few enough. In the last few years, not many people have developed consciences that are tender about the Lord's honor. Prudent consideration of consequences is superabundant, but the spirit that obeys and dares all things for Christ's sake—where is it?

The Abrahams of today will not go out from the people and surroundings with which they are familiar. They will put up with anything sooner than risk their livelihoods. If they do go out, they must know where they are going and how much is to be gleaned in the new country. I am not pronouncing any judgment on their conduct, I am merely pointing out the fact. Our Puritan forefathers had little regard for property or liberty when these stood in the way of conscience; they defied exile and danger sooner than give up a grain of truth. But their descendants prefer peace and worldly amusements, and they pride themselves on their sophistication rather than on heroic faith. The modern believer must have no mysteries. He must have everything planed down to a scientific standard. Abraham *went out, not knowing where he was going,* but people today must have every bit of information with regard to the way, and even then they will not go. If they obey at all, it is because their own superior judgments tend in that direction. But to go forth, not knowing where they are going, and to go at all hazards, is not to their liking at all. They are so highly refined that they prefer to be original and to map out their own way.

My friend, having once discerned the voice of God, obey without question. If you have to stand alone, and if nobody will befriend you, stand alone, and God will befriend you. If you should get an unfavorable word from those you value most, bear it. What, after all, are unfavorable words or good words, compared with keeping a clear conscience by walking in the way of the Lord? The line of truth is as narrow as a razor's edge, and the one who wants to keep to such a line needs to wear the golden sandals of the peace of God. Through divine grace may we, like Abraham, walk hand in hand with the Lord, even where we cannot see our way!

Continuous Obedience

The obedience that faith produces also must be continuous. Having begun the separated life, Abraham continued to dwell in tents, and to sojourn in the land that was far from the place of his birth. His whole life may be summed up in this way: *"By faith Abraham obeyed."* He believed; therefore, he walked before the Lord in a perfect way. He even offered up his son Isaac. "Abraham's mistake," was it? How dare anyone talk in that way! By faith he obeyed, and to the end of his life he was never an original speculator or inventor of ways for self-will, but a submissive servant of that great Lord who condescended to call him *"friend"* (James 2:23). May it be said of you that by faith you obeyed! Do not cultivate doubt, or you will soon cultivate disobedience. Set this up as your standard, and from now on let this be the epitome of your life: "By faith he obeyed."

The Life of Faith and Obedience

We must, therefore, wholeheartedly believe in God and eagerly serve Him. Now, what sort of life will result from our faith and obedience?

Life without Risk

We will live our lives without that great risk that otherwise holds us in peril. A person runs a great risk when he steers himself. Rocks or no rocks, the peril lies in the helmsman. However, the believer is no longer the helmsman of his own vessel; he has taken a Pilot on board. To believe in God and do what He commands is a great escape from the hazards of personal weakness and folly. If we do as God commands, and do not seem to succeed, it is no fault of ours. Failure itself would be success as long as we did not fail to obey.

If we were to pass through life unrecognized, or were only acknowledged by a sneer from the worldly-wise, and if this were regarded as a failure, it could be borne with calm confidence as long

213

as we knew that we had kept our faith in God and our obedience to Him. Providence is God's business; obedience is ours. What comes out of our lives' course must remain with the Lord. To obey is our sole concern. What harvest will come from our sowing we must leave with the Lord of the harvest, but we ourselves must take care of the basket and the seed and scatter our handfuls in the furrows without fail. We can hear, *"Well done, good and faithful servant"* (Matt. 25:23). To be successful servants is not in our power, and we will not be held responsible for it. Our greatest risk is over when we obey. God makes faith and obedience the way of safety.

Life Free from the Heaviest Cares

Next, we will enjoy a life free from life's heaviest cares. If we were in the middle of Africa with Stanley, the newsman who found missionary Dr. David Livingstone, our pressing concern would be to find our way out. Yet when we have nothing to do but to obey, our road is mapped out for us. Jesus says, *"Follow Me"* (Matt. 4:19), and this makes our way plain and lifts a load of cares from our shoulders.

To choose our course by human reasoning is a way of thorns. To obey is like traveling on the king's highway. When we follow our own methods, we have to sail against the wind and try to get back to our original course, and we often miss the port after all. But faith, like a steamship, steers straight for the harbor's mouth and leaves a bright track of obedience behind her as she forges ahead.

When our only concern is to obey, a thousand other cares take flight. If we sin in order to succeed, we have sown the seeds of care and sorrow, and the reaping will be a grievous one. If we forsake the path and try shortcuts, we will have to do a degree of wading through mire and slough, we will spatter ourselves from head to foot, and we will be wearied trying to find our way—all because we could not trust God and obey His instructions. Obedience may appear difficult, and it may bring sacrifice with it, but, after all, it is the nearest and the best road. The ways of obedience are, in the long run, *"ways of pleasantness, and all her paths are peace"* (Prov. 3:17). The person who is always believing and obedient, through the strength of the Holy Spirit, has chosen the *"good part"* (Luke 10:42). It is he who can sing,

> I have no cares, O blessed Lord,
> For all my cares are Thine;

> I live in triumph, too, for Thou
> Hast made Thy triumphs mine.

Or, to change the verse, he is like the shepherd boy in the Valley of Humiliation, from John Bunyan's *The Pilgrim's Progress,* for that lowland is part of the great Plain of Obedience, and he also can sing,

> He that is down need fear no fall,
> He that is low no pride;
> He that is humble ever shall
> Have God to be his Guide.

Although he may not reach the heights of ambition or stand on the dizzying cliffs of presumption, he will know superior joys. He has hit upon the happiest mode of living under heaven—a mode of life corresponding to the perfect life above. He will dwell in God's house and will be continually praising Him.

Life of the Highest Honor

Moreover, the way of obedience is a life of the highest honor. Obedience is the glory of a human life—the glory that our Lord Jesus has given to His chosen, even His own glory. *"Though He was a Son, yet He learned obedience by the things which He suffered"* (Heb. 5:8). He never forged an original course, but He always did the things that pleased the Father. Let this be our glory. By faith we yield our intelligence to the highest intelligence; we are led, guided, and directed, and we follow where our Lord has gone. To us who believe, He is honor. To a soldier it is the greatest honor to have accomplished his sovereign's command. He does not debase his manhood when he subjects it to honorable command. On the contrary, he is even exalted by obeying in the day of danger. It is no dishonor to have it said of us, as Tennyson did of the British cavalry in "The Charge of the Light Brigade,"

> Theirs not to reason why,
> Theirs but to do and die.

The bravest and the most honored of men are those who implicitly obey the command of the King of Kings. The best among His children are those who know their Father's mind the best and who yield to it the most joyful obedience. Within the walls of our Father's house, should we have any other ambition than to be perfectly obedient children and implicitly trusting toward Him?

A Life of Communion with God

Yet, my friend, this is a kind of life that will bring communion with God. God often hides His face behind the clouds of dust that His children make by their self-will. If we transgress against Him, we will soon be in trouble. However, a holy walk—the walk described by our Scripture text as faith that produces obedience—is heaven beneath the stars. God comes down to walk with men who obey. If they walk with Him, He walks with them. The Lord can only have fellowship with His servants as they obey. Obedience is heaven in us, and it is the prelude to our being in heaven. Obedient faith is the way to eternal life; no, it is eternal life revealing itself.

A Life to Imitate

The obedience of faith creates a form of life that may be safely copied. As parents, we wish to live in such a way that our children may imitate us to their lasting profit. Teachers should aspire to be what they want their classes to be. If you have received your own schooling in the obedience of faith, you will be a good teacher. Children usually exaggerate their models, but there is no need to fear that they will go too far in faith or in obedience to the Lord. I like to hear a man say, when his father has gone, "My dear father was a man who feared God, and I desire to follow in his footsteps. When I was a boy, I thought he was rather stiff and puritanical, but now I see that he had a good reason for it all. I feel much the same myself, and would do nothing of which God would not approve."

The bringing up of families is a very important matter. This topic is neglected too much nowadays. However, it is the most profitable of all holy service and is the hope of the future. Great men, in the best sense, are bred in holy households. A God-fearing example at home is the most fruitful of religious agencies.

I knew a humble little church that belonged to one of the strictest sects of Christianity. There was nothing refined about the ministry, but the people were staunch believers. Five or six families who attended that humble ministry learned to truly believe what they believed and to live it out. It was by no means a liberal creed that they received, but what they believed affected their lives. They became substantial in wealth and generous and benevolent in giving.

These families all sprang from plain, humble men who knew their Bibles and believed the doctrines of grace. They learned to fear God, to trust in Him, and to rest in the old faith; and they prospered even in worldly things. Their third generation descendants do not all adhere to their way of thinking, but they have risen through God's blessing on their grandfathers. These men were fed on substantial meat, and they became sturdy old fellows, able to cope with the world and to fight their way. I wish that we had more men today who would maintain truth at all costs. May the Lord give us back those whose examples can be safely copied in all things, even though they may be denounced as being "rigid" or "too precise." We serve a jealous God and a holy Savior. Let us make sure that we do not grieve His Spirit and cause Him to withdraw from us.

A Life That Needs Great Grace

In addition, faith that produces obedience is a kind of life that needs great grace. Those who profess faith but who are not diligent in practicing it will not live in this way. Maintaining the faith that obeys in everything requires watchfulness, prayer, and nearness to God. Beloved, *"He gives more grace"* (James 4:6). The Lord will enable you to add to your faith all the virtues (2 Pet. 1:5).

Whenever you fail in any respect in your life, do not sit down and question the goodness of God and the power of the Holy Spirit. That is not the way to increase the stream of obedience but to diminish the source of it. Believe more instead of less. Try, by God's grace, to believe more in the pardon of sin, more in the renovation by the Holy Spirit, more in the everlasting covenant, more in the love that had no beginning and will never, never cease. Your hope does not lie in rushing into the darkness of doubt but in returning in repentance into the still clearer light of a steadier faith. May you be helped to do so, and may we, and the whole multitude of the Lord's redeemed, by faith go on to obey our Lord in all things!

Remember, *"By faith Abraham obeyed."* Have faith in God, and then obey, obey, obey, and keep on obeying, until the Lord calls you home. Obey on earth, and then you will have learned to obey in heaven. Obedience is the rehearsal of eternal bliss. Practice now, by obedience, the song that you will sing forever in glory. God grant His grace to us!

Chapter 2

At Your Word

*Simon answered and said to Him, "Master, we have toiled
all night and caught nothing; nevertheless at Your word
I will let down the net."*
—Luke 5:5

H ow very much may simple obedience involve the sublime!
Peter went to catch up the net and let it down into the sea,
and he said as naturally as can be, *"At Your word I will let
down the net."* But even though his words were simple, he was
there and then appealing to one of the greatest principles that rules
among intelligent beings, and to the strongest force that sways the
universe: *"At Your word."*

Great God, it is at Your word that seraphim fly and cherubim
bow! Your angels, which excel in strength, do Your commandments,
attending to the voice of Your word (Ps. 103:20). At Your word, space
and time first came into being, as well as everything else that exists.

The Cause of Causes

"At Your word." This phrase is the cause of causes, the beginning of God's creation. *"By the word of the LORD the heavens were
made"* (Ps. 33:6); by that Word the present composition of this round
world was settled as it now stands.

When the earth was formless and dark, Your voice, O Lord,
was heard, saying, *"Let there be light"* (Gen. 1:3), and at Your word
light leaped forth. At Your word day and night took up their places,
and at Your word the waters were divided from the waters by the
firmament of heaven. At Your word the dry land appeared, and the
seas retired to their channels. At Your word the globe was covered
over with green, and vegetable life began. At Your word the sun,
moon, and stars appeared, *"for signs and seasons, and for days and*

years" (v. 14). At Your word the living creatures filled the sea and air and land, and man at last appeared. We are well assured of all this, for by faith we know *"that the worlds were framed by the word of God"* (Heb. 11:3). When we act in conformity with the word of our Lord, we feel that we are in line with all the forces of the universe, traveling on the main track of all real existence. Would you not agree that this is a sublime condition, even though it is seen in the common deeds of our everyday life?

By the Word of His Power

It is not in creation alone that the word of the Lord is supreme. Its majestic power is also manifested in God's continual care toward the world. For the Lord upholds *"all things by the word of His power"* (Heb. 1:3). The Psalms are full of illustrations of this. *"His word runs very swiftly"* (Ps. 147:15). When the lakes and rivers are frozen over from the winter cold, the Lord sends forth His word and melts them (vv. 16–18). Snow and clouds and stormy wind are all fulfilling His word (Ps. 148:8). We see that nature abides and moves by the word of the Lord.

So, too, all matters of fact and history are subject to the supreme Word. Jehovah stands as the center of all things. As Lord of all, He remains at the saluting point, and all the events of the ages come marching by at His word, bowing to His sovereign will. At Your word, O God, kingdoms arise and empires flourish. At Your word races of men become dominant and tread down their fellowmen. At Your word dynasties die, kingdoms crumble, mighty cities become deserts, and armies of men melt away like the frost of the morning. Despite the sin of man and the rage of devils, there is a sublime sense in which all things from the beginning, since Adam crossed the threshold of Eden even until now, have happened according to the purpose and will of the Lord of Hosts. Prophecy utters her oracles, and history writes her pages, at Your word, O Lord.

It is wonderful to think of the fisherman of Galilee letting down his net in perfect consonance with all the arrangements of the ages. Imagine the scene as Peter's net obeys the law that regulates the spheres. His hand consciously does what the star Arcturus and the constellation Orion are doing without thought. This little bell on the Galilean lake rings out in harmony with the everlasting chimes. *"At Your word,"* says Peter as he promptly obeys, therein repeating the watchword of seas and stars, of winds and worlds. It is glorious to be keeping step in this way with the marching of the armies of the King of Kings.

The Password of the Ages

There is another way of applying this concept. *"At Your word"* has been the password of all good men from the beginning until now. Saints have acted on these three words and found their marching orders in them. Go back in your imagination to the time of Noah. Imagine that an ark is being built on dry land, and that a ribald crowd has gathered about the old patriarch, and is laughing at him. Noah is not ashamed, for, lifting his face to heaven, he says, "I have built this great vessel, O Jehovah, at Your word."

Or think of Abraham as he abandons the place of his childhood, leaves his family, and goes with Sarah to a land of which he knows nothing. He crosses the broad Euphrates river and enters into a country possessed by the Canaanites, in which he will roam as a stranger and a sojourner all his days. He dwells in tents, as will Isaac and Jacob. If any scoff at him for thus renouncing the comforts of a settled life, he also lifts his calm face to heaven and smilingly answers to the Lord, "It is at Your word." Yes, and even when his brow is furrowed, and the hot tear is ready to force itself from beneath the Partriarch's eyelid as he lifts his hand with the knife to stab Isaac to the heart, if any charge him with murder, or think that he is mad, he lifts the same calm face toward the majesty of the Most High and says, "It is at Your word." At that word, he joyfully sheathes the sacrificial knife, for he has proven his willingness to go to the utmost at the word of the Lord his God.

If I were to introduce you to a thousand of the faithful ones who have shown the obedience of faith, in every case they would justify their acts by telling you that they did them at God's word. Imagine Moses lifting his rod in the presence of the haughty Pharaoh. He does not lift that rod in vain at Jehovah's word, for the plagues fall thick and heavy upon the Egyptians. They are made to know that God's word does not return to Him void, but accomplishes His purpose (Isa. 55:11), whether it is a threat or a promise.

Then, see Moses lead the people out of Egypt, the whole host with its multitudes! Notice how he brings them to the Red Sea, where the wilderness shuts them in. The heights frown on either side, and the rattle of Egypt's war chariots is behind them. How did

Moses come to play the fool and bring them here? Were there no graves in Egypt that he therefore brought them out to die on the Red Sea shore? Moses' answer is the quiet reflection that he did it at Jehovah's word. And we see that God justifies that word, for the sea opens wide a highway for the elect of God, and they march joyfully through. On the other side, with tambourines and dances they sing to the Lord who has triumphed gloriously (Exod. 15:1).

Now, imagine Joshua surrounding and attacking Jericho. He does not use battering rams. He only uses one great blast of trumpets (Josh. 6:20). His reason for doing so is that God has spoken to him by His word. And so, let us move directly on, for time would fail me to speak of Samson and Jephthah and Barak (Heb. 11:32): these men did what they did at God's word, and, as they did so, the Lord was with them.

The Sublimity of Simple Obedience

Is it bringing things down from the sublime to the ridiculous to talk of Peter and the net that he cast over the side of his little boat? Not at all. We are ourselves ridiculous when we do not make our own lives sublime by the obedience of faith. Certainly, there may be as much sublimity in casting a net as in building an ark, lifting a rod, or sounding a ram's horn; it is clear that, if it is done in faith, the simplest action of life may be sublimely great. The crash of the wave as it covered Peter's net may have been as sublime before the Lord as was the thunderous glory of the Red Sea when the waters returned in their strength. God, who sees the world as *"a drop in a bucket"* (Isa. 40:15), sees wonders in the smallest act of faith.

Do not, I implore you, think that sublimity lies in great quantities, to be measured by a scale, so that a mile is considered sublime and an inch is considered absurd. We do not measure what is moral and spiritual by inches and miles. The common act of fishing at Christ's word links Peter with all the principalities and powers and forces that, in all ages, have known this as their only law: *"He spoke, and it was done; He commanded, and it stood fast"* (Ps. 33:9). We, too, will have fellowship with the sublime if we know how to be perfectly obedient to the Word of the Lord.

The Rule of All Christians

"At Your word" ought to be the rule of all Christians for all aspects of their lives. This rule should direct us in the church and

221

in the world; it should guide us in our spiritual beliefs and in our secular acts. I wish it were so. We hear boasting that the Bible, and the Bible alone, is the religion of Protestants. It is a mere boast. Few Protestants can honestly repeat the assertion. They have other books to which they pay deference, and other rules and guides beyond, above, and even in opposition to, the one Word of God. It ought not to be so. The power of the church and the power of the individual to please God will never be fully known until we get back to the simple yet sublime rule of our text: *"At Your word."*

This rule has many applications, and I am just going to hammer on this phrase as God helps me. To begin, I will somewhat repeat myself by explaining that it ought to apply to the affairs of ordinary life. Next, I will show you how it should also apply to matters of spiritual profit. And then, I will illustrate how it ought to find its chief application in our great life business, which is being *"fishers of men"* (Matt. 4:19).

In the Affairs of Ordinary Life

"At Your word" should apply to all aspects of ordinary life. For example, we should obey God's Word in regard to continuing in honest industry. *"Let each one remain in the same calling in which he was called"* (1 Cor. 7:20). Many people when they experience a trying financial crisis are half ready to resign from their work, or run away from their businesses, because they have toiled all night and have nothing to show for it. It is true that financial darkness may last a long time and not yield quickly to the dawning. Still, Christians must not leave their posts, unless God directs them to do so. Though you may be tried, continue to be diligent in your business, and still *"have regard for good things in the sight of all men"* (Rom. 12:17). Labor on in hope. Say just as Peter did, *"Nevertheless at Your word I will let down the net."*

"Unless the LORD builds the house, they labor in vain who build it" (Ps. 127:1). You know this truth very well. Know this also, that the Lord will not forsake His people. Your best endeavors will not, of themselves, bring you prosperity. Still, do not relax those endeavors. Since God's Word tells you to conduct yourselves like men and to *"stand fast"* (1 Cor. 16:13), then *"gird up the loins of your mind[s], be sober"* (1 Pet. 1:13), and *"be strong"* (1 Cor. 16:13). Do not throw away your shields (see Ephesians 6:16); *"do not cast away your confidence"* (Heb. 10:35), but stand steadily in your rank

until the tide of battle turns. God has placed you where you are. Do not move until His providence calls you. Do not run in the presence of the dark cloud. Open your doors tomorrow morning, display your goods, and do not let despondency drive you to anything that is rash or unseemly. Say, *"Nevertheless at Your word I will let down the net."*

If I am speaking to any who are out of work just now, searching for some place where they can provide bread for themselves and for their families, as is their duty, let them hear and consider this. If any man does not do his best to provide for his own household, he does not come under a gospel blessing, but he is said to have *"denied the faith and* [to be] *worse than an unbeliever"* (1 Tim. 5:8). It is the duty of us all to work at something honorable, so that we may have enough to give to the needy as well as to those dependent on us.

If, after having gone about the city until your feet are blistered, you can find nothing to do, do not sit at home next Monday, sulkily saying, "I will not try again." Apply our Scripture text to this painful trial, and again venture out in hope, saying with Peter, *"We have toiled all night and caught nothing; nevertheless at Your word I will let down the net."* Let people see that a Christian is not readily driven to despair. No, let them see that when the yoke is made heavier, the Lord has a secret way of strengthening the backs of His children to bear their burdens.

If the Holy Spirit makes you calmly resolute, you will honor God much more by your happy perseverance than will the talkative by his fine speeches or the formalist by his outward show. Common life is the true place in which to prove the truth of godliness and bring glory to God. Not by doing extraordinary works, but by the piety of ordinary life, is the Christian known and his faith honored. At God's Word hold on, even to the end. *"Trust in the LORD, and do good; dwell in the land, and feed on His faithfulness"* (Ps. 37:3).

It may be, too, that you have been endeavoring in your daily life to acquire skill in your business, and have not succeeded, or that you have tried to acquire more knowledge, so that you could better fulfill your vocation, but up to this time you have not prospered as you could wish to. Do not, therefore, cease from your efforts. Christians must never be idlers. Our Lord Jesus would never have it said that His disciples are the sort of cowards who, if they do not succeed the first time, will never try again. We are to be patterns of all the moral virtues as well as the spiritual graces. As the

Lord commands, work on with mind and hand, and look to Him for the blessing. At His word, let down the net once more. He may intend to bless you abundantly, when by trial you have been prepared to bear the blessing.

This truth will apply very closely to those who are working hard to train children. It may be that with your own children you have not yet succeeded: the boy's spirit may still be wild and proud, and the girl may not yet have yielded to obedience and submission. Or you may be working in the Sunday school or in an elementary school, trying to impart knowledge and to mold the youthful mind to what is right, and you may have been baffled. But if it is your business to teach, do not be overcome. Stand firm at your work as though you heard Jesus say, *"Whatever you do, do it heartily, as to the Lord and not to men"* (Col. 3:23). Earnestly, then, at His word, again let down the net.

I counsel you, dear friends, in everything to which you set your hands, if it is a good thing, do it with all your might; and if it is not a good thing, have nothing to do with it. It is possible that you are called to teach this generation some moral truth. In most generations individuals have been called to carry out reforms and to promote progress. You are bound to *"love your neighbor as yourself"* (Matt. 22:39); therefore, as you have opportunity, *"do good to all"* (Gal. 6:10). If you have tried and, up to this point, have not won a hearing, do not give up your position. If it is a good thing, and you are a Christian, never let it be said that you are afraid or ashamed. I admire in Palissy, the potter, not only his Christianity, which could not be overcome by persecution, but his perseverance in his own business of making pottery. His last farthing and his last breath would have gone to discovering a glaze or bringing out a color. I love to see such people believers. I would not like to see our Lord followed by a group of cowards who could not fight the common battles of life. How could such weaklings become worthy of the lordlier chivalry that wrestles with *"spiritual hosts of wickedness in the heavenly places"* (Eph. 6:12)? It is for us to be the bravest among the brave in the plains of common life, so that when we are summoned to higher fields, where still greater deeds are needed, we may go there trained for the higher service.

Does it seem to you that it is a little out of place for me, a pastor, to be talking in this way? I do not think so. I notice that in the Old Testament we are told about the sheep and the cattle and the fields and the harvests of good men, and that all of these things had to do with their faith. I notice how the prudent woman, according to Solomon, looked well to her household. (See Proverbs 31:10–31.) And I observe that in the Bible we have the books of Proverbs and Ecclesiastes; there is little spiritual teaching in either of them, but they contain a great deal of good, sound, practical common sense. It is evident to me that the Lord does not intend our faith to be penned up in a pew, but to be lived out in our places of business, and to be seen in every realm of life.

The great principle of our Scripture text came from the lips of a workingman, and to the workingman I return it. It was connected with a net and a boat, the implements of his labor, and with these common things I would link it. And I would say to all who serve the Lord in this present evil world: In the name of God, if you have anything to do, do not be so despondent and despairing as to cease from it, but according to His word, once more go forward in your honest endeavors and, like Peter, say, *"I will let down the net."* This may prove to be a word in season to some who are weary of the hardness of the times. I will rejoice if it strengthens an arm or cheers a heart. Have faith in God, my tried friends. *"Be steadfast, immovable, always abounding in the work of the Lord"* (1 Cor. 15:58).

In Matters of Spiritual Growth

In matters of salvation and spiritual growth, we must, at the word of Christ, *"let down the net"* again. I put this, first, to those of you who have gone to church a great many times—with sincerity, if you are to be believed—hoping to find salvation. You have prayed before the sermon began that the Lord would really bless the sermon to you. Now, I want you to consider my words carefully: I do not understand you at all; I cannot comprehend you, because the way of salvation is open to you at this very moment, and it is, *"Believe on the Lord Jesus Christ, and you will be saved"* (Acts 16:31). You have nothing to wait for, and all your waiting is sinful.

If you say you are waiting for the stirring of the pool (see John 5:2–4), I tell you that there is no pool to be stirred and no angel to stir it. That pool was dried up long ago, and angels never go that way now. Our Lord Jesus Christ closed up the Bethesda pool when He came and said to the man lying there, *"Rise, take up your bed, and walk"* (John 5:8). That is what He says to you. You have no business waiting. However, if you are waiting, I earnestly invite

225

you to believe and live. *"Let down the net"* once more, and let it down this way: say, *"Lord, I believe; help my unbelief!"* (Mark 9:24). Breathe a prayer now to Jesus that He would accept you. Submit yourself to Him and implore Him to become—now, at this moment—your Savior. You will be heard. Plenty of fish are waiting to be taken in the net of faith. At the Lord's word, let it down.

But I will now speak to others who have been letting down their nets, in vain, perhaps, in the form of persistent prayer. Have you been praying for the conversion of a relative or pleading for some other good thing that you believe is according to the will of God, and after long pleading—pleading during the night, for your spirit has been sad—are you tempted never to offer that petition anymore? Now then, at Christ's word, who said, *"Men always ought to pray and not lose heart"* (Luke 18:1), and at the inspired Word of God, which says, *"Pray without ceasing"* (1 Thess. 5:17), *"let down the net,"* and pray again. Pray, not because the circumstances that surround you are more favorable, but simply because God commands you to *"continue earnestly in prayer"* (Col. 4:2). And, who knows? This very time you may meet with success!

Or have you been searching the Scriptures to find a promise that will suit your situation? Do you want to get hold of some good word from God that will comfort you? Schools of such fish are around your boat; the sea of Scripture is full of them—fish of promise, I mean. But the sad thing is that you have not been able to catch one of them. Nevertheless, try again. Search the Scriptures again with prayer, and implore the Holy Spirit to apply a precious portion to your heart, so that you may by faith enjoy the sweetness of it. Perhaps you will obtain your desire this very day and receive a larger blessing than your mind can fully contain, so that in your case also the net will break from the fullness of the favor.

Or it may be that you have been seeking some holy attainment for a long while. You want to conquer a persistent sin, exercise firmer faith, exhibit more zeal, and be more useful, but you have not yet gained your desire. Now then, since it is the Lord's desire that you should be *"complete in every good work to do His will"* (Heb. 13:21), do not cease from your purpose, but at His word let down your net again. Never despair. That temper of yours will be conquered yet; that unbelief of yours will give way to holy faith. *"Let down the net,"* and all the graces may yet be taken in it, to be yours for the rest of your life. At Christ's word alone, labor for the best things, and He will give them to you.

Or are you seeking right now the closer presence of Christ and a nearer fellowship with Him? Are you yearning for a sight of His face, that face that outshines the morning? Do you wish to be brought into His banqueting house to be filled with His love? Have you cried in vain? Then cry once more, *"At Your word,"* for He asks you to come to Him. His loving voice invites you to draw near. At His word press forward once again, let down the net once more, and unspeakable joys await you, surpassing all you have experienced up to now.

So you see that the great principle of our text may justly be applied to our spiritual growth and benefit. God help us by His gracious Spirit to carry it out from day to day.

In the Lifework of Every Christian

This great principle should also be applied to our lifework. And what is the lifework of every Christian? Is it not soulwinning? To glorify God by bringing others to faith in Christ is the great purpose for which we still remain here on earth; otherwise, we would have been caught up to swell the harmony of the heavenly songs. It is expedient for many wandering sheep here below that we should remain here until we have brought them home to the great Shepherd and Overseer of their souls (1 Pet. 2:25).

Our way of winning men for Christ—or, to use His own metaphor, our method of catching men (Luke 5:10)—is by letting down the net of the Gospel. We have learned no other way of "holy fishing." Men with great zeal and little knowledge are inventing ingenious methods for catching men. However, for my part, I believe in nothing but letting down the gospel net by proclaiming the story of God's love toward men in Christ Jesus.

No new Gospel has been committed to us by Jesus, and He has authorized no new way of making it known. Our Lord has called all of us to the work of proclaiming free pardon through His blood to all who believe in Him. Each believer is authorized by Christ to seek the conversion of his friends and associates. May not every person seek to save his brother from the burning *"lake of fire"* (Rev. 20:15)? Must not Jesus smile on anyone's endeavor to deliver his neighbor from going down to eternal death? Has He not said, *"Let him who hears say, 'Come!'"* (Rev. 22:17)?

Whoever hears the Gospel is to invite others to come to Christ. The Word of the Lord is our authorization for keeping to our one work of making known the Gospel. It would be a sorry act of mutiny if we were either to be silent or to preach "a different gospel" (2 Cor. 11:4), which would not be any gospel at all. The Word of the Lord is a warrant that justifies the man who obeys it. "Where the word of a king is, there is power" (Eccl. 8:4). What higher authority can we need?

The Results Are God's Responsibility

"Oh, but," some say, "you ought to advance to something higher than the mere elementary doctrine of grace and give the people something more in keeping with the progress of the times." We will not do so while Jesus commands us to "go into all the world and preach the gospel to every creature" (Mark 16:15). If we do what He commands us, the responsibility of the matter no longer rests with us. Whatever comes of it, we are clear if we have obeyed His orders. A servant is not to justify his master's message, but to deliver it. This makes it a joy to preach, this doing it at His word. Our business is to do what Christ tells us, as Christ tells us, and to do this again and again, as long as we have breath in our bodies. The commanding word continually cries to us, "Preach the Gospel, preach the Gospel to every creature!" Our justification for setting forth "Christ crucified" (1 Cor. 1:23), and incessantly inviting men to believe and live, lies in the same word that commanded Peter to walk on the sea and Moses to draw water out of a rock.

The result of this preaching will justify Christ who commanded it. No man, in the end, will be able to say to the Savior, "You set before your servants an impossible task, and You gave them an instrument to wield that was not at all adapted to produce its purpose." Instead, at the culmination of all things, it will be seen that for the salvation of the elect there was no better way of redemption than a crucified Savior. It will also be seen that there was no better means to make the crucified Savior known than by the simple proclamation of His Word by honest lips in the power of the Spirit of the Lord. The foolishness of preaching will turn out to be the great proof of the wisdom of God (v. 21).

My friends, you who teach or preach from the pulpit or distribute tracts or speak personally to individuals—you do not need to be afraid. Wisdom will exonerate herself from all charges and vindicate her own methods. You may be called a fool today for preaching the Gospel, but that accusation, like rust on a sword, will wear off as you use the weapon in the wars of the Lord. The preaching of the Word soon puts down all outcries against itself; those protests mainly arise because the Word is not preached. No one calls the Gospel weak where it is smiting right and left like a great two-edged sword. Our reply to the outcry about the failure of the pulpit is to get into it and preach the Gospel *"by the Holy Spirit sent from heaven"* (1 Pet. 1:12).

Obedience Is Our Responsibility

Indeed, this word of Christ, whereby He gives us His authorization for letting down the net, is such that it amounts to a command, and we will be found guilty if we do not obey. Suppose Simon Peter had said, "We have toiled all night and have taken nothing. Therefore, despite Your word, I will not let down the net"? Then Simon Peter would have been guilty of disobedience to his Lord and blasphemy against the Son of God.

What can I say to my fellow Christians who profess to be called by God, to be Christ's disciples, and yet never let down the net? Is it true that you are doing nothing for the truth, that you never disseminate the Gospel? Is it true that you call yourselves lights of the world and yet never shine, that you are sowers of the seed and yet forget that you have a seed basket? Am I addressing anyone who is wasting his life in this respect? Is it true that it is professedly your life's purpose to be a fisher of men and yet you have never cast a net or even helped to draw one on shore? Are you living under false pretenses? Are you mocking God by a fruitless claim that you never try to make fruitful? I do not have the strength with which to condemn you, but I pray to God that your own conscience might fulfill that service.

What can be said of the person who has been given a charge by the Lord to make known the glad tidings of salvation from eternal misery and yet is sinfully silent? The Great Physician has entrusted you with the medicine that heals the sick. You see them die around you, but you never speak of the remedy! The great King has given you the meal with which to feed the hungry, and you lock the storehouse door while the crowds are starving in your streets. This is a crime that may well make a man of God weep over you.

For example, the great city of London is growing ungodly to the very core, yet our Lord has given the Gospel into the hands of His churches. What can be the reason for the indifference of the

229

godly? If we keep this Gospel to ourselves, certainly coming ages will harshly condemn us as cruel to our posterity. Succeeding generations will point to our era and say, "What sort of people were these, who had the light but shut it up in a dark lantern?" In a century to come, when others will stand in our cities and walk in our streets, they will say, "A curse upon the memory of the ministers and people who failed in their duty, who came to the kingdom in a solemn time but never realized their calling, and who therefore missed the end and purpose of their being!" May we be spared from such a calamity as this. Yes, we have the authorization for working to spread the truth of God; more than that, we have a statute from the throne, a peremptory command, and it will be to our grief if we do not preach the Gospel.

An All-Powerful Authorization

Now, my friends, this authorization from Christ is one that, if we are in the state of heart that Simon Peter was, will be omnipotent with us. It was very powerful with Simon Peter. He was under the influence of a great disappointment—*"we have toiled all night"*—yet he let down the net. Some say, "We have had all this gospel preaching, we have had all these revivals, all these stirrings, and nothing has come of it." When was that? I hear a good deal of this talk, but what are the facts? "Oh," they say, "you know we had a great deal of revival a little while ago." I do not know anything of the sort. We have had flashes of light here and there, but they have been comparatively so little that it is a pity to make so much of them. Moreover, considering the little that has ever been done for it, the spread of the Gospel has been marvelous.

Look at the current gospel work in India! People say that the Christian faith is not spreading. I say that it is spreading wonderfully compared with the labor that has been expended and the sacrifice that has been made. If in that land you spend a penny and get a thousand English pounds, you have no right to say, "What is that? We want a million." If your desires are that exacting, prove their sincerity by corresponding action. Increase your outlay. The harvest is wonderful considering the little amount of seed that has been sown, but if you wish for more sheaves, sow more. The church has had an enormous return for what little she has done.

In England there have been partial revivals, but to what have they amounted? A flash of light has been seen in a certain district, but darkness has still remained supreme over the length and breadth of the country. The newspapers have reported a great work in a certain spot, but if the papers had reported the places in which there has been no revival, we would have a different view of things! A little corner at the top of a column would have sufficed for the good, and column after column would not have sufficed to make known the black side of the situation.

The church has scarcely ever been in a state of universal revival since the Day of Pentecost. A partial moving among Christians has occurred every now and then, but the whole body throughout has never burned and flamed with the earnestness that the grand cause demands. Oh, that the Lord would set the whole church on fire! We have no cause for disappointment. In proportion to the little effort expended, great things have come to us. Therefore, let us get to our nets again, and say no more about the night in which we have toiled.

Don't Lose Heart

Next, this command overcame Peter's love of ease. Evidently he was tired when he said, *"We have toiled all night."* Fishing is hard work, especially when no fish are caught. It is natural to wish to be excused from further toil when you are already weary with unrewarded labor. I have heard some Christians say, "You know I had my time in the Sunday school years ago, and I used to wear myself out." No doubt their efforts were sincere. But now, they feel authorized to take things easy, for they feel that they do not owe any more to their Lord.

Is it true that any one of us can cease from service when it is plain that we do not cease receiving mercy at the Lord's hands? Are we not ashamed of the situation when it is made clear to us? "Take it easy," people say. Yes, soon, very soon, we will take it easy, for there will be rest enough in the grave. Just now, while the souls of men are perishing, to relax our efforts is wickedness. No, Peter, although you now may be in a dripping sweat from having toiled all night, you must get at it again. He does so. The night's work is nothing; he must work in the day, too, if he is to catch fish.

No Command of Christ Is Out of Season

Moreover, the command of Christ was so supreme over Peter that he was not held back by carnal reason, for reason would say,

"If you could not catch fish in the night, you will certainly not do so in the day." Night was the special time for catching fish on the Gennesaret lake; and by day, when the garish sun was lighting up the waves and letting the fish see every single mesh of the net, they were not likely to come into it. But when Christ commands, the most unlikely time is likely, and the most unpromising sphere becomes hopeful. No act is out of season when Christ commands it. If He says, "Go," go at once, without deliberation. Do not say, *"There are still four months and then comes the harvest"* (John 4:35). Jesus says that the fields *"are already white for harvest!"* (v. 35). Peter lets down the net at once, and wisely does he act at Christ's word.

You Must Personally Let Down the Net

The lesson to you and to me is this: Let us do as Peter did, and let down the net personally, for the apostle said, *"I will let down the net."* Brother, can you not do something with your own heart, lips, and hands? Sister, can you not do something with your own gentle spirit? You may say, "I was thinking about getting half a dozen friends to form a committee to relieve the poor around us." Nothing will ever come of it; the poor will not get a bowl of soup or a hunk of bread. Go about it yourself. You may reply, "But I think I might get a dozen people to come together and organize a society." Yes, and then you would move resolutions and amendments all day long and finish up by passing votes of mutual commendation. You had better get to work yourself, as Peter did.

And you had better do it at once, for Peter immediately let down the net, as soon as he had launched out into the deep. You may never have another opportunity; your zeal may evaporate, or your life may end. Peter, however, only let down one net, and there was the pity of it. If John and James and all the rest had let down their nets, the result would have been much better. "Why?" you ask. Because, since there was only one net, that net was overstrained and it broke. If all the nets had been used, they might have taken more fish, and no net would have been broken.

I was reading some time ago of a catch of mackerel at Brighton, England. When the net was full, the mackerel sticking in all the meshes made it so heavy that the fishermen could not raise it, and the boat itself was in some danger of going down, so they had to cut away the net and lose the fish. If there had been many nets and boats, the fishermen might have buoyed up all of the fish, and so they might have done in this case in our text. As it was, many fish were lost through the breaking of the net.

If a church can be so awakened that each individual gets to work in the power of the Holy Spirit, and then all the individuals combine, how many souls will be captured for Jesus! Multitudes of souls are lost to the blessed Gospel because of our broken nets; the nets get broken because we are not truly united in holy service. By our lack of wisdom we bring about loss to our Master's cause. Ministers would not need to become worn out with work if everyone would do his share; one boat would not begin to sink if each of the other boats took a part of the blessed load.

Now, my friends, if I have accomplished anything by the help of God's Spirit, I hope I have made you ready to accept the following guidance for service, drawn from the text. The way in which to serve God is to do it at His word. I pray that none of us may sink into serving the Lord as a matter of routine. May we never fall into serving Him in our own strength. We must preach, teach, and work in His name because we hear Him calling us to do so. We must act at His word. If this were the case, we would work with much more faith, with much more earnestness, and with much more likelihood of success.

It is a blessed thing to see Christ sitting in the boat while you cast the net. If you catch a glimpse of His approving smile as He watches you, you will work very heartily. You will do what critics sneer at as absurd, but you will do it in all confidence, believing that it must be wise, because Jesus asks you to do it. We must labor in entire dependence on Him, not preaching or teaching because in our judgment it is the right thing to do—Peter did not think so— but because Jesus gives the word, and His word is law. You may not work because you have any expectation of success from the excellence of your work or from the nature of the people among whom you labor, but because Jesus has given you the word.

I remember well how some of my brothers used to talk to me. They said, "You preach the Gospel to dead sinners; you ask them to repent and believe. You might just as well shake a handkerchief ov r a grave and command the corpse to come out of it." Exactly so. They spoke the truth, but then, I would delight to go and shake a handkerchief over graves and command the dead to live if Jesus called me to do so. I would expect to see the cemetery crack and heave from end to end if I were sent on such an errand by the Lord. I would accept the duty joyfully.

The more absurd the wise men of our age make the Gospel out to be, and the more they show that it is powerless to produce the intended purpose, the more we will persevere in our old method of preaching Jesus crucified. Our resolves are not to be shaken by that mode of reasoning. We have never drawn our argument for preaching the Gospel from the work itself but from the orders given us to do it, and we would rather act on the responsibility of Christ than on our own.

I would rather be a fool and do what Christ tells me than be the wisest man of the modern school of thought and despise the Word of the Lord. I would rather lay the responsibility for my life at the feet of Him who commands me to live according to His Word than seek out a purpose in life for myself and feel that the responsibility rested on my own shoulders. Let us be willing to be under orders to Christ, willing to persevere under difficulties, willing to begin anew in His service from this very hour.

Chapter 3

Elijah's Plea

Let it be known this day...that I have done
all these things at Your word.
—1 Kings 18:36

The acts of Elijah were very singular. It had not been known from the foundations of the earth that a man would shut up the doors of rain for more than three years. Yet we read in 1 Kings that Elijah suddenly leaps on the scene, announces the judgment of the Lord, and then disappears for a time. When he reappears, at God's command, he orders Ahab to gather the priests of Baal and to put to the test the question of whether Baal or Jehovah was indeed God. Bullocks would be slain and laid upon the wood, without fire, and the God who would answer by fire would be determined to be the one living and true God, the God of Israel.

We might question within ourselves what right the prophet had to restrain the clouds or to put God's honor to a test. Suppose the Lord had not willed to answer Elijah by fire; did he have any right to make the glory of God hang upon such terms as he proposed? The answer is that he had done all these things according to God's word. It was no whim of his to chastise the nation with a drought. It was no scheme of his, concocted in his own brain, that he should put the divinity of Jehovah or of Baal to the test by a sacrifice to be consumed by miraculous fire. Oh, no! If you read through the life of Elijah, you will see that whenever he took a step, it was preceded by, *"The word of the LORD came to Elijah."* (See 1 Kings 17–21.) He never acted by himself; God was behind him. He moved according to divine will, and he spoke according to divine teaching. He pleaded this fact with the Most High, saying, *"Let it be known this day...that I have done all these things at Your word."*

This makes the character of Elijah stand out, not as an example of reckless daring, but as the example of a man of sound mind.

Faith in God is true wisdom. Childlike confidence in the Word of God is the highest form of common sense. To believe Him who cannot lie and to trust in Him who cannot fail is a kind of wisdom that none but fools will laugh at. The wisest of men must concur with the opinion that it is always best to place your reliance where it will certainly be justified, and always best to believe what cannot possibly be false.

Imagine Elijah before the priests of Baal. He had believed God implicitly, had acted on his belief, and now he naturally expected to be justified in what he hasd done. An ambassador never dreams that his authorized acts will be repudiated by his king. If a man acts as your agent and does as you direct, the responsibility for his actions lies with you, and you must back him up. It would, indeed, be an atrocious thing to send a servant on an errand and, when he had faithfully performed it to the letter, to deny having sent him.

It is not so with God. If we will only trust Him enough to do as He commands, He will never fail us. He will see us through, though earth and hell should stand in the way. It may not be today or tomorrow, but as surely as the Lord lives, the time will come when he who trusted in Him will have joy as a result of His trustworthiness. Obedient believers can take Elijah's plea as a firm basis for prayer. And for those who cannot say that they have acted according to God's Word, it is a solemn matter to consider.

A Firm Basis for Prayer

Perhaps you are a minister of God or a worker in the cause of Christ, and you are going forth and preaching the Gospel with many tears and prayers and are continuing to use every means that Christ has ordained. Are you saying to yourself, "May I expect to have fruit out of all this?" Of course you may. You are not being sent on a frivolous errand. You are not called to sow dead seed that will never spring up. Therefore, when that anxiety weighs heavily on your heart, go to the mercy seat with this as one of your arguments: "Lord, I have acted according to Your Word. Now let it be seen that it is so. I have preached Your Word, and You have said, *'It shall not return to Me void'* (Isa. 55:11). I have prayed for these people, and You have said, *'The effective, fervent prayer of a righteous man avails much'* (James 5:16); let it be seen that this is according to Your Word."

Perhaps you are a teacher. You can say, "I have brought my children in supplication before You, and I have gone forth, after studying Your Word, to teach them, to the best of my ability, the way of salvation. Now, Lord, I claim it of Your truth that You should justify my teaching and my expectation by allowing me to see the souls of my children saved by You, through Jesus Christ, Your Son." Do you not see that you have a good argument, if the Lord has appointed you to do this work? He has, as it were, bound Himself by that very fact to support you in the doing of it.

If you, with holy diligence and carefulness, do all these things according to His Word, then you may come with certainty to the throne of grace and say to Him, "Do as You have said. Have You not said, *'He who continually goes forth weeping, bearing seed for sowing, shall doubtless come again with rejoicing, bringing his sheaves with him'* (Ps. 126:6)? Lord, I have done that. Give me my sheaves. You have said, *'Cast your bread upon the waters, for you will find it after many days'* (Eccl. 11:1). Lord, I have done that; therefore, I implore You to fulfill Your promise to me." You may plead in this fashion with the same boldness that made Elijah say in the presence of all the people, *"Let it be known this day that You are God in Israel and I am Your servant, and that I have done all these things at Your word"* (1 Kings 18:36).

Next, I would apply this teaching to churches. I am afraid that many churches are not prospering. The congregations are thin, the churches are diminishing, the prayer meetings are scantily attended, and spiritual life is low. If I can conceive of a church in such a condition, which, nevertheless, can say to God, "We have done all these things at Your Word," I would expect to see that church soon revived in answer to prayer.

The reason some churches do not prosper is that they have not done according to God's Word. They have not even cared to know what God's Word says. Another book is their standard. Instead of the inspired Word of God, a man is their leader and legislator. Some churches are doing little or nothing for the conversion of sinners. But if anyone, in any church, can go before God and say, "Lord, we have had among us the preaching of the Gospel, and we have earnestly prayed for the blessing. We have gathered about your minister, and we have held him up in the arms of prayer and faith. We have, as individual Christians, sought out our particular realms of service, we have all gone out to bring in souls to You, and we have lived in godliness of life by the help of Your grace. Now, therefore, prosper Your cause," he will find it a good plea. Real prosperity must come to any church that walks according to

237

Christ's rules, obeys Christ's teaching, and is filled with Christ's Spirit. I would exhort all members of churches that are in a poor way right now to see to it that all things are done according to God's Word and then to wait in hope in holy confidence. The fire from heaven must come. The blessing cannot be withheld.

The same principle also may be applied to any individual believers who are in trouble because they have done what is right. It often happens that a man feels, "I could make money, but I must not, for the proposed course of action would be wrong. Such a situation is open, but it involves what my conscience does not approve. I will suffer instead of profiting by doing anything that is questionable." It may be that you are in great trouble, clearly through your obedience to God. In that case, you are the one above all others who may lay this case before the Most High: "Lord, I have done all these things at Your Word, and you have said, *'I will never leave you nor forsake you'* (Heb. 13:5). I implore You to intervene for me." Somehow or other God will provide for you. If He intends for you to be tried further, He will give you strength to bear it (1 Cor. 10:13). But it is likely that now that He has tested you, He will bring you forth from the fire as gold (Job 23:10).

> Do good and know no fear,
> For so thou in the land shall dwell,
> And God thy food prepare.

In addition, I would like to apply this principle to the seeking sinner. You are anxious to be saved. You are attentive to the Word, and your heart says, "Let me know what this salvation is and how to approach it, for I will have it no matter what stands in the way." You have heard Jesus say, *"Strive to enter through the narrow gate"* (Luke 13:24). You have heard His appeal, *"Do not labor for the food which perishes, but for the food which endures to everlasting life"* (John 6:27). You long to enter the narrow gate and to eat of the meat that endures; you would give worlds for such a gift. You have spoken well, my friend. Now, listen. You cannot have heaven through your actions, as a matter of merit. There is no merit possible for you, for you have sinned and are already condemned. But God has laid down certain lines upon which He has promised to meet you and to bless you. Have you followed those lines? If you have, He will not be false to you.

It is written, *"He who believes and is baptized will be saved"* (Mark 16:16). Can you come before God and say, "I have believed and have been baptized"? Then you are on firm pleading ground. It is also written, *"Whoever confesses and forsakes* [his sins] *will have mercy"* (Prov. 28:13). When you have confessed your sins and forsaken them, you have a just claim upon the promise of God, and you can say to Him, "Lord, fulfill this word for Your servant, upon which You have caused me to hope. There is no merit in my faith, my baptism, my repentance, or my forsaking of sin. Yet as You have put Your promise side by side with these things, and I have been obedient to You in regard to them, I now come to You and say, 'Prove Your own truth, for I have done all these things at Your word.'"

No sinner will come before God in the end and say, "I trusted as You asked me to trust, and yet I am lost." It is impossible. Your blood, if you are lost, will be on your own head. But you will never be able to lay your soul's damnation at the door of God. He is not false; it is you who are false.

You see, then, how the principle can be applied in prayer: "I have done these things at Your word; therefore, O Lord, do as You have said."

Have You Been Faithful to God's Word?

We will go over the same ground a little, while I ask you to put yourself through your paces—to examine yourself regarding whether or not you have done all these things at God's Word.

Let every Christian worker who has not been successful answer these questions: Have you done all these things at God's Word? Consider this now. Have you preached the Gospel? Was it the Gospel? Was it Christ you preached or merely something about Christ? Did you give the people bread, or did you give them plates to put the bread on and knives to cut the bread with? Did you give them water to drink, or did you give them the cup that had been near the water? Some preaching is not Gospel; it is a knife that smells of the cheese, but it is not cheese. See to that matter.

If you preached the Gospel, did you preach it properly? That is to say, did you state it affectionately, earnestly, clearly, plainly? If you preach the Gospel using great big university words and dictionary words, everyday people will be lost while they are trying to find out what your frame of reference is. You cannot expect God to bless you unless you preach the Gospel in a very simple way. Have you preached the truth lovingly with all your heart? Have you thrown yourself into it, as if the most important thing to you was the conversion of those you taught? Has prayer been mixed with it? Have you gone into the pulpit without prayer? Have you come out of it without prayer? Have you been to Sunday school without prayer? Have you come away from it without prayer? If so, since you failed to ask for the blessing, you must not wonder if you did not get it.

And another question: Has there been an example to back your teaching? Brothers, have you lived as you have preached? Sisters, have you lived as you have taught in your classes? These are questions we ought to answer, because perhaps God can reply to us, "No, you have not done according to My Word. It was not My Gospel you preached. You were a thinker, and you thought out your own thoughts, and I never promised to bless your thoughts but only My revealed truth. You spoke without love; you tried to glorify yourself by your oratory. You did not care whether souls were saved or not."

Suppose that God can point to you and say, "Your example was contrary to your teaching. You looked one way, but you pulled another way." In that case, there is no integrity in your prayer, is there? Come, let us change our ways. Let us try to rise to the highest pitch of obedience by the help of God's Spirit, not so that we can merit success, but so that we can command it if we act according to God's word. In the third chapter of 1 Corinthians the apostle Paul wrote that he had planted the seeds of the Gospel, his coworker Apollos had watered them, but that only God had given the increase.

And now, let me consider individual churches. I wish that the following questions would be examined by the membership of every church—especially of those churches that are not prospering: Do we as a church acknowledge the headship of Christ? Do we acknowledge the Statute Book of Christ—the one Book that alone and by itself is the religion of a Christian? Do we as a church seek the glory of God? Is that our main and only purpose? Are we travailing in birth (Gal. 4:19) for the souls of the people who live near us? Are we using every scriptural means to enlighten them with the Gospel? Are we a holy people? Is our example such that our neighbors may follow? Do we endeavor, even in the common things of life, to *do all to the glory of God* (1 Cor. 10:31)? Are we prayerful?

(Oh, the many churches that give up their prayer meetings, because prayer is not in them! How can they expect a blessing?) Are we united? Oh, beloved, it is a horrible thing when church members talk against one another and even slander one another, as though they were enemies rather than friends. Can God bless such a church as that? Let us search throughout the camp, lest there be an Achan, whose stolen gold wedge and Babylonian garment, hidden in his tent, binds the hands of the Almighty so that He cannot fight for His people. (See Joshua 7.) Let every church see to itself in this.

Next, I address Christian people who have fallen into trouble through serving God. I am pressing you, but I want to ask you a few questions. Are you quite sure that you have served God? You know there are people who indulge eccentricities and whims. God has not promised to support you in your whims. Certain people are obstinate and will not submit to what everybody must bear who has to earn his bread in a world like this. If you are a mere mule, and get the stick, I must leave you to your reward; but I speak to people of understanding. Be as stern as a Puritan against everything that is wrong, but be supple and yielding to everything that involves self-denial on your part. God will bear us through if the quarrel is His quarrel. But if it is our own quarrel, we may help ourselves. There is a big difference between being pigheaded and being steadfast. To be steadfast, as a matter of principle concerning truth that is taught by God's Word, is one thing. However, to get an odd idea into your head and stubbornly hold to it is quite another.

Besides, some men are conscientious about certain things but do not have an all-around conscience. Certain folks are conscientious about resting on the Sabbath, but the other half of the command is, *"Six days you shall labor"* (Exod. 20:9), and they do not remember that portion of the Law. I like a conscience that works fairly and impartially. But if your conscience gives way for the sake of your own gain or pleasure, the world will think that it is a sham, and they will not be far from the mark. However, if, through conscientiousness, you should be a sufferer, God will bear you through. Only examine and see that your conscience is enlightened by the Spirit of God.

The Way of Salvation

And now I want to address the seeking sinner. Some are longing to find peace but cannot reach it, and I want them to examine whether they have been negligent in some points, so that they are unable to say with Elijah, *"I have done all these things at Your word."*

You cannot be saved by your works. There is nothing you can do to deserve mercy. Salvation must be the free gift of God. But this is the point. God will give pardon to a sinner and peace to a troubled heart along certain lines. Are you wholly on those lines? If so, you will have peace. And if you do not have that peace, something has been omitted.

Faith

The first thing is faith. Do you believe that Jesus Christ is the Son of God? Do you believe that He has risen from the dead? Do you entrust yourself wholly, simply, heartily, once for all, to Him? Then it is written, *"He who believes in Me has everlasting life"* (John 6:47). Go and plead that promise.

Repentance

"I have no peace," says one. Have you sincerely repented of sin? Is your mind totally changed about sin, so that what you once loved you now hate, and what you once hated you now love? Have you had a wholehearted loathing, and giving up, and forsaking of sin? Do not deceive yourself. You cannot be saved in your sins; you are to be saved from your sins. You and your sins must part, or else Christ and you will never be joined. See to this. Labor to give up every sin and turn from every false way. Otherwise, your faith is only a dead faith, and will never save you.

Restitution

It may be that you have wronged a person and have never made restitution. D. L. Moody did great good when he preached restitution. If you have wronged another, you ought to make it up to him. You ought to return what you have stolen, if that is your sin. A person cannot expect peace of conscience until, as far as in him lies, he has made amends for any wrong he has done to his fellowman. See to that, or else, perhaps, this stone may lie at your door, and, because it is not rolled away, you may never enter into peace.

Prayer

It may be, my friend, that you have neglected prayer. Now, prayer is one of those things without which no one can find the Lord. That is how we seek Him, and if we do not seek Him, how will we find Him? If you have been neglectful in this matter of prayer, you cannot say, "I have done all these things 'at Your word.'" May the Lord stir you up to pray mightily, stir you up so that, like Jacob, you will not let Him go until He blesses you! As you wait on the Lord, He will cause you to find rest for your soul.

Good Associations

Possibly, however, you may be a believer in Christ, and you may have no peace because you are associated with ungodly people, going with them to their follies, and mixing with them in their amusements. You see that *"you cannot serve God and mammon"* (Matt. 6:24).

> *Therefore "Come out from among them and be separate, says the Lord. Do not touch what is unclean, and I will receive you." "I will be a Father to you, and you shall be My sons and daughters, says the LORD Almighty."* (2 Cor. 6:17–18)

There is a certain man I know, and I am persuaded that the only thing that keeps him from Christ is the company with which he mingles. I will not say that his company is bad in itself, but it is bad for him. If there is anything that is right in itself, yet becomes ruinous to us, we must give it up. We are not commanded to cut off warts and growths. In the fifth chapter of Matthew, Jesus commands us to cut off right hands and to pluck out right eyes (vv. 29–30)—good things in themselves—if they are stumbling blocks in our way so that we cannot reach Christ.

What is there in the world that is worth keeping if it means the loss of my soul? Away with it. Consequently, there are many things that are lawful to another person, but for you they may not be expedient because they would be injurious. Many things cause no harm to the majority of men, yet to one individual they would be the most perilous things; therefore, he should avoid them. Be a law to yourselves, and stay clear of everything that keeps you away from the Savior.

Obedient in Everything

Perhaps, however, you say, "Well, as far as I know, I do keep out of all bad associations, and I am trying to follow the Lord." Let me press you with a question close to home: Will you be obedient to Jesus in everything?

> For know—nor of the terms complain—
> Where Jesus comes He comes to reign.

If you want to have Christ as your Savior, you must also take Him as your King. It is for this reason that He stresses to you, *"He who believes and is baptized will be saved"* (Mark 16:16). Will baptism save you? Assuredly not, for you have no right to be baptized until you are saved by faith in Jesus Christ. However, remember, if Christ gives you the command—if you accept Him as your King—you are bound to obey Him.

If, instead of saying, "Be baptized," He had simply said, "Put a feather in your cap," you might have asked, "Will putting a feather in my cap save me?" No, but you would be bound to do it if He commanded you. If He had said, "Put a stone in your pocket, and carry it with you," if that were Christ's command, you would need to take the stone and carry it with you. Often, the less importance there seems to be about a command, the more there is that hinges on it.

I have seen a rebellious boy to whom his father has said, "Son, pick up that stick. Pick up that stick." There is no very great importance about the command, and so the youth sullenly refuses to obey. "Do you hear, son? Pick up that stick." No, he will not. Now, if it had been a great thing that he had been asked to do, which was somewhat beyond his power, it would not have been so clear an evidence of his rebellion when he refused to do it, as it was when it was only a little and trifling thing, yet he refused to obey. Therefore, I lay great stress on this point: You who believe in Jesus Christ should act according to His Word. Say, "Lord, what would You have me do? No matter what it is, I will do it, for I am Your servant." I want you, if you desire to be Christ's, to be just like the brave men who rode at Balaclava: "[Yours] not to reason why; / [Yours] but to do and die"—if need be, if Jesus calls you to that. Let this be your song:

> Through floods and flames if Jesus leads,
> I'll follow where He goes.

The kind of faith that at the very outset cries, "I will not do that; it is not essential," and then goes on to say, "I do not agree with that, and I do not agree with the other," is no faith at all. In that case it is you who are master and not Christ. In His own house you are beginning to alter His commands. "Oh," says one, "but as to baptism, I was baptized, you know, a great many years ago, when I was an infant." Do you say so?

You may have heard of Mary, whose mistress said, "Mary, go into the drawing room, and sweep it and dust it." Her mistress went into the drawing room and found it dusty. "Mary, did you not sweep the room and dust it?" she asked. "Well, ma'am, yes, I did. Only, I dusted it first, and then I swept it." That was the wrong order and spoiled the whole thing. And it will never do to put Christ's commands backwards, because then they mean practically nothing. We ought to do what He commands us, exactly as He commands us, when He commands us, in the order in which He commands us. It is ours simply to be obedient. When we are, we may remember that to believe Christ and to obey Christ is the same thing, and that often in Scripture the same word that might be read "believe" might also be read "obey."

He is the *"Author of eternal salvation to all who obey Him"* (Heb. 5:9), and that is to all who believe in Him. Trust Him, then, with your whole heart, and obey Him very willingly. You can then go to Him in your dying hour and say, "Lord, I have done all these things at Your Word. I claim no merit, but I do claim that You keep Your gracious promise to me, for You cannot go back on one word that You have spoken."

God bless you, beloved, for Christ's sake.

Chapter 4

Love's Law and Life

If you love Me, keep My commandments.
—John 14:15

The fourteenth chapter of John is singularly full of certainties, and remarkably studded with *if*s. Concerning most of the great things in this chapter, there never can be an *if;* and yet, the word *if* comes up, I think, no less than seven times in the chapter, not about trifles, but about the most solemn subjects. It is, perhaps, worthy of mention that there is something connected with each of these *if*s—something that results from it or appears to be involved in it or linked with it.

Look at verse two: *"In My Father's house are many mansions; if it were not so, I would have told you. I go to prepare a place for you."* If there were no place for us in the glory land, Jesus would have told us. If any truth that has not been revealed would make our hope a folly, our Lord Jesus would have warned us of it, for He has not come to lure us into a fool's paradise and to deceive us in the end. He will tell us all that it is necessary to know in order for us to have a wise faith and a sure hope.

The Lord has *"not spoken in secret, in a dark place of the earth"* (Isa. 45:19). He has not spoken in contradiction to His revealed Word. Nothing in His secret decrees or hidden designs can shake our confidence or darken our expectation. *"If it were not so, I would have told you."* If there were a secret thing that would injure your prospects, it would have been dragged to light, so that you might not be deceived, for the Lord Jesus has no desire to win disciples by the suppression of distasteful truth. If there were anything yet to be revealed that would render your hope a delusion at the end, you would have been made acquainted with it. Jesus Himself would break the sad news to you. He would not leave you to be horrified by finding it out for yourself. He kindly declares, *"I would have told you."*

Notice the third verse. Again we meet with an *if* and its consequence: *"If I go and prepare a place for you, I will come again and receive you to Myself."* If the Lord Jesus should go away (and this is a supposition no longer, for He has gone), then He would return in due time. Since He has gone, He will come again, for He has made the one dependent on the other. We do not question that He went up into heaven, for He rose from out of the circle of His followers, and they saw Him as He went up into heaven. They had no doubt at all regarding the fact that the cloud had received Him out of their sight. Moreover, they had received assurance out of heaven, by an angelic messenger, that He *"will so come in like manner as you saw Him go into heaven"* (Acts 1:11). His homegoing pledges Him to come and compels us to look for Him. *"If I go and prepare a place for you, I will come again and receive you to Myself."*

The next *if* comes at the beginning of the seventh verse: *"If you had known Me, you would have known My Father also."* If we really do know the Lord Christ, we know God. In fact, there is no way to know God correctly except through His Son Jesus. It is evidently true that men do not hold to pure and simple theism for long. If men well versed in science get away from the Christ, the incarnate God, before long they drift away from God altogether. They begin to slide down the mountain when they abandon the incarnate Deity, and there is no longer any foothold to stop them.

"No one comes to the Father except through [the Son]*"* (John 14:6), and no one keeps to the Father very long who does not also keep to his faith in the Son. Those who know Christ, know God. But those who are ignorant of the Savior are ignorant of God, however much they may pride themselves on their religion. They may know another god, but the only living and true God is unknown except by those who receive Jesus. The divine Fatherhood, of which we hear so much in certain quarters, is only to be seen through the window of incarnation and sacrifice. We must see Jesus before we can gain even so much as a glimpse at the Infinite, the Incomprehensible, and the Invisible. God does not come within finite perception until He enters human flesh, and there we see His glory, *"full of grace and truth"* (John 1:14).

You will find the next *if* a little farther down in the chapter, in the fourteenth verse: *"If you ask any thing in My name, I will do it."* The *if* in this case involves an uncertainty about our prayers—if there is an uncertainty at all. Taking it for granted that we do ask for mercies in the name of Jesus, a glorious certainty is linked to it.

Jesus says, "I will do it." Here our Lord speaks in a sovereign style. We may not say, "I will." The "I wills" pertain to Christ. He can answer, and He has the right to answer. Therefore, He says without reservation, "I will": *If you ask anything in My name, I will do it."*

Oh, that we might put the first *if* out of consideration by continually petitioning the Lord and signing our petitions with the name of Jesus! May we be persistent only in prayers to which we are authorized to attach the words "in Jesus' name." Then, boldly using His name and authority, we will not need to be under any apprehension of failure. The great Father in heaven never denies the power of His Son's name. Neither does the Son Himself draw back from keeping His own pledges. True prayer operates with the same certainty as the laws of nature. *"Delight yourself also in the LORD, and He shall give you the desires of your heart"* (Ps. 37:4). Oh, if only we delighted more in the divine name and character, then our prayers would always speed to the throne!

In the fifteenth verse we discover the *if* of our text, of which I will say nothing for the moment: *"If you love Me, keep My commandments."* Something, you see, is to come out of this *if*, the same as out of all the others. If something, then something: *"If you love Me,"* then carry it out to the legitimate result, which is *"keep My commandments."*

You will find the next *if* in the twenty-third verse: *"Jesus answered and said to him, 'If anyone loves Me, he will keep My word.'"* Respect for His wisdom and obedience to His authority will grow out of love. *"The love of Christ compels us"* (2 Cor. 5:14). We often hear people quote that passage as, "The love of Christ ought to compel us," but that is a corruption of the text. The apostle tells us that the love of Christ does compel us. And if it really enters the heart, it will do so. It is an active, moving power, influencing the inner life and then the external conduct.

> 'Tis love that makes our willing feet
> In swift obedience move.

"If anyone loves Me, he will keep My word." He will believe in the verbal inspiration of his Lord; he will regard His teaching as infallible; he will attend to it and remember it. More than this, he will, by his conduct, carry out the words of his Lord; therefore, he will keep them in the best possible manner by enshrining them in his daily life.

The chapter almost closes at the twenty-eighth verse with: *"If you loved Me, you would rejoice because I said, 'I am going to the Father,' for My Father is greater than I."* When we have an intelligent love for Christ, we rejoice in His gains even though we ourselves appear to be the losers as a result. The physical absence of our Lord from our midst might seem to us to be a great loss, but we rejoice in it because it is for His own greater glory. If He is enthroned in glory, we do not dare lament His absence. Our love agrees to His departure, even rejoices in it, for anything that contributes to His exaltation is sweet to us. Let us, at this moment, because we love Him, rejoice that He has gone to the Father.

If you read the fourteenth chapter of John, you see that, though it is enriched with heavenly certainties, it is also sprinkled with *if*s. Like little pools of sparkling water among the ever abiding rocks, these *if*s gleam in the light of heaven and refresh us even to look upon them.

Let us now consider our text, and may the Holy Spirit lead us into the secret chambers of it! *"If you love Me, keep My commandments."*

We will look at three aspects of this verse. Initially, we will see that the *if* we are considering now is a serious one. Then we will discover that the test that is added concerning it is a very judicious one: *"Keep My commandments."* And we will come to see that this test will be endured by love, for the words are translated in the Revised Version: *"Ye will keep my commandments."* Obedience will follow love as a matter of certainty.

A Very Serious *If*

The *if* in this verse is a very serious one because it goes to the root of the matter. Love belongs to the heart, and every surgeon will tell you that a disease of the heart may not be trifled with. A gifted doctor said to me, "I feel at ease with any matter if it does not concern the head or the heart." Solomon charged us, *"Keep your heart with all diligence, for out of it spring the issues of life"* (Prov. 4:23). If the mainspring fails, all the works of a watch refuse to act. We cannot, therefore, think little of a question that concerns our love, for it deals with a vital part of us. O friends, I hope there is no question about your love for Jesus.

Observe how our Savior puts this *if* in such a way as to teach us that love must be prior to obedience. The text is not, "Keep My commandments, and then love Me." No, we do not expect pure streams until the fountain is cleansed. Nor does He say, "Keep My commandments, and love Me at the same time," as two separate things, although that might correspond with truth in some measure. But love is put first, because it is first in importance and first in experience. *"If you love Me"*—we must begin with love—then *"keep My commandments."*

Love must act as mother, nurse, and food to obedience. The essence of obedience lies in the hearty love that prompts the deed, rather than in the deed itself. I can imagine that a person might, in his outward life, keep Christ's commandments; yet he might never keep them at all in such a way as to be accepted before God. If he became obedient by compulsion, but would disobey if he dared, then his heart is not right before God, and his actions are of little worth. The commandments are to be kept out of love for Him who gave them.

In the realm of obedience, to love is to live: if we love Christ, we will live for Christ. Love for the person of our Lord is the very salt of our sacrifices. To put it in very practical terms, I often say to myself, "Today I have performed all the duties of my office. But have I been careful to remain in my Lord's love? I have not failed to do all that was possible for me. I have gone from early morning until late at night, packing as much work as possible into every hour and trying to do it with all my heart. But have I, after all, done this as unto the Lord and for His sake?" I tremble for fear that I should serve God merely because I happen to be a minister and am called to preach His Word or because the natural routine of the day carries me through it. I am concerned that I may not be impelled by any force but the love of Jesus. This fear often humbles me in the dust and prevents all glorying in what I have done.

Only as we love our Lord can our obedience be true and acceptable. The main concern of our lives should be to do what is right because we love the Lord. We must walk before the Lord as Abraham did, and with the Lord as Enoch did. Unless we are under the constant constraint of love for the Lord Jesus Christ, we will fail terribly.

> Knowledge, alas! is all in vain,
> And all in vain our fear,
> In vain our labor and our pain
> If love is absent there.

See, dear friends, how inward true religion really is, how far it exceeds all external formalism! How deep is the seat of true grace. You cannot hope to do what Christ can smile on until your heart is renewed. A heart at enmity with God cannot be made acceptable by mere acts of piety. The main thing is not what your hands are doing, or even what your lips are saying; it is what you mean and intend in your heart. Which way are your affections tending? The great flywheel that moves the whole machinery of life is fixed in the heart. Therefore, this is the most important of all conditions: *"If you love Me."*

These words have a searching sound. I jump when I hear them. The person who believes in the Lord Jesus Christ for his salvation produces, as the first fruit of his faith, love for Christ. This love must abound in us or nothing is right. Packed away within that box of sweets called "love," you will find every holy thing. But if you have no love, what do you have? Though you wear your fingers to the bone with service, weep out your eyes with repentance, make your knees hard with kneeling, and dry your throat with shouting, if your heart does not beat with love, your religion falls to the ground like a withered leaf in autumn. Love is the chief jewel in the bracelet of obedience. Read the text, and note it well: *"If you love me, keep My commandments."*

What a great amount of religion may be cast out as worthless by this text! Men may keep on going to church, they may be religious throughout their whole lives, and they may be apparently blameless in their moral conduct, yet there may be nothing in them because there is no love for the ever blessed Christ at the foundation of their profession of faith.

When the heathen killed their sacrifices in order to prophesy future events from the entrails, the worst omen they ever got was when the priest, after searching into the victim, could not find a heart, or if that heart was small and shriveled. The soothsayers always declared that this omen was the sure sign of calamity. All the signs were evil if the heart of the offering was absent or deficient. This is especially true with religion and with each religious person. He who searches us, principally searches our hearts. He who tries mankind, chiefly tries the thoughts and intents of the children of men.

The Master is with us, walking with noiseless step, wearing a golden band across His breast and robed in snow-white garments down to His feet. See, He stops before each one of us and gently asks,

"Do you love Me?" Three times He repeats the question. (See John 21:15–17.) He waits for an answer. It is a vital question. Do not refuse a reply. Oh, that the Spirit of the Lord may enable you to answer in sincerity and truth, *"Lord, You know all things; You know that I love You"* (v. 17)!

This matter of love for Jesus is put prior to every other because it is the best reason for our obedience to Him. Notice that He says, *"If you love Me, keep My commandments."* Personal affection will produce personal obedience. Do you not see the meaning of the words? The blessed Jesus says to each of us, *"If you love Me, keep My commandments,"* because, truly, operative love is mainly love toward a person, and love toward our Lord produces obedience to His precepts.

There are some people for whom you would do anything—you want to yield to their wills. If such a person were to say to you, "Do this," you would do it without question. Perhaps a person like this is in the position of being your employer, and you serve him willingly. Perhaps he is a venerated friend, and because you esteem and love him, his word is law to you. The Savior may much more safely than any other be installed in such a position. From the throne of your affections, He says, "If you love Me—if your heart really goes out to Me—then let My Word be a commandment, let My commandment be kept in your memory, and then let it further be kept by being observed in your life."

Do you see the reason the Master begins with the heart? There is no hope of obedience to Him in our actions unless He is enshrined in our affections. Love for the Holy One is the spring and source of all holy living. Dear friends, have you been captured by the beauties of Jesus, and are you held in a divine captivity to the Person of your redeeming Lord, who is worthy to be adored? Then you have within you the impulse that constrains you to keep His commandments.

It was very necessary for our Lord to address His disciples in this way. Yes, it was necessary to speak in this way even to the apostles. He said to the chosen Twelve, *"If you love Me."* We would never have doubted one of them. We now know, by the outcome, that one of them was a traitor to his Lord and sold Him for pieces of silver. But no one suspected him, for he seemed as loyal as any one of them. And if that question, *"If you love Me,"* needed to be raised in the sacred college of the Twelve, how much more must it be allowed to sift our churches and to test us!

My friends, this word is needed among Christians today. Hear its voice: *"If you love Me."* The mixed multitude of people in our churches may be compared to the heap on the threshing floor that John the Baptist described in the third chapter of Matthew. The winnowing fan (v. 12) is clearly needed. Perhaps you have almost taken it for granted that you love Jesus, but it must not be taken for granted. Some of you have been born into a religious atmosphere, you have lived in the midst of godly people, and you have never been out into the wicked world to be tempted by its follies. Therefore, you have come to the careless conclusion that you must assuredly love the Lord. This is unwise and perilous. Never glory in armor that you have not tested, or rejoice in love for Christ that has not been tried and proven. What an awful thing if you should be deceived and mistaken!

It is most kind of the Savior to raise a question about your love and to give you an opportunity to examine yourself and see whether your heart is right. It would be far better for you to err on the side of too much anxiety than on that of carnal security. To be afraid that you are wrong, and therefore to make sure of being right, will bring you to a far better end than being sure that you are right and therefore refusing to examine the ground of your hope. I want you to be fully assured of your love for Jesus, but I do not want you to be deceived by a belief that you have Him if you do not. *"Search me, O God, and know my heart; try me, and know my anxieties"* (Ps. 139:23).

Remember, if anyone does not love the Lord Jesus Christ, he will be *"Anathema Maranatha"* (1 Cor. 16:22 KJV), cursed at His coming. This applies to everyone, even though he may be very eminent. An apostle turned out to be a *"son of perdition"* (John 17:12)—may not you? Any man, even though he may be a learned bishop, a popular pastor, a renowned evangelist, a venerable elder, an active deacon, or the most ancient member of the most orthodox congregation, may yet turn out not to be a lover of the Lord. Though he has gathered to break bread in the sacred name with a select company, if he does not truly love the Lord Jesus Christ, the curse rests on him, whoever he may be. So let us, right now, take from the Master's mouth the heart-searching word, *"If you love Me, keep My commandments."* Let us take it to heart, as if it is addressed to each one of us, personally and alone.

While you are considering this verse, do not compare yourself with others. What do you have to do in this matter with keeping the vineyards of others? See to your own heart. The text does not say, "If the church loves me," or "If such and such a minister loves me," or "If your brothers love me," but it states, *"If you love Me, keep My commandments."* The most important questions for each one to answer are those concerning his personal attachment to his Redeemer and the personal obedience that comes out of it.

I press this inquiry upon you. It may seem like a trite and commonplace question, but it needs to be put again and again before all people in our churches. The preacher needs to be questioned in this way, for he gets into the habit of reading his Bible for other people. The Sunday school teacher needs this inquiry, for he also is apt to study the Scriptures for his class rather than for himself. We all need the truth to come home to us with personal and forcible application, for we are always inclined to shift unpleasant inquiries onto others. When we are conversing with very deaf people, we speak right into their ears, and I wish to address you in a similar way, so that it hits home pointedly to you at this time. Let the text reverberate in your ears, mind, and heart: *"If you love Me, keep My commandments."*

The question is answerable, however. It was put to the apostles, and they could answer it. Peter spoke as all the eleven would have when he said, *"You know that I love You"* (John 21:17). It is not a question concerning mysteries that are out of range and beyond judgment. It deals with a plain matter of fact. A person can know whether he loves the Lord or not, and he ought to know. Yet the person who watchfully guards himself, and is, therefore, half afraid to speak positively, may all the more truly be a lover of the Lord. Holy caution in the heart of someone like this may raise a question where the answer is far more certain than in the hearts of those who never even make the inquiry because they are carnally secure.

Do not be content with merely longing to love Jesus or with longing to know whether you love Him. Not to know whether you love the Lord Jesus is a state of mind so dangerous that I exhort you never to go to sleep until you have escaped from it. A man has no right to smile—I had almost written, he has no right to eat bread or drink water—as long as that question hangs in the balance. It ought to be decided. It can be decided. It can be decided at once.

Not love Jesus? It would be better for me not to live than not to love Him. Not love Christ? May the terrible fact never be hidden from my weeping eyes! Perhaps the dreadful discovery may drive me to better things. If I do love my Lord, I can never rest with the shadow of a doubt darkening the life of my love. A question on such a matter is unbearable.

> Do not I love Thee from my soul?
> Then let me nothing love:
> Dead be my heart to every joy,
> When Jesus cannot move.

> Would not my heart pour forth its blood
> In honor of Thy name,
> And challenge the cold hand of death
> To damp the immortal flame?

> Thou know'st I love Thee, dearest Lord;
> But oh, I long to soar
> Far from the sphere of mortal joys,
> And learn to love Thee more.

My friends, hear the question suggested by this little word, *if*. Consider it well, and do not rest until you can say, *"I love the LORD, because He has heard my voice and my supplications"* (Ps. 116:1).

So much, then, concerning the serious nature of this *if*.

A Judicious *If*

Let me further observe that the test that is proposed in the text is a very judicious one: *"Keep My commandments."* This is the best proof of love.

The test indicated does not suggest a lawless liberty. It is true that we are *"not under law but under grace"* (Rom. 6:14). But we are still *"under law toward Christ"* (1 Cor. 9:21); and if we love Him, we are to keep His commandments. Let us never enter into the counsel of those who do not believe that there are any commandments for believers to keep. Those who do away with duty, also do away with sin, and, consequently, do away with the Savior. It is not written, "If you love Me, do whatever you please." Jesus does not say, "As long as you love Me in your hearts, I do not care anything about your lives." There is no such doctrine as that between the covers of the Holy Book. He who loves Christ is the freest person outside of heaven, but he is also the most under bonds. He is free, for Christ has loosed his bonds, but he is put under bonds to Christ by grateful love. The love of Christ constrains him,

255

from this time forward, to live for the Lord who loved him, lived for him, died for him, and rose again for him.

No, dear friends, we do not desire a lawless life. He who is not under the law as a power for condemnation can yet say that with his heart he *"delight[s] in the law of God"* (Rom. 7:22). He longs for perfect holiness, and in his soul he yields heartfelt homage to the precepts of the Lord Jesus. Love is law; the law of love is the strongest of all laws. Christ has become our Master and King, and *"His commandments are not burdensome"* (1 John 5:3).

Also, our text does not contain any fanatical challenge. We do not read, "If you love Me, perform some extraordinary act." The test required is not an outburst of extravagance or an attempt to realize the ambitious project of a feverish brain. It is nothing of the kind. Hermits, nuns, and religious madcaps find no example or precept here. Some people think that if they love Jesus, they must enter a convent, retire to a cell, dress themselves oddly, or shave their heads. Some men have thought, "If we love Christ, we must strip ourselves of everything we possess, put on sackcloth, tie ropes around our waists, and pine away in the desert." Others have thought it wise to make themselves look absurd by odd dress and behavior. The Savior does not say anything of the kind. Rather, He says, *"If you love Me, keep My commandments."*

Every now and then, we find members of our churches who feel they must leave their trades and their callings to show their love for Jesus. Their children may starve, and their wives may waste away, but their mad whimsies must be carried out for "love of Jesus." Under this influence they rush into all sorts of foolish behavior and soon ruin their reputations, because they will not take the advice of sobriety and cannot be satisfied with the grand test of love that our Lord Himself lays down in this verse. The text does not condemn these frivolous projects specifically, but it does so in general by proposing a more reasonable test: *"If you love Me, keep My commandments."*

Do not spin theories in your excited brain and vow that you will do this desperate thing or the other. The probability is that you are not seeking the glory of the Lord but that you are desiring fame for yourself. You are aiming at supreme devotion so that you may become a distinguished person and so people may talk about your superior sainthood. You may even go so far as to court persecution from selfish motives. The Savior, who is wise, knows what is in men, and He also knows what is the surest test of true love for

Himself: *"If you love Me, keep My commandments."* This is a much more difficult thing than to carry out the dictates of a crazy mind.

Why does the Savior give us this as a test? I think that one reason is that it proves whether you love Christ in His true position or whether your love is for a christ of your own making and your own placing. It is easy to want a half-christ and to refuse a whole Christ. It is also easy to follow a christ of your own making, who is merely an antichrist. The real Christ is so great and glorious that He has a right to give commandments. Moses never used an expression such as our Savior employs here. Moses might have said, "Keep God's commandments," but he never would have said, "Keep my commandments." That dear and divine person whom we call Master and Lord says here, *"Keep My commandments."* What a commanding person He must be! What lordship He has over His people! How great He is among His saints! If you keep His commandments, you are putting Him into the position that He claims. By your obedience you confess His sovereignty and divinity, and you say with Thomas, *"My Lord and my God"* (John 20:28).

I am afraid that a great many people know a christ who is meek and lowly, their servant and savior, but they do not know the Lord Jesus Christ. Alas! My friends, such people set up a false christ. We do not love Jesus at all if He is not our Lord and God. It is all whining pretension and hypocrisy, this love for Christ that robs Him of His deity. I abhor that love for Christ that does not make Him King of Kings and Lord of Lords. Love Him, yet belittle Him? It is absurd. Follow your own will in preference to His will, and then talk of love for Him? Ridiculous! This is only the Devil's counterfeit of love. It is a contradiction of all true love. Love is loyal and crowns its Lord with obedience. If you love Jesus properly, you view His every precept as a divine commandment. You love the true Christ if you love a commanding Christ as well as a saving Christ, and if you look to Him to guide your life as well as to pardon your sin.

This test, again, is very judicious, because it proves the living presence of the object of your love. Love always desires to have its object near, and it has an ability to bring its object near. If you love someone, that person may be far away, yet to your thoughts he is close at hand. Love brings the beloved one so near that the thought of this beloved one exerts influence over a person's life.

Suppose that a gentleman has faithful servants. He goes away and leaves his house in their charge. Even though he has gone abroad, he is at home to his servants, for every day their work is done as if he were there to see it. He is coming home soon, they hardly know when, but they keep all things in readiness for his return, let it happen when it may. They are not "eye" servants, who only attend to their duty when watched; therefore, they do not work any less because he is absent. Even if he does not see them, the eyes of their love always see him; therefore, they work as if he were at home. Their affection keeps him always near.

Imagine that a dear father has died and has left his property to a son who honors his memory. What does the son do? He is generous, like his father. When he is asked why, he replies, "I do exactly what I believe my dear father would do if he were here." Again, he is asked why. He answers, "Because I love him."

When a man is dead, he is still alive to those who love him. In the same manner, the living Christ, who is not dead but has gone away, is made present to us by our real love. The proof of our love is that Jesus is so present that He constrains our actions, influences our motives, and is the cause of our obedience. Jesus seems to be saying, "If you love Me, now that I am gone you will do as you would have done if I were still with you and looking at you. You will continue to keep My commandments as you would in My presence."

It is a most judicious test, once again, because, by keeping our Lord's commandments, we are doing what is most pleasing to Him and will most glorify Him. Some enthusiastic Methodist may cry,

Oh, what shall I do my Savior to praise?

To him I would say, "Listen carefully, my brother. If you love your Savior, keep His commandments. This is all you have to do, and it is a great 'all,' too. Among the rest of His commandments, you may come and be baptized, while you are so earnest to praise your Lord."

"*If you love Me, keep My commandments.*" There is the answer to every rapturous inquiry. Jesus is more glorified by a consistent obedience to His commands than by the most extravagant zeal that we can possibly display. That is only man-made worship because He has never commanded it. If you wish to break the alabaster box and fill the house with sweet perfume, as Mary anointed Jesus in the twelfth chapter of John, and if you wish to crown His head with rarest gems, the method is before you: "*Keep My commandments.*" You cannot do your Lord a greater favor or, in the long run, bring to Him more real an honor than by rendering complete, continual, hearty obedience to every one of His commandments.

Moreover, the Savior knew, when He instructed us to prove this test, that it would prepare us for honoring and glorifying Him in all other ways. Read the context: *"If you love Me, keep My commandments. And I will pray the Father, and He will give you another Helper, that He may abide with you forever"* (John 14:15–16).

You can greatly glorify Christ if you are filled with the Holy Spirit, but you cannot be filled with the Holy Spirit if you do not keep Christ's commandments. The Spirit of God as Comforter will come only to those to whom He comes as Sanctifier. By making us holy, He will qualify us for being useful. The Savior says, *"If you love Me, keep My commandments,"* because we will then obtain that divine Gift by which we can glorify His name. If there is any service to which your love would aspire, obedience to your Lord is the way to it.

But, indeed, I do not need to argue this. When your friend is dying and he asks you to prove your love by such and such a deed, he may ask whatever he will; you give him carte blanche. It may be the simplest thing or the hardest thing, but if he prescribes it as a test of love, you will not refuse him. Or if your wife says to you, "You are going to journey far from me, and I will not see you again for many days. I beg you, therefore, to carry my picture with you," you would not fail to do so. It would be a simple thing, but it would be sacred to you. Baptism and the Lord's Supper will never be slighted by those whose hearts are fully possessed with love for Jesus. They may seem like trifles, but if the Lord Jesus commands them, they cannot be neglected. To stop wearing your wedding ring might be no great crime, yet no loving wife would do it. In the same way, none who regard outward ordinances as love tokens will think of neglecting them. It is not ours to ask for reasons, not ours to dispute whether the deed is essential or nonessential; it is ours only to obey very lovingly. Bridegroom of our hearts, say what You will, and we will obey You! If You will smile and strengthen us, nothing will be impossible if it is great, and nothing will be considered trifling if it is small.

A Compelling *If*

I pray that God will prove the truth of this next statement to you: True love will endure the test. *"If you love me, ye will keep my commandments"* (RV). Again, I have used the translation from the Revised Version here, and I hope it will be written out in capital letters on our revised lives! We will obey, we must obey, since we love Him by whom the command is given.

So then, beloved, let me say this much to you: If you love Christ, set to work to find out what His commandments are. Study the Scriptures regarding every point upon which you have the slightest question. This Sacred Oracle must guide you.

Next, always be true to your convictions about what Christ's commandments are. Carry them out at all costs, and carry them out at once. It would be wicked to say, "Up to this point, I have obeyed, but I will stop here." We are committed to implicit obedience to all of the Master's will, regardless of what it involves. Will you not agree to this at the outset? If you love Him, you will not hesitate.

Also, take note of every commandment as it personally concerns you. Let me mention several commandments, and beg you to obey them as you hear them. *"Go into all the world and preach the gospel to every creature"* (Mark 16:15). Is this not a call to some of you to be missionaries? Do you hear it? Will you not say, *"Here am I! Send me"* (Isa. 6:8)?

Perhaps you are full of enmity; somebody has treated you very badly, and you cannot forget it. I urge you to hear the Lord's command: *"Little children...love one another"* (John 13:33–34). And again,

> *Therefore if you bring your gift to the altar, and there remember that your brother has something against you, leave your gift there before the altar, and go your way. First be reconciled to your brother, and then come and offer your gift.*
>
> (Matt. 5:23–24)

If you are in debt, obey this commandment: *"Owe no one anything except to love one another"* (Rom. 13:8). If you neglect the poor, and live in a stingy way, hear this commandment: *"Give to him who asks you, and from him who wants to borrow from you do not turn away"* (Matt. 5:42). Behind everything is this: *"If you love Me, keep My commandments."* I might mention, one after another, commandments that would be especially applicable, but I pray that the Holy Spirit will *"bring to your remembrance all things"* (John 14:26).

If there is a commandment that you do not relish, it ought to be a warning to you that there is something wrong in your heart that needs to be set right. If you ever quarrel with one of Christ's commands, end that quarrel by especially attending to it beyond every other. Do as the miserly man did when he conquered his greed once and for all. He was a Christian, and he promised he would give a pound to the church. But the Devil whispered, "You need your money. Do not pay." The man stamped his foot and said, "I will give two." Then the Devil said, "Surely you are going mad. Save your money." The man replied that he would not be conquered, that he would give four pounds. "Now," said Satan, "You must be insane." Then the man said, "I will give eight. And if you don't stop your tempting, I will give sixteen, for I will not be the slave of covetousness." The point is to throw your whole soul into that very duty in which you are most tempted to be slack. Jesus does not say, "If you love Me, keep this commandment or that," but "Out of love, obey every command."

Some of you do not love my Lord Jesus Christ. I have not directed this topic to you, but that very fact should make you thoughtful. Consider that I have had nothing to say to you because you do not love the Lord Jesus Christ and therefore cannot keep His commandments. Write down in black and white, "I do not love the Lord Jesus Christ." If this is really so, be honest enough to make a note of it, and think it over. If you love Jesus, you may joyfully write out, "I love the Lord Jesus. Oh, for grace to love Him more!" But if you do not love Him, it will be the honest thing to put it on record. Write it boldly: "I do not love the Lord Jesus Christ." Look at it, and look again. May God the Holy Spirit lead you to repent of not loving Jesus, who is the altogether lovely One and the great Lover of men's souls! Oh, that you may begin to love Him at once!

Chapter 5

The Friends of Jesus

You are My friends if you do whatever I command you.
—John 15:14

Our Lord Jesus Christ is beyond comparison the best of all friends—a friend in need, a friend indeed. "Friend!" said Socrates, "there is no friend!" But Socrates did not know our Lord Jesus, or he would have added, "except the Savior." In the heart of our Lord Jesus there burns such friendship toward us that all other forms of it are as dim candles to the sun. *"Greater love has no one than this, than to lay down one's life for his friends"* (John 15:13).

An ordinary man has gone as far as he possibly can when he has died for his friend. Yet he would have died anyhow, so that in dying for his friend he merely pays, somewhat beforehand, a debt that inevitably must have been discharged. With Christ, there was no need to die at all, and this, therefore, places His love and His friendship in a class by itself. He, who did not need to die, died, and died in agony when He might have lived in glory. Never did man give such proof of friendship as this.

Let our Lord's friendship to us be the model of our friendship to Him. It cannot be so in all respects, because our situations and conditions are different. His must always be the love of the greater to the lesser, the love of the benefactor to one in need, the love of the Redeemer to those who are bought with a price. However, the whole tone and spirit of our Lord's friendship is such that the more closely we can imitate it the better. Such friendship as His should be reflected in a friendship most hearty and self-sacrificing on our part.

In this text from John 15, our Lord does not, I think, speak to us about His being our Friend, but about our being His friends. He is the Friend of sinners. But sinners are not His friends until their hearts are changed. He said, *"You are My friends if you do whatever I command you."* We are not His friends until then. His love for us is entirely of Himself, but friendship requires something from us. Friendship cannot be all on one side. One-sided friendship is more properly called mercy, grace, or benevolence. Friendship in its full sense is mutual. You may do all you please for a man and be perfectly benevolent, and yet he may give you nothing in return. However, real friendship can exist only where there is a response.

Therefore, we do not have before us the question as to whether Christ loves and pities us or not, for in another part of Scripture we read of *"His great love with which He loved us, even when we were dead in trespasses"* (Eph. 2:4–5). He befriended us when we were enemies, but that is not our subject right now. The question is about our being His friends, and this is what we must become if, indeed, there is to be any intimacy of mutual friendship. Friendship cannot be, as I have said, all on one side. It is like a pair of scales: there must be something to balance on the other side. There must be a return of kindly feeling from the person loved. Jesus tells us here that if we are to be His friends, we must do whatever He commands us, and in John 14:15, He says that we must do this out of love for Him.

Beloved, it is the highest honor in the world to be called the friend of Christ. Surely there is no title that excels in dignity what was worn by Abraham, who was called the *"friend of God"* (James 2:23). Lord Brooke was so delighted with the friendship of Sir Philip Sydney that he ordered nothing but this to be engraved on his tomb: "Here lies the friend of Sir Philip Sydney." There is beauty in such a feeling, but still it is a small matter compared with being able to say, "Here lives a friend of Christ." What wondrous condescension that He should call me "friend."

If I am indeed a true believer, not only is He my Friend, without whom I could have no hope here or hereafter, but He has, in the abundance of His grace, been pleased to regard me as His friend. He has been pleased to write down my name in the honored list of intimates who are permitted to speak familiarly with Him, as those do between whom there are no secrets. These intimate friends of Christ open their hearts completely to Him, while He hides nothing from them, saying, *"If it were not so, I would have told you"* (John 14:2).

Beloved, in what a light this sets obedience to Christ's commandments! I cannot help noticing how the doctrine of our text transforms obedience and makes it the joy and glory of life. How precious it is, for it is a better seal of friendship than the possession of the largest gifts and influence. Christ does not say, "You are My friends, if you rise to a position of respectability among men or honor in the church." No, however poor you may be—and those to whom He spoke these words were very poor—He says, *"You are My friends if you do whatever I command you."*

Obedience is better than wealth and better than rank. Jesus values His friends, not by what they have or what they wear, but by what they do. We may credit all of the eleven apostles with having remarkable qualifications for their lifework. Yet their Lord does not say, "You are My friends because I have qualified you for apostleship." Even to these leaders of His sacred flock Jesus says plainly, *"'You are My friends if you do whatever I command you.'* This is the point by which your friendship will be tested: If you are obedient, you are My friends."

He says neither less nor more to any of us today who aspire to the high dignity of being contained within the circle of His personal friendship. You must, my dear fellow believers, yield obedience to your Master and Lord and be eager to do it, or you are not His intimate friends. This is the one essential, which grace alone can give us. Do we rebel against the request? Far from it; our joy and delight lie in bearing our Beloved's easy yoke.

What Kind of Obedience?

Let us look at the subject more closely. Notice that our Lord Himself tells us what obedience He requests from those who call themselves His friends. True friends are eager to know what they can do to please the objects of their love. Let us gladly listen to what our Lord, who is worthy of adoration, speaks to the select circle of His chosen. He asks this of one and all: obedience.

None of us is exempted from doing His commandments. However lofty or however lowly your condition, you must obey. If you have only one talent, you must obey; if you have ten, you must still obey. There can be no friendship with Christ unless we are willing, each one of us, to give Him hearty, loyal service.

Let this thought penetrate the hearts of all upon whom the name of Jesus Christ is named: If you are enrolled among the friends of Jesus, you must be careful about your own personal obedience to His blessed will. Do not forget that even to the "queen," standing on His right *"in gold from Ophir"* (Ps. 45:9), the word is given, *"He is your Lord, worship Him"* (v. 11).

Active Obedience

Also, notice that it must be active obedience. *"If you do."* Some people think it is quite sufficient if they avoid what He forbids. Abstinence from evil is a great part of righteousness, but it is not enough for friendship. If a man can say, "I am not a drunkard, I am not dishonest, I am not unchaste, I am not a violator of the Sabbath, I am not a liar," so far so good, but such righteousness does not exceed that of the scribes and Pharisees, and they cannot enter the kingdom. It is well if you do not willfully transgress, but if you are to be Christ's friends, there must be far more than this. A person would be a poor friend if he only said, "I am your friend, and to prove it, I don't insult you, I don't rob you, I don't speak evil of you." Surely there must be more positive evidence to certify friendship.

The Lord Jesus Christ puts great stress on positive duties. At the Last Day He will say, *"I was hungry and you gave Me food; I was thirsty and you gave Me drink"* (Matt. 25:35). In that memorable twenty-fifth chapter of Matthew, nothing is said about negative virtues, but positive actions are cited and dwelt on in detail. There is an old English saying, "He is my friend who grinds at my mill." That is to say, friendship shows itself in doing helpful acts that prove sincerity. Fine words are mere wind and have no value, if they are not backed up with substantial deeds of kindness. Friendship cannot live on windy talk; it needs matter-of-fact bread. The inspired Word says, "Show me proof of your love; show it by doing whatever I command you."

Continuous Obedience

In addition, it is clear, from the wording of the text, that the obedience Christ expects from us is continuous. He does not say, "If you sometimes do what I command you—if you do it on Sundays, for instance—if you do what I command you in your place of worship, that will suffice." No, we are to abide in Him and keep His statutes even to the end.

I am not now teaching works as the way of salvation but as the evidence of fellowship, which is quite another thing. We must seek, in every place, at all times, and under all circumstances, to do as Jesus commands us out of a cheerful spirit of reverence toward Him. Such tender, loving subjection, as a godly wife gives to her husband, must be gladly yielded by us throughout life if we are His friends.

Universal Obedience

This obedience must also be universal. *"Whatever I command you."* No sooner is anything discovered to be the subject of a command than the one who is a true friend of Christ says, "I will do it," and he does it. He does not pick and choose which precept he will keep and which he will neglect, for this is self-will and not obedience.

I have known some people who have professed faith in Christ to err greatly in this matter. They have been very strict over one point, and they have blamed everybody who did not come up to their strictness, talking as if that one duty fulfilled the whole law. "Straining at gnats," about which Jesus warned the scribes and Pharisees in the twenty-third chapter of Matthew, has been a preoccupation with many. They have bought a choice assortment of strainers of the very finest net to get out all the gnats from their cup, but the next day they have opened their mouths and swallowed a camel without a qualm. This will not do. The test is, *"Whatever I command you."*

I do not mean that little things are unimportant; far from it. If there is a gnat that Christ commands you to strain at, strain it out with great diligence. Do not let even a flea escape you if He commands you to remove it. The smallest command of Christ may often be the most important, and I will tell you why. Some things are great, obviously great, and for many reasons even a hypocritical person who professes to believe in Christ will attend to them. However, the test may lie in the minor points, which hypocrites do not take the trouble to notice, since no human tongue would praise them for doing them.

Here is the proof of your love: Will you do the smaller thing for Jesus, as well as the weightier matter? Too many say, "I do not see any use in it; I can be saved without it; there are a great many different opinions on the point," and so on. All this comes of evil and is not consistent with the spirit of friendship with Christ, for love pleases even in trifles. Is it Christ's will? Is it plainly a precept of His Word? Then it is not yours to reason why or to raise any question.

The reality of your subjection to your Lord and Master may hinge on those seemingly insignificant points. A domestic servant might place the breakfast on the table and feel that she had done her duty. But if her mistress had told her to place the salt on the table, and she had not done so, she would be asked the cause of her neglect. Suppose she replied to her mistress, "I did not think it was necessary. I placed the breakfast before you, but a little salt was too trifling a matter for me to worry about." Her mistress might answer, "But I told you to be sure to put out the salt. Mind you do so tomorrow." The next morning there is no salt, and the maid says that she did not see the use of setting it on the table. Her mistress is displeased and tells her that her wish must be carried out. Will she not be a very foolish and troublesome girl if she refuses to do so because she does not see the use of it? I think it is likely that the young woman would have to find other employment before long, for such conduct is very annoying.

It is the same way with those who profess to have faith but say, "I have attended to the main things, and what I neglect is quite a minor matter." Such are not even good servants; friends they can never be. I implore you, dear believers, strive for universal obedience. *"Whatever He says to you, do it"* (John 2:5). Only by an earnest endeavor to carry out all of His will can you live in happy fellowship with Him, and indeed be His friends.

Obedience As unto the Lord

Note well that this obedience is to be rendered as if it is to Christ Himself. Put the emphasis on the little word *I:* *"You are My friends if you do whatever I command you."* We are to do these things because Jesus commands them. Does not the royal person of our Lord cast a very strong light on the necessity of obedience? When we refuse to obey, we refuse to do what the Lord Himself commands. When the Lord Jesus Christ, the Son of God and our Redeemer, is denied obedience, it is treason. How can rebels against the King be His Majesty's friends? The precepts of Scripture are not the commandments of man or the ordinances of angels. They are the laws of Christ, and how dare we despise them? We are to act justly because Jesus commands us to and because we love to do His pleasure. There can be no friendship without this. Oh, for grace to *"serve the LORD with gladness"* (Ps. 100:2).

Willing Obedience

Moreover, it appears that our Lord wants us to obey Him out of a friendly spirit. To obey Christ as if we were forced to do it under penalty would be of no worth as a proof of friendship. Everyone can see that. He does not speak of slaves but of friends. He does not want us to perform duties out of fear of punishment or love of reward. What He can accept from His friends must be the fruit of love. His will must be our law because His person is our delight. Some professed believers need to be whipped to their duties. They must hear stirring sermons, attend exciting meetings, and live under pressure. But those who are Christ's friends do not need any spur except love. *"The love of Christ compels us"* (2 Cor. 5:14). True hearts do what Jesus asks them to do without having to be flogged and dogged, urged and forced. Coerced virtue is spoiled in the making, as many pieces of earthenware are cracked in the baking. The wine of our obedience must flow freely from the ripe cluster of the soul's love, or it will not be fit for the royal cup. When duty becomes delight and precepts are as sweet as promises, then we are Christ's friends, and not until then.

Those Who Disobey Are Not His Friends

Next, our Lord leads us to conclude from this verse that those who do not obey Him are not His friends. He may still look upon them and be their Friend by changing their hearts and forgiving their sins, but as yet they are not friends of His. A person who does not obey Christ does not give the Savior His proper place, and this is an unfriendly deed. If I have a friend, I am very careful that, if he has honor anywhere, he will certainly have due respect from me. If he is my superior, I am concerned that he should not think that I am intrusive, or imagine that I would take undue advantage of his kindness. My esteem for him will be higher than anyone else's esteem for him. He who is truly Christ's friend delights to honor Him as a great King, but he who will not yield to Him His sovereign rights is a traitor and not a friend.

Our Lord is the *"head over all things to the church"* (Eph. 1:22), and this involves the joyful submission of the members. Disobedience denies to Christ the dignity of that holy headship that is His prerogative over all the members of the body of Christ, and this is not the part of a true friend. How can you be His friend if you will not allow His rule? It is vain to boast that you trust His Cross if you do not reverence His crown.

The person who does not obey Christ's commandments cannot be His friend, because he is not of one mind with Christ—that is evident. *"Can two walk together, unless they are agreed?"* (Amos

3:3). True friendship does not exist between those who differ on first principles. There can be no points of agreement between Jesus Christ and the person who will not obey Him, for he in fact is saying, "Lord Jesus, your pure and holy will is obnoxious to me; your sweet and gracious commands are weariness to me." What friendship can there be here? They are not of one mind. Christ is for holiness; this person is for sin. Christ is for spiritual-mindedness; this person is carnally minded. Christ is for love; this person is for self. Christ is for glorifying the Father; this person is for honoring himself. How can there be any friendship when they are diametrically opposed in design, purpose, and spirit? It is not possible.

The person who does not obey Christ cannot be Christ's friend, though he may profess to be. He may claim to be a Christian in a very self-righteous and loud manner, and for that reason he may be all the more an enemy of the Cross. When others see this man walking according to his own lusts, they cry out, *"You also were with Jesus of Nazareth"* (Mark 14:67), and they attribute all his faults to his religion and immediately begin to blaspheme the name of Christ. Our Lord's cause is hindered more by the inconsistent conduct of His professed friends than by anything else.

Suppose you and I had some very close associate who was found drunk in the street or committing burglary or theft—should we not feel disgraced by his conduct? When he is brought before the magistrate, would you like to have it said that this person is your close friend? No, you would cover your face and beg your neighbors never to mention it. For such a person to be known as your friend would compromise your name and character. I say this even weeping, that Jesus Christ's name is compromised and His honor is tarnished among men by many who wear the name of Christian without having the Spirit of Christ. People like this cannot be His dear companions.

The number of wounds that Jesus has received in the house of His friends is grievous. When Caesar fell, he was slain by the daggers of his friends! In trust he found treason. Those whose lives he had spared did not spare his life. Woe to those who, under the appearance of Christianity, *"crucify again for themselves the Son of God, and put Him to an open shame"* (Heb. 6:6). Nothing burns Christ's cheek like a Judas kiss, and He has had many of them.

Those who do not obey Jesus cannot be owned by Him as His friends, for that would dishonor Him indeed. There was a time—I do not know how it is now—when if any man wanted to be made a count or to get an honorable title, he only had to pay a certain amount at Rome into the papal treasury, and he could be made a noble at once. The titles thus purchased were honorable neither to those who gave nor to those who received them. Whatever His alleged clergy may do, our Lord Himself sells no dignities. The title of "friend of Jesus" is bestowed on those of a certain character, and it cannot be otherwise obtained. His friends are those who obey Him. He grants this title of nobility to all believers who lovingly follow Him, but on His list of friends He enters no others.

Do you not see that His honor requires this? Would you have our Lord stand up and say, "The drunkard is My friend"? Would you want to hear Him say, "That fraudulent bankrupt is My close companion"? Would you want Jesus to claim friendly companionship with the vicious and profane? A man is known by the company he keeps. What would be thought of Jesus if His intimate associates were people of loose morals and unrighteous principles? To go among them for their good is one thing; to make them His friends is another. Where there is no kinship, no likeness, no point of agreement, the fair flower of friendship cannot take root. We may, therefore, also correctly read the text as, "You are not My friends, if you do not do the things that I command you."

Being on Best Terms with Christ

In addition, those who obey Christ best are on the best of terms with Him. "You are My friends," He seems to say, "and you live near Me, enjoying practical, personal friendship and daily communion with Me when you promptly obey." Some of you know by personal experience that we cannot walk in holy relationship with Christ unless we keep His commandments. There is no feeling of communion between our souls and Christ when we are conscious of having done wrong and yet are not sorry for it.

If we know that we have erred, as we often do, if our hearts break because we have grieved our Beloved, and if we go and tell Him our grief and confess our sin, we are still His friends. He kisses away our tears, saying, "I know your weaknesses—I willingly blot out your offenses. There is no breach of friendship between us; I will manifest Myself to you still." However, when we know that we are wrong and feel no softening of heart about it, then we cannot pray, we cannot speak with the Beloved, and we cannot walk with Him as His friends. Familiarity with Jesus ceases when we become familiar with known sin. If, again, we know that something is wrong, and we persevere in it, there cannot be any happy friendship between us and our Savior.

If conscience has told you, dear believer, that a certain thing ought to be given up but you continue in it, the next time you are on your knees to pray, you will feel greatly hampered. When you sit down before your Bible and hope to have communion with Christ as you have formerly enjoyed it, you will find that He has withdrawn Himself and will not be found by you. Is it any wonder? If *"sin lies at the door"* (Gen. 4:7), how can the Lord smile on us? Secret sin will poison communion at the fountainhead. If there is a quarrel between you and Christ and you are hugging closely what He abhors, how can you enjoy friendship? He tells you that sin is a viper that will kill you, but you reply, "It is a necklace of jewels," and you put it around your neck. Do you wonder that because He loves you He is grieved at such mad behavior? Oh, do not bring injury on yourself in this way. Do not pour contempt on His wise commands in this manner.

Some Christians will never get into full fellowship with Christ because they neglect to study His Word and search out what His will is. It ought to be a serious work with every Christian, especially in the beginning of his spiritual walk, to discover what the will of his Lord is on all subjects. Half the Christian people in the world are content to ask, What is the rule of our church? That is not the question. The point is, What is the rule of Christ? Some plead, "My father and mother before me did so." I sympathize to a degree with that feeling. Filial reverence commands admiration. Yet in spiritual things, we are not to *"call anyone on earth...father"* (Matt. 23:9), but are to make the Lord Jesus our Master and exemplar. God has not placed your conscience in your mother's keeping, nor has He committed to your father the right or the power to stand responsible for you. Everyone must *"bear his own load"* (Gal. 6:5) and *"give account of himself to God"* (Rom. 14:12).

Search the Scriptures for yourself, and follow no rule but what is inspired. Take your light directly from the Sun. Let Holy Scripture be your unquestioned rule of faith and practice. If there is any point about which you are uncertain, I charge you, by your loyalty to Christ, if you are His friend, to try to find out what His will is. Once you are sure on that point, never mind the human authorities or dignities who oppose His law. Let there be no question, no hesitation, no delay. If He commands you, carry out His will, though the gates of hell thunder at you.

You are not His friend, or, at any rate, you are not the kind of friend who could enjoy the friendship, unless you resolutely seek to please Him in all things. The intimacy between you and Christ will be disturbed by sin. You cannot lean your head on His chest, as the Beloved Apostle did (see John 13:23), and say, "Lord, I know Your will, but I do not intend to do it." Could you look up into that dear face—that countenance once so marred, now lovelier than heaven itself—and say, "My Lord, I love You, but I will not do Your will completely"? By the very love He has for you, He will chasten you for that rebellious spirit if you indulge it. It is a horrible evil; holy eyes will not endure it. He *"is a jealous God"* (Exod. 34:14) and will not tolerate sin, which is His rival.

"You are My friends if you do whatever I command you." Oh, beloved, see to this! Under all the crosses and losses and trials of life, there is no comfort more desirable than the confidence that you have aimed at doing your Lord's will. If a man suffers for Christ's sake while steadily pursuing the course of holiness, he may rejoice in such suffering. Losses borne in the defense of the right and the true are gains. Jesus is never nearer to His friends than when they bravely bear shame for His sake. If we get into trouble by our own folly, we feel the stinging pain in the deepest part of our hearts. However, if we are wounded in our Lord's battles, the scars are honorable. For His sake we may accept reproach and wear it as a wreath of honor. Jesus delights to be the companion of a person who is cast out by relatives and acquaintances for the truth's sake and for fidelity to His Cross. They may call the faithful one a fanatic and an enthusiast and all such ill-sounding names, but there is no need to fret over these things, for the honor of being Christ's friend infinitely outweighs the world's opinion. When we follow the Lamb wherever He goes, He is responsible for the results, not us.

> Though dark be my way,
> Since He is my guide,
> 'Tis mine to obey,
> 'Tis His to provide.

The consequences that follow when we do right belong to God. Abhor the theory that for the sake of a great good you may do a little wrong. I have heard men say, and Christian men, too, "If I were to follow my convictions strictly, I would have to leave a position of great usefulness; therefore, I remain where I am and quiet my conscience as well as I can. I would lose opportunities of doing good, which I now possess, if I were to put into practice all I believe; therefore, I remain in a position that I could not justify on any other ground."

Is this attitude according to the mind of Jesus? Is this your kindness to your Friend? How many bow in the house of Rimmon and hope that the Lord will have mercy on His servants in this thing? (See 2 Kings 5:18.) We will see if it will be so. We may not *"do evil that good may come"* (Rom. 3:8). If I knew that to do right would shake the whole island of Great Britain, I would be bound to do it. God helping me, I would do it. However, if I heard that a wrong act would apparently bless the whole nation, I would have no right to do wrong on that account. No bribe of supposed usefulness should purchase our conscience. Right is right, and must always end in blessing; wrong is wrong, and must always end in condemnation, though for a while it may wear the appearance of surpassing good.

Did not the Devil lead our first parents astray by the suggestion that great benefit would arise out of their transgression? *"Your eyes will be opened, and you will be like God"* (Gen. 3:5), said the Deceiver. Would it not be a sublime thing for men to grow to be gods? I can imagine Eve saying, "Certainly, I would not lose the opportunity. The race that is yet to be would blame me if I did. I would not want men to remain inferior creatures through my neglect." For the sake of the promised good she ventured upon evil. Thousands of people sin because it seems so advantageous, so wise, so necessary, so sure to turn out well. Hear what Christ says: *"You are My friends if you do whatever I command you."* If you do evil so that good may come, you cannot walk with Him, but if your heart is set on keeping His words, you will find Him loving you and making His home with you (John 14:23).

Obedience Shows Our Friendship with Christ

Now, by our text we are also taught that the friendliest action a person can do for Jesus is to obey Him. Rich men have thought they were doing the friendliest act possible toward Christ by giving immense sums to build churches or to found orphanages or hospitals. If they are believers and have done these things as acts of obedience to Christ's law of stewardship, they have done well—and the more of such generosity the better—but where splendid charitable donations are given out of ostentation or from the idea that some merit will be gained by the consecration of a large amount of wealth, the whole business is unacceptable. *"If a man would give for love all the wealth of his house, it would be utterly despised"* (Song 8:7). Jesus does not ask for lavish expenditure. He asks us to give ourselves to Him. He has made this the token of true love: *"If you do whatever I command you."*

"To obey is better than sacrifice, and to heed than the fat of rams" (1 Sam. 15:22). However much we are able to give, we are obligated to give it, and we should give it cheerfully. But if we suppose that any amount of giving can serve as a substitute for personal obedience, we are greatly mistaken. To bring our wealth and not yield our hearts is to give the box and steal the jewel. How dare we bring our sacrifice in a leprous hand? We ourselves must be cleansed in the atoning blood before we can be accepted, and our hearts must be changed before our offering can be pure in God's sight.

Others have imagined that they could show their friendliness to Christ by some remarkable action of self-mortification. Among Roman Catholics, especially in the old days, it was believed that misery and merit went together, and so men tortured themselves so that they might please God. They went for many days without washing themselves or their clothes; they mistakenly believed that, in this way, they acquired the odor of sanctity. I do not believe that Jesus thinks a person is any more His friend because he is dirty.

Some put on hair shirts, which made raw wounds. I do not think that the kindly Lord Jesus counts this as a friendly act. Ask any humane person whether he would be gratified by knowing that a friend wore a hair shirt for his sake, and he would answer, "Please let the poor creature wear whatever is most comfortable for him, and that will please me best."

The loving Jesus does not take delight in pain and discomfort; forcing one's body to waste away is no doctrine of His. John the Baptist might have been an ascetic, but certainly Jesus was not. He came *"eating and drinking"* (Matt. 11:19), a man among men. He did not come to demand the rigors of a hermitage or a monastery, or else He never would have been seen at feasts. When we hear of the nuns of St. Ann sleeping bolt upright in their coffins, we take no particular satisfaction in their doing so; a kind heart would beg them to go to bed.

I went through a monastery some time ago, and over each bed was a little cat-o'-nine-tails, which I sincerely hope was used to the satisfaction of the possessor. However, I did not copy the idea and buy a couple for my sons. Neither have I sent one to each of my special friends, for I would never ask them to flog themselves as a proof of friendship. Our Lord cannot be gratified by self-inflicted, self-invented tortures. These things are man-made worship, which is no worship. You may fast forty days if you like, but you will gain no merit by it. Jesus Christ has not demanded this as the gauge of friendship, nor will He regard us as His friends for this. He says, *"You are My friends if you do whatever I command you,"* but He does not command you to starve or to wear sackcloth or to shut yourself up in a cell. Pride invents these things, but grace teaches obedience.

Certain people have thought it would be the noblest form of holy service to enter into a brotherhood or sisterhood. They imagined that they would be truly Christ's friends if they joined the "Society of Jesus." I have sometimes asked myself whether it might not be a good thing to form a league of Christian men, all banded together to live alone for Jesus and to give themselves up entirely and wholly to His work. But, assuredly, the formation of guilds, sisterhoods, or brotherhoods, other than the great brotherhood of the church of God, is something that was never contemplated in the New Testament. You will find no foreshadowing of Franciscans and Dominicans there. All godly women were sisters of mercy, and all Christlike men were of the society of Jesus, but we read nothing of monastic or conventual vows.

Anything that is not commanded in Scripture is superstition. We are to worship God according to His will, not according to our wills. Even if I were to consecrate myself entirely to what Roman Catholics called the religious life, by getting away from the associations of ordinary men and trying to spend my whole time in lonely contemplation, there still would be nothing in it, because the Lord Jesus never required it of me. The thing that He does ask is that we will do whatever He commands us.

Why is it that people try to do something that Christ never commanded? A schoolteacher will allow me to use his situation as an example. If he said to a boy in his class, "Now is the time for you to attend to arithmetic," and the boy instead starting practicing his penmanship, would the teacher not ask the boy if he had understood him? If, after a few minutes, he finds the boy writing, does he say, "You have written that line very well"? Not at all. It is a small matter whether the writing has been done well or badly, for to be writing at all when he had been instructed to do his arithmetic is an act of insubordination.

It is the same way with you and me. You and I may do something other than Christ's command, and do it splendidly well, and other people may say, "What pious people they are!" But if we do not do the Lord's will, we will not be His friends. We may wear sandals and coarse clothing and renounce boots and coats, but there is no grace in apparel. Excellence lies in doing what Christ has commanded.

Some people think that it is a very friendly act toward Christ to attend many religious services in a consecrated building. They are at morning prayer and evening worship and feasts and fasts without number. Some of us prefer to have our religious services each day in our own homes, and it will be a dreadful thing when family prayer is given up for public services. However, a number of people think very little of family worship; they think they must go to the church or to some other temple made with hands. But let no one dream he is made Jesus' friend in this way.

We are not to forsake *"the assembling of ourselves together, as is the manner of some"* (Heb. 10:25); it is good for you to meet with God's people as often as you can. Yet even though you may be multiplying your sacraments and increasing your ceremonies, and may be busy with this service and the other service until your heart is worn away with grinding at the mill of outward religion, you are Christ's friends only if you do whatever He commands you. That is a better test than early communion or daily mass.

It comes to this, dear friends: we must steadily, carefully, persistently, and cheerfully do the will of God from the heart in daily life, from our first waking moment until our eyes are closed. Ask concerning everything, What would Jesus have me do about this? What is the teaching of Christ regarding this? For, *"whether you eat or drink, or whatever you do, do all to the glory of God"* (1 Cor. 10:31), and *"whatever you do in word or deed, do all in the name of the Lord Jesus, giving thanks to God the Father through Him"* (Col. 3:17).

You may be a domestic servant and may never be able to give a dollar to church work, but you are Jesus' friend if you do whatever He commands you. You may be a housewife and may not be able to do anything outside of the little family that requires all your attention, but if you are fulfilling your duty to your children, doing what Christ commands you, you are among the friends of Jesus. You may be only a plain workingman or a tradesman with a small shop; you may not be well known; but if you set an example of honesty, uprightness, and piety, doing all things as if you were doing them for Christ because He has saved you, He will call you His friend. What title of nobility can equal this? Friendship with Christ is worth a thousand dukedoms.

Live As If Jesus Were Always Present

The practical outcome of all of this is that we must examine every question regarding duty by the light of the following: Will this be a friendly action toward Christ? If I do this, will I act as Christ's friend? Will my conduct honor Him? Then I am glad. If it will dishonor Him, I will have nothing to do with it. Set each distinct action, as far as you are able, on this scale, and let this be the weight: Is it a friendly action toward my Redeemer?

I wish that we all lived as if Jesus were always present, as if we could see His wounds and gaze into His beautiful countenance. Suppose that tomorrow you are brought into temptation by being asked to do something questionable. Decide what to do in this way: If Jesus could come in at that moment and show you His hands and His feet, how would you act in His sight? Behave as you would act under the realized presence of the Well Beloved. You would not do anything unkind to Him, would you? Certainly you would not do anything to grieve Him if you saw Him before your eyes. Well, keep Him always before you. The psalmist cried, *"I have set the* LORD *always before me"* (Ps. 16:8).

You will need much of the Holy Spirit's anointing to do this. May God give it to you. Live, dear friend, as if Christ would come at once and detect you in the very act. Do only what you would not be ashamed of if, in the next instant, you should see the Lord sitting on the throne of His glory and calling you before His court. If you live in this way, you will delight in an abundance of peace.

> So shall your walk be close with God,
> Calm and serene your frame;
> So purer light shall mark the road
> That leads you to the Lamb.

Obedience will delight you with the blissful presence of your Lord, and in that presence you will find *"fullness of joy"* (Ps. 16:11). You will be the envy of all wise men, for you will be the beloved of the Lord. Your pathway, if it is not always smooth, will be always safe, for Jesus never leaves His friend, and He will never leave you, but will be *"with you always, even to the end of the age"* (Matt. 28:20). May this happy condition be yours and mine.

Chapter 6

The Man Who Will Never See Death

"Most assuredly, I say to you, if anyone keeps My word he shall never see death." Then the Jews said to Him, "Now we know that You have a demon! Abraham is dead, and the prophets; and You say, 'If anyone keeps My word he shall never taste death.' Are You greater than our father Abraham, who is dead? And the prophets are dead. Whom do You make Yourself out to be?"
—John 8:51–53

In the eighth chapter of John, prior to the above passage, we hear the Jews, with malicious voices, assailing our blessed Lord with this bitter question: *"Do we not say rightly that You are a Samaritan and have a demon?"* (John 8:48). How very quietly the Savior answers them! He answers them because He judges that it is necessary to do so. But He does so with great patience and with sound argument: *"I do not have a demon, but I honor My Father"* (v. 49). This is clear proof! No man can be said to have a demon who honors God, for the evil spirit from the beginning has been the enemy of all that glorifies the Father.

Paul, who had not read this passage—for the gospel of John had not yet been written—was nevertheless so filled with his Master's Spirit that he answered in a similar manner when Festus said, *"Paul, you are beside yourself! Much learning is driving you mad!"* (Acts 26:24). He calmly replied, *"I am not mad, most noble Festus, but speak the words of truth and reason"* (v. 25). This was a fine example of our Savior's gentle and forcible reply: *"I do not have a demon, but I honor My Father."*

My friends, whenever you are falsely accused and an evil name is hurled at you, if you must reply, give a *"reason for the hope that is in you, with meekness and fear"* (1 Pet. 3:15). Do not become heated and hurried, for if you do, you will lose strength and will be apt to err. Let your Lord be your model.

The false charge was the occasion of our Lord's utterance of a great truth. The Jews rush on, furious in their rage, but He flashes in their faces the light of truth. To put down error, lift up truth. Thus, their deadly saying was met by a living saying: *"Most assuredly, I say to you, if anyone keeps My word he shall never see death."* Nothing baffles the adversaries of the faith as much as uttering the truth of God with unshakable confidence.

The truth that Jesus stated was full of promise; and if they willfully rejected His promise, it became worse to them than a threat. Christ's rejected promises curdle into woes. If these men, when He said to them, *"If anyone keeps My word he shall never see death,"* still went on reviling Him, then their consciences, when afterward awakened, would have said to them, *"He who does not believe the Son shall not see life, but the wrath of God abides on him"* (John 3:36). If the believer will never see death, then the unbeliever will never see life. Thus the Gospel itself becomes *"the aroma of death leading to death"* (2 Cor. 2:16) to those who refuse it, and the very Word that proclaims eternal life threatens eternal death to the willfully unbelieving.

I pray that we may be put into a frame of mind renewed by grace and may be so helped to keep Christ's commands that we may inherit this wondrous promise: *"If anyone keeps My word he shall never see death."* To this end, may the Holy Spirit especially aid me as I first describe the characteristics of the grace-filled believer, the person who keeps Christ's saying. Next, I will dwell on the glorious deliverance of the believer: he will never see death. And then I want to honor the great Quickener. Evidently, according to the Jews in this text, our Lord was making much of Himself by what He said, and, in truth, the fact that the believer will never see death does greatly magnify the Lord Jesus.

Characteristics of Christlike Believers

Consider the characteristics of the grace-filled believer: *"If anyone keeps My word he shall never see death."* Observe that the one conspicuous characteristic of the person who will never see death is that he keeps Christ's saying, or His word. He may have other characteristics, but they are comparatively unimportant in this respect. He may have a timid nature, he may often be in distress, but if he keeps Christ's saying, he will never see death. He may have been a great sinner in his early life, but because he has been converted and led to keep Christ's saying, he will never see death. He may be a strong-minded person, who keeps a firm grip of eternal realities and therefore is supremely useful, but this promise is none the more true for him, even so. The reason for his safety is the same as it is with the weak and timid person: he keeps Christ's saying; therefore, he will never see death. Divest yourself, therefore, of all inquiries about other matters, and only examine your own heart on this one point: Do you keep Christ's saying? If you do this, you will never see death.

What kind of person keeps Christ's saying? Obviously, he is a person who has a close relationship with Christ. He hears what He says; he notes what He says; he clings to what He says. We meet people nowadays who talk about faith in God, but they do not know the Lord Jesus Christ as the great Sacrifice and Reconciler. Yet without a mediator, there is no coming to God.

Jesus says, *"No one comes to the Father except through Me"* (John 14:6). His witness is true. Beloved, we glorify Christ as God Himself. Truly, we never doubt the unity of the Godhead, but while *"there is one God...*[there is also] *one Mediator between God and men, the Man Christ Jesus"* (1 Tim. 2:5). Forever remember that Christ Jesus, as God-man, as Mediator, is essential to all our communion with the Father. You cannot trust God or love God or serve God in the right way unless you willingly consent to His appointed way of reconciliation, redemption, justification, and access, which is only through the precious blood of Jesus Christ. In Christ we draw near to God. Do not attempt to approach Jehovah, who is *"a consuming fire"* (Heb. 12:29), except through the incarnate God. Tell me, my reader, is your faith fixed on Jesus, whom God has set forth to be the reconciliation for sin? Do you come to God in the way that He has provided? He will not receive you in any other way. If you reject the way of salvation through the blood of the Lamb, you cannot be keeping the saying of Christ. He says, *"He who has seen Me has seen the Father"* (John 14:9), and He says this of no one else.

Next, the person who keeps Christ's saying, making the Lord Jesus his all in all, reverences His Word and keeps it; he respects, observes, trusts, and obeys it. Keeping His saying means, first, that he accepts His doctrine. Whatever Christ has laid down as truth is truth to him.

My reader, is it so with you? Some people's own thoughts are the chief source of their belief. They judge the divine revelation itself and claim the right not only to interpret it, but also to correct and expand it. In the fullness of self-confidence, they make themselves the judges of God's Word. They believe a doctrine because the light of the present age confirms it or invents it. Their foundation is in man's own thought. In their opinion, parts of Scripture are exceedingly faulty and need tinkering with scientific tools. To them, the light of the Holy Spirit is a mere glowworm compared to the light of the present advanced age.

But the person who is to share in the promise now before us is one who believes the Savior's word because it is His word. He takes the sayings of Christ and His inspired apostles as truth, because he believes in the One who spoke them. To him the inspiration of the Holy Spirit is the warrant of faith. This is a very important matter. The foundation of our faith is even more important than the superstructure. Unless you ground your faith on the fact that the Lord has spoken, your faith lacks that worshipful reverence that God requires. Even if you are correct in your beliefs, you are not correct in your spirit unless your faith is grounded on the authority of God's Word. We are to be disciples, not critics. We are through with quibbling, for we have come to believing.

Next, the grace-filled believer trusts Christ's promises. This is a crucial point. Without trust in Jesus we have no spiritual life. Tell me, my reader, do you rely on this saying of the Lord Jesus, *"Most assuredly, I say to you, he who believes in Me has everlasting life"* (John 6:47)? (Do you believe in the promise of pardon to the person who confesses and forsakes his sin—pardon through the precious blood of the great Sacrifice? Are the promises of Christ certainties to you, certainties hallmarked with His sacred, *"Most assuredly, I say to you"*? Can you hang your soul on the sure nail of the Lord's saying? Some of us rest our eternal destiny solely on the truthfulness of Christ. When we take all His promises together, what a fullness of confidence they create in us!

How firm a foundation, you saints of the Lord,
Is laid for your faith in His excellent word!

Furthermore, the grace-filled believer obeys His precepts. No person can be said to be keeping Christ's commands unless he follows them, in practical ways, in his life. Jesus is not only Teacher, but Lord to us. A true keeper of the Word cultivates the spirit of love that is the very essence of Christ's moral teaching. He endeavors to be meek and merciful. He aims at purity of heart and peaceableness of spirit. He follows after holiness, even at the cost of persecution. Whatever he finds that his Lord has ordained, he cheerfully performs. He does not rebel against the Lord's command, thinking that it involves too much self-denial and separation from the world, but he is willing to *"enter by the narrow gate"* (Matt. 7:13) and to follow the *"narrow...way"* (v. 14 KJV) because his Lord commands him. Faith that does not lead to obedience is a dead faith and a false faith. Faith that does not cause us to forsake sin is no better than the faith of devils, even if it is very good faith.

> Faith must obey its Father's will,
> As well as trust His grace:
> A pardoning God is jealous still
> For His own holiness.

Now you see what kind of person keeps Christ's words. The person who obeys Jesus' commands receives, through the Word of God, a new and everlasting life, for the Word of God is a living and incorruptible seed, *"which lives and abides forever"* (1 Pet. 1:23). Wherever the seed of the Word drops into soil that accepts it, it takes root, grows, and bears fruit. *"For God so loved the world that He gave His only begotten Son, that whoever believes in Him should not perish but have everlasting life"* (John 3:16). It is by Christ's sayings, or by the Word of God, that life is implanted in the soul. By that same Word the heavenly life is fed, increased, developed, and, at length, perfected. The power and energy of the Holy Spirit, which work through the Word, are used as the beginning, the sustaining, and the perfecting of the inner life. The life of grace on earth is the blossom, and the life of glory is the fruit. It is the same life all along, from regeneration to resurrection. The life that comes into the soul of the believer when he begins to keep Christ's sayings is the same life that he will enjoy before the eternal throne in the realms of the blessed.

We may know what it means to keep Christ's commands from the fact that He Himself has set us the example. Note well this verse, where Jesus says concerning the Father, *"Yet you have not known Him, but I know Him. And if I say, 'I do not know Him,' I shall be a liar like you; but I do know Him and keep His word"* (John 8:55).

We are to keep our Lord's sayings, even as He kept His Father's sayings. He lived on the Father's Word, and therefore refused Satan's temptation to turn stones into bread. His Father's Word was in

Him so that He always did the things that pleased the Father. When He spoke, He did not speak His own words, but the words of Him who sent Him (John 14:10). He lived so that the divine Word might be carried out completely; even on the cross He took care to make sure that the Scripture was fulfilled. (See John 19:28.)

He said, *"He who is of God hears God's words"* (John 8:47), and *"He who has ears to hear, let him hear!"* (Mark 4:9). God's Word was everything to Him, and He rejoiced over His apostles, because He could say of them, *"They have kept Your word"* (John 17:6). He, whose words you are to keep, showed you how to keep them. Live toward Him as He lived toward the Father. Then you will receive the promise He has made: *"Most assuredly, I say to you, if anyone keeps My word he shall never see death."*

The Glorious Deliverance

Now we turn to the delightful part of our subject, namely, the glorious deliverance that our Lord promises: *"He shall never see death."* Our Lord did not mean that the believer will never die, for He Himself died, and His followers, in long procession, have descended to the grave. Some Christians are comforted by the belief that they will live until the Lord comes and that therefore they will not *"sleep,"* but will only be *"changed"* (1 Cor. 15:51). The hope of our Lord's appearing is a very blessed one, come when He may. However, I do not think that to be alive at His coming is any great object of desire. Is there any real preference in being changed over dying? Do we not read that *"we who are alive and remain until the coming of the Lord will by no means precede those who are asleep"* (1 Thess. 4:15)? This is a great truth. Throughout eternity, if I die, I will be able to say that I had actual fellowship with Christ in the matter of death and descent into the grave, which those happy saints who will survive will never know. It is not a matter of doctrine, but still, if one could have a choice in the matter, it might be gain to die (Phil. 1:21).

> The graves of all His saints He bless'd,
> And soften'd every bed:
> Where should the dying members rest,
> But with the dying Head?

How dear will Christ be to us when, in the ages to come, we will think of His death and will be able to say, "We, too, have died and risen again"! At His coming, you who are alive and remain will certainly not have preference over us, who, like our Lord, will taste death. I am only speaking now of a matter of no great importance, which, as believers, we may use as a pleasant subject of discourse among ourselves. Our Lord has said, *"If anyone keeps My word he shall never see death."* This does not mean the few who will remain at His second advent, but to the entire company of those who have kept His Word, even though they have passed into the grave.

We Will Never See Death

What does this promise mean, then? To begin with, it means that our faces are turned away from death. Suppose that here I am, a poor sinner, convinced of sin, and aroused to a fear of wrath. What is there before my face? On what am I compelled to gaze? The meaning of the original Greek verb is not fully interpreted by the word *see* in *"never see death"*: it is a more intense word. According to a noted biblical scholar, the sight mentioned here is that of "a long, steady, exhaustive vision, whereby we become slowly acquainted with the nature of the object to which our vision is directed." The awakened sinner is made to look at eternal death, which is the threatened punishment of sin. He stands gazing on the result of sin with terror and dismay. Oh, the wrath to come! The death that never dies! While I am still unforgiven, I cannot help gazing on it and foreseeing it as my doom.

When the Gospel of the Lord Jesus comes to my soul and I keep His sayings by faith, I am turned completely around. My back is to death, and my face is toward life eternal. Death is removed, life is received, and more life is promised. What do I see within, around, and before me? Why, life, and only life—life in Christ Jesus, *"who is our life"* (Col. 3:4). In my future course on earth, what do I see? Final falling from grace? By no means, for Jesus said, *"I give them* [My sheep] *eternal life"* (John 10:28). What do I see far away in the eternities? Unending life. *"He who believes in Me has everlasting life"* (John 6:47). Now I begin to realize the meaning of the verses, *"I am the resurrection and the life. He who believes in Me, though he may die, he shall live"* (John 11:25), and *"Whoever lives and believes in Me shall never die"* (v. 26).

The person who has received the words of the Lord Jesus *"shall not come into judgment, but has passed from death into life"* (John 5:24). Consequently, he will never gaze on death. All that lies before the believer is life: *"life...more abundantly"* (John 10:10), life to the full, life eternal (John 17:3). What has become of our death? Our Lord endured it. He died for us. "[He] *Himself bore our sins in His own body on the tree"* (1 Pet. 2:24). In His death, with Him as our representative, we died. There is no death penalty left for the believer, for the least charge cannot be brought against those for whom Christ has died (Rom. 8:33). Therefore, we sing:

> Complete atonement Thou hast made,
> And to the utmost farthing paid
> Whate'er Thy people owed:
> Nor can His wrath on me take place,
> If shelter'd in Thy righteousness,
> And sprinkled with Thy blood.

Shall we die, for whom Christ died in the purpose of God? Can our departure out of the world be sent as a punishment, when our Lord Jesus has so vindicated justice that no punishment is required? When I see my Lord die on the cross, I see that for me death itself is dead.

Free Forever from Spiritual Death

Then there is another meaning to the verse. *"If anyone keeps My word he shall never see death"* means that the person's spiritual death is gone, never to return. Before he knows Christ, he remains in death, and wherever he looks, he sees nothing but death.

Poor souls! You know what I am talking about, you who are anxious about your souls, for you try to pray and find death in your prayers; you try to believe but seem dead regarding faith. I pity you ungodly ones! Although you do not know it, death is everywhere within you. You are *"dead in trespasses and sins"* (Eph. 2:1). Your sins are to you what grave clothes are to a corpse. They seem to be your natural covering; they cling to you; they bind you. Little do you know what corruption is coming upon you, so that God Himself will say of you, "Bury the dead out of my sight."

Yet just as soon as the Gospel of the Lord Jesus comes to a man with power, what is the effect? He is dead no longer; he begins to see life. It may be that at first it is a painful life: a life of deep regrets for the past and dark fears for the future, a life of hungering and thirsting, a life of pining and panting, a life that lacks something—it scarcely knows what—but cannot live without it. This man sees life. The more he keeps his Savior's words, the more he rejoices in Christ Jesus. The more he rests on His promise, the more he loves Him. The more he serves Him, the more his new life will drive death out of sight. Life now abounds and holds sway, and the old death hides away in holes and corners. Though often the believer has to mourn over the old death that struggles to return, still he does not gaze on that death of sin as he once did. He cannot endure it; he takes no pleasure in the contemplation of it; he cries to God for deliverance from it. Grace frees us from the reign of death as well as from the penalty of death. In neither of these senses will the keeper of Christ's words ever look on death.

"But," someone will cry, "will not a Christian die?" Not necessarily, for some will remain at the coming of our Lord, and these believers will not die. Therefore, there is no legal necessity that any should die, since the obligation would then rest alike on all. Still, good men die. Yet they do not die as the penalty of their sin. They are forgiven, and it is not according to God's grace or justice to punish those whom He has forgiven.

O my reader, if you do not believe in the Lord Jesus, death will be a punishment to you. But the nature of death is changed in the case of believers in Jesus. Our deaths will be a falling asleep, not a going to execution. We will depart out of the world to the Father rather than be driven away in wrath. Through the gate of death, we will leave the militant host of earth for the triumphant armies of heaven. What was a cavern leading to blackness and darkness forever has, by the resurrection of our Lord, been made into an open tunnel, which serves as a passage into eternal glory. As a penal infliction upon believers, death was abolished by our Lord; now it has become a stairway from the grace-life below to the glory-life above.

Free from the Influence of Death

Christ's word, "If a man keep my saying, he shall never see death," may further mean that the believer will not live under the influence of death. He will not be perpetually thinking of death, dreading its approach and what follows after it. I must admit that some Christians are in bondage through fear of death, but that is because they do not keep their Master's sayings as they ought to. The effect of His words upon us is frequently such that, instead of being afraid to die, we come to the point of longing to depart. In such a case, we should realize the verses of hymn writer Isaac Watts, who tells us that if we could see the saints above, we would long to join them:

How we should scorn these robes of flesh,
These fetters and this load!
And long for evening to undress,
That we may rest in God.

We should almost forsake our clay
Before the summons come,
And pray and wish our souls away
To their eternal home.

I have to check some dear fellow believers when they say to me, *"Let me die the death of the righteous"* (Num. 23:10). No, do not talk as Balaam did, but rather say, "Let me live, so that I may glorify God and help my sorrowing fellow believers in the Lord's work." I implore you, do not be in a hurry to be gone.

However, this impatience proves that death has lost its terrors for us. We do not see death looming before us as a coming tempest. We do not gaze on it as a fascinating horror that makes our faces pale and casts a lurid glare on all around. We do not see the darkness, for we walk in the light. We do not fear the rumbling of the chariot, for we know the One who rides to us in it.

Free from the Wrath of God

In the next place, we will never see what is the reality and essence of death, namely, the wrath of God in the *"second death"* (Rev. 20:6). We have no cause to fear condemnation, for *"it is God who justifies"* (Rom. 8:33). That final separation from God, which is the real death of human nature, can never come to us. "[Nothing] *shall be able to separate us from the love of God which is in Christ Jesus our Lord"* (v. 39)! The ruin and misery that the word *death* describes, when used in relation to the soul, will never befall us, for we will never perish; neither will anyone snatch us out of Christ's hand (John 10:28).

Free from the Fear of Death

Moreover, when the believer dies, he does not gaze on death. He walks *"through the valley of the shadow of death"* (Ps. 23:4), but he fears no evil and sees nothing to fear. A shadow was cast across his road, but he passed through it and scarcely perceived that it was there. Why was that? Because he had his eye fixed on a strong light beyond, and he did not notice the shadow that otherwise would have distressed him. Believers rejoice so much in the presence of their Lord and Master that they do not observe that they are dying. They rest so sweetly in the embrace of Jesus that they do not hear the voice of wailing. When they pass from one world into another, it is something like going from England to Scotland: it is all one kingdom, and one sun shines in both lands. Often, travelers by railway ask, "When do we pass from England into Scotland?" There is no jerk in the movement of the train, no noticeable boundary. Travelers glide from one country into the other and scarcely know where the boundary lies.

The eternal life that is in believers glides along from grace to glory without a break. We grow steadily on from the blade to the ear, and from the ear to the full corn (Mark 4:28), but no line divides the stages of growth from one another. We will know when we arrive, but the passage may be so rapid that we will not see it. Passing from earth to heaven may seem the greatest of journeys, but it ends *"in the twinkling of an eye"* (1 Cor. 15:52).

> One gentle sigh, the fetter breaks,
> We scarce can say, "He's gone,"
> Before the ransomed spirit takes
> Its mansion near the throne.

Believers will never gaze on death; they will pass it by with no more than a glance. They will go through the Jordan as though it were dry land and scarcely know that they have crossed a river at all. Like Peter, departing believers will scarcely be sure that they have passed through the iron gate, which will open *"of its own accord"* (Acts 12:10); they will know only that they are free. Of each one of them it may be said, as of Peter, he *"did not know that what was done by the angel was real, but thought he was seeing a vision"* (v. 9). Do not fear death, for Jesus says, *"If anyone keeps My word he shall never see death."*

Follow the soul as it enters into the other world: the body is left behind, and the person is a disembodied spirit. However, he does not see death. All the life he needs he has within his spirit by being one with Jesus. Meanwhile, he is expecting that when the trumpet sounds at the Resurrection, his body will be reunited with his spirit, his body having been made to be the dwelling and the instrument of his perfected spirit. While he is absent from the body, he is so present with the Lord that he does not look on death.

But the Judgment Day has come, the Great White Throne is set, and the multitudes appear before the Lamb who will judge! What about the keeper of Christ's sayings? Is he afraid? It is the Day of Judgment, the Day of Wrath! He knows that he will never see death; therefore, he is not in a state of confusion. For him there is no, *"Depart from Me, you cursed"* (Matt. 25:41). He can never come under the eternal sentence. See! Hell opens wide its tremendous mouth. The pit, which long ago was dug for the wicked, yawns and receives them. Down sink the ungodly multitude, a very deluge of souls. *"The wicked shall be turned into hell, and all the nations that forget God"* (Ps. 9:17). In that frightful hour, will the believer's foot slip? No, he will *"stand in the judgment"* (Ps. 1:5) and will never see death.

But the world is burning up: all things are being dissolved, and the elements are melting with fervent heat (2 Pet. 3:10); the stars are falling from heaven like leaves in autumn, and the sun is as black as mourning clothes. Is the believer alarmed now? No! He will never see death. His eyes are fixed on life, and he himself is full of life. He abides in life; he spends his life praising God. He will never gaze on death, for Jesus says, *"Because I live, you will live also"* (John 14:19). O blessed eyes that will never look on death! O happy mind that has been made confident in Jesus Christ of an immortality in which there is no danger!

I pity you who are ungodly. You are made to look on death. It haunts you now; what will it be in the hour of your death? What will you do *"in the floodplain of the Jordan"* (Jer. 12:5)? Nothing remains for you but the wages of sin, which is death (Rom. 6:23). The ruin and misery of your souls will be your endless portion. You will be shut in with the completely destroyed, ruined, and wretched ones forever! This is a dreadful anticipation of judgment that ought to startle you. But as for the believer, *"surely the bitterness of death is past"* (1 Sam. 15:32). We have nothing more to do with death as a penalty or a terror than we have to do with spiritual death as the black suffocation of the heart and the mother of corruption.

Jesus, the Great Quickener

Now, let us move on to rejoice in Jesus as our great Quickener. Those Jews in the eighth chapter of John—what a passion they were in! How unscrupulous was their talk! They could not even quote Christ's words correctly. They said, *"You say, 'If anyone keeps My word he shall never taste death.'"* (v. 52). He did not say so. He said, *"Shall never see death"* (v. 51). We may be said to taste death as our Master did, for it is written that He *"might taste death for everyone"* (Heb. 2:9). And yet, in another sense, we will never taste the wormwood and gall of death (Jer. 9:15), for to us, *"Death is swallowed up in victory"* (1 Cor. 15:54). Death's drop of gall is lost in the bowl of victory.

However, the Lord Jesus did not say that we will never taste death. Neither did He mean that we will not die, in the common sense of the word. He was using one of the meanings of the word *death* that was used by the Hebrew prophets. The Old Testament Scriptures used the word *death* in this way, and these Jews knew its meaning very well. Death did not always mean the separation of the soul from the body, for the Lord's declaration to Adam was, *"In the day that you eat of it you shall surely die"* (Gen. 2:17). Assuredly, Adam and Eve died in the sense intended, but they were not annihilated, nor were their souls separated from their bodies, for they still remained to labor on earth.

"The soul who sins shall die" (Ezek. 18:4) relates to a death that consists of degradation, misery, inability, ruin. Death does not mean annihilation, but something very different. Overthrow and ruin are the death of a soul, just as perfection and joy are its life forever. The separation of the soul from God is the death penalty— and that is death, indeed.

The Jews refused to understand our Lord, yet they clearly saw that what Jesus was claiming glorified Him above Abraham and the prophets. Hidden away in their abusive words, we find a significance that is instructive. It is not the greatness or the goodness of a believer that secures his eternal life; it is his being linked by faith to the Lord Jesus Christ, who is greater than Abraham and the prophets.

A person keeps Christ's commands, and this becomes a bond between him and Christ, and he is one with Christ. Because of their Lord, the saints live, and the living of the saints by Him brings glory and honor to Him. His life is seen in every one of His people. Like mirrors, they reflect His divine life. He has *"life in Himself"* (John 5:26), and He imparts that life to His chosen. As the old creation displays the glory of the Father, so the new creation reveals the glory of the Son. Believers find the highest life in Christ Jesus their Lord, and every particle of this life glorifies Him.

291

It is also to our Lord's glory that we live by His Word. He does not sustain us by the machinery of providence, but by His Word. As the world came into being because God spoke, so we live and continue to live because of Christ's words. What He taught, being received into our hearts, becomes the origin and the nourishment of our eternal life. It is greatly glorifying to Christ that, by His Word, all spiritual life in the countless myriads of believers is given birth and sustained.

It is clear that the Lord Jesus is far greater than Abraham and all the prophets. Their word could not make men live, or even themselves live. But the words of Jesus make alive all who receive them. By keeping them, they live—more than this, they live forever. Glory to the name of Him who quickens those whom He wills!

A sweet inference flows from all this, and with it, I conclude: The glory of Christ depends on the fact that all who keep His sayings will not see death. If you and I keep His commands and we see death, then Jesus is not true. If you, believing in Jesus, gaze on death, it will be proved that He did not have either the power or the will to make His promise good. If the Lord fails in any individual case, He has lost the honor of His faithfulness. Oh, you trembling, anxious souls, lay hold of this:

> His honor is engaged to save
> The meanest of His sheep.

If the saint of God, who has won thousands for Jesus, should perish after all, what a failure of covenant obligations there would be! But that failure would be just as great if one of the least of all those who keep our Lord's sayings should be allowed to perish. Such a loss of honor to our all-glorious Lord is not to be imagined. Therefore, if one of you who are the least in your household do really trust in Him—though you are encumbered with infirmities and imperfections—He must keep you from seeing death. His truth, His power, His unchangeable nature, His love—all are involved in His faithfulness to His promise to each believer. I want you to take this to heart and be comforted.

Even if you are some foul transgressor, the greatest sinner who ever lived, if you will come to Christ, lay hold of His gracious words, keep them, and be obedient to them, you will never see death. There is not a soul in hell who can ever say, "I have kept Christ's sayings, and I have seen death, for here I am." There never would be one such as this, or Christ's glory would be tarnished throughout eternity. Keep His commands, and He will keep you from seeing death!

Book Four

Joy in Christ's Presence

Contents

Chapter 1

Mysterious Visits

You have visited me in the night.
—Psalm 17:3

We ought to be amazed that the glorious God communicates with mankind, who are utterly sinful. *"What is man that You are mindful of him, and the son of man that You visit him?"* (Ps. 8:4). A divine visit is a joy to be treasured whenever we are favored with it. David spoke of it with great solemnity. The psalmist was not content simply to mention it. Rather, he wrote it down in plain terms, so that it might be known throughout all generations: *"You have visited me in the night."*

Beloved, if God has ever visited you, you also will marvel at it, will carry it in your memory, will speak of it to your friends, and will record it in your diary as one of the notable events of your life. Above all, you will speak of it to God Himself and say with adoring gratitude, *"You have visited me in the night."* It should be a solemn part of worship to remember and make known the condescension of the Lord and to say, both in humble prayer and in joyful song, *"You have visited me."*

To you, my dear readers, I will write of my own experience, not doubting at all that it is also yours. If our God has ever personally visited any of us by His Spirit, two results have accompanied the visit: it has been sharply searching, and it has been sweetly comforting.

The Results of God's Visits

Our Hearts Are Searched

When the Lord first draws near to the heart, the trembling soul perceives clearly the searching character of His visit. Remember

297

how Job answered the Lord: *"I have heard of You by the hearing of the ear, but now my eye sees You. Therefore I abhor myself, and repent in dust and ashes"* (Job 42:5–6). We can read of God and hear of God and hardly be affected, but when we feel His presence, it is another matter.

I thought my house was good enough for kings, but when the King of Kings came to it, I saw that it was quite unfit for Him. I never would have known that sin is so *"exceeding sinful"* (Rom. 7:13) if I had not known that God is so perfectly holy. I never would have understood the depravity of my own nature if I had not known the holiness of God's nature.

When we see Jesus, we fall *"at His feet as dead"* (Rev. 1:17). Until then, we are full of vanity and pride. If letters of light traced by a mysterious hand upon the wall caused Belshazzar's knees to knock together and his legs to give way under him (Dan. 5:5–6), what awe overcomes our spirits when we see the Lord Himself! In the presence of so much light, our spots and wrinkles are revealed and we are utterly ashamed. We are like Daniel, who said, *"I was left alone when I saw this great vision, and no strength remained in me; for my vigor was turned to frailty in me, and I retained no strength"* (Dan. 10:8). It is when the Lord visits us that we see our nothingness and ask, "Lord, *'what is man?'"* (Ps. 8:4).

I remember well when God first visited me. It was a night of natural tendencies, of ignorance, of sin. His visit had the same effect on me that it had on Saul of Tarsus when the Lord spoke to him out of heaven. He brought me down off my high horse and caused me to fall to the ground. By the brightness of the light of His Spirit, He made me grope in conscious blindness; and in the brokenness of my heart I cried, *"Lord, what do You want me to do?"* (Acts 9:6). I felt that I had been rebelling against the Lord, kicking *"against the goads"* (v. 5) and doing evil as much as I could, and my soul was filled with anguish at the discovery of this.

The glance of the eye of Jesus was very searching, for it revealed my sin and caused me to go out and weep bitterly. As when the Lord visited Adam and called him to stand naked before Him, so was I stripped of all my righteousness before the face of the Most High. Yet the visit did not end there, for just as the Lord God clothed our first parents in coats of skins, He covered me with the righteousness of the Great Sacrifice and gave me songs in the night. It was night, but the visit was no dream. In fact, there and then I ceased to dream, and I began to deal with the reality of things.

I think you will remember that when the Lord first visited you in the night, it was with you as it was with Peter when Jesus came to him. He had been toiling with his net the whole night, and nothing had come of it. But when the Lord Jesus came into Peter's boat and told him to launch out into the deep and let down his net, he caught such a great multitude of fish that the boat began to sink. The boat went down, down, until the water threatened to engulf it along with Peter, the fish, and everything else. Then Peter fell down at Jesus' knees and cried, *"Depart from me, for I am a sinful man, O Lord!"* (Luke 5:8). The presence of Jesus was too much for him; his sense of unworthiness made him sink like his boat and shrink away from the divine Lord.

I remember that sensation well. Indeed, I was half inclined to cry out, with the demoniac of Gadara, *"What have I to do with You, Jesus, Son of the Most High God?"* (Mark 5:7). My first discovery of Christ's injured love was overpowering, and its very hopefulness increased my anguish, for then I saw that I had slain the Lord who had come to save me. I saw that mine was the hand that had made the hammer fall, the hand that had driven the nails that fastened the Redeemer's hands and feet to the cruel tree.

This is the sight that breeds repentance: *"They will look on* [Him] *whom they pierced....They will mourn for Him"* (Zech. 12:10). When the Lord visits us, He humbles us, removes all hardness from our hearts, and leads us to the Savior's feet.

When the Lord first visited us in the night, it was similar to the way in which John was visited by the Lord on the isle of Patmos. John described it in the following words: *"And when I saw Him, I fell at His feet as dead"* (Rev. 1:17). Yes, even when we begin to see that He has put away our sin and removed our guilt by His death, we feel as if we could never look up again, because we have been so cruel to our Best Friend. It is no wonder if we then say, "It is true that He has forgiven me, but I never can forgive myself. He makes me live, and I live in Him, but at the thought of His goodness I fall at His feet as dead. Boasting is dead, self is dead, and all desire for anything beyond my Lord is dead also." William Cowper poetically described this as

> That dear hour, that brought me to His foot,
> And cut up all my follies by the root.

The process of destroying follies is more hopefully performed at Jesus' feet than anywhere else. Oh, that the Lord would come again to us as He did at first, and like a consuming fire discover and destroy the dross that now alloys our gold! The word *visit* may remind those who travel of the person who searches their baggage. It is in a similar way that the Lord seeks out our secret things. But the word also reminds us of the visits of the physician, who not only finds out our sicknesses, but also aids and cures them. In this way did the Lord Jesus visit us at first.

We Find Sweet Comfort

Since those early days, I hope that you have had many visits from our Lord. Those first visits were, as I said, sharply searching, but the later ones have been sweetly comforting. Some of us have had them especially in the night, when we have been compelled to count the sleepless hours. "Heaven's gate opens when this world's is shut," I have heard it said. The night is still, visitors have gone away, work is done, care is forgotten, and then the Lord Himself draws near. Possibly there may be pain to be endured; your head may be aching, and your heart may be throbbing. But if Jesus comes to visit you, your bed of languishing becomes a throne of glory.

It is true that *"He gives His beloved sleep"* (Ps. 127:2), yet at such times He gives them something better than sleep, namely, His own presence and the *"fullness of joy"* (Ps. 16:11) that comes with it. At night, upon our beds, we have seen the unseen. Sometimes I have tried not to sleep while experiencing an excess of joy, when the company of Christ has been sweetly mine.

Manifestations of Our Lord

"You have visited me in the night." Believe me, there are such things as personal visits from Jesus to His people. He has not utterly left us. Though He may not be seen with our natural eyes near a bush or a running stream, nor on the mountain or by the sea, He still does come and go, observed only by our spirits, felt only by our hearts. He still stands behind our walls and shows Himself through the lattices (Song 2:9).

How can I describe these manifestations of the Lord? It is difficult for me to give you a good idea of them if you do not already know them for yourselves. If you had never tasted sweetness, no one could give you an idea of honey by describing it to you. Yet if the honey is right in front of you, you can *"taste and see"* (Ps. 34:8). To a man born blind, sight must be a thing beyond his imagination; and to one who has never known the Lord, His visits are beyond what that person can conceive of.

More than Assurance of Salvation

For our Lord to visit us is something more than for us to have the assurance of our salvation, although that is very delightful, and none of us would be satisfied unless we possessed it. To know that Jesus loves me is one thing, but to be visited by Him in love is much more.

More than Picturing Christ

Nor is it simply a close contemplation of Christ, for we can picture Him as exceedingly fair and majestic and yet not have Him consciously near us. As delightful and instructive as it is to behold the likeness of Christ by meditation, the enjoyment of His actual presence is something more. I may wear my friend's picture around my neck, and yet I may not be able to say, *"You have visited me."*

The Real Presence of Christ

The actual, though spiritual, coming of Christ is what we so much desire. The Catholic church says much about the real presence, meaning the physical presence, of the Lord Jesus. The priest who celebrates mass tells us that he believes in the real presence, but we reply, "No, you believe in knowing Christ according to the flesh, and in that sense the only real presence of Jesus is in heaven. We, on the other hand, firmly believe in the real presence of Christ that is spiritual, and yet certain."

By spiritual we do not mean unreal. In fact, the spiritual is what is most real to spiritual men. I believe in the true and real presence of Jesus with His people, for such a presence has been real to my spirit. Lord Jesus, You Yourself have visited me. As surely as Jesus came in the flesh to Bethlehem and Calvary, so surely does He come by His Spirit to His people in the hours of their communion with Him. We are as conscious of that presence as we are of our own existence.

The Effects of Christ's Presence

When the Lord visits us in the night, what is the effect upon us? Our hearts meet His heart in a fellowship of love. Such communion first brings peace, then rest, and then joy in our souls. I am not writing of any emotional excitement that turns into fanatical rapture, but I mention a sober fact when I say that the Lord's great heart touches ours, and our hearts rise into empathy with Him.

First, we experience peace. All war is over, and a blessed peace is proclaimed; God's peace guards our hearts and minds through Christ Jesus (Phil. 4:7). At such a time there is a delightful sense of rest; we have no ambitions, no desires. A divine serenity and security envelop us. We have no thought of foes or fears, afflictions or doubts. There is a joyous laying aside of our own wills. We are nothing, and we will nothing; Christ is everything, and His will is the pulse of our souls. We are perfectly content either to be ill or to be well, to be rich or to be poor, to be slandered or to be honored, so that we may simply abide in the love of Christ. Jesus fills the horizon of our beings.

At such a time, a flood of great joy will fill our minds. We will half wish that the morning may never break again, for fear that its light might banish the superior light of Christ's presence. We will wish that we could glide away with our Beloved to the place where He *"feeds...among the lilies"* (Song 2:16). We long to hear the voices of the white-robed armies (Rev. 7:9–10), so that we may follow their glorious Leader wherever He goes.

I am convinced that there is no great distance between heaven and earth, that the distance lies in our finite minds. When the Beloved visits us in the night, He turns our chambers into the vestibules of His palace halls. Earth rises to heaven when heaven comes down to earth.

God Will Visit You

Now, you may be saying to yourself, "I have not enjoyed such visits as these." Yet you may enjoy them. If the Father loves you even as He loves His Son, then you are on visiting terms with Him. Therefore, if He has not called on you, you will be wise to call on Him. Breathe a sigh to Him, and say,

When wilt Thou come unto me, Lord?
Oh come, my Lord most dear!

Come near, come nearer, nearer still,
I'm blest when Thou art near.

"As the deer pants for the water brooks, so pants my soul for You, O God" (Ps. 42:1). If you long for Him, He much more longs for you. No sinner was ever half as eager for Christ as Christ is eager for the sinner; no saint was ever one-tenth as anxious to behold his Lord as his Lord is to behold him. If you are running to Christ, He is already near you. If you sigh for His presence, that sigh is the evidence that He is with you. He is with you even now; therefore, be glad.

Go forth, beloved, and talk with Jesus on the beach, for He often walked along the seashore. Commune with Him amid the olive groves, which were so dear to Him during many nights of wrestling prayer. Have your heart right with Him, and He will visit you often. Soon enough, you will walk every day with God, as Enoch did, and so turn weekdays into Sabbaths, meals into sacraments, homes into temples, and earth into heaven. May it be so with all believers!

Chapter 2

Under His Shadow

*He who dwells in the secret place of the Most High shall abide
under the shadow of the Almighty.*
—Psalm 91:1

I must confess that the outline for this chapter is borrowed. It is
taken from one who will never complain about it, for to the
great loss of the church she has left these lower choirs to sing
above. Frances Ridley Havergal (1836–1879) has been caught up to
add to the music of heaven. Her last poems were published with the
title *Under His Shadow,* and the preface gives the reason for the
name. In the preface she wrote,

> I would like the title to be *Under His Shadow.* I seem to see
> four pictures suggested by that: under the shadow of a rock,
> in a weary plain; under the shadow of a tree; closer still, un-
> der the shadow of His wing; nearest and closest, in the shadow
> of His hand. Surely that hand must be the pierced hand, which
> may oftentimes press us sorely, and yet evermore encircling,
> upholding, and shadowing.

In this chapter, I want to expound on the scriptural plan that
Miss Havergal set down for us. Recall our text: *"He who dwells in
the secret place of the Most High shall abide under the shadow of
the Almighty."* The shadow of God is not the occasional resort of
the saint, but his constant abiding-place. Here we find not only our
consolation, but also our habitation. We ought never to be out of
the shadow of God.

It is to dwellers, not to visitors, that the Lord promises His
protection. *"He who dwells in the secret place of the Most High
shall abide under the shadow of the Almighty,"* and that shadow
will preserve him from the evil and *"terror by night"* (Ps. 91:5),
from the arrows of war and of pestilence, and from destruction (vv.

5–6). Guarded by Omnipotence, the chosen of the Lord are always safe. For, as they dwell in the holy place, very near the mercy seat where the blood was sprinkled long ago, they are covered by the pillar of fire by night and the pillar of cloud by day, which continually hang over the sanctuary. Is it not written, *"In the time of trouble He shall hide me in His pavilion; in the secret place of His tabernacle He shall hide me"* (Ps. 27:5)? What better security can we desire?

As the people of God, we are always under the protection of the Most High. Wherever we go, whatever we suffer, whatever our difficulties, temptations, trials, or perplexities may be, we are always *"under the shadow of the Almighty."* The tenderest care of a guardian is extended over all who maintain their fellowship with God. Their heavenly Father Himself interposes between them and their adversaries. Yet the experiences of the saints differ greatly from person to person. Though they are all under the shadow of God, they enjoy His protection in different ways—in fact, in the four different ways that Frances Havergal mentioned in the preface to her collection of poems.

The Shadow of a Rock

I will begin with the first picture that Miss Havergal mentioned, namely, the rock sheltering the weary traveler. The prophet Isaiah spoke of *"the shadow of a great rock in a weary land"* (Isa. 32:2). Now, I take it that this is where we begin to know our Lord's shadow. At first, He was a refuge to us in time of trouble. The way was weary, and the heat was great; our lips were parched, and our souls were fainting; we looked for shelter, and we found none. We were in the wilderness of sin and condemnation, and who could bring us deliverance, or even hope?

A Hiding Place

Then we cried to the Lord in our trouble, and He led us to the Rock of Ages, which was carved for us long ago. We saw our Mediator coming between us and the fierce heat of justice, and we welcomed the blessed shield. The Lord Jesus was to us a covering for sin; therefore, He was a hiding place from wrath. The sense of divine displeasure, which had beaten upon our consciences, was removed by the removal of the sin itself. Our sin was laid on Jesus, who endured its penalty in our place.

A Complete Shelter

The shadow of a rock is remarkably cooling, and so was the Lord Jesus eminently comforting to us. The shade of a rock is denser, cooler, and more complete than any other shade. Beams of sunlight cannot reach through the rock and into its shade, nor can the heat penetrate as it will sometimes do through the foliage of a forest. Likewise, the peace that Jesus gives *"surpasses all understanding"* (Phil. 4:7); there is no other like it. Jesus is a complete shelter, and blessed are they who are under His shadow. Let us take care that we abide there and never venture forth to answer for ourselves or to brave the accusations of Satan.

The Lord is the Rock of our refuge both from sin and from sorrow of every sort. No sun or heat can afflict us, because we are never out of Christ. The saints know where to fly, and they use their privilege.

> When troubles, like a burning sun,
> Beat heavy on their head,
> To Christ their mighty Rock they run,
> And find a pleasing shade.

Greatness, Not Gentleness

There is, however, something awesome about this great shadow. A very large rock is often so high that it is overwhelming, and we tremble in the presence of its greatness. The idea of littleness hiding behind massive greatness is set forth here, but there is no tender thought of fellowship or gentleness.

Looking only at this picture of the rock, we see the Lord Jesus as our shelter from the consuming heat of well-deserved punishment, but we know little more. Thus, it is very pleasant to remember that this is only one aspect of the fourfold picture. The deep, cool shade of the Rock, my blessed Lord, is inexpressibly dear to my soul as I, a sinner saved, stand in Him. Yet there is more to it than this.

The Shadow of a Tree

Our second picture is found in the Song of Songs: *"As the apple tree among the trees of the wood, so is my beloved among the sons. I sat down under his shadow with great delight, and his fruit was sweet to my taste"* (Song 2:3 KJV). Here we have not so much refuge from trouble as special rest in times of joy.

The spouse was happily wandering through the woods, glancing at many trees and rejoicing in the music of the birds. One tree specially charmed her: the citron with its golden fruit won her admiration, and she sat down under its shadow with great delight. Such was her beloved to her—the best among the good, the fairest of the fair, the joy of her joy, the light of her delight. Such is Jesus to the believing soul.

Rest for Our Souls

The sweet influences of Christ are intended to give us a happy rest, and we ought to avail ourselves of them. *"I sat down under his shadow."* Mary was blessed by taking advantage of the rest that Christ offered, while Martha nearly missed it in all her preparations for the meal. (See Luke 10:38–42.) This is the God-ordained way in which we are to walk, the way in which we *"find rest for [our] souls"* (Matt 11:29).

Dear friends, is Christ to each one of us a place of sitting down? I do not mean a rest of idleness and self-content—God deliver us from that. But there is a rest in the conscious understanding of Christ, a rest of contentment with Him as our all in all. I pray that God will cause us to know more of this rest!

Perpetual Solace

This shadow is also meant to yield perpetual solace, for the spouse in the Song of Songs did not merely come under it, but she sat down as one who meant to stay. Continuance of repose and joy is purchased for us by our Lord's perfected work. Under the shadow she also found food. She had no need to leave it to find a single thing, for the tree yielded not only shade, but also fruit. She did not even need to rise from her rest, but as she sat still she feasted on the delicious fruit. You who know the Lord Jesus know also what this means.

The spouse never wished to go beyond her Lord. She knew no higher life than that of sitting under her Well Beloved's shadow. She passed the cedar, the oak, and every other tree, but the apple tree caught her attention, and there she sat down. *"There are many who say, 'Who will show us any good?'"* (Ps. 4:6). But as for us, O Lord, our hearts are fixed (Ps. 57:7), resting on You. We will go no further, for You are *"our dwelling place"* (Ps. 90:1). We feel at home with You, and we sit down beneath Your shadow.

Some Christians cultivate reverence at the expense of childlike love. They kneel down, but they do not dare to sit down. Our divine Friend and Lover does not want it to be so; He does not wish to have us stand before Him in ceremony, but rather to come boldly to Him (Heb. 4:16).

Delight in Christ's Presence

Let us use His sacred name as a common word, as a household word, and run to Him as to a dear familiar friend. Under His shadow we are to feel that we are at home. After that, He will make Himself at home to us by becoming food for our souls and by giving spiritual refreshment to us while we rest.

The spouse in the Song of Songs did not say that she reached up to the tree to gather its fruit; but she sat down on the ground in intense delight, and the fruit came to her where she sat. It is wonderful how Christ will come down to souls who sit beneath His shadow. If we can only be at home with Christ, He will sweetly commune with us. Has He not said, *"Delight yourself also in the LORD, and He shall give you the desires of your heart"* (Ps. 37:4)?

With the tree, which is our second illustration of the Almighty's shadow, a sense of restful delight in Christ supersedes the sense of awe. Have you ever sat beneath the pleasing shade of that fruitful tree? Have you not only possessed security, but also experienced delight in Christ? Have you sung,

> I sat down under His shadow,
> Sat down with great delight;
> His fruit was sweet unto my taste,
> And pleasant to my sight?

This experience is as necessary as it is joyful—necessary for many reasons. *"The joy of the LORD is* [our] *strength"* (Neh. 8:10), and it is when we delight ourselves in the Lord that we have assurance of power in prayer. Here faith develops, and hope grows bright, while love sheds abroad all the fragrance of her sweet spices. Oh, dear reader, go to the apple tree, and find out who is the fairest among the fair. Make the Light of Heaven the delight of your heart, and then be filled with rest and revel in complete contentment.

The Shadow of His Wings

The third illustration of the shadow of the Almighty is that of the shadow of His wings. This is a precious word: *"Because You have been my help, therefore in the shadow of Your wings I will rejoice"* (Ps. 63:7). Does this Scripture not set forth our Lord as the One in whom we may trust in times of depression?

Earlier in this Psalm, we read that David was banished from the means of grace to *"a dry and thirsty land where there* [was] *no water"* (v. 1). Moreover, he had fallen away from all conscious enjoyment of God. He said, *"Early will I seek You; my soul thirsts for You"* (v. 1). Instead of singing about his present communion with God, he sang of memories.

Like David, we also have come into this condition and have been unable to find any immediate comfort. *"You have been my help"* (v. 7) has been the highest note we could sing, and we have been glad even to reach that. At such times, the light of God's face has been withdrawn, but our faith has taught us to rejoice under the shadow of His wings. There has been no light, we have been completely in the shade, but it has been a warm shade. We have felt that God who has been near must be near us still; therefore, we have been quieted. Our God cannot change (Mal. 3:6); therefore, since He was our help, He must still be our help, even though He casts a shadow over us, for it must be the shadow of His own eternal wings.

The metaphor of wings is, of course, derived from the nestling of little birds under the shadow of their mother's wings, and the picture is unusually touching and comforting. The little bird is not yet able to take care of itself, so it cowers down under the mother, and there it is happy and safe. Disturb a hen for a moment, and you will see all the little chicks huddling together and making a kind of song with their chirps. Then they push their heads into her feathers and seem happy beyond measure in their warm abode.

When we are very ill or extremely depressed, when we are concerned about our sick children or the troubles of a needy household, when the temptations of Satan almost overpower us, how comforting it is to run to our God! As the little chicks run to the hen, we can hide away near His heart, beneath His wings. Oh, tried ones, press closely to the loving heart of your Lord; hide yourselves entirely beneath His wings! Here, awe has disappeared, and rest itself is enhanced by the idea of loving trust. The little birds are safe in their mother's love, and we, too, are secure and happy beyond measure in the loving favor of the Lord.

The Shadow of His Hand

The last illustration of the shadow is that of the hand, and this, it seems to me, points to power and position in service. Read Isaiah 49:2: *"And He has made My mouth like a sharp sword; in the shadow of His hand He has hidden Me, and made Me a polished shaft; in His quiver He has hidden Me."* This undoubtedly refers to the Savior, for notice what comes next:

> And He said to me, *"You are My servant, O Israel, in whom I will be glorified."* Then I said, *"I have labored in vain, I have spent my strength for nothing and in vain; yet surely my just reward is with the LORD, and my work with my God."* And now the LORD says, who formed Me from the womb to be His Servant, to bring Jacob back to Him, so that Israel is gathered to Him (For I shall be glorious in the eyes of the LORD, and My God shall be My strength), indeed He says, *"It is too small a thing that You should be My Servant to raise up the tribes of Jacob, and to restore the preserved ones of Israel; I will also give You as a light to the Gentiles, that You should be My salvation to the ends of the earth."* (Isa. 49:3–6)

Our Lord Jesus Christ was hidden away in the hand of Jehovah, to be used by Him as a polished spear for the overthrow of His enemies and the victory of His people. Yet inasmuch as it is true of Christ, it is also true of all of Christ's servants, *"because as He is, so are we in this world"* (1 John 4:17).

We may be sure that we are included with Christ in the hand of God, for the same expression is found in Isaiah 51:16, where, speaking of His people, He says, *"I have covered you with the shadow of My hand."* Is this not an excellent verse? Every one of you who will be a witness for Jesus will have a share in it. This is where those who are workers for Christ should long to be—*"in the shadow of* [His] *hand"*—in order to achieve His eternal purpose.

What are any of God's servants without their Lord? They are weapons that are out of the warrior's hand, that have no power to do anything. We ought to be like the arrows of the Lord, which He shoots at His enemies. His hand of power is so great, and we as His instruments are so little, that He hides us away in the hollow of His hand, unseen until He shoots us forth. As workers, we are to be hidden away in the hand of God; we are to be unseen until He uses us. To quote another verse, *"In His quiver He has hidden Me"* (Isa. 49:2).

It is impossible for us not to be somewhat well-known if the Lord uses us, but we must not aim at being noticed. On the contrary, if we are used as much as the very chief of the apostles, we must truthfully add, *"though I am nothing"* (2 Cor. 12:11). Our desire should be that Christ should be glorified, and that self should be concealed.

But alas! There is always a way of showing self instead of Christ in what we do, and we are all too ready to fall into it. Suppose I went to visit a poor woman, but I did so with a great deal of arrogance. All that the woman would see was that I had condescended to call upon her. But there is another way of doing the same thing so that the tried child of God will know that a beloved brother or a dear sister in Christ has shown sympathy for her and has come to minister to her heart.

There is a way of preaching in which a great theologian may clearly display his vast learning and talent, and there is another way of preaching in which a faithful servant of Jesus Christ, depending upon his Lord, may speak in his Master's name and leave a rich blessing behind. We ought to choose the way by which Christ may be glorified.

Within the hand of God lies the place of acceptance and safety, the place of power as well as of concealment. God works only with those who are in His hand, and the more we lie hidden there, the more surely He will use us before long. May the Lord do to us according to His Word: *"I have put my words in thy mouth, and I have covered you with the shadow of My hand"* (Isa. 51:16).

In this case, we will feel all the former emotions combined: awe that the Lord would condescend to take us into His hand, rest and delight that He would stoop so low to use us, trust that out of weakness we will now be made strong, and an absolute assurance that the purpose of our existence will be completed, for what is urged onward by the Almighty's hand cannot miss its mark.

These thoughts cover only the surface of this subject, which deserves many more chapters than this one. Therefore, your best course will be to take these few hints and turn them into a long, personal experience of abiding under the shadow of the Almighty. May the Holy Spirit lead you into it and keep you there, for Jesus' sake!

Chapter 3

Under the Apple Tree

I sat down under his shadow with great delight,
and his fruit was sweet to my taste.
—Song of Songs 2:3 KJV

The spouse in the Song of Songs knew her beloved to be like a fruit-bearing tree, and so she sat *"under his shadow"* and fed upon his fruit. She knew him, and she enjoyed his pleasures. It is a pity that we know so much about Christ and yet enjoy Him so little. Our experience ought to keep pace with our knowledge, and that experience should be composed of using what our Lord has given us in practical ways.

The way to learn a truth thoroughly is to learn it by experience, and the way to learn more is to use what you know. Jesus casts a shadow; let us sit under it. Jesus yields fruit; let us taste the sweetness of it. You know a doctrine beyond all doubt when you have proved it for yourself by personal test and trial. The bride in the Song of Songs essentially said, "I am certain that my beloved casts a shadow, for I have sat under it; I am persuaded that he bears sweet fruit, for I have tasted it."

The best way to demonstrate the power of Christ to save is to trust in Him and be saved yourself. Out of all those who are sure of the truth of our holy faith, none is as certain as the one who feels its divine power upon himself. You may reason yourself into a belief of the Gospel, and you may, by further reasoning, keep a strict religious code; but a personal trial and an inward knowledge of the truth are incomparably the best evidences. If Jesus is like an apple tree among the trees of the wood, do not keep away from Him, but sit under His shadow and taste His fruit. He is a Savior; do not believe this fact and yet remain unsaved. As far as Christ is known to you, make use of Him in that measure. This is simple common sense!

Furthermore, we are at liberty to make every possible use of Christ. Both the shadow and the fruit may be enjoyed. Christ in His infinite condescension exists for needy souls. Oh, let me say it over again! It is a bold statement, but it is true: Christ Jesus our Lord exists for the benefit of His people. Just as a physician lives to heal, our Savior exists to save.

The Good Shepherd lives and has even died for His sheep. Our Lord has wrapped us around His heart, and we are intimately interwoven with all His positions of authority, with all His honors, with all His character traits, with all that He has done, and with all that He has yet to do. The sinners' Friend lives for sinners, and sinners may have Him and use what He has provided to the uttermost. He is as free to us as the air we breathe. What are fountains for, but that the thirsty may drink? What is the harbor for, but that storm-tossed ships may find refuge? What is Christ for, but that poor guilty ones like ourselves may come to Him and look and live, and afterward may have all our needs supplied out of His fullness?

Thus, the door is open to us, and we pray that the Holy Spirit may help us to enter in. I want you to notice in our text two things that you may enjoy to the full: first, the heart's rest in Christ, *"I sat down under his shadow with great delight"*; and second, the heart's refreshment in Christ, *"His fruit was sweet to my taste."*

The Heart's Rest in Christ

A Valuable Rest

Let us notice the character of the person who uttered the sentence, *"I sat down under his shadow with great delight."* She was one who knew from experience what weary travel meant; therefore, she valued rest. Keep in mind that the person who has never labored knows nothing of the sweetness of repose. Also, the loafer who has eaten bread he never earned, who has never had a drop of honest sweat, does not deserve rest and does not know what it is. It is to the laborer that rest is sweet. So when we come at last, toil-worn from many miles of weary plodding, to a shaded place where we may comfortably sit down, then we are filled with delight.

The spouse had been seeking her beloved, and in looking for him she had asked where she was likely to find him. *"Tell me,"* she said, *"O you whom I love, where you feed your flock, where you make it rest at noon"* (Song 1:7). This answer was given to her,

"Follow in the footsteps of the flock" (v. 8). She did go her way, but after a while she came to this resolution: "I will sit down *'under his shadow.'"*

Many of you have been painfully wearied by attempting to find peace. Some of you tried ceremonies and trusted in them, and the priest came to your aid, but then he mocked your heart's distress. Others of you sought by various systems of thought to find an anchor; but, as you were tossed from wave to wave, you found no rest upon the seething sea of speculation.

Still others of you tried by your good works to gain rest for your consciences. You multiplied your prayers; you poured out floods of tears; you hoped, through giving to the poor and similar acts of charity, that some merit might come to you; and you hoped that your heart might find acceptance with God, and so have rest. You toiled and toiled, like the men who were in the vessel with Jonah when they rowed hard to bring their ship to land, but could not, *"for the sea was growing more tempestuous"* (Jonah 1:11). There was no escape for you that way, and so you were driven to another way, to rest in Jesus.

My heart looks back to the time when I was under a sense of sin, when I sought with all my soul to find peace but could not discover it, high or low, in any place beneath the sky. Yet when I saw One hanging on a tree as the Substitute for sin, then my heart *"sat down under his shadow with great delight."* I began to reason in this way: Did Jesus suffer in my place? Then I will not suffer punishment. Did He bear my sin? Then I do not bear it. Did God accept His Son as my Substitute? Then He will never strike me down. Was Jesus acceptable to God as my Sacrifice? Then what contents the Lord should certainly content me. Consequently, I will go no farther, but I will sit down under His shadow and enjoy a delightful rest.

Shaded by His Sacrifice

She who said, *"I sat down under his shadow with great delight,"* could appreciate shade, for she had been sunburned. Her exclamation just before this was, *"Do not look upon me, because I am dark, because the sun has tanned me"* (Song 1:6). She knew what heat meant, what the burning sun meant; therefore, shade was pleasant to her.

You can know nothing about the deliciousness of shade until you travel in a thoroughly hot country; then you are delighted with it. Did you ever feel the heat of divine wrath? Did the great Sun—that Sun without *"variation or shadow of turning"* (James 1:17)—ever shoot His hottest rays upon you, the rays of His holiness and justice? Did you cower beneath the scorching beams of that great Light and say, *"We* [are] *consumed by Your anger"* (Ps. 90:7)? If you have ever felt that, you have found it a very blessed thing to come under the shadow of Christ's atoning sacrifice.

A shadow, as you know, is cast by something that comes between us and the light and heat. Our Lord's most blessed body has come between us and the scorching sun of divine justice, so that we sit under the shadow of His mediation with great delight.

And now, if any other sun begins to scorch us, we run to our Lord. If we are oppressed by troubles at home or at work, or if we are tempted by Satan or led astray by inward corruption, we hurry to Jesus' shadow, to hide under Him and to sit down in the cool refreshment with great delight. Because our blessed Lord endured the heat of divine wrath, we may find an inward quiet. The sun cannot scorch us, for it scorched Him. Our troubles need not be troublesome to us, for He has taken our troubles, and we have left them in His hands. *"I sat down under his shadow."*

Take careful notice of these two things concerning the spouse. She knew what it was to be weary, and she knew what it was to be sunburned. To the degree that you know these two things, your esteem for Christ will rise in proportion. You who have never wasted away under the wrath of God have never prized the Savior. Water is of small value in a land of streams and rivers, but if you were making a day's march over burning sand, a cup of cold water would be worth a king's ransom. In the same way, Christ is precious to thirsty souls, but not to anyone else.

Overshadowed by His Love

Now, when the spouse was sitting down, restful and delighted, she was overshadowed. She said, *"I sat down under his shadow."* I do not know a more delightful state of mind than that of feeling overshadowed by our beloved Lord. I was black with sin, but His precious blood overshadowed my sin and hid it forever. My natural condition was that of an enemy to God, but He who reconciled me to God by His blood has overshadowed that also, so that I now forget that I was once an enemy in my joy of being a friend.

I am very weak, but He is strong, and His strength overshadows my feebleness. I am very poor, but He has all the riches of the universe, and His riches overshadow my poverty. I am most unworthy, but He is so worthy that if I use His name I will receive as much as if I were worthy. Indeed, His worthiness overshadows my unworthiness.

It is very precious to put this truth another way and say, "If there is anything good in me, it is not good when I compare myself with Him, for His goodness quite eclipses and overshadows it." Can I say I love Him? I do, but I hardly dare to call it love, for His love overshadows it. Do I think that I serve Him? I want to, but my poor service is not worth mentioning in comparison with what He has done for me. Have I thought that I had any degree of holiness? I must not deny what His Spirit works in me, but when I think of His immaculate life and all His divine perfections, where am I? What am I?

Have you not sometimes felt this? Have you not been so overshadowed by your Lord and hidden in Him that you became as nothing? I myself know what it is to feel that if I die in a poorhouse, it does not matter, as long as my Lord is glorified. Men may slander me (Luke 6:22), if they like, but what difference does it make, since His dear name will one day be written in stars across the sky? Let Him overshadow me; I delight that it should be so.

Spiritual Delight

The spouse told us that when she became quite overshadowed, then she felt great delight. When all you focus on is yourself, you never can have great delight, for you cannot bear to admit that something is greater than yourself. However, the humble believer finds his delight in being overshadowed by his Lord. In the shade of Jesus we have more delight than in any imaginary light of our own. The spouse had great delight. I trust that you, as a Christian, do have such great delight. If you don't, you ought to ask yourself whether you really are one of the people of God.

I like to see a cheerful countenance; yes, and I like to hear of overwhelming joy in the hearts of those who are God's saints! There are people who seem to think that religion and gloom are one and the same and can never be separated. They think that you must pull down the blinds on Sunday and darken the rooms. And if you have a garden, or a rose in bloom, you must try to forget that there are such beauties. They say, "Put your book under your arm, and crawl to your place of worship in as mournful a manner as if you were being marched to the whipping post. Are you not to serve God as miserably as you can?"

You may act this way if you like, but give me a religion that cheers my heart, fires my soul, and fills me with enthusiasm and delight, for that is likely to be the religion of heaven, and it agrees with the experience of the bride in the inspired Song of Songs.

Although I trust that we know what delight means, I question whether we have enough of it to describe ourselves as sitting down in the enjoyment of it. Do you give yourselves enough time to sit at Jesus' feet? That is the place of delight—do you abide in it? Sit down under His shadow. "I have no time," someone may exclaim. Try to make a little. Steal it from your sleep if you cannot get it any other way. Grant leisure to your heart.

It would be a great pity if a man never spent five minutes with his wife, but was forced to be always hard at work. Why, that is slavery, is it not? Will we not then make time to commune with our beloved Lord? Surely, somehow or other, we can squeeze out a little time each day in which we have nothing else to do but to sit down under His shadow with great delight!

When I take my Bible, to feed on it for myself, I generally start to think about preaching on the passage of Scripture, and what I would say about it from the pulpit. I must get away from that and forget that there is a pulpit, so that I may sit personally at Jesus' feet. Oh, there is an intense delight in being overshadowed by Him! He is near you, and you know it. His dear presence is as certainly with you as if you could see Him, for His influence surrounds you.

I have often felt as if Jesus were leaning over me, as a friend might look over my shoulder. My heart grows calm when His cool shade comes over me. If you have been wearied by your family, or troubled over your church, or annoyed with yourself, you will come down from the place where you have seen your Lord and you will feel braced for the battle of life, ready for its troubles and its temptations, because you have seen the Lord. *"I sat down,"* said the spouse, *"under his shadow with great delight."* How great that delight was she could not tell, but she sat down as one overpowered by it, needing to sit still under the load of bliss.

I do not like to talk much about the secret delights of Christians, because there are always some who do not understand my meaning. Even so, I will venture to say this much—that if worldlings could but even guess what are the secret joys of believers, they would give their eyes to share in them with us.

318

We have troubles, and we admit it; we expect to have them. But we also have joys in abundance. You know what this means, do you not? When you have been quite alone with the heavenly Bridegroom, you have wanted to tell the angels about the sweet love of Christ for you, a poor unworthy one. You have even wished to teach fresh music to the golden harps, for even the seraphim do not know the heights and depths of the grace of God as you know them.

The spouse had great delight, and we know that she did for this one reason: she did not forget it. This verse and the whole Song of Songs are a remembrance of what she had enjoyed. She said, *"I sat down under his shadow."* It might have been a month ago, it might have been years ago, but she had not forgotten it. The joys of fellowship with God are written in marble. Memories of communion with Christ Jesus are engraved as in eternal brass.

"I knew a man fourteen years ago," said the apostle Paul (2 Cor. 12:2). Ah, it was worth remembering all those years! He had not told of his delight, but he had kept it stored up. He said, *"I [knew] a man in Christ...fourteen years ago; whether in the body I do not know, or whether out of the body I do not know, God knows"* (v. 2), so great had his delights been.

When we look back, we forget birthdays, holidays, and nights that we have spent in the ways of the world, but we readily recall our times of fellowship with the Well Beloved. We have known our Mounts of Transfiguration, our times of fellowship with the glorified Christ, and like Peter we remember when we were *"with Him on the holy mountain"* (2 Pet. 1:18). Our heads have leaned against the Master's chest (John 13:23), and we can never forget the intense delight; nor will we fail to put on record for the good of others the joys with which we have been indulged.

How beautifully natural this is. There was a tree, and the spouse sat down under the shadow of it. There was nothing strained, nothing formal. In the same way, true piety should always be consistent with common sense, with what seems most fitting, most becoming, most wise, and most natural. We have Christ, whom we may enjoy; let us not despise the privilege.

The Heart's Refreshment in Christ

Let us now look briefly at the heart's refreshment in Christ. *"His fruit was sweet to my taste."* I will not expound fully upon this, but I will give you some thoughts that you can work out for yourself later on.

319

The spouse did not feast upon the fruit of the tree until she was first under the shadow of it. There is no way to know the excellent things of Christ until you trust Him. Not a single sweet apple will fall to those who are outside the shadow. Come and trust Christ, and then you will enjoy all that there is in Christ. O unbelievers, what you miss! If you will only sit down under His shadow, you will have all things; but if you will not, no good thing of Christ's will be yours.

As soon as the spouse was under the shadow, the fruit was all hers. *"I sat down under his shadow,"* she said, and then, *"His fruit was sweet to my taste."* Do you believe in Jesus? Then Jesus Christ Himself is yours. And if you own the tree, you may very well eat the fruit. Since He Himself becomes yours altogether, then His redemption and the pardon that comes from it, His living power, His mighty intercession, the glories of His Second Advent, and all that belongs to Him are given to you for your personal and present use and enjoyment.

"All things are yours" (1 Cor. 3:21), since Christ is yours. Only be careful to imitate the spouse: when she found that the fruit was hers, she ate it. Copy her closely in this. A great fault in many believers is that they do not take the promises for themselves and feed on them. Do not err as they do. Under the shadow you have a right to eat the fruit. Do not deny yourself the sacred provision.

Labor Is Unnecessary

Now, as we read the text, it would appear that the spouse obtained this fruit without effort. Thomas Fuller, an English theologian and author, wrote, "He who would have the fruit must climb the tree." But the spouse did not climb, for she said, *"I sat down under his shadow."* I suppose the fruit dropped down to her. I know that it is so with us. We no longer *"spend money for what is not bread, and [our] wages for what does not satisfy"* (Isa. 55:2), but we sit under our Lord's shadow, we eat what is good, and our souls take delight in the sweetness. Come, Christian, enter into the calm rest of faith by sitting down beneath the cross, and you will be fed so that you are full.

The spouse rested while feasting; she sat and ate. Believer, rest while you are feeding upon Christ! The spouse acknowledged that she sat and ate. Had she not told us in the preceding chapter that the king sat at his table (Song 1:12)? See how similar the church is to her Lord, how similar the believer is to his Savior! We sit down also, and we eat, even as the king does. His joy is in us (John 15:11), and His peace guards our hearts and minds (Phil. 4:7).

The Taste That Satisfies

Notice that, as the spouse fed upon this fruit, she had a relish for it. Not every tongue likes every fruit. Never dispute with other people about tastes of any sort, for agreement is not possible. The dessert that is the most delicious to one person is nauseating to another, and if there were a competition as to which fruit is preferable to all the rest, there would probably be almost as many opinions as there are fruits. But blessed is he who has a relish for Christ Jesus!

Dear reader, is He sweet to you? Then He is yours. There never was a heart that enjoyed the sweetness of Christ unless Christ belonged to that heart. If you have been feeding on Him and He is sweet to you, go on feasting, for He who gave you the taste for His sweetness also gives you Himself to satisfy your appetite.

What are the fruits that come from Christ? Are they not peace with God, renewal of heart, joy in the Holy Spirit, love for the children of God? Are they not regeneration, justification, sanctification, adoption, and all the blessings of the covenant of grace? And are they not each and all sweet to our tastes? As we have fed upon them, have we not said, "Yes, these things are pleasant indeed. There is nothing else like them. Let us live upon them forevermore"?

Therefore, sit down; sit down and feed. It seems strange that we should have to persuade people to do this, but in the spiritual world things are very different from what they are in the natural. If you put a juicy steak and a knife and fork in front of most men, they do not need many arguments to persuade them to eat. Yet they will not eat if they are full, whereas they will eat if they are hungry.

Likewise, if your soul is weary from longing for Christ the Savior, you will feed on Him; but if not, it is useless for me to write to you. However, you who are there, sitting under His shadow, may hear Him speak these words: "Eat, My friend, and drink abundantly." You cannot have too much of these good things. The more of Christ a person has, the better the Christian he is.

Christ, Our All in All

We know that the spouse feasted heartily upon this food from the tree of life, for in later days she wanted more. Read the fourth verse: *"He brought me to the banqueting house, and his banner over me was love"* (Song 2:4). Verse three describes, as it were, her first love for her country love, her rustic love. She went to the woods, and she found him there like an apple tree, and she enjoyed him as one relishes a ripe apple in the country. But she grew in grace, she learned more about her lord, and she found that her beloved was a king.

I would not be at all surprised to find out that she there learned the doctrine of the Second Advent, for then she began to sing, *"He brought me to the banqueting house."* Looking at the biblical application, essentially, she was saying, "He did not merely let me know Him out in the fields as the Christ in His humiliation, but He brought me into the royal palace. Moreover, since He is a King, He brought forth a banner with His own coat of arms, and He waved it over me while I was sitting at the table, and the motto of that banner was love."

She grew very full of emotion. It was such a grand thing to find a great Savior, a triumphant Savior, an exalted Savior! But it was too much for her, and her soul became sick with the excessive glory of what she had learned. Do you see what her heart craved? She longed for her first simple joys, those countrified delights. *"Refresh me with apples"* (v. 5), she said. Nothing but the old joys would revive her.

Did you ever feel like that? I have been satiated with delight in the love of Christ as a glorious exalted Savior when I have seen Him riding on His white horse and going forth to conquer (Rev. 6:2). I have been overwhelmed when I have beheld Him upon the throne, with all the brilliant assembly of angels and archangels adoring Him (Rev. 5:11–13). My thoughts have gone forward to the Day when He will descend with all the splendor of God and will make all kings and princes shrink into nothingness before the infinite majesty of His glory (Rev. 19:11–15).

Then I have felt as though, at the sight of Him, I must fall *"at His feet as dead"* (Rev. 1:17); and I have wanted somebody to come and tell me over again "the old, old story" of how He died so that I might be saved. His throne overpowers me; I want only to gather fruit from His cross. Bring me apples from "the tree" again. I am awestruck while in the palace; let me get away to the woods again.

Give me an apple plucked from the tree. Give me an apple such as this: *"Come to Me, all you who labor and are heavy laden, and I will give you rest"* (Matt. 11:28). Or this: *"This Man receives sinners"* (Luke 15:2). Give me a promise from the basket of the covenant. Give me the simplicity of Christ; let me be a child and feast on apples again, if Jesus is the apple tree. I would gladly meditate upon Christ dying on the cross in my place, Christ overshadowing me, Christ feeding me. This is the happiest state to live in. Lord, give us these apples forever!

You may recall the old story of Jack, a traveling salesman who used to sing,

> I'm a poor sinner, and nothing at all,
> But Jesus Christ is my all in all.

Those who knew him were astonished at his constant composure. They had a world of doubts and fears, and so they asked him why he never doubted.

"Well," said he, "I cannot doubt that I am a poor sinner, and nothing at all, for I know that and feel it every day. And why should I doubt that Jesus Christ is my all in all? For He says He is."

"Oh!" said one of his questioners, "I have my ups and downs."

"I don't," said Jack. "I can never go up, for I am a poor sinner and nothing at all, and I cannot go down, for Jesus Christ is my all in all."

When Jack wanted to join the church, the people said he must tell of his spiritual experience. He said, "All my experience is that I am a poor sinner, and nothing at all, and Jesus Christ is my all in all."

"Well," they said, "when you come before the church meeting, the minister may ask you questions."

"I can't help it," said Jack. "All I know I will tell you; and this is all I know. 'I'm a poor sinner, and nothing at all, but Jesus Christ is my all in all.'"

He was admitted into the church and continued to walk in holiness, but that was still the sum of his experience, and you could not get him beyond it.

"Why," said one brother, "I sometimes feel so full of grace, I feel so advanced in sanctification, that I begin to be very happy."

"I never do," said Jack. "I am a poor sinner and nothing at all."

"But then," said the other, "I go down again and think I am not saved, because I am not as sanctified as I used to be."

"But I never doubt my salvation," said Jack, "because Jesus Christ is my all in all, and He never changes."

That simple story is highly instructive, for it presents a simple man's faith in a simple salvation. This man is an example of a soul under the apple tree, resting in the shade and feasting on the fruit.

An Invitation

At this time I want you to think of Jesus, not as a Prince, but as an apple tree; when you have done this, I pray that you will sit down under His shadow. It is not much to do. Any child can sit down in a shadow when he is hot. Next, I want you to feed on Jesus. Any simpleton can eat apples when they are ripe upon the tree. Come and take Christ, then.

You who have never come before, come now. Come and feel welcome. You who have come often, who have entered into the palace and who are sitting at the banqueting table, you lords and nobles of Christianity, come to the common wood and to the common apple tree where poor saints are shaded and fed. You had better come under the apple tree, like poor sinners such as I am, and be once more shaded with boughs and comforted with apples, or else you may faint beneath the palace glories. The best of saints are never better than when they again drink the milk of the Word and are comforted with the apples that were their first gospel feast.

May the Lord Himself bring forth to you His own sweet fruit!

Chapter 4

Over the Mountains

My beloved is mine, and I am his. He feeds his flock among the
lilies. Until the day breaks and the shadows flee away, turn,
my beloved, and be like a gazelle or a young stag
upon the mountains of Bether.
—Song of Songs 2:16–17

I t is possible that there are believers who are always at their best
and are so happy that they never lose the light of their Father's
countenance. But I am not sure that there are such people, for
those believers with whom I have been most acquainted have had
an experience of both highs and lows. And those of my acquaintances who have boasted of their constant perfection have not been
the most reliable of individuals.

I always hope that there is an attainable spiritual region where
there are no clouds to hide the Sun of our souls. However, I cannot
be very positive about this, for I have not traversed that happy
land. Every year of my life has had a winter as well as a summer,
and every day has had its night. I have seen brilliant sunshine and
heavy rains, and felt warm breezes and fierce winds.

Speaking for the majority of my brothers and sisters in Christ,
I confess that, although the strength is in us, as it is in an oak tree,
we do lose our leaves, and the sap within us does not flow with
equal vigor during all seasons. We have our ups as well as our
downs, our hills as well as our valleys. We are not always rejoicing;
we are sometimes heavyhearted because of our various trials. Alas!
We are grieved to confess that our fellowship with the Well Beloved
is not always that of rapturous delight, but at times we have to seek
Him and cry, *"Oh, that I knew where I might find Him!"* (Job 23:3).

This appears to me to have been, to a degree, the condition of
the spouse when she cried, *"Until the day breaks and the shadows*
flee away, turn, my beloved." These words teach us several things.

Communion May Be Broken

First of all, these words teach us that communion may be broken. The spouse had lost the company of her bridegroom; conscious communion with him was gone, though she loved him and yearned for him. In her loneliness she was sorrowful, but she had by no means ceased to love him, for she called him her beloved and spoke as one who felt no doubt about that love.

Love for the Lord Jesus may be quite as true, and perhaps quite as strong, when we sit in darkness as when we walk in the light. The spouse had not lost her assurance of His love for her and of their mutual interest in one another, for she said, *"My beloved is mine, and I am his."* And yet she added, *"Turn, my beloved."* The condition of our blessings does not always coincide with the state of our joys. A person may be rich in faith and love, and yet have such a low self-image that he is greatly depressed.

It is clear from this sacred Canticle that the spouse loved and was loved, was confident in her lord, and was fully assured of her possession of him, yet for the present there were mountains between them. Yes, we may even be far advanced in the Christian life, and yet be exiled for a while from conscious fellowship with our Lord. There are nights for men as well as for infants, and the strong know as well as the sick and the feeble that the sun is hidden. Therefore, do not condemn yourself because a cloud is over you. Do not cast away your confidence. Rather, let faith be ignited in the gloom, and resolve in love to meet your Lord again, whatever the barriers may be that separate you from Him.

Sorrow and Darkness

When Jesus is absent from a true heir of heaven, sorrow will ensue. The healthier a person's condition, the sooner that absence will be perceived and the more deeply it will be mourned. This sorrow is described in the text as darkness, which is implied in the expression, *"Until the day breaks."* Until Christ appears, no day has dawned for us. We dwell in midnight darkness; the stars of the promises and the moon of experience yield no light of comfort until our Lord, like the sun, arises and ends the night. We must have Christ with us, or we are left to grope for the wall like blind men, and we wander in dismay.

Shadows in the Night

The spouse also spoke of shadows: *"Until the day breaks and the shadows flee away."* Shadows are multiplied when the light of the sun departs, and they are apt to frighten those who are timid. We are not afraid of real enemies when Jesus is with us, but when we miss Him, we tremble at the smallest shadow. How sweet is that song, *"Yea, though I walk through the valley of the shadow of death, I will fear no evil; for You are with me; Your rod and Your staff, they comfort me"* (Ps. 23:4)! But we change our tune when night comes upon us and Jesus is not with us. Then, we fill the night with more terrors. Ghosts, demons, hobgoblins, and things that never existed, except in our imaginations, are apt to swarm about us, and we are in fear where no fear should exist.

Christ Turns His Back

The spouse's worst trouble was that the back of her beloved was turned to her, and so she cried, *"Turn, my beloved."* When his face is toward her, she suns herself in his love; but if the light of his countenance is withdrawn, she is greatly troubled. Our Lord sometimes turns His face from His people, though He never turns His heart from His people. He may even close His eyes in sleep when the vessel is tossed by the tempest (Matt. 8:23–24), but His heart is awake all the while.

Even so, it is terrible enough that we have grieved Him in any degree; it pains us to think that we have wounded His tender heart. He is jealous, but never without cause. If He turns His back upon us for a while, He doubtless has a more than sufficient reason. He would not walk contrary to us if we did not walk contrary to Him (Lev. 26:23–24).

The presence of the Lord makes this life the preface to the celestial life; but His absence leaves us longing for Him, and no comfort remains in the land of our banishment. The Scriptures, the ordinances of the church, private devotion, and public worship are all like sundials—excellent when the sun shines, but of little use in the darkness. O Lord Jesus, nothing can compensate us for the loss of You! Draw near to Your beloved people, for without You our night will never end.

Longings to Restore Communion

When communion with Christ is broken, there is a strong desire in all true hearts to win it back again. If a person loses the joy of communion with Christ, he will never be content until it is restored. Have you ever entertained Prince Immanuel? Has He gone elsewhere? Your heart will be a dreary place until He comes back again.

"Give me Christ, or else I will die," is the cry of every soul who has lost the dear companionship of Jesus. We do not part easily with such heavenly delights. With us it is not a matter of, "Maybe He will return, and we hope He will." Instead, "He must return, or we will become weak and die." We cannot live without Him, and this is a comforting sign, for the soul who cannot live without Him will not live without Him. He comes quickly when life and death depend on His coming. If you must have Christ, you will have Him. This is just how the matter stands: we must drink of this well or we will die of thirst; we must feed upon Jesus or our spirits will starve.

Mountains of Difficulty

I will now go further and say that when communion with Christ is broken, there are great difficulties on the path to its renewal. It is much easier to go downhill than to climb to the same height again. It is far easier to lose joy in God than to find the lost jewel.

The spouse spoke of *"mountains"* dividing her from her beloved. By this, she meant that the difficulties were great. They were not little hills, but mountains, that blocked her way—mountains of remembered sin, alps of backsliding, ranges of forgetfulness, ingratitude, worldliness, coldness in prayer, frivolity, pride, unbelief. I cannot fully describe all the dark geography of this sad experience! Giant walls rose before her like the towering steeps of Lebanon. How could she approach her beloved?

The difficulties that separated her from him were many as well as great. The spouse did not speak of a single mountain, but of *"mountains."* Alps rose upon alps, wall after wall. She was distressed to think that in such a short time so much could come between her and him of whom she had just sung, *"His left hand is under my head, and his right hand embraces me"* (Song 2:6). Alas! We multiply these *"mountains of Bether"* with a sad rapidity!

Our Lord is jealous, and we give Him far too much reason for hiding His face. A fault that seemed so small at the time we committed it is seen in the light of its own consequences, and then it grows and swells until it towers above and hides the face of the Beloved. Then our sun has gone down, and fear whispers, "Will His light ever return? Will it ever be daybreak? Will the shadows ever flee away?" It is easy to grieve away the heavenly sunlight, but ah, how hard to clear the skies and regain the unclouded brightness!

Uncertain Length of Separation

Perhaps the worst thought of all to the spouse was the fear that the dividing barrier might be permanent. It was high, but it might dissolve; the walls were many, but they might fall. But, alas, there were mountains, and these stand fast for ages! She felt like the psalmist when he cried, *"My sin is always before me"* (Ps. 51:3). The pain of our Lord's absence becomes intolerable when we fear that we are hopelessly shut out from Him. A person can bear one night, hoping for the morning, but what if the day should never break?

If we have wandered away from Christ and feel that there are ranges of immovable mountains between Him and us, we feel sick at heart. We try to pray, but devotion dies on our lips. We attempt to approach the Lord at the communion table, but we feel more like Judas than John. At such times, we have felt that we would give our eyes to behold the Bridegroom's face once more and to know that He delights in us as He did in happier days. Still, there stand the awful mountains, black, threatening, impassable; and in the far-off land, the Life of our life is far away and grieved.

Insurmountable Difficulties

The spouse seemed to have come to the conclusion that the difficulties in her way were insurmountable by her own power. She did not even think of going over the mountains to her beloved, but she cried, *"Until the day breaks and the shadows flee away, turn, my beloved, and be like a gazelle or a young stag upon the mountains of Bether."* She did not try to climb the mountains; she knew she could not. If they had been lower, she might have attempted it, but their summits reached to heaven. If they had been less craggy or difficult, she might have tried to scale them; but these mountains were terrible, and no foot could stand upon their barren cliffs.

Oh, the mercy that comes with utter self-despair! I love to see a soul driven into a tight corner and forced to look to God alone.

The end of the creature is the beginning of the Creator. Where the sinner ends, the Savior begins. If the mountains can be climbed, we will have to climb them; but if they are quite impassable, then the soul will cry out with the prophet,

> *Oh, that You would rend the heavens! That You would come down! That the mountains might shake at Your presence; as fire burns brushwood, as fire causes water to boil; to make Your name known to Your adversaries, that the nations may tremble at Your presence! When You did awesome things for which we did not look, You came down, the mountains shook at Your presence.* (Isa. 64:1–3)

Our souls are lame, they cannot go to Christ, and we turn our strong desires to Him and fix our hopes upon Him alone. Will He not remember us in love, and fly to us as He did to His servant of old when He *"rode upon a cherub, and flew; He flew upon the wings of the wind"* (Ps. 18:10)?

A Prayer to the Lord

Now we come to the prayer of our text: *"Turn, my beloved, and be like a gazelle or a young stag upon the mountains of Bether."* Jesus can come to us when we cannot go to Him. The gazelle and the young stag live among the crags of the mountains and leap across the abyss with amazing agility. For swiftness and surefootedness, they are unrivaled.

The psalmist said, *"He makes my feet like the feet of deer, and sets me on my high places"* (Ps. 18:33), alluding to the feet of animals that are created to stand securely on the side of a mountain. And so, the spouse in this golden Canticle sang, *"Behold, he comes leaping upon the mountains, skipping upon the hills. My beloved is like a gazelle or a young stag"* (Song 2:8–9).

Christ Comes to Us

Here I would remind you that this prayer is one that we may justly offer, because it is Christ's way to come to us when our coming to Him is out of the question. "How?" you ask. I answer that He did this long ago, for we remember *"His great love with which He loved us, even when we were dead in trespasses"* (Eph. 2:4–5). When

330

He came into the world in human form, was it not because man could never come to God until God had come to him? Our first parents offered no tears, prayers, or entreaties to God, but the offended Lord spontaneously gave the promise that the Seed of the woman would bruise the Serpent's head (Gen. 3:15). Our Lord's coming into the world was not bought, not sought, not thought of; He came altogether of His own free will, delighting to redeem.

Christ's incarnation was a foreshadowing of the way in which He comes to us by His Spirit. He saw that we were cast out, polluted, shameful, perishing; and as He passed by, His tender lips said, "Live!" In us the Scripture is fulfilled: *"I was found by those who did not seek Me"* (Isa. 65:1). We were too averse to holiness, too much in bondage to sin, ever to have returned to Him if He had not turned to us first.

What do you think of this? Did He not come to us when we were His enemies, and will He not visit us now that we are His friends? Did He not come to us when we were dead sinners, and will He not hear us now that we are weeping saints? If Christ came to the earth in this manner, and if He comes to each one of us in this fashion, we may well hope that now He will come to us in the same way, like the dew that refreshes the grass and *"tarr*[ies] *for no man nor wait*[s] *for the sons of men"* (Mic. 5:7).

Besides, He is coming again in person on the Last Day. Mountains of sin, error, idolatry, superstition, and oppression stand in the way of His kingdom, but He will surely come and overturn, until He reigns over all. He will come in the last days, I say, though He will leap the hills to do it. Because of this, I am sure we may comfortably conclude that He will draw near to us who mourn His absence so bitterly. Therefore, we ought to go to Him and present the petition of our text: *"Turn, my beloved, and be like a gazelle or a young stag upon the mountains."*

He Knows Our Troubles

Our text gives us sweet assurance that our Lord is at home with difficulties that are, to us, quite insurmountable. Just as the gazelle or the young stag knows the mountain passes and the stepping places among the rugged rocks, just as they have no fear among the ravines and the precipices, so our Lord knows the heights and depths, the torrents and the caverns, of our sins and sorrows. He carried the entirety of our transgressions and so became aware of the tremendous load of our guilt. He is quite at home with the infirmities of our human nature; He knew temptation in the wilderness, heartbreak in the Garden, desertion on the cross.

He is quite at home with pain and weakness, for He *"Himself took our infirmities and bore our sicknesses"* (Matt. 8:17). He is at home with despondency, for He was *"a Man of sorrows and acquainted with grief"* (Isa. 53:3). He is at home even with death, for He *"breathed His last"* (Mark 15:37) and passed through the sepulchre to resurrection.

O yawning gulfs and steep mountains of woe, our Beloved, like a deer, has traversed your glooms! O my Lord, You know everything that divides me from You. You also know that I am far too feeble to climb these dividing mountains so that I may approach You. Therefore, I pray, come over the mountains to meet my longing spirit! You know each cavernous abyss and every slippery slope, but none of these can hold You back. Hurry to me, Your servant, Your beloved, and let me again live by Your presence.

He Traverses the Mountains

It is easy, too, for Christ to come over the mountains for our relief. It is easy for the gazelle to cross the mountains; it was created for that purpose. Likewise, it is easy for Jesus, too, for He was ordained long ago to come to man in his worst condition, and to bring with Him the Father's love.

What is it that separates us from Christ? Is it a sense of sin? You have been pardoned once, and Jesus can renew most vividly a sense of full forgiveness. But you say, "Alas! I have sinned again, and fresh guilt weighs on my heart." He can remove it in an instant, for the fountain appointed for that purpose is open and is still full. It is easy for Redeeming Love to forgive the child's offenses, since He has already obtained pardon for the criminal's iniquities. If with His heart's blood He won our pardon from our Judge, He can easily enough bring us the forgiveness of our Father.

Oh, yes, it is easy enough for Christ to say again, *"Your sins are forgiven you"* (Matt. 9:2)! "But," you say, "I feel so unworthy, so unable to enjoy communion with Him." He who healed *"all kinds of sickness and all kinds of disease"* (Matt. 4:23) can heal your spiritual infirmities with a word. Remember the man whose ankle bones received strength, so that he ran and leaped. Remember the woman who was sick with a fever, who was healed at once and arose and ministered to her Lord. *"My grace is sufficient for you, for My strength is made perfect in weakness"* (2 Cor. 12:9).

"But I have such afflictions, such troubles, such sorrows, that I am weighed down and cannot rise into joyful fellowship." Yes, but Jesus can make every burden light and cause each yoke to be easy (Matt. 11:30). Your trials can be made to aid your heavenward course instead of hindering it. I know all about those heavy burdens, and I perceive that you cannot lift them; but skillful engineers can adapt ropes and pulleys in such a way that heavy weights lift other weights. The Lord Jesus is the greatest of engineers, very skilled at the machinery of grace, and He can cause a weight of tribulation to lift from us a load of spiritual deadness, so that we can ascend by what threatened to sink us down like a millstone.

What else hinders our way toward God? I am sure that, even if it were a sheer impossibility, the Lord Jesus could remove it, for *"the things which are impossible with men are possible with God"* (Luke 18:27). But someone objects, "I am so unworthy of Christ. I can understand eminent saints and beloved disciples being greatly indulged, but *'I am a worm, and no man'* (Ps. 22:6); I am utterly below such condescension." Do you really think so? Do you not know that the worthiness of Christ covers your unworthiness? He *"became for us wisdom from God; and righteousness and sanctification and redemption"* (1 Cor. 1:30).

In Christ, the Father does not consider you as low as you think you are. You are not worthy to be called His child, but He does call you so, and He considers you to be among His jewels. Listen, and you will hear Him say, *"I gave Egypt for your ransom, Ethiopia and Seba in your place. Since you were precious in My sight, you have been honored, and I have loved you"* (Isa. 43:3–4). Thus, there remains nothing that Jesus cannot leap over if He resolves to come to you and reestablish your broken fellowship.

He Is among Us

To conclude, our Lord can do all this immediately. As *"in the twinkling of an eye,...the dead will be raised incorruptible"* (1 Cor. 15:52), so in a moment our dead emotions can rise to fullness of delight. He can say to your mountain, *"'Be removed and be cast into the sea,' [and] it will be done"* (Matt. 21:21). Jesus is already among us. We do not have His physical presence, but we perceive His real spiritual presence. He has come. He speaks, saying, *"The winter is past, the rain is over and gone"* (Song 2:11).

333

And so it is; we feel that it is so. A heavenly springtime warms our frozen hearts. Like the spouse, we cry out with wonder, *"Before I was even aware, my soul had made me as the chariots of my noble people"* (Song 6:12). Now in happy fellowship, we see the Beloved and hear His voice. Our hearts are ignited; our affections glow; we are happy, restful, brimming over with delight. The King has brought us into His banqueting house, and His banner over us is love (Song 2:4). It is a good place to be!

O Lord of our hearts, home is not home without You. Life is not life without You. Heaven itself would not be heaven if You were absent. Abide with us. The world is growing dark, the twilight of time is drawing near. Abide with us, for the evening is coming upon us. We are getting older, and we are nearing the night when the dew falls cold and chill. A great future is all around us; the splendors of the last age are descending; and while we wait in solemn, awestruck expectation, our hearts continually cry, *"Until the day breaks and the shadows flee away, turn, my beloved, and be like a gazelle or a young stag upon the mountains of Bether."*

Chapter 5

Christ's Delight in His Church

You are all fair, my love, and there is no spot in you.
—Song of Songs 4:7

Ⅰ ow marvelous are these words! *"You are all fair, my love, and there is no spot in you."* The glorious bridegroom is charmed with his spouse, and he sings soft canticles of admiration. We do not wonder that the bride extols her lord, for he well deserves it, and in him there is room for praise without the possibility of flattery. But does he lower himself to praise this sunburned Shulamite? Yes, for these are his own words, uttered by his own sweet lips.

O believer, do not doubt it, for there are more wonders to reveal! There are greater depths in heavenly things than you have yet dared to hope. The church not only is *"all fair"* in the eyes of her Beloved, but in one sense she always was so.

The Lord delighted in His children before they had either natural or spiritual beings, and from the beginning He could say, *"My delight was with the sons of men"* (Prov. 8:31). Having covenanted to be *"a surety of a better covenant"* (Heb. 7:22), and having determined to fulfill every stipulation of that covenant, He, from all eternity, delighted to survey the purchase of His blood. Certainly, He rejoiced to view His church, according to God's purpose and decree, as already delivered from sin by Him and exalted to glory and happiness.

A Real Delight and Admiration

Now, with joy and gladness let us examine the subject of Christ's delight in His church. Christ has a high esteem for His church. He does not blindly admire her faults, nor does He conceal them from Himself. He is acquainted with her sin, in all its heinousness of guilt; He knows what sort of punishment is deserved.

He does not hesitate to reprove that sin. His own words are, *"As many as I love, I rebuke and chasten"* (Rev. 3:19). He abhors sin in her as much as in the ungodly world—even more, for He sees in her an evil that is not to be found in the transgressions of others, and this evil is the sin against love and grace.

The church is black in her own sight; how much more is she so in the eyes of her omniscient Lord! Yet there it stands, written by the inspiration of the Holy Spirit and flowing from the lips of the Bridegroom: *"You are all fair, my love, and there is no spot in you."* How is this so? Is it a mere exaggeration of love, an enthusiastic canticle, which the sober hand of truth must strip of its glowing fables? Oh, no!

The King is full of love, but He is not so overcome by it that He forgets His reason. The words are true, and He wants us to understand them as the honest expression of His unbiased judgment after having patiently examined His spouse in every way. He would not have us diminish anything; rather, He would have us estimate His opinions by the brightness of His expressions. Therefore, so that there may be no mistake, He states it positively, *"You are all fair, my love,"* and confirms it by a negative, *"There is no spot in you."*

Complete Admiration

When He speaks positively, how complete is His admiration! She is *"fair,"* but that is not a full description; He describes her as *"all fair."* He views her in Himself, washed in His sin-atoning blood and clothed in His meritorious righteousness, and He considers her to be full of loveliness and beauty. No wonder, since they are His own perfect excellencies that He admires.

The holiness, glory, and perfection of His church are His own garments, worn by His own well-beloved spouse, and she is *"bone of* [His] *bones and flesh of* [His] *flesh"* (Gen. 2:23). She is not simply pure or well-proportioned; she is positively lovely and fair! She has actual merit! Her deformities of sin have been removed, but even more, she has obtained a meritorious righteousness through her Lord by which an actual beauty is conferred upon her. Believers are given a righteousness when they become *"accepted in the Beloved"* (Eph. 1:6).

Fairest among Women

The church is not just barely lovely; she is superlatively so. As the bridegroom describes his bride as the *"fairest among women"*

(Song 1:8), so the church has real worth and excellence that cannot be rivaled by all the nobility and royalty of the world. If Jesus could exchange His elect bride for all the queens and empresses of earth, or even for the angels in heaven, He would not, for He puts her first and foremost—*"fairest among women."*

This is certainly not an opinion that He is ashamed of, for He invites all men to hear it. He puts a *"behold"* before it, a special note of exclamation, inviting and arresting attention. *"Behold, you are fair, my love! Behold, you are fair!"* (Song 4:1). He publishes His opinion abroad even now, and one day from the throne of His glory He will avow the truth of it before the assembled universe. *"Come, you blessed of My Father"* (Matt. 25:34) will be His solemn affirmation of the loveliness of His elect.

Repeated Praise

Let us note carefully His repeated praise for His spouse, the church.

> Lo, thou art fair! lo, thou art fair!
> Twice fair thou art, I say;
> My righteousness and graces are
> Thy double bright array.
>
> But since thy faith can hardly own
> My beauty put on thee;
> Behold! behold! Twice be it known
> Thou art all fair to Me!

The bridegroom turns again to his beloved, looks into her doves' eyes a second time, and listens to her lips that drip like a honeycomb (Song 4:11). It is not enough to say, *"Behold, you are fair, my love."* No, he rings that golden bell again, and sings again and again, *"Behold, you are fair."*

After having surveyed her whole person with rapturous delight, he cannot be satisfied until he takes a second gaze and again recounts her beauties. With little difference between his first description and his last, he adds extraordinary expressions of love to prove his increased delight:

O my love, you are as beautiful as Tirzah, lovely as Jerusalem, awesome as an army with banners! Turn your eyes away

337

from me, for they have overcome me. Your hair is like a flock of goats going down from Gilead. Your teeth are like a flock of sheep which have come up from the washing; every one bears twins, and none is barren among them. Like a piece of pomegranate are your temples behind your veil....My dove, my perfect one, is the only one, the only one of her mother, the favorite of the one who bore her. (Song 6:4–7, 9)

Universal Beauty

The beauty that Christ admires in His spouse is also universal; He is as much enchanted with her temples as with her breasts. All her forms of worship, all her pure devotion, all her earnest labor, all her constant sufferings are precious to His heart. She is *"all fair."* Her ministry, her singing of psalms, her intercessory prayer, her benevolence and charity, her alertness to spiritual things—all are admirable to Him, when performed in the Spirit. Her faith, her love, her patience, her zeal, are alike in His esteem as *"rows of jewels"* and *"chains of gold"* (Song 1:10 KJV). He loves and admires everything about her.

In captivity, or in the land of Canaan, she is always fair. On the top of Lebanon, His heart is ravished by one look from her eyes, and in the fields and villages He joyfully receives her love (Song 4:8–15). In the days of His gracious manifestations, He values her above gold and silver. But He has an equal appreciation for her when He withdraws Himself, for it was immediately after He had said, *"Until the day breaks and the shadows flee away, I will go my way to the mountain of myrrh and to the hill of frankincense"* (v. 6), that He exclaimed, *"You are all fair, my love."*

Whenever believers are very near the heart of the Lord Jesus, they are always like *"the apple of His eye"* (Deut. 32:10) and the jewel of His crown. Their names are still on His breastplate (Exod. 28:29), and their souls are still in His gracious remembrance. He never thinks lightly of His people, and certainly throughout His Word there is not one syllable that implies contempt of them. They are the choice treasure and the special portion of the Lord of Hosts. What king will undervalue his own inheritance? What loving husband will despise his own wife? Let others call the church what they may; Jesus does not waver in His love for her, and He does not differ in His opinion of her, for He still exclaims, *"How fair and how pleasant you are, O love, with your delights!"* (Song 7:6).

Let us remember that He who pronounces the church and each individual believer to be *"all fair"* is none other than the glorious Son of God, who is Very God of Very God. Hence, His declaration is final, since Infallibility has uttered it. There can be no mistake when the all-seeing Jehovah is the Judge. If He has pronounced the church to be incomparably fair, she is fair beyond a doubt. And though it is hard for our poor, puny faith to receive, it is nevertheless as divine a truth as any of the indisputable doctrines of revelation.

A Confirmation of Praise

Having thus pronounced the church positively full of beauty, He now confirms His praise by a precious negative: *"There is no spot in you."* It is as if the thought had occurred to the Bridegroom that the critical world would insinuate that He had only mentioned her beautiful parts and had purposely omitted those features that were deformed or defiled. So He sums up everything by declaring her universally and entirely fair, utterly devoid of stain.

A spot is often easily removed, and it may be the very least thing that can disfigure beauty, but the church is delivered in her Lord's sight even from this little blemish. If He had said, "There is no hideous scar, no horrible deformity, no filthy ulcer," we might even then have marveled. But when He testifies that she is free from the slightest spot, all these things are included, and the depth of wonder is increased. If He had only promised to remove all spots, we would have had eternal reason for joy. But when He speaks of it as already done, who can restrain the most intense emotions of satisfaction and delight? O my soul, here is *"marrow and fatness"* (Ps. 63:5) for you; eat your fill, and be abundantly glad!

He Pardons and Loves Us Still

Christ Jesus has no quarrel with His spouse. She often wanders from Him and grieves His Holy Spirit. Nevertheless, He does not allow her faults to affect His love. He sometimes chides, but it is always in the tenderest manner, with the kindest intentions—it is *"my love"* even then. He does not remember our follies; He does not cherish ill thoughts of us, but He pardons and loves after the offense as much as before it.

This is a good thing, for if Jesus were as mindful of injuries as we are, how could He commune with us? Many times a believer will put himself out of communion with the Lord because of some slight change in his circumstances, but our precious Husband knows our silly hearts too well to take any offense at our bad manners.

If He were as easily provoked as we are, who among us could hope for an accepting look or a kind greeting from Him? But He is *"ready to pardon...slow to anger"* (Neh. 9:17). He is like Noah's sons: He goes backward and throws a cloak over our nakedness (Gen. 9:23). Or we may compare Him to Apelles, who, when he painted Alexander, put his finger over the scar on his cheek, so that it might not be seen in the picture. *"He has not observed iniquity in Jacob, nor has He seen wickedness in Israel"* (Num. 23:21), and so He is able to commune with the erring sons of men.

We Are "All Fair"

But the question remains: How can this be? Can this be explained even when sin remains in the hearts of the regenerate? Can our own daily distresses over sin ever allow anything like perfection to become a present attainment? The Lord Jesus says it; therefore, it must be true; but in what sense is it to be understood? How are we *"all fair,"* when we ourselves feel that we are *"dark, because the sun has tanned* [us]*"* (Song 1:6)? We may easily grasp the answer when we consider the analogy of faith.

In the matter of justification, believers are complete and without sin. This is true with respect to the gift of Christ's righteousness that is imparted to believers. His beauty is put upon them, and it makes them very glorious and lovely, so that through Him they are beautiful beyond all others.

Dr. Gill excellently expressed the same idea when he wrote,

> Though all sin is seen by God, in *articulo providentiae,* in the matter of providence, wherein nothing escapes His all-seeing eye; yet in *articulo justificationis,* in the matter of justification, He sees no sin in His people, so as to reckon it to them, or condemn them for it; for they all stand *"holy, and blameless, and above reproach in His sight"* (Col. 1:22).

The blood of Jesus removes all stains, and His righteousness confers perfect beauty. Therefore, in the Beloved, the true believer is as much accepted and approved in the sight of God right now as he will be when he stands before the throne in heaven. The beauty of justification is at its fullness the moment a soul is received into the Lord Jesus by faith. This is righteousness so transcendent that no one can exaggerate its glorious merit. Since this righteousness is that of Jesus, the Son of God, it is therefore divine, and is, indeed, the holiness of God. Hence, Kent was not too daring when he sang,

> In thy Surety thou art free,
> His dear hands were pierced for thee;
> With His spotless vesture on,
> Holy as the Holy One.
> Oh, the heights and depths of grace,
> Shining with meridian blaze;
> Here the sacred records show
> Sinners black, but comely, too!

But perhaps it is best to understand this as it relates to Christ's plans concerning His people. It is His purpose to present them without *"spot or wrinkle or any such thing"* (Eph. 5:27). They will be *"holy, and blameless, and above reproach"* (Col. 1:22) in the sight of the Omniscient God. In view of this, the church is seen as being virtually what she is soon to be in reality.

This is not a frivolous anticipation of the church's excellence, for we should always remember that the Representative, in whom she is accepted, is complete in all perfections and glories at this very moment. The Head of the body is already without sin, being none other than the Lord from heaven. It is in keeping with this truth that the whole body can be pronounced lovely and fair through the glory of the Head. The fact of the church's future perfection is so certain that it is spoken of as if it were already accomplished, and indeed it is so in the mind of Him to whom *"a thousand years* [are] *as one day"* (2 Pet. 3:8).

Let us magnify the name of our Jesus, who loves us so much that He will leap over the years of our pilgrimage that divide us from glory, so that He may give us even now the praise that seems to be appropriate only for the perfection of paradise.

Admiration Sweetened by Love

The lord addressed the spouse as *"my love."* The virgins called her *"fairest among women"* (Song 5:9); they saw and admired her, but it was reserved for her lord to love her.

Who can fully describe the excellence of Christ's love? Oh, how His heart goes out to His redeemed! As for the famed love of David and Jonathan, it is far exceeded in Christ. No tender husband was ever as fond as He is. No illustrations can completely reveal His heart's affection, for it surpasses all the love that man or woman has heard or thought of.

Expressions of Love

Our blessed Lord Himself, when He wanted to declare the greatness of His love, was compelled to compare one inconceivable thing with another in order to express His own thoughts. *"As the Father loved Me, I also have loved you"* (John 15:9). All the eternity, fervency, immutability, and infinity that are to be found in the love of Jehovah the Father toward Jesus the Son, are copied exactly in the love of the Lord Jesus toward His chosen ones. Before the foundation of the world He loved His people; in all their wanderings He loved them, and to the end they will be loved by Him (John 13:1). He has given them the best proof of His affection. He gave Himself to die for their sins and opened the way for them to receive complete pardon as the result of His death.

His Willingness to Die

The willing manner of His death is further confirmation of His boundless love. How Christ delighted in the work of our redemption! *"Behold, I come; in the scroll of the book it is written of me. I delight to do Your will, O my God"* (Ps. 40:7–8). When He came into the world to sacrifice His life for us, it was a freewill offering. *"I have a baptism to be baptized with"* (Luke 12:50). Christ was to be, as it were, baptized in His own blood.

How He thirsted for that time! *"How distressed I am till it is accomplished"* (v. 50). There was no hesitation, no desire to be rid of His responsibility. He went to His crucifixion without once stopping along the way to deliberate about whether He should complete His sacrifice. He paid for the tremendous mass of our fearful debt at once. He asked for neither a delay nor a reduction in suffering or punishment.

From the moment He said, *"Not My will, but Yours, be done"* (Luke 22:42), His course was swift and unswerving, as if He had been hurrying to a crown rather than to a cross. The fullness of time (Gal. 4:4) was His only reminder; He was not forced to discharge the obligations of His church, but even when He was full of sorrow, He joyously faced the law, answered its demands, and cried out, *"It is finished!"* (John 19:30).

Oh, How He Loves!

How hard it is to talk of love in such a way as to convey what is really meant by it! How often have my eyes been full of tears when I have realized the thought that Jesus loves me! How my spirit has been melted within me at the assurance that He thinks of me and carries me in His heart! But I cannot kindle the same emotion in others, nor can I give, in writing, so much as a faint idea of the bliss that is contained in that exclamation, "Oh, how He loves!"

Dear reader, can you say of yourself, "He loved me"? (See Galatians 2:20.) Then look down into this sea of love, and try to guess its depth. Does it not stagger your faith that He loves you so? Or, if you have strong confidence, does it not enfold your spirit in a flame of admiration and adoring gratitude? Even the angels have never known such love as this! Jesus does not engrave their names upon His hands (Isa. 49:16) or call them His bride (Isa. 62:5). No, this highest fellowship He reserves for worms such as ourselves, whose only response is tearful, hearty thanksgiving and love.

Chapter 6

The Beauty of the Church

Behold, you are fair, my love! Behold, you are fair!
—Song of Songs 4:1

As the bird returns often to its nest, and as the traveler hurries to his home, so does the mind continually pursue the object of its choice. We cannot look too often upon the face that we love; we desire always to have our precious things within sight. It is so even with our Lord Jesus. From all eternity, His *"delight was with the sons of men"* (Prov. 8:31). His thoughts rolled onward to the time when His elect would be born into the world; He viewed them in the mirror of His foreknowledge. The psalmist said, *"In Your book they all were written, the days fashioned for me, when as yet there were none of them"* (Ps. 139:16).

When the world was set upon its pillars (1 Sam. 2:8), He was there, and He *"set the boundaries of the peoples according to the number of the children of Israel"* (Deut. 32:8). Many times before His incarnation, He descended to this earth in the likeness of a man. The Son of Man visited His people on the plains of Mamre (Gen. 18:1–33), by the river of Jabbok (Gen. 32:22–30), beneath the walls of Jericho (Josh. 5:13–15), and in the fiery furnace of Babylon (Dan. 3:19–25). Because His soul delighted in them, He could not rest apart from them, for His heart longed for them. They were never absent from His heart, for He had written their names upon His hands (Isa. 49:16) and carried them on His heart (Exod. 28:29).

Christ Remembers His People

Just as the breastplate containing the names of the tribes of Israel was the most brilliant ornament worn by the high priest, so the names of Christ's elect were His most precious jewels, which He always hung nearest His heart. We may often forget to meditate upon the perfections of our Lord, but He never ceases to remember us. He does not care even half as much for any of His most glorious works as He does for His children.

Although His eye sees everything that has beauty and excellence in it, He never fixes His gaze anywhere with the admiration and delight that He spends upon His purchased ones. He charges His angels concerning them (Matt. 4:6), and He calls upon those holy beings to rejoice with Him over His lost sheep (Luke 15:4–7). He talks about them to Himself, and even on the tree of doom He did not cease to soliloquize concerning them (Luke 23:34). He saw the travail of His soul, and He was abundantly satisfied (Isa. 53:11).

Like a fond mother, Christ Jesus sees every dawning of excellence and every bud of goodness in us. He makes much of the beginnings of our graces, and He rejoices in them. As He is to be our endless song, so we are His perpetual prayer. When He is absent from us, He is still thinking of us, and in the black darkness He has a window through which He looks upon us. When the sun sets in one part of the earth, it rises in another place beyond our visible horizon. Likewise, Jesus, our Sun of Righteousness (Mal. 4:2), is pouring light upon His people in a different way, when to our understanding He seems to have set in darkness.

He Cannot Forget His Bride

His eye is always upon the vineyard that is His church: *"I, the LORD, keep it, I water it every moment; lest any hurt it, I keep it night and day"* (Isa. 27:3). He will not trust His angels to do it, for it is His delight to do everything with His own hands. Zion is in the center of His heart, and He cannot forget her, for every day His thoughts are set upon her.

Likewise, in the Song of Songs, when the bride has neglected her beloved and hidden herself from his sight, he cannot be quiet until he looks upon her again. He calls her forth with the most wooing words: *"O my dove, in the clefts of the rock, in the secret places of the cliff, let me see your face, let me hear your voice; for your voice is sweet, and your face is lovely"* (Song 2:14).

She thinks she is unfit to keep company with such a prince, but he entices her from her hiding place. Inasmuch as she comes forth trembling, and bashfully hides her face with her veil, he asks her to uncover her face, to let her husband gaze on her. She is ashamed to do so, for she is dark from the sun's rays, but he insists that she is beautiful to him. He is not content with merely looking, either. He must feed his ears as well as his eyes, and so he praises her speech and entreats her to let him hear her voice.

In the same way, our Lord rejoices in us! Is this not unparalleled love? We have heard of princes who have been smitten by the beauty of a peasant's daughter, but what of that? How amazing that the Son of God dotes on us, looking with eyes of admiration on the poor children of Adam and listening with joy to the lispings of mere flesh and blood. Should we not be exceedingly charmed by such matchless condescension? And should not our hearts as much delight in Him as He does in us? Oh, surprising truth! Christ Jesus rejoices over His poor, tempted, tried, and erring people.

Christ Makes His Love Known to Us

Sometimes the Lord Jesus tells His people His thoughts of love for them. Concerning this, Erskine once said,

> He does not think it enough behind her back to tell it, but in her very presence He says, "Thou art fair, my love." It is true, this is not His ordinary method; He is a wise lover, who knows when to keep back the intimation of love and when to let it out. But there are times when He will make no secret of it, times when He will put it beyond all dispute in the souls of His people.

The Spirit's Witness

The Holy Spirit is often pleased in a most gracious manner to confirm in our spirits the love Jesus has for us. He takes the things of Christ and reveals them to us. No voice is heard from the clouds, and no vision is seen in the night, but we have a testimony surer than either of these. If an angel would fly from heaven and inform the believer personally of the Savior's love for him, the evidence would not be one bit more satisfactory than what is produced in the heart by the Holy Spirit. Ask those of the Lord's people who have lived nearest to the gates of heaven, and they will tell you that they have had seasons when the love of Christ toward them has been so clear and sure that they could no more doubt it than they could question their own existence.

His Presence Brings Confidence

Yes, beloved believer, you and I have had times of refreshment in the presence of the Lord, and then our faith has mounted to the uttermost heights of assurance. We have had confidence to lean our heads against the chest of our Lord, and we have had no more questions about our Master's affection than John had when he lay *"at His feet as dead"* (Rev. 1:17). The dark question, "Lord, am I the one who will betray You?" (Matt. 26:21–22), has been put far from us. He has kissed us with the kisses of His love (Song 1:2), and He has killed our doubts by the closeness of His embrace. His love has been sweeter than wine to our souls.

We felt that we could sing, *"His left hand is under my head, and his right hand embraces me"* (Song 8:3). Then all earthly troubles were as light as the chaff on the threshing-floor, and the pleasures of the world were as tasteless as the white of an egg. We would have welcomed death as the messenger who would introduce us to our Lord, to whom we were eager to go. Christ's love had stirred us to desire more of Him, even His immediate and glorious presence.

Sometimes, when the Lord has assured me of His love, I have felt as if I could not contain more joy and delight. My eyes were filled with tears of gratitude. I fell upon my knees to bless Him, but I rose again in haste, feeling as if I had nothing more to ask for, but that I must stand up and praise Him. At such times I have lifted my hands to heaven, longing to fill my arms with Him, to talk with Him *"as a man speaks to his friend"* (Exod. 33:11), and to see Him in His own person. I have longed to tell Him how happy He has made His unworthy servant and to fall on my face and kiss His feet in unutterable thankfulness and love.

I have feasted on one promise of my Beloved—*"You are Mine"* (Isa. 43:1)—so much that I have wished, like Peter, to build tabernacles in that place and dwell there forever. But, alas, not all of us have yet learned how to preserve that blessed assurance. We stir up our Beloved and awake Him; then He leaves our uneasy hearts, and we grope after Him and make many weary journeys trying to find Him.

An Abiding Sense of His Love

If we were wiser and more careful, we might preserve the fragrance of Christ's words far longer, for they are not like the ordinary manna that soon rotted, but they are comparable to the little bit of it that was put in the golden pot and preserved for many generations. The sweet Lord Jesus has been known to write his love-thoughts on the hearts of His people in so clear and deep a manner, that they have for months, and even for years, enjoyed a continual sense of His affection. A few doubts have flitted across their minds like thin clouds before a summer's sun, but the warmth of their assurance has remained the same for many joyful days. Their paths have been smooth ones; they have fed in the green pastures beside the still waters, for His rod and staff have comforted them, and His right hand has led them.

I am inclined to think that there is more of this in the church than some people will admit to. We have a large number who dwell upon the hills and gaze on the light of the sun. They are the spiritual giants of the day, though the times do not allow them room to display their gigantic strength. In many humble beds, in many crowded workshops, in many modest homes, there are people of the house of David, people after God's own heart, who are anointed with the holy oil.

It is, however, a mournful truth that whole ranks in the army of our Lord are composed of dwarfish "Littlefaiths," as in John Bunyan's *The Pilgrim's Progress*. People of fearful minds and despondent hearts are to be seen everywhere. Why is this? Is it the Master's fault or ours? Surely He cannot be blamed. It is then a matter of inquiry into our own souls: Can I not grow stronger? Must I be a mourner all my days? How can I get rid of my doubts? The answer must be, Yes, you can be comforted, but only the mouth of the Lord can do it, for anything less than this will be unsatisfactory.

Proof for the Asking

I do not doubt that there are ways in which those who are now weak and trembling may attain boldness in faith and confidence in hope. However, I do not see how this can happen unless the Lord Jesus Christ manifests His love to them and tells them of their union with Him. This He will do, if we seek it of Him. The persistent pleader will not lack his reward.

Hurry to Him, O timid one, and tell Him that nothing will content you except a smile from His own face and a word from His own lips! Speak to Him and say, "Lord Jesus, I cannot rest unless I know that You love me! I desire to have proof of Your love by Your own hand and seal. I cannot live on guesses and surmises; nothing but certainty will satisfy my trembling heart. Lord, look upon me, if indeed You love me, and though I am less than the least of all believers, 'say to my soul, "I am your salvation"' (Ps. 35:3)." When this prayer is heard, the castle of despair must totter; there is not one stone of it that can remain upon another if Christ whispers forth His love. As John Bunyan described it in *The Pilgrim's Progress*, even Mr. Despondency and his daughter, Much-afraid, will dance, and Mr. Ready-to-Halt will leap though he has been using crutches.

Oh, for more of these Bethel visits (Gen. 28:10–19), more frequent visitations from the God of Israel! Oh, how sweet to hear Him say to us, as He did to Abraham, *"Do not be afraid, Abram. I am your shield, your exceedingly great reward"* (Gen. 15:1). To be addressed as Daniel was long ago, *"O man greatly beloved"* (Dan. 10:19), is worth a thousand ages of this world's joy. What more can a creature this side of heaven want to make him peaceful and happy than a plain avowal of love from his Lord's own lips? O Lord, let me always hear You. If You will only speak in mercy to my soul, I will ask no more while I dwell in the land of my pilgrimage!

Dear readers, let us work to obtain a confident assurance of the Lord's delight in us, for this will be one of the readiest ways to produce a similar feeling toward Him in our hearts. It enables Him to commune with us. Christ is well pleased with us; let us approach Him with holy familiarity; let us pour out our thoughts to Him, for His delight in us will secure us an audience. The child may stay away from the father when he knows that he has aroused his father's displeasure, but why should we keep at a distance when Christ Jesus is smiling upon us? Rather, since His smiles attract us, let us enter into His courts and touch His golden scepter. O Holy Spirit, help us to live in happy fellowship with Him whose soul is knit to ours!

Chapter 7

Sweet Fellowship with Christ

And of His fullness we have all received, and grace for grace.
—John 1:16

The Lord Jesus forever delights Himself with the sons of men (Prov. 8:31), and He always stands prepared to reveal and communicate that delight to His people. But we are often incapable of returning His affection or enjoying His fellowship, having fallen into a state so base and degraded that we are dead to Him and have no regard for Him. Even so, something has been done for us and in us that allows us to converse with Jesus and to feel at one with Him.

Fellowship with Jesus is begun and maintained by giving and receiving, by communication and reception. I have selected one branch of this mutual communication as the subject for this chapter.

Look closely at the text verse: *"And of His fullness we have all received, and grace for grace."* As the life of grace is first begotten in us by the Lord Jesus, so is it constantly sustained by Him. We are always drawing from this sacred fountain, always deriving sap from this divine root. Jesus communes with us as He bestows His mercies on us, and it is our privilege to have fellowship with Him as we receive them.

Missed Opportunities for Fellowship

There is this difference between Christ and ourselves: He never gives anything to us without manifesting fellowship, but we often receive from Him in such an insufficient manner that communion is not reciprocated. Therefore, we miss the heavenly opportunity of enjoying it. We frequently receive grace without realizing it. The sacred oil maintains our lamps, while we are ignorant of its hidden influence. We may also be the partakers of many mercies

350

that, through our dullness, we do not perceive to be mercies at all. At other times, blessings are recognized as such, but we are reluctant to trace them to their source in the covenant made with Christ Jesus.

We can easily believe that when the poor saints in Jerusalem received the contribution of the Christians in Macedonia and Achaia (Rom. 15:26), many of them acknowledged the fellowship that was demonstrated by the generous offering. But it is also likely that some of them merely looked upon the material nature of the gift and failed to see the spirit behind it.

Indeed, it is possible that, after a period of poverty, some of the receivers would be apt to give greater prominence to the fact that their need was removed than to the sentiment of fellowship with sympathizing Christians. They would rather rejoice over averted famine than the manifestation of fellowship. Undoubtedly, in many instances, the monetary contributions of the church fail to reveal our fellowship to our poor brothers and sisters, and they produce in them no feelings of communion with the givers.

Now, this sad fact is an illustration of the yet more distressing statement that I have made. Just as many of the partakers of the generosity of the church are not alive to the communion contained within the gifts, so the Lord's people are never sufficiently attentive to fellowship with Jesus in receiving His gifts. Instead, many of them forget that His gifts are a privilege, and all of them are not as aware of this as they could be. What is worse, believers often pervert the gifts of Jesus into food for their own sin and immorality!

We are not free from the fickleness of ancient Israel, and our Lord might very well address us in the language of the following passage:

> "When I passed by you again and looked upon you, indeed your time was the time of love; so I spread My wing over you and covered your nakedness. Yes, I swore an oath to you and entered into a covenant with you, and you became Mine," says the Lord GOD. "Then I washed you in water; yes, I thoroughly washed off your blood, and I anointed you with oil. I clothed you in embroidered cloth and gave you sandals of badger skin; I clothed you with fine linen and covered you with silk. I adorned you with ornaments, put bracelets on your wrists, and a chain on your neck. And I put a jewel in your nose, earrings in your ears, and a beautiful crown on your head. Thus

*you were adorned with gold and silver, and your clothing was
of fine linen, silk, and embroidered cloth. You ate pastry of
fine flour, honey, and oil. You were exceedingly beautiful, and
succeeded to royalty. Your fame went out among the nations
because of your beauty, for it was perfect through My splendor
which I had bestowed on you," says the Lord GOD. "But you
trusted in your own beauty, played the harlot because of your
fame, and poured out your harlotry on everyone passing by
who would have it."* (Ezek. 16:8–15)

Should not most of those who claim faith in God confess the
truth of this accusation? Have not most of us sadly departed from
the purity of our love? We rejoice, however, to observe a remnant of
people who live near the Lord and know the sweetness of fellowship. These individuals receive the promise and the blessing, di-
gesting them so that they become good blood in their veins. These
people feed on their Lord so that they *"grow up in all things into
Him"* (Eph. 4:15). Let us imitate those elevated minds and obtain
their high delights.

Maintaining Sweet Fellowship with Jesus

There is no reason that the lowliest of us should not be like
David, who was a *"man after [God's] own heart"* (1 Sam. 13:14). We
may now be dwarfs, but growth is possible. Let us therefore aim at
a higher stature. With the following advice and the Holy Spirit's
help in carrying it through, we can attain the high position of those
who have and maintain sweet fellowship with the Lord.

Embrace Him at All Times

Make every time of need a time of embracing the Lord. Do not
leave the mercy seat (Exod. 25:21–22) until you have clasped Him
in your arms. In every time of need, He has promised to give grace
to help you (Heb. 4:16). What holds you back from obtaining the
promised assistance, as well as sweet fellowship? Do not be like the
beggar who is content with the charity of another, however grudg-
ingly it may be given to him. Rather, since you are a relative of
Christ, seek a smile and a kiss with every blessing He gives you.

Is He Himself not better than His mercies? What are they
without Him? Cry aloud to Him, and let your petition reach His

ears: "O my Lord, it is not enough for me to receive Your bounties, I must have You also. If You do not give me Yourself along with Your favors, they are of little use to me! Oh, smile on me when You bless me, for otherwise I still am not blessed! You put perfume into all the flowers of Your garden, and fragrance into Your spices; if You withdraw Yourself, they are no longer pleasant to me. Come, then, my Lord, and give me Your love with Your grace."

Take heed, Christian, that your own heart is right on key, so that when the fingers of mercy touch the strings they may resound with full notes of communion. How sad it is to receive a favor without rejoicing in it! Yet such is often the believer's case. The Lord casts His lavish bounties at our doors, and we, like lowly peasants, scarcely look out to thank Him. Our ungrateful hearts and unthankful tongues mar our fellowship by causing us to miss a thousand opportunities for exercising it.

Draw on His Supply of Grace

If you wish to enjoy communion with the Lord Jesus in receiving His grace, you must also endeavor to draw supplies from Him at all times. Make your needs public in the streets of your heart, and when the supply of grace is granted, let all the powers of your soul be present when you receive it. Let no mercy come into your house without giving thanks for it. Make note of all of your Master's benefits. Why should the Lord's bounties be hurried away in the dark or buried in forgetfulness? Always keep the gates of your soul open, and sit by the side of the road to watch the treasures of grace that God the Spirit hourly conveys into your heart from Jehovah-Jesus, your Lord.

Never let an hour pass without drawing on the bank of heaven. If all your needs seem satisfied, look steadfastly until the next moment brings another need; then do not delay, but with this proof of necessity, hurry again to your treasury. Your needs are so numerous that you will never lack a reason for petitioning the fullness of Jesus. However, if such an occasion should ever arise, enlarge your heart, and then love will fill the void.

Do not allow any supposed riches of your own to suspend your daily blessings from the Lord Jesus. You have constant need of Him. You need His intercession, His upholding, His sanctification; you need Him to carry out all your works in you and to preserve you until the Day when He appears again. There is not one moment of your life in which you can do without Christ. Therefore, be always at His door, and the needs that you complain of will be reminders to turn your heart toward your Savior.

Thirst makes a person pant for water, and pain reminds man of the physician. Let your needs likewise lead you to Jesus, and may the blessed Spirit reveal Him to you while He lovingly gives you the rich supplies of His love! Go, poor Christian, let your poverty be the rope that pulls you to your rich Brother. Rejoice that your weaknesses make room for grace to rest upon you, and be glad that you have constant needs that perpetually compel you to have fellowship with your Redeemer—who is worthy to be adored.

Study yourself. Seek out your needs, just as the housewife searches for rooms where she may store her things. Look on your needs as rooms to be filled with more of the grace of Jesus, and allow no corner to be unoccupied. Long for more of Jesus. Let everything incite you to seek greater things.

Cry out to the Lord Jesus to fill the dry beds of your rivers until they overflow; then empty the channels that have until now been filled with your own self-sufficiency. Ask Him to fill these also with His superabundant grace. If your heavy trials cause you to sink deeper in the flood of His consolations, be glad of them; and if your vessel sinks to its very bulwarks, do not be afraid. I would be glad to feel the masthead of my soul twenty fathoms beneath the surface of such an ocean. As Rutherford said, "Oh, to be over the ears in this well! I would not have Christ's love entering into me, but I would enter into it and be swallowed up by that love."

Cultivate an insatiable hunger and an unquenchable thirst for this communion with Jesus through His communications. Let your heart cry forever, "Give, give," until it is filled in paradise.

> O'ercome with Jesu's condescending love,
> Brought into fellowship with Him and His,
> And feasting with Him in His house of wine,
> I'm sick of love, and yet I pant for more
> Communications from my loving Lord.

This is the only covetousness that is allowable. But it is not merely beyond rebuke, it is also worthy of commendation. O believers, enlarge your desires and receive more of your Savior's measureless fullness! I charge you to hold continual fellowship with your Lord, since He invites and commands you to partake of His riches in this fashion.

Rejoice in Received Benefits

Let the satisfaction of your spirit overflow in streams of joy because of the benefits that you have received thus far from God's hand. When the believer rests all his confidence in Christ and delights in Him, it is an exercise of communion. Be glad in the Lord, and rejoice in His blessings!

Behold His favors, rich, free, and continual; will they be buried in ingratitude? Will they be covered with a garment of ingratitude? No! I will praise Him. I must extol Him. Sweet Lord Jesus, let me kiss the dust of Your feet. Let me lose myself in thankfulness, for Your thoughts are precious to me: *"How great is the sum of them!"* (Ps. 139:17). I embrace You in the arms of joy and gratitude, and in this I find my soul drawn to You!

This is a blessed method of fellowship. It is kissing the divine lips of grace with the sanctified lips of affection. Oh, for more rejoicing grace, more of the songs of the heart, more of the melody of the soul!

Recognize the Source of Mercies

Seek to recognize Him who is our Head as the only source of your mercies. Whenever chickens drink water, they lift up their heads to heaven after every drink, as if they are giving thanks. In the same manner, we ought to thank God for every blessing we receive, for He is the source of our blessings. If we have anything that is commendable and gracious, it comes from the Holy Spirit, and that Spirit was first bestowed on Jesus, and then through Him on us.

The oil was first poured on the head of Aaron, and from there it ran down upon his garments (Ps. 133:2). Look on your drops of grace, and remember that they come from the Head, Christ Jesus. All your rays come from this Sun of Righteousness, all your showers are poured out from this heaven, all your fountains spring from this great and immeasurable depth. Oh, for grace to see the hand of Jesus in every blessing, in every benefit! In this way communion will be constantly and firmly experienced.

May the Great Teacher, the Holy Spirit, perpetually direct us to Jesus by making the mercies of the covenant the signposts on the road that leads to Him. Happy is the believer who knows how to find the secret abode of his Beloved by tracking the footsteps of

His loving providence. In this is wisdom. Dear Christian, work diligently to follow up every clue that your Master's grace reveals to you!

Maintain a Sense of Dependence

Sweet fellowship with Christ remains when you maintain a sense of your entire dependence upon His good will and pleasure for the continuance of your richest enjoyments. Never try to live on the old manna or to seek help in Egypt. All must come from Jesus, or you are forever ruined. Old anointings will not suffice; your head must have fresh oil poured on it from the golden horn of the sanctuary, or its glory will cease.

Today you may be on the summit of the mount of God, but He who has put you there must keep you there, or you will sink far more quickly than you can imagine. Your mountain stands firm only when He settles it in its place; if He hides His face, you will soon be troubled. If the Savior should see fit, there is not a window through which you now see the light of heaven that He could not darken in an instant. Joshua commanded the sun to stand still (Josh. 10:12–13), but Jesus can shroud it in total darkness. He can withdraw the joy of your heart, the light of your eyes, and the strength of your life. In His hand your comforts lie, and at His will they can depart from you.

Oh, how rich is the grace that supplies us so continually and does not hold back because of our ingratitude! O Lord Jesus, we bow at Your feet, conscious of our utter inability to do anything without You. In every favor that we are privileged to receive, we adore Your blessed name and acknowledge Your inexhaustible love!

Admire God's Undiminished All-Sufficiency

When you have received much, admire the all-sufficiency that still remains undiminished. Thus, you will commune with Christ not only in what you obtain from Him, but also in the superabundance that remains treasured up in Him. Always remember that giving does not impoverish our Lord. When the clouds, those wandering cisterns of the skies, have poured floods upon the dry ground, an abundance remains in the storehouse of rain. Likewise, in Christ there is always an unbounded supply of grace, though the most liberal showers of grace have fallen ever since the foundation of the earth.

The sun is as bright as ever after all its shining, and the sea is quite as full after all moisture has been drawn from it to form clouds. In the same way, our Lord Jesus is always the same overflowing Fountain of fullness. All this is ours, and we may make it the subject of rejoicing fellowship. Come, believer, walk through the length and breadth of the land, for the land is yours as far as the eye can see, and much beyond that is also yours. It is all the gracious gift of your kind Redeemer and Friend. Is there not ample reason for fellowship in this?

Be Assured by Every Mercy

Regard every spiritual mercy as an assurance of the Lord's communion with you. When a young man gives an engagement ring to the girl he wants to marry, she regards it as a symbol of his delight in her. Believer, do the same with the precious presents of your Lord. The common bounties of Providence are shared in by all men, for the good Householder provides water for His swine as well as for His children. Such things, therefore, are no proof of divine indifference.

But you have richer food to eat; *"the children's bread"* (Matt. 15:26) is your portion, and the heritage of the righteous is reserved for you. Therefore, consider every motion of grace in your heart as a pledge and sign of the moving of your Savior's heart toward you. His whole heart is in every mercy that He sends to you. He has impressed a kiss of love upon each gift, and He wants you to believe that every jewel of mercy is a symbol of His boundless love.

View your adoption, justification, and preservation as sweet enticements to fellowship with Christ. Let every note of the promise sound in your ears like the ringing of the bells of the house of your Lord, inviting you to come to the banquets of His love. Joseph sent donkeys laden with the good things of Egypt to his father, and good old Jacob undoubtedly regarded them as pledges of the love of his son's heart. Be sure not to think less of the kindnesses of Jesus.

Know the Value of His Blessings

Study to know the value of His blessings. They are not ordinary things, like costume jewelry or imitation gemstones. Instead, every one of them is so costly that, if all heaven had been drained of treasure, apart from the precious offering of the Redeemer, not even the least of His benefits could have been purchased. When you see your pardon, consider how great a blessing is contained in it! Hell would have been your eternal portion if Christ had not plucked you from the fire!

When you are enabled to see yourself as clothed in the imputed righteousness of Jesus, admire the profusion of precious things of which your robe is made. Think how many times the Man of Sorrows wearied Himself at that loom of obedience on which He wove that matchless garment. And think, if you can, how many worlds of merit were put into the fabric every time a new thread was woven into it!

Remember that all the angels in heaven could not have provided Him with a single thread that would have been rich enough to weave into the texture of His perfect righteousness. Consider the cost of your maintenance for an hour; remember that your needs are so large that all the storehouses of grace that believers could fill could not feed you for a moment.

What an expensive dependent you are! King Solomon made marvelous provision for his household (1 Kings 4:22–23), but all his meat and fine flour would be like a drop in the bucket compared with your daily needs. *"Thousands of rams"* and *"ten thousand rivers of oil"* (Mic. 6:7) would not provide enough to supply the necessities of your hungering soul. Your smallest spiritual need demands infinity to satisfy it. The sum total of your perpetually repeated demands upon the Lord must be amazing!

Arise, then, and bless the Lord for the invaluable riches with which He has endowed you. See what a dowry your Bridegroom has brought to His poor, penniless spouse. He knows the value of the blessings that He brings to you, for He has paid for them out of His heart's richest blood. Do not be so ungenerous as to overlook them as if they were worth only a little. Poor men know more of the value of money than those who have always reveled in an abundance of wealth. Should not your former poverty teach you the preciousness of the grace that Jesus gives? Remember, there was a time when you would have given a thousand worlds, if they had been yours, in order to procure the very least of His abundant mercies.

Remember Your Salvation

Remember how impossible it would have been for you to receive a single spiritual blessing if you had not been in Jesus. The love of God cannot be poured out into anyone's heart unless he is clearly united with God's Son. No exception has ever been made to the universal curse on those of the first Adam's seed who have no interest in the Second Adam. Christ is the only Zoar in which God's Lots can find a shelter from the destruction of Sodom (Gen. 19:15–25). Apart from Him, the blast of the fiery furnace of God's wrath consumes every green herb; it is only in Him that the soul can live.

When a field is on fire, people see sheets of flame shooting up into the sky, and in haste they flee before the devouring element. Yet they have one hope: in the distance there is a lake of water. They reach it, they plunge into it, and they are safe. Although the skies are molten with the heat, the sun darkened with the smoke, and the field utterly consumed in the fire, they know that they are secure while the cooling flood embraces them.

Likewise, Christ Jesus is the only escape for a sinner pursued by the fiery wrath of God, and every believer ought to remember this. Our own works could never shelter us, for they have proved to be only refuges of lies (Isa. 28:17). Even if they had been a thousand times more and better, they would have been only as the spider's web, too frail to hang eternal interests on. There is only one name, one sacrifice, one blood, by which we may escape. All other attempts at salvation are a grievous failure.

How, then, with your innumerable sins, have you escaped the damnation of hell, much less become the recipient of bounties so rich and large? Blessed Window of Heaven, sweet Lord Jesus, let Your church forever adore You as the only channel by which mercies can flow to her. My soul, give Him continual praise, for without Him you would have been poorer than a beggar. Be mindful, O heir of heaven, that you could not have had one ray of hope or one word of comfort if you had not been in union with Christ Jesus! The crumbs that fall from your table are more than grace itself would have given you if you had not been loved and approved in Jesus.

Everything that you have, you have in Him; you have been chosen in Him, redeemed in Him, justified in Him, accepted in Him. You are risen in Him, but without Him you would have died the second death (Rev. 21:8). In Him you are raised to the heavenly places, but out of Him you would have been damned eternally.

Bless Him, then. Ask the angels to bless Him. Rouse all ages to a harmony of praise for His condescending love in taking poor, guilty nothings into oneness with Himself—who is completely worthy of adoration. This is a blessed means of promoting communion.

The sacred Comforter is pleased to take of the things of Christ and reveal them to us as ours, but they are only ours as we are in Him. Holy Jesus, let us never forget that we are members of Your spiritual body and that we are blessed and preserved for this reason.

Think of What Christ Endured

Meditate on the gracious acts that procured such blessings for you. Consider the labors that your Lord endured for you and the sufferings by which He purchased the mercies that He bestows. What human tongue can describe the unutterable misery of His heart or tell so much as one of the agonies that crowded upon His soul? How much less can we comprehend the vast total of Christ's sufferings! But all His sorrows were necessary for your benefit, and without them not one of your innumerable mercies could have been bestowed. Keep in mind that

> There's ne'er a gift His hand bestows,
> But cost His heart a groan.

Look on the frozen ground of Gethsemane, and behold the bloody sweat that stained the soil! Turn to the hall of Gabbatha (John 19:13), and see the victim of justice pursued by His insistent foes! Enter the guardroom of the Praetorians, and view the spitting, and the plucking of His hair! Then conclude your review upon Golgotha, the mount of doom, where death consummated His tortures. If, by divine assistance, you are enabled to enter, in some humble measure, into the depths of your Lord's sufferings, you will be better prepared to hold fellowship with Him the next time you receive His priceless gifts. In proportion to your sense of their costliness will be your capacity for enjoying the love that is centered in them.

Never Forget That Christ Is Yours

Above all, never forget that Christ is yours. Amid the profusion of His gifts, never forget that the chief gift is Himself; and do not forget that, after all, His gifts are but Himself. He clothes you, but it is with Himself, with His own spotless righteousness and character. He washes you, but His innermost self, His own heart's blood, is the stream with which the fountain overflows. He feeds you with the bread of heaven, but do not forget that the bread is Himself, His own body that He gives as the food of souls.

Never be satisfied with something less than a whole Christ. A wife will not be put off with jewels and attire—these will be nothing to her unless she can call her husband's heart and person her own. It was the Passover lamb on which the ancient Israelites feasted on that night that was never to be forgotten. In the same way, feast on Jesus, and on nothing less than Jesus, for anything less than Him will be food too light for your soul's satisfaction. Oh, be careful to eat His flesh and drink His blood (John 6:53–58), and so receive Him into yourself in a real and spiritual manner, for nothing but this will be an evidence of eternal life in your soul!

Is there more that I can add to these instructions for maintaining fellowship with our Lord? One great exhortation remains, which must not be omitted: seek the abundant assistance of the Holy Spirit to enable you to put these things into practice, for without His aid, all that I have written here will be like tormenting the lame with rules for walking, or the dying with regulations for the preservation of health. O Divine Spirit, while we enjoy the grace of Jesus, lead us into the secret abode of our Lord, so that we may eat with Him, and He with us. Grant to us hourly grace, so that we may continue in the company of our Lord from the rising to the setting of the sun!

Chapter 8

Redeemed Souls Freed from Fear

Fear not, for I have redeemed you.
—Isaiah 43:1

I have been lamenting my unfitness for my work, especially for the warfare to which I am called. A sense of heaviness recently came over me, but relief came very quickly, for which I thank the Lord. Indeed, I was greatly burdened, but the Lord comforted me with the words of Isaiah 43:1: *"But now, thus says the LORD, who created you, O Jacob, and He who formed you, O Israel: 'Fear not.'"* I said to myself, "I am what God created me to be, and I am what He formed me to be. Therefore, I must, after all, be the right man for the place in which He has put me." We are in no position to blame our Creator or to suspect that He has missed His mark in forming an instrument for His work. When we understand this, new comfort will come to us.

Not only do the operations of grace in the spiritual world give us consolation, but we are also comforted by what the Lord has done in creation. We are told to cease being afraid, and we do so because we perceive that it is the Lord who made us, and not we ourselves. He will be the One to justify His own creative skills by accomplishing through us the purposes of His love.

The next sentence of Isaiah 43:1 is usually very comforting to my soul. The verse says, *"Fear not, for I have redeemed you."* Think for a few minutes of the wonderful depth of consolation that lies in this fact. We have been redeemed by the Lord Himself, and this is a major reason why we should never again be subject to fear. Oh, that the logic of this fact could be turned into practice, so that from now on we would rejoice, or at least feel the peace of God!

In Times of Trouble

These words of our text verse may be spoken, first of all, concerning those frequent occasions in which the Lord has redeemed

His people out of trouble. Many times might our Lord say to each one of us, *"I have redeemed you."* Out of six, yes, even six thousand trials He has rescued us by the right hand of His power. He has delivered us from our afflictions (Ps. 34:19), and He has *"brought us out to rich fulfillment"* (Ps. 66:12).

In the remembrance of all these redemptions the Lord seems to say to us, "What I have done before, I will do again. I have redeemed you, and I will still redeem you. I have brought you from under the hand of the oppressor; I have delivered you from the tongue of the slanderer; I have borne you up under the load of poverty and sustained you under the pains of sickness; and I am able still to do the same. Why, then, do you fear? Why should you be afraid, since already I have again and again redeemed you? Take heart, and be confident, for even to old age and to death itself I will continue to be your strong Redeemer."

Looking again at our text verse, I suppose it could refer to the great redemption out of Egypt. This statement was addressed to the people of God under captivity in Babylon, and we know that the Lord referred to the Egyptian redemption, for He said, *"I gave Egypt for your ransom"* (Isa. 43:3). Egypt was a great country and a rich country, for we read of *"the treasures in Egypt"* (Heb. 11:26), but God would give all the nations of the earth for His Israel (Isa. 43:4). This was a wonderful comfort to the people of God; they constantly referred to Egypt and the Red Sea, and they made their national anthem out of it.

In all Israel's times of disaster and calamity and trial, they joyfully remembered that the Lord had redeemed them when they were a company of slaves, helpless and hopeless, under a tyrant who cast their firstborn children into the Nile, a tyrant whose power was so tremendous that all the armies of the world could not have wrested their deliverance from his iron hand. The very nod of Pharaoh seemed to the inhabitants of Egypt to be omnipotent; he was a builder of pyramids, a master of all the sciences of peace and the arts of war. What could the Israelites have done against him?

Jehovah came to their relief in their dire extremity. His plagues followed each other in quick succession. The awe-inspiring volleys of the Lord's artillery confounded His foes. At last He killed all the firstborn of Egypt, the most valuable part of all their strength. Then Egypt was glad that Israel departed, and the Lord brought forth His people with silver and gold. All the army of

Egypt was overthrown and destroyed in the Red Sea, and the timbrels of the daughters of Israel sounded joyously on its shores.

This redemption out of Egypt was so remarkable that it is remembered even in heaven. The Old Testament song is woven into that of the new covenant, for the redeemed *"sing the song of Moses, the servant of God, and the song of the Lamb"* (Rev. 15:3). The first redemption was such a wonderful type and prophecy of the other that it will be held in memory forever and ever. Every Israelite must have had confidence in God after what He had done for the people in redeeming them out of Egypt. Every one of the seed of Jacob had an excellent reason to *"fear not."*

Nevertheless, I interpret these words as a reference to the redemption that has been bought for us by Him who loved us and washed us from our sins by His own blood. Let us think of it in this way, too.

In Times of Perplexity

The remembrance of this transcendent redemption ought to comfort us in all times of perplexity. When we cannot see our way or cannot determine what to do, we do not need to be troubled at all concerning it, for the Lord Jehovah can see a way out of every complication.

There was never a problem so difficult to solve as what is answered in redemption. The tremendous difficulty was in this: How can God be just and yet be the Savior of sinners? How can He fulfill His declarations against evil and yet forgive sin? If that problem had been left to angels and men, they could never have worked it out throughout eternity. But God has solved it by freely delivering up His own Son.

In the glorious sacrifice of Jesus we see the justice of God magnified. He placed the whole weight of sin on the blessed Lord, who had become one with His chosen people. Jesus identified Himself with His people; therefore, their sin was laid on Him, and the sword of the Lord awoke against Him. He was not taken arbitrarily to be a victim, but He was a voluntary Sufferer. His relationship amounted to covenant oneness with His people, and *"it was necessary for the Christ to suffer"* (Luke 24:46).

There is a wisdom in this that overcomes all minor perplexities. Take this into account, then, you poor soul in suspense! The Lord says, *"'I have redeemed you.'"* I have already brought you out of the labyrinth in which you were lost because of sin; therefore, I will take you out of the meshes of the net of temptation and will lead you through the maze of trial. *'I will bring the blind by a way they did not know; I will lead them in paths they have not known'* (Isa. 42:16). *'I will bring back from Bashan, I will bring them back from the depths of the sea'* (Ps. 68:22)."

Let us commit our ways to the Lord. Mine is a particularly difficult way, but *"I know that my Redeemer lives"* (Job 19:25), and He will lead me by a right way. He will be our Guide even unto death, and after death He will guide us through those unknown tracks of the mysterious region and will cause us to rest with Him forever.

In Times of Poverty

If we are ever in great poverty, or if we are very limited in means for the Lord's work, let us not be afraid that we will never have our needs supplied. Instead, let us cast off such fears as we listen to the music of these words: *"Fear not, for I have redeemed you."* God Himself looked down from heaven and saw that there was no one who could give Him a ransom for his brother (Ps. 49:7), and each man on his own part was hopelessly bankrupt. Yet despite our spiritual poverty, He found the means of our redemption. What is the significance of this?

Notice how the Holy Spirit makes use of this fact: *"He who did not spare His own Son, but delivered Him up for us all, how shall He not with Him also freely give us all things?"* (Rom. 8:32). We cannot have a need that the Lord will not supply. Since God has given us Jesus, He will give us, not some things, but *"all things."* Indeed, all things are ours in Christ Jesus. No necessity of life can for a single moment be compared to the fearful necessity that .the Lord has already supplied. The infinite gift of God's own Son is far greater than all that can be included in the term *"all things."* Therefore, the poor and needy may take courage that God has said to them, *"Fear not, for I have redeemed you."* Perplexity and poverty are thus effectively met.

When We Feel Insignificant

At times we are troubled by a sense of our personal insignificance. It seems too much to hope that God's infinite mind should enter into our lowly affairs. Though David said, *"I am poor and needy; yet the LORD thinks upon me"* (Ps. 40:17), we are not always quite prepared to say the same. We make our sorrows great under the vain idea that they are too small for the Lord to notice.

I believe that our greatest miseries spring from those little worries that we hesitate to bring to our heavenly Father. Our gracious God puts an end to all such thoughts by saying, *"Fear not, for I have redeemed you."* You are not of such little importance as you suppose. The Lord would never waste His sacred expenditure. He bought you with a price; therefore, He places much confidence in you. Notice what the Lord says: *"Since you were precious in My sight, you have been honored, and I have loved you; therefore I will give men for you, and people for your life"* (Isa. 43:4).

It is amazing that the Lord should think so much of us as to give Jesus for us. *"What is man that You are mindful of him?"* (Ps. 8:4). Yet God's mind is filled with thoughts of love toward man. Do you not know that His only begotten Son entered this world and became a man? The Man Christ Jesus has a name at which every knee shall bow (Phil. 2:10), and He is so dear to the Father that, for His sake, His chosen ones are accepted and are made to enjoy the freest access to Him. We may truly sing,

> So near, so very near to God,
> Nearer we cannot be,
> For in the person of His Son
> We are as near as He.

The very hairs of our heads are all numbered (Matt. 10:30), and we may roll the least burden upon the Lord. We may cast off the cares that we should not hold on to, for *"He cares for [us]"* (1 Pet. 5:7). He who redeemed us never forgets us. His wounds have *"inscribed [us] on the palms of [His] hands"* (Isa. 49:16) and written our names deep in His side. Jesus stoops to our level, for He stooped to bear the cross to redeem us. Do not, therefore, be afraid because of your insignificance.

> *Why do you say, O Jacob, and speak, O Israel: "My way is hidden from the LORD, and my just claim is passed over by my God"? Have you not known? Have you not heard? The everlasting God, the LORD, the Creator of the ends of the earth, neither faints nor is weary. His understanding is unsearchable. He gives power to the weak, and to those who have no might He increases strength.* (Isa. 40:27–29)

The Lord remembers the insignificant ones in Israel. He carries the lambs *"in His bosom"* (Isa. 40:11).

When We Sense Our Fickleness

We are liable to worry a little when we think of our change-ableness. If you are at all like me, you are very far from being always the same. I am sometimes lifted to the very heavens, and then I go down to the deeps. I am at one time bright with joy and confidence, and at another time dark as midnight with doubts and fears. Even Elijah, who was so brave, had his fainting fits. We are to be blamed for this, yet the fact remains: our experience is like an April day, when rain and sunshine take turns. Amid our mournful changes, we rejoice to hear the Lord's own voice saying, *"Fear not, for I have redeemed you."* Everything is not shifting waves; there is rock somewhere. Redemption is an accomplished fact. "The Cross, it stands fast. Hallelujah!"

The price has been paid, the ransom accepted. This has been accomplished and can never be undone. Jesus says, *"I have redeemed you."* Our feelings may change, but this does not alter the fact that we have been bought with a price and made the Lord's own by the precious blood of Jesus. The Lord God has already done so much for us that our salvation is sure in Christ Jesus. Will He begin to build and fail to finish? Will He lay the foundation in the everlasting covenant, dedicate the walls with the infinite sacrifice of the Lamb of God, give up the choicest Treasure He ever had, the chosen and precious One of God, to be the Cornerstone and then not finish the work He has begun? No, if He has redeemed us, He has, in that act, given us the pledge of all things.

See how the gifts of God are tied to this redemption. *"I have redeemed you; I have called you"* (Isa. 43:1).

> *For whom He foreknew, He also predestined to be conformed to the image of His Son, that He might be the firstborn among many brethren. Moreover whom He predestined, these He also called; whom He called, these He also justified; and whom He justified, these He also glorified.* (Rom. 8:29–30)

The Promise of Redemption

Here is a chain in which each link is joined to all the rest, so that they cannot be separated. If God had gone only so far as to make a promise, He would not have gone back on it. If God had gone only so far as to swear an oath by Himself, He would not have failed to keep it. But because He went beyond promise and oath, and by this the Sacrifice was slain and the covenant was ratified, it would be blasphemous to imagine that He would afterward annul His commitment and turn from His solemn pledge. God never goes back on His promises; consequently, His redemption will redeem, and in redeeming it will secure all things for us. *"Who shall separate us from the love of Christ?"* (Rom. 8:35).

With the bloodstain on us, we may well cease to fear. How can we perish? How can we be deserted in the hour of need? We have been bought with too great a price for our Redeemer to let us slip. Therefore, let us march on with confidence, hearing our Redeemer say to us, *"When you pass through the waters, I will be with you; and through the rivers, they shall not overflow you. When you walk through the fire, you shall not be burned, nor shall the flame scorch you"* (Isa. 43:2).

Concerning His redeemed, the Lord will say to the Enemy, *"Do not touch My anointed ones, and do My prophets no harm"* (1 Chron. 16:22). *"The stars from their courses"* (Judg. 5:20) fight for the ransomed of the Lord. If their eyes were opened, they would see the *"mountain...full of horses and chariots of fire all around [them]"* (2 Kings 6:17).

Oh, how my weary heart prizes redeeming love! If it were not for this, I would lie down and die. Friends forsake me, foes surround me, I am filled with contempt and tortured with subtlety and cunning that I cannot defeat. But as the Lord of all brought our Lord Jesus back from the dead by the blood of the everlasting covenant, so by the blood of His covenant does He loose His prisoners and sustain the hearts of those who tremble at His Word. *"O my soul, march on in strength"* (Judg. 5:21), for the Lord has said to you, *"Fear not, for I have redeemed you."*

Chapter 9

Bonds of Unity

I drew them with gentle cords, with bands of love,
and I was to them as those who take the yoke from their neck.
I stooped and fed them.
—Hosea 11:4

Systematic theologians have usually agreed that there are three aspects of union with Christ: natural, spiritual, and covenantal. It is possible that these three terms are comprehensive enough to cover the whole subject, but I know of two other ways in which we are united with Christ. These are the bond of love and the bond of purpose, and I will mention them before the other three.

The Bond of Love

From the beginning, believers were joined to Christ by bonds of everlasting love. Before He took their nature upon Himself or brought them into a conscious enjoyment of Himself, His heart was set on them, and His soul delighted in them. Long before the worlds were made, His omniscient eye beheld His chosen ones and viewed them with delight. Strong were the indissoluble bonds of love, which then united Jesus to the souls whom He determined to redeem. No bars of steel could have been more real and effective bonds.

True love, of all things in the universe, has the greatest cementing force and will bear the greatest strain. Indeed, love will endure the heaviest pressure. Who can tell what trials the Savior's love has borne and how well such love has endured them? No union was ever truer than this. As the soul of Jonathan was knit to the soul of David so that he loved David as his own soul, so was our glorious Lord united and joined to us by ties of fervent, faithful love.

Love has a most potent power in creating and sustaining unity, but it never displays its force as well as when it brings the Creator into oneness with the created, the divine into alliance with the human. This, then, is to be regarded as the dayspring of union—the love of Christ embracing in its folds the whole of the elected family of God.

The Bond of Purpose

There is, moreover, a union of purpose as well as of love. In the union of love, the elect are made one with Jesus by the act and will of the Son. In the union of purpose, they are joined to Him by the ordination and decree of the Father. These divine acts are equally eternal. The Son loved His people and chose them to be His own bride; the Father made the same choice and decreed that the chosen ones would be forever one with His all-glorious Son. The Son loved them, and the Father decreed them His portion and inheritance; the Father ordained them to be what the Son Himself had made them.

In God's purpose, His people have been eternally associated with Christ as parts of one plan. Salvation was the foreordained plan by which God magnified Himself, and it was necessary that a Savior was in that plan—someone associated with the people chosen to be saved. The scope of redemption included both Redeemer and redeemed. They could not be dissociated in the mind and will of the all-planning Jehovah.

The same Book that contains the names of the heirs of life also contains the name of their Redeemer. Jesus could not have been a Redeemer unless souls had been given Him to redeem, nor could believers have been called the *"ransomed of the LORD"* (Isa. 35:10) if He had not undertaken to purchase them. Redemption, when decided upon by the God of heaven, included in it both Christ and His people; therefore, in the decree that established it, they were brought into a near and intimate alliance.

God foresaw the catastrophe of the Fall, and this foresight led Him to provide a gracious way for the elect to escape their inevitable ruin. Thus, other forms of union followed as part of the divine arrangement. These forms of union, besides their immediate purpose in salvation, undoubtedly had a further purpose of illustrating the condescending alliance that Jesus had formed with His chosen. The following are these other forms of union.

Under the Covenant

Jesus is one with His elect through a covenant bond. Every heir of flesh and blood has a personal interest in Adam because he was the covenant head and the representative of the race under the law of works. Under the law of grace, however, every redeemed soul is one with the Lord from heaven, since He is the Second Adam, the Sponsor and Substitute of the elect in the new covenant of love.

The writer of Hebrews declared that Levi was in the loins of Abraham when Melchizedek met him (Heb. 7:9–10). It is equally true that the believer was in the loins of Jesus Christ, the Mediator, when the covenant settlements of grace were decreed, ratified, and made sure forever. Thus, whatever Christ has done, He has done for the whole body of His church. We were crucified in Him and buried with Him (Rom. 6:3–4), and to make it still more wonderful, we are risen with Him and have even ascended with Him to heavenly places (Eph. 2:6).

In this way, the church has fulfilled the law and is *"accepted in the Beloved"* (Eph. 1:6). It is thus that she is regarded with satisfaction by the just Jehovah, for He views her in Jesus and does not look on her as separate from her covenant Head. As the anointed Redeemer of Israel, Christ Jesus has nothing distinct from His church, but all that He has He holds for her.

Adam's righteousness was ours as long as he maintained it, and his sin was ours the moment he committed it. In the same manner, all that the Second Adam is, or does, is ours as well as His, seeing that He is our Representative. Here is the foundation of the covenant of grace. This gracious system of representation and substitution, which moved Justin Martyr to cry out, "O blessed change! O sweet permutation!" is the very groundwork of the Gospel of our salvation and is to be received with strong faith and rapturous joy. In every place, believers are perfectly one with Jesus.

United in Our Natures

For the accomplishment of the great works of atonement and perfect obedience, it was necessary that the Lord Jesus should take upon Himself *"the likeness of sinful flesh"* (Rom. 8:3). Thus, He became one with us in our nature, for in Holy Scripture all partakers of flesh and blood are regarded as of one family. By the fact of common descent from Adam, all men are of one race, seeing that

371

God *"has made from one blood every nation of men to dwell on all the face of the earth"* (Acts 17:26). Hence, in the Bible, man is spoken of universally as *"your brother"* (Lev. 19:17) and *"your neighbor"* (Exod. 20:16), to whom, because of our nature and descent, we are required to render kindness and goodwill.

Now, our Great Melchizedek, in His divinity, is *"without father, without mother, without genealogy, having neither beginning of days nor end of life"* (Heb. 7:3). He is at an infinite distance from fallen manhood both in essence and in rank. Yet as to His manhood, He is to be reckoned as one of us. He was born of a woman. He rested on her breasts and was gently bounced upon her knee. He grew from infancy to youth and then to manhood, and in every stage He was a true and real partaker of our humanity. He is as truly of the race of Adam as He is divine.

Jesus is God without fiction or metaphor, and He is man beyond doubt or dispute. In Christ, the Godhead was not humanized and thereby diluted, and manhood was not transformed into divinity and thereby made more than human. No man was ever more completely human than was the Son of Man, the Man of Sorrows and the One who was acquainted with grief. He is man's Brother, for He bore the whole nature of man. *"The Word became flesh and dwelt among us"* (John 1:14). He who was very God of very God made Himself *"a little lower than the angels"* (Ps. 8:5), and took *"the form of a bondservant, and* [came] *in the likeness of men"* (Phil. 2:7).

This was done with the most excellent intentions with regard to our redemption, inasmuch as it was necessary that man should suffer because he had sinned. However, it undoubtedly had a further purpose: to honor the church and to enable her Lord to sympathize with her. The apostle very beautifully remarked,

> *Inasmuch then as the children have partaken of flesh and blood, He Himself likewise shared in the same, that through death He might destroy him who had the power of death, that is, the devil, and release those who through fear of death were all their lifetime subject to bondage.* (Heb. 2:14–15)

He also wrote, *"For we do not have a High Priest who cannot sympathize with our weaknesses, but was in all points tempted as we are, yet without sin"* (Heb. 4:15).

Thus, in ties of blood, Jesus, the Son of Man, is one with all the heirs of heaven, *"for which reason He is not ashamed to call them brethren"* (Heb. 2:11). Here we have reason for the strongest comfort and delight, seeing that *"both He who sanctifies and those who are being sanctified are all of one"* (v. 11). We can say of our Lord as poor Naomi said of bounteous Boaz, *"This man is a relation of ours, one of our close relatives"* (Ruth 2:20). Overwhelmed by the liberality of our blessed Lord, we are often led to cry with Ruth, *"Why have I found favor in your eyes, that you should take notice of me, since I am a foreigner?"* (v. 10). Are we not ready to die with wonder when, in answer to such a question, He tells us that He is our Brother, bone of our bones and flesh of our flesh?

If in all our trials and distresses we would always treasure in our minds the remembrance of our Redeemer's manhood, we would never bemoan the absence of a sympathizing heart. We would always have His abundant compassion to comfort us. He is no stranger; He is able to enter into the heart's bitterness, for He Himself has tasted bitter hardships. Let us never doubt His power to sympathize with us in our infirmities and sorrows.

One aspect of this subject of our natural union with Christ would be improper to pass over, for it is very precious to the believer. While the Lord Jesus takes upon Himself our nature (Phil. 2:7), He restores in us the image of God that was stained and defaced by the fall of Adam (2 Pet. 1:4). He raises us from the degradation of sin to the dignity of perfection. Thus, in a twofold sense, the Head and members are of one nature, and not like the monstrous image that Nebuchadnezzar saw in his dream, where the head was of fine gold, but the belly and the thighs were of bronze; the legs of iron, and the feet part iron and part clay. (See Daniel 2:32–33.)

Christ's body is no absurd combination of opposites; the Head is immortal, and the body is immortal, too, for thus the record stands: *"Because I live, you will live also"* (John 14:19). *"As is the heavenly Man, so also are those who are heavenly. And as we have borne the image of the man of dust, we shall also bear the image of the heavenly Man"* (1 Cor. 15:48–49). In just a short time, this will be more fully manifested to us, for *"this corruptible must put on incorruption, and this mortal must put on immortality"* (v. 53).

Whatever the Head is, such is the body and every member in particular—a chosen Head and chosen members, an accepted Head and accepted members, a living Head and living members. If the

Head is of pure gold, all the parts of the body are also of pure gold. Thus, the union of our human nature with Christ's divine nature is twofold—a perfect basis for the closest communion.

Stop here for a moment and contemplate the infinite condescension of the Son of God in lifting your wretchedness into blessed union with His glory. You cannot think of these things without ecstatic amazement. You are so lowly that, in remembrance of your mortality, you may *"say to corruption, 'You are my father,' and to the worm, 'You are my mother and my sister'"* (Job 17:14). Yet in Christ, you are so honored that you can say to the Almighty, *"Abba, Father"* (Rom. 8:15), and to the Incarnate God, "You are my Brother (Mark 3:35); you are my Husband" (Hos. 2:16).

If being descendants of ancient and noble families makes men think highly of themselves, surely we have reason to glory over the heads of them all. Lay hold of this privilege; do not let a senseless laziness make you neglect to trace this lineage. Do not allow any foolish attachment to present vanities occupy your thoughts to the point that this glorious privilege is excluded. We have the heavenly honor of union with Christ.

We must now retrace our steps to the ancient mountains and contemplate our union with Christ in one of its earliest forms.

Spiritual Unity

Christ Jesus is also joined to His people in a spiritual union. Borrowing once more from the story of Ruth, we notice that Boaz, although one with Ruth by kinship, did not rest until he had entered into an even closer union with her, namely, that of marriage. In the same manner, added to the natural union of Christ with His people, there is a spiritual union by which He assumes the position of Husband, while the church is His bride.

In love, Christ espoused the church to Himself, as a chaste virgin, long before she fell under the yoke of bondage. Full of burning affection, He toiled as Jacob did for Rachel, until she had been paid for in full. And now, having sought her by His Spirit and having brought her to know and love Him, He awaits the glorious hour when their mutual bliss will be consummated at the Marriage Supper of the Lamb.

The glorious Bridegroom has not yet presented His betrothed, perfected and complete, before the Majesty of heaven. She has not yet actually entered into the enjoyment of her dignities as His wife and queen. Instead, she is still a wanderer in a world of woe, a dweller in the tents of Kedar (Ps. 120:5). But even now she is the bride, the spouse of Jesus, dear to His heart, precious in His sight, and united with His person. In love and tenderness, He says to her,

> Forget thee I will not, I cannot, thy name
> Engraved on My heart doth forever remain:
> The palms of My hands whilst I look on I see
> The wounds I received when suffering for thee.

Toward the church, Christ exercises all the affectionate roles of Husband. He makes rich provision for her needs, pays all her debts, allows her to assume His name and to share in all His wealth. He will never act otherwise to her. He will never mention the word *divorce,* for *"He hates divorce"* (Mal. 2:16). Death severs the conjugal tie between the most loving mortals, but it cannot divide the links of this immortal marriage.

In heaven no one marries, but everyone is as an angel of God (Matt. 22:30); yet there is one marvelous exception to the rule, for in heaven Christ and His church will celebrate their joyous nuptials. This marriage relationship, as it is more lasting, is also more intimate than earthly wedlock. Even the purest and most fervent love of a husband is but a faint picture of the flame that burns in the heart of Jesus. Surpassing all human union is that spiritual cleaving to the church for which Christ left His Father and became one flesh with her.

If this is the union that abides between our souls and the person of our Lord, how deep and broad is the channel of our communion! This is no narrow pipe through which a threadlike stream may wind its way! No, it is a channel of amazing depth and breadth, along which a substantial volume of living water may roll its strength. Behold, He has set before us an open door; let us not be slow to enter. The city of communion has many pearly gates. Every other gate is made up of one pearl, and each gate is thrown open to the uttermost so that we may enter, assured of welcome.

If there were only one small opening through which we could talk with Jesus, it would be a high privilege to thrust a word of fellowship through that narrow door. Indeed, we are blessed in having so large an entrance! If the Lord Jesus had been far away from us, with many a stormy sea between, we would have longed to send a messenger to Him to carry to Him our love and to bring us news from His Father's house. But see His kindness! He has built His house next door to ours. More than that, He settles in with us, and He resides in our poor humble hearts, so that He may have perpetual communion with us.

Oh, how foolish must we be, if we do not live in habitual communion with Him! When the road is long and dangerous and difficult, we do not wonder that friends seldom meet with each other. But when friends live together, when they have the sort of friendship that was between Jonathan and David, will they forget about each other? A wife may, when her husband is on a journey, spend many days without conversing with him. But she could never endure to be separated from him in this manner if she knew that he was still in one of the rooms of their own house. Seek your Lord, for He is near; embrace Him, for He is your Brother; hold Him fast, for He is your Husband; press Him to your heart, for He is of your own flesh.

Vital Union

So far in this chapter, we have considered only the acts of Christ for us, by which He proves His union to us and brings it into effect. We must now come to more personal and tangible forms of this great truth.

Those who are set apart for the Lord are in due time severed from the impure mass of fallen humanity. By sovereign grace, they are engrafted into the person of the Lord Jesus. This, which we call vital union, is a matter of experience rather than of doctrine. It must be learned in the heart, not by the head.

Like every other work of the Spirit, the actual implantation of the soul into Christ Jesus is a mysterious operation. It cannot be understood by carnal reason any more than the new birth can be understood, and the two experiences accompany one another. Nevertheless, the spiritual man discerns it as a most essential thing in the salvation of the soul, and he clearly sees how a living union with Christ is the certain result of the quickening influence of the Holy Spirit. Indeed, in some respects, this living union is identical with the influence of the Spirit.

When, in His mercy, the Lord passed by and saw us in our natural, guilt-ridden state, He first of all said, "Live." He did this first because, without life, there can be no spiritual knowledge, feeling, or motion. Life is one of the absolutely essential things in spiritual matters, and until it is bestowed, we are incapable of partaking in the things of the kingdom.

Now, the life that grace confers upon believers at the moment of their renewal is none other than the life of Christ, which, like the sap from the stem, runs into us, the branches, and establishes a living connection between our souls and Jesus. Faith is the grace that perceives this union and proceeds from it as its first fruit. To use another metaphor, it is the neck that joins the body of the church to its all-glorious Head.

Faith lays hold of the Lord Jesus with a firm and determined grasp. She knows His excellence and worth, and no temptation can induce her to put her trust elsewhere. In turn, Christ Jesus is so delighted with this heavenly grace that He never ceases to strengthen and sustain her by the loving embrace and all-sufficient support of His eternal arms. Here, then, is established a living, tangible, and delightful union, which casts forth streams of love, confidence, sympathy, satisfaction, and joy, from which both the bride and Bridegroom love to drink.

When the eye is clear and the soul can perceive this oneness between itself and Christ, it is as if redeemed and Redeemer share the same pulse, or as if the same blood flows through their veins together. Then the heart is made exceedingly glad; it is as near to heaven as it ever can be on earth, and it is prepared for the enjoyment of the most sublime and spiritual kind of fellowship. This union may be quite as true when we are troubled with doubts concerning it, but it cannot offer consolation to the soul unless it is indisputably proven and assuredly felt. At such a time, it is indeed a honeycomb dripping with sweetness, a precious jewel sparkling with light.

Chapter 10

The Gift of Rest

Come to Me, all you who labor and are heavy laden,
and I will give you rest.
—Matthew 11:28

These words are typically considered as an encouragement to those who labor and are burdened. Therefore, we may have failed to read them as a promise for ourselves. But, beloved friends, we have come to Jesus; therefore, He stands committed to fulfill this priceless pledge to us. We may now enjoy the promise, for we have obeyed the precept. The Faithful and True Witness, whose Word is truth, promised us rest if we would come to Him. Therefore, since we have come to Him and are always coming to Him, we may boldly say, "O God, who is our Peace, make good Your word to us in which you have said, *'I will give you rest.'*"

By faith, we hear our Lord saying to each of us, with a voice of the sweetest music, *"I will give you rest."* May the Holy Spirit bring to each of us the fullness of the rest and peace of God as we consider the promise in these words.

A Promise for Our Spiritual Natures

While studying the Scriptures, we need holy insight to read between the lines and beneath the letter of the Word. We must be enabled by the Holy Spirit to see the deeper meaning to a promise such as, *"I will give you rest."* This promise must mean rest to all parts of our spiritual natures. Our bodies cannot rest if our heads are aching or if our feet are full of pain; if one part of us is disturbed, our bodies are unable to rest. Likewise, the higher nature is one. All its faculties and powers are bound together by such intimate sympathies that every one of them must rest or none can be at ease. But Jesus gives real and universal rest to every part of our spiritual beings.

For the Heart

The heart is by nature as restless as the ocean's waves. It seeks an object for its affection, and when it finds one beneath the stars, it is doomed to sorrow. Either the beloved changes and there is disappointment, or death comes in and there is bereavement. The more tender the heart, the greater its unrest. For some people, the heart is simply the strongest muscle, and these individuals remain undisturbed, because they are callous. But the sensitive, the generous, the unselfish, are often found *"seeking rest, and find*[ing] *none"* (Matt. 12:43). To such individuals, the Lord Jesus says, *"Come to Me,...and I will give you rest."*

Look here, you loving ones, for here is a refuge for your wounded love! You may delight yourselves in the Well Beloved and never fear that He will fail or forget you. Love will not be wasted, however much it may be lavished upon Jesus. He deserves it all, and He requites it all. In loving Him, the heart finds a delicious contentment. When the head rests on His chest, it enjoys an ease that no down-filled pillow could bestow. Madame Guyon rested amid severe persecutions, because her great love for Jesus filled her soul to the brim! O aching heart, come here, for Jesus says, *"I will give you rest."*

For the Conscience

The conscience, when it is at all alive and awake, is much disturbed when the holy law of God has been broken by sin. As you know, once the conscience is aroused, it is not easily quieted. Neither unbelief nor superstition can lull it to sleep; it defies these opiates of falsehood and worries the soul with perpetual annoyance. Like the troubled sea, it cannot rest, but it constantly casts the mire and dirt of past transgressions and iniquities upon the shore of memory.

Is this your situation? Then Jesus says, *"I will give you rest."* If fears and anxieties arise at any time from an awakened conscience, they can only be safely and surely quieted when we run to the Crucified One. In the blessed truth of Christ's substitutionary death, which is acceptable to God and has been fully accomplished by the Lord Jesus, our minds find peace. Justice is honored and law is vindicated in the sacrifice of Christ.

Since God is satisfied, I may be satisfied, too. Since the Father has raised Jesus from the dead and has set Him at His own right hand, there can be no question about His acceptance. Consequently, all who are in Him are accepted, also. We are under no fear now of being condemned; Jesus gives us rest by enabling us to put forth the challenge, *"Who is he who condemns?"* (Rom. 8:34), and to give the reassuring answer, *"It is Christ who died"* (v. 34).

For the Intellect

The intellect is another source of unrest, and in these times there are many things that attempt to trouble the mind. Doubts, stinging like the bites of mosquitoes, are suggested by almost every page of the literature of the day. Most men are drifting like vessels that have no anchors, and they come into collision with us. How can we rest? One scheme of philosophy eats up the other; each new form of heresy devours the last. Is there any foundation? Is anything true? Or is it all fairy tale, and are we doomed to be the victims of an ever changing lie?

O soul, do not seek an answer to this by learning of men, but come and learn of Jesus, and you will find rest! Believe Jesus, and let all the rabbis contradict you if they must. The Son of God was made flesh; He lived, He died, He rose again, He lives, He loves. This is true, and all that He teaches in His Word is assured truth. The rest may blow away like chaff before the wind. A mind in pursuit of truth is like a dove without a proper resting place, until it finds its rest in Jesus.

Concerning All Things

Next, these words mean rest about all things. The person who is uneasy about anything has not found rest. A thousand thorns and briars grow on the soil of this earth, and no man can happily walk life's way unless his feet are *"shod...with the preparation of the gospel of peace"* (Eph. 6:15), which Jesus gives. In Christ, we are at rest concerning our duties, for He instructs and helps us in them. In Him, we are at rest about our trials, for He sympathizes with us in them. With His love, we are at rest as to the movements of Providence, for His Father loves us and will not allow anything to harm us. Concerning the past, we rest in His forgiving love. As to the present, it is bright with His loving fellowship. As to the future, it is brilliant with His expected coming.

This is true of the little things as well as the big. He who saves us from the battle-ax of satanic temptation also extracts the thorn from a domestic trial. We may rest in Jesus concerning our sick child, our business trouble, or grief of any kind. He is our Comforter in all things, our Sympathizer in every form of temptation. Do you have this all-covering rest? If not, why not? Jesus gives it; why do you not partake of it? Do you have something that you could not bring to Him? Then flee from it, for it is not a fit thing for a believer to possess. A disciple should know neither grief nor joy that he could not reveal to his Lord.

This rest must be a very wonderful one, since Jesus gives it. He does not give by ounces and pounds. Instead, He gives golden gifts in immeasurable quantities. It is Jesus who gives *"the peace of God, which surpasses all understanding"* (Phil. 4:7). It is written, *"Great peace have those who love Your law"* (Ps. 119:165); what peace must they have who love God's Son! There are times when Jesus gives us a heavenly paradise of rest; we cannot describe the divine repose of our hearts at such times.

We read in the Gospels that when Jesus hushed the storm, *"there was a great calm"* (Matt. 8:26)—not simply "a calm," but *"a great calm"*—unusual, absolute, perfect, memorable. It reminds us of the stillness that John described in the book of Revelation: *"I saw four angels standing at the four corners of the earth, holding the four winds of the earth, that the wind should not blow on the earth, on the sea, or on any tree"* (Rev. 7:1). Not a ripple stirred the waters, not a leaf moved on the trees.

Assuredly, our Lord has given a blessed rest to those who trust Him and follow Him. They are often unable to inform others as to the depths of their peace and the reasons upon which it is founded. But they know it, and it brings them an inward wealth that causes the fortune of an ungodly millionaire to appear to be poverty itself. May all of us, by happy, personal experience, know to the fullest the meaning of our Savior's promise, *"I will give you rest"*!

But now, in the second place, let us ask, "Why should we have this rest?"

Why We Should Have This Rest

Jesus Gives It

The first answer is in our text. We should enjoy this rest because Jesus gives it. Since He gives it, we ought to take it. Because

He gives it, we may take it. I have known some Christians who have thought that it would be presumptuous on their part to take this rest, so they have kept fluttering about like frightened birds, weary from their long flights but not daring to fold their tired wings and rest. Let us not be so presumptuous as to think that we know better than our Lord. He gives us rest. For that reason, if for no other, let us take it promptly and gratefully. *"Rest in the LORD, and wait patiently for Him"* (Ps. 37:7). Say with David, *"My heart is steadfast, O God, my heart is steadfast; I will sing and give praise"* (Ps. 57:7).

It Will Refresh Us

Next, we should take the rest that Jesus gives because it will refresh us. We are often weary; sometimes we are weary *in* God's work, though I trust we are never weary *of* it. There are many things that cause us weariness: sin, sorrow, the worldliness of some who say they believe, the prevalence of error in the church, and so on. Often we are like a tired child who can hold up his little head no longer. What does he do? Why, he just goes to sleep in his mother's arms! Let us be as wise as the little one and rest in our loving Savior's embrace.

One poet wrote of "tired nature's sweet restorer, balmy sleep," and so it is. Sometimes the very best thing a Christian can do is, literally, to go to sleep. When he wakes, he will be so refreshed that he will seem to be in a new world. But, spiritually, there is no refreshment like what comes from the rest that Christ gives. As we read in Isaiah, *"'This is the rest with which you may cause the weary to rest,' and, 'This is the refreshing'"* (Isa. 28:12).

Dr. Bonar's sweet hymn, which is so suitable for a sinner coming to Christ for the first time, is equally appropriate for a weary believer returning to his Savior's arms. The weary Christian, too, can sing,

> I heard the voice of Jesus say,
> "Come unto Me, and rest;
> Lay down, thou weary one, lay down
> Thy head upon My breast."
> I came to Jesus as I was,
> Weary, worn, and sad:
> I found in Him a resting-place,
> And He has made me glad.

It Improves Our Focus

Another reason we should have this rest is that it will enable us to concentrate all our faculties on the highest purpose. Many, who might be strong servants of the Lord, are very weak because their energies are not concentrated on one purpose. They do not say with Paul, *"One thing I do"* (Phil. 3:13). We are such poor creatures that we often cannot occupy our minds with more than one subject at a time. Why, even the buzzing of a fly or the bite of a mosquito would be sufficient to take our thoughts away from our present holy service! As long as we have any burden weighing on our shoulders, we cannot enjoy perfect rest; and as long as there is any burden on our consciences or our hearts, our souls cannot rest.

How are we to be freed from these burdens? Only by yielding ourselves wholly to the Great Burden-Bearer, who says, *"Come to Me,...and I will give you rest."* When we possess this rest, all our faculties will be centered and focused on one objective, and with undivided hearts we will seek God's glory.

We Will Testify for Him

When we have obtained this rest, we will also be able to testify for our Lord. I remember that, when I first began to teach Sunday school, one day I was speaking to my class on the words, *"He who believes in Me has everlasting life"* (John 6:47). I was rather taken by surprise when one of the boys said to me, "Teacher, do you have everlasting life?" I replied, "I hope so." The student was not satisfied with my answer, so he asked another question, "But, teacher, don't you know?"

The boy was right; there can be no true testimony except one that springs from assured conviction of our own safety and joy in the Lord. We speak what we know; we believe and therefore speak (2 Cor. 4:13). Rest of the heart, which we receive through coming to Christ, enables us to invite others to Him with great confidence, for we can tell them what heavenly peace He has given to us. This will enable us to put the Gospel in a very attractive light, for the evidence of our own experience will help others to trust the Lord for themselves. With the beloved apostle John, we will be able to say to our hearers,

> *That which was from the beginning, which we have heard,*
> *which we have seen with our eyes, which we have looked*

*upon, and our hands have handled, concerning the Word of
life; the life was manifested, and we have seen, and bear witness, and declare to you that eternal life which was with the
Father and was manifested to us; that which we have seen
and heard we declare to you, that you also may have fellowship with us; and truly our fellowship is with the Father and
with His Son Jesus Christ.* (1 John 1:1–3)

It Is Necessary for Growth

In addition, this rest is necessary for our growth. The lily in
the garden is not taken up and transplanted two or three times a
day; that would be the way to prevent all growth. Rather, it is kept
in one place and tenderly nurtured. It is by keeping it quite still
that the gardener helps it to reach perfection. A child of God would
grow much more rapidly if he would simply rest in one place instead of always being on the move. *"In returning and rest you shall
be saved; in quietness and confidence shall be your strength"* (Isa.
30:15). Martha was burdened with preparing the meal, but Mary
sat at Jesus' feet. It is not difficult to tell which of them was more
likely to *"grow in the grace and knowledge of our Lord and Savior
Jesus Christ"* (2 Pet. 3:18).

It Prepares Us for Heaven

Another reason we must have this rest is that it will prepare us
for heaven. I was reading a book the other day in which I found this
expression: "The streets of heaven begin on earth." That is true;
heaven is not as far away as some people think. Heaven is the place
of perfect holiness, the place of sinless service, the place of eternal
glory, and nothing will prepare us for heaven like this rest that Jesus
gives. Heaven must be in us before we are in heaven, and the person
who has this rest has begun his heaven below.

Enoch was virtually in heaven while he walked with God on the
earth, and he had only to continue that holy walk to find himself actually in heaven (Gen. 5:24). This world is part of our Lord's great
house, of which heaven is the upper story. Some of us may hear the
Master's call, "Come up higher," sooner than we think. Then, as we
rest *in* Christ, we will rest *with* Christ. The more we have of this
blessed rest now, the better we will be prepared for the rest that remains for the people of God, that eternal keeping of a Sabbath in the
paradise above (Heb. 4:9–10).

How to Obtain This Rest

By Coming to Christ

Now, how can we obtain this rest? First, we obtain the rest of Christ by coming to Him. He says, *"Come to Me,...and I will give you rest."* I trust that you, my reader, have come to Christ by faith; now prepare yourself for blessed fellowship and communion with Him. Keep on coming to Him, continually coming and never going away.

When you wake up in the morning, come to Christ in an act of renewed communion with Him. All day long, keep on coming to Him even while you are occupied with the affairs of this life. At night, let your last waking moments be spent in coming to Jesus. Come to Christ by searching the Scriptures, for you will find Him there on almost every page. Come to Christ in your thoughts, desires, aspirations, and wishes. In this way, the promise of the text will be fulfilled for you: *"I will give you rest."*

By Yielding to Christ

Next, we obtain rest by yielding to Christ. *"Take My yoke upon you...and you will find rest for your souls"* (Matt. 11:29). Christ calls us to wear His yoke, not to make one for ourselves. He wants us to share the yoke with Him, to be His true yokefellows. It is wonderful that He is willing to be yoked with us; the only greater wonder is that we are so unwilling to be yoked with Him. When we take His yoke upon us, what joy we will have in our eternal rest!

Here we find rest for our souls, a further rest beyond what He gives us when we come to Him. We first rest in Jesus by faith, and then we rest in Him by obedience. The first rest He gives through His death; the further rest we find through imitating His life.

By Learning from Christ

Last, we secure this rest by learning from Christ. *"Learn from Me, for I am gentle and lowly in heart, and you will find rest for your souls"* (Matt. 11:29). We are to be workers with Christ, taking His yoke upon us. At the same time, we are to be students in Christ's school, learning from Him. We are to learn from Christ, and to learn Christ; He is both the Teacher and the Lesson. His gentleness of heart makes Him fit to teach and makes Him the best illustration of His own teaching. If we can become like Him, we will rest as He does. The *"lowly in heart"* will have restful hearts. May we find that full rest, for the Great Rest-Giver's sake!

Chapter 11

Jesus Asleep on a Pillow

*But He was in the stern, asleep on a pillow. And they awoke Him
and said to Him, "Teacher, do You not care that we are perishing?"
Then He arose and rebuked the wind, and said to the sea, "Peace,
be still!" And the wind ceased and there was a great calm.*
—Mark 4:38–39

Our Lord took His disciples with Him into the ship to teach
them a practical lesson. It is one thing to talk to people
about our oneness with them, about how they should exercise faith in time of danger, and about their real safety in apparent
peril. But it is another and far better thing to go into the ship with
them, to let them feel all the terror of the storm, and then to arise
and rebuke the wind and say to the sea, *"Peace, be still!"* Our Lord
gave His disciples a kind of school lesson, an acted sermon, in
which the truth was set forth visibly before them. Such teaching
produced a wonderful effect on their lives. May we also be instructed by it!

In our text there are two great calms. The first is the calm in
the Savior's heart. The second is the calm that He created, through
His words, on the storm-tossed sea.

The Calmness of Our Lord

Within the Lord there was a great calm, and that is why there
was soon a great calm around Him. What is in God comes out of
God. Since there was a calm in Christ for Himself, there was afterward a calm outside for others. What a wonderful inner calm it
was! *"He was in the stern, asleep on a pillow."*

Perfect Confidence in God

He had perfect confidence in God that all was well. The waves
might roar, the winds might rage, but He was not at all disquieted

by their fury. He knew that the waters were in the hollow of His Father's hand, and that every wind was but the breath of His Father's mouth. Therefore, He was not troubled; indeed, He did not have even a thought of concern, for He was as much at ease as He would have been on a sunny day.

His mind and heart were free from every kind of care, for amid the gathering tempest He deliberately lay down and slept like a weary child. He went to the back of the ship, farthest from the spray. He took a pillow and put it under His head, and with definite purpose He fell asleep.

It was His own decision to go to sleep in the storm; He had no reason to stay awake, so pure and perfect was His confidence in the great Father. What an example this is to us! We do not have half the confidence in God that we ought to have—not even the best of us. The Lord deserves our limitless belief, our unquestioning confidence, our undisturbed reliance. Oh, if only we gave these to Him as the Savior did!

Confidence in His Sonship

Along with His faith in the Father, Jesus also had a sweet confidence in His own Sonship. He did not doubt that He was the Son of the Highest. I may not question God's power to deliver, but I may sometimes question my right to expect deliverance. When I do question it, my comfort vanishes. Our Lord had no doubts of this kind. He had long before heard the words, *"This is My beloved Son, in whom I am well pleased"* (Matt. 3:17). He had lived and walked with God in such a way that the witness within Him was continuous; therefore, He had no question about the Father's love for Him as His own Son. His Father was keeping watch over Him—what better thing could a child do than go to sleep in such a happy position? This is what Jesus did.

You and I, too, need to have a greater assurance of our sonship if we wish to have greater peace with God. The Devil knows this, and so he will come to us with his insinuating suggestion, as he did with Jesus, "If you really are a child of God...." (See Matthew 4:3.) If we have the *"Spirit of adoption"* (Rom. 8:15) in us, we will put the Accuser to rout at once. The witness of the Holy Spirit within us, that *"we are children of God"* (v. 16), will counteract his insinuation. Then we will be filled with a great calm because we will have confidence in our Father and assurance of our sonship.

Leaving Everything with God

This blessed Lord of ours had a sweet way of leaving everything with God. He did not stay awake, He did not worry, but He went to sleep. Whatever came, He had left everything in the hands of the great Caretaker. What more is needed? If a watchman were hired to guard my house, I would be foolish if I also sat up for fear of thieves. Why have a watchman if I cannot trust him to watch? *"Cast your burden on the LORD"* (Ps. 55:22), but when you have done so, leave it with the Lord and do not try to carry it yourself. Otherwise, you mock God; you use the name of God, but not the reality of God. Lay down every care, even as Jesus did when He went calmly to the rear part of the ship, quietly took a pillow, and went to sleep.

Some of you may say, "I could do that if my cares were solely for myself." You feel that you cannot cast upon God your burden of concern about your children. But your Lord trusted the Father with those dear to Him. Do you not think that Christ's disciples were as precious to Him as our children are to us? If that ship had been wrecked, what would have become of Peter? What would have become of John, *"that disciple whom Jesus loved"* (John 21:7)? Our Lord regarded with intense affection those whom He had chosen and called, and who had been with Him in His ministry. Even so, He was quite content to leave them all in the care of His Father and go to sleep.

You answer, "Yes, but I am obliged to care, whether I want to or not." Is your case, then, more trying than your Lord's? Do you forget that *"other little boats were also with Him"* (Mark 4:36)? When the storm was tossing His ship, their little ships were even more in jeopardy, and He cared for them all. He was the Lord High Admiral of the Lake of Gennesaret that night. The other ships were a fleet under His convoy, and His great heart went out to them all. Yet He went to sleep, because He had left in His Father's care even the requests for His love and sympathy. We, who are much weaker than He, will find strength in doing the same.

The Wisest Choice

Having left everything with His Father, our Lord did the wisest thing possible. He did just what the hour demanded—He went to sleep! That was the best thing Jesus could do, and sometimes it is the best thing we can do. Christ was weary and worn, and when anyone is exhausted, it is his duty to go to sleep if he can. The Savior had to be up again in the morning, preaching and working miracles, and if He had not slept, He would not have been fit for His holy duty. Also, it was necessary for Him to keep Himself in excellent condition for His service.

Knowing that the time to sleep had come, the Lord slept, which was the right thing to do. Often, when we have fretted and worried, we would have glorified God far more if we had literally gone to sleep. To glorify God by sleep is not as difficult as some might think. To our Lord, it was natural.

You may be worried, sad, or weary. The doctor may have prescribed a medicine for you that does you no good. But if you enter into full peace with God and go to sleep, you will wake up infinitely more refreshed than by using any drug! The sleep that the Lord gives to His beloved (Ps. 127:2) is indeed refreshing and healing. Seek it as Jesus sought it. Go to bed, and you will better imitate your Lord than by troubling other people by your mood.

There is also a spiritual sleep in which we ought to imitate Jesus. How often I have worried about my church, until I have come to my senses and have said to myself, "How foolish I am! Can I not depend on God? Is it not much more His cause than mine?" Then I have taken my load in prayer and left it with the Lord. I have said, "In God's name, this matter will never worry me again," and I have left my urgent concern with Him and have ended it forever.

In this way I have deliberately given up many trying situations into the Lord's care. And when any of my friends have said to me, "What about so and so?" I have simply answered, "I do not know, and I no longer take the trouble to know. The Lord will intervene in some way or other, so I will not worry anymore about it."

No horrible turn of events has ever occurred in a matter that I have left in God's care. Keeping my hands out of such things has been pure wisdom. *"Stand still, and see the salvation of the LORD"* (Exod. 14:13) is God's own precept. Let us follow Jesus' example.

Having a child's confidence in the great Father, He retired to the stern of the ship, selected a pillow, deliberately lay down upon it, and went to sleep. Though the ship was filling with water, though it tossed in the waves, He slept on. Nothing could break the peace of His tranquil soul. Every sailor on board reeled to and fro, staggered like a drunken man, and was at his wits' end. But Jesus was neither at His wits' end nor did He stagger, for He rested in perfect innocence and undisturbed confidence. His heart was and is happy in God; therefore, He remained peaceful. Oh, for grace to imitate Him!

The Failure of the Disciples

But notice, dear friends, the difference between the Master and His disciples. While He was in a great calm, they were in a great storm. Observe their failure here. They were just as human as we are, and so we often act just as they did.

Giving Way to Fear

They gave way to fear. They were very much afraid that the ship would sink and that they would all perish. By yielding to fear in this way, they forgot the solid reasons for courage that were close at hand; for, in actuality, they were safe enough. Christ was aboard that vessel, and if the ship were sinking, He would have sunk with them. A heathen sailor took courage during a storm from the fact that Caesar was on board the ship that was tossed by stormy winds. Should not the disciples have felt secure with Jesus on board? Fear not; you carry Jesus and His cause!

Jesus had come to do a work, and His disciples should have known that He could not perish with that work unaccomplished. Could they not trust Him? They had seen Him multiply the loaves and fishes, cast out devils, and heal all kinds of sicknesses; could they not trust Him to still the storm? Unreasonable unbelief! Faith in God is true wisdom, but to doubt God is irrational. It is the height of absurdity and folly to question omnipotent love.

Wrongful Accusation

The disciples were also unwise in what they said to the Master. He was extremely weary, and He needed sleep, but they hurried to Him and woke Him in a somewhat rough and irreverent manner. They were slow to do so, but their fear urged them. Therefore, they woke Him, uttering ungenerous and unloving words: *"Master, carest thou not that we perish?"* (Mark 4:38 KJV).

Shame on the lips that asked so harsh a question! Did they not greatly blame themselves after thinking about what they had said? Christ had given them no cause for such hard speeches; and, moreover, it was unseemly for them to call Him *"Master"* and then to ask Him, *"Carest thou not that we perish?"* Is He to be accused of such hardheartedness that He would let His faithful disciples perish when He had power to deliver them? Alas, we, too, have been guilty of similar offenses!

I think I have known some of Christ's disciples who have appeared to doubt the wisdom or the love of their Lord. They did not quite say that He was mistaken, but they said that He moved in a mysterious way. They did not quite complain that He was unkind to them, but they whispered that they could not reconcile His dealings with His infinite love. Alas, Jesus has endured much from our unbelief! May this illustration help us to see our failures, and may the love of our dear Lord forgive and cleanse them!

The Calm That Christ Created

So far, I have written about the Master's calm and about the disciples' failure. Now let us focus on the great calm that Jesus created. *"There was a great calm."*

By His Voice

His voice produced this calm. It is said that if oil is poured on water, the water will become smooth. I suppose there is some truth in that statement, but there is all truth in this: If God speaks, the storm subsides into a calm, so that the waves of the sea are still. Our Lord Jesus only has to speak in the heart of any one of us, and immediately *"the peace of God, which surpasses all understanding"* (Phil. 4:7) will possess us.

No matter how dreary your despondency, or how dreadful your despair, the Lord can at once create a great calm of confidence. What a door of hope this opens to any who are in trouble! If I could make a poor man rich by speaking to him, if I could make a sick one well by talking to him, I am sure that I would do so at once. But Jesus is infinitely better than I am; therefore, I know that He will speak peace to the tried and troubled heart.

An Immediate Calm

Note, too, that this calm came at once. Jesus *"arose and rebuked the wind, and said to the sea, 'Peace, be still!' And the wind*

392

ceased and there was a great calm." As soon as Jesus spoke, all was quiet. I have met many people who are troubled, and I have seen a few who have slowly come out into light and liberty. But, more frequently, deliverance has come suddenly. The iron gate has opened of its own accord, and the prisoner has stepped into immediate freedom. (See Acts 12:6–10.) *"The snare is broken, and we have escaped"* (Ps. 124:7). What a joy it is to know that rest is so near even when the tempest rages most furiously!

Faith Is Paired with Rest

Note, also, that the Savior coupled this rest with faith, for He said to the disciples as soon as the calm came, *"Why are you so fearful? How is it that you have no faith?"* (Mark 4:40). Faith and calm go together. If you believe, you will rest; if you will simply cast yourself upon your God, surrendering absolutely to His will, you will have mercy, joy, and light. Even if we have no faith, the Lord will sometimes give us the blessing that we need, for He delights to do more for us than we have any right to expect of Him. However, usually the rule of His kingdom is, *"According to your faith let it be to you"* (Matt. 9:29).

A Delightful Calm

This great calm is very delightful, and concerning this I want to use my personal testimony. I write from my own knowledge when I say that it *"surpasses all understanding"* (Phil. 4:7). The other night I was sitting, meditating on God's mercy and love, when I suddenly found in my own heart a most delightful sense of perfect peace. I had come to Beulah (Isa. 62:4), the land where the sun shines without a cloud. *"There was a great calm."*

I felt as sailors might feel after they have been tossed about in choppy waters, and all of a sudden the ocean becomes as unruffled as a mirror, and the seabirds come and sit in happy circles upon the water. I felt perfectly content, yes, undividedly happy. Not a wave of trouble broke upon the shore of my heart, and even far out to sea in the depth of my being, all was still. I knew no ungratified wish, no unsatisfied desire. I could not discover a reason for uneasiness or a motive for fear. There was nothing close to fanaticism in my feelings, no sign of radical excitement. Rather, my soul was waiting upon God and delighting in Him alone.

Oh, the blessedness of this rest in the Lord! What a paradise it is! This experience was, for me, no different than a fragment of heaven. We often talk about our great spiritual storms. Why should we not speak of our great calms? If ever we get into trouble, how we complain about it! Why should we not sing of our deliverances?

All providence works for our good. Nothing can harm us. The Lord is our shield and our *"exceedingly great reward"* (Gen. 15:1). Why, then, should we fear? *"The LORD of hosts is with us; the God of Jacob is our refuge"* (Ps. 46:7). To the believer, peace is no presumption. He is given the full privilege of enjoying *"perfect peace"* (Isa. 26:3)—a quiet that is deep and founded on truth, a calmness that encompasses all things and is not broken by any of the ten thousand disturbing causes that otherwise might prevent our rest. *"You will keep him in perfect peace, whose mind is stayed on You, because he trusts in You"* (v. 3). Oh, to get into that calm and remain in it until we come to that world where there is no more raging sea!

If we are blessed enough to attain the calm that ruled within our Savior, it will give us power to make external matters calm. One who has peace can make peace. We cannot work miracles out of our own strength, yet the works that Jesus did we will do also (John 14:12). Sleeping His sleep, we will awake in His renewed energy and treat the winds and waves as things subject to the power of faith, and therefore, to be commanded into quiet. We will speak in a way that comforts others: our calm will work marvels in the little ships of which others are captains. We, too, will say, *"Peace, be still!"* Our confidence will prove contagious, and the timid will grow brave. Our tender love will spread to others, and the contentious will cool down to patience.

The catch is that the matter must begin within ourselves. We cannot create a calm until we are calm ourselves. It is easier to rule the elements than to govern the unruliness of our own fickle natures. When grace has made us masters of our fears, so that we can take a pillow and fall asleep amid the hurricane, the fury of the tempest is over. He gives peace and safety when He gives sleep to His beloved (Ps. 127:2).

Chapter 12

Real Contact with Jesus

Jesus said, "Somebody touched Me,
for I perceived power going out from Me."
—Luke 8:46

Our Lord was very frequently in the midst of a crowd. His preaching was so clear and so forcible that He always attracted a vast number of hearers. Moreover, the rumor of the loaves and fishes no doubt had something to do with increasing His audiences, for the expectation of seeing a miracle would be sure to add to the numbers of the hangers-on. Our Lord Jesus Christ often found it difficult to move through the streets because of the masses who pressed against Him. This was encouraging to Him as a preacher, yet only a small amount of real good came from all the excitement that gathered around His personal ministry.

Perhaps He looked upon the great mass of people and said, *"What is the chaff to the wheat?"* (Jer. 23:28), for here it was piled upon the threshing floor, heap upon heap. After His death, His disciples might have counted only a few converts, for those who had spiritually received Him were but few. Many were called, but few were chosen (Matt. 22:14). Yet wherever one was blessed, our Savior took note of it; it touched a chord in His soul. He never could be unaware when power had gone out from Him to heal a sick one, or when power had gone forth with His ministry to save a sinful soul.

Of all the crowd that gathered around the Savior on the day of which our text speaks, I find nothing said about one of them except this solitary *"somebody"* who had touched Him. The crowd came and the crowd went, but little is recorded of it all. Just as the ocean leaves very little behind it when it has reached full tide and recedes again to deeper waters, so the vast multitude around the Savior left only this one precious deposit—one *"somebody"* who had touched Him and had received miraculous power from Him.

On Sunday mornings, crowds come pouring into churches like a mighty ocean, and then they all withdraw again. Here and there a *"somebody"* is left weeping for sin, a *"somebody"* is left rejoicing in Christ, a *"somebody"* is left who can say, "I have touched the hem of His garment, and I have been made whole." (See Matthew 9:20–21.) May God find these few people when they reach out for Him, and all the praise will be His!

Jesus said, *"Somebody touched Me."* From this, we observe that we should never be satisfied unless we come into personal contact with Christ, so that we touch Him as this woman touched His garment. Second, if we can make such personal contact, we will have a blessing: *"I perceived power going out from Me."* Third, if we do receive a blessing, Christ will know it. However obscure our case may be, He will know it, and He will have us make it known to others. He will speak and ask the questions that will draw us out and manifest us to the world.

Our Main Goal: Personal Contact with Christ

First, then, let it be our chief aim and objective to come into personal contact with the Lord Jesus Christ. Peter said, *"The multitudes throng and press You"* (Luke 8:45), and that is true of the multitude to this very day. But of those who come where Christ is in the assembly of His people, a large proportion come only because it is their custom to do so.

Perhaps such people hardly know why they go to a place of worship. They go because they have always gone, and they think it is wrong not to go. They are just like doors that swing upon their hinges; they take no interest in what is going on, and they do not and cannot enter into the heart and soul of the service. They are glad if the sermon is rather short, for then there is less boredom for them. They are glad if they can look around and gaze at the congregation, for then there is something to interest them. But drawing near to the Lord Jesus is not what they hope to do. They have not looked at church attendance in that light.

They come and they go, and they will keep coming and going, until eventually they will come for the last time and they will find out in the next world that the means of grace were not instituted to be matters of custom. They will suddenly discover that to have heard Jesus Christ preached, and to have rejected Him, is no trifle, but a solemn thing for which they will have to answer in the presence of the great Judge of all the earth.

There are others who come to the house of prayer and enter into the service in a self-righteous fashion. They may come to the Lord's Table. They may even join the church. They are baptized, yet not by the Holy Spirit. They take Communion, but they do not take the Lord Himself; they eat the bread, but they never eat His flesh; they drink the wine, but they never drink His blood. (See John 6:53–56.) They have been immersed in water, but they have never been buried with Christ in baptism, nor have they risen again with Him into newness of life (Rom. 6:4). To them, reading, singing, kneeling, hearing, and so on, are enough. They are content with the shell, but they know nothing of the blessed spiritual kernel, the true *"marrow and fatness"* (Ps. 63:5).

These are the majority, no matter what church you may choose. They press in around Jesus, but they do not touch Him. They come, but they do not come into contact with Jesus. They are outward, external hearers only, but there is no inward touching of the blessed person of Christ, no spiritual contact with the ever blessed Savior, no stream of life and love flowing from Him to them. It is all mechanical religion. They know nothing of vital godliness.

"Somebody," said Christ, *"touched Me,"* and that is the soul of the matter. Dear reader, when you are alone in prayer, never be satisfied with having prayed. Do not give up until you have touched Christ in prayer. If you have not reached Him, sigh and cry until you do! Do not think you have already prayed, but try again. Also, when you go to church, do not be satisfied with just listening to the sermon. Do not be content unless you gain access to Christ the Master and touch Him.

When you come to the Communion table, do not consider it an ordinance of grace to you unless you have gone right through the veil (Heb. 6:19–20) and into Christ's own arms, or at least have touched His garment. The life and soul of Communion is to touch Jesus Christ Himself, and unless *"somebody"* has touched Him, the ceremony is just a dead performance, without life or power.

The woman of our text verse was not only among those who were in the crowd, but she also touched Jesus. Therefore, dear readers, let me hold her up as our example in some respects, though in other respects I pray that you might excel her.

Under Many Difficulties

First, she felt that it was of no use being in the crowd or being on the same street with Christ, or near to the place where He was, unless she could reach Him. She knew she had to touch Him (Matt. 9:21). You will notice that she did so under many difficulties. There was a great crowd (Luke 8:42). She was a woman. She was also a woman weakened by a long-term disease that had drained her strength and had left her more fit for lying in bed than for struggling in the seething tumult (v. 43). Yet notwithstanding that, her desire was so intense that she pressed on, probably enduring many shoves and bruises. At last, this poor trembling woman got near to the Lord.

Beloved, it is not always easy to touch Jesus. It is very easy to kneel down to pray, but not so easy to reach Christ in prayer. Perhaps the cries of your own child have often hindered you when you were striving to approach Jesus. Perhaps a knock comes at the door when you most wish to be alone. When you are sitting in the house of God, the person seated in front of you may unconsciously distract your attention. It is not easy to draw near to Christ, especially when you come directly from your workplace with a thousand thoughts and cares about you. You cannot always unload your burden outside and go into the sanctuary with your heart prepared to receive the Gospel.

Ah, it is a terrible fight sometimes, a real fight with evil, with temptation, and I do not know what else. But, beloved, fight it out! Do not let your times of prayer be wasted or your opportunities for hearing be thrown away, but like this woman, be resolved that, in all your weakness, you will lay hold of Christ. And then, if you are resolved about it and you still cannot get to Him, He will come to you. When you are struggling against unbelieving thoughts, He will turn and say, "Make room for that poor feeble one, so that she may come to Me, for My desire is toward the work of My own hands. Let her come to Me, and let her desire be granted to her."

In Secret

Observe, also, that this woman touched Jesus very secretly (Luke 8:44). Perhaps you are drawing near to Christ at this very moment, and yet you have gained so little contact with Christ that the joyous flush and the sparkle in the eye, which we often see in the child of God, have not yet come to you. But though your touch is in secret, it is true. Although you cannot yet tell another about it, it is accomplished. You have touched Jesus.

Beloved, it is not always the closest fellowship with Christ of which we talk the most. Deep waters are still and calm. I suppose that we sometimes come nearer to Christ when we think we are at a distance than we do when we imagine we are near Him, for we are not always exactly the best judges of our own spiritual states. We may be very close to the Master, yet we may be so anxious to get closer that we feel dissatisfied with the measure of grace that we have already received. To be satisfied with self is not a sign of grace, but to long for more grace is often a far better evidence of the healthy state of the soul.

Friend, go to the Master in secret. If you do not dare to tell your wife or your child or your father that you are trusting in Jesus, it need not be told as yet. You may do it secretly, as the believer did to whom Jesus said, *"When you were under the fig tree, I saw you"* (John 1:48). Nathanael had retired to the shade so that no one might see him, but Jesus saw him and took note of his prayer. Likewise, Jesus will see you in the crowd or in the dark, and He will not withhold His blessing.

Under a Sense of Unworthiness

This woman also came into contact with Christ under a very deep sense of unworthiness. I imagine she thought, "If I touch the Great Prophet, it will be remarkable if He does not strike me down with some sudden judgment," for her sickness had designated her as an unclean woman. She had no right to be in the crowd. If the Levitical law had been strictly carried out, I suppose she would have been confined to her house. But she was wandering about, and she needed to go and touch the holy Savior.

Ah, poor heart, you feel that you are not fit to touch the hem of the Master's robe, for you are so unworthy. You have never felt so undeserving as you do now. When you think back on last week and its struggles, when you think of the present state of your heart and all its wanderings from God, you feel as if there never was a sinner as worthless as you. "Is grace for me?" you ask. "Is Christ for me?" Oh, yes, unworthy one, He is! Do not go away without touching Him.

Jesus Christ does not save the worthy, but the unworthy. Your plea must not be righteousness, but guilt. And, though you are ashamed of yourself, Jesus is not ashamed of you, for you are a child of God. Though you feel unfit to come, let your unfitness only urge you on with a greater earnestness of desire. Let your sense of need make you more fervent to approach the Lord, who can supply your need.

Thus, you see, the woman came under difficulties, she came secretly, she came as an unworthy one, but still she obtained the blessing.

Trembling in Faith

This woman trembled as she touched the Master; it was only a hurried touch, but still it was the touch of faith. Oh, to lay hold of Christ! Be thankful if you get near Him even for a few minutes. "Abide with me," should be your prayer; but oh, if He only gives you a glimpse of Himself, be thankful! Remember that a single touch healed the woman (Luke 8:44). She did not embrace Christ for hours. With only a touch, she was healed.

Beloved, may you catch a glimpse of Jesus now! Though it is only a glimpse, it will delight and comfort your soul. Perhaps you are waiting for Christ, desiring His company, and while you are turning this over in your mind you are asking, "Will He ever shine upon me? Will He ever speak loving words to me? Will He ever let me sit at His feet? Will He ever permit me to rest my head in His lap?" Come and try Him. Though you may shake like a leaf, come.

Sometimes they come best who come most tremblingly, for when the creature is lowest, then the Creator is highest; when in our own esteem we are less than nothing, then Christ is fairer and lovelier in our eyes. One of the best ways to reach heaven is on our hands and knees. At any rate, there is no fear of falling when we are in that position.

Let your lowliness of heart, your sense of utter nothingness, be a sweet means of leading you to receive more of Christ, instead of disqualifying you. The emptier I am, the more room there is for my Master. The more I lack, the more He will give me. The more I feel my sickness, the more I will adore and bless Him when He makes me whole.

You see, the woman really did touch Christ, and so I come back to that. Whatever infirmity there was in the touch, it was a real touch of faith. She did reach Christ Himself. She did not touch Peter; that would have been of no use to her. She did not touch John or James; that would have been no good to her. She touched the Master Himself.

Do not be content unless you can do the same. Put out the hand of faith, and touch Christ. Rest on Him. Rely on His bloody sacrifice, His dying love, His rising power, His ascended plea. As you rest in Him, your vital touch, however feeble, will certainly give you the blessing your soul needs.

This leads me to say what the results of this touch were.

The Result: Healing and Wholeness

The woman in the crowd did touch Jesus, and having done so, she received power from Him. The healing energy streamed at once through the finger of faith into the woman. In Christ there is healing for all spiritual diseases. There is a speedy healing, a healing that will not take months or years but that is complete in one second.

In Christ there is a sufficient healing, though your diseases might be multiplied beyond all comparison. In Christ there is an all-conquering power to drive out every illness. Though, like this woman, you baffle physicians and your case is considered desperate beyond all others, a touch from Christ will heal you.

What a precious, glorious Gospel we have to preach to sinners! If they touch Jesus when the Devil himself is in them, that touch of faith will drive the Devil out. Even though you may have been like the man into whom a legion of devils had entered, the words of Jesus cast them all into the deep, and you sat at His feet, clothed and in your right mind. (See Mark 5:1–15.) There is no excess or extravagance of sin that the power of Jesus Christ cannot overcome.

If you can believe, you will be saved, no matter what you have done in the past. If you can believe, even though you have been lying in scarlet dye until your whole being has been stained red by sin, the precious blood of Jesus will make you white as snow. Though you have become black as hell itself and fit to be cast into the pit, if you trust Jesus, your simple faith will give to your soul the healing that will make you fit to walk the streets of heaven and to stand before Jehovah-Rapha's face, magnifying *the LORD who heals you* (Exod. 15:26).

And now, child of God, I want you to learn the same lesson. You may have said of yourself, "Alas, I feel very dull; my spirituality is at a very low ebb. The spirit is willing, but the flesh is weak (Matt. 26:41). Most likely I will have no holy joy today!" Why not? The touch of Jesus could make you alive if you were dead, and surely it will stir the little life that is in you, though it may seem to you that it is dying!

Struggle hard, my friend, to come to Jesus! May the eternal Spirit help you, and may you yet find that your dull, dead times can soon become your best times. Oh, what a blessing it is that God *"lifts the beggar from the ash heap"* (1 Sam. 2:8)! He does not raise us when He sees that we are already up. Instead, when He finds us lying low, then He delights to lift us and set us *"among princes"* (v. 8). In a single moment, you may mount up from the depths of heaviness to the very heights of ecstatic worship, if you can only touch Christ crucified. View Him there, with streaming wounds, with thorn-crowned head, as He dies for you in all the majesty of His misery!

But then, you say, "I have a thousand doubts right now." Ah, but your doubts will soon vanish when you draw near to Christ. Anyone who feels the touch of Christ never doubts, at least not while the touch lasts, for observe this woman! She felt in her body that she was made whole, and so will you, if you come into contact with the Lord. Do not wait for proof, but come to Christ for proof. If you cannot even dream of a good thing in yourself, come to Jesus Christ as you did at the first. Come as if you never had come at all. Come to Jesus as a sinner, and your doubts will flee away.

Another complains, "But I know about all the sins I have committed since my conversion." Well, return to Jesus when your guilt seems to return. The fountain is still open, and that fountain, you will remember, is open not only for sinners, but also for saints. The Scriptures say, *"In that day a fountain shall be opened for the house of David and for the inhabitants of Jerusalem"* (Zech. 13:1). That is, there is a fountain for you, for believers in Jesus. The fountain is still open. Come to Jesus anew, and whatever your sins, doubts, or burdens may be, they will all depart as soon as you touch your Lord.

He Knows When You Touch Him

My next observation is, if somebody touches Jesus, the Lord will know it. You may be a stranger to many people, but that does not matter. Your name is *"Somebody,"* and Christ knows you. If you receive a blessing, there will be two who will know it—you and Christ. Oh, if you will look to Jesus today, it might not be known to others, and your neighbors might not hear of it, but still it will be registered in the courts of heaven. All the bells of the New Jerusalem will ring, and all the angels will rejoice as soon as they know that you are born again (Luke 15:10).

"Somebody!" I do not know your name, but—*"Somebody!"*—God's electing love rests on you; Christ's redeeming blood was shed for you; and the Spirit has brought about a work in you; otherwise, you would not have touched Jesus. Jesus knows all of this.

It is a consoling thought that Christ knows not only the prominent children in the family, but also the little ones. This truth stands fast: *"The Lord knows those who are His"* (2 Tim. 2:19), whether they have just come to know Him now, or whether they have known Him for fifty years. *"The Lord knows those who are His."* If I am a part of Christ's body, I may be just the foot, but the Lord knows the foot. The head and the heart in heaven feel when the foot on earth is bruised.

If you have touched Jesus, I tell you that amid the glories of angels and the everlasting hallelujahs of all the blood-bought believers, He has found time to hear your sigh, to receive your faith, and to give you an answer of peace. All the way from heaven to earth there has rushed a mighty stream of healing power, which has come from Christ to you. Since you have touched Him, the healing power has touched you.

Make It Known to Others

Now, since Jesus knows of your salvation, He wishes other people to know of it, too. That is why He has put it into my heart to say, "Somebody has touched the Lord." Where is that somebody? Somebody, where are you? You have touched Christ, though with a weak finger, and you are now saved. Make it known to your fellow Christians. It is due them to let them know. You cannot guess what joy it gives other believers when they hear of sick ones being healed by the Master.

Perhaps you have known the Lord for months and you have not yet made an open acknowledgment of it. Do not hold back any longer, but go forth tremblingly, as this woman did. Perhaps you may say, "I do not know what to say." Well, you must tell what this woman told the Lord; she told Him the whole truth. Your fellow believers do not want anything else. They do not desire any sham experience. They do not want you to manufacture feelings like somebody else's that you have read of in a book. Go and tell what you have felt. No one will ask you to tell what you have not felt or what you do not know. But if you have touched Christ and you have been healed, go and tell your brothers and sisters in Christ what the Lord has done for your soul.

And, when you draw near to Christ and have a sweet season of communion with Him, tell it to your fellow believers. After hearing a sermon, take home spiritual food for those in your family who could not attend church that day. God grant that you may always have something sweet to tell about what you have known of precious truth.

Whoever you may be, though you may be nothing but a poor "somebody," if you have touched Christ, tell others about it. In this way, they may come and touch Him, too.

Chapter 13

A Word from the Beloved's Mouth

*He who is bathed needs only to wash his feet, but is completely
clean; and you are clean, but not all of you.*
—John 13:10

Gideon's fleece was so full of dew that he could wring out the
moisture. In the same manner, sometimes a verse of Scripture will be very full of meaning when the Holy Spirit visits
His servants through its words. This statement of our Savior to His
disciples has been to me like bread dipped in honey, and I do not
doubt that it will prove equally as sweet to you.

The Ancient Blessing

Observe carefully, dear reader, the high praise that is given to
the Lord's beloved disciples: *"You are clean."* This is the ancient
blessing, lost so quickly by our first parents. The loss of this virtue
shut man out of Paradise and continues to shut men out of heaven.
The lack of cleanness in their hearts and upon their hands condemns sinners to banishment from God and defiles all their offerings. To be clean before God is the desire of every repentant person,
and it is the highest aspiration of the most advanced believer. It is
what all the ceremonies and cleansings of the law can never bestow
and what Pharisees, with all their pretensions, cannot attain. To be
clean is to be like the angels, like glorified saints, even like the Father Himself.

Acceptance with the Lord, safety, happiness, and every blessing always accompany cleanness of heart. The one who has a clean
heart cannot miss out on heaven. A clean heart seems too high a
condition to be ascribed to mortals, yet by the lips of Him who could
not err, the disciples were said to be *"clean."* There was no qualify-
ing phrase, no condition for their cleanness. They were perfectly

justified in the sight of eternal equity and were regarded as free from every impurity.

Is this blessing yours? Have you ever believed so that you might receive Christ's righteousness? Have you taken the Lord Jesus to be your complete cleansing, your sanctification, your redemption? Has the Holy Spirit ever sealed in your peaceful spirit the gracious testimony, *"You are clean"*? The assurance is not confined to the apostles, for you also are *"complete in Him"* (Col. 2:10) and *"perfect in Christ Jesus"* (Col. 1:28), if you have by faith received the righteousness of God.

The psalmist said, *"Wash me, and I shall be whiter than snow"* (Ps. 51:7). If you have been washed, you are clean before the Lord to the highest and purest degree, and you are clean now. Oh, that all believers would live up to this privilege! But, unfortunately, too many are as depressed as if they were still miserable sinners; they forget that they are forgiven in Christ Jesus and therefore ought to be happy in the Lord. Remember, beloved believer, because you are one with Christ, you are not with sinners *"poisoned by bitterness"* (Acts 8:23) but with the saints in the *"land flowing with milk and honey"* (Num. 16:13).

Your cleanness is not measured by any scale or ruler; it is not a variable or vanishing quantity. Instead, it is present, constant, and perfect. You are clean through the Word, through the application of *"the blood of sprinkling"* (Heb. 12:24) to your conscience, and through the imputation of the righteousness of the Lord Jesus Christ.

Lift up your head, therefore, and sing with a joyful heart, because your transgression has been pardoned, your sin has been covered, and Jehovah sees no iniquity in you. Do not let another moment pass until by faith in Jesus you have grasped this privilege. Do not be content merely to believe that the priceless gift may be had, but lay hold of it for yourself. You will find that the song praising Christ's substitutionary death for you is an excellent song, if you are able to sing it.

The One Who Gives the Praise

Much of the force of our text, *"You are clean,"* lies in the One giving the praise. To receive the approval of our fellowmen is consoling, but in the end it is of small consequence. The human standard of purity is itself grossly incorrect, and therefore to be judged by it is a poor test, and to be acquitted by it is a slender comfort. However, the Lord judges no one according to the flesh. He came forth from God and is Himself God, infinitely just and good. Hence, His tests are accurate, and His verdict is absolute (John 8:15–16).

I have come to know that whoever He pronounces clean is clean indeed. Our Lord is omniscient, so He can at once detect the least evil in His disciples. If unpardoned sin remains with an individual, He has to have seen it. If any former condemnation were lingering upon someone, He would detect it at once, for no speck could escape His all-discerning eye. Even so, He said without hesitation to all the disciples but Judas, *"You are clean."*

Perhaps they did not catch the full glory of this pronouncement. They might have missed much of the deep, joyous meaning that is now revealed to us by the Spirit. Otherwise, what bliss to have heard with their own ears from those sacred lips so plain, so positive, so sure a testimony of their character before God! Yet our hearts do not need to be filled with regret because we cannot hear that ever blessed voice with our earthly ears, for the testimony of Jesus in the Word is quite as sure as the witness of His lips when He spoke among the sons of men. And that testimony is, *"Everyone who believes is justified from all things"* (Acts 13:39).

Yes, this promise is as certain as if you heard the Redeemer Himself say it. You are free from all condemning sin if you are looking with your whole heart to Jesus as your all in all. What a joy is yours and mine! He who is to judge the world in righteousness has Himself confirmed that we are clean. However black and terrible the condemnation of guilt is, the forgiveness of our sins is that much brighter and more comforting. Let us rejoice in the Lord, whose indisputable judgment has given forth a blessing so joyous, so full of glory.

> Jesus declares me clean,
> Then clean indeed I am,
> However guilty I have been,
> I'm cleansèd through the Lamb.

Those Who Were Praised

It may encourage you to call to mind the people who were praised. They were not cherubim and seraphim, but men, and notably they were men filled with weakness. There was Peter, who a

407

few minutes afterward was brash and presumptuous. But it is not necessary to name them one by one, for they all forsook their Master and fled in His hour of peril. Not one among them was more than a mere child in grace. They had little about them that was apostolic except their commission. They were very evidently men who had the same passions that we do, yet their Lord declared them to be clean, and clean they were.

This is nourishment for those souls who are hungering for righteousness and worrying because they feel so much of the burden of indwelling sin: cleanliness before the Lord is not destroyed by our sins and weaknesses or prevented by our inward temptations. We stand in the righteousness of Another. No amount of personal weakness, spiritual anxiety, soul conflict, or mental agony can mar our acceptance in the Beloved (Eph. 1:6). We may be weak infants or wandering sheep, and for both reasons we may be very far from what we wish to be. But, as God sees us, we are viewed as washed in the blood of Jesus, and we, even we, are *"completely clean."*

What a forcible expression, *"completely clean"*—every inch, from every point of view, in all respects, and to the uttermost degree! Dear friend, if you are a believer, this fact is true even for you. Do not hesitate to drink of it, for it is water out of your own well, given to you in the covenant of grace. Do not think that it is presumptuous to believe this statement, as marvelous as it is. You are dealing with a wonderful Savior, who does only wonderful things. Therefore, do not stand back on account of the greatness of the blessing, but rather believe even more readily because the message is so similar to everything the Lord says or does.

Yet when you have believed for yourself and have cast every doubt to the wind, you will not wonder less, but more. Your never ceasing cry will then be, *"Why is this granted to me?"* (Luke 1:43). How is it that I, who wallowed with swine, should be made as pure as the angels? Since I have been delivered from the foulest guilt, is it indeed possible that I am now the possessor of a perfect righteousness? Sing, O heavens, for the Lord has done it, and He shall have everlasting praise!

When the Praise Was Given

The time when the praise was given is also a lesson to us. The word of loving judgment is in the present tense: *"You are clean."* It is not, "You were clean," which might be a condemnation for willful neglect, a prophecy of wrath to come, or a rebuke for purity that has been shamelessly defiled. Nor is it, "You might have been clean," which would have been a stern rebuke for privileges rejected and opportunities wasted. Nor is it even, "You will be clean," though that would have been a delightful prophecy of good things to come at some distant time. But it is, *"You are clean,"* at this moment, wherever you are. Even Peter, who had just spoken so rudely, was then clean.

This is a great comfort amid our present sense of imperfection! Our cleanness is a matter of this present hour. We are, in our present condition and position, *"completely clean."* Why then postpone our joy? The reason for it is in our possession, so let our joy overflow even now.

Much of our heritage is certainly to come in the future, but if no other blessing were tangible to our faith in this immediate present, this one blessing alone should awaken all our powers to the highest praise. Even now we are clothed with the fair white linen that is the righteousness of believers, for we are washed in the blood of Christ and pardoned by His name. May the Holy Spirit bear witness with every believer that *"you are clean."*

Chapter 14

Comfort and Consolation

I will not leave you orphans; I will come to you.
—John 14:18

In the absence of our Lord Jesus Christ, the disciples were like children deprived of their parents. During the three years in which He had been with them, He had solved all their difficulties, borne all their burdens, and supplied all their needs. Whenever a case was too hard or too heavy for them, they took it to Him. When their enemies nearly overcame them, Jesus came to the rescue and turned the tide of battle.

They were all happy and safe enough while the Master was with them; He walked in their midst like a father amid a large family of children, making the whole household glad. But He was about to be taken from them by a shameful death, and they probably felt that they would be like little children deprived of their natural and beloved protector. Our Savior knew the fear that was in their hearts, and before they could express it, He removed it by saying, "You will not be left alone in this wild and barren world; though I may be absent in the flesh, I will be present with you in a more effective way. I will come to you spiritually, and you will derive from My spiritual presence even more good than you could have had from My bodily presence, had I still continued in your midst."

Observe, first, that an evil is averted here: *"I will not leave you orphans."* In the second place, a consolation is provided: *"I will come to you."*

An Evil Averted

Without their Lord, and apart from the Holy Spirit, believers would be like other orphans, unhappy and desolate. Give them

410

what you may, their loss cannot be recompensed. No number of lamps can make up for the sun's absence; shine as they may, it is still night. No circle of friends can compensate for the loss of a woman's husband; without him, she is still a widow. Without Jesus, it is inevitable that believers would be like orphans, but Jesus has promised that we will not be so. He declares that we will have the one thing that can remove the desolation: *"I will come to you."*

What Makes One an Orphan

Now remember, an orphan is someone whose parents are dead. This in itself is a great sorrow, for the father can no longer love his children and protect and provide for them as he once did. But we are not orphans in that sense, for our Lord Jesus is not dead. It is true that He died, for one of the soldiers pierced His side with a spear, and blood and water came out from the wound (John 19:34). This was certain proof that the fountain of life had been broken up. He died, certainly, but He is not dead now. Do not go to the grave to seek Him. Angel voices say, *"He is not here; for He is risen"* (Matt. 28:6). He could not be held captive by the bonds of death.

We do not worship a dead Christ, nor do we even think of Him now as a corpse. Oh, it is so good to think of Christ as living, remaining in a real and true existence. He is no less alive because He died, but all the more truly full of life because He has passed through the gates of the grave and is now reigning forever. See, then, the bitter root of the orphan's sorrow is gone from us, for our Jesus is not dead now. No mausoleum enshrines His ashes, no pyramid entombs His body, no monument records the place of His permanent sepulchre.

> He lives, the great Redeemer lives,
> What joy the blest assurance gives!

We are not orphans, for *"the Lord is risen indeed!"* (Luke 24:34).

Not Left Alone

One of the greatest sorrows that an orphan has that springs out of the death of his parent is that he is left alone. He cannot now make appeals to the wisdom of the parent who could direct him. He cannot run, when he is weary, to climb on his father's knee as he

411

once did. He cannot lean his aching head against his parent's chest. "Father," he may say, but no voice answers him. "Mother," he may cry, but that fond title, which would awaken the mother if she slept, cannot arouse her from the bed of death. The child is alone, far from those two hearts that were his best companions. The parents are gone. Such little ones know what it is to be deserted and forsaken.

But we are not so; we are not orphans. It is true that Jesus is not here in body, but His spiritual presence is quite as blessed as His bodily presence would have been. Actually, it is better, for if Jesus Christ were here in person, we could not all come and touch the hem of His garment—not all at once, at any rate. There might be thousands waiting all over the world to speak with Him, but how could they all reach Him if He were merely here in body? Everyone might be waiting to tell Him something, but in the body He could receive only one or two at a time.

But there is no need for you to say a word; Jesus hears your thoughts and attends to all your needs in the same moment. There is no need to press to reach Him because the crowd is large, for He is as near to me as He is to you, and as near to you as to believers all over the world. He is present everywhere, and all His beloved may talk with Him. You can tell Him at this moment the sorrows that you dare not open up to anyone else. In declaring them to Him, you will feel that you have hardly breathed them into the air before He has heard you. He is a real person, one so real that it is as if you could grip His hand and see the loving sparkle of His eye and the sympathetic look of His countenance.

Is it not this way with you? You know that you have *a friend who sticks closer than a brother"* (Prov. 18:24). You have a near and dear One. You are not an orphan; the *"Wonderful, Counselor, Mighty God, Everlasting Father, Prince of Peace"* (Isa. 9:6) is with you. Your Lord is here, and He comforts you, as a mother comforts her child.

Not without Provisions

The orphan, too, has lost the hands that always took care to provide food, clothing, and a comfortable home. Poor, feeble one, who will provide for his needs? His parents are gone; who will take care of the little wanderer now?

But it is not so with us. Jesus has not left us as orphans. His care for His people is no less now than it was when He sat at the table with Mary, Martha, and Lazarus. Instead of the provisions being less, they are even greater. Since the Holy Spirit has been given to us, we have richer fare and are more indulged with spiritual comforts than believers were before the Master's bodily form departed. Is your soul hungry? Jesus gives you the bread of heaven. Is your soul thirsty? The waters from the rock do not cease to flow.

Come to Jesus, and make your needs, your burdens, known to Him. You have only to make your needs known to have them all supplied. Christ waits to be gracious to you. He stands with His golden hand open to supply the needs of every living soul. "Oh," says one, "'I am poor and needy'"; then go on with the quotation: "Yet the LORD thinks upon me" (Ps. 40:17). Another says, "I have asked the Lord three times to take away 'a thorn in the flesh' (2 Cor. 12:7) from me." Remember what He said to Paul: "My grace is sufficient for you" (v. 9). You are not left without the strength you need.

The Lord is still your Shepherd. He will provide for you until He leads you through death's dark valley and brings you to the shining pastures upon the hilltops of glory. You are not destitute; you do not need to compromise with this world by bowing to its demands or trusting its vain promises, for Jesus "will never leave you nor forsake you" (Heb. 13:5).

Not without Suitable Instruction

The orphan, too, is left without the instruction that is most suitable for a child. We may say what we will, but there is no one as fit to form a child's character as the parent. It is a very sad loss for a child to have lost either father or mother, for the most skillful teacher, though he may do much, can hardly make up for the way a parent's love can mold a child's mind.

But, dear friends, we are not orphans; we who believe in Jesus are not left without an education. Jesus is not here Himself, it is true. I imagine some of you wish you could go to church on Sundays and listen to Him! Would it not be wonderful to look up at the pulpit and see the Crucified One, and to hear Him preach? Ah, so you think, but the apostle said, "Even though we have known Christ according to the flesh, yet now we know Him thus no longer" (2 Cor. 5:16).

It is profitable that you should receive the Spirit of Truth, not through the golden vessel of Christ in His actual presence, but through the poor earthen vessels of humble servants of God. At any rate, whether a preacher speaks or an angel from heaven speaks, the speaker does not matter; it is the Spirit of God alone who is the power of the Word and who makes that Word vital and life-giving for you.

Now, you have the Spirit of God. The Holy Spirit is given so that you may understand every truth of the Scriptures. You may be led into the deepest mysteries by His teaching. You may be enabled to know and to comprehend those things in the Word of God that have puzzled you for a long time. When you humbly look up to Jesus, His Spirit will still teach you. Even if you could scarcely read a word of the Bible, you would be better instructed than doctors of divinity if you went to the Holy Spirit and were taught by Him in the things of God. Those who go only to books and to the letter of the law, and who are taught by men, are fools in the sight of God; but those who go to Jesus and sit at His feet and ask to be taught by His Spirit will be *"wise for salvation"* (2 Tim. 3:15). Blessed be God, we are not left as orphans; we have an Instructor with us still.

Not Lacking a Defender

There is one point in which the orphan is often sorrowfully reminded of his orphanhood, namely, in lacking a defender. It is so natural in little children, when some big bully harasses them, to say, "I'll tell my father!" How often we hear little ones say, "I'll tell Mother!" Sometimes, not being able to do this is a much greater loss than we can guess. Cruel thieves might come and snatch away from orphans the little that a father's love had left behind, and in the court of law there has been no defender to protect the orphan's possessions. Had the father been there, the child would have had his rights; but in the absence of the father, the orphan is eaten up like bread, and the wicked of the earth devour his possessions.

In this sense, believers are not orphans. The Devil would rob us of our heritage if he could, but there is an *"Advocate with the Father"* (1 John 2:1) who pleads for us. Satan would snatch from us every promise and tear from us all the comforts of the covenant, but we are not orphans. When the Enemy brings a suit against us and thinks that we are the only defendants in the case, he is mistaken, for we have an Advocate on high. Christ comes in and

414

pleads, as the sinners' Friend, for us; and when He pleads at the bar of justice, there is no fear that His plea will be ineffective or that our inheritance is not safe. He has not left us as orphans.

You who love the Master, you are not alone in this world. Even if you have no earthly friends, if you have no one to whom you can take your cares, if you are quite lonely, Jesus is with you, is really with you, with you in a practical way, able to help you, and ready to do so. You have a good and kind Protector close at hand at this present moment, for Christ has said, *"I will not leave you orphans."*

Consolation Provided

The second comment I wish to make about our text is that it provides consolation for us. Not only are we saved from being without our Father, but the Lord Jesus also said, *"I will come to you."*

Jesus Comes to Us by the Spirit

What does this mean? From the context, we may suppose that it means, *"'I will come to you'* by My Spirit." Beloved, we must not confuse the persons of the Godhead. The Holy Spirit is not the Son of God; Jesus, the Son of God, is not the Holy Spirit. They are two distinct persons of the one Godhead. But there is such a wonderful unity, and the blessed Spirit acts so marvelously as the Agent of Christ, that it is quite correct to say that when the Spirit comes, Jesus comes, too. Thus, *"I will come to you"* means, "I, by My Spirit, who will take My place and represent Me, will come to be with you."

See then, Christian, you have the Holy Spirit in you and with you to be the Representative of Christ. Christ is with you now, not in person, but by His Representative—an efficient, almighty, divine, everlasting Representative, who stands for Christ and is like Christ in your soul. Because you have Christ by His Spirit in this way, you cannot be an orphan, for the Spirit of God is always with you.

It is a delightful truth that the Spirit of God always dwells in believers—not sometimes, but always. He is not always active in believers, and He may be grieved until His perceptible presence is altogether withdrawn, but His secret presence is always there. At no single moment is the Spirit of God wholly gone from a believer. The believer would die spiritually if this could happen, but this cannot be, for Jesus has said, *"Because I live, you will live also"* (John 14:19).

Even when the believer sins, the Holy Spirit does not utterly depart from him, but He is still in him to make him regret the sin into which he has fallen. The believer's prayers prove that the Holy Spirit is still within him. *"Do not take Your Holy Spirit from me"* (Ps. 51:11) was the prayer of a believer who had fallen very far but with in whom the Spirit of God still resided, notwithstanding all the foulness of his guilt and sin.

Visits from the Spirit

In addition to this, Jesus Christ by His Spirit makes certain kinds of visits to His people. The Holy Spirit becomes wonderfully active and powerful at certain times of refreshment. We are then especially and joyfully aware of His divine power. His influence streams through every part of our natures and floods our dark souls with His glorious rays, as the sun shining at midday. Oh, how delightful this is! Sometimes we have felt His presence at the Communion table. I am equally sure that Jesus Christ has come to us at prayer meetings, during the preaching of the Word, in times of private meditation, and as we have searched the Scriptures.

Let us ask the Lord to permit us once again to feel the truth of the promise, *"I will not leave you orphans; I will come to you."*

All His Words Are Instructive

And now, let me remind you that every word of our text verse is instructive: *"I will not leave you orphans; I will come to you."* Observe that the *"I"* is there twice. We can hear Jesus saying, *" 'I will not leave you orphans.'* Your fathers and mothers may, but I will not. Friends who once loved you may become hard-hearted, but I will not. Judas may play the traitor, and Ahithophel may betray his David, but *'I will not leave you orphans.'* You have had many disappointments, great heartbreaking sorrows, but I have never caused you any. I, the Faithful and True Witness, the immutable, the unchangeable Jesus, the same yesterday, today, and forever—*'I will not leave you orphans; I will come to you.' "*

Grasp onto that word, *"I,"* and let your soul say, *" 'Lord, I am not worthy that You should come under my roof'* (Matt. 8:8). If You had said, 'I will send an angel to you,' it would have been a great mercy, but You say, *'I will come to you.'* If You had asked some of my fellow Christians to come and speak a word of comfort to me, I would have been thankful, but You have put it in the first person: *'I will come to you.'* O my Lord, what should I say, what should I do, but feel a hungering and a thirsting for You, which nothing can satisfy until You fulfill Your own word: *'I will not leave you orphans; I will come to you'*?"

And then notice the people to whom it was addressed: "*'I will not leave you orphans.'* You, Peter, who will deny Me; you, Thomas, who will doubt Me—*'I will not leave you orphans.'*" You who are so insignificant in Israel that you sometimes think that you are so worthless, so unworthy, He will not leave you comfortless, not even you! "O Lord," you say, "if You would look after the rest of Your sheep, I would bless You for Your tenderness to them, but I—I deserve to be left. If I were forsaken by You, I could not blame You, for I have played the harlot against Your love. Yet You continue to say to me, *'I will not leave you.'*"

Heir of heaven, do not lose your part in this promise. Say to Him, "Lord, come to me, and though You refresh all my fellowmen, refresh me with some of the drops of Your love. O Lord, fill the cup for me; my thirsty spirit pants for it. Fulfill Your word to me, as I stand like Hannah in Your presence. Come to me, Your servant, unworthy to lift so much as my eyes toward heaven and only daring to say, *'God, be merciful to me a sinner!'* (Luke 18:13). Fulfill Your promise even to me, *'I will not leave you orphans; I will come to you.'*"

The Sufficiency of His Words

Take whichever of the words you will, and they each sparkle and gleam in this manner. Observe, too, the richness and sufficiency of the text: *"I will not leave you orphans; I will come to you."* He does not promise, "I will send you sanctifying grace, sustaining mercy, or precious mercy," but He says the only thing that will prevent you from being orphans: *"I will come to you."*

Ah, Lord! Your grace is sweet, but You are better. The vine is good, but the clusters are better. It is well enough to have a gift from Your hand, but oh, to touch the hand itself! It is well enough to hear the words of Your lips, but oh, to kiss those lips as the spouse did in the Song of Songs (Song 1:2)! This is better still!

You know that you cannot prevent an orphan from remaining an orphan. You may feel great kindness toward the child, supply

417

his needs, and do all you possibly can for him, but he is still an orphan. He must get his father and mother back, or else he will still be an orphan. Knowing this, our blessed Lord does not say, "I will do this and that for you," but *"I will come to you."*

Do you not see, dear friends, here is not only all you can want, but also all you think you can want, wrapped up in a sentence, *"I will come to you"*? *"It pleased the Father that in Him all the fullness should dwell"* (Col. 1:19). Thus, when Christ comes, *"all the fullness"* comes as well. *"In Him dwells all the fullness of the Godhead bodily"* (Col. 2:9). Thus, when Jesus comes, the very Godhead comes to the believer. Observe, then, the language and the sufficiency of the promise.

A Continual Promise

I want you to notice, further, the continued freshness and force of the promise. If you owe someone fifty dollars and you give him a written promise to pay tomorrow, he will come to your house tomorrow and get the fifty dollars. What good is the written promise after that? It has no further value; it is discharged. How would you like to have a written promise that would always stand good? That would be a great gift. "I promise to pay forever, and this bond, though paid a thousand times, will still hold good." Who would not like to have a check of that sort? Yet this is the promise that Christ gives you: *"I will not leave you orphans; I will come to you."*

The first time a sinner looks to Christ, Christ comes to him. And then what? Why, the next minute it is still, *"I will come to you."* But suppose someone has known Christ for fifty years, and he has had this promise fulfilled a thousand times a year. Is the promise done with then, after fifty thousand times? Certainly not! It stands just as fresh as when Jesus first spoke it: *"I will come to you."*

When we understand this, we will take our Lord at His word. We will go to Him as often as we can, for we will never weary Him. And when He has kept His promise most, then we will go to Him and ask Him to keep it more still. And after ten thousand proofs of the truth of it, we will only have a greater hungering and thirsting to get it fulfilled again. This is our blessed provision: *"I will come to you."* In the last moment, when your pulse beats faintly and you are just about to pass away and enter into the invisible world, you may have this on your lips and say to your Lord, "My Master, still fulfill the word in which You have caused me to hope: *'I will not leave you orphans; I will come to you.'"*

Entirely Valid

Let me remind you that the text is at this moment valid, and for this reason I delight in it. *"I will not leave you orphans."* That means now, *"I will not leave you orphans* [now].*"* Are you comfortless right now? It is your own fault. Jesus Christ does not leave you so, nor does He make you so. There are rich and precious things in this word: *"I will not leave you orphans; I will come to you,"* that is, *"I will come to you* [now].*"*

You may be going through a very dry spiritual time, and you may be longing to come nearer to Christ. Then plead the promise before the Lord. Plead the promise as you sit where you are: "Lord, You have said You will come to me; come to me now." There are many reasons, believer, why you should plead in this way. You want Him, you need Him, you require Him; therefore, plead the promise and expect its fulfillment.

And oh, when He comes, what a joy it is! He is as a bridegroom coming out of his chamber with his garments fragrant with *"myrrh and aloes and cassia"* (Ps. 45:8). How the oil of joy will perfume your heart! How soon will your sackcloth be put away, and garments of gladness will adorn you! With great joy in your heart, your heavy soul will begin to sing when Jesus Christ whispers that you are His and that He is yours (Song 6:3)! Come, my Beloved, do not hesitate; *"be like a gazelle or a young stag upon the mountains"* (Song 2:17), and prove Your promise: *"I will not leave you orphans; I will come to you."*

Many Do Not Share in This Promise

And now, let me remind you that there are many who have no share in the promise of our text. What can I say to such people? I pity you who do not know what the love of Christ means. Oh, if you could only see the joy of God's people, you would not rest an hour without it.

His worth, if all the nations knew,
Sure the whole world would love Him too.

Remember, if you want to find Christ, He is to be found in the way of faith. Trust Him, and He is yours. Depend on the merit of His sacrifice; cast yourself entirely upon that, and you are saved, and Christ is yours.

Chapter 15

The Sin-Bearer

[Christie] Himself bore our sins in His own body on the tree, that we,
having died to sins, might live for righteousness; by whose stripes
you were healed. For you were like sheep going astray, but have now
returned to the Shepherd and Overseer of your souls.
—1 Peter 2:24–25

This wonderful passage is part of Peter's address to servants, and in his day nearly all servants were slaves. Peter began by saying,

Servants, be submissive to your masters with all fear, not only
to the good and gentle, but also to the harsh. For this is com-
mendable, if because of conscience toward God one endures
grief, suffering wrongfully. For what credit is it if, when you
are beaten for your faults, you take it patiently? But when you
do good and suffer, if you take it patiently, this is commend-
able before God. For to this you were called, because Christ
also suffered for us, leaving us an example, that you should
follow His steps: "Who committed no sin, nor was deceit
found in His mouth"; who, when He was reviled, did not re-
vile in return; when He suffered, He did not threaten, but
committed Himself to Him who judges righteously; who Him-
self bore our sins in His own body on the tree, that we, having
died to sins, might live for righteousness; by whose stripes you
were healed. (1 Pet. 2:18–24)

If we are in a humble condition of life, we will find our best comfort in thinking of the humble Savior bearing our sins in all patience and submission. If we are called to suffer, as servants often were in Roman times, we will be comforted by a vision of our Lord buffeted, scourged, and crucified, yet silent in the majesty of His endurance. If these sufferings are entirely undeserved and we are grossly slandered, we will be comforted by remembering Him who committed no sin and in whose lips no guile was found. Our Lord Jesus is Head of the Guild of Sufferers: He did good, and suffered for it, but He took it patiently. Our support in carrying our cross, which we are appointed to bear, is only to be found in Him who *"bore our sins in His own body on the tree."*

We ourselves now know by experience that there is no place for comfort like the Cross. It is a tree stripped of all foliage, apparently dead; yet we sit under its shadow with great delight, and its fruit is sweet to our taste (Song 2:3). Truly, in this case, like cures like. By the suffering of our Lord Jesus, our suffering is made easy. The servant is comforted since Jesus took upon Himself the form of a servant (Phil. 2:7); the sufferer is encouraged *"because Christ also suffered for us"* (1 Pet. 2:21); and the slandered one is strengthened because Jesus also *"was reviled"* (v. 23).

As we hope to pass through the tribulations of this world, let us stand fast by the Cross; for if that is gone, the star is extinguished whose light cheers the downtrodden, shines on the injured, and brings light to the oppressed. If we lose the Cross, if we miss the substitutionary sacrifice of our Lord Jesus Christ, we have lost everything.

The verses that I quoted at the beginning of this chapter speak of three things: the bearing of our sins, the changing of our condition, and the healing of our spiritual diseases. Each of these deserves our most careful notice.

The Bearing of Our Sins

Literally

The first thing is the bearing of our sins by our Lord, who *"Himself bore our sins in His own body on the tree."* These words plainly assert that our Lord Jesus really did bear the sins of His people. How literal the language is! Words mean nothing if Christ's substitutionary sacrifice is not indicated here, and I do not know the meaning of Isaiah 53 if this is not its meaning. Read the prophet's words: *"The LORD has laid on Him the iniquity of us all"* (Isa. 53:6); *"for the transgressions of My people He was stricken"* (v. 8); *"He shall bear their iniquities"* (v. 11); *"He was numbered with the transgressors, and He bore the sin of many"* (v. 12).

I cannot imagine that the Holy Spirit would have used language so expressive if He had not intended to teach us that our

Savior really did bear our sins and suffer in our place. What else can be intended by texts like these: *"Christ was offered once to bear the sins of many"* (Heb. 9:28); *"He made Him who knew no sin to be sin for us, that we might become the righteousness of God in Him"* (2 Cor. 5:21); *"Christ has redeemed us from the curse of the law, having become a curse for us (for it is written, 'Cursed is everyone who hangs on a tree')"* (Gal. 3:13); *"Christ also has loved us and given Himself for us, an offering and a sacrifice to God for a sweet-smelling aroma"* (Eph. 5:2); *"once at the end of the ages, He has appeared to put away sin by the sacrifice of Himself"* (Heb. 9:26)? These Scriptures either teach the bearing of our sins by our Lord Jesus, or they teach nothing.

In these days, among many errors and denials of truth, there has sprung up a teaching of "modern thought" that explains away the doctrine of substitution and vicarious sacrifice. Some have gone so far as to say that the transference of sin or righteousness is impossible, and others of the same school have stigmatized the idea as immoral.

It does not much matter what these modern haters of the Cross may dare to say. Assuredly, what they deny, denounce, and deride is the cardinal doctrine of our most holy faith and is as clearly in Scripture as the sun is in the heavens. Beloved, as we suffer through the sin of Adam, so are we saved through the righteousness of Christ. Our fall was caused by another, and so is our rising again. We are under a system of representation and imputation, no matter what anyone says against it. To us, the transference of our sin to Christ is a blessed fact clearly revealed in the Word of God and graciously confirmed in the experience of our faith.

In that same chapter of Isaiah we read, *"Surely He has borne our griefs and carried our sorrows"* (Isa. 53:4), and we perceive that this was a fact, for He was really, truly, and emphatically sorrowful. Therefore, when we read that He *"bore our sins in His own body on the tree,"* we dare not take it lightly. We believe that in very deed He was our Sin-Bearer. Possible or impossible, we sing with full assurance, "He bore on the tree the sentence for me."

If the sorrow had been figurative, the sin-bearing might have been a mere myth, but the one fact is parallel with the other. There is no mere illustration in our text; it is a bare, literal fact: "[Christ] *Himself bore our sins in His own body on the tree."* Oh, if only people would quit raising trivial objections to this great truth! To question and debate the Cross is like the crime of the Roman soldiers when they divided His garments among themselves and cast lots for His clothing (John 19:24).

Personally

Next, note how personal are the terms used here! The Holy Spirit is very explicit: *"Who Himself bore our sins in His own body."* It was not by delegation, but *"Himself,"* and it was not in someone's imagination, but *"in His own body."* Observe, also, the personal aspect from our side of the question: He *"bore our sins"*—my sins and your sins. As surely as it was Christ's own self that suffered on the cross, so truly were they our own sins that Jesus bore *"in His own body on the tree."*

Our Lord has appeared in court for us, accepting our place at the stand: *"He was numbered with the transgressors"* (Isa. 53:12). Moreover, He has appeared at the place of execution for us and has borne the death penalty upon the gallows of doom in our place. In propria persona, our Redeemer has been arraigned, though innocent; has come under the curse, though forever blessed; and has suffered to the death, though He had done nothing worthy of blame. *"He was wounded for our transgressions, He was bruised for our iniquities; the chastisement for our peace was upon Him, and by His stripes we are healed"* (v. 5).

Continually

The sin-bearing on our Lord's part was also continual. This passage in 1 Peter has been forced beyond its meaning; people have used it to assert that our Lord Jesus bore our sins nowhere but on the cross. But the words do not say this. *"The tree"* was the place where, beyond all other places, we see our Lord bearing the chastisement for our sins. But before this, He had felt the weight of the enormous load. It is wrong to base a great doctrine upon the incidental form of one passage of Scripture, especially when that passage of Scripture bears another meaning.

In the Revised Version, the marginal note for this passage reads, *"Who his own self carried up our sins in his body to the tree."* Our Lord carried the burden of our sins up to the tree, and there and then He made an end of it. He had carried that load long before, for John the Baptist said of Him, *"Behold! The Lamb of God who takes away* [the verb is in the present tense] *the sin of the world!"* (John 1:29). Our Lord was then bearing the sin of the world as the Lamb of God. From the day when He began His divine ministry, and even before that, He *"bore our sins."*

He was *"the Lamb slain from the foundation of the world"* (Rev. 13:8); when He went up to Calvary, bearing His cross, He was bearing our sins on the tree. Especially in the agony of His death, He stood in our place, and upon His soul and body burst the tempest of justice that had gathered through our transgressions.

Finally

This sin-bearing is final. He *"bore our sins in His own body on the tree,"* but now He bears them no longer. The sinner and the sinner's Surety are both free, for the law is vindicated, the substitutionary sacrifice is complete. He dies no more; death no longer has dominion over Him, for He has ended His work and has cried, *"It is finished!"* (John 19:30). As for the sins that He bore in His own body on the tree, they cannot be found, for they have ceased to exist.

This is according to that ancient promise: *"'In those days and in that time,' says the LORD, 'the iniquity of Israel shall be sought, but there shall be none; and the sins of Judah, but they shall not be found'"* (Jer. 50:20). The work of the Messiah was *"to finish the transgression, to make an end of sins, to make reconciliation for iniquity, to bring in everlasting righteousness"* (Dan. 9:24). Now, if sin is brought to an end, nothing more needs to be done; if transgression is finished, there is no more to be said about it.

Effectively

Let us look back with holy faith and see Jesus bearing the stupendous load of our sins up to the tree and on the tree. His sacrifice discharged the whole mass of our moral liability both in reference to guiltiness in the sight of God and to the punishment that follows! It is a law of nature that nothing can be in two places at the same time, and if sin was borne away by our Lord, it cannot rest upon us. If by faith we have accepted the Substitute whom God Himself has accepted, then it is not possible for the penalty to be demanded twice, first of the Surety and then of those for whom He stood.

The Lord Jesus bore the sins of His people away, even as the scapegoat carried the sin of Israel to an uninhabited land. (See Leviticus 16:10.) Our sins are gone forever. *"As far as the east is from the west, so far has He removed our transgressions from us"* (Ps. 103:12). He has cast all our iniquities into the depths of the sea; He has hurled them behind His back, where they will be seen no more.

Beloved friends, we very calmly and coolly talk about this thing, but it is the greatest marvel in the universe. It is the miracle of earth, the mystery of heaven, the terror of hell. If we could fully realize the guilt of sin, the punishment due for it, and the literal substitution of Christ, it would give us an intense enthusiasm of gratitude, love, and praise. This is enough to make us all shout and sing, as long as we live, "Glory, glory to the Son of God!"

What an amazing thing that the Prince of Glory, in whom there is no sin, who was indeed incapable of evil, should condescend to come into such contact with our sin by being made *"to be sin for us"* (2 Cor. 5:21)! Our Lord Jesus did not handle sin with golden tongs, but He bore it on His own shoulders. He did not lift it with golden staffs, as the priests carried the ark, but He Himself bore the hideous load of our sin *"in His own body on the tree."* This is the mystery of grace that *"angels desire to look into"* (1 Pet. 1:12).

The Change in Our Condition

In the second place, notice the change in our condition that the text describes as the result of the Lord's bearing of our sins: *"That we, having died to sins, might live for righteousness."* The change is a dying and a reviving, a burial and a resurrection. We are brought from life to death and from death to life.

Dead to the Punishment for Sin

We are legally dead to the punishment for sin from this point onward. If I were condemned to die for an offense, and someone else died in my place, then I died in the one who died for me. The law could not lay the charge against me a second time, bring me before the judge again, condemn me, and lead me out to die. Where would be the justice of such a procedure? I am dead already; how can I die again?

Likewise, I have borne the wrath of God in the person of my glorious and ever blessed Substitute; how then can I bear it again?

What was the use of a Substitute if I am to bear it also? If Satan were to come before God to lay an accusation against me, the answer would be, "This man is dead. He has borne the penalty, and is dead to sins, for the sentence against him has been executed upon Another." What a wonderful deliverance for us! Bless the Lord, O my soul!

Actually Dead to Sins

But Peter also meant to remind us that, through the influence of Christ's death upon our hearts, the Holy Spirit has made us now to be actually dead to sins. In other words, we no longer love them, and they have ceased to hold dominion over us. Sin is no longer at home in our hearts; if it enters there, it is as an intruder. We are no longer its willing servants. Sin calls to us by temptation, but we give it no answer, for we are deaf to its voice. Sin promises us a high reward, but we do not consent, for we are dead to its allurements.

We sin, but our will is not to sin. It would be heaven to us to be perfectly holy. Our hearts and lives pursue perfection, but sin is abhorred by our souls. *"Now if I do what I will not to do, it is no longer I who do it, but sin that dwells in me"* (Rom 7:20). Our truest and most real self hates sin, yet we fall into it. Even so, we run from the evil of sin with the greatest speed, for the new life within us has no dealings with sin; it is dead to sin.

The Greek word used here cannot be fully translated into English. It signifies "being unborn to sins." We were born in sin, but by the death of Christ and the work of the Holy Spirit in us, that birth is undone. We are actually "unborn" to sins. What was in us by sin, even at our birth, is through the death of Jesus counteracted by the new life that His Spirit imparts. We are unborn to sins. I like the phrase, as unusual as it may seem. Does it seem possible that birth can be reversed—that the born can be unborn? Yet it is so. The true ego, the "I," is now unborn to sins, for we are *"born, not of blood, nor of the will of the flesh, nor of the will of man, but of God"* (John 1:13). We are unborn to sins and born to God.

Brought into Life

Our Lord's sin-bearing has also brought us into life. Dead to evil according to law, we also live *"in newness of life"* (Rom. 6:4) in

427

the kingdom of grace. Our Lord's objective is *"that we...might live for righteousness."* Not only are our lives to be righteous, which I trust they are, but we are made alive and made sensitive and vigorous in righteousness. Through our Lord's death, our eyes, our thoughts, our lips, and our hearts are renewed unto righteousness. Certainly, if the doctrine of His atoning sacrifice does not bring life to us, nothing will. When we sin, it is the sorrowful result of our former death; but when we work righteousness, we throw our whole souls into it. *"We...live for righteousness."*

Because our divine Lord has died, we feel that we must use ourselves for His praise. The tree that brought death to our Savior is a tree of life to us. Sit under this true Tree of Life, and you will shake off the weakness and disease that came in by that Tree of Knowledge of Good and Evil. David Livingstone, the Scottish missionary to Africa, used certain medicines that were known as Livingstone's Rousers. But the glorious truths that are extracted from the bitter wood of the cross are far better rousers! Dear readers, let us show in our lives what wonders our Lord Jesus has accomplished for us by His agony and bloody sweat, by His cross and passion!

The Healing of Our Diseases

The apostle then wrote of the healing of our diseases by Christ's death: *"By whose stripes you were healed. For you were like sheep going astray, but have now returned to the Shepherd and Overseer of your souls."* We were healed, and we remain so. It is not a thing to be accomplished in the future; it has been done already. Peter described our disease in verse twenty-five. What was the nature of our sickness, then?

We Were Like Animals

First, it was brutishness. *"You were like sheep."* Sin has made us so that we are only fit to be compared to beasts, and to those of the least intelligence. The Scripture compares the unregenerate man to *"a wild donkey's colt"* (Job 11:12). Amos compared Israel to the *"cows of Bashan"* (Amos 4:1), and he said to them, *"You will go out through broken walls, each one straight ahead of her"* (v. 3). The psalmist compared himself to a huge animal: *"I was so foolish and ignorant; I was like a beast before You"* (Ps. 73:22). We are nothing better than beasts until Christ comes to us.

But we are not beasts after that! A living, heavenly, spiritual nature is created within us when we come into contact with our Redeemer. We still carry around with us the old brutish nature, but by the grace of God it is put in subjection and kept there. Our fellowship now is with the Father and with His Son Jesus Christ. We *"were like sheep,"* but we are now men redeemed unto God.

We Were Prone to Wander

We are cured also of our tendency to wander, which is so common in sheep. *"You were like sheep going astray"*—always going astray, loving to go astray, delighting in it, never so happy as when we were wandering away from the fold. We wander still, but not as sheep wander. We now seek the right way and desire to *"follow the Lamb wherever He goes"* (Rev. 14:4). If we wander, it is through ignorance or temptation. We can truly say, *"My soul follows close behind You"* (Ps. 63:8). Our Lord's cross has securely nailed our hands and feet. Now we cannot run greedily after iniquity. Instead, we say, *"Return to your rest, O my soul, for the LORD has dealt bountifully with you"* (Ps. 116:7).

We Were Unable to Return

Another disease of ours was an inability to return: *"You were like sheep going astray, but have now returned."* Dogs, and even swine, are more likely to return home than wandering sheep. But now, beloved, though we wandered, we have returned and still do return to our Shepherd. Like Noah's dove, we have found no rest anywhere outside of the ark; therefore, we return to Him, and He graciously pulls us in to Himself. If we wander at any time, we bless God that there is something sacred within us that will not let us rest, and that there is a far more powerful Something above us that draws us back.

We are like the needle in a compass: touch the needle with your finger, force it to point to the east or to the south, and it may do so for a moment; but take away the pressure, and in an instant it returns to the magnetic north. We must go back to Jesus in the same way; we must return to the *"Overseer of* [our] *souls."* Our souls cry, *"Whom have I in heaven but You? And there is none upon earth that I desire besides You"* (Ps. 73:25). Thus, by the virtue of our Lord's death, an immortal love is created in us that leads us to seek His face and renew our fellowship with Him.

We Were Ready to Follow Others

Our Lord's death has also cured us of our readiness to follow other leaders. If one sheep goes through a gap in the hedge, the whole flock will follow. We have been accustomed to following ringleaders in sin or in error. We have been too ready to follow custom and to do what is considered proper and respectable. But now we are resolved to follow none but Jesus, according to His Word: *"My sheep hear My voice, and I know them, and they follow Me"* (John 10:27); *"yet they will by no means follow a stranger, but will flee from him"* (v. 5).

I am resolved to follow no human leader. Faith in Jesus creates a sacred independence of mind. We have learned such dependence upon our crucified Lord that we have none to spare for men.

We Were Exposed to Wolves

Finally, when we were wandering, we were like sheep exposed to wolves, but we are delivered from this by being near the Shepherd. We were in danger of death, in danger from the Devil, in danger from a thousand temptations, which, like ravenous beasts, prowled around us. Having ended our wandering, we are now in a place of safety. When the lion roars, we are driven closer to the Shepherd, and we rejoice that His staff protects us. He says, *"My sheep hear My voice, and I know them, and they follow Me. And I give them eternal life, and they shall never perish; neither shall anyone snatch them out of My hand"* (John 10:27–28).

What a wonderful work of grace has been brought about in us! We owe all this not to the teaching of Christ, though that has helped us greatly; not to the example of Christ, though that is inspiring us to diligently imitate Him; but to His stripes: *"By whose stripes you were healed."*

Dear reader, we preach Christ crucified because we have been saved by Christ crucified. His death is the death of our sins. We can never give up the doctrine of Christ's substitutionary sacrifice, for it is the power by which we hope to be made holy. Not only are we washed from guilt in His blood, but by that blood we also overcome sin. As long as breath or pulse remains in us, we can never conceal the blessed truth that He *"bore our sins in His own body on the tree, that we, having died to sins, might live for righteousness."* May the Lord help us to know much more of this than I can write, for Jesus Christ's sake!

Book Five

Holy Spirit Power

Contents

Chapter 1

The Comforter

But the Helper ["Comforter"* KJV], the Holy Spirit, whom the Father*
will send in My name, He will teach you all things, and bring to
your remembrance all things that I said to you.
—John 14:26

ood old Simeon referred to Jesus as *"the Consolation of Is-*
rael" (Luke 2:25), and He was. Before His actual appearance, His name was Day Star, which means "cheering the
darkness," and is prophetic for the rising sun. Israel looked to Him
with the same hope that cheers the nightly watcher as he faithfully
waits for the sun to rise in the morning. When Jesus was on the
earth, He must have been the consolation of all those who were
privileged to be His companions. We can imagine how readily the
disciples would run to Christ to tell Him of their sorrows, and how
sweetly, with that matchless intonation of His voice, He would
speak to them and bid their fears be gone. Like children, they
would consider Him as their Father.

Every need, every groan, every sorrow, and every agony would
at once be carried to Him, and He, like a wise physician, had a balm
for every wound. He had a solution for their every care, and He
readily dispensed mighty remedies for all of their fevered troubles.
It must have been sweet to have lived with Christ. Sorrows were
masked joys because they presented an opportunity to go to Jesus
to have them removed. Oh, if only we could have placed our weary
heads upon Jesus' chest, have heard His kind voice, and seen His
gentle look as He said, *"Come to Me, all you who labor and are*
heavy laden, and I will give you rest" (Matt. 11:28).

When He was about to die, great prophecies and great purposes were to be fulfilled. Jesus had to go to the cross. He had to
suffer so that He could be our redemption from sin. He had to
slumber in the dust a while so that He might perfume the chamber
of the grave.

His resurrection took place so that one day, we, *"the dead in Christ"* (1 Thess. 4:16), might rise first and stand in glorious bodies upon the earth. He ascended on high so that He might make captivity captive (Ps. 68:18). He chained the fiends of hell, lashing them to His chariot wheels and dragging them high upon heaven's hill. This was to make them feel a second overthrow from His right arm when He dashed them from the pinnacles of heaven down to deeper depths beneath.

Jesus said, *"It is to your advantage that I go away; for if I do not go away, the Helper ["Comforter" KJV] will not come to you; but if I depart, I will send Him to you"* (John 16:7). Hear how kindly Jesus spoke, *"And I will pray the Father, and He will give you another Helper ["Comforter" KJV], that He may abide with you forever"* (John 14:16). He would not leave those few poor sheep alone in the wilderness. He would not desert His children and leave them fatherless. Before He left, He gave soothing words of comfort.

There are different meanings of the Greek word that is translated *"Helper"* or *"Comforter."* Early translators employed transliteration, having left the original word in the Greek but transcribed it into our alphabet to form the word *Paraclete. Paraclete* is the Holy Spirit, and it is the original Greek word, but it has other meanings besides *"Helper"* or *"Comforter."* Sometimes it means "monitor" or "instructor." Frequently it means "advocate," but the most common meaning of the word is *"Helper"* or *"Comforter."* However, we cannot pass over those other interpretations without saying something about them.

The Holy Spirit as Teacher

Jesus had been the official instructor of His saints while He was on earth. They called no man Rabbi except Christ. (See Matthew 23:8–10.) They did not sit at the feet of men to learn their doctrines, but they heard them directly from the lips of Him who spoke as no man has ever spoken. When Christ was to leave, where would they find another infallible teacher? Should they go to a pope in Rome to be their infallible oracle? Should they lean on the councils of the church to decide all complex questions? Christ said no such things. *"I will pray the Father, and He will give you another Helper ["Comforter" KJV], that He may abide with you forever."*

We can insert the word *Instructor* for *"Helper"* or *"Comforter"*; Christ was to send us another Instructor to be the person to explain

Scripture, to be the authoritative Oracle of God, who will make all dark things light, who will unravel mysteries, who will untwist all knots of revelation, and who will make you understand what you could not discover had it not been for His influence. No man ever learns anything correctly unless he is taught by the Spirit. No man can know Jesus Christ unless he is taught by God.

No doctrine of the Bible can be safely, thoroughly, or truly learned without the one authoritative Teacher. Do not tell me of systems of divinity, schemes of theology, infallible commentators, the most learned people, or the most arrogant doctors, but tell me of the great Teacher who will instruct the sons of God and make us wise to understand all things.

The Holy Spirit is the Teacher. It does not matter what this or that man says. I rest on no man's boasting authority, nor should you. You are not to be carried away by the craftiness of men or by their deceitful words. The Holy Spirit is resting in the hearts of His children.

The Holy Spirit as Advocate

Another translation of *Paraclete* is "Advocate." Have you ever thought of how the Holy Spirit can be called an advocate? You know Jesus Christ is called *"Wonderful, Counselor, Mighty God"* (Isa. 9:6), but how can the Holy Spirit be called Advocate? I suppose it is because He is our advocate on earth to plead against the enemies of the Cross. How was it that Paul could so ably plead before Felix and Agrippa? (See Acts 24:10–21; 26:2–29.) How was it that the apostles stood boldly before the magistrates and confessed their Lord? (See, for example, Acts 4:5–21.) How has it come to pass that God's ministers have been made as fearless as lions, their brows firmer than brass, their hearts sterner than steel, and their words like the language of God? It is simply that it was not the men who pleaded, but it was God the Holy Spirit pleading through them.

Besides this, the Holy Spirit is the Advocate in men's hearts. I have known of men rejecting a doctrine until the Holy Spirit began to illumine them. We who are the advocates of the truth are often very poor pleaders. We spoil our cause by the words we use, but it is a mercy that the Holy Spirit will advocate successfully through us and overcome each sinner's opposition.

Did you ever know Him to fail, even once? Has God not convinced you of sin in the past? Did the Holy Spirit not prove to you that you were guilty even though no minister could ever cause you to admit your self-righteousness? Did He not advocate Christ's righteousness? Did He not tell you that your works were dirty rags? Did He not convince you of the judgment to come? He is the mighty Advocate when He pleads in the soul. He makes us aware of sin, of righteousness, and of the judgment to come (John 16:8).

> Blessed Advocate, plead in my heart, and plead with my conscience. When I sin, make my conscience bold to tell me. When I err, make my conscience speak at once, and when I turn aside to crooked ways, advocate the cause of righteousness and suggest I sit down in disgrace, knowing my guiltiness in the sight of God.

There is even another sense in which the Holy Spirit advocates. He advocates our cause to Jesus Christ *"with groanings which cannot be uttered"* (Rom. 8:26). When my soul is ready to burst within me, my heart is swelled with grief, or the hot tide of my emotions is near overflowing from my veins, I long to speak, but the very desire chains my tongue. I wish to pray, but the fervency of my feeling curbs my language. There is a groaning within me that cannot be uttered.

Do you know who can utter that groaning, who can understand it, and who can put it into heavenly language and utter it in a celestial tongue so that Christ can hear it? It is God the Holy Spirit. He advocates our cause with Christ, and Christ then advocates it with the Father. He is the Advocate, and He makes intercession for us *"with groanings which cannot be uttered."*

The Holy Spirit as Comforter

Having explained the Spirit's offices as Teacher and Advocate, we come now to the word used in the King James Version of our text—*"Comforter."* Let us look at three aspects of this word: the Comforter, the comfort, and the comforted.

The Comforter

First, God the Holy Spirit is our very loving Comforter. If I am in distress and want consolation, and some passerby hears of my sorrow, steps in, sits down, and tries to cheer me, he may speak soothing words, but he does not love me. He is a stranger, who does not know me at all; he has only come to try his skill. What is the consequence? His words run over me like oil on a slab of marble. They are like pattering rain on a rock; they do not ease my grief, and I stand unmoved because he has no love for me.

But let someone who loves me as dearly as his own life come and plead with me. Truly these words are music, and they taste like honey. This friend knows the password for the doors of my heart, and my ear is attentive to His every word. I catch the intonation of each syllable as it falls, for it is like the harmony of the harps of heaven. His is the voice of love, and it speaks a language of its own. It is an idiom and an accent that none can mimic. Wisdom cannot imitate it, and oratory cannot attain it. It is love alone that can reach the mourning heart. Love is the only handkerchief that can wipe away the mourner's tears.

Is not the Holy Spirit our loving Comforter? Do you not know how much the Holy Spirit loves you? Can you not measure the love of the Spirit? Do you not know how great the affection of His soul is toward you? Go and measure heaven, weigh the mountains in scales, take the ocean's water and count each drop, and count the sand upon the sea's wide shore. When you have accomplished all of this, you can tell how much He loves you. He has greatly loved you, loved you for a long time, and will always love you. Surely He is the person to comfort you because He loves you. Admit Him into your heart so that He may comfort you in your distress.

Also, He is our *faithful* Comforter. Love sometimes proves unfaithful. How bitter it is to have a friend turn from me in my distress. Oh, woe of woes to have one who loves me in my prosperity forsake me in the dark day of my trouble. God's Spirit is not like this. He ever loves, and He loves to the end.

Trust Him. Maybe a little while ago you found the sweet, loving Comforter, and you obtained relief from Him. When others failed you, He sheltered you in His bosom and carried you in His arms. Oh, why distrust Him now? Away with your fears. He is your faithful Comforter.

You may say, "But I have sinned." So you have, but sin cannot sever you from His love; He still loves you. Do not think that the scars of your old sins have marred your beauty or that He loves you less because of that blemish. He loved you when He foreknew your sin, and He does not love you any less now. Come to Him in all boldness of faith, and tell Him that you are sorry that you grieved

Him. He will forget your wandering and will receive you again. The kisses of His love will be bestowed upon you, and the arms of His grace will embrace you. He is faithful, so trust Him. He will never deceive you. He will never leave you.

How *wise* a comforter is the Holy Spirit. Job had comforters, and I think he spoke the truth when he said, *"Miserable comforters are you all!"* (Job 16:2). Did people not comprehend his grief and sorrow? They thought that he was not really a child of God. They thought that he was self-righteous, and they gave him the wrong treatment. It is bad when a doctor mistakes a disease and gives a wrong prescription.

Sometimes when we go and visit people, we mistake their disease. We want to comfort them on a point where they do not require any such comfort at all, and they would be better left alone than spoiled by such unwise comforters. But how wise the Holy Spirit is. He takes the soul, lays it on the table, and dissects it in a moment. He finds out the root of the matter, sees where the complaint is, and either applies the knife where something is required to be taken away or puts a bandage where the sore is. He never makes mistakes. From every comforter but the Holy Spirit I turn, for He alone gives the wisest consolation.

Mark how *safe* a comforter the Holy Spirit is. All comfort is not safe. There is a very melancholy young man over there. He became so because he stepped into the house of God and heard a powerful preacher. The Word was blessed and convinced him of sin. When he went home, his father and the rest found that there was something different about him. "Oh," they said, "John is mad. He is crazy." His mother said, "Send him into the country for a week. Let him go dancing or to the theater."

Did John find any comfort there? No. They made him feel worse, for while he was there, he thought hell might open and swallow him up. Did he find any relief in the pleasures of the world? No, he thought they were an idle waste of time. They are miserable comfort, but they are the comfort of the world.

When a Christian becomes distressed, many may recommend this remedy or another. Ah, there have been many who have been destroyed by elixirs that were given to lull them to sleep. Many have been ruined by the cry of peace when there was none (Jer. 6:14). They hear gentle things when they ought to be stirred to the quick. Cleopatra's serpent was brought in a basket of flowers, and men's ruin often lurks in fair and sweet speeches. But the Holy

Spirit's comfort is safe, and you may rest on it. Let Him speak the Word, and there is a reality about it. Let Him give the cup of consolation, and you may drink it to the bottom, for in its depths there is nothing to intoxicate or ruin. It is all safe.

Moreover, the Holy Spirit is our *active* Comforter. He does not comfort by words alone but by deeds. As in James 2:16, some people comfort others by saying, *"'Be warmed and filled,' but* [they] *do not give them the things which are needed for the body."* Therefore, *"what does it profit?"* (v. 16). As this verse says, words give nothing. But the Holy Spirit gives. He intercedes with Jesus, gives us promises, gives us grace, and in these ways, He comforts us. Remember, He is always a *successful* comforter. He never attempts what He cannot accomplish.

You never have to send for Him. Your God is always near you, and when you need comfort in your distress, the Word is near you. It is in your mouth and in your heart (Rom. 10:8). He is an ever--present help in the times of trouble (Ps. 46:1).

The Comfort

Now, some persons make a great mistake about the influence of the Holy Spirit. A foolish man had a desire to preach in a certain pulpit. Even though he was quite incapable of the duty, he called upon the minister and assured him solemnly that the Holy Spirit revealed to him that he was to preach in his pulpit. "Very well," said the minister, "I suppose I must not doubt your assertion, but it has not yet been revealed to me that I am to let you preach. You must go your way until it is."

I have heard many fanatical people say that the Holy Spirit has revealed this and that new idea to them. This is revealed nonsense. The Holy Spirit does not reveal anything fresh now. He brings old things to our remembrance. *"But the Helper, the Holy Spirit, whom the Father will send in My name, He will teach you all things, and bring to your remembrance all things that I said to you."* The canon of revelation is closed. No more is to be added.

God does not give a fresh revelation, but He reveals the old one. When it has been forgotten and laid in the dusty chamber of our memory, He retrieves it and cleans the picture, but He does not paint a new one. There are no new doctrines, but the old ones are often revived. It is not by any new revelation that the Spirit comforts. He does so by telling us old things over again. He brings a fresh

439

lamp to manifest the treasures hidden in Scripture. He unlocks the strong chests where the truth has long been, and He points to secret chambers filled with untold riches. However, He coins no more, for enough is done.

There is enough in the Bible for you to live on forever. If your life should outnumber the years of Methuselah, there would be no need for a fresh revelation. If you should live until Christ comes upon the earth, there would be no necessity for the addition of a single word. If you should go down as deep as Jonah into *"the belly of hell"* (Jonah 2:2 KJV) or descend into *"the sorrows of hell"* (Ps. 18:5 KJV) as David said he did, there would be enough in the Bible to comfort you without a supplementary sentence. But Christ says, *"All things that the Father has are Mine. Therefore I said that He will take of Mine and declare it to you"* (John 16:15).

The Holy Spirit whispers to the heart. He says things such as, "Be of good cheer. There is One who died for you. Look to Calvary; behold His wounds; see the torrent gushing from His side—there is your purchaser, and you are secure. He loves you with an everlasting love, and this chastisement is meant for your good. Each stroke is working for your healing. By the blueness of the wound your soul is made better." *"For whom the LORD loves He chastens, and scourges every son whom He receives"* (Heb. 12:6).

Do not doubt His grace because of your tribulation, but believe that He loves you as much in seasons of trouble as in times of happiness. And what, when weighed on the scales of Jesus' agonies, is all your distress?

Especially at times when the Holy Spirit takes back the veil of heaven and lets the soul behold the glory of the upper world, then that saint can say,

> Oh, You are a Comforter to me. Let cares like a wild deluge come and storms of sorrow fall. May I but safely reach my home, My God, my heaven, my all.

Were I to tell of the manifestations of heaven, some of you could follow. You, too, have left sun, moon, and stars at your feet, while in your flight you outstripped the tardysluggish lightning. You have seemed to enter the gates of pearl and to tread the golden streets while borne aloft on wings of the Spirit. But here, we must not trust ourselves because we could become lost in reverie and forget our theme.

The Comforted

Who are the comforted people? I like to cry out at the end of my sermons, "Divide. Divide," because there are two parties. Some are the comforted, and others are the comfortless. Some have received the consolation of the Holy Spirit, and others have not. Let me try to sift my readers to see which are the chaff and which are the wheat. May God grant some of the chaff to be transformed into His wheat.

You may say, "How am I to know whether I am a recipient of the comfort of the Holy Spirit?" You may know it by one rule: If you have received one blessing from God, you will receive all other blessings as well. Let me explain myself. If I were an auctioneer and could sell the Gospel off in lots, I would dispose of it all. If I could say, "Here is justification through the blood of Christ, free, given away, gratis," many would say, "I will have justification. Give it to me. I wish to be justified, and I wish to be pardoned."

Suppose I offered sanctification, the giving up of all sin, a thorough change of heart, leaving off drunkenness and swearing. Many would say, "I don't want that. I would like to go to heaven, but I do not want that holiness. I would like to be saved, but I would like to have my drink still. I would like to enter glory, but I must be able to curse on the road."

If you have one blessing, you will have all. God will never divide the Gospel. He will not give justification to one and sanctification to another, or pardon to one and holiness to another. No, it all goes together. *"Whom He predestined, these He also called; whom He called, these He also justified; and whom He justified, these He also glorified"* (Rom. 8:30).

Oh, if I could lay down nothing but the comforts of the Gospel, you would fly to them as flies do to honey. When you become ill, you send for the clergyman. You all want your minister to come then and give you consoling words. However, if he is an honest man, he will not give some of you a particle of consolation. He will not begin to pour oil when the knife would be better.

I want to make a man feel his sins before I dare tell him anything about Christ. I want to probe into his soul and make him feel that he is lost before I tell him anything about the purchased blessing.

Have you been convicted of sin? Have you ever felt your guilt before God? Has your soul been humbled at Jesus' feet? Have you been made to look to Calvary alone for your refuge? If not, you have no right to consolation. The Spirit comes to convict before He comforts, and you must have the other operations of the Holy Spirit before you can derive anything from His comfort.

What do you know about the Comforter? Let this solemn question penetrate your soul. If you do not know the Comforter, I will tell you whom you will know. You will know the Judge. If you do not know the Comforter on earth, you will know the Condemner in the next world. He will cry, *"Depart from Me, you cursed, into the everlasting fire prepared for the devil and his angels"* (Matt. 25:41).

If we were to live here forever, you might slight the Gospel. If you had a lease on life, you might despise the Comforter, but you must die. Probably, some have gone to their long last home, and some will soon be among the glorified above or among the damned below. Which will it be? Let your soul answer. If you fell down dead tonight, where would you be—in heaven or in hell?

Do not be deceived. Let conscience have its perfect work, and if, in the sight of God, you are obliged to say, "I tremble and fear that my portion would be with unbelievers," listen one moment. *"He who believes and is baptized will be saved; but he who does not believe will be condemned"* (Mark 16:16).

Weary sinner, the Devil's castaway, reprobate one, wicked one, harlot, robber, thief, adulterer, fornicator, drunkard, swearer, Sabbath-breaker, I am addressing you as well as the redeemed. I exempt no man. God has said that there is no exemption here. *"If you confess with your mouth the Lord Jesus and believe in your heart that God has raised Him from the dead, you will be saved"* (Rom. 10:9). Sin is no barrier, and your guilt is no obstacle. Though as black as Satan or as deceptive as a fiend, whosoever believes will have every sin forgiven, will have every crime effaced, will have every iniquity blotted out, will be saved in the Lord Jesus Christ, and will stand in heaven safe and secure. This is the glorious Gospel. May God make it hit home in your heart and give you faith in Jesus.

> We have listened to the preacher—
> Truth by him has now been shown;
> But we want a Greater Teacher,
> From the everlasting throne:
> Application is the work of God alone.

Chapter 2

The Power of the Holy Spirit

Now may the God of hope fill you with all joy and peace
in believing, that you may abound in hope
by the power of the Holy Spirit.
—Romans 15:13

Power is the special and distinctive prerogative of God and God alone. *"God has spoken once, twice I have heard this: that power belongs to God"* (Ps. 62:11). God is God, and power belongs to Him.

He delegates a portion of it to His creatures, yet it is still His power. The sun, *"which is like a bridegroom coming out of his chamber, and rejoices like a strong man to run its race"* (Ps. 19:5), has no power to perform its motions except as God directs. The stars, although they travel in their orbits and none could stop them, have neither might nor force except what God gives them. The tall archangel, near His throne, outshines a comet in its blaze, and though he is one of those who excel in strength and listen to the voice of the commands of God (Ps. 103:20), he has no might except what his Maker gives to him. As for Leviathan, who makes the sea boil like a pot so that one would think the deep were white, or Behemoth, who drinks up the Jordan in one gulp and boasts that he can snuff up rivers, and those majestic creatures that are found on earth, they owe their strength to Him who fashioned their bones of steel and made their tendons of brass.

Think of man. If he has might or power, it is so small and insignificant that we can scarcely call it such. Yes, even when it is at its greatest, when he sways his scepter, when he commands hosts, when he rules nations, the power still belongs to God.

This exclusive prerogative of God is to be found in each of the three persons of the glorious Trinity. The Father has power, for by His Word were the heavens made and all the host of them. By His strength, all things stand and fulfill their destiny through Him. The Son has power, for like His Father, He is the Creator of all things. *"All things were made through Him, and without Him nothing was made that was made"* (John 1:3). *"And He is before all things, and in Him all things consist"* (Col. 1:17). The Holy Spirit also has power. This is the power that I will discuss.

We will look at the power of the Holy Spirit in three ways: the outward and visible displays of it, the inward and spiritual manifestations of it, and the future and expected works of it. The power of the Spirit will then, I trust, be made clearly present to your souls.

The power of the Spirit has not been dormant. It has exerted itself. Much has been done by the Spirit of God already. More has been done than could have been accomplished by any being except the infinite, eternal, almighty Jehovah, with whom the Holy Spirit is one person. There are four works that are the outward and manifest signs of the power of the Spirit: creation works, resurrection works, works of attestation or of witness, and works of grace.

The Outward Displays of the Holy Spirit's Power

The Works of Creation

The Spirit has manifested the omnipotence of His power in Creation. Though not very frequently in Scripture, sometimes Creation is ascribed to the Holy Spirit as well as to the Father and the Son. The creation of the heavens above us is said to be the work of God's Spirit. This you will see at once by referring to Job 26:13, *"By His Spirit He adorned the heavens; His hand pierced the fleeing [*"crooked"* KJV] serpent."* All of the stars of heaven are said to have been placed by the Spirit. One particular constellation called the Crooked Serpent is specially pointed out as His handiwork. He makes loose the bands of Orion, binds the sweet influences of Pleiades, and guides Arcturus with his sons (Job 38:31–32 KJV). He made all the stars that shine in heaven.

Also, those continued acts of Creation that are still performed in the world, such as the bringing forth of man and animals with their births and generations, are ascribed to the Holy Spirit. If you look at Psalm 104, you will read, *"You hide Your face, they are troubled; You take away their breath, they die and return to their dust. You send forth Your Spirit, they are created; and You renew the face of the earth"* (Ps. 104:29–30).

The creation of man is the work of the Spirit. The creation of all life is as much to be ascribed to the power of the Spirit as the first adorning of the heavens or the fashioning of the constellations.

Look at the first chapter of Genesis and you will see that peculiar operation of power upon the universe that was put forth by the Holy Spirit. You will then discover His special work. There we read, *"The earth was without form, and void; and darkness was on the face of the deep. And the Spirit of God was hovering over the face of the waters"* (Gen. 1:2).

There was one particular instance of Creation in which the Holy Spirit was especially involved. It was the formation of the body of our Lord Jesus Christ. Though our Lord Jesus Christ was born of a woman and made in the likeness of sinful flesh, the power that produced Him was entirely in God the Holy Spirit. As the Scriptures express it, *"The Holy Spirit will come upon you, and the power of the Highest will overshadow you; therefore, also, that Holy One who is to be born will be called the Son of God"* (Luke 1:35). He was begotten, as the Apostles' Creed says, of the Holy Spirit. The corporeal frame of the Lord Jesus Christ was a masterpiece of the Holy Spirit.

I suppose Christ's body excelled all others in beauty and was like that of the first man. I suppose it was the very pattern of what the body is to be in heaven when it will shine forth in all its glory. That fabric, in all its beauty and perfection, was modeled by the Spirit. In His book were all the members written when as of yet there were none of them (Ps. 139:16 KJV). The Holy Spirit fashioned and formed Christ, and here again, we have another instance of the creative energy of the Spirit.

The Works of Resurrection

A second manifestation of the Holy Spirit's power is to be found in the resurrection of the Lord Jesus Christ. If you have ever studied this subject, you have perhaps been rather perplexed to find that sometimes the resurrection of Christ is ascribed to Himself. By His own power and Godhead, He could not be held by the bond of death (Acts 2:24), but since He willingly gave up His life, He had the power to take it again (John 10:17). In another portion of Scripture you find the power ascribed to God the Father: *"He raised Him from the dead"* (Acts 13:34). God the Father exalted Him. There are many similar passages. However, again, it is said in Scripture that Jesus Christ was raised by the Holy Spirit.

445

Now, all these things are true. He was raised by the Father because the Father said for Him to be loosed. Justice was satisfied. God's law required no more satisfaction. God gave an official message that delivered Jesus from the grave. Christ was raised by His own majesty and power because He had a right to come out. He could no longer be held by the bonds of death. However, He was raised after three days by the Spirit and the energy that His mortal frame received. If you want proof of this, open your Bibles and read the following:

> For Christ also suffered once for sins, the just for the unjust, that He might bring us to God, being put to death in the flesh but made alive by the Spirit. (1 Pet. 3:18)

> But if the Spirit of Him who raised Jesus from the dead dwells in you, He who raised Christ from the dead will also give life to your mortal bodies through His Spirit who dwells in you. (Rom. 8:11)

The resurrection of Christ, then, was effected by the agency of the Spirit. This is a noble illustration of His omnipotence.

If you could have stepped as angels into the grave of Jesus and seen His sleeping body, you would have found it to be as cold as any other corpse. If you had lifted up His hand, it would have fallen by His side. You would have seen that the blood did not fall from His pierced hands. They were cold and motionless. If you had looked at His eyes, they would have been glazed. You would have seen the death-thrust that must have annihilated life.

Could that body live? Could it start up? Yes, and it is an illustration of the might of the Spirit. For when the power of the Spirit came on Him, as when it fell upon the *"dry bones"* (Ezek. 37:4) of the valley, He arose in the majesty of His divinity. Bright and shining, He astonished the watchmen so that they fled away. He rose no more to die but to live forever, King of Kings and Prince of the kings of the earth.

The Works of Attestation

The third of the works of the Holy Spirit that have so wonderfully demonstrated His power are the attestation works. By these I mean the works of witnessing. When Jesus Christ went for baptism in the river Jordan, the Holy Spirit descended upon Him like a dove and proclaimed Him God's beloved Son (Matt. 3:16–17). This is what I call an attestation work. Afterward, when Jesus Christ raised the dead; healed the leper; spoke to diseases, which caused them to flee quickly; and propelled demons to rush in thousands from those who were possessed by them, it was all done by the power of the Spirit. The Spirit lived in Jesus without measure. By that power, all these miracles were worked. These were attestation works.

After Jesus Christ had ascended to heaven, the master attestation of the Spirit happened when He came like a *"rushing mighty wind"* (Acts 2:2) upon the assembled apostles. Split tongues as of fire sat upon them, and He attested to their ministry by giving them the ability *"to speak with other tongues, as the Spirit gave them utterance"* (v. 4). Also, miraculous deeds happened through them and how they taught. Look at how Peter raised Dorcas, how Paul breathed life into Eutychus, and how great deeds took place through the apostles as well as through their Master. Mighty signs and wonders were done by the Holy Spirit, and many believed because of them. (See, for example, Romans 15:18–19.)

Who would doubt the power of the Holy Spirit after that? What will those Socinians, who deny not only the divinity of Christ but also the existence of the Holy Spirit and His absolute personality, do when we confront them with Creation, resurrection, and attestation? They must rush from the very teeth of Scripture. As Matthew 21:44 says, *"And whoever falls on this stone will be broken; but on whomever it falls, it will grind him to powder."* The Holy Spirit has the omnipotent power of God.

The Works of Grace

Other outward and visible signs of the power of the Spirit are works of grace. Picture a city where a soothsayer has power. Philip enters it and preaches the Word of God. Right away, Simon Magus loses his power and seeks for the power of the Spirit to be given to him. He fancies that it might be purchased with money. (See Acts 8:9–24.)

In modern times, picture a country where the inhabitants live in miserable wigwams and feed on reptiles. Observe them bowing down before their idols and worshipping their false gods. They are so into superstition and so degraded and debased that you question whether they have souls or not. Look! Moffat goes with the Word of God in his hand and preaches as the Spirit gives him utterance.

447

That Word is accompanied with power. The inhabitants cast aside their idols, and they hate and abhor their former lusts. They build houses in which to dwell. They also become clothed and are now in their right minds. They break the bow and cut the spear into parts. The uncivilized become civilized, and the savage becomes polite. He who knew nothing begins to read the Scriptures, and out of the mouths of barbarians, God affirms the power of His mighty Spirit.

Picture a household in a city where the father is a drunkard, the most desperate of characters. See him in his madness. You might just as well meet an unchained tiger than meet such a man. He seems as though he could tear a man who offends him to pieces. Look at his wife. She, too, has a spirit in her, and when he treats her wrongly, she can resist him. Many brawls have been seen in that house, and often has the neighborhood been disturbed by the noise created there. As for the poor little children, see them in their rags and nakedness, poor untaught things. Untaught did I say? They are taught and well taught in the Devil's school, and they are growing up to be the heirs of damnation.

However, someone whom God has blessed by His Spirit is guided to the house. He may be but a humble city missionary, but he speaks to people like them. "Oh," he says, "come and listen to the voice of God." Whether it is by God's own agency or a minister's preaching, the Word, which is *"living and powerful"* (Heb. 4:12), cuts into the sinner's heart.

The tears run down his cheeks as have never been seen before. He shakes and quivers. The strong man bows down. The mighty man trembles, and those knees that never shook begin to knock together. That heart that never cowered before now begins to shake before the power of the Spirit. He sits down on a humble bench as a penitent. He lets his knees bend while his lips utter a child's prayer. But while it is a child's prayer, it is a prayer of a child of God. He becomes a changed character.

Mark the reformation in his house. His wife becomes a respected lady. His children are a credit to the family name. In due time, they grow up like olive branches around his table and adorn his house like polished stones. Pass by the house. There is no noise or brawl, but there are songs of Zion. See him, for there is no drunken revelry. He has drained his last cup, and now forswearing it, he comes to God and is His servant.

Now, you will not hear at midnight the shout of revelry, but there should be a noise. It will be the sound of the solemn hymn of praise to God. Is there not such a thing as the power of the Spirit? Yes, there is. We have all witnessed it.

I know a village that was once, perhaps, the most profane in England. It was a village inundated by drunkenness and debauchery of the worst kind. It was nearly impossible for an honest traveler to stop in the public house without being annoyed by blasphemy. It was a place known for radicals and robbers.

One man, the ringleader of all, listened to the voice of God. That man's heart was broken. The whole gang came to hear the Gospel preached, and they sat and seemed to revere the preacher as if he were a god and not a man. These men were changed and reformed. Everyone who knew the place affirmed that such a change could be brought about only by the power of the Holy Spirit.

Let the Gospel be preached and the Spirit poured out. You will see that it has such power to change the conscience, to improve the conduct, to raise the depraved, and to chastise and curb the wickedness of the race, that you must glory in it. There is nothing like the power of the Spirit. Only let it come, and indeed, everything can be accomplished.

The Inward Power of the Holy Spirit

Now, the second point is the inward and spiritual power of the Holy Spirit. What you have already read about may be seen, but what you are about to read must be felt. No man will fully grasp what I say unless he has felt it.

First, the Holy Spirit has a power over men's hearts, which can be very hard to affect. If you want to get them for any worldly object, you can do it. A cheating world can win a man's heart, and a little gold can win a man's heart. A trump of fame and a little clamor of applause can win a man's heart. But there is not a minister breathing who can win a man's heart by himself. He can win his ears and make them listen, and he can win his eyes and fix them upon him. He can win his attention, but the heart is very slippery.

The heart is a fish that all gospel fishermen have trouble holding. You may sometimes pull it almost all the way out of the water, but slimy as an eel, it slips between your fingers, and you have not captured it after all. Many men have fancied that they have caught the heart, but they have been disappointed. A strong hunter is needed to overtake the red deer on the mountains. It is too fast for a human foot to approach.

The Spirit alone has power over a man's heart. Do you ever try your power on a heart? If any man thinks that a minister can convert the soul by himself, I wish he would try. Let him go and be a Sunday school teacher. He will take his class, have the best books that can be obtained, establish the best rules, draw his lines of protection about the house of his spirit, and take the best boy in his class. If he is not tired in a week, I would be very much mistaken. Let him spend four or five Sabbaths trying, but he will say, "The young fellow is incorrigible."

Let him try another. And he will have to try another, and another, and another before he will manage to convert one. He will soon find that it is as the Lord says in Zechariah 4:6: *"Not by might nor by power, but by My Spirit."* Man cannot reach the soul, but the Holy Spirit can.

"My beloved put his hand by the latch of the door, and my heart yearned for him" (Song 5:4). The Holy Spirit can give a sense of blood-bought pardon that will dissolve a heart of stone. He can

> Speak with that voice which
> wakes the dead,
> And bids the sinner rise:
> And makes the guilty conscience dread
> The death that never dies.

He can make Sinai's thunders audible. He can make the sweet whisperings of Calvary enter into the soul. He has power over the heart of man, and a glorious proof of the omnipotence of the Spirit is that He has rule over the heart.

But if there is one thing more stubborn than the heart, it is the will. "My Lord Willbewill," as Bunyan calls him in his *Holy War,* is a fellow who will not easily be bent. The will, especially in some men, is a very stubborn thing, and in all men, if the will is once stirred up to opposition, there is nothing that can be done with them.

Somebody believes in free will. Many dream of free will. Free will. Where is that to be found? Once there was free will in the Garden of Eden, and a terrible mess free will made there. It spoiled all Paradise and turned Adam out of the Garden. Free will was once in heaven, but it turned the glorious archangel out, and a third part of the stars of heaven fell into the Abyss.

Yet some boast of free will. I wonder whether those who believe in it have any more power over people's wills than I have. I know that I have none. I find the old proverb very true, "One man can bring a horse to water, but a hundred cannot make him drink." I do not think any man has power over his fellow creature's will, but the Spirit of God does.

"Your people shall be volunteers in the day of Your power" (Ps. 110:3). He makes the unwilling sinner so willing that he is impetuous after the Gospel. He who was obstinate now hurries to the Cross. He who laughed at Jesus now hangs on His mercy, and he who would not believe is now made by the Holy Spirit to do so willingly and eagerly. He is happy to do it and rejoices at the sound of Jesus' name. He delights to run in the way of God's commandments. The Holy Spirit has power over the will.

There is one more thing that I think is worse than the will. You may guess what I mean. The will is somewhat worse than the heart to bend, but there is one thing that excels the will in its naughtiness: the imagination. I hope that my will is managed by divine grace. However, I am afraid that my imagination is not at times. Those who have a fair share of imagination know what a difficult thing it is to control. You cannot restrain it. It will break the reins. You will never be able to manage it.

The imagination will sometimes fly up to God with such a power that eagles' wings cannot match it. It sometimes has such might that it can almost see the King in His beauty and the land that is very far off. With regard to myself, my imagination will sometimes take me over the gates of iron, across that infinite unknown, to the very gates of pearl and discovery of the glorified.

It is just as potent in the other direction. My imagination has taken me down to the vilest kennels and sewers of the earth. It has given me thoughts so dreadful that while I could not avoid them, I was thoroughly horrified by them. These thoughts come, and the time when the plagues break out the worst is often when I feel in the holiest frame of mind, the most devoted to God, and the most earnest in prayer. However, I rejoice and think of one thing: I can cry out when this imagination comes upon me.

In Leviticus, when the maiden cried out against an evil act that was committed, her life was to be spared. So it is with the Christian. If he cries out, there is hope. Can you chain your imagination? No, but the power of the Holy Spirit can. It will do it, and it does do it at last. It does it even on the earth.

The Future and Desired Effects

Jesus Christ exclaimed, *"It is finished!"* (John 19:30). This concerned Christ's own labor, but the Holy Spirit cannot say that. The Holy Spirit still has more to do, and until the consummation of all things, when the Son Himself becomes subject to the Father, *"It is finished!"* will not be said by the Holy Spirit.

What, then, does the Holy Spirit have to do? First, He has to perfect us in holiness. A Christian needs two kinds of perfection. One is the perfection by the justification of Jesus, and the other is the perfection of sanctification worked by the Holy Spirit. At present, corruption still rests in the heart of even the regenerate; the heart is partially impure and there are still lusts and evil imaginations.

However, my soul rejoices to know that the day is coming when God will finish the work that He has begun. He will present my soul not only perfect in Christ, but also perfect in the Spirit, without spot, blemish, or any such thing. Is it true that my poor, depraved heart is to become as holy as that of God? Is it true that this poor spirit that often cries, *"O wretched man that I am! Who will deliver me from this body of death?"* (Rom. 7:24), will get rid of sin and death? Is it true that I will have no evil things to vex my ears and no unholy thoughts to disturb my peace? Oh, happy hour.

Oh, to be washed white, clean, pure, and perfect. Not an angel will be more pure than I will be and not God Himself more holy. I will be able to say, in a double sense, "Great God, I am clean. Through Jesus' blood I am clean, and through the Spirit's work I am clean, too." Must we not extol the power of the Holy Spirit in making us fit to stand before our Father in heaven?

The Works of Latter-Day Glory

Another great work of the Holy Spirit that is not accomplished is the bringing on of the latter-day glory. In a few more years, I do not know when or how, the Holy Spirit will be poured out in a far different style from the present. *"There are diversities of activities"* (1 Cor. 12:6), and during the last few years, the diversified operations have consisted in very little pouring out of the Spirit. Ministers have gone on in dull routine, continually preaching, preaching, preaching, and little good has been done.

The hour is coming when the Holy Spirit will be poured out again in such a wonderful manner that *"many shall run to and fro, and knowledge shall increase"* (Dan. 12:4), and the knowledge of the Lord will cover the earth *"as the waters cover the sea"* (Isa. 11:9). When His kingdom will come and His will shall be done on earth as it is in heaven (Matt. 6:10), we are not going to be dragging on forever like Pharaoh with the wheels off his chariot.

Perhaps there will be no miraculous gifts, for they will not be required. Yet there will be such a miraculous amount of holiness, such an extraordinary fervor of prayer, such a real communion with God, so much vital religion, and such a spread of the doctrines of the Cross that everyone will see that the Spirit is truly poured out like water, and the rains are descending from above. Let us pray for this, continually labor for it, and seek it from God.

Great Resurrection Power

One more work of the Spirit that will especially manifest His power is the general resurrection. From Scripture, we have reason to believe that while it will be effected by the voice of God and of His Word (the Son), the resurrection of the dead will be brought about by the Spirit. The same power that raised Christ from the dead will also quicken your mortal bodies (Rom. 8:11). The power of the resurrection is perhaps one of the finest proofs of the works of the Spirit.

My friends, if this earth could have its mantle torn away for a little while, if the green sod could be cut from it, and we could look about six feet deep into its bowels, what a world it would seem. What would we see? Bones, carcasses, rottenness, worms, corruption. And you would say, "Can these dry bones live?" (See Ezekiel 37:1–5.) Yes, *"in a moment, in the twinkling of an eye, at the last trumpet. For the trumpet will sound, and the dead will be raised incorruptible, and we shall be changed"* (1 Cor. 15:52).

He speaks, and they are alive. See them scattered; bone comes to bone. See them naked; flesh comes upon them. See them lifeless; *"Come from the four winds, O breath, and breathe on these slain, that they may live"* (Ezek. 37:9). When the wind of the Holy Spirit comes, they live; they stand on their feet as a great army (v. 10).

Practical Power of the Holy Spirit

I have attempted to speak of the power of the Spirit, and I trust that I have shown it to you. We must now have a moment or two for practical inference. Christian, the Spirit is very powerful. What do you infer from that fact? Infer that you never need to distrust the power of God to carry you to heaven. This sweet verse has been placed on my soul:

> His tried Almighty arm
> Is raised for your defense;
> Where is the power can reach you there?
> Or what can pluck you thence?

The power of the Holy Spirit is your bulwark, and all His omnipotence defends you. Can your enemies overcome omnipotence? They can then conquer you. Can they wrestle with Deity and hurl Him to the ground? They might then conquer you. For the power of the Spirit is our power, and the power of the Spirit is our might.

Once again, if this is the power of the Spirit, why should you doubt anything? There is your son and your wife for whom you have pleaded in prayer so frequently. Do not doubt the Spirit's power. He may tarry, but wait for Him. There is your husband, holy woman, and you have wrestled for his soul. Though he is ever so hardened and quite a desperate wretch who treats you poorly, there is power in the Spirit. You, who have come from barren churches with scarcely a leaf on the tree, do not doubt the power of the Spirit to raise you up. For they will be as a pasture for flocks, a den of wild donkeys (Isa. 32:14), open but deserted until the Spirit is poured out from on high. *The parched ground shall become a pool, and the thirsty land springs of water; in the habitation of jackals, where each lay, there shall be grass with reeds and rushes"* (Isa. 35:7).

You who remember what your God has done for you personally, never distrust the power of the Spirit. You have seen the wilderness blossom like Carmel. You have seen the desert blossom like the rose. Trust Him for the future. Then go out and labor with the conviction that the power of the Holy Spirit is able to do anything. Go to your Sunday school, your tract distribution, your missionary enterprise, and your preaching with the conviction that the power of the Spirit is our great help.

What is there to be said to you about this power of the Spirit? To me, there is hope for some of you. I cannot save you, and I cannot get at you. I may make you cry sometimes. However, you just wipe your eyes, and it is all over. But I know my Master can reach and save you. That is my consolation. Chief of sinners, there is hope for you. This power can save you as well as anybody else. It is able to break your heart of iron and to make your eyes of stone run with tears. His power is able.

If He wills to change your heart, to turn the current of all your ideas, to make you at once a child of God, or to justify you in Christ, there is power enough in the Holy Spirit. He does not withhold from you, but you are *"restricted by your own affections"* (2 Cor. 6:12). He is able to bring sinners to Jesus.

He is able to make you willing in the day of His power. Are you willing? Has He gone so far as to make you desire His name, to make you wish for Jesus? Then, sinner, while He draws you, say, "Draw me, for I am wretched without you." Follow Him, and while He leads, tread in His footsteps.

Rejoice that He *"has begun a good work in you"* (Phil. 1:6), for there is an evidence that He will continue it even to the end. And, hopeless one, put your trust in the power of the Spirit. Rest on the blood of Jesus, and your soul is safe, not only now but throughout eternity. God bless you.

Chapter 3

The Holy Spirit, the Great Teacher

However, when He, the Spirit of truth, has come,
He will guide you into all truth; for He will not speak on His own
authority, but whatever He hears He will speak;
and He will tell you things to come.
—John 16:13

To a great extent, this generation has gradually and impercep-
tibly become godless. One of the diseases of present mankind
is the secret but deep-seated godlessness by which man has
departed from the knowledge of God. Science has discovered second
causes for us. Thus, many have forgotten the first Great Cause—the
Author of all. They have been able to pry so far into secrets that the
great axiom of the existence of God has been too much neglected.

Even among professing Christians, while there is a great
amount of religion, there is too little godliness. There is much external formalism but too little inward acknowledgment of God, too
little living on God, living with God, and relying on God.

The sad fact is that when you enter many of our places of worship you will certainly hear the name of God mentioned, but except
in the benediction, you will scarcely know that there is a Trinity. In
many places dedicated to the Lord, the name of Jesus is too often
kept in the background. The Holy Spirit is almost entirely neglected, and very little is said concerning His sacred influence.

To a large degree, even religious men have become godless in
this age. We sadly require more preaching regarding God—more
preaching of those things that look not so much at the creature to
be saved as at the Almighty to be extolled.

My firm conviction is that we will see a proportionately greater
display of God's power and a more glorious manifestation of His
might in our churches as we have more regard for the sacred Godhead, the wondrous Three in One. May God send us a Christ-exalting,

Spirit-loving ministry. Men who will proclaim God the Holy Spirit in all His offices and extol God the Savior as the Author and Finisher of our faith. Men should not neglect that Great God, the Father of His people, who before all worlds elected us in Christ His Son, justified us through His righteousness, and will inevitably preserve us and gather us together in the consummation of all things at the Last Great Day.

The subject of our text is God the Holy Spirit. May His sweet influence rest upon us. The disciples had been instructed by Christ concerning certain elementary doctrines, but Jesus did not teach His disciples more than what we might call the ABC's of religion. He gave His reasons for this in John 16:12, *"I still have many things to say to you, but you cannot bear them now."*

Jesus' disciples were not then possessors of the Spirit. They had the Spirit as far as the work of conversion was concerned, but they did not have Him in the matters of bright illumination, profound instruction, prophecy, and inspiration. Jesus said that He would send the Comforter and that when He had come, He would guide them into all truth. The same promise that He made to His apostles stands for all of His children. In reviewing it, we will take it as our portion and heritage. We should not consider ourselves intruders on the property of the apostles or on their exclusive rights, for we conceive that Jesus says even to us, *"When He, the Spirit of truth, has come, He will guide you into all truth."*

Concentrating on our text, we see five things. First, an attainment is mentioned: a knowledge of all truth. Second, a difficulty is suggested: we need guidance into all truth. Third, a person is provided: the Spirit will come and guide you into all truth. Fourth, a manner is hinted at: He will *guide* you into all truth. Fifth, a sign is given as to the working of the Spirit: we may know whether He works by His guiding of us into all truth (this is one thing—not truths, but truth).

Attainment of Truth

An attainment is mentioned. This is a knowledge of all truth. We know that some conceive doctrinal knowledge to be of very little importance and of no practical use. I do not think so. I believe that the science of Christ crucified and the judgment of scriptural teachings are exceedingly valuable. I think it is right that the Christian ministry should not only be arousing but instructing. It should not merely be awakening but also enlightening, and it should appeal not only to the passions but to the understanding. I am far from thinking that doctrinal knowledge is of secondary importance. I believe it to be one of the first things needed in the Christian life—to know the truth and then to practice it. I scarcely need to tell you how desirable it is for us to be well taught in the things of the kingdom.

Human nature itself, when it has been sanctified by grace, gives us a strong desire to know all truth. The natural man separates himself and interferes by meddling with all knowledge. God has put an instinct into man by which he is rendered unsatisfied if he cannot probe mystery to its bottom. He can never be content until he can unriddle secrets. What we call curiosity is something that is given to us from God. It impels us to search into the knowledge of natural things.

That curiosity, which is sanctified by the Spirit, is also brought to bear in matters of heavenly science and celestial wisdom. David said, *"Bless the LORD, O my soul; and all that is within me, bless His holy name!"* (Ps. 103:1). If there is a curiosity within us, it ought to be employed and developed in a search after truth. *"All that is within me,"* sanctified by the Spirit, should be developed. And truly, the Christian man feels an intense longing to bury his ignorance and to receive wisdom. If he desired terrestrial knowledge while in his natural state, how much more ardent is his wish to unravel, if possible, the sacred mysteries of God's Word? A true Christian is always intently reading and searching Scripture so that he may be able to certify himself as to its main and cardinal truths.

Not only is this attainment to be desired because nature teaches us so, but a knowledge of all truth is very essential for our comfort. I believe that many persons have been distressed half of their lives from the fact that they did not have clear views of truth. For instance, many poor souls, under conviction, abide three or four times longer in sorrow of the mind than they would if they had someone to instruct them in the great matter of justification. There are believers who are often troubling themselves about falling away, but if they knew in their souls the great consolation that we *"are kept by the power of God through faith for salvation"* (1 Pet. 1:5), they would no longer be troubled about it.

I have found some who are distressed about the unpardonable sin. However, if God instructs us in that doctrine and shows us that no truly awakened conscience can ever commit that sin, because, when it is committed, God gives us up to a seared conscience, we would never fear or tremble afterward, and all that distress would be alleviated. Depend on this, the more you know of God's truth—all other things being equal—the more comfortable you will be as a Christian. Nothing can give a greater light on your path than a clear understanding of divine things.

It is a mangled gospel, too commonly preached, that causes the downcast faces of Christians. Give me the congregation whose faces are bright with joy, and let their eyes glisten at the sound of the Gospel. I will then believe that they are receiving God's own words. Instead of joyful faces, you will often see melancholy congregations whose faces are not much different than the bitter countenances of poor creatures swallowing medicine. This is because the Word spoken terrifies them by its legality instead of comforting them by its grace.

We love a cheerful Gospel, and we think that all the truth will tend to comfort the Christian. Again, I hold that this attainment of the knowledge of all truth is very desirable for the usefulness that it will give us in the world at large. We should not be selfish. We should always consider whether a thing will be beneficial to others. A knowledge of all truth will make us very serviceable in this world. We will be skillful physicians who know how to take the poor, distressed soul aside, place a hand on his eye, and take the scales off for him so that heaven's light may comfort him. (See Acts 9:17–18.) There will be no person, however perplexing his condition may be, to whom we will not be able to speak and comfort.

He who holds the truth is usually the most useful man. As a good Presbyterian brother said to me the other day, "I know God has blessed you exceedingly in the gathering of souls, but it is an extraordinary fact that nearly all the men I know, with scarcely an exception, have been made useful in gathering in souls and have held the great doctrines of the grace of God." Almost every man whom God has blessed with the building up of the church into prosperity and every man around whom the people have rallied has been a man who has held firmly to free grace from first to last through the finished salvation of Christ.

A Difficulty Suggested

A difficulty is suggested. The difficulty is that truth is not so easy to discover. We need a guide to conduct us into all truth.

There is no man born in this world by nature who has the truth in his heart. There is no creature that was ever fashioned, since the Fall, who has a knowledge of truth innate and natural. Many philosophers have disputed whether there are such things as innate ideas at all, but it is of no use disputing whether there are any innate ideas of truth. There are none.

There are ideas of everything that is wrong and evil, but in our flesh, no good thing dwells. We are born in sin and shaped in iniquity. Our mothers conceived us in sin (Ps. 51:5). There is nothing good in us and no tendency toward righteousness. Then, since we are not born with the truth, we have the task of searching for it. If we are to be blessed by being eminently useful as Christians, we must be well instructed in matters of revelation. The difficulty is that we cannot follow the winding paths of truth without a guide. Why is this?

First, it is because of the very great intricacy of truth itself. Truth itself is no easy thing to discover. Those who fancy that they know everything and constantly dogmatize with a spirit that says, "We are the men, and wisdom will die with us," of course see no difficulties in the system they hold. However, I believe that the most earnest student of Scripture will find things in the Bible that puzzle him. However earnestly he reads it, he will see some mysteries that are too deep for him to understand. He will cry out, "Truth, I cannot find you. I don't know where you are. You are beyond me, and I cannot fully view you."

Truth is a path so narrow that two can rarely walk together on it. We usually tread the narrow way in single file. Two men can seldom walk arm in arm in the truth. We believe the same truth in the main, but we cannot walk together in the path, for it is too narrow. The way of truth is very difficult. If you step an inch to the right, you are in a dangerous error, and if you swerve a little to the left, you are equally in the mire. On one hand, there is a huge precipice and on the other a deep swamp. Unless you keep to the true line, to the width of a hair, you will go astray. Truth is a narrow path indeed. It is a path the eagle's eye has not seen and a depth the diver has not visited.

Truth is like the veins of metal in a mine. It is often excessively thin and does not run in one continuous layer. Lose it once, and you may dig for miles and not discover it again.

The eye must perpetuously watch the direction of the waterway of truth. Grains of truth are like the grains of gold in the rivers of Australia. They must be shaken by the hand of patience and washed in the stream of honesty, or the fine gold will be mingled with sand. Truth is often mingled with error, and it is hard to distinguish it. However, *"when He, the Spirit of truth, has come, He will guide you into all truth."*

Another reason that we need a guide is the harm caused by error. It easily steals upon us, and if I may so describe our position, we are often in a tremendous fog. We can scarcely see an inch before us. We come to a place where there are three turns. We think we know the spot. There is the familiar lamppost, and now we must take a sharp turn to the left. But not so. We ought to have gone a little to the right.

We have been at the same place so often that we think we know every stone on the path. There's our friend's shop over the way. It is dark, but we think we must be quite right, and all the while we are quite wrong and find ourselves half a mile out of the way.

So it is with matters of truth. We think that we are surely on the right path, and the voice of the Evil One whispers, "That is the way; walk in it." You do so, and you find to your great dismay that instead of the path of truth, you have been walking in the path of unrighteousness and erroneous doctrines.

The way of life is a labyrinth. The grassiest paths and the most bewitching are the farthest away from right. The most enticing are those that are garnished with improper truths. I believe that there is not a counterfeit coin in the world that is as close to a genuine one as some errors are as close to the truth. One is base metal, and the other is true gold. Still, in externals, they differ very little.

We also need a guide because we are so prone to go astray. If the path of heaven is as straight as Bunyan pictures it, with no turning to the right or left, and no doubt it is, we are so prone to go astray. We could go to the right to the Mountains of Destruction or left to the dark Wood of Desolation. In Psalm 119:176, The psalmist said, *"I have gone astray like a lost sheep."* That means very often. For if a sheep is put into a field twenty times and does not get out twenty-one times, it will be because it cannot. It will be because the place is boarded up, and it cannot find a hole in the hedge.

If grace did not guide a man, he would go astray, though there were signposts all the way to heaven. Even if it was boldly written, "This is the way to refuge," he would still turn aside. The avenger of blood would overtake him if some guide did not, like the angels in Sodom, put his hand on his shoulders and cry, *"Escape for your life! Do not look behind you nor stay anywhere in the plain. Escape to the mountains, lest you be destroyed"* (Gen. 19:17). These, then, are the reasons why we need a guide.

A Person Provided

A person is provided. This is none other than God, and this God is none other than a person. This person is *"He, the Spirit,"* the *"Spirit of truth,"* not an influence or an emanation but actually a person. *"When He, the Spirit of truth, has come, He will guide you into all truth."* Now, we wish you to look at this guide to consider how adapted He is to us.

In the first place, He is infallible. He knows everything and cannot lead us astray. If I pin my sleeve to another man's coat, he may lead me part of the way rightly, but, by and by, he will go wrong himself, and I will be led astray with him. But if I give myself to the Holy Spirit and ask His guidance, there is no fear of my wandering.

Again, we rejoice in this Spirit because He is ever-present. We fall into a difficulty sometimes and say, "Oh, if I could take this to my minister, he would explain it. But I live so far off, and I am not able to see him." A passage of Scripture perplexes us, and we turn the text round and round and cannot make anything out of it. We look at the commentators, but many of them avoid the hard passages to some degree.

But when we have no commentator or minister, we still have the Holy Spirit. Let me tell you a little secret: Whenever you cannot understand a text, open your Bible, bend your knees, and pray over that text. If it does not split into atoms and open itself, try again. If prayer does not explain it, it is one of the things God did not intend you to know, and you may be content to be ignorant of it.

Prayer is the key that opens the cabinets of mystery. Prayer and faith are sacred picklocks that can open secrets and obtain great treasures. There is no college for holy education like that of the blessed Spirit, for He is an ever-present tutor. We only have to call on Him in prayer, and He is at our side, the great Expositor of truth.

But there is one thing about the suitability of this Guide that is remarkable, and I do not know whether it has struck you—*to* a truth, but it is only the Holy Spirit who can guide us *into* a truth. John 16:13 says, *"into."* Mark that word.

Now, for instance, it is a long while before you can lead some people to election, but when you have made them see its correctness, you have not led them *into* it. You may show them that it is plainly stated in Scripture, but they will turn away and hate it. You take them to another great truth, but they have been brought up in a different fashion and cannot answer your arguments. They say, "The man is right, perhaps," and they whisper, so low that conscience itself cannot hear, "but it is so contrary to my prejudices that I cannot receive it." Even after you have led them *to* the truth and they see that it is true, how hard it is to lead them *into* it.

Many of my hearers are brought *to* the truth of their depravity, but they are not brought *into* it and are not made to feel it. Some of you are brought to know the truth that God keeps us from day to day. However, you rarely get into it so as to live in continual dependence on God the Holy Spirit and draw fresh supplies from Him. Get inside it.

A Christian should do with truth as a snail does with his shell: live inside it as well as carry it on his back and perpetually have it with him. The Holy Spirit, it is said, will lead us into all truth. You may be brought to a chamber where there is an abundance of gold and silver, but you will be no richer unless you achieve an entrance. It is the Spirit's work to unbar the two-leaved gates and to bring us into the truth so that we may get inside it. As dear old Rowland Hill said, "Not only hold the truth, but have the truth hold us."

A Method Suggested

A method is suggested: *"He will guide you into all truth."* Now, I must give an illustration. I must compare truth to some cave or grotto of which you have heard. Its wondrous stalactites hang from the roof, and others start from the floor. It is a cavern that glitters with spar and abounds in marvels. Before entering the cavern, you inquire for a guide. He comes with his flaming torch and leads you down to a considerable depth. You find yourself in the midst of the cave, and he leads you through different chambers. Here, he points to a little stream rushing from amid the rocks, indicating its rise and progress. There, he points to some peculiar rock and tells you its name. Then, he takes you into a large natural hall and tells you how many persons once feasted in it, and so on.

Truth is a grand series of caverns, and it is our glory to have so great and wise a Conductor. Imagine that we are coming to the darkness of it. He is a light shining in the midst of us to guide us; by the light, He shows us wondrous things.

The Holy Spirit teaches us in three ways: suggestion, direction, and illumination. First, He guides us into all truth by suggesting it. There are thoughts that dwell in our minds that were not born there but were brought from heaven and put there by the Spirit. It is not our imaginations that angels whisper into our ears and that devils do the same.

Both good and evil spirits hold conversations with men, and some of us have experienced this. We have had strange thoughts that were not the offspring of our souls but that came from angelic visitors. Direct temptations and evil insinuations have also occurred that were not brewed in our own souls but that came from the pestilential cauldron of hell. The Spirit does speak in men's ears. Sometimes He speaks in the darkness of the night. In ages gone by, He spoke in dreams and visions, but now He speaks by His Word.

Have you not at times had a thought, concerning God and heavenly things, in the middle of your business and you could not tell from where it came? Have you not been reading or studying the Scripture when a text came to your mind? You could not help it, but even though you put it down, it was like cork in water and would swim up again to the top of your mind. Well, that good thought was put there by the Spirit. He often guides His people into all truth by suggesting, just as the guide in the grotto does with his torch. The cavern guide does not say a word, perhaps, but he walks into a passage himself, and you follow him. As the Spirit suggests a thought, your heart follows it.

I can well remember the manner in which I learned the doctrines of grace in a single instant. Born, as all of us are by nature, an Arminian, I still believed the old things that I had heard continually from the pulpit, and I did not see the grace of God. I remember sitting in the house of God one day, hearing a sermon that was as dry as possible and as worthless as all such sermons are. A thought struck my mind, "How did I come to be converted?" I prayed. I then wondered, "How did I come to pray?" I was induced to pray by reading the Scriptures. "How did I come to read the Scriptures?" And then, in a moment, I saw that God was at the bottom of it all and that He is the Author of faith (Heb. 12:2). It was then that the whole doctrine opened up to me from which I have not departed.

Sometimes, however, He leads us by direction. The guide points and says, "There, gentlemen, go along that particular path. That is the way." In the same way, the Spirit gives direction and tendency to our thoughts. He is not suggesting a new one, but He is letting a particular thought, once started, take such and such a direction. He is not so much putting a boat on the stream as He is steering it when it is there. When our thoughts are considering sacred things, He leads us into a more excellent channel from that in which we started.

Time after time you have begun a meditation on a certain doctrine and have unaccountably been gradually led away into another. You saw how one doctrine leaned on another, as is the case with the stones in the arch of a bridge, all hanging on the keystone of Jesus Christ crucified. You were brought to see these things not by a new suggested idea but by direction given to your thoughts.

Perhaps the best way that the Holy Spirit leads us into all truth is by illumination. He illuminates the Bible. Now, do any of you have an illuminated Bible? "No," says one, "I have a leather Bible." Another says, "I have a marginal reference Bible." That is all very well, but do you have an illuminated Bible? "Yes," says yet another, "I have a large family Bible with pictures in it." There is a picture of John the Baptist baptizing Christ by pouring water on His head. There are many other illustrations as well, but that is not what I mean by, "an illuminated Bible." "I have a Bible with splendid engravings in it," says another. I know you may have, but do you have an illuminated Bible? Finally, someone says, "I do not understand what you mean by an illuminated Bible." Well, it is the Christian man who has an illuminated Bible. He does not buy it illuminated originally, but when he reads it,

> A glory gilds the sacred page,
> Majestic like the sun;
> Which gives a light to every age,
> It gives, but borrows none.

There is nothing like reading an illuminated Bible. You may read to all eternity and never learn anything from it unless it is illuminated by the Spirit. Then, the words shine forth like stars. The book seems as if it is made of gold leaf. Every single letter glitters like a diamond. Oh, it is a blessed thing to read an illuminated Bible lit up by the radiance of the Holy Spirit.

Have you read the Bible and studied it only to find that your eyes are still unenlightened? Go and say, "Oh, Lord, gild the Bible for me. I want an expounded Bible. Illuminate it, and shine on it, for I cannot read it profitably unless you enlighten me."

Blind men may read the Bible with their fingers, but blind souls cannot. We need a light to read the Bible by, for there is no reading it in the dark. Thus, the Holy Spirit leads us into all truth by suggesting ideas, directing our thoughts, and illuminating the Scriptures when we read them.

An Evidence

The question arises, "How may I know whether I am enlightened by the Spirit's influence and led into all truth?" First, you may know the Spirit's influence by its unity. He guides us into all truth. Second, you may know His influence by its universality. He guides us into all truth.

Regarding unity, if you are judging a minister as to whether he has the Holy Spirit in him or not, you may know him in the first place by the constant unity of his testimony. A man cannot be enlightened by the Holy Spirit if he sometimes says yes and sometimes says no. The Spirit never says one thing at one time and another thing at another time. Indeed, there are many good men who say both yes and no, but their contrary testimonies are not both from God the Spirit. God the Spirit cannot witness to black and white, to a falsehood and a truth.

It has always been held as a first principle that truth is one thing. Some persons say, "I find one thing in one part of the Bible and another thing in another part, and though it contradicts itself, I must believe it." All quite right, friend, if it did contradict itself, but the fault is not in the wood but in the carpenter. Just as many carpenters do not understand dovetailing, so it is that many preachers do not understand dovetailing. It is very nice work, and it is not easily learned. It takes some apprenticeship to make all doctrines fit neatly together.

Second, you may know if you are led by the Spirit's influence and guided into all truth by its universality. The true child of God will not be led into some truth, but into all truth. When he first starts, he will not know half of the truth. He will believe it but will not understand it. He will have a small bit of it but not the sum total in all its breadth and length.

There is nothing like learning through experience. A man cannot become a theologian in a week. Certain doctrines take years to develop themselves. Like aloe that takes a hundred years to be readied, there are some truths that must long lie in the heart before they really come out and make themselves appear, so that we can speak of them as what we do know and testify of what we have seen (John 3:11).

The Spirit will gradually lead us into all truth. For instance, if it is true that Jesus Christ is to reign on the earth personally for a thousand years, as I am inclined to believe it is, if I am under the Spirit, that will be more and more revealed to me until I declare it with confidence. Some men begin very timidly. At first, a man says, "I know we are justified by faith, and I have peace with God, but so many have cried out against eternal justification that I am afraid of it." However, he is gradually enlightened and led to see that in the same hour when all his debts were paid, a full discharge was given. He sees that in the moment when sin was canceled, every elect soul was justified in God's mind even though they were not justified in their own minds until afterward. The Spirit will lead you into all truth.

Now, what are the practical inferences from this great doctrine? The first is with reference to the Christian who is afraid of his own ignorance. There are many who are enlightened and have tasted of heavenly things, but they are afraid that they are too ignorant to be saved. The Holy Spirit can teach anyone, regardless of how illiterate or uninstructed he might be.

I have known some men who were almost idiots before conversion, but afterward, they had their faculties wonderfully developed. Some time ago, there was a man who was so ignorant that he could not read, and never in his life did he speak anything with proper grammar unless it was by mistake. Moreover, he was considered to be what the people in his neighborhood called "daft." But when he was converted, the first thing he did was pray. He stammered out a few words, and in a little time, his powers of speaking began to develop themselves. Then, he thought he would like to read the Scriptures. After long, long months of labor, he learned to read. What was the next thing? He thought he could preach, and he did preach a little in his own homely way in his house. He thought, "I must read a few more books." His mind expanded, and he became a useful minister, settled in a country village, laboring for God.

Little intellect is needed to be taught of God. If you feel your ignorance, do not despair. Go to the Spirit, the great Teacher, and ask His sacred influence. It will come to pass that *"He will guide you into all truth."*

Whenever any of our fellow Christians do not understand the truth, let us take a hint as to the best way of dealing with them. Do not dispute with them. I have heard many controversies, but I have never heard of any good coming from one of them. Few men are taught by controversy. The axiom rings true: "A man convinced against his will is of the same opinion still." Pray for them that the Spirit of truth may lead them *"into all truth."* Do not be angry with your brother, but pray for him. Cry, "Lord, open his eyes that he *'may see wondrous things from Your law'* (Ps. 119:18)."

Finally, some of you know nothing about the Spirit of Truth or about the truth itself. It may be that some of you are saying, "We care little about which of you are right. We are happily indifferent to it." Poor sinner, if you knew the gift of God and who it was that spoke the truth, you would not say, "I don't care about it." If you only knew how essential the truth is to your salvation, you would not talk in such a way. The truth of God is that you are a worthless sinner who must believe that God, from all eternity, apart from all of your merits, loved you and bought you with the Redeemer's blood. He justified you in the forum of heaven and will justify you by and by in the forum of your conscience through the Holy Spirit by faith. If you knew that there is a heaven for you beyond the chance of a failure and a crown for you, the luster of which can never be dimmed, then you would say, "Indeed the truth is precious to my soul."

Why, these men of error want to take away the truth that alone can save you, the only Gospel that can deliver you from hell. They deny the great truths of free grace—those fundamental doctrines that alone can snatch a sinner from hell. Even though you do not feel interested in them now, I still would say that you ought to desire to see them promoted. May God have you know the truth in your hearts. May the Spirit *"guide you into all truth."* For if you do not know the truth here, learning of it will be sorrowful in the dark chambers of the pit where the only light will be the flames of hell. May you know the truth here.

"The truth shall make you free" (John 8:32), and *"if the Son makes you free, you shall be free indeed"* (v. 36), for He says, *"I am the way, the truth, and the life"* (John 14:6). Believe on Jesus, you chief of sinners. Trust His love and mercy, and you will be saved, for God the Spirit gives faith and eternal life.

Chapter 4

The Withering Work of the Spirit

The voice said, "Cry out!" And he said, "What shall I cry?" "All flesh is grass, and all its loveliness is like the flower of the field. The grass withers, the flower fades, because the breath of the LORD blows upon it; surely the people are grass. The grass withers, the flower fades, but the word of our God stands forever."
—Isaiah 40:6–8

Having been born again, not of corruptible seed but incorruptible, through the word of God which lives and abides forever, because "All flesh is as grass, and all the glory of man as the flower of the grass. The grass withers, and its flower falls away, but the word of the LORD endures forever." Now this is the word which by the gospel was preached to you.
—1 Peter 1:23–25

This passage from Isaiah may be used as a very eloquent description of our mortality. If a sermon was preached from it on the frailty of human nature, the brevity of life, and the certainty of death, no one could dispute the appropriateness of the text. Yet I venture to question whether such a discourse would strike the central teaching of the prophet.

Something more than the decay of our material flesh is intended here. The carnal mind, the flesh in another sense, was intended by the Holy Spirit when He had His messenger proclaim these words. By the context, it does not seem to me that a mere expression of the mortality of our race was needed. It would hardly keep pace with the sublime revelations that surround it, and it would, in some measure, be a digression from the subject at hand.

The notion that we are simply reminded of here, our mortality, does not square with the New Testament exposition of it in Peter, which I have also placed before you as a text. There is another, more spiritual meaning here beyond what would be contained in the great and very obvious truth: all of us must die.

Look at the fourth chapter of Isaiah with care. What is the subject of it? It is the divine consolation of Zion. Zion had been tossed back and forth with conflicts. She had been smarting from the sting of sin. The Lord, to remove her sorrow, had His prophets announce the coming of the long-expected Deliverer, the end and accomplishment of all her warfare, and the pardon of her iniquity. There is no doubt that this is the theme of the prophecy, and there is no sort of question about the next point.

This point is that Isaiah goes on to foretell the coming of John the Baptist as the forerunner of the Messiah. We have no difficulty in the explanation of the passage, *"The voice of one crying in the wilderness: 'Prepare the way of the LORD; make straight in the desert a highway for our God'"* (Isa. 40:3). The New Testament refers this again and again to the Baptist and his ministry. The object of the coming of the Baptist and the mission of the Messiah, of whom he spoke, was the manifestation of divine glory.

Observe Isaiah 40:5, *"The glory of the LORD shall be revealed, and all flesh shall see it together; for the mouth of the LORD has spoken."* Well, what next? Was it necessary to mention man's mortality in this connection? I think not. However, there is much more in the way of appropriateness to the succeeding verses if we see their deeper meaning. Do they not mean this?

In order to make room for the display of the divine glory in Christ Jesus and His salvation, there would come a withering of all the glory man boasts of himself. The flesh should be seen for its truly corrupt and dying nature so that the grace of God alone may be exalted. This would be seen under the ministry of John the Baptist first and should be the preparatory work of the Holy Spirit in men's hearts, in all time, so that the glory of the Lord will be revealed and human pride will be forever confounded.

The Spirit blows on the flesh, and what seems vigorous becomes weak. What was fair to look on is smitten with decay, and the true nature of the flesh is discovered. Its deceit is laid bare, and its power is destroyed. There is space for the dispensation of the ever-abiding Word and for the rule of the Great Shepherd whose words are spirit and life (John 6:63).

There is also a withering brought by the Spirit that is the preparation for the sowing and implanting by which salvation is brought about. The withering before the sowing was marvelously fulfilled in the preaching of John the Baptist. Appropriately, he carried on his ministry in the desert, for a spiritual desert was all around him. His was *the voice of one crying in the wilderness* (Isa. 40:3). It was not his work to plant. His job was to cut down.

The fleshly religion of the Jews was then in its prime. Pharisaism stalked the streets in all its pomp. Men complacently rested in outward ceremonies only, and spiritual religion was at the lowest conceivable ebb. Here and there a Simeon and an Anna may have been found, but for the most part, men knew nothing of spiritual religion. They said in their hearts, *"'We have Abraham as our father'* (Matt. 3:9), and this is enough." What a stir John made when he called the lordly Pharisees a *"generation of vipers"* (v. 7 KJV) and said, *"Repent, for the kingdom of heaven is at hand!"* (v. 2). How he shook the nation with the declaration, *"Even now the ax is laid to the root of the trees"* (v. 10). Stern as Elijah, his work was to level the mountains and to lay low every lofty imagination.

The word *repent* was as a scorching wind to the foliage of self-righteousness. It was a killing blast for the confidence of ceremonialism. His food and his dress called for fasting and mourning. The outward token of his ministry declared the death amid which he preached, as he baptized in the waters of the Jordan those who came to him. This was the meaning of the emblem that he set before the crowd. His typical act was as thorough in its teaching as were his words. Plus, he warned them of a yet more searching and trying baptism with the Holy Spirit and with fire, and of the coming of One whose *"winnowing fan is in His hand, and He will thoroughly clean out His threshing floor"* (v. 12). The Spirit in John the Baptist blew as the rough north wind, searching and withering, and it made him a destroyer of the vain glories of a fleshly religion. This was done so that the spiritual faith might be established.

When our Lord Himself actually appeared, He came into a withered land whose glories had all departed. Old Jesse's stem was bare, and our Lord was the branch that grew out of his root. The scepter had departed from Judah, and the lawgiver from between his feet, when Shiloh came (Gen. 49:10). An alien sat on David's throne, and the Romans called the covenant land their own. The lamp of prophecy burned dimly, if it had not utterly gone out. No Isaiah had come forth at that time to console them, not even a Jeremiah to lament the abandonment of their faith.

The whole economy of Judaism was like worn-out clothes. It had become old and ready to vanish. The priesthood was in disarray.

Luke tells us that Annas and Caiaphas were high priests that year—two in a year or at once—a strange setting aside of the laws of Moses. All the dispensation that gathered around the visible, or as Paul called it, an *"earthly sanctuary"* (Heb. 9:1), was coming to a close.

When our Lord had finished His work, the veil of the temple was torn in two, the sacrifices were abolished, the priesthood of Aaron was set aside, and carnal ordinances were abrogated, for the Spirit revealed spiritual things. When He came who was made a priest, *"not according to the law of a fleshly commandment, but according to the power of an endless life"* (Heb. 7:16), there was *"an annulling of the former commandment because of its weakness and unprofitableness"* (v. 18).

Such are the facts of history, but I am not about to expand on them. I am coming to your own personal histories, to the experience of every child of God. In every one of us, it must be fulfilled that all that is of the flesh in us, when we see it as nothing but grass, must be withered, and the loveliness of it must be destroyed.

The Spirit of God, like the wind, must pass over the field of our souls and cause our beauty to be as a fading flower. He must so convince us of sin and so reveal ourselves to ourselves that we will see that *"the flesh profits nothing"* (John 6:63). Our fallen nature is corruption itself, and *"those who are in the flesh cannot please God"* (Rom. 8:8). The sentence of death on our former legal and carnal life must be brought home to us, so that the incorruptible seed of the Word of God, implanted by the Holy Spirit, may be in us and abide in us forever.

Implanting work always follows where withering work has been performed.

Causing the Ungodliness of the Flesh to Fade

The work of the Holy Spirit on the soul of man in withering up what is of the flesh is very unexpected. You will observe in our Scripture that even the speaker himself, though doubtless one taught of God, said, *"What shall I cry?"* Even he did not know that there must first be an experience of preliminary visitation for the comforting of God's people. Many preachers of God's Gospel have forgotten that *"the law was our tutor to bring us to Christ, that we might be justified by faith"* (Gal. 3:24). They have sown on the unbroken, fruitless ground and have forgotten that the plow must break the clods. We have seen too much of trying to sew without the sharp needle of the Spirit's convincing power.

Preachers have labored to make Christ precious to those who think of themselves as rich and wealthy in goods. It has been labor in vain. It is our duty to preach Jesus Christ even to self-righteous sinners, but it is certain that they will never accept Jesus Christ while they hold themselves in high esteem. Only the sick will welcome the physician. It is the work of the Spirit of God to convince men of sin, and until they are convinced of sin, they will never be led to seek the righteousness that God gives by Jesus Christ.

I am persuaded that wherever there is a real work of grace in any soul, it begins with a pulling down. The Holy Spirit does not build on the old foundation. Wood, hay, and straw will not do for Him to build upon (1 Cor. 3:12–13). He will come as the fire and cause all of nature's proud idols to blaze. He will break our bows, cut our spears apart, and burn our chariots with His fire. When every sandy foundation is gone, and not until then, He will lay in our souls the great stone Foundation, *"chosen by God and precious"* (1 Pet. 2:4).

Do you not see that it is divinely wise that you be stripped before you are clothed? Would you wear Christ's lustrous righteousness, which is whiter than any person could make it, on the outside and conceal your own filthy rags inside? No, they must be put away. Not a single thread of your own must be left upon you. God may not cleanse you until He has made you see some of your defilement, for you would never value the precious *"blood of Jesus Christ His Son* [that] *cleanses us from all sin"* (1 John 1:7), if you had not first of all been made to mourn the fact that you are altogether an unclean thing.

The convincing work of the Spirit, wherever it comes, is unexpected. Even to the child of God in whom this process still has to go on, it is often startling. We begin to rebuild what the Spirit of God has destroyed. Having begun in the Spirit, we act as if we will be made perfect in the flesh, and then, when our mistaken upbuilding has to be leveled with the earth, we are almost as astonished as we were when the scales first fell from our eyes. Newton was in this sort of condition when he wrote,

> I asked the Lord that I might grow
> In faith and love and every grace,
> Might more of His salvation know,
> And seek more earnestly His face.

'Twas He who taught me thus to pray,
And He, I trust, has answered prayer;
But it has been in such a way
As almost drove me to despair.

I hoped that in some favored hour,
At once He'd answer my request,
And by His love's constraining power
Subdue my sins, and give me rest.

Instead of this, He made me feel
The hidden evils of my heart;
And let the angry powers of hell
Assault my soul in every part.

Marvel not, for the Lord is accustomed to answering His people. The voice that says, *"Comfort, yes, comfort My people!"* (Isa. 40:1), achieves its purpose by first making them hear the cry, *"All flesh is grass, and all its loveliness is like the flower of the field"* (v. 6).

If we consider well the ways of God, we should not be astonished that He begins with His people by revealing the terrible things before righteousness.

Observe the method of Creation. I will not venture upon any dogmatic theory of geology, but there seems to be every probability that this world has been readied and destroyed many times before the last arranging of it for the habitation of men. *"In the beginning God created the heavens and the earth"* (Gen. 1:1). Then came a long interval, and at length, at the appointed time, during seven days, the Lord prepared the earth for the human race.

Consider the state of matters when the Great Architect began His work. What was there in the beginning? Originally, nothing. When He commanded the ordering of the earth, how did it happen? *"The earth was without form, and void; and darkness was on the face of the deep"* (v. 2). There was no trace of another's plan to interfere with the Great Architect. *"With whom did He take counsel, and who instructed Him, and taught Him in the path of justice? Who taught Him knowledge, and showed Him the way of understanding?"* (Isa. 40:14).

He received no contribution of columns or pillars toward the temple that He intended to build. The earth was, as the Hebrew puts it, *tohu* and *bohu,* disorder and confusion. So it is in the new creation as well. When the Lord creates us anew, He borrows nothing from the old man, but He makes all things new. He does not repair and add a new wing to the old house of our depraved nature, but He builds a new temple for His own praise. We are spiritually without form and empty. Darkness is on the faces of our hearts, and His Word comes to us saying, *"Let there be light"* (Gen. 1:3), and there is light preceding long life and every precious thing.

Take another instance from the ways of God. When man has fallen, when does the Lord bring him to the Gospel? The first whisper of the Gospel was, *"I will put enmity between you and the woman, and between your seed and her Seed; He shall bruise your head, and you shall bruise His heel"* (Gen. 3:15). That whisper came to man as he was shivering in the presence of his Maker, having nothing more to say by way of excuse, but standing guilty before the Lord. When did the Lord God clothe our parents? It was not until He first had asked the question, *"Who told you that you were naked?"* (v. 11). Not until the fig leaves had utterly failed did the Lord bring in the covering skin of the sacrifice and wrap them in it.

If you will pursue the meditation on the acts of God with men, you will constantly see the same thing. God has given us a wonderful type of salvation in Noah's ark, but Noah was saved in that ark in connection with death. He himself, as it were, was enclosed alive in a tomb, and all the world outside was left to destruction. All other hope for Noah was gone, and then, the ark rose upon the waters.

Remember the redemption of the children of Israel from Egypt. It occurred when they were in the saddest situation, and their cries went up to heaven because of their bondage. No arm was bringing salvation until with a high hand and an outstretched arm, the Lord brought forth His people. Before salvation, there comes the humbling of the creature, the overthrow of human hope.

As in the backwoods of America before the cultivation of land, the planting of cities, the arts of civilization, and the transactions of commerce, the woodman's ax must cut and sever the stately trees. Centuries must fall. The roots must be burned. The old reign of nature must be disturbed because the old must go before the new can come. Even the Lord takes away the first so that He may establish the second.

The first heaven and the first earth must pass away, or there cannot be a new heaven and a new earth. Now, as it has been outwardly, we ought to expect that it would be the same within us.

When these witherings and fadings occur in our souls, we should only say, *"It is the LORD. Let Him do what seems good to Him"* (1 Sam. 3:18).

Our Scripture shows that this withering process happens universally over the hearts of all those on whom the Spirit works. The withering is a withering of what? Of part of the flesh and some portion of its tendencies? No. Observe, *"All flesh is grass, and all its loveliness"*—the very choice and pick of it—*"is like the flower of the field."* What happens to the grass? Does any of it live? *"The grass withers."* All of it. The flower, will that not live? So fair a thing, does it not have immortality? No, it *"fades."* It utterly falls away.

So wherever the Spirit of God breathes on the soul of man, there is a withering of everything that is of the flesh. It is seen that *"to be carnally minded is death"* (Rom. 8:6). Of course, we all know and confess that where there is a work of grace, there must be a destruction of our delight in the pleasures of the flesh. When the Spirit of God breathes on us, what was sweet becomes bitter, and what was bright becomes dim. A man cannot love sin and yet possess the life of God. If he takes pleasure in the fleshly joys he once delighted in, he is still what he was. He minds the things of the flesh; therefore, he loves according to the flesh (v. 5), and he will die. The world and its lusts are as beautiful as the meadows in spring to the sinful, but to the renewed soul, they are a wilderness and uninhabited.

Of those very things we once delighted in we say, *"'Vanity of vanities,' says the Preacher, 'all is vanity'"* (Eccl. 12:8). We cry to be delivered from the poisonous joys of earth. We hate them and wonder how we could have ever enjoyed them. Do you know what this kind of withering means? Have you seen the lusts of the flesh and the pleasures fade away before your eyes? This must happen, or the Spirit of God has not visited your soul.

Whenever the Spirit of God comes, He destroys the goodness and flower of the flesh. Our self-righteousness withers along with our sinfulness. Before the Spirit comes, we think of ourselves as the best. We say, "We have kept all the commandments since childhood," and we arrogantly ask, "What do we lack? Have we not been moral? Have we not been religious?" We confess that we may have committed faults, but we think they are very excusable. We venture in our wicked pride to imagine that we are not so bad, as the Word of God would lead us to think, after all.

When the Spirit of God blows on the attractiveness of your flesh, its beauty will fade as a leaf, and you will have quite another idea of yourself. You will then find no language too severe in which to describe your past character. Searching deep into your motives and investigating what moved you to your actions, you will see so much evil that you will cry with the tax collector, *"God, be merciful to me a sinner!"* (Luke 18:13).

While the Holy Spirit has withered the self-righteousness in us, He has not half completed His work. There is much more to be destroyed. Along with everything else, our boasted power of resolution must also go. Most people conceive that they can turn to God whenever they resolve to do so. "I am a man of such strength of mind," says one, "that if I made up my mind to be religious, I could be so without difficulty." "Ah," says another fleeting spirit, "I believe that one of these days I can correct the errors of the past and begin a new life." These resolutions of the flesh are good flowers, but they must all fade. Even when the Spirit of God visits, we find that we do not act as we should. We discover that our wills are turned off to all that is good, and we naturally refuse to come to Christ so that we may have life. Resolutions are poor and frail when they are seen in the light of God's Spirit.

Still, the man will say, "I believe I have within myself an enlightened conscience and an intelligence that will guide me accurately. The light of nature I will use, and I do not doubt that I will find my way back again if I wander." Man, your wisdom that is the very flower of your nature—what is it but folly? However, you do not see this. Unconverted and unrenewed, you are in God's sight no wiser than the colt of a wild ass (Job 11:12). I wish you were humbled in your own esteem as a little child at the feet of Jesus and made to cry, "Teach me."

When the withering wind of the Spirit moves over the carnal mind, it reveals the death of the flesh in all respects, especially in the matter of power toward what is good. We then learn that Word of our Lord, *"Without Me you can do nothing"* (John 15:5). When I was seeking the Lord, I not only believed but also felt in my very soul that I could not pray without divine help. I could not even feel accurately, or mourn, or groan as I would have. I longed to desire more of Christ, but I could not even feel that I needed Him as I ought to have felt it.

This heart was then as hard, as adamant, and as dead as those that rot in their graves. Oh, what I would, at times, have given for a tear. I wanted to repent, but I could not. I longed to believe, but I could not. I felt bound, hampered, and paralyzed.

477

This is a humbling revelation of God's Holy Spirit but a needful one. The faith of the flesh is not the faith of God's elect. The faith that justifies the soul is the gift of God and not of ourselves (Eph. 2:8). Repentance that is the work of the flesh will need to be repented of. The flower of the flesh must wither. Only the seed of the Spirit will produce fruit unto perfection. The heirs of heaven are born not of blood, nor of the will of the flesh, nor of man, but of God (John 1:13). If the work in us is not the Spirit's working, but our own, it will droop and die when we require its protection most. Its end will be as the grass that is here today and gone tomorrow.

Besides the universality of this withering work within us, notice also the completeness of it. The grass, what does it do? Droop? No, it *"withers."* The flower of the field, what does it do? Does it hang its head a little? No, according to Isaiah, it *"fades,"* and according to Peter, it *"falls away."* There is no reviving it with showers, for it has come to its end. The awakened are led to see that in their flesh dwells no good thing.

What dying and withering work some of God's servants have had in their souls! Look at John Bunyan as he describes himself in his *Grace Abounding.* For how many months and even years was the Spirit engaged in writing death on all that was the old Bunyan in order that he might become by grace a new man, fitted to track the pilgrims along their heavenly ways.

We have not all endured the ordeal so long, but in every child of God, there must be a death to sin, to the law, and to self, which must be fully accomplished before he is perfected in Christ and taken to heaven. Corruption cannot inherit incorruption. It is through the Spirit that we mortify the deeds of the body, and therefore live.

Can the fleshly mind not be improved? By no means, *"because the carnal mind is enmity against God; for it is not subject to the law of God, nor indeed can be"* (Rom. 8:7). Can you not improve the old nature? No, *"you must be born again"* (John 3:7). Can it not be taught heavenly things? No, *"the natural man does not receive the things of the Spirit of God, for they are foolishness to him; nor can he know them, because they are spiritually discerned"* (1 Cor. 2:14).

There is nothing to be done with the old nature but to put it in the grave. It must be dead and buried. When this is so, the incorruptible seed that lives and abides forever will then develop gloriously. The fruit of the new birth will come to maturity, and grace will be exalted in glory. The old nature never does improve. It is as earthly, sensual, and devilish in the saint who is eighty years old as it was when first he came to Christ.

It is unimproved and unimprovable toward God. It is enmity itself. Every imagination of the thoughts of the heart is continuously evil. In the old nature, *"the flesh lusts against the Spirit, and the Spirit against the flesh; and these are contrary to one another"* (Gal. 5:17). There cannot be peace between them.

Withering work in the soul is very painful. As you read these verses, do they not strike you as having the tone of a funeral? *"All flesh is grass, and all its loveliness is like the flower of the field. The grass withers, the flower fades."* This is mournful work, but it must be done. I think that those who experience a great deal of it when they first come to Christ have much reason to be thankful. Their course in life will, in all probability, be much brighter and happier.

I have noticed that persons who are converted very easily and who come to Christ with relatively little knowledge of their own depravity have to learn it afterward. They seem to remain babes in Christ for a long time, and they are perplexed with matters that would not have troubled them if they had experienced a deeper work at first. No, if grace has begun to build in your soul and any of the old walls of self-trust have been left standing, they will have to come down sooner or later.

You may congratulate yourself on their remaining, but it is a false congratulation. Your glorying is not good. I am sure that Christ will never put a new piece on an old garment or new wine in old bottles. He knows it would be worse in the long run. All that is of nature's spinning must be unraveled. The natural building must come down—planks and plaster, roof and foundation—and we must have a house that is not made with the hands.

It was a wonderful mercy for the city of London that the great fire cleared away all of the old buildings that were the resting place of the plague. A far healthier city was then built. Thus, it is a great mercy for a man when God sweeps away all of man's own righteousness and strength, when He makes him feel that he is nothing and can be nothing, and when He drives him to confess that Christ must be all in all. Then, his only strength lies in the eternal might of the ever-blessed Spirit.

Although this is painful, it is inevitable. I have already shown you how necessary it is that all of the old should be taken away. However, let me further remark that it is inevitable that the old should go because it is in itself corruptible. Why does the grass wither? Because it is a withering thing. It must die. How could it spring out of the earth and be immortal? It is not a flower that never fades. It does not bloom in Paradise. It grows in soil on which the curse has fallen. Every supposed good thing that grows out of yourself is mortal, just like you, and it must die.

The seeds of corruption are in all the fruits of manhood's tree. Even if they are as fair to look on as Eden's clusters, they must decay.

Moreover, it would never be acceptable to have something of the flesh and something of the Spirit in our salvation. If it were so, there would be a division of the honor—up to now the praises of God, beyond this will be my own praises. If I were to win heaven partly through what I had done and partly through what Christ had done, and if the energy that sanctified me was in a measure my own and in a measure divine, the reward should be divided. Thus, the songs of heaven, while they would be partly to the Almighty, must also be partly to the creature. But this will not be.

Down, proud flesh. Down, I say. Though you clean and purge yourself as you do, you are corrupt to the core. Though you labor to the point of weariness, you build wood that will be burned and stubble that will be turned to ashes. Give up your own self-confidence, and let the work and the merit be where the honor will be, namely, with God alone. It is inevitable, then, that there should be all this withering.

The Implantation

According to Peter, although the flesh withers and the flower falls away, in the children of God, there is something of another kind that does not wither. *"Having been born again, not of corruptible seed but incorruptible, through the word of God which lives and abides forever....'The word of the LORD endures forever.'"*

The Gospel is of use to us because it is not of human origin. If it were of the flesh, all it could do for us would not land us beyond the flesh. However, the Gospel of Jesus Christ is superhuman, divine, and spiritual. In its conception, it was of God. Its great gift, even the Savior, is a divine gift, and all of its teachings are full of Deity.

If you believe a gospel that you have thought out for yourself or a gospel that comes from the brain of man, it is of the flesh. It will wither, and you will die and be lost through trusting in it. The only word that can bless you and that can be a seed in your soul must be the living and incorruptible Word of the eternal Spirit.

Now, this is the incorruptible Word: *"The Word became flesh and dwelt among us"* (John 1:14). *"God was in Christ reconciling the world to Himself, not imputing their trespasses to them"* (2 Cor. 5:19). This is the incorruptible Word: *"Whoever believes that Jesus is the Christ is born of God"* (1 John 5:1). *"He who believes in Him is not condemned; but he who does not believe is condemned already, because he has not believed in the name of the only begotten Son of God"* (John 3:18). *"God has given us eternal life, and this life is in His Son"* (1 John 5:11).

Now, this is the seed, but before it can grow in your soul, it must be planted there by the Spirit. Will you receive it? Then, the Holy Spirit implants it in your soul. Leap up to it and say, "I believe it, and I grasp it. I fix my hope on the incarnate God. The substitutionary sacrifice and the complete atonement of Christ is all my confidence. I am reconciled to God by the blood of Jesus." Then, you possess the living seed within your soul.

What is the result of it? According to the text, a new life comes into us as the result of the indwelling of the living Word and our being born again by it. It is a new life. It is not the old nature putting out its better parts and not the old Adam refining, purifying itself, and rising to something better. No, the flesh withers, and its flower fades. It is an entirely new life. You are just as much new creatures at your regeneration as if you had never existed and had been created for the first time. *"Therefore, if anyone is in Christ, he is a new creation; old things have passed away; behold, all things have become new"* (2 Cor. 5:17).

The child of God is beyond and above other men. Other men do not possess the life that he has received. They have a body and a soul, but he is spirit, soul, and body. A fresh principle, a spark of the divine life, has dropped into his soul. He is no longer a natural or carnal man, but he has become a spiritual man. He is understanding spiritual things and possessing a life far superior to anything that belongs to the rest of mankind. May God, who has withered what is of the flesh in your souls, speedily grant you the new birth through the Word.

Now, wherever this new life comes through the Word, it is incorruptible. It *"lives and abides forever."* To get the good seed out of a true believer's heart and to destroy the new nature in him is a thing that is attempted by earth and hell, but it is never achieved.

481

Pluck the sun out of the sky, and even then, you will not be able to pluck grace out of a born-again heart. It can neither corrupt itself nor be corrupted. *"We know that whoever is born of God does not sin"* (1 John 5:18). *"I give them eternal life, and they shall never perish; neither shall anyone snatch them out of My hand"* (John 10:28). *"But whoever drinks of the water that I shall give him will never thirst. But the water that I shall give him will become in him a fountain of water springing up into everlasting life"* (John 4:14).

You have a natural life that will die; it is of the flesh. You have a spiritual life, and of that it is written, *"And whoever lives and believes in Me shall never die. Do you believe this?"* (John 11:26). You now have within you the noblest and truest immortality. You must live as God lives—in peace, joy, and happiness.

Remember, if you do not have this, you *"shall not see life"* (John 3:36). What, then? Will you be annihilated? No, but the wrath of the Lord will be upon you (v. 36). You will exist, but you will not live. You will know nothing of life, for life is the gift of God in Christ Jesus. But an everlasting death that is full of torment and anguish will be on the one who does not believe.

If you do not believe, you will be *"cast into the lake of fire. This is the second death"* (Rev. 20:14). You will be one of those whose *"worm does not die, [and whose] fire is not quenched"* (Mark 9:44). May God, the ever-blessed Spirit, visit you. If He is now striving with you, do not quench His divine flame.

Do not toy with any holy thought you have. If you must confess that you are not born again, be humbled by it. Go and seek mercy from the Lord. Plead for Him to deal graciously with you and save you. Many who have had nothing but moonlight have received it, and before long, they have had sunlight.

Above all, remember what the quickening seed is, and reverence it when you hear it preached: *"This is the word which by the gospel was preached to you."* Respect it and receive it. Remember that the quickening seed is all wrapped up in this sentence: *"Believe on the Lord Jesus Christ, and you will be saved"* (Acts 16:31). *"He who believes and is baptized will be saved; but he who does not believe will be condemned"* (Mark 16:16). The Lord bless you, for Jesus' sake.

Chapter 5

The Covenant Promise of the Spirit

*I will put My Spirit within you and cause you to walk in My
statutes, and you will keep My judgments and do them.*
—Ezekiel 36:27

T he tongues of men and of angels might fail. To call this verse
a golden sentence would be much too commonplace, and to
liken it to a pearl of great price would be too poor a comparison. We cannot feel, much less speak, too much in praise of the
great God who has put this clause into the covenant of His grace. In
that covenant, every sentence is more precious than heaven and
earth, and this line is not the least among His choice words of
promise: *"I will put My Spirit within you."*

A Gracious Word

I would begin by saying that it is a gracious word, but it was
spoken to a graceless people. It was spoken to a people who had
followed their own ways and refused the way of God. They were a
people who had already provoked something more than ordinary
anger in the Judge of all the earth.

For He Himself said in Ezekiel 36:18, *"I poured out My fury on
them."* These people, even under chastisement, caused the holy
name of God to be profaned among the heathen wherever they
went. They had been highly favored, but they abused their privileges and behaved worse than those who never knew the Lord.
They sinned flagrantly, willfully, wickedly, proudly, and presumptuously; by this, they greatly provoked the Lord.

Yet He made such a promise to them as this, *"I will put My
Spirit within you."* Surely, *"where sin abounded, grace abounded
much more"* (Rom. 5:20). Clearly, this is a word of grace, for the
law says nothing of this kind. Turn to the Law of Moses, and see if

there is any word spoken there that concerns the putting of the Spirit within men to cause them to walk in God's statutes. The law proclaims the statutes, but the Gospel alone promises the Spirit by which the statutes will be obeyed.

The law commands and makes us know what God requires of us, but the Gospel goes further and inclines us to obey the will of the Lord. It also enables us to walk in His ways. Under the dominion of grace, *"God...works in you both to will and to do for His good pleasure"* (Phil. 2:13).

So great a blessing as this could never come to any man by merit. A man might act as if he deserves a reward of a certain kind in a measure suited to his commendable action. However, the Holy Spirit can never be the wage for human service. The idea verges on blasphemy.

Can any man deserve Christ dying for him? Who would dream of such a thing? Can any man deserve the Holy Spirit dwelling in him and working holiness in him? The greatness of the blessing lifts it high above the range of merit. If the Holy Spirit is bestowed, it must be by an act of divine grace—grace infinite in bounty, exceeding all that we could have imagined. "Sovereign grace o'er sin abounding" is here seen in clearest light.

"I will put My Spirit within you" is a promise that drips with grace as the honeycomb drips with honey. Listen to the divine music that pours from this word of love. I hear the soft melody of grace, grace, grace, and nothing else but grace. Glory be to God, who gives to sinners the indwelling of His Spirit.

A Divine Word

"I will put My Spirit within you" is also a divine word. Who but the Lord could speak in this way? Can one man put the Spirit of God within another? Could all of the church combined breathe the Spirit of God into a single sinner's heart? To put any good thing into the deceitful heart of man is a great achievement, but to put the Spirit of God into the heart is truly done only by the finger of God.

"The LORD has made bare His holy arm" (Isa. 52:10) and displayed the fullness of His mighty power. To put the Spirit of God into our nature is a work peculiar to the Godhead. To do this within the nature of a free agent, such as man, is marvelous.

Who but the God of Israel can speak after this royal style and beyond all dispute declare, *"I will put My Spirit within you"*? Men must always surround their resolutions with conditions and uncertainties, but since omnipotence is behind every promise of God, He speaks like a king in a style that is fit only for the eternal God. He purposes and promises, and just as surely, He performs. The promise of our sacred verse is certain to be fulfilled. It is certain because it is divine.

Oh, sinner, if we poor creatures had the work of saving you, we would break down in the attempt; but behold, the Lord Himself comes on the scene, and the work is done. All the difficulties are removed by this one sentence, *"I will put My Spirit within you."* We have worked with our spirits, have wept over you, have begged you, but still we have failed. However, there comes One into the matter who cannot fail. With Him, nothing is impossible (Luke 1:37). He begins His work by saying, *"I will put My Spirit within you."* The word is of grace and of God. Regard it, then, as a pledge from the God of grace.

An Individual and Personal Word

To me, there is much charm in the further thought that this is an individual and personal word. The Lord means, *"I will put My Spirit within you"* as individuals, one by one. This must be so since the context requires it.

We read in Ezekiel 36:26, *"I will give you a new heart."* Now, a new heart can only be given to one person. Each man needs a heart of his own, and each man must have a new heart for himself. The verse continues, *"And put a new spirit within you."* Within each one, this must be done: *"I will take the heart of stone out of your flesh and give you a heart of flesh"* (v. 26).

These are all personal, individual operations of grace. God deals with men one by one in the solemn matters of eternity, sin, and salvation. We are born one by one, and we die one by one. Even so, we must be born again one by one, and each one must receive the Spirit of God for himself. Without this gift of the Spirit, a man has nothing. Man cannot be caused to walk in God's statutes except by the infusion of grace into him as an individual.

Is there a single man or woman who feels himself or herself to be all alone in the world and therefore hopeless? You can believe that God will do great things for a nation, but how should the solitary be thought of? You are an odd person, one that could not be written down in any list. You are a peculiar sinner with inherent tendencies all your own. God says, *"I will put My Spirit within you."* That means within your heart. Yes, even yours. You who have long been seeking salvation but who have not known the power of the Spirit, this is what you need.

You have been striving in the energy of the flesh, but you have not understood where your true strength lies. God says to you in Zechariah 4:6, *"'Not by might nor by power, but by My Spirit,' says the LORD of hosts,"* and again, *"I will put My Spirit within you."* Oh, that this word might be spoken by the Lord to that young person who is ready to despair or to that sorrowful one who has been looking within for power to pray and to believe.

You are without strength or hope in and of yourself, but this meets your case in all points. *"I will put My Spirit within you"* means within you as an individual. Ask the Lord for it. Lift up your heart in prayer to God, and ask Him to pour on you the Spirit of grace and of supplication. Plead with the Lord, saying, "Let your good Spirit lead me, even me." Cry, "Pass me not, my gracious Father, but fulfill in me this wondrous word of yours, *'I will put My Spirit within you.'"*

A Separating Word

This is also a separating word. I do not know whether you will see this readily, but it must be so. This word separates a man from his peers. Men, by nature, are of another spirit than that of God, and they are under subjection to that evil spirit, *"the prince of the power of the air"* (Eph. 2:2). When the Lord comes to gather His own, fetching them out from among the heathen, He effects the separation by fulfilling this word, *"I will put My Spirit within you."* After this is done, the individual becomes a new man.

Those who have the Spirit are not of the world or like the world. They soon have to come out from among the ungodly and be separate, for differences of nature create conflict. God's Spirit will not dwell with the evil spirit. You cannot have fellowship with Christ and with Belial, with the kingdom of heaven and with this world.

I wish that the people of God would again awaken to the truth that to gather a people from among men is the great purpose of the present dispensation. It is still true, as James said at the Jerusalem council, *"Simon has declared how God at the first visited the Gentiles to take out of them a people for His name"* (Acts 15:14).

We are not to cling to the old wreck with the expectation that we will pump the water out of her and get her safely into port. No, the cry is very different: "Take to the lifeboat! Take to the lifeboat!" You are to leave the wreck. Then, you are to carry away from the sinking mass what God will save. You must be separate from the old wreck, so it will not suck you down to sure destruction.

Your only hope of doing good to the world is by being *"not of the world"* (John 17:16), just as Christ was not of the world. If you sink to the world's level, it will not be good for it or for you. What happened in the days of Noah will be repeated. When the sons of God entered into alliance with the daughters of men, and there was a league between the two races, the Lord could not endure the evil mixture. He drew up the passageway of the lower deep and swept the earth with a destroying flood.

Surely, in that Last Day of destruction, when the world is overwhelmed with fire, it will be because the church of God will have degenerated and the distinctions between the righteous and the wicked will have been broken down. The Spirit of God, wherever He comes, speedily makes and reveals the difference between Israel and Egypt. And in proportion as His active energy is felt, there will be an ever-widening gulf between those who are led by the Spirit and those who are under the dominion of the flesh. This is a separating word. Has it separated you? Has the Holy Spirit called you apart and blessed you? Do you differ from your old companions? Do you have a life that they do not understand? If not, may God, in mercy, put into you that most heavenly deposit, *"I will put My Spirit within you."*

A Uniting Word

It is also a very uniting word. It separates from the world, but it joins to God. *"I will put My Spirit within you."* It is not merely a spirit or the spirit, but His Spirit. Now, when God's own Spirit comes to reside within our mortal bodies, we are near kindred to the Most High. As 1 Corinthians 6:19 asks, *"Do you not know that your body is the temple of the Holy Spirit?"* Does this not make a man outstanding? Have you never stood in awe of your own self? Have you thought enough about how this poor body is sanctified, dedicated, and elevated into a sacred condition by being set apart as a *"temple of the Holy Spirit"*?

We are brought into the closest union with God that we can well conceive of. The Lord is our light and our life while our spirits are subordinate to the divine Spirit. *"I will put My Spirit within you."*

God Himself then dwells in you. The Spirit of Him who raised Christ from the dead is in you. Your life is hidden with Christ in God and the Spirit seals you, anoints you, and abides in you. By the Spirit, we have access to the Father (Eph. 2:18). By the Spirit, we perceive our adoption and learn to cry, *"Abba, Father"* (Rom. 8:15). By the Spirit, we are made *"partakers of the divine nature"* (2 Pet. 1:4) and have communion with the threefold, holy Lord.

A Condescending Word

I cannot help adding that it is a very condescending word. *"I will put My Spirit within you."* Is it really true that the Spirit of God, who displays the power and energetic force of God, by whom God's Word is carried into effect, who moved on the face of the waters and brought order and life from chaos and death, is the One who lowers Himself to reside in men? God in our nature is a very wonderful conception. God in the babe at Bethlehem, God in the carpenter of Nazareth, God in the Man of Sorrows, God in the Crucified, and God in Him who was buried in the tomb—this is all marvelous.

The Incarnation is an infinite mystery of love, but we believe it. Yet if it were possible to compare one great wonder with another, I would say that God's dwelling in His people and that repeated ten thousand times over is more marvelous. That the Holy Spirit should dwell in millions of redeemed men and women is a miracle not surpassed by that of our Lord's adoption of human nature.

Our Lord's body was perfectly pure, and the Godhead, while it dwelt in His holy manhood, did at least dwell with a perfect and sinless nature. However, the Holy Spirit bows Himself to dwell in sinful men. He dwells in men who, after their conversions, still find the flesh warring against the spirit and the spirit against the flesh (Rom. 7:23). He dwells in men who are not perfect even though they strive to be so. These men have to mourn their shortcomings and even have to confess with shame a measure of unbelief. *"I will put My Spirit within you"* means that the Holy Spirit is in our imperfect nature. Wonder of wonders! Yet it is as surely a fact as it is a wonder.

Believers in the Lord Jesus Christ, you have the Spirit of God, for *"if anyone does not have the Spirit of Christ, he is not His"*

(Rom. 8:9). You could not bear the suspicion that you are not His. Therefore, as surely as you are Christ's, you have His Spirit abiding in you.

The Savior has gone away on purpose so that the Comforter may be given to dwell in you, and He does dwell in you. Is it not so? If it is so, admire this condescending God, and worship and praise His name. Sweetly submit to His rule in all things. Grieve not the Spirit of God (Eph. 4:30). Watch carefully so that nothing comes into you that may defile the temple of God. Let the faintest warning of the Holy Spirit be law to you. It was a holy mystery that the presence of the Lord was especially within the veil of the tabernacle and that the Lord God spoke by *"the Urim and the Thummim"* (Exod. 28:30) to His people. It is an equally sacred marvel that the Holy Spirit now dwells in our spirits, abides within our nature, and speaks to us what He hears of the Father.

By divine impressions that the opened ear can comprehend and the tender heart can receive, He continues to speak. May God help us to know His *"still small voice"* (1 Kings 19:12) so as to listen to it with reverent humility and loving joy. Then, we will know the meaning of the words, *"I will put My Spirit within you."*

A Spiritual Word

It is also a very spiritual word. *"I will put My Spirit within you"* has nothing to do with our wearing a peculiar garb; that would be a matter of little worth. It has nothing to do with affectations of speech; those might readily become a deceptive peculiarity. Our text has nothing to do with outward rites and ceremonies either, but it goes much further and deeper. It is an instructive symbol when the Lord teaches us our deaths with Christ by burial in baptism (Rom. 6:4). It is also to our great profit that He ordains bread and wine to be tokens of our communion with Him in the body and blood of His dear Son (Luke 22:19–20). However, these are only outward things, and if they are unattended by the Holy Spirit, they fail to achieve the purpose of their design.

There is something infinitely greater in this promise, *"I will put My Spirit within you."* I cannot give you the whole force of the Hebrew words meaning *"within you,"* unless I paraphrase them a little.

This paraphrase reads, "I will put My Spirit in the midst of you." The sacred deposit is put deep down into our life's secret place. God does not put His Spirit on the surface of the man, but He puts Him into the center of his being. The promise means, "I will put My Spirit in your hearts, in the very core of you." This is an intensely spiritual matter, without anything material and visible being mixed in it. It is spiritual, you see, because it is the Spirit who is given, and He is given internally—within our spirits.

An Effectual Word

Observe once more that this word is a very effectual one. *"I will put My Spirit within you and cause you to walk in My statutes, and you will keep My judgments and do them."* The Spirit is operative. First, He is operative on the inner life in that He causes you to love the law of the Lord. Then, He moves you openly to keep His statutes concerning Himself and His judgments between you and your fellowman. If a man is whipped into obedience, it is of little worth, but when obedience springs out of a life within, it is a priceless breastplate of jewels. If you have a lantern, you cannot make it shine by polishing the glass outside. You must put a candle within it, and this is what God does.

He puts the light of the Spirit within us, and then, our light shines. He puts His Spirit so deep down in the heart that the whole nature feels it, and it works upward like a spring from the bottom of a well. Moreover, it is so deeply implanted that there is no removing it. If it were in the memory, you might forget it. If it were in the intellect, you might err in it, but within you it touches the whole man and has dominion over you without fear of failure.

When the very kernel of your nature is quickened into holiness, practical godliness is adequately secured. Blessed is he who knows by experience our Lord's words, *"The water that I shall give him will become in him a fountain of water springing up into everlasting life"* (John 4:14).

Quickening

Let me show you how the good Spirit manifests the fact that He dwells in men. Quickening is one of the first effects of the Spirit of God being put within us. We are dead by nature to all heavenly and spiritual things, but when the Spirit of God comes, we begin to live. The man visited of the Spirit begins to feel. The terrors of God make him tremble; the love of Christ makes him weep. He begins to fear, and he begins to hope: a great deal of the first and a very little of the second, it may be. He learns spiritually to sorrow. He is grieved that he has sinned and that he cannot cease from sinning. He begins to desire what once he despised, especially desiring to find the way of pardon and reconciliation with God.

I cannot make you feel. I cannot make you sorrow because of your sin, and I cannot make you desire eternal life. However, it is all done as soon as this is fulfilled by the Lord: *"I will put My Spirit within you."* The quickening Spirit brings life to those dead in trespasses and sins. This life of the Spirit shows itself by causing the man to pray.

The cry is the distinctive mark of the living child. He begins to cry in broken words, *"God, be merciful to me a sinner!"* (Luke 18:13). At the same time that he pleads, he feels the soft relentings of repentance. He has a new mind toward sin, and he grieves that he should have grieved his God. With this comes faith, perhaps feeble and trembling, only a touch of the hem of the Savior's robe, but still, Jesus is his only hope and his sole trust. To Him he looks for pardon and salvation. He dares to believe that Christ can save even him. Life comes into the soul when trust in Jesus springs up in the heart.

Remember, just as the Holy Spirit gives quickening at first, He must also revive and strengthen it. Whenever you become dull and faint, cry for the Holy Spirit. Whenever you cannot feel as devoted as you wish to feel and you are unable to rise to any heights of communion with God, plead our Scripture in faith, and beg the Lord to do as He has said: *"I will put My Spirit within you."* Go to God with this covenant clause, even if you have to confess, "Lord, I am like a log. I am a helpless lump of weakness. Unless You come and quicken me, I cannot live for You." Plead persistently the promise, *"I will put My Spirit within you."*

All that the life of the flesh will produce is corruption. All of the energy that comes from mere excitement will die down into the black ashes of disappointment. The Holy Spirit alone is the life of the regenerated heart.

Do you have the Spirit? If you do have Him within you, do you have only a small measure of His life? Do you wish for more? Then, go to where you went at first. There is only one river of the water of life; draw from its floods. You will be lively enough, bright enough, strong enough, and happy enough when the Holy Spirit is mighty within your soul.

Enlightening

When the Holy Spirit enters, after quickening, He gives enlightening. We cannot make men see the truth. They are so blind, but when the Lord puts His Spirit within them, their eyes are opened. At first, they may see rather hazily, but they do see. As the light increases and the eyes are strengthened, they see more and more clearly. What a mercy it is to see Christ, to look to Him, and to be enlightened. By the Spirit, souls see things in their reality. They see the actual truth of them and perceive that they are facts. The Spirit of God illuminates every believer and enables believers to see even more marvelous things out of God's law. However, this never happens unless the Spirit opens the eyes. The apostle speaks of being brought *"out of darkness into His marvelous light"* (1 Pet. 2:9).

It is a marvelous light that comes to the blind and dead. It is marvelous because it reveals truth with clearness. When you get into a puzzle over the Word of the Lord, do not give up in despair, but in faith cry, "Lord, put your Spirit within me." Here lies the only true light of the soul.

Conviction

The Spirit also works conviction. Conviction is more persuasive than illumination. It is the setting of a truth before the eye of the soul so as to make it powerful on the conscience. I have spoken to many who know what conviction means, yet I will explain it from my own experience.

From my reading, I knew what sin meant. Yet I never knew sin in its heinousness and horror until I found myself bitten by it as by a fiery serpent. I felt its poison boiling in my veins. When the Holy Spirit made sin appear as sin to me, I was overwhelmed by the sight. I would rather have fled from myself to escape the intolerable vision. A naked sin that is stripped of all excuse and set in the light of truth is worse to see than the Devil himself.

When I saw sin as an offense against a just and holy God, committed by such a proud and yet insignificant creature as myself, I was alarmed. Did you ever see and feel yourself to be a sinner? "Oh, yes," you say, "we are sinners." Do you mean it? Do you know what it means? Many of you are no more sinners in your own estimation than you are barbarians. The beggar who exhibits a fake sore does not know disease. If he did, he would have enough of it without pretenses.

To kneel down and say, "Lord, have mercy on us miserable sinners," and then, to get up and feel yourself a very decent sort of person, worthy of commendation, is to mock almighty God. It is by no means a common thing to get hold of a real sinner, one who is truly so in his own esteem. However, it is as pleasant as it is rare, for you can bring to the real sinner the real Savior, and He will welcome him. I do not wonder that Hart said, "A sinner is a sacred thing. The Holy Spirit has made him so."

The point of contact between a sinner and Christ is sin. The Lord Jesus gave Himself for our sins. He never gave Himself for our righteousness. He comes to heal the sick, and the point He looks to is our sickness. No one ever knows sin as his own personal ruin until the Holy Spirit shows it to him. Conviction regarding the Lord Jesus comes in the same way. We do not know Christ as our Savior until the Holy Spirit is put within us. Our Lord says, *"He will take of what is Mine and declare it to you"* (John 16:14). You never see the things of the Lord Jesus until the Holy Spirit shows them to you.

To know Jesus Christ as your Savior, as one who died for you in particular, is a knowledge that only the Holy Spirit imparts. Comprehending present salvation personally as your own comes by your being convinced of it by the Spirit. Oh, to be convinced of righteousness and acceptance in the Beloved (Eph. 1:6). This conviction comes only from Him who has called you, even from Him of whom the Lord says, *"I will put My Spirit within you."*

Purification

Furthermore, the Holy Spirit comes into us for purification. *"I will put My Spirit within you and cause you to walk in My statutes, and you will keep My judgments and do them."* When the Spirit comes, He infuses a new life, and that new life is a fountain of holiness. The new nature cannot sin because it is born of God, and it is a living and incorruptible seed (1 Pet. 1:23). The Holy Spirit is the life of holiness. This life produces good fruit, and good fruit only.

At the same time, the coming of the Holy Spirit into the soul gives a mortal stab to the power of sin. The *"old man"* (Rom. 6:6) is not absolutely dead, but it is crucified with Christ. It is under sentence, and before the eye of the law, it is dead. As a man nailed to a cross may linger long but cannot live, so the power of evil dies hard, but it must die. Sin is an executed criminal. Those nails that fasten it to the cross will hold it until no breath remains in it. God the Holy Spirit gives the power of sin its death wound. The old nature struggles in its dying agonies, but it is doomed, and it must die.

You will never overcome sin by your own power or by any energy other than that of the Holy Spirit. Resolves may bind it, as Samson was bound with cords, but sin will snap the cords in half. The Holy Spirit lays the ax at the root of sin, and it must fall. The Holy Spirit within a man is *"the spirit of judgment and...the spirit of burning"* (Isa. 4:4). Do you know Him in that character?

As the Spirit of judgment, the Holy Spirit pronounces sentence on sin, and it goes out with the brand of Cain on it. He does more. He delivers sin over to burning. He executes the death penalty on what He has judged. How many of our sins have we had to burn alive! It has cost us no small pain to do it. Sin must be taken out of us by fire if no gentler means will serve, and the Spirit of God is a consuming fire. Truly, *"our God is a consuming fire"* (Heb. 12:29).

Some paraphrase this verse as, "God out of Christ is a consuming fire," but that is not Scripture. It is, *"our God,"* our covenant God, who is a consuming fire to refine us from sin. Has the Lord not said, *"I will...thoroughly purge away your dross, and take away all your* [sin]*"* (Isa. 1:25)? This is what the Spirit does, and it is by no means easy work for the flesh, which would spare many flattering sins if it could.

The Holy Spirit wets the soul with purity until He saturates it. Oh, to have a heart saturated with holy influences until it is as Gideon's fleece, which held so much dew that Gideon could wring out a bowlful from it. (See Judges 6:36–38.) Oh, if only our whole natures were filled with the Spirit of God, and we were sanctified wholly—body, soul, and spirit. Sanctification is the result of the Holy Spirit being put within us.

Preservation

The Holy Spirit also acts in the heart as the Spirit of preservation. Where He dwells, men do not go back into ruin. He works in them a watchfulness against temptation day by day. He helps them to wrestle against sin. A believer would rather die ten thousand deaths than sin. He works in a believer's union to Christ, which is the source and guarantee of acceptable fruitfulness. He creates in the saints those holy things that glorify God and bless the sons of men.

All true fruit is the *"fruit of the Spirit"* (Gal. 5:22). Every true prayer must be *"praying in the Holy Spirit"* (Jude 20). He helps our weaknesses in prayer (Rom. 8:26). Even the hearing of the Word of the Lord is of the Spirit, for John says, *"I was in the Spirit on the Lord's Day, and I heard behind me a loud voice"* (Rev. 1:10). Everything that comes of the man or is kept alive in the man is first infused and then sustained and perfected by the Spirit. *"It is the Spirit who gives life; the flesh profits nothing"* (John 6:63).

We never go an inch toward heaven in any other power than that of the Holy Spirit. We do not even stand fast and remain steadfast except as we are upheld by the Holy Spirit. The vineyard that the Lord has planted, He also preserves. As it is written, *"I, the LORD, keep it, I water it every moment; lest any hurt it, I keep it night and day"* (Isa. 27:3). Did I hear that young man say, "I would like to become a Christian, but I fear I could not hold out? How am I to be preserved?" This is a very proper inquiry, for *"he who endures to the end will be saved"* (Matt. 10:22).

Temporary Christians are no Christians. Only the believer who continues to believe will enter heaven. How, then, can we hold on in such a world as this? Here is the answer. *"I will put My Spirit within you."* When a city has been captured in war, those who formerly possessed it seek to win it back again, but the king who captured it sends an army to live within the walls. He says to the captain, "Take care of this city that I have conquered, and do not let the enemy take it again." Likewise, the Holy Spirit is the army of God within our redeemed humanity, and He will keep us to the end. *"The peace of God, which surpasses all understanding, will guard your hearts and minds through Christ Jesus"* (Phil. 4:7). For preservation, then, we look to the Holy Spirit.

Guidance

The Holy Spirit is also within us for guidance. The Holy Spirit is given to lead us into all truth (John 16:13). Truth is like a vast cave, and the Holy Spirit brings torches and shows us all the splendor of the roof. Since the passage seems intricate, He knows the way, and He leads us into the deep things of God. He opens up to us one truth after another by His light and His guidance. Thus, we are *"taught by the LORD"* (Isa. 54:13).

He is also our practical guide to heaven, helping and directing us on the upward journey. I wish Christian people would more often inquire of the Holy Spirit as to guidance in their daily lives. Do you not know that the Spirit of God dwells within you? You need not always be running to this friend and to that to get direction. Wait on the Lord in silence. Sit still in quiet before the revelation of God. Use the judgment God has given you, but when that does not suffice, resort to Him whom Bunyan calls "the Lord High Secretary," who lives within, who is infinitely wise, and who can guide you by making you to *"hear a word behind you, saying, 'This is the way, walk in it'"* (Isa. 30:21).

The Holy Spirit will guide you in life, He will guide you in death, and He will guide you to glory. He will guard you from modern error and from ancient error, too. He will guide you in ways that you do not know. Through the darkness, He will lead you in a way you have not seen. These things He will do for you, and He will not forsake you.

Oh, this precious Scripture. I seem to have before me a great cabinet full of jewels, rich and rare. May the Holy Spirit Himself come and hand these out to you, and may you be adorned with them all the days of your life.

Consolation

Finally, *"I will put My Spirit within you"* is by way of consolation, for His choice name is "The Comforter." Our God would not have His children unhappy; therefore, He Himself in the third person of the blessed Trinity has undertaken the office of Comforter.

Why does your face wear such a mournful expression? God can comfort you. You who are under the burden of sin, it is true no man can help you into peace, but the Holy Spirit can. God, grant Your Holy Spirit to every seeker who has failed to find rest. Put Your Spirit within him, and he will rest in Jesus. And you, dear people of God, who are worried, remember that worry and the Holy Spirit are very contradictory one to another. *"I will put My Spirit within you"* means that you will become gentle, peaceful, submitted, and acquiescent in the divine will. Then, you will have faith in God that all is well. David says, *"God my exceeding joy"* (Ps. 43:4), and such He is to us. "Yes, mine own God is He."

Can you say, "My God, my God"? Do you want anything more? Can you conceive of anything beyond your God? Omnipotent to work all forever! Infinite to give! Faithful to remember! All that is good! He is light only, for *"in Him is no darkness at all"* (1 John 1:5). I have all light, yes, all things, when I have my God. The Holy Spirit makes us comprehend this when He is put within us.

Holy Comforter, abide with us, for then, we enjoy the light of heaven. Then, we are always peaceful and even joyful, for we walk in unclouded light. In Him our happiness sometimes rises into great waves of delight as if it leaped up to the glory. The Lord wants to make this Scripture your own, *"I will put My Spirit within you."*

Chapter 6

Honey in the Mouth

He will glorify Me, for He will take of what is Mine and declare it to you. All things that the Father has are Mine. Therefore I said that He will take of Mine and declare it to you. A little while, and you will not see Me; and again a little while, and you will see Me, because I go to the Father.
—John 16:14–16

Here you have the Trinity, and there is no salvation apart from the Trinity. It must be the Father, the Son, and the Holy Spirit. *"All things that the Father has are Mine,"* says Christ, and the Father has all things. They were always His, are still His, always will be His, and they cannot become ours until they change ownership, until Christ can say, *"All things that the Father has are Mine."*

It is by virtue of the representative character of Christ standing as the Surety of the Covenant that the *"all things"* of the Father are passed over to the Son and that they might be passed over to us. *"For it pleased the Father that in Him all the fullness should dwell"* (Col. 1:19). *"And of His fullness we have all received"* (John 1:16). But yet, we are so dull that even though the conduit is laid to the great fountain, we cannot get at it. We are lame. We cannot reach there. In comes the third person of the divine Unity, the Holy Spirit, and He receives of the things of Christ and then delivers them over to us. So we do actually receive through Jesus Christ, by the Spirit, what is in the Father.

Ralph Erskine, in his preface to a sermon on John 16:15, has a notable piece. He speaks of grace as honey for the cheering of the saints, for the sweetening of their mouths and hearts. He says that in the Father,

The honey is in the flower, which is at such a distance from us that we could never extract it. [In the Son] the honey is in the comb, prepared for us in our Emmanuel, God-Man, Redeemer, the Word that was made flesh, saying, "'*All things that the Father has are Mine*'—Mine for your use and profit": it is in the comb. But then, next, we have honey in the mouth; the Spirit taking all things, and making application thereof, by showing them unto us, and making us to eat and drink with Christ, and share of these *"all things"*; yea, not only eat the honey, but the honeycomb with the honey; not only His benefits, but Himself.

It is a very beautiful division of the subject. Honey is in the flower in God, as is mystery—really there. There never will be any more honey than there is in the flower. There it is. But how will you and I get at it? We do not have the wisdom to extract the sweetness. We are not like the bees that are able to find it.

Yet you see in Christ it becomes the honey in the honeycomb, and He is sweet to our taste as honey dropping from the comb. Sometimes we are so faint that we cannot reach out a hand to grasp that honeycomb. There was a time when our palates were so depraved that we preferred bitter things and thought them sweet.

Now that the Holy Spirit has come, we have the honey in our mouths and the taste that can enjoy it. Yes, we have now enjoyed it so long that the honey of grace has entered into our constitution, and we have become sweet unto God. His sweetness has been conveyed to us by this strange method.

I scarcely need to remind you to keep the existence of the Trinity prominent in your life. Remember, you cannot pray without the Trinity. If the full work of salvation requires a Trinity, so does that very breath by which we live. You cannot draw near to the Father except through the Son and by the Holy Spirit. There is a trinity in nature undoubtedly. Certainly the need of a Trinity in the realm of grace constantly turns up. When we get to heaven, we will understand, perhaps, more fully what is meant by the Trinity in unity. But if that is a thing never to be understood, we will at least comprehend it more lovingly.

We will rejoice more completely as the three tones of our music rise in perfect harmony to Him who is One and Indivisible and yet is Three—the forever blessed Father, Son, and Holy Spirit—one God.

I cannot reveal the following point to you; He must do it. We must have the Scripture acted out upon ourselves. *"He will glorify Me, for He will take of what is Mine and declare it to you."* May it be so just now.

What the Holy Spirit Does

"He will take of what is Mine and declare it to you." It is clear that the Holy Spirit deals with the things of Christ. Do not let us strain at anything new. The Holy Spirit could deal with anything in heaven above or in the earth beneath: the story of the ages past, the story of the ages to come, the inward secrets of the earth, and the evolution of all things, if there is an evolution. He could do it all.

Like the Master, the Holy Spirit could handle any topic He choses, but He confines Himself to the things of Christ and therein finds unutterable liberty and boundless freedom.

The Holy Spirit still exists and works and teaches in the church. However, we have a test by which to know whether what people claim to be revelation is revelation or not: *"He will take of what is Mine."* The Holy Spirit will never go farther than the Cross and the coming of the Lord. He will go no farther than what concerns Christ. *"He will take of what is Mine."* His one vocation is to deal with the things of Christ. If we do not remember this, we may be carried away by capricious ideas, as many have been.

When a minister has spent all Sunday morning whittling away a Scripture to the small end of nothing, what has he done? Here is a minister who professes to have been called by the Holy Spirit to the job of taking of the things of Christ. A whole morning was spent with precious souls who were dying while he spoke to them, handling a theme that was not in the least relevant to the needs of his hearers.

Oh, imitate the Holy Spirit. If you profess to have Him dwelling in you, be moved by Him. Let it be said of you in your measure, as of the Holy Spirit without measure, *"He will take of what is Mine and declare it to you."*

But, next, what does the Holy Spirit do? Why, He deals with feeble men. Yes, He dwells with us poor creatures. I can understand the Holy Spirit taking the things of Christ and rejoicing in them, but the marvel is that He should glorify Christ by coming and showing these things to us. And yet, it is among us that Christ is to receive His glory. Our eyes must see Him. An unseen Christ is not very glorious, and the unknown things of Christ, the untasted and unloved things of Christ seem to have lost their brilliance to a high degree.

The Holy Spirit, therefore, feeling that to show a sinner the salvation of Christ glorifies Him, spends His time—and has been spending these centuries—in taking of the things of Christ and showing them to us. It is a great condescension on His part to show them to us, but it is a miracle, too.

If it were reported that suddenly stones had life, hills had eyes, and trees had ears, it would be a strange thing. However, for us who were dead and blind and deaf in an awful sense (for the spiritual is more emphatic than the natural), for us to be so far gone and for the Holy Spirit to be able to show the things of Christ to us is to His honor. But He does do it. He comes from heaven to dwell with us. Let us honor and bless His name.

I never could make up my mind which to admire most as an act of condescension: the incarnation of Christ or the indwelling of the Holy Spirit. The incarnation of Christ is marvelous in that He should dwell in human nature. Observe that the Holy Spirit dwells in human nature in its sinfulness, not in perfect human nature, but in imperfect human nature. He continues to dwell, not in one body that was fashioned strangely for Himself and was pure and without taint, but He dwells in our bodies. *"Do you not know that your body is the temple of the Holy Spirit who is in you?"* (1 Cor. 6:19). In addition, this He has done these multitudes of years, not in one instance nor in thousands of instances only, but in a number that no man can count.

He continues to come into contact with sinful humanity. He does not show the things of Christ to the angels or to the seraphim, to the cherubim or to the host who have washed their robes and made them white in the blood of the Lamb, but He will show them to us.

He takes of the words of our Lord—those that Christ spoke personally and those that Christ spoke by His apostles. Let us never allow anybody to divide between the Word of the apostles and the Word of Christ. Our Savior has joined them together: *"I do not pray for these alone, but also for those who will believe in Me through their word"* (John 17:20).

If any begin rejecting the apostolic Word, they will be outside the number for whom Christ prays. They shut themselves out by that very fact. I wish that they would solemnly recollect that the Word of the apostles is the Word of Christ. He did not tarry long enough after He had risen from the dead to give us a further exposition of His mind and will, and He could not have given it before

His death because it would have been unsuitable. *"I still have many things to say to you, but you cannot bear them now"* (John 16:12).

After the descent of the Holy Spirit, the disciples were prepared to receive what Christ spoke by His servants Paul, Peter, James, and John. Certain doctrines that we are sometimes taunted about as not being revealed by Christ but by His apostles were all revealed by Christ, every one of them. They can all be found in His teaching, but they are very much in parable form. It was after He had gone up into glory and had prepared a people by His Spirit to understand the truth more fully that He sent His apostles. He said, "Go, and open up to those whom I have chosen out of the world the meaning of all I said." (See Matthew 28:18–20.) The meaning is all there, just as all the New Testament is in the Old.

The words of the Lord Jesus and the words of His apostles are to be explained to us by the Holy Spirit. We will never get at the center of their meaning apart from His teaching. We will never get at their meaning at all if we begin disputing the words, saying, "Now, I cannot accept the words." If you will not have the shell, you will never have the chick. It is impossible.

"The words are not inspired," some say. If we have no inspiration in the words, we have got an intangible inspiration that oozes away between our fingers and leaves nothing behind. We must go and say,

> Great Master, we thank You for the Book with all our hearts, and we thank You for putting the Book into words. But now, good Master, we will not quibble over the letter, as did the Jews and the rabbis and the scribes of old and so miss Your meaning. Open wide the door of the words that we may enter into the secret closet of the meaning, and teach us this, we pray You. You have the key. Lead us in.

Dear friends, whenever you want to understand a text of Scripture, try to read the original. Consult anybody who has studied what the original means, but remember that the quickest way into a text is praying in the Holy Spirit. Pray the chapter over. I do not hesitate to say that if a chapter is read on one's knees, looking up at every word to Him who gave it, the meaning will come to you with infinitely more light than by any other method of studying it. *"He will glorify Me, for He will take of what is Mine and declare it to you."*

He will redeliver the Master's message to you in the fullness of its meaning, but I do not think that is all that the text means. *"He will take of what is Mine."* In the next verse, the Lord goes on to say, *"All things that the Father has are Mine."* I do think that it means, therefore, that the Holy Spirit will show us the things of Christ.

Christ speaks as if He did not have any things just then that were especially His own, for He had not died, nor had He risen. He was not pleading then as the great Intercessor in heaven. All of that was to come. But still, He says, "Even now, all things that the Father has are mine: all His attributes, all His glory, all His rest, all His happiness, all His blessedness. All *that* is mine, and the Holy Spirit will show that to you."

But I almost might read my text in another light, for He has died, risen, gone on high, and yes—He is coming again. His chariots are on the way. Now, there are certain things that the Father has and that Jesus Christ has that are truly the things of Christ, emphatically the things of Christ. My prayer is that all preachers of the Gospel might have this Scripture fulfilled in them, *"He will take of what is Mine and declare it to you."*

Suppose that we are going to preach the Word soon, and the Holy Spirit reveals to us our Master in His Godhead. Oh, how we would preach Him as divine. How surely He can bless our congregations! How certainly He must be able to subdue all things unto Himself, seeing that He is very God of very God!

It is equally sweet to see Christ as man. Oh, to have the Spirit's view of Christ's manhood! May I distinctly be able to recognize that He is bone of my bone and flesh of my flesh; that in His infinite tenderness He will pity me and deal with my poor people and with the troubled consciences that are around me; and that I have still to go to them and tell them of the One who is touched with the feeling of their infirmities, having been tempted in all points just as they still are (Heb. 4:15)! Oh, if we once, no, if every time before we preach, we could get a view of Christ in His divine and human natures and come down fresh from that vision to speak about Him, what glorious preaching it would be for our people!

It is a glorious thing to get a view of the offices of Christ by the Holy Spirit, but especially of His office as the Savior. I have often prayed to Him, "You must save my people. It is no business of mine. I never set up in that line or put over my door that I was a savior, but You have been apprenticed to this trade. You have learned it by experience, and You claim it as Your own honor. You are exalted on high to be a Prince and the Savior. Do Your own work, my Lord."

I took this Scripture and used it during a service, and I know that God blessed it when I said to them, "May the Holy Spirit show you that Christ is the Savior! A physician does not expect you to make any apologies when you call on him because you are ill, for he is a physician, and he wants you to come to him in order that he may prove his skill. Christ is the Savior, and you need not apologize for going to Him because He cannot be the Savior if there is not somebody to be saved."

The fact is, Christ cannot get hold of us anywhere except by our sin. The point of contact between the sick one and the physician is the disease. Our sin is the point of contact between us and Christ. Oh, that the Spirit of God would take of Christ's divine offices, especially that of the Savior, and show them to us!

Did the Holy Spirit ever show you these things of Christ, namely, His covenant engagements? When He struck hands with the Father, it was so that He would bring many sons to glory; it was so that, of those whom the Father gave Him, He would lose none, but they would be saved. He is under bonds to His Father to bring His elect home. When the sheep have to pass again under the hand of Him who counts them, they will go under the rod one by one, each one having the blood-mark. He will never rest until the number in the heavenly fold tallies the number in the Book of Life.

So I believe, and it has been delightful for me to have been shown this when I have gone to preach. On a dull, dreary, wet, foggy morning, only a few are present. Yes, but they are picked people, whom God has ordained to be there, and there will be the right number there.

I preach, and there will be some saved. We do not go at it by chance but guided by the blessed Spirit of God. We go with a living certainty, knowing that God has a people that Christ is bound to bring home, and bring them home He will. While He will see the *"labor of His soul, and be satisfied"* (Isa. 53:11), His Father will delight in every one of them. If you get a clear view of that, it will give you backbone and make you strong. *"'He will take of what is Mine'* and will show you My covenant engagements, and when you see them, you will be comforted."

But the Holy Spirit favors you by taking what is peculiarly Christ's—namely His love—and showing that to you. We have seen it, and we have seen it sometimes more vividly than others. If the full blaze of the Holy Spirit were to be concentrated on the love of

Christ and our eyesight enlarged to its maximum capacity, it would be such a vision that heaven could not exceed it.

We should sit with our Bibles before us in our studies and feel Christ. *"I know a man in Christ who fourteen years ago; whether in the body I do not know, or whether out of the body I do not know, God knows; such a one was caught up to the third heaven"* (2 Cor. 12:2). Oh, to see the love of Christ in the light of the Holy Spirit! When it is so revealed to us, it is not merely the surface that we see but the love of Christ itself.

You know that you have never really seen anything yet, strictly speaking. You see only the appearance of the thing—the light reflected by it. That is all you see, but the Holy Spirit shows us the naked truth and the essence of the love of Christ. That essence shows love without beginning, without change, without limit, and without end. That love is set upon His people simply from motives within Himself and from no outside motive. What must it be, what tongue can tell? Oh, it is a ravishing sight!

I think that if there could be one sight more wonderful than the love of Christ, it would be the blood of Christ.

> Much we talk of Jesu's blood,
> But how little's understood!

It is the climax of God. I do not know of anything more divine. It seems to me as if all the eternal purposes worked up to the blood of the Cross and then worked from the blood of the Cross toward the outstanding consummation of all things.

Oh, to think that He should become man. God has made spirit, pure spirit, embodied spirit, as well as the material. Somehow, as if He would take all up into one, the Godhead links Himself with the material. He wears dust about Him even as we wear it. Taking it all up, He then goes in that fashion and redeems His people from all the evil of their souls, their spirits, and their bodies. He pours out a life that, while it was human, was so in connection with the divine that we speak correctly of "the blood of God."

Turn to the twentieth chapter of Acts, and read how the apostle Paul put it, *"Shepherd the church of God which He purchased with His own blood"* (Acts 20:28). I believe that Dr. Watts is not wrong when he says, "God who loved and died." It is an incorrect accuracy, a strictly absolute accuracy of incorrectness. So it must be whenever the finite talks of the Infinite. It was a wonderful sacrifice that could absolutely obliterate, annihilate, and extinguish sin and all the traces that could possibly remain of it. He has finished the transgression, made an end of sins, made reconciliation for iniquity, and brought in everlasting righteousness (Dan. 9:24).

You have seen this, have you not? But you have to see more of it yet, and when we get to heaven, we will then know what that blood means. With what vigor we will sing, *"To Him who loved us and washed us from our sins in His own blood"* (Rev. 1:5). Will anybody be there to say, "Is not that the religion of the slaughterhouse?" They blasphemously call it this. They will find themselves where they will wish they had believed "the religion of the slaughterhouse." I think that it will burn like coals into the soul of any man who has ever dared to talk like that. He did his own willful deeds in spite of the blood of God, and by these will be cast away forever.

May the Holy Spirit show you Gethsemane, Gabbatha (John 19:13), and Golgotha. Then, may it please Him to give you a sight of what our Lord is now doing. Oh, how it would cheer you up at any time when you were depressed to see Him standing and pleading for you. Do you not think that if your wife were ill, your child were sick, there was scant food in the cupboard, and you were to go out the back door and see Him with the breastplate on, all the stones glittering, your name there, and Him pleading for you, you would not go in and say, "There, wife, it is all right. He is praying for us"? Oh, it would be a comfort if the Holy Spirit showed you a pleading Christ. (See Romans 8:34.)

Then, realize that He is reigning as well as pleading. He is at the right hand of God the Father (Acts 2:33), who *"has put all things under His feet"* (1 Cor. 15:27), and He waits until the last enemy will lie there. Now, you are not afraid, are you, of those who have been snubbing you and opposing you? Remember, He has said, *"All authority has been given to Me in heaven and on earth. Go therefore and make disciples of all the nations...;and lo, I am with you always, even to the end of the age"* (Matt. 28:18–20).

Best of all, may the Holy Spirit give you a clear view of His coming. This is our most brilliant hope, to say, "He is coming." The bolder the Adversary grows, the less faith there is, and when zeal seems almost extinct—these are the tokens of His coming. The Lord always said so and that He would not come unless there was a falling away first (2 Thess. 2:3). So the darker the night grows and the fiercer the storm becomes, the better will we remember that He of the Lake of Galilee came to His disciples on the waves in the night when the storm was wildest. (See Matthew 14:22–39.)

Oh, what will His enemies say when He comes, when they behold the nailprints of the Glorified and the Man with the thorn-crown? When they see Him really come, those who have despised His Word and His ever-blessed blood, how they will flee before that face of injured love.

We, on the contrary, through His infinite mercy, will say, "This is what the Holy Spirit showed us, and now we behold it literally. We thank Him for the foresights that He gave us of the joyful vision."

There is one point that I want you to consider: When the Holy Spirit takes of the things of Christ and shows them to us, He has a purpose in so doing.

It is with you, with regard to the Spirit showing you things, as it was with Jacob. You know Jacob was lying down and went to sleep, and the Lord said to him, *"The land on which you lie I will give to you"* (Gen. 28:13). Wherever you go, throughout the whole of Scripture, if you can find a place where you can lie down, that is yours. If you can sleep on a promise, that promise is yours.

"Lift your eyes now," said God to Abraham, *"and look from the place where you are; northward, southward, eastward, and westward; for all the land which you see I give to you and your descendants forever"* (Gen. 13:14–15). The Lord increases our holy vision of delighted faith, for there is nothing you see that you cannot also enjoy. All that is in Christ is there for you.

The Holy Spirit Comes to Glorify Christ

"He will glorify Me." The Holy Spirit never comes to glorify us, or to glorify a denomination, or, I think, even to glorify a systematic arrangement of doctrines. He comes to glorify Christ. If we want to be in accord with Him, we must minister in a manner that will glorify Christ.

If it is not distinctly my aim to glorify Christ, I am not in accord with the aim of the Holy Spirit, and I cannot expect His help. We would not be pulling the same way. Therefore, I will have nothing of which I cannot say that is said simply, sincerely, and only that I may glorify Christ.

How, then, does the Holy Spirit glorify Christ? It is very beautiful to think that He glorifies Christ by showing Christ's things. If you wanted to do honor to a man, you would perhaps take him a present to decorate his house. But here, if you want to glorify Christ, you must go and take the things out of Christ's house, "the things of Christ."

Whenever we are praising God, what do we do? We simply say what He is. "You are this, and You are that." There is no other praise. We cannot fetch anything from elsewhere and bring it to God, but the praises of God are simply the facts about Himself.

If you want to praise the Lord Jesus Christ, tell the people about Him. Take of the things of Christ, and show them to the people. Thus, you will glorify Christ. Alas, I know what you will do. You will weave words together, and you will form and fashion them in a marvelous manner until you have produced a charming piece of literature. When you have carefully done that, put it in the fire under the oven, and let it burn. Possibly, you may help to bake some bread with it. It is better for us to tell what Christ is than to invent ten thousand fine words of praise in reference to Him. *"He will glorify Me, for He will take of what is Mine and declare it to you."*

Again, I think that the blessed Spirit glorifies Christ by showing us the things of Christ as Christ's. Oh, to be pardoned! Yes, it is a great thing, but to find that pardon in His wounds, that is a greater thing. Oh, to get peace! Yes, but to find that peace in the blood of His Cross. Have the blood-mark very visibly on all your mercies. They are all marked with the blood of the Cross, but sometimes we think so much of the sweetness of the bread or of the coolness of the waters that we forget from where and how they came to be. They lack their choicest flavor.

That it came from Christ is the best thing about the best thing that ever came from Christ. That He saves me is somehow better than my being saved. It is a blessed thing to go to heaven, but I do not know that it is not a better thing to be in Christ and so, as the result of it, to get into heaven.

It is He Himself and what comes from Him that becomes best of all because it comes from Himself. The Holy Spirit will glorify Christ by making us see that these things from Christ are indeed of Christ, completely from Christ, and still in connection with Christ, and we enjoy them only because we are in connection with Christ.

Then, it is said in the text, *"He will glorify Me....He will take of what is Mine and declare it to you."* Yes, it does glorify Christ for the Holy Spirit to show Christ to us. Often I have wished that men of great minds might be converted. I have wished that we could have a few Miltons and like men to sing of the love of Christ, a few mighty men who teach literature and philosophy to devote their talent to the preaching of the Gospel.

Why is it not so? Well, it is because the Holy Spirit does not seem to think that that would be the way to glorify Christ supremely. He prefers, as a better way, to take us commonplace people and to show us the things of Christ. He does glorify Christ. Blessed be His name that ever my bleary eyes should look on His infinite loveliness; that ever such a wretch as I, who can understand everything but what I ought to understand, should be made to comprehend the heights and depths and to know with all saints the love of Christ that passes knowledge (Eph. 3:18–19).

You see that clever boy in school; well, it is not much for the master to have made a scholar of him. But here is one who shines as a scholar, and his mother says that he was the slowest learner in the family. All his schoolfellows say, "Why, he had the hardest time with his lessons! He seemed to have no brains, but our master somehow got some brains into him and made him know something that he appeared, at one time, incapable of knowing." Somehow, it does seem to be as if our very folly, impotence, and spiritual death will go toward the increase of that great glorifying of Christ at which the Holy Spirit aims if the Holy Spirit shows to us the things of Christ.

Then, since it is for the honor of Christ for His things to be shown to men, He will show them to us so that we may go and show them to other people. This we cannot do except when He is with us to make the others see. But He will be with us while we tell what He has taught us, and the Holy Spirit will really be showing to others while He is showing to us. A secondary influence will flow from this service, for we will be helped to use the right means to make others see the things of Christ.

The Comforter

It is the Comforter who does this, and we will find our richest, surest comfort in this work of the Holy Spirit who will take of the things of Christ and show them unto us.

First, He does so because there is no comfort in the world like seeing Christ. He shows us the things of Christ. Oh, if you are poor and if the Holy Spirit shows you that Christ had no where to lay

His head, what a sight for you. If you are sick and the Holy Spirit shows you what sufferings Christ endured, what comfort comes to you. If you are made to see the things of Christ, each thing according to the condition that you are in, how speedily you are delivered out of your sorrow.

If the Holy Spirit glorifies Christ, that is the cure for every kind of sorrow. He is the Comforter. Many years ago, after the terrible accident in the Surrey Gardens, I had to go away into the country and keep quite still. The very sight of the Bible made me cry. I could only stay alone in the garden, and I was heavyhearted and sad. People had been killed in the accident, and there I was, half-dead myself.

I remember how I got back my comfort, and I preached on the Sunday after I recovered. I had been walking around the garden, and I was standing under a tree. If it is there now, I would know it. There I remembered these words: *"Him God has exalted to His right hand to be Prince and Savior"* (Acts 5:31). "Oh," I thought to myself, "I am only a common soldier. If I die in a ditch, I do not care. The King is honored. He wins the victory."

I was like those French soldiers in the old times who loved the emperor; and you know how, when they were dying, if the emperor rode by, the wounded man would raise himself up on his elbow and cry once more, *Vive l'Empereur!* The emperor was engraved on his heart. And so, I am sure, it is with every one of you, my comrades, in this holy war. If our Lord and King is exalted, then, let other things go whichever way they like. If He is exalted, never mind what becomes of us.

We are but pygmies, and it is all right if He is exalted. God's truth is safe, and we must be perfectly willing to be forgotten, derided, slandered, or anything else that men please. The cause is safe, and the King is on the throne. Hallelujah! Blessed be His name!

Book Six

The Second Coming of Christ

Contents

Chapter 1

He Is Coming with Clouds

Behold, He is coming with clouds, and every eye will see Him, even
they who pierced Him. And all the tribes of the earth will mourn
because of Him. Even so, Amen.
—Revelation 1:7

In reading the entire first chapter of Revelation, we observe how
the beloved John saluted the seven churches in Asia with,
"Grace to you and peace" (v. 4). Blessed men scatter blessings.
When the benediction of God rests on us, we pour out benedictions
on others.

From this blessing, John's gracious heart rose into adoration
of the great King of Kings. As the hymn puts it, "The holy to the
holiest lead." Those who are good at blessing men will be quick at
blessing God.

It is a wonderful doxology that John has given us: *"To Him*
who loved us and washed us from our sins in His own blood, and
has made us kings and priests to His God and Father, to Him be
glory and dominion forever and ever. Amen" (Rev. 1:5–6). I like the
alliteration of the fifth verse in the Revised Version: *"Unto him*
that loveth us, and loosed us from our sins by his blood." Truly our
Redeemer has loosed us from sin, but the mention of His blood
suggests washing rather than loosing. We can keep the alliteration
and yet retain the meaning of cleansing if we read the passage, *"To*
Him who loved us and [laved, which means washed] *us." Loved* us
and *laved* us—carry those two words with you. Let them lie on your
tongue to sweeten your breath for prayer and praise. *"To Him who*
loved us and [laved] *us...be glory and dominion forever and ever."*

Then, John told of the dignity that the Lord has put upon us in
making us kings and priests, and from this he ascribed royalty and
dominion to the Lord Himself. John had been extolling the great
King, whom he called *"the ruler over the kings of the earth"* (v. 5).

Such indeed He *"was and is and is to come!"* (Rev. 4:8). When John had touched upon that royalty that is natural to our divine Lord, and that dominion that has come to Him by conquest and by the gift of the Father as the reward of all His travail, he then went on to note that Christ has *"made us kings"* (Rev. 5:10). Our Lord diffuses His royalty among His redeemed.

We praise Him because He is in Himself a king, and next, because He is a kingmaker, the fountain of honor and majesty. He has enough of royalty for Himself, but also He hands a measure of His dignity to His people. He makes kings out of such common stuff as He finds in us poor sinners. Will we not adore Him for this? Will we not *"cast* [our] *crowns"* (Rev. 4:10) at His feet? He gave our crowns to us; will we not give them back to Him?

"To Him be glory and dominion forever and ever. Amen" (Rev. 1:6). King by divine nature! King by filial right! Kingmaker, lifting up the beggar from the dunghill to set him among princes! King of Kings by the unanimous love of all your crowned ones! *"You are he whom your brothers shall praise"* (Gen. 49:8)! Reign forever! To You be hosannas of welcome and hallelujahs of praise. Lord of heaven and earth, let all things that are, or ever will be, give to You all glory in the highest.

Beloved, do your souls not catch fire as you think of the praises of Immanuel? Gladly I would fill the universe with His praises. "Oh, for a thousand tongues to sing" the glories of the Lord Jesus! If the Spirit who dictated the words of John has taken possession of our spirits, we will find adoration to be our highest delight. Never are we so near to heaven as when we are absorbed in the worship of Jesus, our Lord and God. Oh, that I could now adore Him as I will do when, delivered from this encumbering body, my soul will behold Him in the fullness of His glory!

It would seem that John's adoration was increased by his expectation of the Lord's Second Coming, because he cries, *"Behold, He is coming with clouds."* John's adoration awoke his expectation, which all the while was lying in his soul as an element of the vehement heat of reverent love that he poured forth in his doxology. *"Behold, He is coming,"* he said, and thus he revealed one source of his reverence. *"Behold, He is coming,"* and this exclamation was the result of his reverence. He adored until his faith realized his Lord and became a second and nobler sight.

I think, too, that his reverence was deepened and his adoration was made more fervent by his conviction of the speediness of his

Lord's coming. *"Behold, He is coming."* John meant to assert that He is even now on His way. As workmen are moved to be more diligent in service when they hear their master's footfall, so saints are undoubtedly quickened in their devotion when they are conscious that He whom they worship is drawing near. He has gone away to the Father for a while, and so He has left us alone in this world; but He has said, *"I will come again and receive you to Myself"* (John 14:3). We are confident that He will keep His word. Sweet is the remembrance of that loving promise.

That assurance was pouring its savor into John's heart while he was adoring. It became inevitable, as well as most right and proper, that his doxology at its close would have introduced him to the Lord Himself and caused him to cry out, *"Behold, He is coming."* Having worshiped among the pure in heart, he saw the Lord. Having adored the King, he saw Him assume the judgment seat and appear in the clouds of heaven.

When once we enter upon heavenly things, we do not know how far we can go or how high we can climb. John, who began with blessing the churches, now beholds his Lord. May the Holy Spirit help us to think reverently of the wondrous coming of our blessed Lord, when He will appear to the delight of His people and the dismay of the ungodly!

I would like to glean three points from the text. They will seem unremarkable to some of you. Indeed, they are the commonplace of our divine faith, yet nothing can be of greater importance. The first is that our Lord Jesus is coming: *"Behold, He is coming with clouds."* The second is that Christ's coming will be seen by all: *"Every eye will see Him, even they who pierced Him."* Finally, this coming will cause great sorrow: *"All the tribes of the earth will mourn because of Him."*

The Lord Jesus Christ Is Coming Again

May the Holy Spirit help us as we remember that our Lord Jesus Christ is coming! This announcement is thought worthy of a note of admiration. *"Behold, He is coming."* As in the old books the printers put hands in the margin pointing to special passages, such is this *"Behold."* It is a nota bene, calling on us to "note well" what we are reading. Here is something that we are to hold and behold. We now hear a voice crying, "Come and see!" The Holy Spirit never uses superfluous words or redundant notes of exclamation; when

He cries, *"Behold,"* it is because there is reason for deep and lasting attention.

Will you turn away when He bids you pause and ponder, linger and look? You who have been beholding vanity, come and behold the fact that Jesus comes. You who have been beholding this and looking at that and thinking of nothing worthwhile, forget these passing sights and spectacles, and for once behold a scene that has no parallel. It is not a monarch in her jubilee, but the King of Kings in His glory. *"This same Jesus"* (Acts 1:11) who went up from Olivet into heaven is coming again to earth *"in like manner"* (v. 11) as His disciples saw Him go up into heaven. Come and behold this great sight. If ever there were a thing in the world worth looking at, it is this. Behold! See if there was ever glory like His glory!

Listen to the midnight cry, *"Behold, the bridegroom is coming!"* (Matt. 25:6). It has practical implications for you. *"Go out to meet him!"* (v. 6). This voice is to you, O sons of men. Do not carelessly turn aside, for the Lord God Himself demands your attention. He commands you to *"Behold."* Will you be blind when God bids you to see? Will you shut your eyes when your Savior cries, *"Behold"*? When the finger of inspiration points the way, will your eyes follow where it directs you? *"Behold, He is coming."* O beloved, look here, I implore you.

A Vivid Realization

If we read our text carefully, this *"Behold"* shows us first that this coming is to be vividly realized. I imagine I see John. He is in the Spirit, but suddenly he seems startled into a keener and more solemn attention. His mind is more awake than usual, though he was always a man of bright eyes that saw afar. (We compare him to the eagle for the height of his flight and the keenness of his vision.) Yet all of a sudden, even he seems startled with a more astounding vision. He cries out, "Behold! Behold!" He has caught sight of his Lord. He does not say, "He will come by and by," but "I can see Him; He is coming now." He had evidently realized the Second Advent. He had so conceived of the Second Coming of the Lord that it had become a matter of fact to him, a matter to be spoken of and even to be written down. *"Behold, He is coming."*

Have you and I ever realized the coming of Christ so fully as this? Perhaps we believe that He will come. I hope that we all do. If we believe that the Lord Jesus has come the first time, we believe also that He will come the second time. But are these equally assured truths to us? Perhaps we have vividly realized the first appearing from Bethlehem to Golgotha, and we have traced the Lord from Calvary to Olivet, understanding that blessed cry, *"Behold! The Lamb of God who takes away the sin of the world!"* (John 1:29). Yes, *"the Word became flesh and dwelt among us, and we beheld His glory, the glory as of the only begotten of the Father, full of grace and truth"* (v. 14). But have we with equal firmness grasped the thought that *"He will appear a second time, apart from sin, for salvation"* (Heb. 9:28)? Do we now say to each other when we gather in happy fellowship, "Yes, our Lord is coming"?

His coming should be to us not only a prophecy assuredly believed among us, but a scene that is pictured in our souls and anticipated in our hearts. My imagination has often set forth that awesome scene; but better still, my faith has realized it. I have heard the chariot wheels of the Lord's approach, and I have endeavored to set my house in order for His reception. I have felt the shadow of the great cloud that will attend Him diminishing my love for worldly things. I hear even now in my spirit the sound of the last trumpet, whose tremendous blast startles my soul to serious action and brings purpose to my life. I pray to God that I would live more completely under the influence of that grand event!

Brothers and sisters, I invite you to this realization. One of Christ's followers said to his friends after the Lord had risen, *"The Lord is risen indeed"* (Luke 24:34). I want you to feel just as certain that the Lord is coming. I desire that, as we meet our fellow Christians, we would say to one another, *"Behold, He is coming."* We are sure that He will come and that He is on the way, but the benefit of a more vivid realization would be incalculable.

A Zealous Proclamation

This coming is to be zealously proclaimed, for John did not just calmly say, *"He is coming,"* but he vigorously cried, *"Behold, He is coming."* Just as the herald of a king prefaces his message by a trumpet blast that calls attention, so John cried, *"Behold."* As the town crier of old was accustomed to saying, "O yes! O yes!" or to use some other striking formula by which he called on men to pay attention to his announcement, so John has stood in the midst of us and cried, *"Behold, He is coming."* He called attention by that emphatic word, *"Behold."* It was no ordinary message that John

517

brought, and he would not have us treat his word as a commonplace saying. He threw his heart into the announcement. He proclaimed it loudly, he proclaimed it solemnly, and he proclaimed it with authority: *"Behold, He is coming."*

A Frequent Proclamation

Beloved, no truth ought to be more frequently proclaimed, next to the first coming of the Lord, than His Second Coming. You cannot thoroughly set forth all the ramifications of the First Advent if you forget the Second. At the Lord's Supper, there is no discerning the Lord's body unless you recognize His first coming, but there is no drinking of His cup to its fullness unless you hear Him say, *"Till I come"* (Rev. 2:25). You must look forward as well as backward.

It must be this way with all our ministries; we must look to Christ on the cross and on the throne. We must vividly realize that He who has once come is coming again; otherwise, our testimonies will be marred and one-sided. We will make lame work of preaching and teaching if we leave out either Advent.

An Assuring Proclamation

Next, this truth is to be unquestionably asserted. *"Behold, He is coming."* It is not, "Perhaps He will come," or "Possibly He may yet appear." *"Behold, He is coming"* should be dogmatically asserted as an absolute certainty that has been realized by the heart of the man who proclaims it.

All the prophets said that He will come. From Enoch down to the last who spoke by inspiration, they declared, *"Behold, the Lord comes with ten thousands of His saints"* (Jude 14). You will not find one who has spoken by the authority of God who does not, either directly or by implication, assert the coming of the Son of Man, when the multitudes born of woman will be summoned to His bar to receive their just rewards. All the promises are tied to this prophecy: *"Behold, He is coming."*

We have His own word for it, and this makes assurance doubly sure. He has told us that He will come again. He often assured His disciples that if He went away from them, He would come again to them. (See, for example, John 14:28.) He left us the Lord's Supper as a parting token to be observed until He comes (1 Cor. 11:26). As often as we break bread, we are reminded that, though it is a most blessed ordinance, it is a temporary one that will cease to be celebrated when our absent Lord is once again present with us.

What, dear ones, is there to hinder Christ from coming? When I have studied and thought over this word, *"Behold, He is coming,"* I have said to myself, Yes, indeed He will; who could hold Him back? His heart is with His church on earth. In the place where He fought the battle, He desires to celebrate the victory. His *"delight [is] with the sons of men"* (Prov. 8:31). He and all His saints are waiting for the Day of His appearing. The very earth, in her sorrow and her groaning, travails for His coming, which is to be her redemption. (See Romans 8:19–22.) The creation is made subject to futility for a little while, but when the Lord comes again, the creation itself also *"will be delivered from the bondage of corruption into the glorious liberty of the children of God"* (v. 21).

We might question whether He would come a second time if He had not already come the first time. However, if He came to Bethlehem, be assured that His feet will stand again on Olivet. (See Acts 1:9–12.) If He came to die, do not doubt that He will come to reign. If He came to be *"despised and rejected by men"* (Isa. 53:3), why should we doubt that *"when He comes,...*[He will] *be admired among all those who believe"* (2 Thess. 1:10)? His sure coming is to be unquestionably asserted.

An Attention-Demanding Proclamation

Dear friends, this fact that He will come again is to be taught as demanding our immediate interest. *"Behold, He in coming with clouds."* Behold, look at it, meditate on it. It is worth thinking of. It concerns you personally. Study it again and again. *"He in coming."* He will be here so soon that it is put in the present progressive tense: *"He is coming."* That shaking of the earth, that blotting out of the sun and moon, that fleeing of heaven and earth before His face—all these are so nearly here that John described them as accomplished. *"Behold, He is coming."*

There is a sense hovering in the background that Christ is already on the way. All that He is doing in providence and grace is a preparation for His coming. All the events of human history, all the great decisions of His stately majesty whereby He rules all things—all these are tending toward the Day of His appearing. Do not think that He delays His coming and then suddenly He will rush here in

519

hot haste. He has arranged for it to take place as soon as wisdom allows. We do not know what may make the present delay imperative, but the Lord knows, and that suffices.

You grow uneasy because nearly two thousand years have passed since His ascension and Jesus has not yet come; but you do not know what had to be arranged for and how much a lapse of time was absolutely necessary for the Lord's designs. Those are no little matters that have filled up the great pause; the intervening centuries have teemed with wonders. A thousand things may have been necessary in heaven itself before the consummation of all things could be reached. When our Lord comes, it will be seen that He came as quickly as He could in His infinite wisdom. He cannot behave Himself otherwise than wisely, perfectly, divinely. He cannot be moved by fear or passion so as to act hastily as you and I too often do. He dwells in the leisure of eternity and in the serenity of omnipotence. He does not have to measure out days, months, and years, and to accomplish so much in such a space or else leave His life's work undone. Rather, according to the power of an endless life, He proceeds steadily on. To Him, *one day is as a thousand years* (2 Pet. 3:8). Therefore, be assured that the Lord is even now coming. He is making everything move in that direction. All things are working toward that grand climax. At this moment, and every moment since He went away, the Lord Jesus has been coming back again. *Behold, He is coming.* He is on the way! He is nearer every hour!

A Manifest Proclamation

And we are told that His coming will be attended by a peculiar sign: *Behold, He is coming with clouds.* We will have no need to question whether it is the Son of Man who has come or whether He is indeed come. His return is to be no secret matter; His coming will be as clear as the clouds seen in the sky. In the wilderness the presence of Jehovah was known by a visible pillar of cloud by day and an equally visible pillar of fire by night (Exod. 13:21–22). That pillar of cloud was the sure token that the Lord was in His Holy Place, dwelling between the cherubim. Such is the token of the coming of the Lord Jesus Christ.

> Every eye the cloud shall scan,
> Ensign of the Son of Man.

It is written, *"Then the sign of the Son of Man will appear in heaven, and then all the tribes of the earth will mourn, and they will see the Son of Man coming on the clouds of heaven with power and great glory"* (Matt. 24:30). The passages of Scripture in which it is indicated that our Lord will come either sitting on a cloud (Rev. 14:14–16), *"with clouds"* (Rev. 1:7), or *"in the clouds"* (Mark 13:26) are abundant. Is it not to show that His coming will be majestic? He makes the clouds His chariots. He comes with hosts of attendants—of a nobler sort than earthly monarchs can summon to do them homage.

With clouds of angels, cherubim, seraphim, and all the armies of heaven, He comes. With all the forces of nature, thunderclouds, and blackness of tempest, the Lord of all makes His triumphant entrance to judge the world. The clouds are the dust of His feet in that terrible day of battle when He will rid Himself of His adversaries, shaking them out of the earth with His thunder, and consuming them with the devouring flame of His lightning. All of heaven will gather with its utmost pomp at the great appearing of the Lord, and all the terrible grandeur of nature will then be seen at its fall. Not as the Man of Sorrows, *"despised and rejected by men"* (Isa. 53:3), will Jesus come. Rather, as Jehovah came upon Sinai in the midst of thick clouds and a terrible darkness, so will He come, whose coming will be the final judgment.

A Mighty Proclamation

The clouds are meant to set forth the might, as well as the majesty, of His coming. *"Ascribe strength to God; His excellence is over Israel, and His strength is in the clouds"* (Ps. 68:34). This was the royal token given by Daniel the prophet: *"I was watching in the night visions, and behold, One like the Son of Man, coming with the clouds of heaven!"* (Dan. 7:13). Not less than divine is the glory of the Son of God, who once had *"nowhere to lay His head"* (Matt. 8:20). The most sublime objects in nature will most aptly minister to the manifest glory of the returning King. *"Behold, He is coming,"* not with the swaddling cloths of His infancy, the weariness of His manhood, or the shame of His death, but with all the glorious tapestry of heaven's high chambers. The hangings of the divine throne room will aid His stately entrance.

A Terrifying Proclamation

The clouds also denote the terror of His coming to the ungodly. His saints will be caught up together with Him in the clouds, *"to meet the Lord in the air"* (1 Thess. 4:17); but the clouds will turn their blackness and horror of darkness to those who remain on earth. Then, the impenitent will behold this dread vision: *"They will see the Son of Man coming in the clouds with great power and glory"* (Mark 13:26). The clouds will fill them with dread, and the dread will be abundantly justified, for those clouds are big with vengeance and will burst in judgment on their heads. His Great White Throne, though it is bright and lustrous with hope for His people, will, with its very brightness and whiteness of immaculate justice, strike dead the hopes of all those who trusted that they might live in sin and yet go unpunished. *"Behold, He is coming with clouds."*

I am in happy circumstances at present because my subject requires no effort of imagination from me. To indulge on such a theme would be a wretched desecration of so sublime a subject, which should come home to all hearts in its own simplicity. Think clearly for a moment until the meaning becomes real to you. Jesus Christ is coming in unmatched, majestic splendor. When He comes, He will be enthroned far above the attacks of His enemies, the persecutions of the godless, and the sneers of skeptics. He is coming in the clouds of heaven, and we will be among the witnesses of His appearing. Let us dwell on this truth.

Everyone Will See His Appearing

My second observation about the text is that our Lord's coming will be seen by all. *"Behold, He is coming with clouds, and every eye will see Him, even they who pierced Him."* To my way of thinking, the word *every* allows no exceptions, leaving no one excluded. *"Every eye will see Him."*

By Physical Eyes

First, I gather from this expression that it will be a literal appearing and an actual sight. If the Second Advent were to be a spiritual manifestation to be perceived by the minds of men, the phraseology would have been, "Every mind will perceive Him." But it is not so; we read, *"Every eye will see Him."* Now, the mind can behold the spiritual, but the eye can see only what is distinctly material and visible. The Lord Jesus Christ will not come spiritually, for in that sense He is already here; but He will come really and substantially, for *"every eye will see Him,"* even those unspiritual eyes that gazed on Him with hate and pierced Him. Do not dreamily say to yourself, "Oh, there is some spiritual meaning about all this." Do not destroy the teaching of the Holy Spirit by the idea that there will be a spiritual manifestation of the Christ of God, but that a literal appearing is out of the question. That would be altering the record. The Lord Jesus will come to earth a second time as literally as He has come a first time. The same Christ who ate *"a piece of a broiled fish and some honeycomb"* (Luke 24:42) after He had risen from the dead; the same Jesus who said, *"Handle Me and see, for a spirit does not have flesh and bones as you see I have"* (v. 39)—*"this same Jesus,...in like manner"* (Acts 1:11), with a material body, is to come in the clouds of heaven. In the same way that He went up, He will come down. He will be literally seen. The words cannot be honestly read in any other way.

"Every eye will see Him." Yes, I do literally expect to see my Lord Jesus with these eyes of mine, even as that saint Job expected, who long ago fell asleep, believing that *"after my skin is destroyed, this I know, that in my flesh I shall see God"* (Job 19:26). He believed his eyes, and not another's, would allow him to see for himself. There will be a real resurrection of the body—though the moderns doubt it—such that we will see Jesus with our own eyes. We will not find ourselves in a shadowy, dreamy land of floating fiction where we may perceive but cannot see. We will not be airy nothings—mysterious, vague, and impalpable. Rather, we will literally see our glorious Lord, whose appearing will be no phantom show or shadow dance. Never a day will be more real than the Day of Judgment; never a sight will be more true than the Son of Man upon the throne of His glory. Will you take this statement to heart so that you may feel the force of it? We are getting too far away from facts nowadays and too much into the realm of myths and notions. *"Every eye will see Him."* In this there will be no delusion.

Seen by All Kinds of Men

Note well that He is to be seen by all kinds of men: *"Every eye will see Him"*—the king and the peasant, the most learned and the most ignorant. Those who were blind before will see when He appears. I remember a man born blind who loved our Lord most intensely, and he was happy to glory in this, that his eyes had been reserved for his Lord. He said, "The first whom I will ever see will be the Lord Jesus Christ. The first sight that greets my newly opened eyes will be the Son of Man in His glory." There is great comfort in this to all who are now unable to behold the sun. Since *"every eye will see Him,"* you also will see the King in His beauty.

Small pleasure is this to eyes that are full of filthiness and pride. You do not care for this sight, yet you must see it whether you like it or not. So far, you have shut your eyes to good things, but you must see Him when He comes. All who dwell on the face of the earth—if not all at the same moment, yet still with the same certainty—will behold the once-crucified Lord. They will not be able to hide themselves or to hide Him from their eyes. They will dread the sight, but it will come upon them, even as the sun shines on the thief who delights in the darkness. They will be obliged to admit in dismay that they behold the Son of Man. Overwhelmed with the sight, they will not be able to deny it.

He will be seen by those who have been long since dead. What a sight that will be for Judas, for Pilate, for Caiaphas, and for Herod! What a sight it will be for those who, in the course of their lives, said that there was no Savior and no need of one, or that Jesus was a mere man and His blood was not a propitiation for sin! Those who scoffed and reviled Him have long since died, but they will all rise again to this heritage among the rest: they will see Him whom they blasphemed sitting in the clouds of heaven.

Prisoners are troubled at the sight of the judge. The trumpet of the court brings no music to the ears of guilty criminals. But you must hear it, O impenitent sinners! Even in your graves you must hear the voice of the Son of God and live and come forth from the tombs to receive the things done in your bodies, whether they were good or bad (2 Cor. 5:10). Death cannot hide you, nor can the vault conceal you, nor will rottenness and corruption deliver you. You are bound to see with your own eyes the Lord who will judge both you and your fellowmen.

Seen by Those Who Pierced Him

It is emphasized in the text that He will be seen by *"they who pierced Him."* In this are included all of the company who nailed Him to the tree, along with those who took the spear and made the gash in His side—indeed, all who had a hand in His cruel crucifixion. It includes all of these, but it encompasses many more besides. *"They who pierced Him"* are by no means few.

Who have pierced Him? Why, those who once professed to love Him and have gone back to the world. Those who once ran well, what has hindered them (Gal. 5:7)? Now they use their tongues to speak against the Christ whom once they professed to love. Those whose inconsistent lives have brought dishonor on the sacred name of Jesus have also pierced Him. Those who refused His love, stifled their consciences, and refused His rebukes have pierced Him. Alas, so many of you are piercing Him now by your shameful neglect of His salvation! Those who have gone every Sunday to hear of Him but have remained *"hearers only, deceiving* [them]*selves"* (James 1:22), destroying their own souls rather than yield to His infinite love, have pierced His tender heart.

Dear ones, I wish I could plead effectively with you so that you would not continue any longer among the number of those who have pierced Him. If you will look at Jesus now and mourn for your sin, He will cleanse and remove your sin. Then, you will not be ashamed to see Him in that Day. Even though you did pierce Him, you will be able to sing, *"To Him who loved us and washed us from our sins in His own blood"* (Rev. 1:5). But remember, if you persevere in piercing Him and fighting against Him, you will still have to see Him in that Day to your terror and despair. He will be seen by you and by me, however badly we may behave. And what horror will that sight cost us!

I am often ill; who knows how soon I will come to my end? I would use all that remains in me of physical strength and providential opportunity to spread the Gospel. We never know how soon we may be cut off, and then, we are gone forever from the opportunity of benefiting our fellowmen. It would be a pity to be taken away with one opportunity of doing good left unused. Thus, I earnestly plead with you under the shadow of this great truth: I urge you to be ready, since we will both behold the Lord in the Day of His appearing. Yes, I will stand in that great throng. You also will be there. How will you feel? You are not accustomed, perhaps, to attending a place of worship, but you will be there. The occasion will be very solemn to you. You may absent yourself from the assemblies of the saints now, but you will not be able to absent yourself from the gathering of that Day. You will be there, one in that great multitude. You will see Jesus the Lord as truly as if you were the only person before Him, and He will look on you as certainly as if you were the only one who had been summoned to His bar.

Kindly think about this. Let your heart dwell on it. Silently repeat to yourself the words, *"Every eye will see Him, even they who pierced Him."*

His Coming Will Bring Sorrow

My third comment on this text is a painful one, but it needs to be enlarged upon: His coming will cause great sorrow. What does the text say about His coming? *"All the tribes of the earth will mourn because of Him."*

A General Sorrow

"All the tribes of the earth." Thus, this sorrow will be very general. You thought, perhaps, that when Christ came, He would come to a glad world, welcoming Him with song and music. You may have thought that there might be a few ungodly people who would be destroyed with the breath of His mouth, but that the bulk of mankind would receive Him with delight. See how different it will be: *"all the tribes of the earth will mourn"*—all sorts of people who belong to the earth, those from all nations, tribes, and tongues. They will weep and wail and gnash their teeth at His coming. Oh, what a sad prospect! There are no palatable things to prophesy for those who have *"pierced Him."*

A Great Sorrow

Next, this sorrow will be very great. They will *"mourn."* I cannot put into English the full meaning of that most expressive word. Sound it out at length, and it conveys its own meaning. It is as when men wring their hands and burst out into a loud cry, or as when Eastern women in their anguish rend their garments and lift up their voices with the most mournful notes. *"All the tribes of the earth will mourn,"* wail as a mother laments over her dead child, wail as a man might wail who found himself hopelessly imprisoned and doomed to die. Such will be the hopeless grief of *"all the tribes of the earth"* at the sight of Christ in the clouds. If they remain impenitent, they will not be able to be silent; they will not be able to repress or conceal their anguish. Rather, they will wail and openly vent their horror. What a sound that will be that will go up before high heaven when Jesus sits on the cloud and in the fullness of His power summons them to judgment! Then, they *"will mourn be-cause of Him."*

Will your voice be heard in that wailing? Will your heart be breaking in that general dismay? How will you escape? If you are one of the *"tribes of the earth"* and remain impenitent, you will mourn with the rest of them. Unless you now fly to Christ, hide yourself in Him, and so become one of the kindred of heaven; unless you repent and become one of His chosen, blood-washed ones who will praise His name for washing them from their sins, there will be wailing at the judgment seat of Christ, and you will be joining in it.

From this text it becomes quite clear that men will not be universally converted when Christ comes, because, if they were so, they would not wail. Then, they would lift up the cry, "Welcome, Son of God!" The coming of Christ would be as the hymn puts it:

> Hark, those bursts of acclamation!
> Hark, those loud triumphant chords!
> Jesus takes the highest station.
> Oh, what joy the sight affords!

These acclamations come from His people. But according to the text, the multitude of mankind will weep and wail, and therein they will not be among His people. Do not, therefore, look for salvation at some future day, but believe in Jesus now; find in Him your Savior. If you joy in Him now, you will much more rejoice in Him in that Day; but if you will have cause to wail at His coming, it will be well to wail at once.

False Expectations

Note one more truth. It is quite certain that when Jesus comes in these latter days, men will not be expecting great things of Him. You know the talk nowadays about "a larger hope." Those who put forth this vain philosophy deceive the people with the idle dream of repentance and restoration after death, a fiction unsupported by the least bit of Scripture. If the tribes of the earth expected that they would die out and cease to be when Christ comes, they would be rejoicing because they had escaped the wrath of God instead of wailing. Would not each unbeliever say, "It were a consummation devoutly to be wished"? If they thought that at His coming there would be a universal restoration and a general delivery of souls long shut up in prison, would they wail? If Jesus were supposed to come to proclaim a general restoration, they would not wail but would shout for joy.

Since His coming to the impenitent is ominous with black despair, they will wail because of Him. If His first coming did not give you eternal life, His Second Coming will not. If you did not hide in His wounds when He came as your Savior, there will be no hiding place for you when He comes as your Judge. They will weep and wail because, having rejected the Lord Jesus, they have turned their backs on the last possibility of hope.

Why do they *"mourn because of Him"*? Will it not be because they will see Him in His glory and they will recollect that they slighted and despised Him? They will see Him come to judge them, as they remember that once He stood at their door with mercy in His hands and said, "Open to me," but they would not admit Him. They refused His blood; they refused His righteousness; they trifled with His sacred name; now, they must give an account for this wickedness. They put Him away in scorn; now, when He comes, they find that they can trifle with Him no longer. The days of child's play and of foolish delay are over; now, they solemnly have to give an accounting of their lives. See, the books are opened! They are covered with dismay as they remember their sins and know that they were written down by a faithful pen. They must give an account. Unwashed and unforgiven, they cannot render that account without knowing that the sentence will be, *"Depart from Me, you cursed"* (Matt. 25:41). This is why they weep and wail because of Him.

O souls, my natural love of ease makes me wish that I could present pleasant things to you, but they are not in my commission. However, I scarcely need to wish to put forth a soft gospel, for so many are already doing it to you at your cost. Since I love your immortal souls, I dare not flatter you. As I will have to answer for it in the last great Day, I must tell you the truth.

> You sinners, seek His face,
> Whose wrath you cannot bear.

Seek the mercy of God right now. I have written this to implore you to be reconciled to God. *"Kiss the Son, lest He be angry, and you perish in the way, when His wrath is kindled but a little. Blessed are all those who put their trust in Him"* (Ps. 2:12).

However, if you will not have my Lord Jesus, He is coming all the same. He is on the road now, and when He comes, you *"will mourn because of Him."* Oh, that you would make Him your friend, and then meet Him with joy! Why would you choose eternal death? He gives life to all those who trust Him. Believe, and live.

May God save your souls right now, and He will have the glory.

Chapter 2

The Reward of the Righteous

When the Son of Man comes in His glory, and all the holy angels
with Him, then He will sit on the throne of His glory. All the nations
will be gathered before Him, and He will separate them one from
another, as a shepherd divides his sheep from the goats. And He
will set the sheep on His right hand, but the goats on the left. Then
the King will say to those on His right hand, "Come, you blessed of
My Father, inherit the kingdom prepared for you from the
foundation of the world: for I was hungry and you gave Me food;
I was thirsty and you gave Me drink; I was a stranger and you took
Me in; I was naked and you clothed Me; I was sick and you visited
Me; I was in prison and you came to Me."
—Matthew 25:31–36

To rise above this present evil world to something nobler and better is exceedingly beneficial to our souls. *"The cares of this world, the deceitfulness of riches, and the desires for other things"* (Mark 4:19) are apt to choke everything good within us, and we grow fretful and despondent, perhaps proud and carnal. It is wise for us to cut down these thorns and briars because heavenly seed sown among them is not likely to yield a harvest. I do not know a better sickle with which to cut them down than with thoughts of the kingdom to come.

Sometimes people who live at a low level of elevation develop a sickly appearance, because the atmosphere in the valley is permeated with noxious vapors, and the air is close and stagnant. When they travel to a higher altitude, they are glad to escape the adverse conditions they live in below. Up in the mountains, they breathe clear, fresh air as it blows from the virgin snows of the high summits. It would be healthier for those who live in the valleys if they could frequently leave their homes among the marshes and the mists and spend time in the clear atmosphere above.

It is to such an exploit of climbing that I invite you now. May the Spirit of God bear us on eagles' wings so that we may leave the mists of fear, the fevers of anxiety, and all the evils that gather in this valley of earth, and get ourselves up to the mountains of future joy and blessedness where it will be our delight to dwell forever, world without end! May God disentangle us now for a little while, cut the cords that keep us here below, and permit us to climb! Some of us are like chained eagles fastened to the rocks; however, unlike the eagles, we begin to love our chains and would, if it really came to the test, be afraid to have them snapped. Even if our bodies cannot immediately escape from the chains of mortal life, may God grant us grace that our spirits may escape. Leaving the body like a servant at the foot of the hill, may our souls, like Abraham, go to the top of the mountain and have communion with the Most High.

While examining this text, I direct your attention, first, to the circumstances that surround the rewarding of the righteous; second, to their portion; and third, to the inheritors themselves.

Circumstances of Our Reward

We read, *"When the Son of Man comes in His glory."* It appears that we must not expect to receive our reward until by and by. Like the hireling, we must complete our workday, and then, at evening we will receive our pay. Too many Christians look for a present reward for their labors. If they meet with success, they begin doting on it as though they had received their recompense. Like the seventy disciples who returned saying, *"Lord, even the demons are subject to us"* (Luke 10:17), they rejoice too exclusively in present prosperity, whereas the Master bade His disciples not to look on miraculous success as being their reward since that might not always be the case. Christ said, *"Nevertheless do not rejoice in this, that the spirits are subject to you, but rather rejoice because your names are written in heaven"* (v. 20).

Success in the ministry is not the Christian minister's true reward. It is an earnest, a pledge, but the wages still wait. You must not look on the esteem of your fellowmen as being the reward of excellence, because often you will meet with the reverse: you will find your best actions misconstrued and your motives misinterpreted. If you are looking for your reward here, I may warn you of the apostle's words: *"If in this life only we have hope in Christ, we are of all men the most pitiable"* (1 Cor. 15:19). Other men receive their rewards in the present. Even the Pharisees get theirs—*"Assuredly, I say to you, they have their reward"* (Matt. 6:2, 5, 16)—but we have none here.

To be despised and rejected of men is the Christian's lot. Even among his fellow Christians, he will not always stand in good repute. It is not unqualified kindness or total love that we receive, even from the saints. If you look to Christ's bride herself for your reward, you will miss it. If you expect to receive your crown from the hand of your brothers in the ministry who know your labors and who ought to sympathize with your trials, you will be mistaken. *"When the Son of Man comes in His glory"* is your time of recompense—not today, tomorrow, or at any time in this world. Do not consider anything that you acquire or any honor that you gain to be the reward of your service to your Master; that dividend is reserved for the time *"when the Son of Man comes in His glory."*

Observe with delight the majestic Person by whose hand the reward is given. It is written, *"When the* [King] *comes."* Beloved, we love the King's court attendants; we delight to be numbered with them ourselves. It is no mean thing to do service to Him whose head,

> Though once 'twas crowned with thorns,
> Is crowned with glory now.

However, it is a delightful thought that the service of rewarding us will not be left to the courtiers. The angels will be there, and the beloved of the King will be there; but heaven was not prepared by them, nor can it be given by them. Their hands will not yield us a coronation. We will join their songs, but their songs will not be our reward. We will bow with them, and they with us. However, it will not be possible for them to give us the recompense of the reward: that starry crown is all too weighty for an angel's hand to bring, and the benediction all too sweet to be pronounced even by celestial lips. The King Himself must say, *"Well done, good and faithful servant"* (Matt. 25:23).

What do you say to this, my dear one? You have felt a temptation to look to God's servants, to the approval of the minister, to the kindly look of parents, to the word of commendation from your coworker. You value all these—and I do not blame you—but these may fail you. Therefore, never consider them as being the reward. You must wait until the time when the King comes. Then, it will neither be your brothers, your pastors, your parents, nor your fellow workers, but the King Himself who will say to you, *"Come, you blessed."*

How this sweetens heaven! It will be Christ's own gift. How this makes the benediction doubly blessed! It will come from His lips, which drip like myrrh and flow with honey. Beloved, Christ who became a curse for us will give the blessing to us. Roll this as a sweet morsel around your tongues.

The character in which our Lord Jesus will appear is significant. Jesus will truly then be revealed as *"the King." "Then the King will say."* It was to Him as King that the service was rendered, and it is from Him as King that the reward must therefore come. Thus, on the very threshold of His return, questions of self-examination arise: Since the King will not reward the servants of another prince, am I therefore His servant? Is it my joy to wait at the threshold of His gates and sit like Mordecai at the courts of Ahasuerus? Say, soul, do you serve the King? My meaning here is not the kings and queens of earth—let them have loyal servants for their subjects—but saints are servants of the Lord Jesus Christ, the King of Kings. Are you one? If you are not, when the King comes in His glory, there can be no reward for you.

I long in my own heart to recognize Christ's kingly office more than I have ever done. It has been my delight to preach Christ dying on the cross, for *"God forbid that I should boast except in the cross of our Lord Jesus Christ"* (Gal. 6:14). However, for myself I want to realize Him on His throne, reigning in my heart, having a right to do as He wills with me. I want to be in the condition of Abraham, who, when God spoke—though it was to tell him to offer up his own Isaac—never asked a question but simply said, *"Here I am"* (Gen. 22:11). Beloved, seek to know and feel the controlling power of the King; otherwise, when He comes, since you have not known Him as King, He cannot know you as servant. It is only to the servant that the King can give the reward that is spoken of in this text.

Now, let's move on. *"When the Son of Man comes in His glory."* The fullness of this description is impossible to conceive.

> Imagination's utmost stretch
> In wonder dies away.

However, this we know—and it is the sweetest thing we can know—that if we have been partakers with Jesus in His shame, we also will be sharers with Him in the radiance that will surround Him. Are you, beloved, one with Christ Jesus? Are you of His flesh and of His bones? Does a vital union knit you to Him? Then, you are today with Him in His shame; you have taken up His cross and gone with Him *"outside the camp, bearing His reproach"* (Heb. 13:13). Undoubtedly, you will be with Him when the cross is exchanged for the crown. But judge yourself: if you are not with Him in the regeneration, neither will you be with Him when He comes in His glory.

If you recoil from the *"fellowship of His sufferings"* (Phil. 3:10), you will not understand *"the power of His resurrection"* (v. 10), or experience the joy *"when the Son of Man comes in His glory, and all the holy angels with Him."* What, are angels with Him? Yet He does not take up angels; He takes up the seed of Abraham. Are the holy angels with Him? Come, my soul, then, you cannot be far from Him. If His friends and His neighbors are called together to see His glory, what do you think will happen if you are married to Him? Will you be distant? Though it will be the Day of Judgment, yet you cannot be far from that heart that, having admitted angels into intimacy, has admitted you into union. Has He not said to you, *"I will betroth you to Me in faithfulness, and you shall know the LORD"* (Hos. 2:20)? Have not His own lips said, "I am married to you, and My delight is in you"? (See Jeremiah 3:14; Isaiah 62:4.) If the angels, who are but the friends and the neighbors, will be with Him then, it is abundantly certain that His own beloved Hephzibah (Isa. 62:4), in whom is all His delight, will be near to Him and will be a partaker of His splendor. When He comes in His glory and when His communion with angels is distinctly recognized, then, His unity with the church will become apparent.

"Then He will sit on the throne of His glory." Here is a repetition of the same reason why this should be your time and mine to receive the reward from Christ if we are found among His faithful servants. When He sits on His throne, it would not be fitting that His own beloved ones should be in the mire. When He was in the place of shame, they were with Him; now that He is on the throne of gold, they must be with Him there, too. There would be no oneness—union with Christ would be a mere matter of talk—if it were not certain that, when He is on the throne, they will be there, too.

Further, I want you to notice one particular circumstance regarding the time of the reward. It occurs after He divides the sheep from the goats. My reward, if I am a child of God, cannot come to me while I am in union with the wicked. Even on earth, you will have the most enjoyment of Christ when you are most separated from this world. Be assured, although the separated path does not seem an easy one and it will certainly entail persecution and the loss of many friends, yet it is the happiest journey in the world. You conforming Christians who can enter into the world's mirth to a certain degree, you cannot know—and never will know as you now are—the inward joys of those who live in lonely but lovely fellowship with Jesus. The nearer you get to the world, the further you must be from Christ. I believe the more thoroughly a bill of divorce is given by your spirit to every earthly object on which your soul can set itself, the closer will be your communion with your Lord. *"Forget your own people also, and your father's house; so the King will greatly desire your beauty; because He is your Lord, worship Him"* (Ps. 45:10–11).

It is significant that not until the King separates the sheep from the goats does He say, *"Come, you blessed."* Though the righteous will have enjoyed a blessedness as disembodied spirits, yet even when they are bodily raised from the grave, their joy will not be fully accomplished until the Great Shepherd appears to separate them once and for all by *"a great gulf"* (Luke 16:26), which cannot be passed, from all association with the nations that forget God.

Now then, beloved, these circumstances all put together come to this: the reward for following Christ is not today, is not among the souls of men, is not from men, is not from the excellent of the earth, and is not even bestowed by Jesus while we are here. The glorious crown of life that the Lord's grace will give to His people is reserved for the Second Advent, *"when the* [King] *comes in His glory, and all the holy angels with Him."* Wait with patience, wait with joyful expectation, for He will come. Blessed be the Day of His appearing.

The Portion of the Reward

We have now to turn to the second point, which concerns the portion of the reward itself. Every word is suggestive. I will not attempt an exhaustive study, but merely to glance at them all.

At His Right Hand

The reward of the righteous is set forth by the loving benediction pronounced to them by the Master, but their very position gives some foreshadowing of it. He put the sheep on His right hand. Heaven is a position of the most elevated dignity authoritatively conferred and of divine satisfaction manifestly enjoyed. God's saints are always at His right hand according to the judgment of faith, but hereafter it will be more clearly manifested. God is pleased to be close to His people and to place them near to Himself in a place of protection.

Sometimes, it seems as if the saints were at His left hand; some of them certainly have less comfort than worldlings. *"I have seen the wicked in great power, and spreading himself like a native green tree"* (Ps. 37:35). *"Their eyes bulge with abundance; they have more than heart could wish"* (Ps. 73:7). Meanwhile, His people are often made to drink from bitter waters.

The world is upside down now, but the Gospel has begun to turn it up the right way. However, when the day of grace is over and the day of glory comes, then will it be righted indeed; then, those who wandered about in sheepskins and goatskins (Heb. 11:37) will be clothed in glittering apparel, being transfigured like the Savior on Mount Tabor. Then, those *"of whom the world was not worthy"* (v. 38) will come to a world that will be worthy of them. Then, those who were hurried to the stake and to the flames will triumph with chariots of fire and horses of fire, and increase the splendor of the Master's regal appearing.

Yes, beloved, you will eternally be the object of divine satisfaction, not in secret communion, but your state and glory will be revealed before the sons of men. Your persecutors will gnash their teeth when they see you occupying places of honor at His right hand, while they, though far greater than you on earth, are condemned to take the lowest spot. How the rich man will bite his fire-tormented tongue in vain as he sees Lazarus, the beggar on the dunghill, made to sit at the right hand of the King eternal and immortal! (See Luke 16:20–25.) Heaven is a place of dignity. "There we will be as the angels," says one, but I believe we will be even more superior than they. Is it not written of Him who in all things is our Representative, *"He has put all things under His feet"* (1 Cor. 15:27)? Even the very seraphs, who are themselves so richly blessed, what are they but *"ministering spirits sent forth to minister for those who will inherit salvation"* (Heb. 1:14)?

A Welcome Word

Now, turning to the welcome uttered by the Judge, we find that the first word is *"Come."* It is the symbol of the Gospel. The law said, "Go." The Gospel says, "Come." The Spirit says it in invitation; the bride says it in intercession; believers say it by constantly, laboriously endeavoring to spread abroad the Good News.

Since Jesus says, *"Come,"* we learn that the very essence of heaven is communion. *"Come."* You came near enough to say, *"Lord, I believe; help my unbelief!"* (Mark 9:24). You looked to Him on the cross and were enlightened. You had fellowship with Him in bearing His cross. You filled up what was *"lacking in the afflictions of Christ, for the sake of His body, which is the church"* (Col. 1:24). Still come! Always come! Forever come! Come up from your graves, you risen ones. Come up from among the ungodly, you consecrated ones. Come up from where you cast yourselves down in your humiliation before the Great White Throne. Come up to wear His crown and to sit with Him upon His throne! Oh, that word has heaven lurking within it. It will be to you your joy forever to hear the Savior say to you, *"Come."*

I assert before you that my soul has sometimes been so full of joy I could hold no more when my beloved Lord has said to my soul, *"Come."* He has taken me into His banqueting house; His banner of love has waved over my head (Song 2:4); and He has taken me away from the world, its cares and its fears, its trials and its joys, up to *"the top of Amana, from the top of Senir and Hermon"* (Song 4:8), where He has manifested Himself to me.

When this *"Come"* will sound in your ears from the Master's lips, there will not be the flesh to drag you back; there will be no sluggishness of spirit, no heaviness of heart. You will come eternally then; you will not climb to descend again, but rise up and up in one blessed *excelsior* forever and ever. This first word *"Come"* indicates that heaven is a state of communion.

Then, it is, *"Come, you blessed,"* which is a clear declaration that this is a state of happiness. They cannot be more blessed than they are: they have their hearts' desire. Though their hearts have been enlarged and their desires have been expanded by entering into the infinite and getting rid of the cramping influences of corruption and of time, yet even when their desire knows no limitations, they will have all the happiness that the utmost expansion of their souls can by any possibility conceive.

We know this much—and this is all we know—they are supremely blessed. Their blessedness does not come from any secondary joy but from the great primary Source of all good. *"Come, you blessed of My Father."* They drink the unadulterated wine at the winepress itself, where it joyously leaps from the bursting clusters. They pluck celestial fruits from the fruitful boughs of the immortal Tree. They sit at the fountainhead and drink the waters as they spring with unrivaled freshness from the depths of the heart of Deity. They will not be basking in the beams of the sun, but they will be like Uriel, the angel in the sun. They will dwell in God, and so their souls will be satisfied with favor and will be full, more than full, with His presence and benediction.

Inherit the Kingdom

Now, I would like you to notice that, according to the words of the text, the blessed will recognize their right to be there; therefore, it will be a state of perfect freedom, ease, and fearlessness. The Scripture says, *"Inherit the kingdom."* A man does not fear to lose what he gains by inheritance from his parent. If heaven had been the subject of earning, we might have feared that our merits had not really deserved it and, therefore, suspected that one day a writ of error would be issued and that we would be ejected. But we do know whose sons we are; we know whose love it is that makes our spirits glad; and when we *"inherit the kingdom,"* we will enter it not as strangers or as foreigners, but as sons coming to their birthright. Looking over all its streets of gold and surveying all its walls of pearl, we will feel that we are at home in our own house and have an actual right, not through merit but through grace, to everything that is there. It will be a state of heavenly bliss; the Christian will feel that law and justice are on his side and that those stern attributes have brought him there as well as mercy and loving-kindness.

The word *"inherit"* here connotes full possession and enjoyment. We have inherited in a certain sense before; but now, like heirs who begin to spend their own money and to farm their own acres when they have arrived at full maturity, so will we enter into our heritage. We are not fully grown as yet and, therefore, are not admitted to full possession. But wait awhile; those gray hairs indicate, my friend, that you are growing older. Those whose hair still looks youthful may have to tarry for a little longer. Yet I do not know; the Lord may soon permit any of us to sleep with our fathers. However, sooner or later as He wills, we will one day come into possession of the land.

Now, if it is sweet to be an heir while you are not of age, what is it like to be an heir when you have arrived at mature adulthood? Is it not delightful to sing the hymn and to behold the land of pure delight, whose everlasting spring and never withering flowers are just across the narrow stream of death? Oh, you sweet fields and you saints immortal who lie down there! When will we be with you and be satisfied? If the mere thought of heaven ravishes the soul, what must it be like to be there, to plunge deep into the stream of blessedness, to dive and find no bottom, to swim and find no shore? To sip of the wine of heaven as we sometimes do now makes our hearts so glad that we do not know how to express our joy. Oh, what it will be to drink deep and drink again, sitting forever at the table, knowing that the feast will never be over, the cups will never be empty, and there will be no worse wine brought out later, but rather better and better still in infinite progression, if such a thing is possible!

The word *"kingdom,"* which stands next, indicates the richness of the heritage of saints. It is no petty estate, no alms rooms, no happy corner in obscurity. I heard a good man say he would be content to have a corner behind the door. I will not be. The Lord says we will inherit a kingdom. We should not be satisfied to inherit less, because less than that would not suit our characters. He *"has made us kings and priests to His God"* (Rev. 1:6), and we must reign forever and ever or be as wretched as deposed monarchs. A king without a kingdom is an unhappy man. If I were a poor servant, a room in a rescue mission would be a blessing, because it would coincide with my condition and degree. However, if by grace I am made a king, I must have a kingdom, or I will not have attained a position equal to my nature. He who makes us kings will give us a kingdom to fit the natures that He has bestowed on us.

Beloved, strive more and more after what the Spirit of God will give you, a kingly heart. Do not be among those who are satisfied and contented with the miserable nature of ordinary humanity. The world can be only a child's glass bead to a truly royal spirit; these glittering diadems are only nursery toys to God's kings. The true jewels are up there; the true treasury wealth looks down on the stars. Do not be stingy with your soul! Acquire a kingly heart. Ask the King of Kings to give it to you, and beg of Him a royal spirit. Act royally on earth toward your Lord and toward all men, for His sake. Go about the world not as lowly men in spirit and action, but as kings and princes of a race superior to the dirt-scrapers who are on their knees crawling in the mud after yellow earth. Then, when your soul is royal, remember with joy that your future inheritance will be all that your kingly soul yearns for in its most royal moments. It will be a state of unutterable richness and wealth of soul.

A Prepared Kingdom

Looking at the word *"prepared,"* we may conceive this to mean a condition of surpassing excellence. It is a prepared kingdom. It has been prepared for such a long time, and He who prepared it is so wondrously rich in resources that we cannot possibly conceive how excellent it must be. If I might so express an idea, God's common gifts, which He throws away as though they were nothing, are priceless. But what will be the nature of these gifts, on which the infinite mind of God has been set for ages and ages in order that they may reach the highest degree of excellence?

Long before Christmas chimes were ringing, a mother was so glad to think that her boy was coming home after his first quarter away at school that she began preparing and planning all sorts of joys for him. Well might his holidays be happy when his mother had been contriving to make them so. In an infinitely nobler manner, the great God has prepared a kingdom for His people; He has thought, "That will please them, and that will bless them, and this will make them superlatively happy." He has prepared the kingdom to perfection.

If that were not enough, as the glorious Man Christ Jesus went up from earth to heaven, you know what He said when He departed: *"I go to prepare a place for you"* (John 14:2). We know that the infinite God can prepare a place fitting for a finite creature, but the words smile so sweetly at us as we read that Jesus Himself, who is a man and therefore knows our hearts' desires, has had a finger in it; He has prepared it, too. It is a kingdom prepared for you, on which the thoughts of God have been set to make it excellent *"from the foundation of the world."*

Chosen Inheritors

We must not pause. This is a *"kingdom prepared for you."* Mark that! I must confess that I do not like certain expressions I hear sometimes that imply that heaven is prepared for some who will never reach it, prepared for those who will be driven as ac-cursed ones into the place of torment. I know there is a sacred verse that says, "[Let] *no one...take your crown*" (Rev. 3:11), but that refers to the crown of ministerial success rather than of eter-nal glory. An expression that grated on my ears, from the lips of a certain good man, went something like this: "There is a heaven prepared for all of you; but if you are not faithful, you will not win it. There is a crown in heaven laid up for you; but if you are not faithful, it will be without a wearer." I do not believe it; I cannot believe it. That any crown of eternal life that is laid up for the *"blessed of* [the] *Father"* would ever be given to anybody else or left without a possessor, I do not believe. I dare not conceive of crowns in heaven with nobody to wear them.

Do you think that in heaven, when the whole number of saints is complete, you will find a number of unused crowns? "Ah, who are these crowns for? Where are the heads for these?" "They are in hell!" Then, brother, I have no particular desire to be in heaven. If all of the family of Christ are not there, my soul will be wretched and forlorn because of their sad loss, for I am in union with them all. If one soul that believed in Jesus does not get there, I would lose respect for the promise and respect for the Master, too. He must keep His word to every soul that rests in Him.

If your God has actually prepared a place for His people, made provision for them, and then been disappointed, He is no God to me. I could not adore a disappointed God. I do not believe in such a God. Such a being would not be God at all. The notion of disap-pointment in His eternal preparations is not consistent with Deity. Talk thus of Jupiter and Venus if you please, but the infinite Jeho-vah is dishonored by being mentioned in such a connection. He has prepared a place for you. Here is personal election. He has made a distinct ordinance for every one of His people so that where He is, there they will be also (John 14:3).

Time of the Preparation

"Prepared...from the foundation of the world." Here is eternal election appearing before men were created, preparing crowns be-fore heads were made to wear them. Thus, before the starry skies began to gleam, God had carried out the decree of election in a measure that will be perfected, when Christ comes again, to the praise of the glory of His grace, *"who works all things according to*

the counsel of His will" (Eph. 1:11). Our portion, then, is one that has been prepared from all eternity for us according to the election of God's grace, one suitable to the loftiest character to which we can ever attain, that will consist in nearness to Christ, communion with God, and standing forever in a place of dignity and happiness.

The Righteous Inheritors

Finally, we want to consider carefully the people who will inherit the kingdom. These righteous inheritors are recognizable by a secret and by a public character. Their name is *"blessed of* [the] *Father."* The Father chose them, gave His Son for them, justified them through Christ, preserved them in Christ Jesus, adopted them into the family, and now has accepted them into His own house.

Their nature is described in the word *"inherit."* Since none can inherit but sons, they have been born again and have received the nature of God. *"Having escaped the corruption that is in the world through lust"* (2 Pet. 1:4), they have become *"partakers of the divine nature"* (v. 4) and are thus sons. Their appointment is mentioned: *"Inherit the kingdom prepared for you from the foundation of the world."* Their name is *"blessed"*; their nature is that of a child; their appointment is that by God's decree.

Behavior of the Righteous

For a moment, we want to look at the actions of the inheritors, their outward behavior. They appear to have been distinguished among men for deeds of charity, and these were not in any way associated with ceremonies or outward observances. It is not said that they preached—they did so, some of them. It is not said that they prayed—they must have done so, or they would not have been spiritually alive. The actions that are selected as typical are actions of charity to the indigent and forlorn.

Why focus on charitable acts? I think so that the general audience assembled around the throne would know how to appreciate this evidence of their newborn nature. The King might think more of their prayers than of their benevolent acts, but the multitude would not. He speaks so as to gain the verdict of all assembled. Even their enemies could not object to His calling those blessed who had performed these actions.

If there is any action that wins for men the universal consent to their goodness, it is an action by which men would be served. *"Against such there is no law"* (Gal. 5:23). I have never heard of any state in which there was a law against clothing the naked and feeding the hungry. Humanity, even when its conscience is so seared that it cannot see its own sinfulness, can still detect the virtuousness of feeding the poor. Undoubtedly, this is one reason that these actions were selected.

Evidences of Grace

Moreover, they may have been chosen as evidences of grace because, as actions, they are a wonderful means of separating between the hypocrite and the true Christian. Dr. Gill had an idea—and perhaps he was right—that this is not a picture of the general judgment but of the judgment of the professing church. If so, it is all the more reasonable to conclude that these works of mercy are selected as appropriately discerning between the hypocrite and the sincere. I fear that there are some of you who loudly profess your faith who could not stand the test. "Good, praying people," they call you, but what do you give to the Lord? Your religion has not touched your pockets.

This does not apply to some of you, for there are many of whom I would venture to speak before the bar of God, that I know your substance to be consecrated to the Lord and His poor, and I have sometimes thought that beyond your means you have given both to the poor and to God's cause. However, there are others of a very different disposition. Now, I will give you in plain English a lesson that none can fail to understand. You may talk about your religion until you have worn your tongue out, and you may get others to believe you; you may remain in the church twenty years, and nobody ever detect in you or even suspect you of anything like an inconsistency; but if it is in your power and you do nothing to relieve the necessities of the poor members of Christ's body, you will be damned as surely as if you were drunkards or whoremongers. If you have no care for God's church, this text applies to you, and will as surely sink you to the lowest hell as if you had been common blasphemers. That is very plain English, but it is the clear meaning of my text, and it is at my peril that I flinch from telling you of it.

"I was hungry and you gave Me"—what? Good advice, yes, but no meat. *"I was thirsty and you gave Me"*—what? A tract, and no

drink. *"I was naked and you"*—gave me what? Your good wishes, but no clothes. *"I was a stranger and you"*—what? You pitied me, but you did not take me in. *"I was sick and you"*—what? You said you could recommend a doctor for me, but you did not visit me. *"I was in prison"*—God's servant, a persecuted one, put in prison for Christ's sake—and you said that I should be more cautious, but you did not stand by my side and take a share of the blame and bear with me reproach for the truth's sake. You see, this is a very terrible *"winnowing fan"* (Matt. 3:12) to some of you begrudging ones whose main object in life is to get all you can and hold it fast, but it is a fan that frequently must be used. Whoever else tries to spare you, by the grace of God, I will not; but I will labor to be ever more bold in denouncing sin.

"Well," says one, "what is all of that to those who are so poor that they have nothing to give away?" My dearly beloved, do you notice how beautifully the text takes care of you? It hints that there are some who cannot give bread to the hungry and clothes to the naked, but what about them? They are the people spoken of as *"the least of these My brethren"* (Matt. 25:40), who receive the blessing of kindness. This passage comforts the poor and by no means condemns them.

Certain of us honestly give to the poor all we can spare, and then, of course, everybody comes to such a person. When we then say, "Really, I cannot give any more," somebody snarls and says, "Do you call yourself a Christian?" "Yes, I do. I should not call myself a Christian if I gave away other people's money; I should not call myself a Christian if I gave away what I do not have; I should call myself a thief, pretending to be charitable when I could not pay my debts." I have very great pity indeed for those people who get into the bankruptcy court. I do not mean I pity the debtors, for I seldom have much sympathy with them; I have a good deal of feeling for the creditors who lose by having trusted dishonest people.

If any man thinks that he would live beyond his means in order to get a charitable character, my dear brother, you are wrong. That action is in itself wrong. What you have to give must be what is your own. "But I would have to tighten my way of living," says one, "if I did it." Well, pinch yourself! I do not think there is half the pleasure in doing good until you get to the pinching point. This remark, of course, applies only to those of us of moderate means, who can soon distribute our charitable gifts and get down to the pinching point where we begin to feel, "Now, I must do without that; now I must curtail this thing in order to do more good." Oh, you cannot know! It is then when you really can feel, "Now, I have not given God merely the cheese parings and candle ends that I could not use, but I have really cut out for my Master a good piece of the loaf; I have not given Him the old crusts that were getting moldy, but I have given Him a piece of my own daily bread; and I am glad to do it, if I can show my love to Jesus Christ by denying myself."

If you are doing this—if you are feeding the hungry and clothing the naked out of love for Jesus—I believe that these actions are given as examples because they are such blessed detectives between the hypocrites and the truly godly people. When you read *"for"* in this passage, you must not understand that their reward is because of this, but that they have proved to be God's servants by this. So while they do not merit it because of these actions, these actions show that they were saved by grace, which is evidenced by the fact that Christ has wrought such works in them. If Christ does not work such things in you, you have no part in Him; if you have not produced such works as these, you have not believed in Jesus.

Now, somebody says, "Then, I intend to give to the poor in the future in order that I may have this reward." Ah, but you are very much mistaken if you do that.

The Duke of Burgundy was waited on by a poor man, a very loyal subject, who brought him a very large root that he had grown. He was a very poor man indeed, and every root he grew in his garden was of consequence to him. But merely as a loyal offering, he brought to his prince the largest his little garden produced. The prince was so pleased with the man's evident loyalty and affection that he gave him a very large sum. Seeing this, the duke's steward thought, "Well, I see this pays; this man got fifty pounds for his large root. I think I will make the duke a present." So he bought a horse, and he reckoned that he should have in return for it ten times as much as it was worth. He presented it to the duke with that view in mind. The duke, like a wise man, quietly accepted the horse and gave the greedy steward nothing. That was all.

Likewise, you say, "Well, here is a Christian man, and he gets rewarded; he has been giving to the poor, helping the Lord's church, and he is saved; these benevolent acts pay, so I will make a little investment, too." But, you see, the steward did not give the horse out of any idea of loyalty, kindness, or love for the duke, but out of very great love for himself; therefore, his investment brought no return. If you perform deeds of charity with the idea of getting to heaven by them, it is yourself that you are feeding and yourself that you are clothing. All your virtue is not virtue—it is rank selfishness; it smells strongly of selfhood, and Christ will never accept it. You will never hear Him say "thank you" for it. You served yourself, and no reward is due.

You must first come to the Lord Jesus Christ and look to Him to save you. You must forever renounce all ideas of doing anything to save yourself. But once having been saved, you will be able to give to the poor and needy without selfishness mixing with your motives, and you will receive a reward of grace for the love-token that you have given.

It is necessary to believe in Christ in order to be capable of true virtue of the highest order. It is necessary to trust Jesus and to be fully saved yourself before there is any value in your feeding the hungry or clothing the naked.

May God give you grace to go to my wounded Master and to rest in the precious Atonement, which He has made for human sin. When you have done that, being loved so greatly, may you show that you love in return; being purchased so dearly, may you live for Him who bought you. Let the actions by which you prove your love gleam and glisten like God-given jewels: visiting the sick, comforting the needy, relieving the distressed, and helping the weak. May God accept these offerings as they come from gracious souls. To Him be praise evermore.

Chapter 3

The Ascension and the Second Advent

And while they looked steadfastly toward heaven as He went up,
behold, two men stood by them in white apparel, who also said,
"Men of Galilee, why do you stand gazing up into heaven? This
same Jesus, who was taken up from you into heaven, will so come
in like manner as you saw Him go into heaven."
—Acts 1:10–11

F our great events shine brightly in our Savior's story. All
Christian minds delight to dwell on His birth, His death, His
resurrection, and His ascension. These make four rungs in
that ladder of light, the foot of which is on the earth, and the top of
which reaches to heaven. We could not afford to dispense with any
one of those four events, nor would it be profitable for us to forget
or to underestimate the value of any one of them.

That the Son of God was born of a woman creates in us the
intense delight of a brotherhood springing out of a common humanity. That Jesus once suffered to the death for our sins, and
thereby made a full atonement for us, is the rest and life of our
spirits. The manger and the cross together are divine seals of love.
That the Lord Jesus rose again from the dead is the guarantee of
our justification, as well as a transcendently delightful assurance of
the resurrection of all His people and of their eternal life in Him.
Has He not said, *"Because I live, you will live also"* (John 14:19)?
The resurrection of Christ is the morning star of our future glory.
Equally delightful is the remembrance of His ascension. No song is
sweeter than this: *"You have ascended on high, You have led cap-*
tivity captive; You have received gifts among men, even from the re-
bellious, that the LORD God might dwell there" (Ps. 68:18).

Each one of those four events points to a future event, and
they all lead up to it: the fifth link in the golden chain is our Lord's
second and most glorious Advent. Nothing is mentioned between

His ascent and His descent. True, a rich history comes between, but it lies in a valley between two stupendous mountains. We step from alp to alp as we journey in meditation from the Ascension to the Second Advent. I say that each of the previous four events points to it. Had He not come a first time in humiliation, born under the law, He could not *"appear a second time, apart from sin, for salvation"* (Heb. 9:28) in amazing glory.

Because He died once, we rejoice *"that Christ, having been raised from the dead, dies no more. Death no longer has dominion over Him"* (Rom. 6:9). Therefore, He comes to destroy that last enemy (1 Cor. 15:26), which He has already conquered through His death (Heb. 2:14). It is our joy, as we think of our Redeemer as risen, to feel that, in consequence of His rising, the trump of the archangel will assuredly sound for the awaking of all His slumbering people, when *"the Lord Himself will descend from heaven with a shout"* (1 Thess. 4:16). As for His ascension, He could not descend a second time if He had not first ascended. But having perfumed heaven with His presence and prepared a place for His people, we may aptly expect that He *"will come again and receive* [us] *to* [Himself]; *that where* [He is], *there* [we] *may be also"* (John 14:3). I want you, therefore, as you pass with joyful footsteps over these four grand events, as your faith leaps from His birth to His death, from His resurrection to His ascension, to be looking forward and hastening unto this crowning fact of our Lord's history: before long, He will come *"in like manner"* as He was seen going into heaven.

A Clarifying Depiction

At this present moment, we will start from the Ascension. If I had sufficient imagination, I would like to picture our Lord and the eleven walking up the side of Olivet, communing as they went, a happy company with a solemn awe upon them but with an intense joy in having fellowship with each other. Each disciple was glad to think that his dear Lord and Master, who had been crucified, was now among them, not only alive, but also surrounded with a mysterious safety and glory that none could disturb. The enemy was as still as a stone. No dog moved his tongue; His bitterest foes made no sign during the days of our Lord's afterlife below.

The company moved onward peacefully toward Bethany, which they all knew and loved. The Savior seemed drawn there at the time of His ascension, even as men's minds return to old and well-loved scenes when they are about to depart from this world. His happiest moments on earth had been spent beneath the roof where Mary, Martha, and their brother Lazarus lived. Perhaps it was best for the disciples that He should leave them at that place where He had been most hospitably entertained, to show that He departed in peace and not in anger. There they had seen Lazarus raised from the dead by Him who was now to be taken up from them: the memory of the triumphant past would help the tried faith of the present. There they had heard the voice saying, *"Loose him, and let him go"* (John 11:44); there they might aptly see their Lord loosed from all bonds of earthly gravitation that He might go to His Father and their Father. The memories of the place might help to calm their minds and arouse their spirits to that fullness of joy that ought to attend the glorifying of their Lord.

But they had come to a standstill, having reached the crest of the hill. The Savior stood conspicuously in the center of the group. Following a most instructive discourse, He pronounced a blessing on them as He lifted His pierced hands. While He was pronouncing words of love, He began to rise from the earth. To their astonishment, He had risen above them all! In a moment He had passed beyond the olives, which, with their silvery sheen, seemed to be lit up by His milder radiance. While the disciples were looking, the Lord had ascended into midair, and speedily He had risen to the regions of the clouds. Suddenly, as they stood spellbound with astonishment, a bright cloud like a chariot of God bore Him away. That cloud concealed Him from mortal gaze. *"Even though we have known Christ according to the flesh, yet now we know Him thus no longer"* (2 Cor. 5:16). They were riveted to the spot, and very naturally so. They lingered for a long time in that place. They stood with streaming eyes, awestruck, still looking upward.

It was not the Lord's will that they should remain inactive for long; their reverie was interrupted. They might have stood there until wonder saddened into fear. As it was, they remained long enough, for the angel's words may be accurately translated, "Why have you stood gazing up into heaven?"

Their lengthened gaze needed to be interrupted. Therefore, two shining ones, such as before met the women at the sepulcher (Luke 24:1–8), were sent to them. These messengers of God appeared in human form so that they might not alarm them, and in white raiment as if to remind them that all was bright and joyous.

These white-robed ministers stood with the disciples as if they would willingly join their company. Since none of the eleven would break the silence, the men in white raiment began the discourse. Addressing them in the usual celestial style, they asked a question that contained its own answer and then went on to tell their message. As they had once said to the women, *"Why do you seek the living among the dead? He is not here, but is risen!"* (Luke 24:5–6), so did they now say, *"Men of Galilee, why do you stand gazing up into heaven? This same Jesus, who was taken up from you into heaven, will so come in like manner as you saw Him go into heaven."* The angels showed their knowledge of them by calling them *"Men of Galilee,"* and reminded them that they were still on earth by recalling their place of birth.

Brought back to their senses, their reverie over, the apostles at once girded up their loins for active service. They did not need to be told twice but hastened to Jerusalem. The vision of angels had singularly brought them back into the world of actual life again, so that they obeyed Christ's command, *"Tarry in the city of Jerusalem"* (Luke 24:49). They seemed to say, "The taking up of our Master is not a thing to weep about. He has gone to His throne and to His glory, and He said it was expedient for us that He should go away. He will now send us the promise of the Father; we scarcely know what it will be like, but let us, in obedience to His will, make our way to the place where He charged us to await the gift of power."

Do you not see them going down the side of Olivet, taking that Sabbath-day journey into the cruel and wicked city without a thought of fear, having no dread of the bloodthirsty crew who slew their Lord, but happily remembering their Lord's exaltation and in the expectation of a wonderful display of His power? They held fellowship of the most delightful kind with one another. Shortly, they entered into the Upper Room where, in protracted prayer and communion, they waited for the promise of the Father.

I fear I have no imagination; I have barely mentioned the incidents in the simplest language. Yet try to realize the scene because it will be helpful to do so since our Lord Jesus is to come *"in like manner"* as the disciples saw Him ascend.

My first topic for discussion will be the gentle chiding administered by the shining ones: *"Men of Galilee, why do you stand gazing up into heaven?"* Second, I will consider the cheering description of our Lord that the white-robed messengers used: *"This same Jesus."*

Finally, I wish to examine the practical truth that they taught: *"This same Jesus, who was taken up from you into heaven, will so come in like manner as you saw Him go into heaven."*

A Gentle Chiding

First, then, is a gentle chiding. It was not sharply uttered by men dressed in black who used harsh speech to upbraid the servants of God severely for what was rather a mistake than a fault. No, the language is strengthening, yet tender; the form of a question allows them to reprove themselves rather than to be reproved; and the tone is that of brotherly love and affectionate concern.

Doing What Seems Right

Notice that what these saintly men were doing seems at first sight to be very right. I think, if Jesus were among us now, we would fix our eyes on Him and never withdraw them. He is altogether lovely, and it would seem wicked to yield our eyesight to any inferior object as long as He was able to be seen. When He ascended into heaven, it was the duty of His friends to look upon Him. It can never be wrong to look up; we are often directed to do so. It is even a holy saying of the psalmist: *"I will direct* [my prayer] *to You, and I will look up"* (Ps. 5:3), and *"I will lift up my eyes to the hills; from whence comes my help?"* (Ps. 121:1). If it is right to look up into heaven, it must be still more right to look up while Jesus rises to the place of His glory. Surely it would have been wrong if they had looked anywhere else.

It was due to the Lamb of God that they beheld Him as long as their eyes could follow Him. He is the Sun; where should eyes be turned but to His light? He is the King; where should courtiers within the palace gate turn their eyes but to their king as he ascends to his throne? The truth is that there was nothing wrong in their looking up into heaven.

However, they went a little farther than looking—they stood *"gazing."* A little excess in right action may be faulty. It may be wise to look but foolish to gaze. There is a very thin line sometimes between what is commendable and what is censurable. There is a golden mean that is not easy to keep. The exact path of right is often as narrow as a razor's edge, and he who does not err either on the right hand or on the left must be wise.

Look is ever the right word. After all, it is *"Look to Me, and be saved"* (Isa. 45:22). Look, yes, look steadfastly and intently. Your posture should always be that of one *"looking unto Jesus"* (Heb. 12:2) throughout life.

However, there is a gazing that is not commendable, when the look becomes not that of reverent worship, but of presumptuous curiosity; when the desire to know what should be known mingles with a prying into what it is for God's glory to conceal. Beloved, it is of little use to look up into an empty heaven. If Christ Himself is not visible in heaven, then, we gaze in vain, since there is nothing for a saintly eye to see. When the person of Jesus was gone out of the azure vault above them and the cloud had effectively concealed Him, why should they continue to gaze when God Himself had drawn the curtain? If infinite wisdom had withdrawn the object on which they desired to gaze, what would their gazing be but a sort of reflection on the wisdom that had removed their Lord?

Yet it did seem very right. Thus, certain things that you and I do may appear right, yet we may need to be chided into doing something better. They may be right in themselves, but they are not appropriate for the occasion, not seasonable, not expedient. They may be right up to a point, and then, they may touch the boundary of excess. A steadfast gaze into heaven may be to a devout soul a high order of worship, but if looking upward fills up much of our working time, it might become the most idle form of folly.

Doing What Comes Naturally

However, I cannot help adding that it was very natural. I do not wonder that the whole eleven stood gazing up, for if I had been there, I am sure I would have done the same. How struck they must have been with the ascent of the Master out of their midst! You would be amazed if someone from among your own number began to ascend into heaven, would you not? Our Lord did not gradually melt away from sight as a phantom or dissolve into thin air as a mere apparition. The Savior did not disappear in that way at all. He rose, and they saw that it was His very self that was rising. His own body, the material in which He had veiled Himself, actually, distinctly, and literally rose to heaven before their eyes. I repeat, the Lord did not dissolve and disappear like a vision of the night, but He evidently rose until the clouds intervened and they could see Him no more.

I think I would have stood looking at the very place where His cloudy chariot had been. I know it would be idle to continue to do so, but our hearts often urge us on to acts that we could not justify logically. Hearts are not to be argued with. Sometimes you stand by a grave where one is buried whom you dearly loved. You go there often to weep; you cannot help it. The place is precious to you. Yet you could not prove that you do any good by your visits. Perhaps you even injure yourself thereby and deserve to be gently chided with the question, Why?

It may be the most natural thing in the world, and yet it may not be a wise thing to do. The Lord allows us to do what is innocently natural, but He will not have us carry it too far because then, it might foster an evil nature. Hence, He sends an interrupting messenger—not an angel with a sword, or even a rod, but He sends some man in white raiment. I mean one who is both cheerful and holy, and who, by his conduct or his words, suggests to us the question, *"Why do you stand gazing?"* What will be the benefit? What will it avail? Thus, our understanding is called into action, and we, being men of thought, answer within ourselves, "This will not do. We must not stand here gazing forever." Therefore, we arouse ourselves to get back to the Jerusalem of practical life, where we hope to do service for our Master in the power of God.

Notice, then, that the disciples were doing what seemed to be right and what was evidently very natural. But note also that it is very easy to carry the apparently right and the absolutely natural too far. Let us take heed to ourselves and often ask our hearts, Why?

Acting without Reason

Next, notice that what they did was not justifiable, based on strict reason. While Christ was going up, it was proper that they should adoringly look at Him. He might almost have said, "If you see Me when I am taken up, a double portion of My spirit will rest on you." (See 2 Kings 2:9–10.) They did well to look where He led the way. However, when He was gone, to remain gazing was an act that they could not exactly explain to themselves and could not justify to others. Try asking the question like this: "What purpose will be fulfilled by your continuing to gaze into the sky? He is gone; it is absolutely certain that He is gone. He is taken up, and God Himself has manifestly concealed all trace of Him by bidding yonder cloud to sail in between Him and you. Why do you still gaze? He told you, *'I go to My Father'* (John 14:12). Why stand and gaze?"

We may, under the influence of great love, act unwisely. I well remember seeing the action of a woman whose only son was emigrating to a distant land. I stood in the station, noticing her many tears and her frequent embraces of her boy; but the train came, and he entered the carriage. After the train had pulled out from the station, she was foolish enough to break away from friends who sought to detain her. She ran along the platform, leaped down on the railroad tracks, and pursued the flying train. It was natural, but it would have been better left undone. What was the use of it?

We should abstain from acts that serve no practical purpose, for in this life we have neither time nor strength to waste in fruitless action. The disciples would be wise to cease gazing, for nobody would be benefited by it, and they would not themselves be blessed. What is the use of gazing when there is nothing to see? Well did the angels ask, *"Why do you stand gazing up into heaven?"*

Again, ask another question: What precept were they obeying when they stood gazing up into heaven? If you have a command from God to do a certain thing, you need not inquire into the reason of the command; it is disobedient to question God's will. However, when there is no precept whatever, why persevere in an act that evidently does not promise to bring any blessing? Who had ordered them to stand gazing up into heaven? If Christ had done so, then, in Christ's name, let them stand like statues and never turn their heads. But since He had not told them to do so, why did they do what He had not directed and leave undone what He had commanded? He had strictly charged them that they should tarry at Jerusalem until they were *"endued with power from on high"* (Luke 24:49). Thus, what they did was not justifiable.

Acting Unproductively

Here is the practical point for us: What they did, we are very apt to imitate. "Oh," you say, "I would never stand gazing up into heaven." I am not sure of that. Some Christians are very curious but not obedient. Clear precepts are neglected, but they seek to solve difficult problems. I remember a person who always was dwelling on the vials and seals and trumpets; he was great at apocalyptic symbols. But he had seven children, and he had no family prayer. If he had left the vials and trumpets and tended to his boys' and girls' upbringing, it would have been far better.

I have known men marvelously learned in Daniel and specially instructed in Ezekiel, but singularly forgetful of the twentieth chapter of Exodus and not very clear about the eighth chapter of Romans. I do not speak with any blame of such folks for studying Daniel and Ezekiel—quite the opposite. Yet I wish they had been more zealous for the conversion of the sinners in their homes and neighborhoods and more careful to assist the poor saints. I admit the value of the study of the feet of the image in Nebuchadnezzar's vision and the importance of knowing the kingdoms that make up the ten toes, but I do not see the propriety of allowing such studies to override the commonplace activities of practical godliness. If the time spent over obscure theological propositions were given to a mission in the dim alley near the man's house, more benefit would come to man and more glory to God.

Do not misunderstand, beloved. I would have you understand all mysteries, if you could. But do not forget that our chief business here below is to cry, *"Behold! The Lamb of God!"* (John 1:29). By all means, read and search until you know all that the Lord has revealed concerning things to come, but first of all see to it that your children are brought to the Savior's feet and that you are workers together with God in the building of His church. The dense mass of misery and ignorance and sin that is round about us on every side demands all our powers. If you do not respond to the call, though I am not a man in white apparel, I venture to say to you, "You men of Christendom, why do you stand gazing up into the mysteries when so much is to be done for Jesus and you are leaving it undone?" Oh, you who are curious but not obedient, I fear I address you in vain, but I have done so nevertheless. May the Holy Spirit apply this to your hearts.

Others are contemplative but not active; they are much given to the study of Scripture and to meditation but not *"zealous for good works"* (Titus 2:14). Contemplation is so scarce these days that I could wish there were a thousand times as much of it. However, in the case to which I refer, everything runs in the one channel of thought: all time is spent in reading, in enjoyment, in rapture, and in pious leisure.

Religion should never become the subject of selfishness, yet I fear some treat it as if its chief end were personal spiritual gratification. When a man's religion totally lies in his saving only himself and in enjoying holy things for himself, there is a disease within him. When his judgment of a sermon is based on the one question,

"Did it feed me?" it is a swinish judgment. There is such a thing as getting a swinish religion in which you are yourself first, yourself second, yourself third, yourself to the utmost end. Did Jesus ever think or speak in that fashion? Contemplation of Christ Himself may be carried out so as to lead you away from Him. The recluse meditates on Jesus, but he is as unlike the busy, self-denying Jesus as any can be. Meditation, unattended by active service in the spreading of the Gospel among men, well deserves the rebuke of the angel, *"Men of Galilee, why do you stand gazing up into heaven?"*

Acting Impatiently

Moreover, some are anxious and deliriously impatient for some supernatural intervention. We get at times into a sad state of mind because we do not see the kingdom of Christ advancing as we desire. I suppose it is with you as it is with me: I begin to fret and am deeply troubled. I feel that there is good reason I should be upset, because *"truth is fallen in the street"* (Isa. 59:14) and the *"day of trouble and rebuke and blasphemy"* (Isa. 37:3) is upon us. Then, I pine because the Master is away, and I cry, "When will He be back again? Oh, why are His chariots so long in coming? Why does He tarry through the ages?" Then, if you are like me, your desires sour into impatience, and you begin gazing up into heaven, looking for His coming with a restlessness that does not allow you to discharge your duties as you should. Whenever anybody gets into that state, this is the word: *"Men of Galilee, why do you stand gazing up into heaven?"*

Acting from Wrong Desires

In certain cases this uneasiness has drawn to itself a wrong expectation of immediate wonders and an intense desire for sign-seeing. Ah, me, what fanaticism comes of this! In America years ago, a man came forward who declared that on a certain day the Lord would come. This man led a great company to believe his crazy predictions. Many took their horses and fodder for two or three days and went out into the woods, expecting to be all the more likely to see what was to be seen when once away from the crowded city. All over the States, there were people who had made ascension dresses in which to soar into the air in proper costume.

556

They waited, and they waited, and I am sure that no text could have been more appropriate for them than this: *"Men of* [America], *why do you stand gazing up into heaven?"* Nothing came of it, yet there are thousands in England and America who need only a fanatical leader for them to run into similar folly.

The desire to know the times and seasons is a craze with many poor bodies whose insanity runs in that particular groove. All natural occurrences are *"signs of the times"* (Matt. 16:3)—signs, I may add, that they do not understand. Earthquakes are special favorites with them. "Now," they cry, "the Lord is coming," as if there had not been earthquakes of the sort we have heard of lately hundreds of times since our Lord went up into heaven. When the prophetic earthquakes occur in various places (Matt. 24:7), we will know of it without the warnings of these brothers. How many people have been infatuated by the number of the Beast and have been ready to leap for joy because they have found the number 666 in some famous person's name. Why, everybody's name will yield that number if you treat it judiciously and use the numerals of Greece, Rome, Egypt, China, or Timbuktu. I feel weary with the silly way in which some people make toys out of Scripture and play with texts as with a deck of cards.

Whenever you meet with a man who promotes himself as a prophet, keep out of his way in the future. When you hear of signs and wonders, turn to your Lord, and *"by your patience possess your souls"* (Luke 21:19). *"The just shall live by faith"* (Rom. 1:17). There is no other way of living among wild enthusiasts.

Believe in God, and do not ask for miracles and marvels or the knowledge of times and seasons. To know when the Lord will restore the kingdom is not in your scope. Remember this verse: *"It is not for you to know times or seasons"* (Acts 1:7). If I were introduced into a room where a large number of parcels were stored and told that there was something good for me, I would begin to look for anything with my name on it. If I came on a parcel and saw in big letters, "It is not for you," I would leave it alone. Here, then, is a package of knowledge marked, *"It is not for you to know times or seasons which the Father has put in His own authority"* (v. 7). Cease to meddle with matters that are concealed, and be satisfied to know the things that are clearly revealed.

A Cheering Description

Next, I want you to notice the cheering description that these bright spirits gave concerning our Lord. They described Him as *"this same Jesus."* I appreciate the description all the more because it came from those who knew Him: He was *"seen by angels"* (1 Tim. 3:16). They had watched Him all His life long, and they knew Him. When they, having just seen Him rise to His Father and His God, said of Him, *"This same Jesus,"* then, I know by an infallible testimony that He was the same, and that He is the same.

Jesus Is Alive

Jesus is gone, but He still exists. He has left us, but He is not dead. He has not dissolved into nothing like the mist of the morning. *"This same Jesus"* is gone up unto His Father's throne, and He is there today as certainly as He once stood at Pilate's bar. As surely as He did hang upon the cross, so surely does He, the selfsame Man, sit upon the throne of God and reign over creation.

I like to compare the positive identity of the Christ in the seventh heaven with the Christ in the lowest depths of agony. The Christ they spat on is now the Christ whose name the cherubim and seraphim are singing day without night. The Christ they scourged is He before whom principalities and powers delight to cast their crowns. Think of it, and be glad. Do not stand gazing up into heaven after a myth or a dream. Jesus lives; mind that you live also. Do not loiter as if you had nothing at all to do or as if the kingdom of God had come to an end because Jesus is gone from the earth as to His bodily presence. It is not all over; He still lives, and He has given you work to do until He comes. Therefore, go and do it.

"This same Jesus." I love that word *Jesus,* because it means "Savior." Oh, you anxious sinners, the name of Him who has gone into His glory is full of invitation to you! Will you not come to *"this same Jesus"*? This is He who opened the eyes of the blind and brought forth the prisoners out of incarceration. He is doing the same thing today. Oh, that your eyes may see His light! He who touched the lepers and raised the dead is the same Jesus still, *"able to save to the uttermost those who come to God through Him"* (Heb. 7:25). Oh, that you may look and live! You have only to come to Him by faith, as she did who touched the hem of His garment. You have but to cry to Him as the blind man did whose sight He restored, for He is the same Jesus, bearing about with Him the same tender love for guilty men and the same readiness to receive and cleanse all who come to Him by faith.

The Same Jesus Will Return

"This same Jesus." Why, that must have meant that He who is in heaven is the same Christ who was on earth, but it must also mean that He who is to come will be the same Jesus who went up into heaven. There is no change in our blessed Master's nature, nor will there ever be. There is a great change in His condition:

> The Lord shall come, but not the same
> As once in lowliness He came,
> A humble man before His foes,
> A weary man, and full of woes.

He will be *"this same Jesus"* in nature, though not in condition; He will possess the same tenderness when He comes to judge, the same gentleness of heart when all the glories of heaven and earth encircle His brow. Our eyes will see Him in that Day, and we will recognize Him, not only by the nailprints, but by the very look of His countenance, by the character that gleams from that marvelous face. We will say, "It is Jesus! 'Tis He! The same Christ who went up from the top of Olivet from the midst of His disciples!" Go to Him with your troubles as you would have done when He was here. Look forward to His Second Coming without dread. Look for Him with that joyous expectancy with which you would welcome Jesus of Bethany, who loved Mary, Martha, and Lazarus.

Preceding that sweet title came this question: *"Why do you stand gazing up into heaven?"* They might have said, "We stay here because we do not know where to go. Our Master is gone." But, oh, it is the same Jesus, and He is coming again; so go down to Jerusalem and get to work directly. Do not worry yourselves. No grave accident has occurred. It is not a disaster that Christ has gone, but an advance in His work. Despisers tell us nowadays, "Your cause is done, for Christianity has become obsolete! Your divine Christ is gone; we have not seen a trace of His miracle-working hand, nor heard a whisper of that voice that no man could rival." Our response should be that we are not standing, gazing into heaven; we are not paralyzed because Jesus is away. He lives; our great Redeemer lives. Although it is our delight to lift up our eyes because we expect His coming, it is equally our delight to turn our heavenly gazing into an earthward watching and to go down into the city, there to tell that Jesus is risen, that men are to be saved by faith in

Him, and that *"whoever believes in Him should not perish but have everlasting life"* (John 3:16).

We are not defeated—far from it. His ascension is not a retreat, but an advance. His tarrying is not for lack of power, but because of the abundance of His long-suffering. The victory is not questionable. All things work for it: all the hosts of God are mustering for the final charge. *"This same Jesus"* is mounting His white horse to lead forth the armies of heaven, conquering and to conquer.

A Great Practical Truth

My third point concerns the great practical truth found in the text. This truth is not one that is to keep us gazing into heaven, but one that is to make each of us go to his own house to render earnest service. What is this truth?

Jesus Is in Heaven

First, this truth is that Jesus is gone into heaven. Jesus is gone! Jesus is gone! It sounds like a bell ringing. Jesus is taken up from you into heaven—that sounds like marriage chimes. He is gone, but He is gone up to the hills from where He can survey the battle—up to the throne from which He can send us help. The reserve forces of the Omnipotent stood waiting until their Captain came; now that He has come into the center of the universe, He can send legions of angels or raise up hosts of men for the help of His cause.

I see every reason for going out into the world and getting to work because He is ascended into heaven. Moreover, *"all authority has been given to [Him] in heaven and on earth"* (Matt. 28:18). Is this not a good argument to spur you on: *"Go therefore and make disciples of all the nations, baptizing them in the name of the Father and of the Son and of the Holy Spirit"* (v. 19)?

Jesus Will Come Again

Second, Jesus will come again. This is another reason for girding our loins, because it is clear that He has not quit the fight or deserted the field of battle. Our great Captain is still heading the conflict. He has ridden into another part of the field, but He will be back again, perhaps *"in the twinkling of an eye"* (1 Cor. 15:52). You do not say that a commander has given up the campaign because it is expedient that he should withdraw from your part of the field. Our Lord did the best thing for His kingdom in going away. It was expedient to the highest degree that He should go and that we should each one receive the Spirit. There is a blessed unity between Christ the King and the most common soldier in the ranks. He has not taken His heart, His care, or His interest from us. He is bound up heart and soul with His people and their holy warfare, and this is the evidence of it: *"Behold, I am coming quickly, and My reward is with Me, to give to every one according to his work"* (Rev. 22:12).

Returning in the Same Manner

Moreover, we are told in the text—and this is a reason why we should get to our work—that He is coming *"in like manner"* as He departed. Certain of the commentators do not seem to understand English at all. *"This same Jesus, who was taken up from you into heaven, will so come in like manner as you saw Him go into heaven."* This, they say, relates to His spiritual coming at Pentecost. Give anybody a grain of sense, and do they not see that a spiritual coming is not a coming *"in like manner"* as He went up into heaven? There is an analogy, but certainly not a likeness, between the two things. Our Lord was taken up; they could see Him rise. He will come again, and *"every eye will see Him"* (Rev. 1:7). He went up not in spirit, but in bodily form: likewise, He will come down bodily.

"This same Jesus...will so come in like manner." He went up as a matter of fact—not in poetic figure and spiritual symbol, but as a matter of fact. *"This same Jesus"* literally went up, and He will literally come again. He will descend in clouds even as He went up in clouds, and *"He shall stand at last on the earth"* (Job 19:25) even as He stood before.

He went up to heaven unopposed; no high priests, scribes, Pharisees, or even one of the rabble opposed His ascension. It is ridiculous to suppose that they could have. When He comes a second time, none will stand against Him. His adversaries will perish; as the fat of rams, they will melt away in His presence. When He comes, He will break rebellious nations with a rod of iron (see Revelation 2:26–27), for His force will be irresistible in that Day.

Beloved, do not let anybody spiritualize all this away from you. Jesus is coming as a matter of fact; therefore, go to your sphere of service as a matter of fact. Get to work and teach the ignorant, win the wayward, instruct the children, and everywhere tell out the sweet name of Jesus. As a matter of fact, give of your substance, but do not talk about your giving. As a matter of fact, consecrate your daily life to the glory of God. As a matter of fact, live wholly for your Redeemer. Jesus is not coming in a sort of mythical, misty, hazy way. He is literally and actually coming, and He will literally and actually call on you to give an account of your stewardship. Therefore, today, literally and not symbolically, personally and not by proxy, go out through the portion of the world that you can reach *and preach the gospel to every creature*￼ (Mark 16:15), as you have opportunity.

Be Ready to Meet Him

This is what the men in white apparel meant—be ready to meet your coming Lord. What is the way to be ready to meet Jesus? It is the same Jesus who went away from us who is coming; so then, let us be doing what He was doing before He went away. If it is the same Jesus who is coming, we cannot possibly put ourselves into any posture of which He will better approve than by going about doing good. If you would meet Him with joy, serve Him with earnestness. If the Lord Jesus Christ were to come today, I would like Him to find me at my studying, praying, or preaching. Would you not like Him to find you in your Sunday school class or out there at the corner of the street preaching or doing whatever you have the privilege of doing in His name? Would you meet your Lord in idleness? Do not think of it.

One morning I called to see a sister. When I arrived, she was cleaning the front steps with some bleach. She apologized very much and said that she felt ashamed of being caught in such a position. I replied, "Dear friend, you could not be in a better position than you are, for you are doing your duty as a good housewife. May God bless you." She had no money to spare for a servant, and she was doing her duty by keeping the home tidy. I thought she looked more beautiful with her pail beside her than if she had been dressed according to the latest fashion. I said to her, "I assure you that I would like my Lord to come and find me, just as I have found you, doing my daily work with all my heart and fulfilling the duty of the hour. May the Lord Jesus Christ, when He comes suddenly, find you just as you are, doing your duty!"

I want you all to get to your pails without being ashamed of them. Serve the Lord in some way or other. Serve Him always; serve Him intensely; serve Him more and more. Go tomorrow and serve the Lord at the counter, in the workshop, or in the field. Go and serve the Lord by helping the poor and the needy, the widow and the fatherless. Serve Him by teaching the children, but especially by endeavoring to train your own children. Go and hold a temperance meeting; show the drunkard that there is hope for Him in Christ. Go to the midnight meeting, and let the fallen woman know that Jesus can restore her.

Do what Jesus has given you the power to do. Then, Christian disciples, you will not stand gazing up into heaven, but you will wait on the Lord in prayer, receive the Spirit of God, and declare to all around the doctrine of "believe and live." Then, when Christ comes, He will say to you, *"Well done, good and faithful servant....Enter into the joy of your lord"* (Matt. 25:23). So may His grace enable us to do.

Chapter 4

Coming Judgment of the Secrets of Men

God will judge the secrets of men by Jesus Christ,
according to my gospel.
—Romans 2:16

I t is impossible for any of us to tell what it cost the apostle Paul to write the first chapter of the epistle to the Romans. *"It is shameful even to speak of those things which are done by* [the wicked] *in secret"* (Eph. 5:12), but Paul felt that it was necessary to break through his shame and to speak out concerning the hideous vices of the heathen. He has left on record an exposure of the sins of his day, which crimsons the cheeks of the modest when they read it and makes the ears of him who hears it tingle.

Paul knew that this chapter would be read, not in his age alone, but in all ages, and that it would go into the households of the most pure and godly as long as the world stands. Yet he deliberately wrote it, and wrote it under the guidance of the Holy Spirit. He knew that it must be written to put to shame the abominations of an age that was almost past shame. Monsters that revel in darkness must be dragged into the open so that they may be withered up by the light.

After Paul had thus written in anguish, he thought about his chief comfort. While his pen was black with the words he had written in the first chapter, he was driven to write about his greatest delight. He held on to the Gospel with a greater tenacity than ever. As in the text verse, he needed to mention the Gospel. He did not speak of it here as "the Gospel" but as *"my gospel."* *"God will judge the secrets of men by Jesus Christ, according to my gospel."*

Paul must have felt that he could not live in the midst of such depraved people without holding the Gospel with both hands and grasping it as his very own. *"My gospel,"* he said. Not that Paul was the author of it, not that Paul had an exclusive monopoly on its blessings, but that he had received it from Christ Himself and re-garded himself as responsibly entrusted with it so that he could not disown it even for an instant. So fully had he taken it into himself that he could not do less than call it *"my gospel."* In other places he spoke of *"our gospel"* (2 Cor. 4:3; 1 Thess. 1:5; 2 Thess. 2:14), thus using a possessive pronoun to show how believers identify them-selves with the truth that they preach.

Paul had a Gospel, a definite form of truth, and he believed in it beyond all doubt. Therefore, he spoke of it as *"my gospel."* We can hear the voice of faith that seems to say, "Though others reject it, I am sure of it and allow no shade of mistrust to darken my mind. To me it is *'good tidings of great joy'* (Luke 2:10). I hail it as *'my gospel.'* If I am called a fool for holding on to it, I am content to be a fool and to find all my wisdom in my Lord."

> Should all the forms that men devise
> Assault my faith with treacherous art,
> I'd call them vanity and lies,
> And bind the Gospel to my heart.

Is not this word, *"my gospel,"* the voice of love? Does he not by this word embrace the Gospel as the only love of his soul, for the sake of which he had suffered the loss of all things and counted them but rubbish (Phil. 3:8), for the sake of which he was willing to stand before Nero and proclaim the message from heaven, even in Caesar's palace? Though each word should cost him a life, he was willing to die a thousand deaths in the holy cause. *"My gospel,"* said he, with a rapture of delight, as he pressed to his bosom the sacred deposit of truth.

"My gospel." Does this not show his courage? It is as much as to say, *"I am not ashamed of the gospel of Christ, for it is the power of God to salvation for everyone who believes"* (Rom. 1:16). He said *"my gospel,"* as a soldier speaks of "my colors" or of "my king." He resolves to bear this banner to victory and to serve this royal truth even to the death.

"My gospel." There is a touch of discrimination about the ex-pression. Paul perceived that there were other gospels being pro-moted, and he made short work of them when he said, *"But even if we, or an angel from heaven, preach any other gospel to you than what we have preached to you, let him be accursed"* (Gal. 1:8).

The apostle had a gentle spirit. He prayed heartily for the Jews who persecuted him and yielded his life for the conversion of the

Gentiles who maltreated him, but he had no tolerance for those who preached a false gospel. He exhibited great breadth of mind, and to save souls he became *"all things to all men"* (1 Cor. 9:22). However, when he contemplated any alteration or adulteration of the Gospel of Christ, he thundered without measure. When he feared that something else might spring up among the philosophers or among the Judaizers that would hide a single beam of the glorious Sun of Righteousness, he used no measured language, but cried concerning the author of such a darkening influence, *"Let him be accursed"* (Gal. 1:8).

Every heart that would see men blessed whispers an "Amen" to the apostolic benediction. No greater curse can come upon mankind than the obscuring of the Gospel of Jesus Christ. Paul said of himself and his true brothers and sisters, *"We are not, as so many, peddling the word of God"* (2 Cor. 2:17). He cried to those who turned aside from the one true Gospel, *"O foolish Galatians! Who has bewitched you?"* (Gal. 3:1). He spoke of all new doctrines as *"a different gospel, which is not another; but there are some who trouble you"* (Gal. 1:6–7).

As for myself, looking at the matter afresh, amid all the filthiness that I see in the world of this day, I lay hold of the pure and blessed Word of God and call it all the more earnestly, *"my gospel"*—mine in life and mine in death, mine against all comers, mine forever, with God helping me. With emphasis I say, *"my gospel."*

Now let us notice what it was that brought up this expression, *"my gospel."* What was Paul preaching about? Certainly not about any of the gentle and tender themes that we are told nowadays should occupy all our time. Rather, he was speaking of the terrors of the law, and in that connection he spoke of *"my gospel."*

Let us at once turn our attention to this text. It needs no dividing, for it divides itself. First, let us consider that on a certain Day, God will judge mankind; second, on that Day God will judge the secrets of men; third, when He judges the secrets of men, it will be by Jesus Christ; and, fourth, this judgment is according to the Gospel.

God Will Certainly Judge

We begin with the solemn truth that on a certain Day God will judge men. A judgment is going on daily. God is continually holding court and considering the behavior of the sons of men. Every evil deed that they do is recorded in the register of doom, and each good action is remembered and laid up in store by God. That judgment is reflected in a measure in the consciences of men. Those who know the Gospel, and those who do not know it, have a certain measure of light alike, by which they know right from wrong—their consciences are all the while accusing or else excusing them.

This session of the heavenly court continues from day to day like that of our local magistrates. This does not prevent, but rather necessitates, the holding of an ultimate great judgment. As each man passes into another world, there is an immediate judgment passed upon him, but this is only the foreshadowing of what will take place at the end of the age.

There is a judgment also passing upon nations. Since nations will not exist as nations in another world, they have to be judged and punished in this present state. The thoughtful reader of history will not fail to observe how sternly justice has dealt with empire after empire when they have become corrupt. Colossal dominions have withered when sentenced by the King of Kings. Ask yourself, "Where is the empire of Assyria today? Where are the mighty cities of Babylon? Where are the glories of the Medes and Persians? What has become of the Macedonian power? Where are the Caesars and their palaces?" These empires were forces established by cruelty and used for oppression; they fostered luxury and licentiousness. When they were no longer tolerable, the earth was purged from their polluting existence. What horrors of war, bloodshed, and devastation have come upon men as the result of their iniquities!

The world is full of the monuments both of the mercy and the justice of God. In fact, the monuments of His justice, if rightly viewed, are proofs of His goodness: it is mercy on the part of God to put an end to evil systems when, like a nightmare, they weigh heavily on the shoulders of mankind.

The omnipotent Judge has not ceased from His sovereign rule over kingdoms, and our own country may yet have to feel His chastisements. What is there about London that it should be more enduring than Rome? Why should the palaces of our monarchs be eternal if the palaces of Russia have fallen? The almost boundless power of the Pharaohs has passed away, and Egypt has become the lowliest of nations. Why should not England come under similar condemnation? What are we? What is there about our boastful race, whether on this side of the Atlantic or the other, that we should monopolize the favor of God? If we rebel and sin against Him, He will not hold us guiltless, but will deal out impartial justice to an ungrateful race.

Still, though such judgments proceed every day, yet there is to be a Day in which God will judge the sons of men in a more distinct, formal, public, and final manner. We might have guessed this by the light of nature and of reason. Even heathen people have had a dim notion of a day of doom. However, we are not left to guess it; we are solemnly assured of it in Holy Scripture. Accepting this Book as the revelation of God, we know beyond all doubt that a Day is appointed in which the Lord *"will judge the secrets of men."*

Judging in this context means all that concerns the proceedings of trial and verdict. God will judge the race of men. That is to say, first, there will be a session of majesty and the appearing of a Great White Throne, surrounded with the pomp of angels and glorified beings. Then, a summons will be issued, bidding all men to come to judgment, to give their final accounts. The heralds will fly through the realms of death and summon those who sleep in the dust, for the quick and the dead *"must all appear before the judgment seat of Christ"* (2 Cor. 5:10). John said,

> And I saw the dead, small and great, standing before God, and books were opened. And another book was opened, which is the Book of Life. And the dead were judged according to their works, by the things which were written in the books. The sea gave up the dead who were in it, and Death and Hades delivered up the dead who were in them. And they were judged, each one according to his works.   (Rev. 20:12–13)

Those who have been buried for so long that their dust is mingled with the soil and have undergone a thousand transmutations will nevertheless be made to appear personally before the judgment seat of Christ. What an inquest that will be! You and I and all the myriads of our race will be gathered before the throne of the Son of God. Then, when all are gathered, the indictment will be read, and each one will be examined concerning *"the things done in the body, according to what he has done, whether good or bad"* (2 Cor. 5:10). Then, the books will be opened, and everything recorded there will be read before the face of heaven. Every sinner will then hear the story of his life published to his everlasting shame. The good will ask no concealment, and the evil will find none. Angels and men will then see the truth of things, and the saints will judge the world.

The great Judge Himself will then give the decision: He will pronounce sentence upon the wicked and execute their punishment. No partiality will be seen. There will be no private conferences to secure immunity for nobles, no hushing up of matters so that great men may escape contempt for their crimes. All men will stand before the one great judgment bar. Evidence will be given concerning them all, and a righteous sentence will go forth from the mouth of Him who does not know how to flatter the great.

This will be so, and it ought to be so. God should judge the world because He is the universal Ruler and Sovereign. There has been a day for sinning; there ought to be a day for punishing. A long age of rebellion has been endured; there must be a time when justice asserts her supremacy. We have seen an age in which reformation has been commanded, in which mercy has been presented, in which dissuasion and entreaty have been used. There ought at last to come a day when God *"will judge the living and the dead"* (2 Tim. 4:1) and measure to each the final result of life.

It ought to be so for the sake of the righteous. They have been slandered, despised, and ridiculed. Worse than that, they have been imprisoned, beaten, and put to death times without number. The best have had the worst of it, and there ought to be a judgment to set these things right.

Besides, the festering iniquities of each age cry out to God that He should deal with them. Will such sin go unpunished? To what end is there a moral government at all, and how is its continuance to be secured if there are not rewards and punishments and a day of reckoning? For the display of His holiness, for the overwhelming of His adversaries, for the rewarding of those who have faithfully served Him, there must be and will be a Day in which God will judge the world.

Why does it not come at once? When will it come? The precise date we cannot tell. Neither man nor angel knows that Day, and it is idle and profane to guess at it since even the Son of Man does not know the time (Mark 13:32).

It is sufficient for us that the Judgment Day will surely come; it ought to be sufficient also to believe that it is postponed on purpose to give breathing time for mercy and space for repentance. Why should the ungodly want to know when that Day will come? What is that Day to them? To them it will be darkness, not light. It will be the Day of their being consumed as completely dry stubble. Therefore, bless the Lord that He delays His coming, and know that *"the longsuffering of our Lord is* [for the] *salvation"* (2 Pet. 3:15) of many.

Moreover, the Lord keeps the scaffold standing until He has built up the fabric of His church. Not yet are the elect all called out from among the guilty sons of men. Not yet have all the redeemed with blood been redeemed with power and brought forth out of the corruption of the age into the holiness in which they walk with God. Therefore, the Lord waits.

However, do not deceive yourselves. The great Day of His wrath is coming, and your days of reprieve are numbered. *"With the Lord one day is as a thousand years, and a thousand years as one day"* (v. 8). Perhaps you may die before the appearing of the Son of Man, but, even so, you will see His judgment seat, for you will rise again as surely as He rose. When the apostle Paul addressed the Grecian sages at Athens, he said,

> *God...now commands all men everywhere to repent, because He has appointed a day on which He will judge the world in righteousness by the Man whom He has ordained. He has given assurance of this to all by raising Him from the dead.*
>
> (Acts 17:30–31)

Do you not see, O you impenitent ones, that a risen Savior is the sign of your doom? As God has raised Jesus from the dead, so He will raise your bodies, that in these you may come to judgment. Before the judgment seat every man and woman will give an account of the things done in the body, whether they are good or whether they are evil. (See Romans 14:12.) Thus the Lord has decreed, and thus it shall be so.

The Secrets of Men Will Be Judged

Now, I want to call your attention to the idea that *"God will judge the secrets of men."* This will happen to all men of every nation, of every age, of every rank, and of every character. The Judge will, of course, judge their outward acts, but these may be said to have preceded them to judgment. Their secret acts are specially mentioned, because these will make judgment all the more searching.

By *"the secrets of men,"* the Scripture means those secret crimes that hide themselves away by their own infamy, which are too vile to be spoken of, which cause a shudder to go through a nation if they are dragged, as they ought to be, into the daylight. Secret offenses will be brought into judgment. The deeds of the night and of the closed room, the acts that require a finger to be placed on the lips and a conspiracy of silence to be sworn, revolting and shameless sins that must never be mentioned lest the man who committed them be excluded from his fellowmen as an outcast and abhorred even by other sinners—all these will be revealed.

All that any of you have done or are doing, if you are bearing the Christian name and yet practicing secret sin, will be laid bare before the universal gaze. If you sit among the people of God but you are living in dishonesty, untruthfulness, or uncleanness when no other eye can see, it will all be known. Shame and confusion of face will eternally cover you. Contempt will be the inheritance to which you awake when hypocrisy is no more possible. *"Do not be deceived, God is not mocked; for whatever a man sows, that he will also reap"* (Gal. 6:7). He will bring the secrets of men into judgment.

Our text especially refers to the hidden motives of every action. A man may do what is right from a wrong motive, and so the deed may be evil in the sight of God, though it seems right in the sight of men. Oh, think what it will be to have your motives all brought to light, to have it proven that you were godly for the sake of gain, that you were generous out of ostentation or zealous for love of praise, that you were careful in public to maintain a religious reputation but that all the while everything was done for self and self only! What a penetrating light God will turn upon our lives, when the darkest chambers of human desire and motive will be as clear as public acts! What a revelation it will be that makes manifest all thoughts, imaginings, lusts, and desires! All anger, envy, pride, and rebellion of the heart—what a disclosure will these make! All the sensual desires and imaginings of even the most self-controlled—what a foulness will these appear! What a day it will be when the secrets of men will be set in the full blaze of noon!

God will also reveal secrets that were secrets even to the sinners themselves, for there is sin in us that we have never seen and iniquity in us that we have never yet discovered. For our own comfort's sake, we have managed to blind our eyes somewhat, and we take care to avert our gaze from things that are inconvenient to see. However, we will be compelled to see all these evils in that Day, when the Lord *"will judge the secrets of men."*

I do not wonder that when a certain rabbi read Ecclesiastes 12:14, *"For God will bring every work into judgment, including every secret thing, whether good or evil,"* he wept. It is enough to make the best man tremble. Were it not for You, Jesus, whose precious blood has cleansed us from all sin, where would we be? Were it not for Your righteousness, which covers those who believe in You, who among us could endure the thought of that tremendous Day? In You, Jesus, we are made righteous; therefore, we do not fear the hour of trial. But were it not for You, our hearts would fail us for fear!

Now, if you ask me why God should specially judge the secrets of men—since this is not done in human courts, and cannot be, for secret things of this kind do not come under the cognizance of our short-sighted tribunals—I answer, it is because there is really nothing secret from God. We make a difference between secret and public sins, but He does not, for all things are naked and open to His eyes. All deeds are done in the immediate presence of God, who is personally present everywhere. He knows and sees all things as one, and every secret sin is but conceived to be secret through the deluded fantasy of our ignorance. God sees more of a secret sin than any man can see of what is done before his face. *"'Can anyone hide himself in secret places, so I shall not see him?' says the LORD"* (Jer. 23:24).

The secrets of men will be judged because often the greatest of moral acts are done in secret. The brightest deeds that God delights in are those that are done by His servants when they have shut the door and are alone with Him, when they have no motive but to please Him, when they studiously avoid publicity lest they should be turned aside by the praise of men, when the right hand does not know what the left hand does (Matt. 6:3), and when the loving, generous heart devises liberal things (Isa. 32:8) and does them confidentially so that it should never be discovered how the deed was done. It would be a pity that such deeds should be left out at the great audit.

Thus, too, secret vices are also of the very blackest kind, and to exempt them would be to let the worst of sinners go unpunished. Should it be that these polluted beings would escape because they have purchased silence with their wealth? I say solemnly, *"God forbid"* (Rom. 3:6 KJV). And He does forbid it. What they have done in secret will be proclaimed from the housetops.

Besides, the secret things of men enter into the very essence of their actions. An action is, after all, good or bad very much according to its motive. It may seem good, but the heart's incentive may taint it. Thus, if God did not judge the secret part of an action, He would not judge righteously. He will weigh all our actions, detect the designs that led to them, and reveal the motives that prompted them.

Is it not certainly true that the secret thing is the best evidence of the man's condition? Many men will not do in public what would bring them shame, not because they are not black-hearted enough for it, but because they are too cowardly. What a man does when he thinks that he is entirely by himself is the best revelation of the man. What you will not do because it would be told of you if you did ill is a poor index of your real character. What you will do because you will be praised for doing well is an equally faint test of your heart. Such virtue is mere self-seeking, or mean-spirited subservience to your fellowman. However, what you do out of respect to no authority but your own conscience and your God, what you do unobserved, without regard to what man will say concerning it—such actions reveal you and discover your real soul. Hence, God lays a special stress and emphasis here upon the fact that He will in that Day *"judge the secrets of men by Jesus Christ."*

Oh, friends, if it does not make you tremble to think of these things, it ought to do so. I feel the deep responsibility of emphasizing such matters, and I pray that God in His infinite mercy will apply these truths to our hearts that they may be forceful in our lives. These truths ought to startle us, but I am afraid we come in contact with them with small result. We have grown familiar with them, and they do not penetrate us as they should. We have to deal, beloved, with an omniscient God, with One who never forgets what is known, with One to whom all things are always present, with One who will conceal nothing out of fear or favor of any person, with One who will shortly bring the splendor of His omniscience and the impartiality of His justice to bear upon all human lives. God help us, wherever we rove and wherever we rest, to remember that each thought, word, and act of each moment lies in that fierce light that shines on all things from the throne of God.

Judged by Jesus Christ

Another solemn revelation of our text lies in the fact that *"God will judge the secrets of men by Jesus Christ."* Jesus Christ will sit

573

on the throne as God's Vice General and as the Judge, acting for God. What a name for a judge—the Savior-Anointed, Jesus Christ! He is to be the Judge of all mankind. Our Redeemer will be the determiner of our destiny.

In the first place, I do not doubt that this will be for the display of His glory. What a difference there will be then between the babe of Bethlehem's manger, who was hunted by Herod and carried down by night into Egypt for shelter, and the King of Kings and Lord of Lords before whom every knee must bow (Phil. 2:10)! What a difference between the weary man, full of woes, and He who will then be clothed with glory, sitting on a throne encircled with a rainbow! From the derision of men to the throne of universal judgment, what an ascent!

I am unable to convey to you my own heart's sense of the contrast between the Son of Man who *"is despised and rejected by men"* (Isa. 53:3) and the universally acknowledged Lord, before whom Caesars and pontiffs will bow in the dust. He who was judged at Pilate's bar will summon all to His bar. What a change from the shame and spitting, from the nails and the wounds, from the mockery and the thirst, from the dying anguish, to the glory in which will come He whose eyes are as a flame of fire and out of whose mouth there goes a two-edged sword (Rev. 1:14, 16)! *"He shall judge between the nations, and rebuke many people"* (Isa. 2:4), even He whom the nations abhorred. He will break them in pieces like a potter's vessel, even those who cast Him out as unworthy to live among them.

Oh, how we ought to bow before Him now as He reveals Himself in His tender sympathy and in His generous humiliation! Let us *"kiss the Son, lest He be angry"* (Ps. 2:12). Let us yield to His grace, that we may not be crushed by His wrath. You sinners, bow before those pierced feet, or else they will tread on you like clusters in the winepress. Look up to Him with weeping, confess your forgetfulness of Him, and put your trust in Him, lest He look down on you in indignation. Remember that He will one day say, *"Bring here those enemies of mine, who did not want me to reign over them, and slay them before me"* (Luke 19:27).

The holding of the judgment by the Lord Jesus will greatly enhance His glory. It will finally settle one controversy that is still upheld by certain erring spirits: no doubt will remain as to our Lord's deity in that day—no question that *"this same Jesus"* (Acts 1:11) who was crucified is both Lord and God. God Himself will judge, but He will perform the judgment in the person of His Son Jesus Christ, truly man, but nevertheless most truly God. Being God, He is divinely qualified to *"judge the world with righteousness, and the peoples with His truth"* (Ps. 96:13).

You again ask, "Why is the Son of God chosen to be the final Judge?" I give as a further answer that He receives this high office not only as a reward for all His pains and as a manifestation of His glory, but also because men have been under His mediatorial sway, and He is their Governor and King. At the present moment, we are all under the sway of the Prince Immanuel, *"God with us"* (Matt. 1:23). We have been placed by an act of divine clemency, not under the immediate government of an offended God, but under the reconciling rule of the Prince of Peace. Jesus said: *"All authority has been given to Me in heaven and on earth"* (Matt. 28:18). *"For the Father judges no one, but has committed all judgment to the Son, that all should honor the Son just as they honor the Father"* (John 5:22–23). We are commanded *"to preach to the people, and to testify that it is He who was ordained by God to be Judge of the living and the dead"* (Acts 10:42). Jesus is our Lord and King, and it is right that He should conclude His mediatorial sovereignty by rewarding His subjects according to their deeds.

I have something to express to you that ought to reach your hearts even if other thoughts have not done so. I think that God has chosen Christ, the Man Christ Jesus, to judge the world so that there may never be a quibble raised concerning that judgment. Men will not be able to say, "We were judged by a superior being who did not know our weaknesses and temptations; therefore, He judged us harshly and without a generous consideration of our condition." No, *"God will judge the secrets of men by Jesus Christ,"* who *"was in all points tempted as we are, yet without sin"* (Heb. 4:15). He is our brother, bone of our bone and flesh of our flesh, partaker of our humanity; therefore, He understands and knows what is in men. He has shown Himself to be skillful in all the surgery of mercy throughout the ages. At last He will be found equally skillful in dissecting motives and revealing the thoughts and intents of the heart. Nobody will ever be able to look back on that imposing tribunal and say that He who sat upon it was too stern because He knew nothing of human weakness. It will be the loving Christ, whose tears and bloody sweat and gaping wounds attest to His brotherhood with mankind. It will be clear to all intelligence that however dreadful His sentences, He could not be unmerciful.

"*God will judge* [us] *by Jesus Christ,*" in order that the judgment may be indisputable.

But pay close attention, for I write with a great weight on my soul. This judgment "*by Jesus Christ*" puts beyond possibility all hope of any post-intervention. If the Savior condemns, who can plead for us? In a parable found in the thirteenth chapter of Luke, Jesus told of an owner of a vineyard who was about to cut down a barren fig tree when the dresser of the vineyard pleaded, "Let it alone another year." But what can come of that tree when the vinedresser himself says to the master, "It must fall; I myself must cut it down"? When your Savior becomes your Judge, you will be judged indeed. If He should say, "*Depart from Me, you cursed*" (Matt. 25:41), who can call you back? If He who bled to save men at last comes to this conclusion—that there is no more to be done but they must be driven from His presence—then, bid farewell to all hope. To the guilty, the judgment will indeed be a great day of dread, decision, and despair.

An infinite horror will seize their spirits as the words of the loving Christ freeze the very marrow of their bones and fix them in the ice of eternal despair. There is, to my mind, a climax of solemnity in the fact that "*God will judge the secrets of men by Jesus Christ.*"

Does not this also show how certain the sentence will be? This Christ of God is too much in earnest to play with men. If He says, "*Come, you blessed of My Father*" (Matt. 25:34), He will not fail to bring them to their inheritance. If He is driven to say, "*Depart from Me, you cursed*" (v. 41), He will see it is done, and into everlasting punishment they must go. Even when it cost Him His life, He did not draw back from doing the will of His Father, nor will He shrink in that Day when He pronounces the sentence of doom. Oh, how evil must sin be since it constrains the tender Savior to pronounce a sentence of eternal woe!

I am sure that many of us have been driven lately to an increased hatred of sin, and our souls have recoiled within us because of the wickedness amid which we dwell. It has made us feel as if we would gladly borrow the Almighty's thunderbolts with which to smite iniquity. Such haste on our parts may not be seemly, since it implies a complaint against divine long-suffering. But Christ's dealing with evil will be calm and dispassionate, and all the more crushing. Jesus, with His pierced hand that attests to His supreme love for men, will wave the impenitent away. Those lips that bade the weary to rest in Him will solemnly say to the wicked, *"Depart from Me, you cursed, into the everlasting fire prepared for the devil and his angels"* (Matt. 25:41). To be trampled beneath the foot that was nailed to the cross will be to be crushed indeed. Yet so it is that *"God will judge the secrets of men by Jesus Christ."*

In God's judging men *"by Jesus Christ,"* it seems to me as if God intended to give a display of the unity of all His perfection. In this same Man, Christ Jesus, the Son of God, you behold justice and love, mercy and righteousness, combined in equal measure. He turns to the right and says, *"Come, you blessed"* (Matt. 25:34), with infinite grace; with the same lips, as He glances to the left, He says, *"Depart from Me, you cursed"* (v. 41). Men will then see at one glance how love and righteousness are one, and how they meet in equal splendor in the person of the Well Beloved, whom God has therefore chosen *"to be Judge of the living and the dead"* (Acts 10:42).

According to the Gospel

I will finish this subject with my last point, which is that all of this is according to the Gospel. What I am attempting to express is that there is nothing in the Gospel contrary to this solemn teaching. Men gather to us to hear us preach of infinite mercy and tell of the love that blots out sin. The task is joyful when we are called to deliver such a message. But remember, nothing in that message makes light of sin. The Gospel offers you no opportunity of continuing in sin and escaping without punishment. Its own cry is, *"Unless you repent you will all likewise perish"* (Luke 13:3).

Jesus did not come into the world to make sin less terrible. Nothing in the Gospel excuses sin; nothing in it affords toleration for lust or anger, dishonesty or falsehood. The Gospel is as truly a two-edged sword against sin as ever the law can be. There is grace for the man who repents from his sin, but there is tribulation and wrath for every man who does evil. *"If he does not turn back, He will sharpen His sword; He bends His bow and makes it ready"* (Ps. 7:12).

The Gospel is all tenderness to the repenting, but all terror to the obstinate offender. It has pardon for the chief of sinners and mercy for the vilest of the vile, if they will forsake their sins; but it is according to our Gospel that he who goes on in his iniquity will be cast into hell and *"he who does not believe will be condemned"*

(Mark 16:16). With deep love for the souls of men, I bear witness to the truth that he who does not turn with repentance and faith to Christ will go away into punishment as everlasting as the life of the righteous. This is according to our Gospel. Indeed, we would not have needed such a Gospel if there had not been such a judgment. The background of the Cross is the judgment seat of Christ. We would not have needed so great an atonement, so vast a sacrifice, if there had not been a supreme sinfulness in sin, a transcendent justice in the judgment, and an incomparable terror in the sure rewards of transgression.

"According to my gospel," said Paul; he meant that the judgment is an essential part of the Gospel creed. If I had to sum up the Gospel, I would have to tell you certain facts: Jesus, the Son of God, became man; He was born of the Virgin Mary; He lived a perfect life; He was falsely accused of men; He was crucified, died, and was buried; the third day He rose again from the dead; He ascended into heaven and sits on the right hand of God, from where He will also come to judge *"the living and the dead"* (Acts 10:42). These are the elementary truths of our Gospel. We believe in the resurrection of the dead, the final judgment, and the life everlasting.

The judgment is according to the Gospel. In times of righteous indignation, its terrible significance seems to be the Gospel in itself to the pure in heart. I mean this: As I have read information concerning oppression, slavery, the treading down of the poor, and the shedding of blood, I have rejoiced that there is a righteous Judge. I have read of secret wickedness among the rich men of this city, and I have said to myself, "Thank God, there will be a Judgment Day." Thousands of men have been hanged for lesser crimes than those that are now being committed by gentlemen whose names are on the lists of rank and beauty. Ah, me, how heavy is my heart as I think of it! But one day, the Lord will be revealed *"in flaming fire taking vengeance on those who do not know God, and on those who do not obey the gospel of our Lord Jesus Christ"* (2 Thess. 1:8). The secret wickedness of London cannot go on forever. Even they who truly love men and most desire salvation for them cannot but cry out, "How long? How long, O God? Will You endure this forever?" God has appointed a Day when He will judge the world; we sigh and cry until it ends the reign of wickedness and give rests to the oppressed.

Beloved, we must preach the coming of the Lord, and preach it more than we have done, because it is the driving power of the

Gospel. Too many have kept back these truths, and thus the bone has been taken out of the arm of the Gospel. Its point has been broken; its edge has been blunted. The doctrine of judgment to come is the power by which men are to be aroused. There is another life, the Lord will come a second time, judgment will arrive, and the wrath of God will be revealed. Where this is not preached, I am bold to say, the Gospel is not preached. It is absolutely necessary to the preaching of the Gospel of Christ that men be warned as to what will happen if they continue in their sins.

Surgeon, are you too delicate to tell the man that he is ill? Do you hope to heal the sick without their knowing it? If you therefore flatter them, what happens? They laugh at you, they dance on their own graves, and at last they die! Your delicacy is cruelty; your flatteries are poisons; you are a murderer. Should we ministers keep men in a fool's paradise? Should we lull them into soft slumbers from which they will awake in hell? Are we to become helpers of their damnation by our smooth speeches? In the name of God, we dare not. It becomes every true minister of Christ to cry aloud and spare not, for God has set a Day in which He will *judge the secrets of men by Jesus Christ, according to my gospel.*

As surely as Paul's Gospel was true, the judgment will come. Therefore, flee to Jesus this day, O sinners. O you saints, come hide yourselves again beneath the crimson canopy of the atoning sacrifice, so that you may now be ready to welcome your descending Lord and escort Him to His judgment seat. O my beloved, may God bless you, for Jesus' sake.

Chapter 5

The Two Appearings and the Discipline of Grace

For the grace of God that brings salvation has appeared to all men, teaching us that, denying ungodliness and worldly lusts, we should live soberly, righteously, and godly in the present age, looking for the blessed hope and glorious appearing of our great God and Savior Jesus Christ, who gave Himself for us, that He might redeem us from every lawless deed and purify for Himself His own special people, zealous for good works.
—Titus 2:11–14

Upon reading this text, we see at a glance that Paul believed in the divinity of our Savior. He did not preach a savior who was a mere man. He believed the Lord Jesus Christ was truly man, but he also believed He was God over all; thus, Paul used the striking words, the *"glorious appearing of our great God and Savior Jesus Christ."* There is no appearing of God the Father; no such expression is found in Scripture. This appearing is the appearing of that second person of the blessed Trinity, who has already appeared once and who will *"appear a second time, apart from sin, for salvation"* (Heb. 9:28) in the latter days.

Paul believed in Jesus as *"our great God and Savior."* It was his high delight to extol the Lord who once was crucified in weakness. He calls Him here, *"our great God,"* thus especially dwelling on His power, dominion, and glory. This is all the more remarkable because he immediately went on to say, *"Who gave Himself for us, that He might redeem us from every lawless deed."* He who gave Himself, He who surrendered life itself upon the accursed tree, He who was stripped of all honor and glory and entered into the utmost depths of humiliation—He was most assuredly the great God, all of that notwithstanding. O beloved, if you take away the deity of

Christ, what in the Gospel is left that is worth preaching? None but *"our great God"* is equal to the work of being our Savior.

We learn also at that Paul believed in a great redemption. *"Who gave Himself for us, that He might redeem us from every lawless deed."* That word *redemption* sounds in my ears like a silver bell. We are ransomed, purchased back from slavery, at an immeasurable price—not merely by the obedience of Christ, or the suffering of Christ, or even the death of Christ, but by Christ's giving Himself for us. All that there is in the great God and Savior was laid down in order *"that He might redeem us from every lawless deed."*

The splendor of the Gospel lies in the redeeming sacrifice of the Son of God. It is the gem of all the Gospel gems. As the moon is among the stars, so is this great doctrine among all the lesser lights that God has kindled to gladden the night of fallen man. Paul never hesitated; he had a divine Savior and a divine redemption, and he preached these with unwavering confidence. Oh, that all preachers were like him!

It is also clear that Paul looked on the first appearing of the Savior and Redeemer from all iniquity as a display of the grace of God. He said, *"For the grace of God that brings salvation has appeared to all men."* In the person of Christ, the grace of God is revealed, as when the sun rises and makes glad all lands. It is not a private vision of God to a favored prophet on a lone mountaintop, but it is an open declaration of the grace of God to every creature under heaven, a display of the grace of God to all eyes that are open to see it.

When the Lord Jesus Christ came to Bethlehem, and when He closed a perfect life by His death on Calvary, He manifested the grace of God more gloriously than has been done by creation or providence. This is the clearest revelation of the everlasting mercy of the living God. In the Redeemer we behold the unveiling of the Father's face or, might I say, the laying bare of the divine heart. This is the *"Dayspring from on high* [who] *has visited us"* (Luke 1:78), the *"Sun of Righteousness* [who arose] *with healing in His wings"* (Mal. 4:2).

The grace of God has shone forth conspicuously and made itself visible to men of every rank in the person and work of the Lord Jesus. This was not given to us because of any deserving of ours; it is a manifestation of free, rich, undeserved grace, and of that grace in its fullness. The grace of God has been made manifest to the entire universe in the appearing of Jesus Christ our Lord.

The grand object of the manifestation of divine grace in Christ Jesus is to deliver men from the dominion of evil. The world in Paul's day was steeped in immorality, debauchery, ungodliness, bloodshed, and cruelty of every kind. I do not have the space at this point to give you even an outline sketch of the Roman world when Paul wrote this letter to Titus. We are bad enough now, but the outward manners and customs of that period were simply horrible. The spread of the Gospel has brought about a change for the better. In the days of the apostles, the favorite spectacles for holiday entertainment were the butcheries of men. Such was the general depravity that vices that we hardly dare to mention were defended and gloried in. In the midnight of the world's history, our Lord appeared to put away sin. The Lord Jesus Christ, who is the manifestation of the divine grace to men, came into the world to put an end to the unutterable tyranny of evil. His work and teaching are meant to uplift mankind at large, as well as to redeem His people from all iniquity and to sanctify them to Himself as His peculiar heritage.

Paul looked on recovery from sin as being a wonderful proof of divine grace. He was not talking about a kind of grace that would leave men in sin, yet save them from its punishment. No, this salvation is salvation from sin. He was not referring to a free grace that winks at iniquity and makes nothing of transgression; rather, he was talking about a far greater grace that denounces the iniquity, condemns the transgression, and then delivers the victim of it from the habit that has brought him into bondage. Paul declared that the grace of God has shone upon the world in the work of Jesus in order that the darkness of its sin and ignorance may disappear and the brightness of holiness, righteousness, and peace may rule the day. May God send us to see these blessed results in every part of the world! May God make us to see them in ourselves! May we ourselves feel that the grace of God has appeared to us individually!

Our apostle wanted Titus to know that this grace was intended for all ranks of men: for the Cretans, who were *"always liars, evil beasts, lazy gluttons"* (Titus 1:12), and even for the most despised bondservants (Titus 2:9–10), who were treated worse than dogs under the Roman Empire. To each one of us, whether rich or poor, prominent or obscure, the Gospel has come. Its design is that we may be delivered by it from all *"ungodliness and worldly lusts."*

This being the general thrust of the text, I ask you to examine it more closely, while I try to show how the apostle stimulates us to holiness and urges us to overcome all evil. May the Holy Spirit bless our meditations!

Our Position: In Between

First of all, we find in this text Paul's description of our position. The people of God stand between two appearances. In the eleventh verse we read, *"The grace of God that brings salvation has appeared to all men."* Then, in the thirteenth verse, we find, *"Looking for the blessed hope and glorious appearing of our great God and Savior Jesus Christ."* We live in an age that is an interval between two appearings of the Lord from heaven. By the first coming of our Lord, believers in Jesus are shut off from the old system of doing things. *"These times of ignorance God overlooked, but now commands all men everywhere to repent"* (Acts 17:30).

We are divided from the past by a wall of light, of which some of the building stones are Bethlehem, Gethsemane, and Calvary. We date from the birth of the Virgin Mary's Son: we begin with *Anno Domini* (in the year of our Lord). All the rest of time is before Christ and is marked off from the Christian era. Bethlehem's manger is our beginning. The chief landmark for all time to us is the wondrous life of Him who is *"the light of the world"* (John 9:5). We look to the appearing of the grace of God in the form of the lowly One of Nazareth, for our trust is there. We confide in *"the Word* [who] *became flesh and dwelt among us, and we beheld His glory, the glory as of the only begotten of the Father, full of grace and truth"* (John 1:14). The dense darkness of the heathen ages begins to be broken when we reach the first appearing, and the dawn of a glorious day begins.

Beloved, we look forward to a second appearing. Our outlook for the close of this present era is another appearing—an appearing of glory rather than of grace. After our Master ascended from the brow of Olivet, His disciples remained for a while in mute astonishment; but soon an angelic messenger reminded them of prophecy and promise by saying, *"Men of Galilee, why do you stand gazing up into heaven? This same Jesus, who was taken up from you into heaven, will so come in like manner as you saw Him go into heaven"* (Acts 1:11). We believe that our Lord in the fullness of time *"will descend from heaven with a shout, with the voice of an archangel, and with the trumpet of God"* (1 Thess. 4:16).

> The Lord shall come! The earth shall quake;
> The mountains to their center shake;
> And withering from the vault of night,
> The stars shall pale their feeble light.

This is the terminus of the present age. We look from that noble year of our Lord, in which He came the first time, to that greater year of our Lord, in which He will come a second time in all the splendor of His power to reign in righteousness and break the evil powers as with a rod of iron.

See, then, where we are: we are encompassed about, behind and before, with the appearings of our Lord. Behind us is our trust; before us is our hope. Behind us is the Son of God in humiliation; before us is the great God our Savior in His glory. To use an ecclesiastical term, we stand between two epiphanies: the first is the manifestation of the Son of God in human flesh in weakness and humility; the second is the manifestation of the same Son of God in all His power and glory. In what a position, then, do we saints stand! We have an era all to ourselves, which begins and ends with the Lord's appearings.

In This Present Age

Our position is further described in the text, if you look at it, as being in this present world or age. We are living in the age that lies between the two blazing beacons of the divine appearings, and we are called to hasten from one to the other. The sacramental host of God's elect is marching on from the one appearing to the other with hasty feet. We have everything to hope for, in the last appearing, as we have everything to trust in, in the first appearing. Now we have to wait with patient hope through the weary interval that intervenes.

Paul called it *"the present age."* This marks its fleeting nature. It is present, but it is scarcely future, because the Lord may come so soon and thus end it all. It is present now, but it will not be present long. It is but a little time, and He who is coming will come and will not tarry. Now, it is *"the present age."* Oh, how present it is! How sadly it surrounds us!

However, by faith we count these present things to be as insubstantial as a dream. We look to the things that are not seen and not present as being real and eternal. We pass through this world as men on a pilgrimage. We traverse an enemy's country. Going from one manifestation to another, we are as birds migrating on the wing from one region to another: there is no rest for us by the way. We are to keep ourselves as loose as we can from this country through which we make our pilgrim's way, because we are *"strangers and foreigners"* (Eph. 2:19), and *"here we have no continuing city"* (Heb. 13:14). We hurry through this Vanity Fair: before us lies the Celestial City and the coming of the Lord who is the King thereof. As voyagers cross the Atlantic, and so pass from shore to shore, so do we speed over the waves of this ever-changing world to the gloryland of the bright appearing of our Savior Jesus Christ.

Already I have given to you, in this description of our position, the very best argument for a holy life. If it is true, my beloved, then, you are not of the world even as Jesus is not of the world. If this is so—that before you blazes the supernatural splendor of the Second Advent and behind you burns the everlasting light of the Redeemer's first appearing—what manner of people ought you to be?

If you are but journeying through this present world, do not allow your hearts to be defiled with its sins; do not learn the manner of speech of these aliens through whose country you are passing. Is it not written, *"A people dwelling alone, not reckoning itself among the nations"* (Num. 23:9)? *"Come out from among them and be separate, says the Lord. Do not touch what is unclean, and I will receive you. I will be a Father to you, and you shall be My sons and daughters, says the LORD Almighty"* (2 Cor. 6:17–18).

Those who lived before the coming of Christ had responsibilities upon them, but not such as those that rest on you who have seen the face of God in Jesus Christ, and who expect to see that face again. You live in light that makes their brightest knowledge a comparative darkness; therefore, *"walk as children of light"* (Eph. 5:8). You stand between two mornings, between which there is no evening. The glory of the Lord has risen upon you once in the incarnation and atonement of Christ Jesus; that light is shining more and more. Soon there will come the perfect day that will be ushered in by the Second Advent. The sun will no more go down, but it will unveil itself and shed an indescribable splendor upon all hearts that look for it.

Therefore, *"let us put on the armor of light"* (Rom. 13:12). What a grand expression! Helmet of light, breastplate of light, shoes of light—everything of light. What a knight must he be who is clad not in steel, but in light, light that flashes confusion on his foes! There ought to be a holy light about you, O believer in Jesus, for there is the appearing of grace behind you and the appearing of glory before you. Two manifestations of God shine on you. Like a wall of fire, the Lord's appearings are round about you; there ought to be a special glory of holiness in the midst. *"Let your light so shine before men, that they may see your good works and glorify your Father in heaven"* (Matt. 5:16). That is the position of the righteous according to the text, and it furnishes a loud call to holiness.

The Instructions

Second, I have to call your attention to the instruction that is given to us by *"the grace of God that...has appeared to all men."* A better translation of this verse might be: "The grace of God that brings salvation has appeared to all men, disciplining us in order that we may deny ungodliness and worldly lusts." Those of you who know a little Greek will note that the word that is rendered *"teaching"* in this version is a scholastic term and has to do with the education of children—not merely the teaching of them, but the training and bringing up of them. The grace of God has come to be a schoolmaster to us, to teach us, to train us, to prepare us for a more developed state. Christ has manifested in His own person the wonderful grace of God that is to deal with us as with sons, to educate us unto holiness, and so to prepare us for the full possession of our heavenly heritage. We are the many sons who are to be brought to glory by the discipline of grace (Heb. 2:10).

Grace Has a Discipline

So then, first of all, grace has a discipline. We generally think of the law when we talk about tutors (see Galatians 3:24) and discipline, but grace itself has a discipline and a wonderful training power, too. The manifestation of grace is preparing us for the manifestation of glory. *"What the law could not do"* (Rom. 8:3), grace is able to do and is doing. The free favor of God instills new principles, suggests new thoughts, and creates in us love for God and hatred of what is opposed to God by inspiring us with gratitude. Happy are they who attend the school of the grace of God!

This grace of God entering into us shows us what was evil even more clearly than the commandment does. We receive a vital, testing principle within, whereby we discern between good and evil. The grace of God provides us with instruction, but also with chastisement; as it is written, *"As many as I love, I rebuke and chasten"* (Rev. 3:19). As soon as we come under the conscious enjoyment of the free grace of God, we find it to be a holy rule, a fatherly government, a heavenly training. We do not find self-indulgence, much less licentiousness. On the contrary, the grace of God both restrains and constrains us. It makes us free to holiness and delivers us from *"the law of sin and death"* (Rom. 8:2) by *"the law of the Spirit of life in Christ Jesus"* (v. 2).

Chosen Disciples of Grace

In addition to grace having its discipline, grace has its chosen disciples. You cannot help noticing that while the eleventh verse says, *"The grace of God that brings salvation has appeared to all men,"* it is clear that this grace of God has not exercised its holy discipline on *"all men."* Therefore, the text changes its *"all men"* into *"us"* and *"we"* in the twelfth verse. Usually in Scripture when you find a generality, you soon find a particularity near it. This text follows that pattern: *"Teaching us that, denying ungodliness and worldly lusts, we should live soberly, righteously, and godly in the present age."* Thus, grace has its own disciples.

Are you a disciple of the grace of God? Did you ever submit yourself to it? Have you learned to spell that word, *f–a–i–t–h?* Do you have childlike trust in Jesus? Have you learned to wash in the basin of atonement? Have you learned those holy exercises that are taught by the grace of God? Can you say that your salvation is of grace? Do you know the meaning of that text, *"By grace you have been saved through faith, and that not of yourselves; it is the gift of God"* (Eph. 2:8)? If so, then, you are His disciples, and the grace of God that has appeared so conspicuously has come to discipline you.

As disciples of grace, endeavor to adorn its doctrine. According to the previous verses, even a slave might do this (Titus 2:9–10). He might be an ornament to the grace of God. Let grace have such an effect upon your life and character that all may say, "See what grace can do! See how the grace of God produces holiness in believers!" All along I wish to be driving home the same point at which the apostle is aiming: we are to be holy because grace exercises a purifying discipline and because we are disciples of that grace.

The Results of the Discipline of Grace

According to the apostle, the discipline of grace has three results: denying, living, and looking. You see the three words before you; the first is *"denying."* When a young man comes to college, he usually has much to unlearn. If his education has been neglected, a sort of instinctive ignorance covers his mind with briars and brambles. If he has gone to some faulty school where the teaching is flimsy, his tutor has first of all to extract from him what he has been badly taught. The most difficult part of training young men is not to put the right things into them, but to get the wrong thing out of them. A man proposes to teach a language in six months; in the end a great thing is accomplished if one of his pupils is able to forget all his nonsense in six years.

The Discipline of Denying

When the Holy Spirit comes into the heart, He finds that we know so much already of what it would have been good to have left unknown: we are self-conceited and puffed up; we have learned lessons of worldly wisdom and carnal policy. These we need to unlearn and deny. The Holy Spirit works this denying in us by the discipline of grace.

What do we have to deny? First, we have to deny *"ungodliness."* This is a lesson that many of you have a great need to learn. Listen to men who are employed as manual laborers. "Oh," they say, "we have to work hard; we cannot think about God or religion." This is ungodliness! The grace of God teaches us to deny this, and we come to loathe such atheism. Others who are striving in the world of commerce cry out such excuses as, "If you had as much business to look after as I have, you would have no time to think about your soul or another world. Trying to battle with the competition of the times leaves me no opportunity for prayer or Bible reading; I have enough to do with my schedules and ledger." This also is ungodliness! The grace of God leads us to deny this; we abhor such forgetfulness of God.

A great work of the Holy Spirit is to make a man godly, to make him think of God, to make him feel that this present life is not all, but to realize that there is a judgment to come, wherein he must *"give account of himself to God"* (Rom. 14:12). God cannot be forgotten with impunity. If we treat Him as if He were nothing and leave Him out of our calculations for life, we will make a fatal mistake. O my friend, there is a God, and as surely as you live, you are accountable to Him. When the Spirit of God comes with the grace of the Gospel, He removes our ingrained ungodliness and causes us to deny it with joyful earnestness.

We next deny *"worldly lusts,"* the lusts of *"the present age,"* which I described to you just now as coming in between the two appearings. This present age is as full of evil lusts as that in which Paul wrote concerning the Cretans. *"All that is in the world; the lust of the flesh, the lust of the eyes, and the pride of life"* (1 John 2:16) is yet with us. Wherever the grace of God comes effectually, it makes the person who lived loosely deny the desires of the flesh; it causes the man who lusted after gold to conquer his greediness; it brings the proud man away from his ambitions; it trains the idler to diligence; and it sobers the wanton mind that cared only for the frivolities of life. Not only do we leave these lusts, but we deny them. We have an abhorrence of those things in which we formerly placed our delight. Our cry is, *"What have I to do anymore with idols?"* (Hos. 14:8). To the worldling we say, "These things may belong to you; but as for us, we cannot own them: *'Sin shall not have dominion over* [us]' (Rom. 6:14). We are not of the world; therefore, its ways and fashions are none of ours."

The period in which we live should not have paramount influence over us, for our truest life is with Christ in eternity and *"our citizenship is in heaven"* (Phil. 3:20). The grace of God has made us deny the prevailing philosophies, glories, maxims, and fashions of this present world. In the best sense we are nonconformists. We desire to be crucified to the world and the world to us. This was a great thing for grace to do among the degraded sensualists of Paul's day, and it is no less a glorious achievement in these times.

The Discipline of Living

But, beloved, you cannot be complete with a merely negative religion; you must have something positive. Thus, the next word is about living: *"We should live soberly, righteously, and godly in the present age."* Observe, dear friends, that the Holy Spirit expects us to live in this present world; therefore, we are not to exclude ourselves from it. This age is the battlefield in which the soldier of Christ is to fight. Society is the place in which Christianity is to exhibit the grace of Christ. If some good sisters were to retire into a large house and live secluded from the world, they would be shirking their duty rather than fulfilling it. If all the good, true men were to form a select colony and do nothing else but pray and hear sermons, they would simply be refusing to serve God in His own appointed way. No, you have to live soberly, godly, and righteously in this world, such as it is at present. It is of no use for you to scheme to escape from it. You are bound to confront this torrent and withstand all its waves. If the grace of God is in you, that grace is meant to be displayed, not in a select and secluded retreat, but in this present world. You are to shine in the darkness like a light.

This lifestyle is described in a threefold way. First, you are to live *"soberly,"* that is, for yourself. You are to live *"soberly"* in all your eating and your drinking and in the indulgence of all bodily appetites—that goes without saying. Drunkards and revilers, fornicators and adulterers, cannot inherit the kingdom of God (1 Cor. 6:9–10). You are to live soberly in all your thinking, all your speaking, all your acting. There is to be sobriety in all your worldly pursuits. You are to have yourself well in hand; you are to be self-restrained.

I know some brothers who are not often sober. I do not accuse them of being drunk with wine. Rather, they are mentally intoxicated: they have no reason, no moderation, no judgment. They are all spur and no rein. Right or wrong, they must have what they have set their hearts on. They never look around to take the full bearing of a matter. They never evaluate calmly, but with closed eyes they rush in like bulls. Alas, for these unsober people! They are not to be depended on; they are impulsive and unreliable. The man who is disciplined by the grace of God becomes thoughtful, considerate, self-controlled. He is no longer tossed about by passion or swayed by prejudice.

There is only one insobriety into which I pray we may fall. Truth to say, it is the truest sobriety. Of this the Scripture says, *"Do not be drunk with wine, in which is dissipation; but be filled with the Spirit"* (Eph. 5:18). When the Spirit of God takes full possession of us, then, we are borne along by His sacred energy and are filled with a divine enthusiasm that needs no restraint. However, when we are exposed to all other influences, we must guard ourselves against yielding too completely, so that we may thus live *"soberly."*

As to his fellowmen, the believer is to live *"righteously."* I cannot understand any Christian who can do a dirty, dishonest thing in business. Craftiness, cunning, overreaching, misrepresentation, and deceit are no instruments for the hands of godly men. I am told that my principles are too angelic for business life, that a man cannot be a match for his fellowmen in trade if he is too puritanical. Others are up to tricks, and he would be ruined if he could not trick them in return. O my dear believers, do not talk in this way. If you mean to go the way of the Devil, say so and take the consequences. However, if you profess to be servants of God, deny all partnership with unrighteousness. Dishonesty and falsehood are the opposites of godliness. A Christian man may be poor, but he must live righteously; he may lack sharpness, but he must not lack integrity. A Christian profession without uprightness is a lie. Grace must discipline us to righteous living.

We are told in the text that we are to live *"godly"* toward God. Every man who truly has the grace of God in him will think much of God and will *"seek first the kingdom of God and His righteousness"* (Matt. 6:33). God will enter into all his plans, God's presence will be his joy, God's strength will be his confidence, God's providence will be his inheritance, God's glory will be the chief end of his being, and God's law will be the guide of his conversation. Now, if the grace of God that has appeared so plainly to all men has really come with its sacred discipline upon us, it is teaching us to live in this threefold manner.

The Discipline of Looking

In addition, there is looking as well as living. One work of the grace of God is to cause us to be *"looking for the blessed hope and glorious appearing of our great God and Savior Jesus Christ."* What is that *"blessed hope"*? First, that when He comes, we will rise from the dead if we have fallen asleep; and that, if we are alive and remain, we will be changed at His appearing. (See 1 Thessalonians 4:15–17; 1 Corinthians 15:51–53.) Our hope is that we will be approved of Him and will hear Him say, *"Well done, good and faithful servant"* (Matt. 25:21). This hope is not of debt, but of grace; although our Lord will give us a reward, it will not be according to the law of works.

"But we know that when [Jesus] is revealed, we shall be like Him, for we shall see Him as He is" (1 John 3:2). When Jesus shines forth as the sun, *"then the righteous will shine forth as the sun in the kingdom of their Father"* (Matt. 13:43). Our gain by godliness cannot be counted into the palm of a hand; rather, it lies in

the glorious future. Yet to one with faith, it is so near that at this moment I almost hear the chariot of the Coming One. The Lord is coming, and in His coming lies the great hope of the believer—his great stimulus to overcome evil, his main incentive to perfect holiness in the fear of the Lord. Oh, to be found blameless in the day of the manifestation of our Lord! May God grant us this! Do you see, beloved, how the discipline of the doctrine of grace runs toward separating us from sin and making us live unto God?

Words of Encouragement

Finally, our text sets forth certain encouraging truths for us. I will only briefly hint at them even though the passage is rich beyond measure with hope for the future.

We Struggle Not Alone

In this great battle for right and truth and holiness, what could we do, my friends, if we were left alone? Our first encouragement is that grace has come to our rescue. In the day when the Lord Jesus Christ appeared among men, He brought for us the grace of God to help us to overcome all iniquity. He who struggles now against inbred sin has the Holy Spirit within him to help him. He who goes forth to fight against evil in other men by preaching the Gospel has that same Holy Spirit going with the truth to make it *"like a fire...and like a hammer"* (Jer. 23:29). I would throw down my weapons and retreat from so hopeless a fight were it not that *"the LORD of hosts is with us; the God of Jacob is our refuge"* (Ps. 46:7). The grace of God that brings salvation from sin has flashed forth conspicuously like the lightning that is seen from one part of the heaven to the other, and our victory over darkness is insured. However hard the conflict with evil, it is not desperate. We may hope on and hope ever.

A certain warrior was discovered in prayer, and when his king sneered, he answered that he was pleading with his majesty's strongest ally. (I question whether God is the ally of anybody when he goes forth with gun and sword.) However, in using those *"weapons of our warfare [that] are not carnal but mighty in God for pulling down strongholds"* (2 Cor. 10:4), we may truly count on our noble Ally. Speak the truth, for God speaks with you! Work for God, for God *"works in you both to will and to do for His good pleasure"* (Phil. 2:13). The appearance of the grace of God in the person of Christ is encouragement enough to those who are under the most difficult circumstances and have to contend for righteousness against the deadliest odds. Grace has appeared; therefore, let us be of good courage!

His Promise to Return

A second encouraging truth is that another appearing is coming. He who bowed His head in weakness and died in the moment of victory is coming in all the glory of His endless life. Do not question it. The world is not going to darken into an eternal night; the morning comes as well as the night. Though sin and corruption abound and the love of many grows cold (Matt. 24:12), these are but the tokens of the near advent of Him who said that it would be so before His appearing. The right with the might and the might with the right will be: as surely as God lives, it must be so. We are not fighting a losing battle. The Lord must triumph.

If His suffering life and cruel death had been the only appearing, we might have feared. But it is not: it is but the first and the preparatory part of His manifestation. He comes! He comes! None can hinder His coming! Every moment brings Him nearer; nothing can delay His glory. When the hour strikes, He will appear in the majesty of God to put an end to the dominion of sin and bring in endless peace. Satan will be bruised under our feet shortly. *"Therefore comfort one another with these words"* (1 Thess. 4:18), and then, prepare for further battle. Sharpen your swords, and be ready for close fighting! Trust in God, and keep your powder dry. Let this ever be our war cry, "He must reign!" We look for the *"glorious appearing of our great God and Savior Jesus Christ."*

We Serve a Glorious Master

Another encouragement is that we serve a glorious Master. The Christ whom we follow is not a dead prophet like Mohammed. Truly *"we preach Christ crucified"* (1 Cor. 1:23); but we also believe in Christ risen from the dead, in Christ ascended on high, in Christ soon to come a second time. He lived, and He lives as the great God and our Savior.

If you are indeed soldiers of such a Captain, throw fear to the wind. Can you be cowards when the Lord of Hosts leads you? Dare you tremble when at your head is the *"Wonderful, Counselor, Mighty God, Everlasting Father, Prince of Peace"* (Isa. 9:6)? The trumpet is already at the lip of the archangel; who will not act like a man? The great drum that makes the universe to throb summons you to action.

> Stand up, stand up for Jesus,
> Ye soldiers of the cross;
> Lift high His royal banner;
> It must not suffer loss.

His Cross is the old Cross still, and none can overthrow it. Hallelujah to the name of Jesus!

Precious Memories

Then come the tender thoughts with which I finish, the memories of what the Lord has done for us to make us holy: *"Who gave Himself for us."* We have special redemption, redemption with a wondrous price: *"Who gave Himself for us."* Put away that trumpet and that drum; take down the harp and gently touch its sweetest strings. Tell how the Lord Jesus loved us and gave Himself for us. Beloved, if nothing else can touch your hearts, this must: *"Do you not know that...you are not your own? For you were bought at a price"* (1 Cor. 6:19–20).

Christ gave Himself for us with two objectives. The first is redemption, that He might redeem us from all iniquity, so that He might break the bonds of sin asunder and so that He might cast the cords of depravity far from us. He died—do not forget that—died that your sins might die, died that every lust might be dragged into captivity under His chariot wheels. He gave Himself for you that you might give yourselves for Him.

Second, He died that He might purify us—purify us to Himself. How clean we must be if we are to be clean unto Him. The holy Jesus will commune only with what He has purified after the manner of His own nature, purified to Himself. He has purified us to be wholly His. No human hand may use the golden cup; no human incense may burn in the consecrated censer. We are purified to Himself, as the Hebrew would put it, to be His *cegullah*, His "unique possession." The phrase *"special people"* really means that believers are Christ's own people, His choice and select portion.

Saints are Christ's crown jewels; His box of diamonds; His very, very, very own. He carries His people as lambs in His bosom; He engraves their names on His heart. They are the inheritance to which He is the heir, and He values them more than all the universe. He would lose everything else sooner than lose one of them. He desires that you who are being disciplined by His grace should know that you are altogether His. You are Christ's. Each one of you is to know, "I do not belong to this world or even to myself; I belong only to Christ. I am set aside by Him for Himself only, and His I will be." The silver and the gold are His, and the cattle upon a thousand hills are His; but He makes small account of them. *"The Lord's portion is His people"* (Deut. 32:9).

Zealously Serving by Good Works

The apostle finishes by saying that we are to be a people *"zealous for good works."* I desire before God that all Christian men and women were disciplined by divine grace until they became *"zealous for good works"*! In holiness, zeal is sobriety. We are not only to approve of good works and speak for them, but we are also to be red-hot for them. We are to be on fire for everything that is right and true. We must not be content to be quiet and inoffensive, but we need to be *"zealous for good works."* May the Lord's grace set us on fire in this way.

There is plenty of fuel in the church; what is lacking is fire. A great many people, all very respectable, are, in their sleepy way, doing as little as they can for any good cause. This will never do. We must wake up!

The quantity of ambulance work that Christ's soldiers have to do is overwhelming! One half of Christ's army has to carry the other half. May our fellow saints get off the sick list! Oh, that all of us were ardent, fervent, vigorous, and zealous! Come, Holy Spirit, and quicken us! We cannot go about to get this by our own efforts and energies, but God will work it by His grace. Grace given us in Christ is the fountainhead of all holy impulse. O heavenly grace, come like a flood at this time and bear us away!

May those of you who have never felt the grace of God be enabled to believe in the Lord Jesus Christ as to His first appearing! Then, trusting in His death on the cross, you will learn to look for His Second Coming upon His white steed, and you will rejoice therein. To His great name be glory forever and ever!

Chapter 6

Preparation for the Coming of the Lord

And now, little children, abide in Him, that when He appears, we
may have confidence and not be ashamed before Him at His coming.
                        —1 John 2:28

M y first, most fervent desire is that my readers would come
to Christ. I stretch myself to lift Him up just *"as Moses*
lifted up the serpent in the wilderness" (John 3:14), and to
invite men to look to Him and live. There is no salvation except by
faith in the Lord Jesus Christ. He said, *"Look to Me, and be saved,*
all you ends of the earth! For I am God, and there is no other" (Isa.
45:22).

When you have looked to Jesus, my next concern is that you
may be found in Christ, the City of Refuge. I long to speak of you as
people *"in Christ Jesus"* (Rom. 8:1). You must be in living, loving,
lasting union with the Son of God, or else you are not in a state of
salvation. What begins with coming to Christ continues in your
growing into Him and receiving of His life, as the engrafted branch
is bound to the vine. You must be in Christ as the stone is in the
building (1 Pet. 2:5), as the member is in the body (1 Cor. 12:18).

When I have good hope that my readers have come to Christ
and are in Christ, a further concern springs up in my heart: that
they may *"abide in Him."* My longing is that, despite temptations
to go away from Him, you may always remain at His feet; that,
notwithstanding the evil of your nature, you may never betray your
Master but may faithfully hold to Him. I would have you mindful of
this precept: *"As you have therefore received Christ Jesus the Lord,*
so walk in Him" (Col. 2:6). Oh, that you may be *"rooted and built*
up in Him" (v. 7), always in union with Him! Then, I may be able
to present you to our Lord in the Day of His appearing *"with ex-*
ceeding joy" (Jude 24).

I want to pay attention to this third concern of all those who
minister for Christ. John said, *"Little children, abide in Him."* How

sweetly those words must have flowed from the lips and the pen of such a venerable saint! In this I think the beloved disciple echoed the Lord Jesus, who had told His disciples:

> *Abide in Me, and I in you. As the branch cannot bear fruit of itself, unless it abides in the vine, neither can you, unless you abide in Me....If you abide in Me, and My words abide in you, you will ask what you desire, and it shall be done for you.*
>
> (John 15:4, 7)

That word *abide* was a very favorite one with the Lord Jesus, and it became equally dear to that *"disciple whom Jesus loved"* (John 21:20). *Abide* was one of John's special words.

May the Lord help us to consider these blessed words! Better still, may He write them on our hearts, and may we fulfill their teaching!

First, notice what John exhorted them to do: *"abide in Him."* Second, note how he addressed them: *"little children."* Finally, consider what motive he gave them: *"that when He appears, we may have confidence and not be ashamed before Him at His coming."*

Abide in Christ

First, then, observe what John was exhorting them to do: *"abide in Him."* By this he meant one thing, but that thing is so comprehensive that we may better understand it by viewing it from many sides.

Fidelity to Christ's Teachings

John meant fidelity to the truth taught by our Lord. We are sure he meant this, because a little previously he had said, *"If what you heard from the beginning abides in you, you also will abide in the Son and in the Father"* (1 John 2:24). Beloved, you have believed in the Lord Jesus Christ unto the salvation of your souls. You have trusted in Him as the Son of God, the appointed Mediator, and the effectual Sacrifice for your sin. Your hope has come from a belief in Christ as God has borne witness to Him. Abide in the truth that you received from the beginning, for in your earliest days it wrought salvation in you. The foundation of your faith is not a changeable doctrine; you rest on a sure word of testimony.

Truth, in its very nature, is fixed and unalterable. You know more about it than you did, but the truth itself is still the same and must be the same. Take care that you abide in it. You will find it difficult to do so, for there is an element of changeableness about yourself; this you must overcome by grace.

You will find many elements of seduction in the outside world. There are men whose business it is to shake the faith of others and thereby to gain a repute for cleverness and depth of thought. Some seem to think it an ambition worthy of a Christian to be always questioning, or, as Paul put it, to be *"always learning and never able to come to the knowledge of the truth"* (2 Tim. 3:7). Their chosen career is to throw doubt into minds that have been made blessed by a gracious certainty. Therefore, you will often be led to test your foundation, and at times, tremble as you cling to it.

Pay attention, then, to this word from the mouth of the apostle: *"abide in Him."* Keep to where you were as to the truth that you believe. What has justified you will sanctify you. What has, in a measure, sanctified you will yet perfect you. Make no change as to the eternal truths on which you base your hope. As a stone, you are built on the foundation; abide there. As a branch, you have been grafted into the stem; abide there. As a member, you are in the body; abide there. It is all over with you if you do not. Abide in that holy mold of doctrine into which you were at first delivered. Let no man deceive you with vain words, though there are many abroad in these days who would *"deceive, if possible, even the elect"* (Matt. 24:24). Abide in Jesus by letting His words abide in you. Believe what you have found to be the means of your quickening. Believe it with a greater intensity and a greater practicality. *"Do not cast away your confidence, which has great reward"* (Heb. 10:35).

Constancy of Trust

Next, John meant *"abide in Him"* as to the loyalty of your trust. When you first enjoyed a hope, you rested on Christ alone. I think I heard the first babbling of your infant faith when it said,

> I'm a poor sinner and nothing at all,
> But Jesus Christ is my all in all.

At first, you had no experience on which you could rely and no inward graces on which you could depend; you rested wholly on

Christ and His finished work. In no degree did you rest on the works of the law, your own feelings, your own knowledge, or even your own resolves. Christ was all. Do you not remember how you used to tell others that the Gospel precept was *"Only believe"* (Mark 5:36)? You cried to them, "Trust in Jesus. Get out of yourselves. Find all your needs provided for in Him."

Now, beloved, you have experience; thank God for it. Now you have the graces of the Spirit; thank God for them. Now you know the things of God by the teaching of the Holy Spirit; be grateful for that knowledge. However, do not fly in the face of your Savior now by putting your experience, your graces, or your knowledge where He and He alone must be. Depend today as simply as you depended then. If you have some idea that you are hastening toward perfection, take care that you do not indulge a vain conceit about yourself. But even if it is true, still do not mix your perfection with His perfection, or your advance in grace with the foundation that He has laid for you in His blood and righteousness. *"Abide in Him."*

Jesus is the good ship into which you have entered so that He may bear you safe to the desired haven. Abide in the vessel. Neither venture to walk on the water, like Peter, nor think to swim by your own strength; instead, *"abide in Him,"* and you will weather every storm. Only as you keep to your first simple confidence in the perfect work of the Lord Jesus can you have peace and salvation. As it is written, *"You will keep him in perfect peace, whose mind is stayed on You, because he trusts in You"* (Isa. 26:3).

Christ, Our Constant Object

Moreover, abide in the Lord Jesus Christ by making Him the constant ambition of your life. As you live by Christ, so live for Christ. Ever since you trusted in Christ's dying for you, you have felt that if He died for you, then, you died in Him, and that henceforth your life might be consecrated to Him. *"You are not your own"* (1 Cor. 6:19), but you are Christ's, and Christ's only. The first purpose of your being is to honor and serve Him *"who loved* [you] *and gave Himself for* [you]*"* (Gal. 2:20). You have not followed after wealth, honor, or self-gratification, but you have followed Jesus. Take heed that you *"abide in Him"* by continuing to serve Him.

Do not love the world or the things in the world. If anyone loves the world, the love of the Father is not in him. For all

599

that is in the world; the lust of the flesh, the lust of the eyes,
and the pride of life; is not of the Father but is of the world.
And the world is passing away, and the lust of it; but he who
does the will of God abides forever.   (1 John 2:15–17)

You may wisely continue where you are, for you have chosen
the right pursuit, and you have entered upon the right road. The
crown that glitters in your eye at the end of the race is worthy of all
your running. You could not have a nobler motivating power than
the constraining love of Christ. To live for Christ is the highest lifestyle; continue in it more and more. If the Lord changes your circumstances, still live for Christ. If you go up, take Christ up with
you. If you go down, Christ will go down with you. If you are in
health, live for Christ earnestly. If you are bound to a sickbed, live
for Christ patiently. Go about your business, and sing for Jesus; or
if He bids you stay at home and cough away your life, then, do so
for Jesus. Just let everything be for Him. For you, *excelsior* means
higher consecration, more heavenly living.

Persevering in Obedience

Surely, we should also understand that, by abiding in Him, we
are to persevere in our obedience to our Lord. The verse that follows our text is, *"If you know that He is righteous, you know that*
everyone who practices righteousness is born of Him" (1 John 2:29).
Whatever your Lord bids you to do, continue to do. Call no man
"Master" (see Matthew 23:9–10), but in all things submit your
thoughts, your words, and your acts to the rule of the Lord Jesus.
Obey Him by whose obedience you are justified. Be precise and
prompt in your execution of His commands. If others consider you
morbidly conscientious, do not heed their opinions, but *"abide in*
Him." The Master's rule is always binding on all His disciples, and
they depart from Him in heart when they stray from His rule.

Obedience to the precept is as much included in our honor of
Christ as faith in the doctrine. If you have been upright in your
dealings, be upright now; be accurate to the penny in every payment. If you have been loving and generous, be loving and generous
now; your Lord's law is love. If you have closely imitated the Lord
Jesus, go on to copy Him still more precisely. Seek no new model;
pray that the Holy Spirit would work the same thing in you. As a
soldier, your Captain's Word is law.

Yours is not to reason why,
Yours is but to do and die.

"Abide in Him." I know you might be rich by doing that un-Christlike act: scorn to win wealth in such a way. I know you may involve yourself in persecution if you follow your Lord closely. Accept such persecution gladly, and rejoice in it for His name's sake. I know that a great many would say that for charity's sake you must make compromises by being in conformity with evil doctrines and worldly practices, but you know better. It is yours to follow the Lamb wherever He goes. This is what His beloved apostle meant when he said, *"Abide in Him."*

Vitally United with Christ

However, I have not completed the full description yet. I fear I am not able to do so by reason of my shallow knowledge and forgetfulness. Continue in virtual union with your Lord. All the life you have is life derived from Him; seek no other. You are not a Christian unless Jesus is the Christ of God to you. You are not alive unto God unless you are one with the risen Lord. You are not saved unless He is your Savior, nor righteous unless He is your righteousness. You have not a single pulse of heavenly desire or a breath of divine life in you except what was first given to you from Him and is daily given to you by Him. Abide in this vital union. Do not try to lead an independent life. *"Abide in Him"* from day to day in complete dependence on the life that is stored up in Him on your behalf.

Be Directed by Him

Let your life *"abide in Him"* in the sense of being directed by Him. The head directs all the members. The order that lifts the hand, spreads the palm, closes the fist, or lowers the arm comes from the brain, which is the headquarters of the soul. Abide in your Lord by implicitly acknowledging His headship. Let every regulation of your life come from *"Him who is the head"* (Eph. 4:15), and let it be obeyed as naturally as the desires of the mind coming from the brain are obeyed by every part of the body.

There is no war between the hand and the foot because they abide in the head. Thus, they are ruled without force and guided without violence. If the leg were to set up an independent authority over itself instead of obeying the head, what strange walking we should see! Have you ever met with afflicted people in whom the nerves have lost their function and the muscles seem to jerk at random, throwing out a leg or an arm without reason? Such movements are painful to see, and we know that such men are diseased. Do not desire to be without law to Christ. *"Let this mind be in you which was also in Christ Jesus"* (Phil. 2:5). In that respect, *"abide in Him."*

Christ, Our Element of Life

"Abide in Him" as the element of your life. Let Him encompass you as the air surrounds you on all sides. As a fish, whether it be the tiniest sprat or the biggest whale, abides in the sea, so you abide in Christ. The fish does not seek the sky or the shore; it could not live out of the element of water. Just so, I beseech you, do not seek to live in the world and in its sins, because as a Christian you cannot live there—Christ is your life. There is room enough for you in the Lord Jesus Christ because He is the infinite God. Do not go outside of Him for anything. Do not seek pleasure or treasure outside of Christ, for such pursuits would be ruinous. Have no needs or desires that are apart from the Lord's will. Let Him draw a line around you, and abide within that circle.

At Home in Him

"Abide in Him" in the sense of being at home in Him. What a world of meaning I intend by that phrase, "being at home in Christ." Yet this is the sense of the word, *"abide in Him."* Recently, I spoke to a friend who had bought a pleasant house with a large garden. He told me, "I now feel as if I have a home. I had lived in London for years and had moved from one house to another with as little regret as a man feels in changing a bus. But I have always longed for the comfortable feeling that I felt in my father's house in the country. Why, there we loved the cozy rooms, the lookouts from the little windows, and the corner cupboards in the kitchen. As for the garden and the field, they yielded us constant delight, for there was that bush in the garden where the robin had built her nest and the tree with the blackbird's nest. We knew where the pike stayed in the pool, where the tortoise had buried itself for the winter, and

where the first primroses would be found in the spring. A vast difference exists between a house and a home." That is what John meant with regard to Christ: we are not merely to call on Him, but to *"abide in Him."*

Do not go to Jesus one day and to the world the following day. Do not be a day-to-day lodger with Him, but *"abide in Him."* My friend spoke of changing from one bus to another, and I fear that some change from Christ to the world when the day changes from Sunday to Monday; but it should not be so.

Say with Moses, *"LORD, You have been our dwelling place in all generations"* (Ps. 90:1). Lord, Your Cross safeguards the family of love. Within the thorn-hedge of Your suffering love, our whole estate is surrounded. Your name is named on our abiding place. We are not tenants with a lease to You, but we have a secure dwelling in You. Lord Jesus, we are at home nowhere but in You; in You we abide. Wherever else we lodge, in due time, we are required to move. Whatever else we have, we lose it or leave it; but You are the same, and You do not change. We can truly say and sing:

> Here would I make a settled rent
> While others go and come:
> No more a stranger or a guest,
> But like a child at home.

What a comfort to have our Lord Himself to be our chosen dwelling place in time and in eternity!

Now, I think I have come nearer to the full sense of the text. *"Abide in Him"* means hold fast to Him, live in Him, let all your noblest powers be drawn forth in connection with Him as a man at home replenishes his strength. Feel at ease in fellowship with Him. Say, *"Return to your rest, O my soul, for the LORD has dealt bountifully with you"* (Ps. 116:7).

Remain with Him

Why did John urge us to abide in Christ? Is there any likelihood of our going away from Him? Yes, for in this very chapter, John mentioned apostates who had degenerated from disciples into antichrists. Of them he said, *"They went out from us, but they were not of us; for if they had been of us, they would have continued with us"* (1 John 2:19). *"Abide in Him,"* then, and do not turn aside to crooked ways as many professing Christians have done. The Savior once asked His apostles, *"Do you also want to go away?"* (John 6:67), and they answered Him with that other question, *"Lord, to whom shall we go? You have the words of eternal life"* (v. 68). I hope your heart is so conscious that He has the words of eternal life that you could not dream of going elsewhere.

"But surely it is implied in these warnings that saints do leave their Lord and perish?" I answer, "No." Carefully observe the provision that is made against that fatality—provision to enable us to carry out the precept of the text. Just look at the verse that immediately precedes our text. What do you see? *"You will abide in Him"* (1 John 2:27). Then, the passage continues, *"And now, little children, abide in Him."* There is a promise made to those who are in Christ that they *"will abide in Him."*

However, that promise does not render the precept unnecessary, for the Lord deals with us as with reasonable beings, not as with sticks and stones. He secures the fulfillment of His own promise that we *"will abide in Him"* by impressing on our hearts His sacred precept, whereby He bids us to *"abide in Him."* The force He uses to effect His purpose is instructive, heartwarming, and persuasive. We abide in Christ, not by a physical law, as a mass of iron abides on the earth, but by a mental and spiritual law, by which the greatness of divine love and goodness holds us fast to the Lord. You have the guarantee that you will abide in Christ in the covenant agreement, *"I will put My fear in their hearts so that they will not depart from Me"* (Jer. 32:40). What a blessed promise that is! You are to take care that you abide in Christ as much as if all depended on yourself, yet you can look to the promise of the covenant and see that the real reason for your abiding in Christ lies in the operation of His unchanging love and grace.

The Holy Spirit, Our Abiding Helper

Moreover, beloved, if you are in Christ Jesus, you have the Holy Spirit given to you to enable you to *"abide in Him."* Read the entire verse that precedes our text:

> *But the anointing which you have received from Him abides in you, and you do not need that anyone teach you; but as the same anointing teaches you concerning all things, and is true, and is not a lie, and just as it has taught you, you will abide in Him.* (1 John 2:27)

The Holy Spirit brings the truth home to your heart with savor and unction, endearing it to your innermost soul. The truth has so saturated you through the anointing that you cannot give it up. Has not your Lord said, *"The water that I shall give him will become in him a fountain of water springing up into everlasting life"* (John 4:14)?

Thus, you see that what is commanded in one Scripture is promised and provided for in another. God's commands are enabling to His people. As He bids you to abide in Him, He causes you to abide in Him to His praise and glory by that very bidding.

Little Children

Second, notice how John addressed these believers. He said, *"And now, little children."* This indicates the apostle's love for them. John lived to a great age. Tradition has it that they used to carry him into the assembly, and, when he could do nothing else, he would lift his hand and simply say, "Little children, love one another" (See 1 John 4:4, 7.) Here, to show his tender concern for those to whom he wrote, he called them *"little children."* He could not wish them a greater blessing out of the depth of his heart's affection than that they should faithfully abide in Christ.

In Right Relationship with the Lord

By the address of *"little children,"* John reminded them of their near and dear relationship to their Father in heaven. You are the children of God, but as yet you are little ones; therefore, do not leave your Father's house or run away from your Elder Brother's love. Because you are little children, you are not old enough to travel alone; therefore, stay at home and abide in your Lord.

Did he not also hint at their feebleness? Even if you were grown and strong, you would not be wise to gather all together and wander away into the far country; but since you are so young, so dependent, so feeble, it is essential that you *"abide in Him."* Would a baby forsake his mother? What can you do apart from God? Is He not your life, your all?

Did not the apostle also gently allude to their fickleness? You are very changeable, like little babies. You are apt to be hot and cold in half an hour. You are this and that, and fifty other things, in the course of one revolving moon. But, little children as you are, be faithful to one point—abide in your Savior. Do not change toward your Redeemer. Stretch out your hands, clasp Him, and cry,

> My Jesus, I love Thee,
> I know Thou art mine,
> For Thee all the follies
> Of sin I resign.

Surrender yourself to Him by an everlasting covenant never to be canceled. Be His forever and ever.

Daily Dependence

Did not this remind them of their daily dependence on the Lord's care, just as little children depend on their parents? Beloved, the Lord has to nurse you. He feeds you with the *"pure milk of the word"* (1 Pet. 2:2). He comforts you as a mother does her child (Isa. 66:13). He carries you in His bosom (Isa. 40:11). He bears you all your days. Your new life is as yet weak and struggling; do not carry it into the cold atmosphere of distance from Jesus. *"Little children,"* since you derive all from Jesus, *"abide in Him."* To go elsewhere will be to wander into a howling wilderness. The world is empty; only Christ has fullness. Away from Jesus, you will be like a child deserted by his mother, left to languish and starve, or as a little lamb on the hillside without a shepherd, tracked by the wolf, whose teeth will soon extract its heart's blood. Abide, child, with your mother! Abide, lamb, with your Shepherd!

All Believers Are Included

We may all fit John's description at this time. The beloved John speaks to us as to little children, for none of us are much more. We are not such wonderfully knowing people as are certain of our neighbors. We are not such learned scientists or astute minds as they are. Nor do we have their marvelous moral consciousness, which is superior to inspiration itself. Therefore, we are bound by our very feebleness to venture less than they do. Let the men of the world choose what paths they will; we feel bound to abide in Christ because we know no other place of safety. They may push off into the sea of speculation; our smaller boats must hug the shore of certainty. To us, however, it is no small comfort that the Lord has revealed to babes the things that are hidden *"from the wise and prudent"* (Matt. 11:25). Those who become as little children enter into the kingdom of heaven (Matt. 18:3).

Cling to the Lord Jesus in your feebleness, in your fickleness, in your nothingness. Take Him to be everything to you. *"The rock badgers are a feeble folk, yet they make their homes in the crags"* (Prov. 30:26); follow their example, *"little children."* Abide in the cleft of the Rock of Ages, and let nothing tempt you to abandon your stronghold. You are no lion, able to fight your foes and deliver yourself by brute strength; you are only a little rabbit, and you will be wise to hide rather than fight. *"Little children, abide in Him."*

Right Motives

I now come to my last point, which is most important because it is the steam that drives the engine. We will consider what motivation John gave us for this pleasant, necessary duty of abiding in Christ.

Kindly look at the text, for there is in it a little word to be noticed. The apostle exhorted us by a motive in which he took his share. Let me read it: *"Now, little children, abide in Him, that when He appears,* [you] *may have confidence."* No, no. Look at that little word. It actually says, *"that...we may have confidence."* The beloved John needed to have confidence at the appearing of the Lord—confidence derived from the same source as that to which he directed his little children. They must abide in Christ so that they might have confidence, and the dearest of the apostles must practice the same abiding. How wisely, and yet how sweetly, he put himself on our level in this matter!

Drawn from Jesus

Notice, further, that the motive is one drawn from Jesus. John did not drive believers with the lash of the law, but he drew them *"with gentle cords, with bands of love"* (Hos. 11:4). I never like to see God's children whipped with rods gathered from the thorny sides of Sinai. We have not come to Mount Sinai but to Mount Zion (Heb. 12:18–24). When a man tries to pommel me to my duty by the law, I kick like a bull unaccustomed to the yoke. Rightly so, because *"we are not under law but under grace"* (Rom. 6:15). The motive that sways a freeborn heir of heaven proceeds from grace, not from law; from Jesus, not from Moses. Christ is our example and our motive, also. Blessed be His name!

Two Perspectives of Christ's Coming

The motive is drawn from our Lord's expected advent. Notice how John expressed it. He used two phrases for this same thing: *"when He appears"* and *"at His coming."* The Second Advent may be viewed from two perspectives: first, as the appearing of One who is here already but is hidden; second, as the coming of One who is absent. In the first sense, we know that our Lord Jesus Christ abides in His church, according to His word, *"Lo, I am with you always, even to the end of the age"* (Matt. 28:20). Yet though spiritually present, He is unseen. All of a sudden, our Lord will be *"manifested,"* as the Revised Version translates it in 1 John 2:28. The spiritual and secret presence of Christ will become a visible and manifest presence in the Day of His appearing.

John also used the term, *"at His coming,"* or "His presence." This is the same thing from another point of view. In a certain evident sense, our Lord is absent: *"He is not here; for He is risen, as He said"* (Matt. 28:6). He has gone His way to the Father. In that respect He will *"appear a second time, apart from sin, for salvation"* (Heb. 9:28). *"This same Jesus, who was taken up from you into heaven, will so come in like manner as you saw Him go into heaven"* (Acts 1:11). There is thus a difference of perspective between the descriptions of the Second Advent as *"His appearing"* (2 Tim. 4:1) and *"His coming."* John pleaded the glorious manifestation of our Lord under both of these views as a reason for abiding in Him.

Confidence, the Reward of Abiding

As to our Lord's appearing, John would have us abide in Christ so that we may have confidence when He appears. Confidence at His appearing is the high reward of constant abiding in Christ. The apostle keeps Christ's appearing most prominent as a motivation. A thousand things are to happen at our Lord's appearing, but John did not mention one of them. He did not hold it up as a thing to be desired that we may have confidence amid the wreck of matter and the crash of worlds—when the stars will fall like autumn leaves; when the sun will be turned into darkness and the moon into blood; when the graves will be opened and the dead rise; when the heavens, being on fire, will be dissolved and the elements will melt with fervent heat; or when the earth and the works therein will also be burned up. Those will be ominous times, days of terror and dismay. However, it is none of these that he referred to particularly, for he regarded all these events as swallowed up in the one great fact of the *"glorious appearing of our great God and our Savior Jesus Christ"* (Titus 2:13).

His desire was that we may have confidence if Christ appears suddenly. What did John mean by having confidence *"when He appears"*? Just this: if you abide in Him when you do not see Him, you will be very bold should He suddenly reveal Himself. Before He appears, you have dwelt in Him, and He has dwelt in you; what fear could His appearing cause you? Your faith has so realized Him that, if suddenly He were to appear to your senses, it would be no surprise to you and would assuredly cause you joy rather than dismay. You would feel that, at last, you could enjoy what you had for so long expected, and you could see somewhat more closely your Friend with whom you had long been familiar. I trust, beloved, that some of us live in such a style that if our Lord were to appear suddenly, it would cause no alarm to us. We have believed Him to be present, though unseen, and it will not affect our conduct when He steps from behind the curtain and stands in the open light.

If the Lord Jesus were now to stand next to us, we would remember that we had His presence before and had lived in it, and now we would only be more assured of what we knew before by faith. We would behold our Lord with confidence, freedom, assurance, and delight, feeling perfectly at home with Him. The believer who abides in his Lord would be only a little startled by His sudden appearing. If he is serving his Lord now, he would go on serving Him. He loves Him now, and he would go on loving Him. As he would have a clearer view of Christ, he would feel only a more intense consecration to Him.

The Greek word *parrhesia,* translated here as *"confidence,"* means freedom of speech or outspokenness. If our divine Lord were to appear momentarily, we would not lose our speech through fear but would welcome Him with glad acclaim. To desert our Lord would rob us of that ease of mind that is implied by free speech, but to cling to Him will secure us confidence.

We now speak to Him in secret, and He answers us. We will not cease to speak in tones of reverent love when He appears. I have preached concerning my Lord, though He is not seen, the truths that I will not blush to acknowledge before His face. If my Lord and Master were, at this instant, to appear in His glory, I would confidently hand Him the volumes of my sermons as proof that I have not departed from His truth but have heartily continued in Him. I ought to improve in many things, but I could not improve on the Gospel that I have preached. I am prepared to live by it, to die by it, or to meet my Lord on it if He should this day appear.

O beloved, if you are in Christ, see to it that you so *"abide in Him"* that, should He suddenly appear, you would behold Him with confidence. If we abide in Christ and He were to unveil His majestic face, we might be overcome with rapture; but our confidence in Him would grow stronger, our freedom with Him would be even more enlarged, and our joy in Him would be made perfect. Has He not prayed for us that we may be with Him and behold His glory (John 17:24)? Can we be afraid of the answer to His loving prayer? If you abide in Christ, the manifestation of Christ will be your manifestation, which will be a matter of delight and not of fear.

Beloved, if you do not *"abide in Him,"* you will have no confidence. If I were to compromise the truth, and then, my Lord were to appear, could I meet Him with confidence? If, to preserve my reputation or to be thought liberal-minded, I played fast and loose with the Gospel, how could I see my Lord's face with confidence? If any of you have failed to serve your Master, if you have preferred gain to godliness and pleasure to holiness, if He were suddenly to shine forth in His glory, what confidence could you have in meeting Him?

Not Ashamed at His Return

One day a godly man was asked, "If the Lord were now to appear, how would you feel?" He replied, "My brother, I would not be afraid, but I think I would be ashamed." He meant that he was not afraid of condemnation, but he blushed to think how little he had served his Lord. In his case it was genuine humility. I pray that you get beyond being afraid, and that the Lord may make you to *"abide in Him"* so that you will *"not be ashamed before Him at His coming."*

Another aspect of *"not be[ing] ashamed before Him at His coming"* is that, having regarded Him as being absent, you should not have so lived that you would be ashamed of your past if He suddenly appeared in person. What must it be like to be driven away from His presence with shame into everlasting contempt? The text may have such an implication.

What have you been doing while He has been absent? This is a question for a servant to answer at his Lord's arrival. You are left in His house to take care of it while He is in the far-off country. If you have been beating His servants and eating and drinking with the drunken, you will be greatly ashamed when He returns. His coming will be in itself a judgment. *"Who can endure the day of His coming? And who can stand when He appears?"* (Mal. 3:2). Blessed is that man who, with all his faults, has been so sanctified by grace that he will not be ashamed at his Lord's coming. Who is that man? It is the man who has learned to abide in Christ.

Prepare Yourself

What is the way to prepare for Christ's coming? By the study of the prophecies? Yes, if you are sufficiently instructed to be able to understand them. "To be prepared for the Lord's coming," some enthusiasts might say, "should I not spend a month in retirement and remove myself from this wicked world?" You may, if you like, and especially you will do so if you are lazy. However, the one scriptural prescription for preparing for His coming is to *"abide in Him."* If you abide in the faith of Him, holding His truth, following His example, and making Him your dwelling place, then, your Lord may come at any hour, and you will welcome Him. The cloud, the Great White Throne, the blast of trumpets, the angelic attendants of the last judicial court, the trembling of creation, and the rolling up of the universe as worn-out apparel will have no alarms for you because you will not be ashamed at His coming.

Always Be Ready

The date of Christ's return is concealed. (See Mark 13:32.) No one can tell when He will come. Watch for Him, and be always ready, so that you may not be ashamed at His advent. Should a Christian go into worldly gatherings and amusements? Would he not be ashamed if his Lord came and found him among the enemies of the Cross? I dare not go where I would be ashamed to be found should my Lord come suddenly. Should a Christian man ever be in a rage? Suppose his Lord should come right then and there; would the man not be ashamed at His coming? Another person says about an offender, "I will never forgive her; she will never darken my doors again." Would not that one be ashamed if the Lord Jesus came and found her unforgiving? Oh, may we *"abide in Him"* and never be in such a state that His coming would be unwelcome to us!

Beloved, so live daily in duty and in devotion that your Lord's coming will be timely. Go about your business and *"abide in Him."* Then, His coming will be a glorious delight to you. We are never in a better state for seeing our Master than when we are faithfully doing His work. There is no need for a pious dressing up. He who abides in Christ always wears garments of glory and beauty. He may go with his Lord into the wedding whenever the midnight cry is heard. *"Abide in Him,"* and then, none can make you ashamed. *"Who shall bring a charge against God's elect?"* (Rom. 8:33).

He will come. Behold, He is coming even now. Do you not hear the sound of His chariot wheels? He may arrive before the sun goes down. *"Therefore you also be ready, for the Son of Man is coming at an hour you do not expect"* (Matt. 24:44). When the world is eating and drinking, marrying and giving in marriage, He will bring destruction on the ungodly. Be so engaged, day by day, that you will not be taken unawares.

What it will be to be caught up together with the saints in the clouds, to meet the Lord in the air! What it will be to see Him come in the glory of the Father, and all His holy angels with Him! What it will be to see Him reign upon the earth, with His ancients, gloriously! Can you imagine the millennial splendor, the age of gold, the serene days of peace? As for the judgment of the world, *"do you not know that the saints will judge the world?...Do you not know that we shall judge angels?"* (1 Cor. 6:2–3). We will appear as assessors with Christ, and *"the God of peace will crush Satan under* [our] *feet"* (Rom. 16:20).

Glory awaits us, and nothing but glory, if we abide in Christ. Therefore, keep your garments unspotted, your waist girded, your lamps trimmed, and your lights burning. Be among those who look for your Lord, in order that, when He comes, you may have confidence and not shame.

May the Holy Spirit, without whom this cannot happen, be freely given to us this day, in order that we may abide in the Lord! And you who have never trusted in Christ for salvation, may you come to Him and then *"abide in Him"* from this good hour! To His name be glory!

Chapter 7

Watching for Christ's Coming

Blessed are those servants whom the master, when he comes, will find watching. Assuredly, I say to you that he will gird himself and have them sit down to eat, and will come and serve them. And if he should come in the second watch, or come in the third watch, and find them so, blessed are those servants.
—Luke 12:37–38

Since I am about to address another aspect of Christ's Second Coming, I trust that you, dear reader, are attuned to the subject now and that you will not have to make any very great exertion of mind to plunge into midstream and be carried away with the full current of thought concerning our Savior's Second Advent.

This is a very appropriate subject when we consider the Lord's Table because the Lord's Supper not only looks backward and is a memorial of His agony, but it also looks forward and is an anticipation of His glory. Paul wrote to the church at Corinth, *"For as often as you eat this bread and drink this cup, you proclaim the Lord's death till He comes"* (1 Cor. 11:26). By looking forward in a right state of heart to that Second Coming of Christ, which is the joy of His church, you will also be in a right state of heart for coming to the Communion table. May the Holy Spirit make it to be so!

According to our Lord's example, the posture at the Communion table was not that of kneeling, but of reclining. The easiest position that you can assume is the most fitting for the Lord's Supper. Yet remember that the Supper was no sooner finished than, *"when they had sung a hymn, they went out to the Mount of Olives"* (Mark 14:26) to the agonies of Gethsemane.

It often seems to me as if now, after finding rest at the table by feeding upon Christ (whose real presence we have with us not in a physical way, but in a spiritual sense), we could sing a hymn and then go out to meet our Lord at His Second Coming. We would not be going to the Mount of Olives to see Him in a bloody sweat (Luke 22:44), but to hear that word of the angel, *"This same Jesus, who was taken up from you into heaven, will so come in like manner as you saw Him go into heaven"* (Acts 1:11). I do not think we should feel at all surprised if we were to leave the table of fellowship the next time we share in it and go out to meet our Lord at once.

We should always be waiting for His appearing, ever expecting Him, not knowing at what hour the Master of the house will come (Mark 13:35). The world does not expect Him; it goes on with its *"eating and drinking, marrying and giving in marriage"* (Matt. 24:38). However, His own family should expect Him. When He will return, I trust that He will not find the door shut against Him, but that we will be ready to open to our Lord immediately when He knocks. That is the object of these few words, to stir you up to be ever watching for Christ's Second Coming.

The Lord Will Return

First, the Lord will come again. He who has come once is to come again; He will come a second time. We can be assured that the Lord will come again because He has promised to return. We have His own word for it. That is our first reason for expecting Him. Among the last of the words that He spoke to His servant John are these: *"Surely I am coming quickly"* (Rev. 22:20). You may read it, *"'I am coming quickly.'* I am even now upon the road. I am traveling as fast as wisdom allows. I am always coming, and coming quickly." Our Lord has promised to come, and to come in person.

Some try to explain the Second Coming as though it refers to the time when a believer dies. You may, if you like, consider that Christ comes to His saints in death. In a certain sense, He does; but that sense will never bear out the full meaning of the teaching of the Second Advent with which the Scripture is full. Rather, *"the Lord Himself will descend from heaven with a shout, with the voice of an archangel, and with the trumpet of God"* (1 Thess. 4:16). He who went up to heaven will come down from heaven, and *"He shall stand at last on the earth"* (Job 19:25). Every redeemed soul can say with Job, *"After my skin is destroyed, this I know, that in my flesh I shall see God, whom I shall see for myself, and my eyes shall behold, and not another"* (vv. 26–27). Christ will as certainly be here again in glory as He once was here in shame, for He has promised to return.

Redemption Requires Christ's Return

Moreover, the great plan of redemption requires Christ's return. It is a part of the plan that, as He came once as a sin-offering, He should *"appear a second time, apart from sin, for salvation"* (Heb. 9:28); that is, as He came once to redeem, He should come a second time to claim the inheritance that He has so dearly bought. He came once so that His heel might be bruised; He will come again to break the Serpent's head (Gen. 3:15) and to dash His enemies in pieces as potters' vessels with a rod of iron (Ps. 2:9). He came once to wear the crown of thorns; He must come again to wear the diadem of universal dominion. He comes to the Marriage Supper; He comes to gather His saints together; He comes to glorify them with Himself on this same earth where once He and they were *"despised and rejected by men"* (Isa. 53:3).

Be sure of this: the whole drama of redemption cannot be perfected without this last act of the coming of the King. The complete history of Paradise Regained requires that the New Jerusalem should come down from God out of heaven, prepared as a bride adorned for her husband (Rev. 21:2). It also requires that the heavenly Bridegroom should come riding forth on His white horse, conquering and to conquer (Rev. 6:2), King of Kings and Lord of Lords, amid the everlasting hallelujahs of saints and angels. It must be so. The man of Nazareth will come again. No one will spit in His face then, but every knee will bow before Him (Phil. 2:10). The Crucified will come again, and although the nailprints will still be visible, no nails will then fasten His dear hands to the tree. Instead, He will grasp the scepter of universal sovereignty, and He will reign forever and ever. Hallelujah!

In His Own Time

When will He come? Ah, that is the question, the question of questions! He will come in His own time. He will come in due time.

Calling on me, a brother minister said, as we sat together, "I would like to ask you a lot of questions about the future."

"Oh, well!" I replied, "I cannot answer you, for I know no more about it than you do."

"But," said he, "what about the Lord's Second Advent? Will there not be the Millennium first?"

I said, "I cannot tell with certainty whether the Millennium will be first, but this I know: the Scripture has left the whole matter with an intentional indistinctness, in order that we may be always expecting Christ to come and that we may be watching for His coming at any and every hour. I think that the Millennium will begin after His coming, and not before it. I cannot imagine the kingdom with the King absent. It seems to me to be an essential part of the millennial glory that the King would then be revealed. At the same time, I am not going to lay down anything definite on that point. He may not come for a thousand years; He may come tonight. The teaching of Scripture is: *'The Son of Man is coming at an hour you do not expect'* (Matt. 24:44). It is clear that if it were revealed that a thousand years must elapse before He would return, we might very well go to sleep for the entire time because we would have no reason to expect that He would come when Scripture told us He would not."

"Well," answered my friend, "but when Christ comes, that will be the general judgment, will it not?" I then quoted these texts: *"The dead in Christ will rise first"* (1 Thess. 4:16), and *"But the rest of the dead did not live again until the thousand years were finished. This is the first resurrection"* (Rev. 20:5).

I replied, "There is a resurrection from among the dead to which the apostle Paul labored to attain (Phil. 3:8–11). We will all rise, but the righteous will rise a thousand years before the ungodly. There is to be that interval of time between the one and the other; whether that is the millennial glory or not, I will not say, although I think it is. But this is the main point: the Lord will come. We know not when we are to expect His coming. We are not to lay down, as absolutely fixed, any definite prediction or circumstance that would allow us to go to sleep until that prediction was fulfilled or that circumstance was apparent."

"Will not the Jews be converted to Christ and restored to their land?" inquired my friend.

I responded, "Yes, I think so. *'They will look on* [Him] *whom they pierced. Yes, they will mourn for Him as one mourns for his only son'* (Zech. 12:10); God will give them the kingdom and the glory, for they are His people, whom He *'has not cast away'* (Rom. 11:2). The Jews, who are the natural olive branches, will yet be grafted into their own olive tree again (see Romans 11:23–24), and then will be accomplished *'the fullness of the Gentiles'* " (v. 25).

"Will that be before Christ comes, or after?" asked my friend.

I answered, "I think it will be after He comes; but whether it is or not, I am not going to commit to any definite opinion on the subject."

I admonish you, my dear friends, to read and search the Scriptures for yourselves.

Still, this one thing stands first and is the only thing that I will insist upon now: the Lord will come. He may come now; He may come tomorrow; He may come in the first watch of the night or the second, or He may wait until the morning watch. Whenever He is coming again, the one word that He gives to you all is, "Watch! Watch!" Thus, whenever He does come, you may be ready to open to Him and to say in the language of the hymn,

> Hallelujah! Welcome,
> Welcome, Judge divine!

So far, I know that we are scriptural and, therefore, perfectly safe in our statements about the Lord's Second Advent.

Ideas of Delay Can Be Harmful

Friends, I would be earnest on this point: the notion of the delay of Christ's coming is always harmful, however you arrive at it, whether it be by studying prophecy or in any other way. If you come to be of the opinion of the servant mentioned in the following text, you are wrong:

> But if that servant says in his heart, "My master is delaying his coming," and begins to beat the male and female servants, and to eat and drink and be drunk, the master of that servant will come on a day when he is not looking for him, and at an hour when he is not aware, and will cut him in two and appoint him his portion with the unbelievers.   (Luke 12:45–46)

Do not, therefore, get the idea that the Lord delays His coming, and that He will not or cannot come as yet. It would be far better for you to stand on tiptoe in expectation and to be rather disappointed to think that He does not come. I do not wish you to be shaken in mind so as to act fanatically or foolishly, as certain people did in America when they went out into the woods with ascension dresses on, so as to go straight up all of a sudden. Fall into none of those absurd ideas that have led people to leave a chair vacant at the table or to set an empty plate because the Lord might come and want it. Try to avoid all other superstitious nonsense. To stand stargazing at the prophecies with your mouth wide open is the wrong thing to do. Far better will it be to go on working for your Lord, getting yourself and your service ready for His appearing, and cheering yourself, all the while telling yourself, "While I am at work, my Master may come. Before I get weary, my Master may return. While others are mocking me, my Master may appear. Whether they mock or applaud is nothing to me. I live before the great Taskmaster's eye and do my service, knowing that He sees me, and expecting that, by and by, He will reveal Himself to me. Then, He will reveal me and my right intentions to men who have misrepresented me."

That is the first point, beloved: the Lord will come. Settle that in your minds. He will come in His own time, and we are always to be looking for His appearing.

Commanded to Watch for Him

Second, the Lord bids us to watch for Him. That is the heart of the text: *"Blessed are those servants whom the master, when he comes, will find watching."*

Now, what is this watching? The first essential part of this watching is that we are not to be taken up with present things. You remember that the Scripture tells us not to take thought about what we will eat or drink (Luke 12:22); we are not to be absorbed in that. We who are Christians are not to live the fleshly, selfish life that asks, "What will I eat and drink? How can I store up my goods? How can I get food and clothing here?" You are something more than dumb, driven cattle that must think of hay and water. You have immortal spirits. Rise to the dignity of your immortality. Begin to think of the kingdom: the kingdom so soon to come; the kingdom that your Father has given you (Luke 12:32) and that, therefore, you must certainly inherit; the kingdom that Christ has prepared for you, for which He is making you *"kings and priests"* (Rev. 1:6) to God so that you may reign with Him forever.

Be Heavenly Minded

Oh, be not earthbound! Do not cast your anchor here in these troubled waters. Do not build your nest in any of these trees; they are all marked for the ax and are coming down. Your nest will come down, too, if you build it here. *"Set your mind on things above, not on things on the earth"* (Col. 3:2). Look up yonder,

> Up where eternal ages roll
> Where solid pleasures never die
> And fruits eternal feast the soul.

There project your thoughts and your anxieties, and have a care about the world to come. Do not be anxious about the things that pertain to this life. *"Seek first the kingdom of God and His right-eousness, and all these things shall be added to you"* (Matt. 6:33).

Be Ready to Serve

Reading further, you will notice that watching implies keeping ourselves in a serviceable condition: *"Let your waist be girded"* (Luke 12:35). You know how the Orientals wear flowing robes, which can get in their way. Thus, if a man has physical work at hand, he just tucks in his robe under his belt, ties his belt in tightly, and gets ready for the task. Turning the Oriental into the Western figure, we would say in English, "Roll up your shirtsleeves, and prepare for work." That is the way to wait for the Lord, ready for service, so that He may never find you idle when He comes.

Earlier, I described to you a true event in which I interrupted a saintly lady scrubbing her front stoop when I called on her. She was energetically fulfilling her God-given responsibility as keeper of the home. That picture brought forth a desire in my heart to be found by my Master, when He returns, doing the task at hand. May you also desire to be doing your duty. You are to be engaged about those vocations to which God has called you. You are to be doing it all out of love for Christ and as service to Him. Oh, that we might watch in that style, with our waist girded, doing *"all in the name of the Lord Jesus"* (Col. 3:17)!

Work, wait, and watch! Can you put those three things together? Work, wait, and watch! This is what your Master asks of you. Work, wait, and watch!

Be a Welcoming Light

He would have us wait with our lights burning. If the Master comes home late, let us sit up late for Him. It is not for us to go to bed until He comes home. Have the lights all trimmed; have His room well lit up; have the entrance hall ready for His approach. When the King comes, have your torches flaming, so that you may go out to meet the royal Bridegroom and escort Him to His home. If we are to watch for the Lord, it must be with our lamps burning brightly in welcome.

Are you making your light shine among men? Do you think that your conduct and character are examples that will do your neighbors good, and are you trying to teach others the way of salvation? Some professing Christians are like *"a lamp...under a basket"* (Matt. 5:15). May we never be such! May we stand with our lamps trimmed, our lights burning, and as those who wait for their Lord—not walking in darkness or concealing our light, but letting it shine brightly!

That is the way to watch for Christ: with your belt tight about you because you are ready for work, and your lamp shining with brightness because you are anxious to illuminate the dark world in which you live.

Be Doing What Jesus Would Do

To put it very plainly, I think that watching for the Lord's Second Coming means acting just as you would like to be acting if He were to come. Recently, I saw in the orphanage classroom that little motto, "What would Jesus do?" That is a very splendid motto for a whole life: "What would Jesus do in such a situation or in this case?" And do just that.

Another good motto for guidance is this: "What would Jesus think of me if He were to come right now?" There are some places into which a Christian should not go because he would not like his Master to find him there. There are some kinds of amusements into which a believer should never enter because he would be ashamed for his Master to come and find him there. There are some conditions of angry temper, pride, petulance, or spiritual sloth in which you would not like to be if you knew that the Master was coming. Suppose an angel's wing should brush your cheek just as you have spoken some unkind word and a voice should say, "Your Master is coming." You would tremble, I am sure, to meet Him in such a condition.

Oh, beloved, let us try every morning to get up as if that were the morning Christ would come. When we go up to bed at night, may we lie down with this thought: "Perhaps I will be awakened by the ringing of the silver trumpets heralding His Coming. Before the sun arises, I may be startled from my dreams by the greatest of all cries, 'The Lord is come! The Lord is come!'" What a check, what an incentive, what a bridle, what a spur such thoughts as these would be to us! Take this as the guideline for your whole life: Act as if Jesus would return during your performing the deed in which you are engaged; if you would not wish to be caught in that act by the Lord's Coming, stop doing it.

Be a Vigilant Keeper of the Watch

The second verse of our text speaks about the Master coming in the second or the third watch. We are to act as those who keep the watches of the age for Christ. Among the Roman army, it was as it is on board ship: there were certain watches. A Roman soldier stood on guard for three hours; when his watch was completed, another sentry came who took his place. The first man retired and went back to the barracks, and the fresh sentinel stood in his place during his allotted time.

Beloved, we have succeeded a long line of watchmen. Since the days of our Lord when He sent out the chosen Twelve to stand upon the citadel and tell how the night waxed or waned, how the watchmen have come and gone! Our God has changed the watchmen, but He has kept the watch. He still sets watchmen on the walls of Zion, who cannot hold their peace day or night, but must watch for the coming of their Master, watch against evil times, watch against error, and watch for the souls of men. At this time, some of us are called to be specially on the watch, and dare we sleep? After such a line of lynx-eyed watchmen, who counted not their lives dear unto them that they might hold their post and watch against the Foe, will we be cowards and be afraid, or will we be sluggards and go to our beds? By Him *"who lives, and was dead, and...*[is] *alive forevermore"* (Rev. 1:18), we pray that we may never be guilty of treason to His sacred name and truth. May we watch on to the last moment when the clarion cry will ring out, *"Behold, the bridegroom is coming; go out to meet him!"* (Matt. 25:6).

Brothers and sisters, you are set to watch tonight just as they did in the brave days of old! Whitefield's and Wesley's men were watchmen, along with those before them in the days of Luther and of Calvin, and back even to the days of our Lord. They kept the watches of the night, and you must do the same until,

> Upstarting at the midnight cry,
> "Behold your heavenly Bridegroom nigh,"

you go forth to welcome your returning Lord.

Be Ready to Welcome Him

We are to wait with one object in view, namely, to open the door to Him and to welcome Him, so *"that when he comes and knocks* [we] *may open to him immediately"* (Luke 12:36).

Perhaps you know what it is to go home to a loving, tender wife and children who are watching for you. You have been on a journey, absent for some time; you have written them letters, which they have greatly valued; you have heard from them; but all that is nothing like your personal presence. They are looking for your arrival. If, perchance, your mode of transportation should break down or be late and you arrived at eleven or twelve o'clock at night, you would not expect to find the house all shut up and no-body watching for you. No, you had told them that you would come, and you were quite sure that they would watch for you.

Sometimes I, too, feel rebuked for not watching for my Master, especially when I realize that my dogs are sitting at the door at this very time, waiting for me. Long before I reach home, there they are. At the first sound of the carriage wheels, they lift up their voices with delight because their master is coming home. Oh, if we loved our Lord as dogs love their masters, how we would catch the first sound of His Coming as we are waiting, always waiting, and never truly happy until at last we will see Him! Pardon me for us-ing a dog as a picture of what you ought to be, but when you have attained to a state above that one, I will find another illustration to portray my meaning.

Blessings and Rewards for Watchmen

Now, finally, there is a reward for those who are watching for Christ's return. Their reward is this: *"Blessed are those servants whom the master, when he comes, will find watching."*

Watchmen have a present blessedness. It is a very blessed thing to be on the watch for Christ; it is a blessing to us now. How it detaches you from the world! You can be poor without murmur-ing; you can be rich without worldliness. You can be sick without sorrowing; you can be healthy without presumption. If you are always waiting for Christ's Coming, untold blessings are wrapped up in that glorious hope. *"Everyone who has this hope in Him purifies himself, just as He is pure"* (1 John 3:3). Blessings are heaped up one upon another in that state of heart in which a man is always looking for his Lord.

But what will be the blessedness when Jesus does come? Well, a part of that blessedness will be in future service. Sunday school teachers, preachers, and ministers, you must not think that when you are done working here, the Master will say, "I have discharged you from My service. Go, sit on a heavenly mount, and sing yourselves away forever and ever." Never!

I am only learning how to preach now; I will be able to preach by and by. You are just learning to teach now; soon you will be able to teach. To angels, principalities, and powers, you will make known the manifold wisdom of God. I sometimes aspire to the thought of a congregation of angels and archangels who will sit and wonder as I tell what God has done for me. I will be to them an everlasting monument of the grace of God to an unworthy wretch, on whom He looked with infinite compassion and saved with a wonderful salvation.

All those stars, those worlds of light, who knows how many of them are inhabited? I believe there are regions beyond imagination to which every child of God will become an everlasting illumination, a living example of the love of God in Christ Jesus. The people in those far-distant lands could not see Calvary as this world has seen it, but they will hear of it from the redeemed. Remember how the Lord will say, *"Well done, good and faithful servant; you were faithful over a few things, I will make you ruler over many things"* (Matt. 25:21). The servant is to keep on doing something, you see. Instead of having some little bit of a village to govern, he is to be made ruler over some great province. So it is in this passage.

Reading further in Luke, we find: *"Truly, I say to you that he will make him ruler over all that he has"* (Luke 12:44). That is, the man who has been a faithful and wise steward of God here will be called of God to more eminent service hereafter. If a person serves his Master well, when his Master comes, He will promote him to still higher service.

Do you not know how it used to be in the Spartan army? A man who had fought well and been a splendid soldier was often covered with wounds on his chest. The next time a war began, the

623

leaders would say, "Poor fellow, we will reward him! He will lead the way in the first battle. He fought so well before when he met one hundred with a little troop behind him; now, he can meet ten thousand with a much larger troop." "Oh," you object, "that is giving him more work!"

That is God's way of rewarding His people, and a blessed thing it is for the industrious servant. His rest is in serving God with all his might. This will be our heaven, not to go there to roost, but to be always on the wing, forever flying and forever resting at the same time. We will *do His word, heeding the voice of His word* (Ps. 103:20). *"His servants shall serve Him. They shall see His face"* (Rev. 22:3–4). Blended together, these two things make a noble ambition for every Christian.

May the Lord keep you waiting, working, and watching so that when He comes, you may have the blessedness of entering upon some larger, higher, nobler service than you could accomplish now, for which you are preparing by the lowlier and more arduous service of this world! God bless you, beloved.

If any of you do not know my Lord, and therefore do not look for His appearing, remember that He will come whether you look for Him or not. When He comes, you will have to stand at His bar. One of the events that will follow His Coming will be your being summoned before His judgment seat. How will you answer Him then? How will you answer Him if you have refused His love and turned a deaf ear to the invitations of His mercy? If you have delayed and delayed, how will you answer Him? How will you answer Him in that day if you stand speechless? Your silence will condemn you, and the King will say, *"Bind him hand and foot, take him away, and cast him into outer darkness"* (Matt. 22:13).

May God grant that we may believe in the Lord Jesus unto life eternal, and then wait for His appearing from heaven, for His love's sake!